ANATOLE FRANCE

FRANCE IN THE VILLA SAÏD (1913)

ANATOLE FRANCE

1844-1896

By EDWIN PRESTON DARGAN

PROFESSOR OF FRENCH LITERATURE

AT THE UNIVERSITY OF CHICAGO

Published in co-operation with
The Modern Language Association of America

NEW YORK TORONTO

OXFORD UNIVERSITY PRESS

1937

PRINTED IN THE UNITED STATES OF AMERICA

The author highly appreciates and hereby acknowledges assistance extended by the American Council of Learned Societies, which by a 'grant in aid of publication' has greatly facilitated the production of the present study. And he is most grateful to the Committee on Research Activities of the Modern Language Association, which saw fit to make a recommendation to this effect.

CONTENTS

CONTENTS

ILLUSTRATIONS

MAPS

INTRODUCTION

§ 1

THIS work was undertaken some ten years ago as an attempt at a 'psychological biography.' It was believed that a study of France's mind and art would show an interesting personal development and that something might be discovered to throw light upon the chief currents of his era. These intentions have not been renounced —rather they constitute the two focal points in line with which a good deal of the material that I have used has been, like so many unassorted filings, polarized and systematized. But it was soon apparent that there was more to the problem than this. Anatole's mind could not be studied *in vacuo*.

Readings in France's works and in the vast literature about him, together with summers spent in the Parisian collections and in conversations with those who knew him, brought it home to me that regarding the essential facts of this author's life there is a considerable amount of disagreement and that already the 'legend' has often displaced reality.[1] Therefore my study must be properly biographical before it could be even tentatively psychological. There were too many debatable areas over which our subject himself has thrown but a fitful light and concerning which the multitude of witnesses has often, indeed, darkened counsel. Early in the proceedings I submitted a list of seventeen such questions to two of the leading 'Franciens' and watched them very obligingly scurry around the Collection Lion in an endeavour to do the right thing by the inquisitive American. It is a tribute to the enterprise and knowledge of these gentlemen that ten of the questions were soon answered. But alas ! Not all were so readily soluble, still other interrogation-points have arisen, and to this day the neophyte in matters Anatolian may cut his teeth upon such *cruces* as these.— Who was Grand'maman Nozière ? When did A.F. set up a bachelor establishment ? What were the circumstances surrounding his divorce ?

§ 2

ON similar enigmas I have tried to assemble the available evidence. But of course no really definitive biography of France can be written until his scattered correspondence — still more scattered as a result of the Caillavet-Pouquet sale in 1932—has been collected and published; and until many people now living are no more. At present, for instance, it would be a venturesome thing to write dogmatically about 'Anatole and Madame de Caillavet.' While waiting, we do what we can. . . One of my objectives, and the one that took the most time, was to go through the greater part of the literature on the general subject; the extent of this may be surmised by a glance at my Bibliography which includes perhaps half of the titles actually examined. Unless it be Proust, no other modern Frenchman has been more written about than Anatole France; and it is sad to consider how much of the writing is now practically waste paper. During the year of his Jubilee and death, the world was deluged with a flood of mediocre articles and doubtfully blessed with what Professor Gauss of Princeton once called a succession of 'fly-by-night' books. Yet most of these have been scrutinized for what little they might add in the way of facts or well-grounded opinions. Of course, there are also real authorities and sound pieces of reconstruction built on one or the other of France's many facets; these have been used frequently, and the numerous references to them will be found at the end of this volume.* In a pioneering synthesis of this kind, there would be no excuse for the omission of references. Anatole himself once declared to a young friend: 'An historical work without notes becomes a work of fiction.'[2]

More rewarding than anything, naturally, has been the long study of France's own work, especially that portion of it which is not known to the general public and which lies for the most part ossified in old periodicals. 'Now since these bones have rested quietly in the grave under the drums and tramplings'—of half a century—it has seemed well worth while to venture into the Valley of Jehoshaphat and hale them forth. No student of France has hitherto used his articles in *l'Univers illustré* as fully as they are used here. Other comparatively new features of this work are the following: (1) the attempt made to straighten out the ties that bind Anatole's youth to that of 'le Petit Pierre'; (2) the detailed study of his life and personality during his second period; here as elsewhere, accurate *dating* is of more importance than some writers have realized; (3) the examination (as a specimen)

* As a rule, footnotes are reserved for translations — usually of verse. Unless otherwise indicated, these are by the present author.

of the manuscript of *Thaïs,* found in the Appendices; (4) some fresh light on France's divorce decree, although part of that is still *sub judice;* (5) a study of the effects upon his mind and heart of the ravages of his middle years. (Chapters XIII and XIV, though perhaps less interesting than some others to the general reader, illustrate several of the above points and contain material not hitherto consecutively developed.) Also, distinctive approaches may be discerned in the two general intentions mentioned in my first paragraph above: to these we now recur.

§ 3

WHAT may be said, then, about France's evolution or his 'education' in the broader sense of the word? He had a slowly maturing mind and a talent that came late to the realization of its true *moyens.* It was ultimately an intelligence which, though not among the deepest, was surely among the most comprehensive of his time. His range of interests was scarcely surpassed by that of Sainte-Beuve himself. Although we become weary of France's repetitions, we are comforted by the feeling that when we pick up a work of his, we are straightway launched on a stream of culture that is mile-wide and almost endless. 'One escapes in his books,' said Stuart Sherman, 'from the shallow and savorless modernity of contemporary literature. He is a cosmopolitan not merely of the present year of grace; he was a citizen of the world before the Christian era.'[3]

Anatole's predilections, as will later appear, were with the pagans and their philosophy; to the end his ideal of life was to converse serenely 'under the rose' with ancient sages.[4] Yet how could anybody confine within one period this 'Don Juan des idées et des sentiments'?[5] A Grecian one day, he was a boulevardier the next; attached to La Pucelle in the morning, he would prefer Rabelais at night. The fourth and the eighteenth centuries alternated in his affections. In the manner of Dryden's Buckingham, hints one reviewer, he 'could be by turns priest, scholar, courtesan, proconsul, slave, peasant, poet, Satan himself.'[6] He boxed the compass politically, historically, æsthetically, scientifically. His humanism was broad enough to include not only the wealth of a hundred museums, but the basic ideas of a dozen sciences from astronomy to zoology. He displays before us the leading tenets of all previous epochs, deliberately making them clash with our own. It has been well said that Anatole brings together the full and swirling currents of the French mind; he combines

> the fluidity of Renan; the Parnassian taste, which is so impeccable and hard to satisfy; Diderot's bold freedom and natural sensuality; the sure but soft elegance of Fénelon and of Racine; and the abundant and well-sustained irony of Montaigne or of Rabelais. And with all this, M. France still remains himself.[7]

Let us not yet inquire, with Mr. Chevalier, whether our author's range of feeling was on a par with his myriad-mindedness; let us not yet curiously analyse the *mollesse* which many have found in his character. Let us simply posit, with M. Barthou, (a life-long devotee of Anatole's) as the two abiding features of his talent, a constant preoccupation with the past and a perpetual inability to get away from himself.[8]

§ 4

BUT what was this ego from which he scarce sought release and to which he manifested the most charming fidelity?[9] Was it really the dissociated personality that many critics apperceive? For here, too, we find the most diverse opinions, suggesting corresponding and basic diversities in the composition of Anatole. If he was 'everything by starts,' they would have us believe, he was also 'nothing long.' He was tender—but he was also cruel. He was selfish—but extremely benevolent. He was conservative—but a pronounced radical. He was a careless dilettante—yet remarkably learned. He believed in the future of humanity—yet emphatically he believed in nothing of the sort. Around his irony, or his dilettantism, or his sensuality, or his pessimism, or his conservatism, disparate structures have been erected. Each is unfinished, but each is oriented towards the Truth—a rising sun.

No such statue of Memnon will at present be attempted; from up and down the land let us first gather the component parts; you may ultimately see them grow into something. It is with the *formation* of that something that I am primarily occupied. Yet even now this much may be postulated: despite the tangled threads in France's personality, despite the contradictions in his ever more discursive and speculative thought, there is the dominant's persistence, there are all the time definite trends, recurrences, preferences, that must emerge clearly in the making of such a man. For if we cannot quite agree with those who claim that Anatole's life and work were well integrated throughout, we may at least chime in with Gregh's poetic tribute to this mind:

> C'était un de ceux en qui le monde
> S'ordonne, se construit et devient plus humain.* [10]

§ 5

LET us remember that France lived and wrote a long, long time. As in the case of Montaigne, of Voltaire, or of H. G. Wells, his message must have undergone changes in the lengthy transmission. The term 'evolution,' for all its banality and its perilous connotations, is hardly avoidable and has in fact already been used by several people.[11] It involves certain complications.

For one thing, whatever reversions and overlapping may presently be found, the master's development must evidently be considered as divisible into phases and stages. Our study should be dynamic rather than static.[12] Again, whether or not the reader accepts the division shortly to be proposed, one central event is now well-assured: shortly after his *mezzo del cammin,* France's life was almost broken in two; after the fissure it was patched together and went along on another plane. The break, in the realm of ideas, has long been perceptible and has frequently been viewed as primarily an intellectual emergence or manifestation. After reviewing the evidence and consulting some of those who knew him round 1890, I am led to believe that it was rather the rift in his personal life and its re-formation round a new centre that made of him a new-old Anatole. This question will be discussed in the final chapters below.

Now with reference to divisions and dates, several respectable schemes have already been proposed. Of these I shall consider two. On the intellectual basis, M. Gaffiot would distinguish three clear-cut periods:

> Up to 1879, it is evolutionary Pantheism that dominates in him; from 1879 to 1892, it is rather scepticism; from 1892 on, it is a pessi-

* For he was one of those in whom the world
Is ranged and humanized and rounded to a whole.

mistic and socialistic *critique,* becoming aggravated, in 1895 (*sic*) at the time of the Dreyfus Affair.[13]

The year '1879' should be pushed backward, the year '1895' should decidedly move on. Consequently, the central date best worth retaining in this outline is—approximately—that of 1892.

Another proposal also suggests three periods, but they are more convincingly chosen: the epoch of *Sylvestre Bonnard*—dilettantism *à la* Renan; the epoch of 'Jérôme Coignard'—the controversy with Brunetière (1889), having first brought A.F.'s scepticism into the open; the Dreyfus episode (1897 *et seq.*), combined with the Voltairianism of the *Histoire contemporaine,*—A.F. becoming 'militantly anti-clerical and socialistic.'[14]

The above description of France's first period together with the definition and dating of the final period seem to me acceptable, if we are to content ourselves with three large divisions. The year 1889 is doubtless important; one might also suggest 1893, for reasons that will appear later;[15] but almost every year in that central epoch is important; and what can be done about it? My solution has been to stop the *Bonnard* era in 1886, when France joined the staff of *Le Temps,* and to begin then the Age of Great Upheavals, closing the same when the Academy opened its doors. (This is the limit of the present work.) Nor am I quite satisfied with a tripartite arrangement. *Five* divisions seem better—something like this:

First (1844-62), the eighteen years of Anatole's childhood and adolescence, including the notable effects of his mother's influence, his father's book-shop, his education in a clerical school, the upbuilding of his inner life. Second, the period of young manhood and early productivity (1862-86), with the development of his two strongest tastes—antiquity on the one hand, the old Régime and French classicism on the other. Third, the Epicurean phase (1886-96),[16] reaching its height in the *Jardin d'Epicure,* but already discernible from many articles published in *Le Temps.* Fourth (1897-*c.* 1910), the socialistic and sceptical period. Fifth (1912-1924), old age, with its sourer vintage and its harking back to the memories of childhood.

Of course these boundaries are not fixed. France was sceptical in his teens, conservative in the midst of his socialism, and a lover of antiquity until his dying day. Our treatment, then, will require a certain amount of weaving back and forth. Since we are much occupied with the formation of Anatole's mind, no excuse is needed for dwelling upon his youthful years. They were, says a recent eulogist, 'the most decisive, the most self-determining' of his whole career, 'and his character was permanently marked by them.'[17] In comparison with these, the years that France lived in the twentieth century were retrogressive and were productive of few important novelties.[18]

A few words regarding the title and the scope of this volume. I have considered and rejected such titles as the 'Youth' and the 'Education' of A.F. In spite of M. Seillière's practice, the youth of a writer cannot reasonably be prolonged through his fifty-second year: Anatole's maturity was delayed, but not to that extent. The widest sense of the word 'Education' seems applicable and has, in fact, been thus applied in the text, whether with reference to the preceptorial role of Madame de Caillavet or to other formative influences.[19] France himself speaks of three kinds of 'écoles' to which he was subjected; and of these only one was academic. But had such a title been chosen the ghost of Henry Adams must have crossed my path. The final unpretentious selection at least indicates that I attempt to cover Anatole's development *in extenso* through 1896.

There are several reasons for halting this biography in that year. It represents a kind of crescendo in France's progress. By then the man and the mask that he wore had been thoroughly fashioned: his 'Education' was an accomplished fact. It is also a fact that because of the present unavailability of much correspondence and other documents, the road in front would bristle with even more difficulties than the road behind. Again, there are human limitations of time and patience; these may affect both author and reader. . . Furthermore, there may evolve a certain thesis from the following pages: to wit, that the greater part of A.F.'s utterances after our line of division was anticipated by what he had written earlier. Hence the need for examining closely a number of his obscurer articles, especially throughout his second or journalistic period. As for his celebrated third period, I make here and now this reservation regarding the treatment: my final chapters are provisional only, for doubtless important revelations are still to be made in this connexion.

§ 6

But in our interweaving and interlocking various outstanding themes will, as illustrations, be carried through to the bitter end. Such are France's devotion to Racine and to Virgil, such his relations with Leconte de Lisle and with the publisher, Lemerre. In fact, at this point it may be well to distinguish between these major themes—'la volupté,' the hatred of asceticism, Joan of Arc may stand as further examples in the realm of main forces or ideas—and what I shall classify as minor *motifs* in his works.[20] Such *motifs* are the recurrent Venus Genetrix, the wavy forelock of the Romantics, the phrase about everybody 'seeking salvation as best he can.' In either case, the hall-mark of a persistent idea is its repetition. Probably no other great writer ever repeated himself so frequently and so nonchalantly. 'Sa contemplation,' said Lemaître elegantly, 'est pleine de ressouvenirs'—involving not merely one memory, but the recollections of many memories.[21] But Lemaître speaks too mildly when he continues: 'For M. France, things have a way of being repeated two or three times.' This is a gross understatement. There are cases of reiteration even unto the twentieth or the thirtieth echo. At times Anatole seems afflicted with the disease called 'echolalia.' How often do we listen to the majestic reverberations of that major theme, 'In Praise of Latin'? How often do we hear the thin *motif* of the False Dauphin wind through the corridors of the Conciergerie? Has any one counted the number of appearances of the Baron Vivant-Denon? Or of Noah's Ark? Or of the vagabond dressed in bed-ticking? In the pictorial world, there must be a dozen fine copies of the well-known masterpiece, 'Dido Meets Aeneas in Hades.'

We do not always complain. For one thing, as an artist in stylistic harmonies, Anatole will vary his effects, his modulations. And although some of his echoes become irritating to sensitive ears, yet for the student of mental states they are usually revealing—they indicate fixations. Let some one but mutter in France's hearing the name of Minerva or of La Pucelle or of St. Mary the Egyptian. Instantly the spring is touched. The well-oiled shutters roll open, the preliminary click is heard, the Voice once more exclaims: 'Why all this fuss about a mere virginity!'[22]

§ 7

Besides repetitions, there are continually in this writer's work and talk echoes of the two kinds emphasized by M. Barthou—either from the historic past or from the past of Anatole France. His most fascinating pages proceed from one or the other of these inspirations, rather than from the spectacle of contemporary society.

By temperament he was a scholar rather than a novelist. He mirrored the manifold past, of which he was a 'sort of synthesis'; hence *par excellence* he 'had the faculty of abolishing time, of being everywhere, questioning all the vanished moments of terrestrial life.'[23] That gift allowed him to view present-day things *sub specie æternitatis*. How often, in his articles, does he prelude the consideration, say of book-dealers or of the art of cooking, by philosophizing on the subject and by carrying it back to its historical origins! Lemaître and others have declared that his mind was one of the richest 'resultants' of all preceding lore, particularly as filtered through the sieve of nineteenth-century investigation. Barrès pointed out that 'he trod again the highroad of the century,' from its romantic perturbations to the leanings toward history and science; and another writer argued that France finally merited the Nobel prize because his works contain all the intellectual history of our time. Not merely one century but all centuries, insists Maurras; for 'who, better than France, could speak of the army of stars and the most ancient science of the heavens?'—tempering his speech, however, by the 'newly born disciplines.' M. Mornet has demonstrated at length France's loyalty to the new knowledge, even when it involves desperate contradictions and agonies of thought.[24]

But there is nothing arid or harsh about all this. Anatole wears his learning like a gentleman. Any study of his sources, for example those of *La Rôtisserie de la Reine Pédauque,* will show him adapting with a light touch, with a flair for short cuts, his prosier predecessors. Together with his artistic sense, it may have been his supple Alexandrianism, as some have hinted, that enables him to reflect easily so many moods and modes of civilization, ancient or modern. His rendering, his appeal, after all, are those of his own time.[25]

Victor Hugo once wrote:

Mon âme aux mille voix que le Dieu que j'adore
Mit au centre de tout comme un écho sonore . . . * [26]

But in the case of Anatole, his equally vibrant soul gave forth an *écho suave.*

§ 8

THE primary sources for investigating France's life and mind are of two main sorts. First, there are his own works, especially the four semi-autobiographical volumes; then there are the volumes of recollections, for the most part published shortly after his death by those who had known him in his last years. The former may be called the 'Gospels'; the latter, the 'reminiscential volumes' or more briefly the 'ana.'

In this section let us consider the Gospels. It is true that these four are far from exhausting France's personal memories. It will appear later that biographical material can be drawn from periodical articles, from such works as *Les Désirs de Jean Servien,* and even from the *Histoire contemporaine.*[27] In all his writings, says Michaut, 'there is scarcely any ego but *his* ego; so his whole work seems a tissue of memories and confidences.' Barthou agrees that from the time of *Sylvestre Bonnard* France 'never stopped confessing and depicting himself.'[28] This is thoroughly in line with Anatole's professions of subjectivity. Furthermore, *Dichtung und Wahrheit* are so closely interwoven in his experience that we may, with some qualifications, accept Gottschalk's statement: 'Every change which occurs in the personality of the writer finds soon afterward its counter-effect in his utterances.'[29]

The four titles particularly in question are the following.—The *Livre de Pierre,* most of which ran serially in *La Nouvelle Revue*[30] and which was published as the first part of the famous *Livre de mon ami* in 1885. The first sections of *Pierre Nozière:* these are in the vein of *Le Livre:* most of them were written in the eighties and had appeared in various periodicals before their late gathering in book-form (1899).[31] And those autumnal fruits, *Le Petit Pierre* (1918) and *La Vie en fleur* (1922), which show the writer, as he himself had once predicted,[32] still haunted by childhood memories.

* My soul with its thousand voices whom the God I adore has installed, like a sonorous echo, in the centre of all things.

Even admitting a certain amount of fictional arrangement, we have here a goodly amount of autobiography, since Anatole felt recurrently a strong nostalgia for his youth. Never, in fact, has a French author left a fuller record of his childhood ; and probably only once or twice has such a record possessed a greater psychological and literary importance. France's chief predecessors in this line were Rousseau and Renan. Anatole's abiding interest in that type of reminiscence which deals with a writer's youth is proven not only by his admiration of Coppée's *Toute une jeunesse* but especially by a fine page which preludes his review of Renan's *Souvenirs*.[33] He declares here that such autobiographers are at their best when revealing

> their early sentiments and the magnificent freshness of their souls. Rousseau made his childhood interesting in spite of certain confessions which he had better not have written. Chateaubriand magically unrolls before us the melancholy hours, the sharp and solitary yearnings that he knew at Combourg. The most charming story by George Sand tells about her early years at Nohant. Dickens moves us to tears in showing us the lad who became in time the most affectionate and tender among writers. . .

And now it is the turn of Renan and *his* memories. Thus France challenges comparison with the masters in that field.

It is not surprising that the four Gospels have been termed France's *Souvenirs d'enfance et de jeunesse*. But it is plausibly argued[34] that while Renan is Celtic in spirit, France, here as elsewhere, is truly the 'enfant latin.'

To what extent may these volumes be accepted as a truthful record ? How far may their youthful hero, 'Pierre Nozière,' be viewed as a replica of Anatole France and the life of the Nozières as a 'reconstitution' of that led by the Thibault family ? The author himself insists in several passages that as an amused and elderly stranger he can now contemplate this boy-self with perfect detachment.[35] More than once he raises the question of exactitude ; and although he admits that chronology has troubled him, yet he believes that on the whole he has given a faithful account of his past. The *Livre de mon ami,* notably, is declared to be a 'récit exact de mon enfance.'[36] But his fullest statement about these matters is to be found in the 'Postface' to *La Vie en fleur*.[37]

There he says first that all these recollections are 'true with regard to the principal events, characters and customs.' Changes of names and occupations were made for obvious reasons; circumstances were sometimes invented in order better to display a character—'psychological verity' being the main issue. His memory, usually faithful in detail, has sometimes let whole episodes escape. Then imagination has come to his aid. But 'no one has ever lied in a truer fashion.' A reviewer has objected that in becoming 'Dr. Nozière,' le Père France lost a book-shop; [38] yet (Anatole continues) the old gentleman remains none the less his father for all that. The apologia concludes with an argument which will become very familiar as we proceed. There is in the Gospels some degree of art, that is to say artifice. If humanity needs truth, it needs still more the kind of falsehood that consoles and encourages. We are led to infer that Anatole is doing his bit in that direction. But the insistence on his verity in character-drawing is unmistakable.

Now the important thing we want to know is, How far did the author of the 'Pierre' books fulfil his general intention? Our procedure in the following chapters will to some extent depend upon the answer. Let us hear the critics and get some sidelights.

Some very good judges (e.g., M. Vandérem) hold that the author comes nearer to reality in his reminiscences than elsewhere in his work. So M. Souday believes that here we have 'France in a state of nature, free from literary intoxication.' An entire section in M. Corday's volume is devoted to showing close correspondences between Pierre's youth and that of Anatole. Masson thinks that it is the intellectual rather than the sentimental development of either lad that is unfolded in the Gospels; and that however much 'falsehood' may be involved, it works always toward that higher verity which is artistic *vraisemblance*. [39]

Others are lured by the author to speak of Pierre-Anatole as one and the same. Which is the boy who was born a looker-on; or which one is described as an 'astonishing, caressing and ironic youngster, both precocious and naïve, with his great eyes well-opened on the world.'? [40] M. Vandérem finds that not only does France depict boys in his own meditative image; he is a still 'stricter realist' in reviving a gallery of older persons, delicate faded figures reanimated authentically from a corridor of the French past. An American, arguing that Anatole's 'books of reminiscence reveal the life springs of his work' and that *Le Livre* particularly contains a good deal of factual truth, is disposed to apply the higher, psychological test to the Gospels as a whole. 'They record the spiritual history of the author's early life and of a few persons intimately connected with it, and not the physical details and incidents.' Thereby they retain a universal value. An Englishman, Edmund Gosse, is both *pro* and *con*. Admitting the charge of 'doctored autobiography,' he is willing for France to aid memory by imagination, thus attaining in the Gospels 'a charm of intimacy hardly to be found elsewhere.'[41]

There is evidently something to be said *per contra*. Le Moy finds some cases of genuine inaccuracy even in *Le Livre*; he holds that none of the four volumes are faithful memoirs.[42] Another writer wonders (and we may well wonder) whether certain sages like M. Dubois really spoke so wisely as they are made to do; or whether the flowers of this wisdom were not culled somewhere near the Jardin d'Epicure rather than in the fresh pastures of youth.[43] Indeed, I do not feel that the conversations were meant to be historically accurate dialogue; a more serious blemish, on the artistic side, would be the quantity of repetitions to be found in the various volumes.

The most thorough-going opponent of France's veracity is M. Ballaguy, who holds, too severely, I believe, that none of the Gospels deserve much credence. Yet we shall find, in the first Chapter below, that this article on 'Aïeux et parents d'Anatole France'[44] makes many useful rectifications. There were certainly cases where France's memory was at fault. M. Roujon is also a sceptic—at least with regard to the last two volumes of memoirs. How could the elderly writer, with his 'eye on posterity,' recapture his youthful vision? Consequently these 'impressions of childhood are revised and often distorted by an old man whose very subtlety forbade him to find again his first innocence. *Le Livre de mon ami* gives much fresher and more direct testimony.'[45]

There may be two opinions about that. In old age, memories of childhood are often more clear-cut than in the middle years; something like the Eternal Return is achieved. Yet certainly we should distinguish among the several volumes, both as to the quality of the retrospect and as to the nature of the contents. All the Gospels are coloured, to a greater or less degree, by the feelings peculiar to the epoch—peaceful middle age or the lingering look of the seventies—when they were written.[46] As in France's stories for children, the feeling is rarely that of a child—I mean, that although emotions may be recaptured, they are also recoloured by experience. And this in spite of his best endeavours; for he was quite conscious of the difficulty and tried to steer an even course between spontaneity and a belated puerility.[47] What, then, about the comparative value of the volumes?

The *Livre de Pierre* is on all accounts the most rewarding. We need not take too literally France's phrase about the book as 'an exact account of my childhood'—that is like the 'all is true' of Balzac or any other novelist. We may dismiss, as Michaut has done, the reproach that the work does not constitute a full autobiography[48]—such, clearly, was not the author's intention. But broadly, as Giraud says, 'one can draw from it with both hands';[49] and neither Giraud nor any other psychological biographer has failed to do so. *Pierre Nozière,* in its early sections, is of the same inspiration, and tells us much about the lad's environment. It has a good deal of charming 'espièglerie.' It is, however, a less satisfactory book, because of its piecemeal composition: 'Notes on my Old Plutarch' can scarcely be thought of as really belonging. Yet many of the originals whom Pierre-Anatole knew are here drawn to the life.

When the last two Gospels appeared, they were reviewed by some with condescension, by others with amiability. Was not the aged gentleman tempting fortune with his sequels? Yet few traces of senility are discernible in *La Vie en fleur* written at the age of seventy-seven. The more amiable critics[50] found that in both these volumes France was still *en veine* and 'inexhaustible'; that the return to childhood was successfully accomplished, for in a sense he still could hear the horns of Elfland blowing. Some emphasize the completeness of the psychological reversion and insist that *Le Petit Pierre* is much richer in content than *Pierre Nozière;* but others complain of 'an artificiality and a self-consciousness from which *Le Livre de mon ami* was free.'[51]

Personally, I do not feel that France here became too 'literary.' In *Le Petit Pierre,* one may allow for the presence of a number of wise saws, together with a precocious scepticism, which was definitely a trait of Anatole himself.[52] But one also finds a 'tendresse presque féminine'[53] alternating with an elderly whimsicality and delightful flights, like that of the escaping parrot whom all pursued. The same sort of young-old *fantaisiste* appears in *La Vie en fleur:* shall we say on that account that the truth is not in him? Edmund Gosse, deploring that the line was not more closely drawn between the actual and the fictitious, still recognizes that 'the story is a document,' however much 'arranged'; he recognizes, too, the sparkling vivacity with which certain episodes, away from Pierre's home, are told.[54] In fact, a salient feature of *La Vie en fleur* is that the young man is now going out in the world, frequenting parties and beginning (fictionally) his adolescent amours.

Something like the following seems a reasonable conclusion regarding the documentary value of the Gospels. They all contain mention of certain personages and events which are either not verifiable or are invented out of whole cloth. They all include conversations which are doubtless in part deftly fabricated. And the author (for dramatic purposes) presents as crucial or as epoch-making his meetings with certain acquaintances—Marcelle, Hamoche, the Princess Bagration—who were probably less influential on his formation than he would have us believe. The two final volumes are subject to more suspicion in these respects than is the *Livre de Pierre;* hence in the subsequent treatment more has been drawn from the earlier work.

Yet there is this to be said: as our knowledge of Anatole's youth, proceeding from other sources, deepens and widens, it becomes plain that the Gospels offer a great deal of disguised autobiography. More and more 'originals' of his portraits are being identified; more and more episodes are verified. Here is one test that seems applicable. When things happen *outside* of the Gospels—when they find place likewise in France's newspaper articles or in his recorded chats with friends—then such events are in principle substantiated. They move from the plane of semi-fiction to the plane of fact. Thus the existence of Mme. Mathias and of M. Dubois is rendered authentic. Furthermore, repetitions anywhere of the same type of occurrence, or retouches of the same portrait (as in the case of M. Debas) tend in the direction of greater *vraisemblance.* Many of the Gospel narratives are almost literally true.

But I have tried to be careful. When in doubt, I generally use the name 'Pierre' with reference to events that cannot be clearly assigned to the experience of Anatole. It may be that some day they can be more closely correlated with that experience. Often, too, it is less a question of actual happenings than of similar psychological reactions. There the author and 'Pierre,' with all allowance for the distance of the impressions, must frequently be one and the same soul. And it is an ampler 'psychograph' that I am trying in the long run to construct.

§ 9

It may appear to some readers that I treat too fully, *re* Anatole's works, the opinions of preceding critics, particularly the French. I would reply that a foreigner, however practised in French literature, is more content to have the trend of native opinion behind him; and that furthermore the age of rampant individualism in criticism is about over, unless one chances to be a very great critic indeed. Rather than record my immediate and personal responses to masterpieces, it seemed to me of better worth, in each instance, to assemble and weigh at some length the previous *dicta* of thoughtful men. Afterwards, where possible, one could endeavour to strike a balance and to offer one's own considered views. Let us relinquish to more cock-sure critics their immediate reactions. My belief is that, in matters of taste and judgment, something like a true verdict may be reached only through the accumulation, the sifting and pondering of the better sort of suffrages.

It remains to indicate the contributions to our subject made by the leading volumes of reminiscences that have appeared since the time of France's death. These 'ana' vary greatly in content and point of view. When they consist, as they often do, of conversations reported by those who knew France only in his old age, they are subject to checks similar to those suggested above for the Gospels. Repetitions of data, among the reminiscential volumes, make for *vraisemblance;* and so, less tangibly, do the statements that chime in with one's general conception of the character and the situation. In the case of France's thought and tendencies, one should always trust to well-known and abiding trends rather than to particular contradictions, *boutades,* and remarks made half-jestingly. The writers of these 'ana' do not always discriminate, nor is their penetration always sufficient.[55]

The most serious accusation to be levelled against some of the Boswells, or Eckermanns, is the accusation of bad faith toward their master. It is thus eloquently expressed by M. Corday:

Trusting to the simple probity of his guests, he spoke freely before them, he paid them the affectionate compliment of thinking aloud in their presence. But these ungrateful intimates betrayed him. Whether through folly or perfidy, they have often echoed only the more paradoxical side of his conversation. When he gave free wing to his fancy, instead of completely boxing the compass with him [this was his habit, on any given subject], they played up only what they wanted to play up, or else they quoted only his most extreme sallies. . . When he painted one of those familiar portraits, in which he alternated light and shadow, they displayed only the shadow. How many hearts have they thus wounded! . . .[56]

There is little doubt as to what volume is meant. It is the notorious *Anatole France en Pantoufles*—'Anatole France Himself'—by Jean-Jacques Brousson. This *succès de scandale* was the result of the writer's intimacy with France, as secretary and disciple, for a period of seven years (1902-1909). We need not go here into the causes that ruptured the intimacy, nor into the strange account of the rupture found in another of Brousson's books.[57] It so happens that in the *Pantoufles* volume (and to a lesser extent in the author's other lucubrations), there is a good deal bearing on the childhood and youth of Anatole. Are we to accept these statements as truly representing France's own utterances and his then state of mind?

Only with many grains of salt. In the first place, with regard to questions of fact, evidence has accumulated to show that Brousson often distorted the simplest events and their sequence.[58] With regard to the interpretation of Anatole France's character and motives, the question is more complicated. Insincerity, sensuality, and selfishness are often attributed to him; and often, it would appear, with some reason. Yet the total effect of the work is undeniably to exaggerate the lower sides of France's manifold nature. At the same time, there are occasions where measured doses of Brousson, as an astringent and alterative, are recommended to offset the over-sentimentalizing and glorification of still other Boswells. The *Pantoufles,* then, together with other such 'ana' by Brousson, will occasionally be cited below; the reader is cautioned to bear in mind these preliminary reserves.

While suggesting like strictures with regard to France's character, Le Goff's *Anatole France à La Béchellerie* lacks the bitterness and prejudices of Brousson. Beneath the mask of indulgence which the old man wore (he is viewed in the last ten years of his life), the furrows of irony, mockery, and malice are readily discernible. This in spite of the fact that Le Goff is apparently an adherent of *l'Action française,* trying to understand a political free lance, and comparatively a simple soul, trying to understand a complex one. Anatole often monologues here, and his outpourings are too lengthy for us to accept them as *verbatim* transcriptions. But they do make him stand out as a living figure. There is much more about the Great War than about his own youth. There is probably some exaggeration regarding his hostility to the French Revolution.

One thing that makes us suspect some 'doctoring' in these volumes of table-talk is that similar anecdotes are told about different people. For example, in Le Goff as in Gsell's *Propos,* diverse Anglo-Saxon visitors to the Master are represented in the same gawky roles. Gsell deals with an earlier period : *Les Matinées de la Villa Saïd : Propos d'Anatole France.* Although the record of these chats has not been seriously challenged,[59] Gsell is occasionally inaccurate, more often trivial or gossipy ; as in Le Goff, no adequate conception of France's more serious thinking is to be found. It is again the 'Monsieur Bergeret' of Brousson who glides around in slippered ease, amusing, sly, and malicious. This popular effigy, largely built up out of these three volumes, represents the avatar that we may speak of as Anatole Himself.

But among the reminiscential volumes, there are more serious contributions. Apart from the biography of Jacques Roujon—a depressing appraisal, on the whole, which contains little on A.F.'s youth—there is notably the series of *Conversations* as recorded, stenographically, by 'Nicolas Ségur.'[60] While not minimizing the sensual and iconoclastic penchants of France, Ségur's books and articles, according to his expressed intention, are less concerned with anecdotes than with general ideas. In this domain he believes that the Master's views are usually acceptable ; in fact, he has a great admiration and affection for his subject. He hints that the other memoirists have done for France *au moral* a portrait analogous to the one that Van Dongen perpetrated *au physique*—a ribald likeness that Anatole France himself qualified as a 'deliquescent Camembert.'[61] Ségur wishes rather to reveal the man who was 'worthy of his work.' He comes nearer to this goal than any other writer of 'ana.' Sometimes he is partisan; sometimes it has been questioned whether 'Les Mélancolies de l'intelligence' (used as a sub-title) are not to be attributed at least as much to Ségur as to France.[62] Is it true that the latter was never gay? Did his clairvoyance leave no shred of illusion? At any rate, Ségur agrees with the others in emphasizing Anatole's marvellous conversational powers.

A stronger degree of partisanship is apparent in the last two volumes to be considered—Michel Corday's *Anatole France, d'après ses confidences et ses souvenirs*[63] and the *Promenades d'Anatole France* by Sándor Kéméri (Mme. Bölöni). From the standpoint of a great admirer, who insists on such points as Anatole France's 'modesty' and his self-detachment, M. Corday has yet done his best to give us a faithful transcript from his many note-books, written *sur le vif* and shortly after leaving the Presence of his god. 'It is thus France's own testimony about himself that I propose to publish, as simply as possible, without retouches.'[64] At times Anatole's *dicta* are taken almost too naïvely, too literally. But this is better than an excess of subjective interpretation. On the subject of France's youth, Corday is both full and accurate, since he submitted his notes to the Master. Along the same lines, Mme. Bölöni's volume is occasionally useful, though she is chiefly occupied with the period just following Mme. de Caillavet's death. (She accompanied France as a travelling companion and secretary during those difficult years.) In her case, admiration reaches the point of sentimental hero-worship.

The value attached in the subsequent pages to a number of standard biographical studies and monographs may be roughly estimated from the frequency with which they are cited. Yet it has not proved practicable to make complete references for all material drawn from M. Carias or Professor Shanks, from Mme. Pouquet, MM. Michaut, Giraud, and Roujon; nor from such monographs as those by Maurice Kahn, Girard, and Le Moy. Let this be taken as a general acknowledgment to these and similar authorities. Altogether, about six hundred titles have been more or less used. For the text of France's writings, I have as far as feasible made reference by volume and page to the 'definitive' edition of the *Œuvres complètes,* so competently edited by M. Carias. Unfortunately, this edition is not quite so complete as one could wish ; in many cases, it will appear, I have been obliged to go to other sources ; and in some instances it has seemed better to cite from the original form of France's works.

My treatment is not fictionized. Such a method in the present case would seem both unnecessary and unwarranted. Anyhow, I am of the persuasion of Mr. De Voto, rather than that of M. Maurois and his ilk. In biographical as in historical writing, the truth is the all-important consideration. To reach it, no pains should be avoided, few compromises should be made. Neither writer nor reader should fear occasional tedium, if thereby a fuller veracity is attained. And the scholar thus toiling reaps this compensation — that the truth, if not 'stranger than fiction,' is often more richly rewarding. Such I certainly feel to be the case in the career of Anatole France.

I think, however, that the hybrid genre of the 'vie romancée' has left two useful legacies. In straight biography or in 'psychography,' the use of dialogue is permissible for the sake of vividness, where it is based on authentic sources. The same conditions would apply to the psychological monologue, which professes to give the inner thoughts of the person concerned. To be sure, one cannot always tell whether the alleged meditation is perfectly paralleled by Anatole's written expression. One is the bud, the other is the flower.

Some day the alternations of France's fame after the close of his third phase (1896) may be written. At present I am occupied rather with the rise of that fame. Yet it should be said here — it can readily be seen now — that the adorations and prostrations which continued until about the opening of the war, and which often took on the character of a mild mania, were naturally followed, even before his death, by a series of violent reactions, especially among *les jeunes*. Our Bibliography lists a certain amount of this sort of literature.[65] The causes for its existence are well analyzed by M. Barthou.[66] It is not to be expected or desired that the pendulum should ever swing back to the high point of adulation that it once attained. But it is to be hoped, in view of France's qualities and influence, that something like an impartial evaluation of the man may ultimately be achieved. This volume is an incomplete effort in that direction.

§ 10

I AM indebted to various people and institutions, whether in this country or in France, for certain kindly services, often spontaneously rendered.

The American Council of Learned Societies generously awarded me a grant which facilitated a trip to Paris in the summer of 1930. Without this help, a good deal of first-hand and other information in the volume would be lacking. Officials of the Bibliothèque de l'Arsenal were very obliging in tracing down some rare editions. At the New York Public Library, every effort was made to find the vanished numbers of *l'Univers illustré;* these were courteously loaned, on two occasions, by the Widener Library, at Harvard. The Librarian of the University of Chicago, Dr. M. L. Raney, kindly co-operated with regard to purchasing photostats of the *Temps* articles, together with other material.

To Professor Louis Cons, of Columbia University, is due the credit—or the onus—of originally suggesting something like the present work. I hardly know whether to bless or blame him. Mr. Gabriel Wells, the well-known New York book-dealer, and his able coadjutor, Mr. William H. Royce, have very graciously communicated valuable manuscript material: the precious *brouillon* of *Thaïs;* the volume that I call 'Anatole's Scrap-Book'; and certain letters written by France during the Great War. Professor André Morize, of Harvard, was good enough to send on, of his own motion, a quantity of bibliographical references; and Professor B. E. Young, of Indiana State University, thoughtfully forwarded his collection of newspaper clippings on the death and funeral of France. I thank the editors of *The Virginia Quarterly Review* for permission to use sections of an article published by them.[67] Professor H. C. Lancaster, of the Johns Hopkins University, has furnished the most practical and friendly assistance.

My debts to compatriots of the Master are numerous and are hereby gratefully acknowledged. I owe to the late Mme. France the privilege of a visit to 'La Béchellerie'; and to M. Lucien Psichari the pleasure of going through the Villa Saïd in his company, together with some interesting data about his grandfather's library. M. Marcel Bouteron, with his usual kindness, arranged several fruitful introductions, especially one to M. Charles Grandjean, who was, in the eighties, an intimate of France's circle. I thank the latter gentleman for the courtesy and charm with which he received a foreigner, as well as for the intelligent candor with which he spoke of those by-gone days. M. Georges Huard took a good deal of trouble to convey information supplementing his excellent monographs. The late M. Noël Charavay showed and told me some very interesting things. I am appreciative of the constant interest in this undertaking shown by Dr. Horatio S. Krans, Director of the American University Union in Paris. I received more than one hint from M. Edouard Champion and regret very much that circumstances have always prevented my consulting his notable collection.

En revanche, the tale of what I have drawn from the Collection Jacques Lion and from its friendly proprietor could not be adequately told. Not only has M. Lion furnished in person or by correspondence accurate documentation to clear up many moot points ; he also allowed me to work alone in the midst of his treasures during the greater part of two summers. For this privilege I can never be sufficiently grateful ; failing that, I could never have learned many things that are here recorded. Furthermore, a number of the photographs here reproduced were taken by M. Lion himself ; due acknowledgment is accordingly made of this and other favours. Another authority on France, M. Léon Carias, careful editor and biographer, has been so kind as to reply to many queries, either *viva voce* or by letter. Naturally, neither of these helpful gentlemen, nor any one but myself, should be held responsible for inevitable errors.

I am obliged to present or former students at the University of Chicago, as follows : to Mr. W. L. Crain, who arranged for the photographing of the *Temps* articles and did quite valuable spade work in that connexion ; to Mr. J. D. Brennard, who supplied some important documentation ; to Prof. L. B. Walton (of Duke University), who among other good deeds furnished a basic bibliography on Anatole France in Germany. The following seminary students here have written term-papers or dissertations which I have found useful in several cases : Misses Labadie, Hildebran, Sproull, Nottingham, Shipman, and Rachel Wilson ; Messrs. J. B. Allin, J. C. Davis, William Schuyler, W. G. Wing, and others. Thanks are also due to various individuals or publishers for permission to reproduce illustrations or to quote passages of some length. As follows :

To Dodd, Mead and Company for quotations from Mrs. John Lane's translation of France's *Marguerite;* also from J. L. May's *Anatole France, the Man and his Work* and from H. L. Stewart's *Anatole France, the Parisian.* To Harper and Brothers for quotations from L. P. Shanks' *Anatole France: The Mind and the Man.* To Henry Holt and Company for quotations from Stuart Sherman's *On Contemporary Literature.* To Robert McBride and Company for quotations from G. Turquet-Milnes' *Some Modern French Writers.* To the Oxford University Press for quotations from Haakon Chevalier's *The Ironic Temper; Anatole France and his Time.* To Simon and Schuster for quotations from Will Durant's *Adventures in Genius.*

For the illustrations I am again grateful to Jacques Lion for these reproductions from his private collection: 'France in the Villa Saïd' (frontispiece); 'A.F. in 1873.' Also to MM. Lion and Carias for the following *planches* from the latter's volume on *Anatole France* (Rieder): 'Parents and "Pierre" at 6'; 'A.F. in 1862'; 'How A. F. entered the Academy ("Gyp").' To Mme. Jeanne Pouquet for 'Madame de Caillavet'; 'A.F. in 1883'; 'At the time of *Le Lys Rouge,*' from *Le Salon de Madame de Caillavet* (Hachette). To Gabriel Wells of New York City for the MS. called 'A Page of Retrospect.' To M. Pierre Calmettes for 'Villa Saïd: "La cité des livres,"' from *La Grande Passion d'Anatole France* (Editions Seheur).

The maps (respectively of the forties and of the eighties) have been adapted in order better to exhibit 'Pierre's Paris' and 'Anatole's Paris.' I regret that M. Giraud's volume on *A.F.*—an expansion of his earlier essay—has appeared too recently to be utilized in full.

Last, but by no means least, I pay tribute to the co-operation of my daughter and secretary, Avise Dargan Coates. Without her tireless aid, the light of day could scarcely have shone on these pages; *quorum magna pars fuit.*

E. P. D.

September 22, 1936

ANATOLE FRANCE

1844–1896

CHAPTER I

Childhood's Circle

§ 1

IT is related that on a mild afternoon near the beginning of the present century three people were strolling along the right bank of the Seine, not far from the friendly Louvre. The trio consisted of a whimsical elderly gentleman, with a long horse-like head; a vivacious blonde lady, accustomed to the directing of destinies; and a smouldering secretary.[1] They became known to literary fame as Anatole France, Mme. Arman de Caillavet, and Jean-Jacques Brousson.

Presently the three half-crossed the river and in their customary way paused in the middle of the Pont des Arts, with the statue of Henri IV behind them. As usual, Mme. de Caillavet, Anatole's most constant Egeria, ordered the two men to admire the sunset. Leaning on her shepherdess' crook, facing the Trocadéro, she remarked repeatedly that from this point one views the finest sunset in the world. But Anatole mocked and gibed at the repetitions of Egeria, at the hulking Trocadéro in front, at the heavy gallant, Henri Quatre, seated behind. He burlesqued the lady, declaiming, 'Stay, traveller! Remove thy hat! Observe that this is the rarest place in the world for sunsets.' Until finally Mme. de Caillavet, who had seemed unconscious of the teasing, retorted:

'Yes, I love this spot. I can see the Louvre, the Tuileries garden, the Institute, . . . and the little house where the greatest writer of France was born.'

Egeria was both right and wrong. She was correct in assuming that Anatole loved the storied vista more than he would then admit and loved particularly to recreate with his inward eye the scenes that enveloped his childhood sixty years before. How often did he declare that Paris was a fairer, sweeter city in those days than in the twentieth century! It was a *ville-lumière,* as Hugo dubbed it, an enchantment whose light was comparable to that of ancient Greece. And for a youth who adored all varieties of light, it became a passion to watch the swift rippling of the Seine, to follow quaint and crooked streets not yet industrialized or Haussmannized, to note across the river the superb sky-line, including then the time-worn Tuileries. It was his pleasure to let the eye rest, so near home, on the cherished book-stalls and the shade-trees that grew along the Quais. It was his secret, when boyish ambition was awakened, to draw on a sketch-map a bold line leading from that home to the very dome of the Institute,[2] whither the hand of Mme. de Caillavet was one day to propel him.

§ 2

BUT could Egeria, on that sunny afternoon, actually have seen Anatole's birthplace? Let us consider the facts.

The house in which the lad was really born (19 Quai Malaquais) sheltered the family for only a few months after that event.[3] Then they moved to a near-by apartment at 15 Quai Malaquais, where they lived for nine years.[4] Both of these houses were much altered at the time (1862) when the adjoining Ecole des Beaux-Arts extended a wing to the Quai Malaquais; so it is doubtful whether Mme. de Caillavet could have seen more than a memory of the birth-place. If she had in mind the nine-year abode of the Thibault family, it is again doubtful whether that could be called a 'little house'; the four-room apartment and the bookstore below were small enough, to be sure, but they formed part of a large mansion. It was occupied mainly by the shops and families of booksellers, among whom the 'Père France' was notable. His dark shop, together with that of a dealer in old prints, occupied the ground-floor, while the family lived above. Like Samuel Johnson, Anatole had a book-dealer for his father, and the wide and curious learning of the son had thus a natural origin.

These houses, immediately facing the river, were in those days in a 'green and peaceful' neighbourhood,[5] as yet undisturbed by the noisy concomitants of industrialism. Many associations gather round these dwellings. Quite close (at number 9) was the Hôtel de Transylvanie which figures in *Manon Lescaut*. Numbers 5 and 7—the former a fine seventeenth-century mansion—were in 1911 taken over by the Librairie Honoré Champion,[6] whose founder had much earlier (1873) first followed Anatole's father at No. 15, before pursuing him to the Quai Voltaire. Adjoining the France abode (Quai Malaquais) was the handsome Hôtel de Chimay. Anatole relates how he would salute in passing the various tenants and merchants clustering round this building.[7] It is described as a stately abode, 'nobly opening its sculptured portals upon its *cour d'honneur.'* In 1884, the dramatist Pailleron lived in a wing of the Hôtel de Chimay; his apartment, Anatole tells us, was fantastically furnished, and he entertained lavishly.[8]

Shades of still earlier periods haunted other houses on the Quai. Such historic figures as Queen Marguerite and Marshal Saxe, Henriette de France, Mazarin, and Mirabeau had lived near-by. No wonder that Anatole was from childhood swathed in an historical atmosphere; nor that in his old age he hesitated to tread his own Quai Malaquais because it was haunted by 'too many phantoms.'[9]

Next door to the Hôtel was the home of the Thibault family. This building was owned by a certain Pellapra, who appears as 'M. Bellaguet' in the books dealing with Pierre Nozière. But these Gospels are a little ambiguous about Bellaguet. If he had a fine and venerable appearance, he was both wealthy and unscrupulous; in fact, to the day of his funeral he 'enjoyed the consideration reserved for successful dishonesty.'[10] At any rate, he was not too proud to concern himself personally with his tenants, among whom he lived in a patriarchal manner.

The birthplace itself had been inhabited by such celebrities as George Sand—it sheltered the first phase of her amour with Musset—as well as by Arsène Houssaye and Auguste Barbier, the author of vigorous political verse. In view of the refusal of the present owner to permit the installation of a memorial tablet for France, it was decided to commemorate his juvenile sojourn at No. 15. The celebration took place on May 20, 1933.[11] It is true that little or nothing remains of the birthplace, and some aver that the present number 19 has slightly shifted from its former site. But it is appropriate that a tablet should be put up in the neighbourhood; for Anatole France himself made much of the historical and biographical significance of such *plaques*.

§ 3

WHILE Louis-Philippe was still king of the French and Louis-Napoleon was a prisoner at Ham, when Chateaubriand was composing his *Mémoires d'Outre-tombe* and Dickens was about to produce *David Copperfield,* when railways and postage-stamps were just coming in, there was born, on April 16, 1844, a frail man-child presently baptized Jacques-Anatole-François Thibault.[12] The birth-scene was humorously described by the victim. 'I was,' Pierre declared from hearsay, 'as red as a tomato and an ugly little beast.'[13] On June 9, the baptism took place, at the community church of Saint-Germain-des-Près,[14] the sponsors being Jacques Charavay and Henriette Larade, of whom we shall hear more. The name was simplified in quite a natural manner. The elder Thibault was also called 'François,' which, in accordance with an old Angevin practice, was softened into 'France' by friends and customers. Following this example, Anatole adopted the middle and more euphonious terms of his complete appellation.[15] At home and school he was so accustomed to being called 'le petit France,' that he was fourteen years old before he knew his real name; this was reserved for official and legal occasions—to such an extent that at the time of his second marriage, Anatole Himself had to ask how 'Thibault' was spelled![16]

In 1853, the family moved to the Quai Voltaire, where Anatole passed the most memorable years of his youth, and where his father's book-shop became moderately famous among literati.[17] This house (No. 9, Quai Voltaire) had been the final home of the elegant antiquary, the Baron Vivant-Denon;[18] Père France sold his stock and retired, in 1866; subsequently (1890) the shop was occupied by the Librairie Champion, which presently moved in turn to the Quai Malaquais.[19] The Quai Voltaire house, too, though the elderly France spoke of it to Corday as 'intacte dans l'ensemble,' has probably been modernized since the Thibault family lived there. It is now turned into a furniture and antiquity store; but there was much of that atmosphere around the place when Anatole was growing up. 'I have preserved,' he says, 'a warm memory of that handsome Quai Voltaire, where I learned my taste for the arts.'[20]

§ 4

Let us now turn to the inmates of the home.

In the Gospels according to Anatole, the members of the 'Nozière' family are somewhat embellished, legitimately enough, in their status and circumstances. But elsewhere in his writings France does not disguise the fact that he was brought up by rather humble folk. His origins have recently been 'discovered' and discussed. Yet France himself once revealed: 'Je suis né dans Paris de parents angevins et beaucerons.'[21] People have tried to make out a set of Angevin traits—gentleness, addiction to revery and irony—both for him and for his father. What is clearer is that the Thibault family, even before the Revolution and the Empire, were certainly living in Anjou; they were tillers of the soil or tenders of the vineyards in the department of Maine-et-Loire, near Brissac. They dwelt for the most part near the hamlet of Saulgé-l'Hôpital, on the left bank of the Loire.[22] In this pleasant rolling countryside François-Noël was born of a stock that for four generations at least had usually been in close contact with the soil of France. Around Angers and Saumur, the name Thibault is still found; some cousins of Anatole wrote to their famous relative from the former town, and he has been reproached with not answering their letters. But in his old age he could not answer, or even open, one-tenth of the letters that he received. It may be conceded, however, that since he never visited his ancestral home, he did not have the local piety evinced by his father, who corresponded and kept up affectionate relations with his brother in Anjou,[23] was generous in money-matters, and hospitably received in Paris visits from his nephews and nieces.

Anatole did none of these things; and he has accordingly been accused, unjustifiably I believe, of a kind of snobbery. In view of his own statements, it cannot be proven that he sought to conceal his peasant origins, nor is it likely that *Le Livre de mon ami* was written to varnish his parents with a bourgeois respectability. 'France quite understood,' says M. Bourget, who knew him well in those days, 'what he owed to the good people who surrounded his childhood and youth.'[24] Others bear witness that in his later years he spoke most affectionately of his relatives; and on the whole, says Corday, his portraits are very close resemblances.[25] If in *Le Livre* he hints that his people came from 'Le Bocage' or even the Valois, if he romances about Claude Nozière the smuggler, all this is within his right as a story-teller. If elsewhere he allows it to be thought that his mother came from Bruges instead of Chartres, surely this slip is due to his 'nonchalance' rather than to deliberate deception.

Far from being snobbish, the urbane Anatole would talk to any one (except, perhaps, the cousins from Angers), and to the surprise of the *gens du monde* he often preferred plainer company than theirs. As *Crainquebille* and other testimony show, he lived reasonably close to the heart of the people and was unaffectedly democratic both in his childhood and in his later years. Some of his best friends, like Charavay and Coppée, were 'peuple.' This acceptance of his class, however, did not prevent France from embroidering at times the plain canvas of reality. The last chapter in the *Livre de Pierre* deals with his supposed visit to 'le bas Maine' and to the ancestral house 'which sheltered for more than two hundred years my paternal family' ; there was also an ancestral ghost, and we have the story of the noted smuggler. 'I come from peasants,' Anatole admits, but the whole suggestion of the passage is that they were rather distinguished peasants. Yet this episode is purely 'literary,' being lifted and adapted from a tale by Emile Souvestre.[26]

§ 5

THERE is a legend that the grandfather of Anatole was wounded at Waterloo. He was actually a shoemaker[27] who lived in the market-town of Saulgé-l'Hôpital and who married a girl from his own commune. This grandmother could have had little in common with the fictive and delightful 'Grand'Maman Nozière,' whom we shall consider later. The real grandparents had six children, of whom the youngest (b.1805) was François-Noël Thibault, Anatole's father.[28] An elder brother, Louis, settled in the neighbourhood as a *garde champêtre*. The family as a whole clung to the soil, to the military service, and to the Royalist cause. For eight years of his youth Noël Thibault toiled as a hired 'hand' on farms around Lignières ; then about 1826 he went up to Paris for his service, which he prolonged, as 'guardsman' under Charles X.[29] He may have been attached to the bodyguard of the eccentric Duchesse de Berry and long preserved a fragment of the Bourbon flag which she had torn into relics after the Revolution of July.[30] The 'armurier Leclerc,' in *Pierre Nozière,* gives an account of his learning to read amid the confusion of the barracks. This passage probably refers to Noël Thibault. Both men were in garrison at Courbevoie and both used (originally) a simple peasant language, *not* of the kind attributed to 'Dr. Nozière.' It is curious to remember that Anatole's father was illiterate until after he had attained manhood and that he re-

PARENTS, AND 'PIERRE' AT SIX

mained an ardent upholder of the Catholic Church and the Bourbon cause. Only once does he seem to have wavered in this allegiance : in 1848, he was smitten with a brief fervour for the Second Republic.[31] Even after that event he found it difficult to forget his grudge against Louis-Philippe and the bourgeois monarchy. He was a firm believer in hierarchies within the social order.[32]

When this conservative peasant finally settled in Paris and sought a means of livelihood, his new zeal for learning led him into the book-business. He was associated first with the very reputable firm of Techener and, in the 1830's, managed their branch establishment on the Place de l'Oratoire du Louvre. This 'Librairie historique d'ouvrages . . . relatifs à la Révolution' was presently conducted under France's own name. It is thought that his patron, the Comte de La Bédoyère, who had also served in the Garde of Charles X, provided the funds for this purpose.[33] After moving twice, the book-shop came to rest at 15 Quai Malaquais. This was a veritable 'maison de libraires.' There were, in the building, at least two others of the trade ; one of them, curiously enough, was named Mathias.

Self-taught as he was, the elder France became something of an authority on the Revolution, compiling and printing catalogues and even monographs bearing on that subject.[34] A dozen of his catalogues still exist at the Bibliothèque Nationale, while a list of the monographs which he published runs to forty-five titles, mostly bearing on Revolutionary and colonial history.[35] It is probable that for quite a while he read more books than he sold ; his son, writing under a pseudonym, boldly calls the father an 'érudit libraire' and elsewhere declares that he was 'très instruit' ; yet illogically he concedes Noël France's 'insufficient education' ; his orthography always remained shaky.[36] As late as 1862, le Père France wrote to the Comte de Chambord a letter expressing his staunch Legitimist principles.[37] He sold his business in 1866, retired to Neuilly, comfortably off, in 1878, and died there in 1890. In 1840 he had married Antoinette Gallas, who was a native of Chartres and not of Bruges as certain legends have it.

There were a few characteristics which Anatole shared with his father : an interest in the visionary and the supernatural ; a penchant for books, bibliographies, and catalogues ; a taste for collections of various kinds ; a vague impracticality in affairs[38] and a corresponding zest for the world of ideas. But they were seldom the same ideas. Of 'Pierre Nozière' his grandmother said, 'He will be quite a different customer (*gaillard*) from his father.' The remark is equally applicable to Anatole. The son has gone so far as to say that he generally arrived at his own views by opposing those of his father—a method which has been much favoured since the reign of Samuel Butler the Second. The picture given of Dr. Nozière (in the *Livre de Pierre*) elevates the father's station and improves the family circumstances; Anatole admits elsewhere[39] that 'things were on a narrower and more humble scale with us' than 'Pierre' recorded; in his fragmentary 'Autobiographie' he speaks of the time when his father's fortune was 'dure et petite'; yet one witness unjustifiably declares that Anatole 'always affected to ignore the difficult beginnings' of Père France.[40] It seems clear that the various passages concerning Pierre's father probably give the essential traits of Noël Thibault; there has also sprung up a considerable amount of biographical literature about the actual bookseller and his very definite personality.[41]

His outstanding characteristic is that although he was attached to Anjou he had no apparent 'douceur angevine' in his composition. On the other hand, Anatole had this suavity and cared little for those people or things that were deprived of it.[42] Weary of the life-struggle, the father surveyed the human scene through the coloured lenses of irony and pity—and bequeathed them to his son. Some maintain that he also left Anatole a kind of tenacity—the kind that 'holds to the All-Good' in the matter of books.[43] However that may be, the elder Thibault constantly viewed with a distrustful eye the antics, the gesture, the development of his offspring. In *Le Livre de mon ami* he is represented as having grave doubts as to the character and sanity of 'le petit bonhomme.' If Little Peter, imitating St. Nicholas, threw to the poor all his worldly goods, Father closed the window and cried, 'What a fool that child is!' If Peter dressed up in cap and bells and invaded his parents' room, Father decided: 'That child does no good here. He must be sent to boarding-school.' And sent to school he was, after long perorations on the part of Dr. Nozière. It is authentic that the excellent doctor and the estimable Thibault varied their usual taciturnity with long discourses that must have driven their joint offspring wild—and wilder as he grew older. But how amply he avenged himself in his own elderly monologues!...Dr. Nozière was persuaded that his only and lonely child became 'exalted' by himself and needed companionship.

'You are right, my dear,' responded his prudent wife.

Then the doctor, after starting from the history of primitive man and apostrophizing a very ancient tooth, gravely enjoined on his eight-year-old, for reasons pertaining to race-development, the necessity of knowledge and of love.

'Yes indeed, dear,' said Mother a little absently, 'but I really think we should confide him to a woman's care at first.'

The only trait added in *Pierre Nozière* is that, although the lad perpetually questioned his father on all manner of things, there was little confidence between the two, and less as the years went on. They were contrasted temperamentally as well as in matters of opinion. 'Instinctively, in everything,' says *le Petit Pierre,* 'I was opposed to him.' [44] For example, where the old gentleman was addicted to romantic vagueness, Anatole preferred classical symmetry and precision.[45] And if Father adored Chateaubriand, Son came to dislike the Vicomte with an undying prejudice.

Not only were both parents too pious for Anatole, not only did they surround him with restrictions, but Noël in particular was for long disappointed with his son's indifferent attitude, with what seemed his stupid dilettantism and lack of any definite progress at school. We learn from *La Vie en fleur* more of the father's doubts: 'He was persuaded that I would never amount to anything, whether in letters or in science.' [46] Evidently, 'paternal reason' was a considerable force, and it was a force arrayed against the expansions and reticences of youth.

When in his plain-spoken old age Anatole discussed his upbringing, he emphasized the anxious restrictions with which his mother vexed him, but he also pointed out the contrast between the two parents, the father being unsympathetic, not to say unintelligent, the mother more tender and hopeful regarding the boy's possibilities.[47] If, on the one hand, Anatole shared for a while his father's respect for the nobility (*re* Alfred de Vigny), yet Noël Thibault's mania for Chateaubriand was not appreciated. Manifold copies of his works were strewn *ad nauseam* about the house. The stiff old bookseller knew Chateaubriand's fine phrases by heart, declaimed them, recited long passages from *Les*

Martyrs or from the *Itinéraire de Paris à Jérusalem.*[48] Such passages were also used as household oracles. 'Like his favourite author, he spoke of the slightest domestic incidents in the tone of a prophet of Israel.' He treasured the famous cane with which the Vicomte climbed Mount Sinai. It became a fetish, a magic wand. And like the Vicomte — or Moses — descending from Sinai, Noël fulminated from the Ten Tables of the Domestic Law against burnt cutlets and hard-boiled eggs. But while Father grew eloquent, or remarked that his son was a sleepy-head, or received him unpleasantly after an unfavourable school-report, Mother placidly closed her ears to the eloquence, petted the sleepy-head, consoled him about his school-reports, and bravely believed in his future. Noël for a time disowned the youth 'because he made verses,' and the budding poet joyously set up a *mansarde* for himself. Is it surprising that the critical spirit of the younger France was early awakened ?

It is true that in after years Noël recommended his son's articles in *Le Temps*. Even before that, his connexions with the editors of diverse small journals had opened a pathway for Anatole's first critical articles. According to Carias, the father took due pride in many of the son's productions.[49] And the mature Anatole in several passages combined a sort of *amende honorable* to his father with a stencilled portrait of the book-dealer's personality.[50] 'He was stiff, dry, rigid under his black cravat, rather inflexible. But without bending to the opinions of others, he yet knew how to keep the sympathy and the good will of his visitors.'[51] Again in his brief 'Autobiographie,' Anatole describes his father, keynoting the description around the essential 'nobility' of his soul and of his person. The latter is the more conspicuous. It is symbolized partly by the high stock which the old man wore, the sign of a certain pride and high-mindedness characteristic of that whole generation. It was the stock of Lamartine. But it was the waving forelock of Chateaubriand. This *coup de vent,* as he calls it, this carefully trained lock rising high from the forehead, had marked not only the Great Sachem of Romanticism ; it had distinguished the men of 1793, of Marengo and Austerlitz, it had felt 'the breath of terror and of glory.' Hence his father and 'our fathers' in general had lived on the heights, as attested by their Romantic attitudes, their ample and rhetorical speech.[52] The elder France is summed up as a very grave and doctrinaire sort of person — and his offspring adds: 'serious people have always judged me severely.'

One wonders a little whether the stiffness and the severity of Noël France were not in part assumed. Without going so far as to call him a 'tender' or an 'irresolute' man,[53] it would seem that his penchant for self-cultivation and contemplation—with all the lowering effect upon the family fortunes—would not make for a fundamental harshness of disposition. Perhaps he was still a Romantic *au fond,* with a didactic camouflage. At any rate, Anatole ultimately rendered justice to his father's character and efforts, without which the son could hardly have achieved his own peculiar destiny.

§ 6

But we are dealing now with an earlier period when the father was less honoured and the mother was all in all to the boy. In the *Livre de Pierre* she figures as the wisest and best of mothers. Remember that he was an only child; and he was born when his father was thirty-eight. Madame France was then in her thirty-third year. But, first, what is her actual life-history?

Little is known of her background and parentage. Many have spoken of her Flemish origins,[54] and some have even declared that she was born at Bruges. This is an error. Wherever her family came from, it is now certain that she was born at Chartres, on November 1, 1811. Her grandfather kept a mill on the banks of the Eure. Her mother, then aged twenty, was Amable-Antoinette Gallas. The daughter in turn was named Antoinette Gallas. No father's name is found on her birth-certificate, where it plainly appears that she was illegitimate.[55] She is in fact described as a 'fille naturelle,' and the girl-mother as 'non-mariée'—circumstances which will sufficiently account for the silence and mystery with which Anatole enveloped his mother's origins.[56] Although recognized by *her* mother in the year after her birth, the life of the younger Antoinette was necessarily obscure (the two women seem to have lived mostly in the ancestral mill), until in 1840 she was married to Noël France-Thibault. As dowry, she may have brought him a small farm, but according to 'Pierre,' this or another such disappeared as a consequence of Father's unfortunate speculation in the mineral waters of Saint-Firmin.[57]

Antoinette Thibault was clearly a 'good manager'—she had to be that. Apart from occasional squalls, of which Anatole was usually the storm-centre, her married life seems to have been tranquil and happy. We glimpse her absorbed in the household accounts, or planning purchases for the winter.[58] We find her preparing modest but appetizing meals, or caring for the pots of flowers which were her only luxury. 'She was always toiling for our good,' the elderly Anatole pensively remembers.[59] She was constantly occupied with the adornment of her son, whether with getting a lace collar for a childish portrait or with making over his school clothes out of the well-worn garments of his elders. There is the story of the red *paletot* or surcoat, so painfully confected out of an old dress; although Mother thought he looked altogether lovely in this (or in anything else), Anatole's schoolmates teased him for two years about it, and many were the heartburnings at home. In *Pierre Nozière,* this seems to be converted into the tale of the ill-fitting 'tunic.'[60]

Dark, vivacious, with the speaking eyes which Anatole inherited, usually gay and good-humoured, 'Maman' was subject to spells of over-anxiety and maternal concern.[61] Yet this absorbing affection was for long reciprocated, because it was long deserved. France once declared that he never experienced a real passion, except in his childish 'adoration pour maman.'[62] Very significantly, he admitted that when later he approached other women, he sought in them the image of his excellent mother.[63] For she was not only 'simple and good'; she was the great consoler and *confidante;* although her incessant hovering had irritated him in the days of his young manhood, after her death he knew not where to turn. In 1910, said an eye-witness, 'he is still seeking her, his homesick heart demands her. He sees her rise before him'—with all her incomparable qualities. And he makes *us* see her too, as M. Barthou epitomizes her—'living and keen and active, with a spark of mischievousness, but so *sympathique* . . . and radiating the divine confidence which every good Frenchwoman has in her own family-life.'[64] It is well attested that on Anatole's death-bed, her name was the last to pass his lips.[65]

Recurring to the Gospels, we find that Pierre's mother, as depicted in his *Livre,* bears many resemblances to the above portrait. Madame Nozière, too, is full of gaiety and fancy, combined with a shrewd practicality. (The last quality was an essential defence for any one placed between the two Thibaults.) In the boy's earliest childhood she caressingly called him 'petit bêta' and gave him an unforgotten rose. She loved to dress him like the Children in the Tower and to tell him that story (together with many others later assembled in *Nos Enfants*). In the telling she showed 'the divine patience and the joyous simplicity of souls whose only concern in this world is love.' Pierre's confidence in her was adorable and absolute. She told him how 'bad children' were to be pitied, not blamed. She corrected him with winning touches of drollery and laughter; she knew how to reduce his vanity. She spoke delightfully and taught him good French as a truly 'maternal' tongue.

Elsewhere in his work, Anatole's feeling for 'Maman' is reflected, I believe, in the whole tender chapter concerning Alfred de Vigny's mother,[66] as well as in the *Poèmes dorés,* where the parting of David Copperfield from *his* mother is beautifully rendered:

Et le fouet du départ a claqué ; jeune et pâle,
La mère a prolongé son doux geste d'adieu.

. . . .

Et sur sa tête nue, à l'exilé si chère,
Pas un seul des cheveux blonds et fins n'a bougé.

Son enfant ne doit plus la revoir en ce monde ;
Mais après cet adieu simple et mystérieux,
Certe ! il emporte d'elle une image profonde,
Calme, et faite pour vivre à jamais dans ses yeux.[67] *

Gentle to all (but singing to Anatole only), dainty, devout and winsome, she was a woman to leave an imperishable memory. M. Bourget recalls her as 'si fine de physionomie, si douce de manières'[68]—and centring on her son all her joy and faith. How she believed in his future, how she saw him with the transfiguring gaze of love! It was she alone who urged him to 'be a writer,' when neither father nor friend encouraged the awkward schoolboy.

In *Pierre Nozière* there is little added, but this little again stresses the mingling, in the mother's character, of practical sense and imagination. 'Fancy' is perhaps the better word, as regards

* The coachman has cracked his whip for the last time; the young pale mother prolongs her gentle gesture of farewell. . . And on her bare head, so dear to the exiled lad, not a lock of her fine blond hair has stirred. Her child will see her no more in this world; but after that simple and mysterious farewell he will surely carry for ever in his mind's eye a deep, quiet and immortal image of her.— 'La Dernière Image.'

both mother and son. Indeed they both protested that they had *no* imagination![69] This point will demand later inquiry. Here we may listen to Pierre explaining his mother's supposed defect:

> She thought that imagination appeared only in novel-writing. She did not know that she had really a very quaint and delightful imagination, which did not depend upon phrases. *Maman* was a home-keeping lady . . . and the kind of imagination that she had was the kind that animates and colors a humble *ménage*. She could put life and speech into pots and pans.[70]

Consequently, the kind of stories she told were not so much fairy-tales (which some have suggested) as plain tales of child-life placed in ordinary circumstances and adorned with ample morals. Plain tales—but as Anatole said she had a way with her, and he tried to follow this 'excellent manner' in retelling them.

Anatole's affection for his mother has been preserved in several of those rather insipid and conventional 'vœux' with which the French celebrate their fêtes.[71] But a more personal note appears in the letters written her in his eighth year: 'What am I without you? You must bend down so I can kiss you. I want to do so well that you will always be the happiest mother and I the happiest child.' He did so exceedingly well that he compiled for her that same year a little volume of *Nouvelles Pensées et Maximes chrétiennes—par Anatole*. Undoubtedly she laid the foundation for his long-continued interest in religion and saints' lives. She was a profoundly pious woman.

But Brousson, alas! Brousson . . . interrupts the chorus of love and praise; and in this case his evidence is supported by that of others. The carping iconoclasm of France's old age did not spare even his mother. It says much for the force of his long admiration that some of it still survived even at the period of disillusionment. He still feels that his mother alone was truly close to him, mainly because of her fundamental good sense, so different from Father's diatribes. While he dogmatized, she showed evidence of an 'esprit très voltairien' (Anatole over-reaches himself here); while Father declaimed, Mother was sublime simplicity in everything, in the kitchen, in literature...

'The son,' interrupted Brousson, 'practices in literature the maternal method.'

'Flatterer !' murmured Anatole, appeased ; but he insisted that she was at her best when preparing meals in a well-kept kitchen, thus preserving him from the horrors of a school-refectory. In another connexion, he formally admits that his style owes much to her simple grace :

> Yes, it is from her that I get my style. She was an excellent story-teller, who brought out the salient points and made the commonest things *radiant*. Her conversation, my friend, was a country garden, containing everything, roses and strawberries, 'mixing the useful with the sweet.'

What, then, was the fly in the amber ? Why was such a mother not perfect ? The answer is given by one sentence and one chapter in Brousson.[72] (They may both be taken with some grains of salt.) The sentence is : 'Up to the time of my marriage, my mother always tucked me into bed.' The chapter-heading is 'Amour Tyrannique' and it develops the natural consequence of this loving devotion. 'She adored her only son, her Anatole, as her own precious masterpiece.' She wanted him to be famous and honoured, especially in bourgeois circles. She loved him, in short, too well : 'literally she poisoned my life. She stupefied me, she bewildered me. She made me hesitant and timid.' Indeed, she held him in such bonds that he scarcely dared speak for himself, or take an evening off, or have a love-affair. She spied upon his adolescent amours, always sitting up for him, if necessary until dawn, with the implacable candle in her hand and the tyranny of tears in reserve. And this lasted, we are told, until his thirty-fifth year. There are other indications of a considerable maternal fussiness.[73] Verily, there is a Nemesis for mothers, and excessive devotion causes its own undoing. Mme. Thibault was the first of the women who made of Anatole, his whole life long, a sort of spoiled and helpless child.

This darker side of the mother's character is borne out to a certain extent by passages in *Le Petit Pierre*.[74] There we learn that whenever the lad overstayed his time out-of-doors, he found his mother in the wildest state of excitement. These attacks went so far as to affect her health and her disposition. Else, how could she let Anatole see that she was jealous even of his genius ? It has been well said that her 'over-zealous watchfulness' fostered his natural timidity and his habit of shirking the responsibilities of real life.[75] It is questionable whether he ever outgrew the latter habit.

§ 7

THE 'strange case' of Grand'Maman Nozière has not yet been adjudicated. Certain biographers[76] accept her literally as the paternal grandmother who supposedly lived in Paris and gave Anatole some of his notorious eighteenth-century tastes. But the letters published by M. Le Moy show that Grandmother Thibault at least did not live in Paris and was not at all that kind of person ; in fact, it is alleged that A.F. once spoke of her as 'une sorte de vivandière.'[77] It seems more likely, from various indications, that the grandmother of the *Livre de Pierre* was drawn from Anatole's mother's mother[78]—'Madame' Gallas of Chartres, who settled in Paris and married a rascal called Hyacinthe Dufour. Or she may be a composite portrait. Let us consider the possibilities.

On the one hand, there is the real Madame Gallas—subsequently Madame Dufour—who must have been a rather plain sort of person. She had various analogies with Madame Mathias, the child's nurse : for one thing, she frequently took the boy walking ; she lived separated from Dufour, who had ruined her fortunes ; and she had an unequal character, 'a Dantesque face and a weak nature.' Otherwise she was described to Sándor Kéméri as 'simple, gentle, and intelligent.' Undoubtedly, there was such a person in the house ; Madame Dufour lived there when she was not in the country. But she also told Anatole stories—and was a 'charmante conteuse.' Thereby she leads us on to her counterfeit presentment.[79]

For, on the other hand, there is a glorified grandmother who told tales of the Revolution and kept dried flowers in a copy of Legouvé's works given her as a young girl.[80] It was the first old lady who took Anatole for walks, notably on the occasion when they saw the dandified figure of Barbey d'Aurevilly.[81] It was the latter creation who was further exalted into the character of 'Grand'Maman Nozière'—a very important personage. During the Revolution, she had passed through experiences which are magnified into adventures, not only in *Le Livre,* but in such stories as 'Madame de Luzy' or 'Le Petit Soldat de plomb.'[82] To her is attributed the flippant but aristocratic manner of the Old Régime. It is she who is supposed to have inoculated France with his Voltairianism—to offset the piety of his parents.[83] 'Such a grandmother is so evidently an indispensable figure in the entourage of the young Anatole that one accepts her without hesitation'—but nevertheless certain critics reject her or hold that she is 'purely fictitious.'[84]

I do not believe that she is wholly fictitious. The data given above would indicate that she is an artistic enlargement of the figurine, Madame Gallas. Anatole makes her an embodiment of his earliest eighteenth-century predilections. As such, she looms large in his consciousness. If we cannot say with Giraud that 'the spirit of Grand'Maman Nozière seems to have outweighed all other influences,'[85] yet this blended grandmother was definitely a factor in the boy's early environment. We shall therefore condense Pierre's account of her life and death.

In the *Livre de mon ami* we learn of the effect which the death of the grandmother had on the Nozière household. Pierre recalled her as essentially frivolous, gay, indulgent in moral matters, and smiling at the seriousness and piety of his parents. Under the Terror and under the Empire she had experienced several adventures, one of which is narrated with gusto.[86] Her ideas 'danced in her head,' where there were likewise all sorts of freaks and fancies. She married twice; of her second husband, nominally a Nozière, she said that he had 'all the virtues and vices which make an accomplished spouse.' But her grandson says calmly, 'she never really admired men—she admired no one but me.' And this was another element in making a spoiled child of the youthful Pierre.

On the paternal side, there was an aunt, 'Tante Chausson,' thus named both in the memoirs and in actuality.[87] *Née* Renée Thibault, she had married and settled in Angers. She was a withered and avaricious old soul, who occasionally descended on her relatives in Paris. At least one member of the family was right glad when she flitted back to Angers. Hers was a nature not fertile, Pierre remarks, 'in fresh, pure and abundant consolations.' Obviously she considered him a pampered child, and in this as in other matters he felt it his duty to contradict her opinions—the same system which Pierre had applied to Father. When occasion offered, it was doubtless a great pleasure as well as an 'act of piety to deceive Aunt Chausson.'

§ 8

THEN there are the nurses and other servants who composed the remainder of the Thibault-Nozière household. Since Anatole's parents were busy people, it is plain that either 'Grand'Maman' or one of the successive nurses had to accompany the boy on his outings. One morning he would play on the Quai Malaquais, with his dark curly head attracting the attention of the passers-by ; on the next day he might be taken for a walk, 'which was my greatest pleasure.'[88] A taste for gentle strolling was communicated to Pierre by his earliest nurse, 'Nanette.'[89] With frequent intervals of repose, these two would wander along the banks of the Seine, no farther than the Jardin des Plantes and the Pont d'Austerlitz. Scarcely larger than little Pierre, Nanette was a 'holy woman' in a fluted bonnet. They had about the same ideas of the world, and they loved each other dearly. Seated on a bench, 'she would meditate gently about obscure and familiar things.' Presently, when Pierre was not yet six years old, she disappeared like the quaint old fairy that she was. No original for Nanette has been discovered.

There followed Madame Mathias, 'aux yeux de braise, au cœur de cire.' (These 'smouldering eyes' are her *motif,* just as we shall find golden eyes characteristic of Marcelle, the godmother.) Pierre remembers more about Madame Mathias, since he was older then, and they went further afield—they actually played in the Tuileries ! But it does not appear that either of these nurses was one of those gorgeously caparisoned *bonnes* whose flaunting ribbons associate them with the families of the well-to-do. In sober fact, just as Eve came from Adam's rib, so Madame Mathias sprang from the humbler side of Madame Gallas—another left-handed birth. Her character was but slightly changed in the process. Her name was evidently borrowed from that of a bookseller at 15 Quai Malaquais. She first entered the Nozière household as a helper to the old cook, Mélanie, with whom she got along very badly. For the Mathias had a 'difficult character, both violent and sensitive.' She soon became interested in 'petit Pierre,' since the boy had a way of attracting his elders. She tried to correct him for his misdeeds by reading out pretended newspaper accounts of them. Thus: 'At the Tuileries yesterday, young Peter Nozière behaved badly—but he has promised to reform.' She succeeded only in arousing Pierre's scepticism.[90]

It was clear that Madame Mathias had lived and loved. Taking her small charge along, she conversed and condoled with the old spectacle-maker, who later killed himself. She had known mystery and tragedy; they had made her hollow-cheeked, sullen, feared by most people. Only Pierre (*æt.* eight) loved and understood her. He understood her better than did his father although the latter was no bad observer for a meditative man. The nurse's essential kindness was revealed to Pierre by the fact that contradicting her austere visage, 'passing almost unperceived on that scene of violent desolation,' was a small soft innocent nose. And falling into his favourite vein, the grown-up Anatole apostrophizes Madame Mathias. How he could wish to see her again, knitting stockings, with spectacles too huge for the tiny nose! How he remembers her death in the Spring-time, when her modest coffin carried away all their world of common associations! But not quite all, for the character of Madame Mathias reappears, as a domestic aunt, in the *Désirs de Jean Servien*. Both of these women were of the people and left with the composite Jean-Pierre-Anatole a fondness for the sights and sounds beloved of the populace.

There are two accounts of the 'past' of Madame Mathias. One of them is narrated outside of the Gospels and thus seems to place the woman in real life. According to this simpler version,[91] a domestic incident once reminded Madame Mathias of her former husband. She told Anatole that he was a 'very agreeable' fellow. But in *Pierre Nozière* this kernel develops into an explanation of her character.

One day, then, Pierre learned the mystery which made his nurse resemble 'a house ravaged by a fire of long ago.' Through tortuous ways, the twain passed into strange Olympic regions where 'priests of stone' were seated around a square, where a great church darkened the humble shop of a public writer. This person also wore the Romantic *coup de vent* in his hair;[92] he turned out to be the husband of Madame Mathias, who had deserted her, of whom she had never spoken, and whom she still loved dearly, the braggart, the ne'er-do-well, the ex-captain, flotsam from the wreckage of the Empire. And she adored him still! She spoke to him with ardent eyes, with a caressing voice that Pierre had never heard. They talked a little of long-past days; he gracefully admitted that Nature had broken the mould in which men like him were fashioned; and on parting he proudly accepted a few francs which his wife was just as proud to give him.

We shall find that M. Mathias, *alias* 'Hyacinthe Dufour,' was based on a real personage. He will afford proof that Madame Mathias was a partial incarnation of Anatole's maternal grandmother.

Two servants who figure in the later Gospels had probably a slighter influence upon Pierre-Anatole. For a time he felt akin to the cook Mélanie, because they had a like simplicity of soul; he even declares that he owes to her 'the foundation of my moral ideas,' but that is certainly an exaggeration. At any rate, she taught him to appreciate the rude savour of the popular French of field and market. When she retired to a farm, he was much afflicted, and he occasionally visited her in her dotage.[93]

Mélanie was succeeded by a livelier person, Justine of the Scarlet Cheeks, who often escorted the boy to school. Travellers along the Loire valley know that near the embankment of the river there are still found caverns whose denizens are styled troglodytes. Such was the origin of Justine. In fact, Dr. Nozière sonorously called her 'la fille des troglodytes.' Her baptismal name was properly Radégonde—the name of a saint that will become a familiar *motif* as we proceed—but mother Nozière changed this appellation to the smoother 'Justine.' If her youthful vigour attracted her small charge, it was not without dire consequences for the household. There her nickname was 'La Catastrophe,' because she generally wrecked everything with which she came in contact. She fought the pots and pans; she dismembered the statuary; she filled the place with loud and fiendish laughter—altogether, she disrupted the former peace of the establishment. No wonder that in the pages of the later Gospels she is still the source of unextinguishable mirth.

All these domestic characters are almost certainly real;[94] and they lingered long in Anatole's memory. Half a century later, after his great bereavement, he recalled with a special tenderness not only his parents but the humbler folk who had surrounded his youth.[95]

Such was the 'first circle' that Sainte-Beuve rightfully considers so important in any writer's formation. These personages live again with surprising vigour in the pages of Pierre's reminiscences. Together with his fairy godmother and certain others, they show the keenness of his early sentimental life. 'From his childhood on, Anatole France had a rare susceptibility to emotion.'[96] From the first he was captivated by beauty or charm and repelled by their opposites. Again, such vivid memories are proof of an unusual and tenacious talent. Anatole once said, and he probably meant us to apply the saying to his own skill : 'The gift of bringing back the past is as extraordinary as the gift of seeing the future.' Both talents were his, in ample measure.

CHAPTER II

Childhood's World

§ 1

ANATOLE was once urged by a certain young lady to write his memoirs. A meagre compliance with the request is to be found in the few pages of the fragmentary 'Autobiographie' already mentioned, written not long before his death.[1] 'J'aime à me souvenir,' he declared in answer to the young lady's urging; the word 'souvenir,' if adequately interpreted, reveals the peculiar charm and value of the *Livre de Pierre,* as a mingling of *Dichtung und Wahrheit.* One critic after another[2] emphasizes the fascination of these memories. Either France is styled the 'poète du souvenir' ; or it is here that he best reveals himself as an 'intimate' artist ; or he displays the spectacle of life as it first affects the nervous system of an impressionable child ; or in short, 'the power of remembrance is the distinctive gift of Anatole France.' Sándor Kéméri shows us how even the elderly Anatole connected his emotional memories with the masterpieces which he contemplated.[3] Mr. J. M. Murry believes that because of the gap between the wisdom of age and the follies of childhood—and, we should add, because of the sympathy which bridges that gap—A.F. has resurrected in Little Pierre Nozière the most living and enchanting portrait of all his gallery.[4]

France's own testimony is very similar. Speaking in the character of Jacques Tournebroche, he remarks in *La Rôtisserie* that he finds in his recollections, rather than in reading, an inexhaustible reservoir.[5] The author later assembled with loving care an edition of the notable *Poèmes du souvenir* (1910) ; and he once declared about autobiographies in general that usually their first chapters are the most interesting, for in them is preserved the true romance.[6] Yet he is modest about his own recollections, wondering whether posterity will care for 'these trifles' and debating whether he did well to publish them in his lifetime. For as a rule, 'presque tous les mémoires sont des mémoires d'outre-tombe.'[7]

A la Rousseau, Anatole admits that his youthful period was 'marked only by sentiments and thoughts'—nothing much really happened.[8] Viewing himself candidly as an ordinary, hence a representative man (a point which is repeated),[9] he will venture 'to tell us of his experiences and how he has conceived of this world.' He conceived of all his youth, at least, as an enchanted realm—the realm of Queen Mab. So the various volumes of 'souvenirs' cover the facts as with a rosy gauze, introduce an atmosphere of fairyland into the house of his parents, and transfer narrator and reader back into the dream-world in which the boy lived.

We recall the salient examples of this process that Anatole has already pointed out: Rousseau embellishing his *Confessions;* Chateaubriand, with his wistful and winning melancholy, revisioning the years at Combourg; Dickens reliving the early experiences of David Copperfield; since France's time we have the case of Proust using the power of unconscious memory to recreate his boyhood. We shall presently see that there were other autobiographies, more nearly contemporary with Anatole's. Therefore we approach the *Livre de mon ami,* aware that the dreams of youth are long, long dreams; for the book is full of terms like *images, souvenirs, ombres, fantômes,* all trembling back from the twilight-sleep of the past.

These recurrent visions prove that the boy's universe was then 'in its magnificent new birth, clothed with the freshest colours.' Back through the layers of memory, he went to the very dawn of life. This was in Mother's room, of course, a large bedroom with green wall-paper.[10] Pierre recalls how in his little cot, he was drawn near his mother's bed, 'whose immense curtains filled me with fear and admiration.' In this trundle-bed (Anatole confides in his journalistic days),[11] he had marvellous dreams, evoked by the Angevin folk-tales which his father, leaning over the cot, would whisper to him. . . Presently Pierre's imagination turned a small sofa into a horse, a jealously guarded private steed. This was kept by a fair lady in black, who spoke to him familiarly of countries where the mountains are made of caramels and the rivers run lemonade. There was also an even lovelier lady in white. Perfect would have been their betrothal but for the hovering of a villain in black side-whiskers, a sort of Mr. Murdstone, who compelled the lady to exile her small adorer to the dining-room. None too soon the side-whiskered intruder was sent away, and the small boy's amours with the white lady were disturbed no more. 'That is probably why I have no further recollection of them.' But such incidents connect with the admissions of Anatole

Himself, who plainly states that his precocious sensuality was aroused by the caresses of these or similar ladies.[12]

Among the earliest *souvenirs* of these 'primitive times' are the memory of his mother's simple black fichu and that of a seamy stove-pipe hat worn by an elderly visitor. This garment was of particular interest, for out of it came, by some conjuring trick, little dry cakes that had their attraction.[13]

Pierre's father had a small museum of savage trophies and stuffed animals—all of which seemed 'monstrous.' He and his mother preferred a quieter salon, papered with roses; he remembers his joy when in a fanciful humour she gave him one of these paper flowers. Another day, alas!, she dressed him like one of the Children in the Tower; they went visiting, and at the turning of a stone stair-case a dog's bark released a torrent of nervous fear. *He* was the child in the picture; *this* was the Tower; and the shadows in the place were 'animated by my creative terror.'

Like Chateaubriand and like Proust, France weaves back and forth between the then and the now; the closer he weaves the weft of the past, the more beautiful and shimmering is the fabric. Soon we reach one of the pensive passages or interludes which serves as a *Rückblick* on his childish cosmos. 'My life was a small thing, to be sure; but it really was a life, a centre, the midst of the world.' Therefore he was happy in the centre of things. Now let us see how Anatole transfers his emotions and repeats his phrases in *A Travers Champs*.[14] The small hero of this story is enthroned on a rock by his adoring sister:

> He experiences a pious joy at becoming an idol. Heaven is above his head, the woods and the fields are at his feet. *He is in the midst of the world*. He alone is great, he alone is beautiful.

This conception was dissolved by the sudden laughter of the boy's sister. Petit Pierre, too, once imagined himself as the focus around which the universe was framed; and the author of *Le Jardin d'Epicure* laments the common illusion, thanks to which 'each one of us esteems himself the centre of the cosmos.' Riquet, M. Bergeret's dog, likewise believes that he is in the midst of creation, with everything else ranged around him. But in Anatole's own life, he was (*æt.* six) dislodged from his proud eminence at 'le centre du monde' by the rude Fontanet, who robbed him of his sweetmeats.[15]

§ 2

PIERRE's world is peopled primevally by tender giants, 'immutable and eternal' ; they are his parents and his nurses. Around him is a 'grande douceur,' into which he sinks and snuggles. He is charmed by his home, by the light and air around, by flowers and perfumes. He loved his dog, Puck or 'Caire,' who grew up with him.[16] He dreamed of ever-fresh toys. He made many drawings, some of which are still preserved.[17] In fact, he wondered at 'the number of lines and faces that could be got out of a pencil.'[18] Already his plastic sense led him to see, as presently to recall, many things in the form of images. His own pictures are not notable, except for the fact that he drew soldiers by preference. Presently real leaden soldiers beguiled his hours. In truth, the later pacifist once cared more for military toys than for anything else. Eagerly he drew up his squadrons on the dining-room table ; sincerely he regretted the absence of genuine guns and pistols ; ardently he yearned for the day when he might wear the epaulets of a general. And through the familiar Luxembourg he saw soldiers defiling, he created endless marching columns, with their proper equipment. The possession of a drum exalted him to the seventh heaven of delight.[19]

But there were also other kinds of toys. Most important of all was the Noah's Ark which contributed so largely to form his conception of the world. He played childish comedies, with his five fingers for the actors ; he mimicked the neighbours and the scenes of actual life which he had observed. In short, he went through the usual gestures of an 'only child, accustomed to playing alone and always living in some dreamland.' It is fairly certain that the experiences of Anatole with toys and games ran very close to those of Pierre.[20]

The boy's playthings also helped to imbue him with the feeling for form and colour, 'le sens profond des images.'[21] Destiny made him an artist, but caprice made him dream of military glory or of the exemplary life of a saint. Under the latter inspiration, he gave his goods to the needy ; that is, he actually threw out of the window twelve shining new coins, marbles, and tops, and a nice sabot. Probably he was following the maxim recorded in *La Vie en fleur* : 'It was necessary that each of us should give his superfluous goods to the poor.'[22] Evidently, he would be the 'Good

Boy' of the story-books. Later it became clear that the Jardin des Plantes was the Terrestrial Paradise ; above it there was a purer sky, and legendary beasts were strolling round ; thither as to a hermitage he would retire ; and he would put on his visiting cards, 'Hermit and Calendar Saint.'

When Pierre was nine, Grand'Maman Nozière died. He remembers no impression of sadness but rather of a romantic strangeness ; he felt that all the sights and sounds in the neighbourhood were affected by her death. Her weird pale face was unforgettable. Soon he plunged into depths of memory that gave her figure a fresh life. 'I recalled with great vividness all that I had seen her do or heard her say.' This was shortly after the lad had entered the dame-school, which he did at the age of eight.

§ 3

THERE are several indications that about this time Pierre-Anatole was beginning to grow up. He was no longer the young child of the 'primitive ages.' Not only did he go out to school, but his games became more boisterous,[23] and his strength was probably greater. Justine had found him thin and pale and puny. Whether he was sharper than usual, or whether he was rather 'ordinary' is a matter for debate even in his own mind.[24] We have a picture of him at the age of six, a 'speaking' miniature of a lad startlingly alert, with his brilliant coffee-coloured eyes already turned knowingly upon the world. 'Never,' says Sándor Kéméri, 'have I seen in a child's picture a pair of eyes so filled with questioning and with timidity.'[25] He is wearing a delicate lace collar, the story of which he later told the Princess Bibesco.[26] It was rented from a *mercerie* each time that he had to pose. . . How reconcile this childish brilliance with his later phases of hebetation at school ? Was dullness a defensive armour that he assumed ? Of that period Anatole declares, 'I was not at all an exceptional boy — I was timid and sleepy.' The fact is that he was a slight, fragile youth, 'too soon made glad' or the reverse, swayed by an excitable fancy. His parents were anxious about his health and his mother cosseted her only child.

Another event that marked his emergence from the budding stage of childhood was that after the death of 'M. Bellaguet,' the family apartment was remodelled and Pierre was allowed a room to himself. This room, which contained an 'historic' bed and which afforded more privacy than he had yet known, had a great effect upon his inner life:

> Poor room of my childhood, it was between your four walls that there came to haunt me the coloured images of knowledge, the illusions that accumulated between myself and Nature . . . the terrifying simulacra of love and beauty.[27]

But all this is going rather fast. Recollections of Pierre's later boyhood are not so numerous as those of his tenderer years, yet he seems to have kept long the utter integrity and naïveté of children. He certainly knew the spirit of play, the magic charm that transforms a sideboard into a travellers' inn and a narrow passage into the highroad of adventure. There was for some time no rift between the dream and reality.

§ 4

Like a stone he fell snugly in the centre of his pool, and there radiated from him circles widening to the utmost marge: circles of experiences, of acquaintances, of exploration and adventure in Paris. Let us take the people of his immediate neighbourhood, real or fictional. Each of these, according to the embellished Gospels, added a definite experience to 'Pierre's' inner life, his conception of the cosmos. But first the facts, the 'originals' of certain characters, so far as they may be ascertained.

When Anatole was baptized, the Abbé Molinier officiated, and the godparents were M. Jacques Charavay and Henriette-Stéphanie Larade. The Abbé became 'Moinier' in the first chapter of *Petit Pierre* and also appears under the same name in *La Vie en fleur*. Jacques Charavay was converted into 'M. Danquin,' who figures in the last two Gospels. According to the implacable M. Ballaguy,[28] the circumstances and position of the Danquin family, like those of the Nozières, have been much improved in the telling. For one thing, Charavay could not have seen Napoleon, as the fictive godfather claims he did. But such details, one feels, do not shake the verisimilitude of the Danquin portrait.

This godfather is drawn by Pierre as a *bon bourgeois* of definite tastes and personality.[29] Interchanges of visits and of invitations to meals between the two households were frequent. On one such occasion we find Danquin, offended by a prank of Pierre's, recommending strongly that the boy be sent to boarding-school—thus corroborating Father's idea. The *parrain* had a high conception of the historic role of France and adored Napoleon; he cared for paleontology and discoursed on ancient jaw-bones; but most of all he was interested in his food. Pierre would often go to the Danquin household, on the Rue Saint-André-des-arts, where the couple was said to live childless and 'dans l'aisance.' (Neither of these statements would apply to the Charavay family, which furthermore did not live in the street mentioned.)[30] There the young visitor learned a little about dancing, but more about practical gastronomy. In fact, Danquin had in his head 'a gastronomic map of France,' with the specialties of each town clearly indicated. He would serve liberally at these copious dinners. For the rest, he was a 'reasonable' human being, opposed to Romantic ardours, disliking the third Napoleon, and firm in his militaristic patriotism. He is described as short and fat, with curly gray hair and round, heavy cheeks. But when Pierre last saw his godfather, he was in poor health, with diminished *embonpoint*. It seems that gastronomy, coupled with heart-trouble, had been too much for this excellent man.

The true godmother of Anatole was not literally, it seems,[31] the alluring 'Marcelle Dupont,' but (again) a much humbler person. Mme. Larade is not credited with gallant adventures, but rather with an obscure scribbler as a husband.[32] Her circumstances were limited and she had few acquaintances in Paris. But for all that she made a deep impression upon Pierre-Anatole. Let us turn to the *Livre de mon ami* and observe how she is glorified.

Pierre was only five and still had a 'charming idea of the world,' when Marcelle, the beautiful godmother, Marcelle of the Golden Eyes, came into his life. For once 'the reality was equal to a child's dream of beauty.' Her eyes, her singing voice, her fresh lips, all left with him a simple and luminous *souvenir*. France himself once wrote in Marcelle's honour some unpublished verses which celebrate the *marraine* as hovering over the bath-tub of his babyhood.[33] She had been a school-friend of Pierre's mother and had once, apparently, flirted with his father. Her husband, Dupont, was a poor stick, a 'magot' or monkey-face,[34] and Marcelle must have looked further afield for her conquests. She was made, simply and solely, for inspiring and conferring love. So Anatole rewards her with this perfect apostrophe :

Poor soul, poor wandering soul, dear phantom, marraine and fairy, thou art blest by the most faithful of thy lovers, by the only one, perhaps, who *still remembers*. Blest for the gift you gave my cradle, for having revealed to me . . . the delicious torments that Beauty accords to those who are eager to understand her. The child you lifted from the ground became the most favoured of your friends. For to him, you opened, O generous woman, together with your two arms, the infinite world of dreams.

§ 5

It was, then, Marcelle, the fairy godmother, who gave Pierre the early comprehension of beauty ; among other acquaintances, an old antiquity-dealer is said to have bestowed upon the boy his second greatest gift—'the love of intellectual things and the zeal for writing.' With Père Le Beau [35] the *cacoethes scribendi* took the form of compiling book-catalogues ; and Anatole (*æt.* 10) conceived the idea that cataloguing was the finest occupation in the world. A very old man and slightly puerile, Le Beau had a perfect understanding with the lad. His language was 'simple, short, picturesque, like a child's tale.' He was a full-faced person with curly white hair which wound like honeysuckle around his hat. Also he possessed a collection, or rather a wild medley of objects, which may have contributed to form Pierre's taste for *bibelots*—'articles of virtue and bigotry.' In this den the boy's imagination was awakened like that of Raphaël de Valentin by the antiquity-shop in *La Peau de chagrin* : 'I found there an enchanted race of mischievous sprites.' One day the boy discovered Le Beau correcting proofs ; immediately, he knew that *this* was the finest vocation in the world, and he longed for the time to come when he should do likewise . . . Anatole thus summarizes what Le Beau encouraged in him :

He accustomed my childish mind to old and rare forms of objects, he directed it towards the past and inspired it with certain curiosities ; through his regular mental work he set me the example of wanting to learn things even from boyhood. Thanks to him I have become a great reader, a zealous commentator of ancient texts.

Now who was Père Le Beau? There is one obvious answer. For once the paternal example was effective.[36] Noël France certainly compiled catalogues—that of the La Bédoyère Collection is a case in point—and certainly also he taught the trade to his son. Physically, however, there would be little resemblance between the elder France and Le Beau. The portrait of the latter was probably modelled upon one of the eccentric bibliophiles who haunted the book-shop. Or else he is copied after another rabid collector, the Colonel Maurin, whose material on the Revolution presently passed on to the Charavays.[37] It remains to be seen whether Pierre's abstract zeal for catalogue-making was still in force when this occupation became young Anatole's business.

So Pierre was surrounded mainly by old people or by women. But fortunately there was one exception. He attended school together with an alert and capable lad known to fame as 'Fontanet.' Apparently, it was an attraction of opposites, and the association was a salutary thing for the home-keeping youth. Fontanet made gentle fun of Pierre. Fontanet was practical, enterprising, noted for leadership. It was he who teased the mistress of the school and laughed at her poetry. His name in real life was Louis Cazeaux—a name mentioned in *l'Orme du Mail*.[38] As Fontanet, he will reappear frequently in these pages.

§ 6

THUS far the *Book of My Friend*—meaning Myself. Turning to *Pierre Nozière,* we find another portrait-gallery of figures associated with Anatole's youth and with life 'in the Quarter.' There was, on the Quai Malaquais, an open-air booth where a certain vender of spectacles displayed his wares. Mme. Mathias, leading little Pierre, would often stop for a chat with this M. Hamoche, whose rusty collection of medals and minerals intrigued the interest of the child. He was a little bald man, haggard and worn, with strange yellowing clothes. Part of his life had been spent in California during the heyday of the Gold Rush. But M. Hamoche had brought back nothing save misery and misfortune. So he taught Pierre two things. First, that the world is wide. 'It was not bounded, as I thought, by the Place Saint-Sulpice and the Pont d'Iéna. He showed me that the earth is great enough to get lost in and is full of vague and terrible things.' And he taught also the significance of misfortune, making Pierre lose, he says, 'my early confidence in the goodness of nature. I have never recovered it since.' [39] Especially was this lesson driven home when the spectacle-vender fell ill and threw himself from the window of his attic. This is represented as a definite date in the boy's development, for the structure of his world had changed and his old cosmogony was 'thrown into the vast abyss of human errors, along with the Ptolemaic system.' From that time on he could no longer believe that life is a game and the earth a box of Nuremberg toys.

One cannot tell about the reality of Hamoche; and as in some other cases, Pierre probably exhibits his acquaintance with this character as more epoch-making than it actually was. But among the 'braves gens' [40] who undoubtedly constituted Anatole's early circle, there is another and a more definite influence. A sturdier merchant of the Quarter brought him a happier outlook than did Hamoche and shared in giving him an enduring taste which he has often commemorated. This was a taste for the old books which the *bouquinistes* displayed under the boy's eyes, both on the Quai Malaquais and the Quai Voltaire:

> With what joy do I recall the long hours spent before these stalls, under the soft gray sky! . . . There is no more peaceful pleasure than that of stirring the dust in the two-cent boxes and evoking magically a thousand terrible or charming phantoms from the past.

The *bouquinistes* of that time were 'fort honnêtes gens'; among them he singles out a certain Debas who for half a century had kept his stall opposite Anatole's second home. Worn by wind and rain, he looked like a stone statue in the portal of a church. He was essentially a devoted Franciscan, a little brother of the poor. Numberless were his deeds of charity: writing letters for the illiterate, making toys for their children, succouring the sick. Conserving his interest in the life of the humble, Anatole seems to approve these activities. Debas was also a 'man of Plutarch' in his open-air democracy, his dislike of 'tyrants,' among whom he included the third Napoleon. We see him standing there stoically in the early days of the Second Empire, plying a trade and professing a creed that have long outlasted its tinsel glories.

This account is on the whole supported by an article in the *Vie littéraire* of 1893.[41] Here France relates that Octave Uzanne, the bibliophile, has just told him of the death of Debas. The two writers regret that they will not find again, opposite the Hôtel de Chimay, the stationary figure of the little man in the long black blouse. He sold them principally classics—at least, nothing under two hundred years old. The book-dealer was a wonderful talker, in fact something of a button-holer. He was also an idealist and rather a reactionary in politics. An abbé once told him : 'Vous n'avez de bas que le nom.' Evidently, then, this character, along with M. Dubois, the major-domo Morin, and a few others, was portrayed by Pierre under his real name.[42]

The portrait of Debas is retouched in *Le Petit Pierre* where he is made more comic, more garrulous, and something of a bore with his moralizings. On this account he was nicknamed 'Simon de Nantua,' after a saintly and perambulant pack-merchant ; Debas, too, went about considerably. As a good Samaritan, he was repairing the stove of the Nozières when the parrot Navarin escaped, and he shared in the fantastic pursuit of the bird.[43]

Other neighbours and originals, of minor significance, appear occasionally in the Gospels. At 15 Quai Malaquais, there were numerous small rooms and apartments which 'M. Bellaguet' rented at low prices. Among the tenants were Madame Petit, who likewise was a spectacle-vender, and M. Ménage, whose studio excited Pierre's ebullient fancy. More than that was probably stirred by Madame Moser, a 'pretty lady' kept, it was said, by an ambassador. She liked to draw Pierre into her room and entertain him with sweetmeats and songs. Other inmates were the elegant Madame Petitpas and the fat publisher, M. Caumont, who looked so ridiculous in his guard's uniform. In the next house lived M. Morin, a sort of major-domo for Bellaguet and a person of consequence in the Quarter. Morin would let the boy accompany him into the apartments of certain notables and feast his eyes on their sumptuous furnishings.[44]

It was, I believe, the Quai Voltaire home that housed, along with the Thibaults, 'Madame Laroque' and her daughter. The former was an old friend of the family and counted for something in Anatole's first travels.[45] Farther away, in the old Rue du Bac, lived a little tailor, M. Augris, who fashioned his garments badly. In order to save material, this worthy regularly cut too short Pierre's coats and trousers. He would seem to have affiliations with another cheap tailor who maltreated the famous 'tunique' of which we shall hear again. At any rate, Augris was the real name of a real person ; and the same statement is true of the majority of the humble neighbours described in the Gospels. M. Corday says :

> They certainly existed, all these figures in Pierre's childhood : the woman who sold spectacles . . . , the antiquity-dealers, the *bouquinistes,* the old armourer who polished up his rapiers. . .
>
> These depictions of the co-tenants and their abodes are exact. For the small boy penetrated into everybody's home. . .
>
> And he has kept the names of certain neighbours like the book-dealer Caumont . . . [like] Debas [and] Augris.[46]

§ 7

Even certain animals of the Gospels had genuine originals—the dog finally known as 'Caire' and perhaps the parrot 'Navarin.'[47] The latter was the property of Madame Laroque. Between the bird and Pierre a state of guerilla warfare existed. When Anatole sentimentally declares, 'I have always loved animals,' we should be on guard. It depended a good deal on the animal. Among those who really won his approval were the originals of the cat 'Hamilcar' in *Sylvestre Bonnard* and of the dog 'Riquet' in the Bergeret series.[48]

Some personages of the Danquin circle are described in *La Vie en fleur*—for example, Marc Ribert, Madame Gobelin and her daughter, and especially Marie Bagration. But these belong to the days when the adolescent Pierre was 'stepping out,' and will therefore be considered later. Here we may pause to consider a case-history which has its complications. On the same level with Grand'Maman Nozière, 'Uncle' Hyacinthe Dufour[49] presents to the world his ambiguous front. Who was this personage and who his semi-fictional derivatives ?

In *Le Crime de Sylvestre Bonnard,* we read the story of a boy's absurd obsession with an ordinary doll. Sylvestre was old enough to be ashamed of himself, but whenever he passed the shop he yearned for that doll ; 'it took on in my imagination a kind of life which made it mysterious and terrible, but all the more desirable and dear.'[50] It is plain that, but for a directing Providence, Sylvestre Bonnard would have developed into a monomaniac on the subject. Fortunately, there is a God from the Machine. Enter

Uncle Victor, ex-captain of Napoleon's army, a 'brigand de la Loire,' swaggerer, rake and roisterer, who still wore the befrogged *redingote* of the Empire and still denounced the Bourbons. Sylvestre, stimulated by the soldier's brandy, confessed one day his passion, as they were going by the store.

'Uncle,' said he, 'won't you buy me that doll ?'

Jovian thunders emanated from the martial chest of Victor, who considered the request both unmanly and unmilitary :

'Buy a boy a doll, *sacré bleu !* Do you want to disgrace us ? . . . Ask for a sabre or a gun, and I will spend my last cent for you. But a doll, *mille tonnerres !* . . . Never !'

Upon what real prototype was Uncle Victor modelled ? In *Le Petit Pierre,* we find a dissipated ex-soldier of the Empire, Hyacinthe Dufour ; he too is styled 'Uncle,' having married, fictionally, a rich aunt by the mother's side. But according to the record he was the real ('second') husband of Grand'Maman Gallas, and hence the father-in-law of Noël France.[51] His alleged exploits are largely taken from Louis Blanc's *Histoire de dix ans.*[52] He was the 'terror and the shame' of his family. He too swaggers along the Boulevards, bedecked in a long frock-coat with violets on his chest. He too teaches high-sounding moral lessons, which he is not concerned with putting into practice ; he has even more idle vices than Uncle Victor and passes through a succession of trades, none of which detains him long. His only positive asset was a beautiful handwriting which he presently used in copying out Anatole's *Légende de Sainte-Radegonde.* The fact that he became a public letter-writer or copyist and that his devoted, long-deserted wife gave him her all, both in money and service, must remind us of the husband of Mme. Mathias, who shared certain traits with Mme. Gallas-Dufour.[53] Thus we may trace the evolution of a type in a portrait-painter's hands. The one real personage, Dufour, is not depicted until towards the end of Anatole's life, but his image had been known from boyhood and had given rise successively to several semi-fictional portraits : the 'embellished' figure of Uncle Victor in *Sylvestre Bonnard ;* that of Mathias in *Pierre Nozière ;* and possibly certain features of the Marquis Tudesco in the *Désirs de Jean Servien.*

Such a process as this would seem to warrant Michaut's assertion that 'nothing in France's work is more instructive than the invention of characters. We see the elements that make up his personages form, dissolve and form again. It is a slow continuous elaboration; it is not at all an immediate and spontaneous creation.'[54]

§ 8

FINALLY, the youth had his contacts with actual literary and historical figures. There is no doubt that the great *tragédienne,* Rachel, then near her decline, once stopped him on the stairs and laid her hand upon his head.[55] Thus early was awakened Anatole's abiding penchant for actresses, especially for those who could adequately interpret Racine. We are told, too, that M. Ingres, the venerable painter, was a neighbour and once ordered the youth to yield him his seat at a theatre. The behest was promptly obeyed by Pierre, who greatly admired the neo-classical art of Ingres.[56] Jules Sandeau was occasionally glimpsed on the Quai. In the company of Grandmother Dufour, Pierre caught sight of that ancient dandy and relic of Romanticism, Barbey d'Aurevilly.[57] Adorned with his velvet hat, his lace cuffs, and his plum-coloured satin trousers, he strolled along haughtily. Another Romantic chieftain was still visible near the Quai Malaquais. Did Anatole (then aged four) really see Chateaubriand just before his death or did he remember how others had described that tottering figure? At any rate the description exists and has been thus revamped: 'A man with a vast cranium, massive and naked as a block of Breton granite, and whose eyes, deeply sunk in orbits like ogives, not so long before shot flames and now scarcely retained a feeble light,—an old man, morose, sickly, superb.'[58] In spite of his little self, Anatole could not fail to be impressed by the Vicomte. Another wanderer on the Quays was plebeian and smiling where Chateaubrian was patrician and severe. The song-writer Béranger was also visible, with white locks but with a red rose in his buttonhole, still jaunty, the incarnation of something undying in the popular heart. 'Those,' said Pierre magniloquently, 'are the two portents under which I was born.'[59]

Portents indeed; and others of historical significance penetrated to the quiet Quarter. When Anatole was four or five, there took place the Revolution of 1848, with its oratorical idealism presently shattered by craft and dissension. Some fragments of the Revolutionary banners were found at 15 Quai Malaquais. Father for a time wore the uniform of the National Guard, with shako and golden cock complete ; Mother and her women-friends in the building made lint for the wounded.[60] She also probably recalled to Pierre in later years the bloody days of the barricades, but for all that the events of the Revolution seemed to the lad 'infinitely mysterious.' Very likely they were mysterious to the parties most concerned. Anatole dates from these years the awakening of his sardonic sense of history, largely through the caricatures of *Charivari* and the caustic remarks of Godfather Danquin. Girardin was represented as a clown, Thiers as a dwarf, while the oncoming third Napoleon was not inaptly likened to a 'melancholy parrot.'[61]

At this point a short excursion into the history of French literature may be allowed. In that domain, when Anatole France was born, and for some years later, it was definitely ebb-tide. The great wave of Romanticism, a mile long, had towered and broken ; it now receded, having left its thin white line upon the shore. The failure of Hugo's drama, *Les Burgraves* (1843), is usually believed to mark the turning-point. Sainte-Beuve, three years earlier, had urged the disbanded Romanticists to close ranks and make a front again ; but the fact is that a new movement was getting under way. A socialistic and humanitarian impulse was fostered by Lamartine and Proudhon and George Sand—a generous hope nearly attained and then crushed by the events of 1848-49. More enduring was the sociological realism of Balzac, who, in 1844, was writing his last grim novels and preparing the first complete edition of *La Comédie humaine*. The periodical form of serialized fiction, known as the *roman-feuilleton,* was practised by nearly every novelist, including the elder Dumas and Eugène Sue. Hugo, still the seer, was probing his inner and private life, before retiring to his high belvedere at Guernsey. There was no other great poetry in sight. There was no criticism, save that of Sainte-Beuve, who had not yet reached full stature. Especially was there little trace of that inquiring analytical spirit which came later to feast on many cultures, which earned the name of Alexandrianism, and of which Anatole France offers the most complete and illustrious example.

CHAPTER III

The Book-Shop ; Open-Air Schooling

§ I

THE ripples of the lad's experiences widened out from his home into the Quarter, into Paris at large, and into certain educational establishments.

Concerning the value of these different types of training, the author has no doubt whatever. Quite the lowest in the scale was his formal education which will be dealt with in our next chapter. The main advantage of such teaching was that you could get away from it by cutting classes and taking to the streets ('l'école buissonnière'). Anatole's street-schooling (i.e., 'l'école en plein vent') was among the best possible varieties and 'taught me much high wisdom.' It gave him his taste for vagabondage and probably favoured his natural discursiveness, together with his tendency to view life as a spectacle. Still more profitable was home-schooling or 'l'école domestique.' That is a branch of education on which we have already sat long with Pierre. It is evident that he has carefully thought out his three departments of learning and holds firmly by the rather paradoxical order of merit which he assigns to each.[1]

So first, some additional points about the home. It was when Anatole was in his tenth year that the family moved to No. 9 Quai Voltaire, a 'house whose tranquil façade and high arched windows recalled in its aristocratic simplicity' [2] — the Age of Louis XIV. Gone were the childish days of the trundle-bed and Mother's room in the old 'decrepit' house of the Quai Malaquais ; gone were the shadowy monsters that glided around his couch. In either establishment the lad was acquainted with the *res angusta domi,* for, as already hinted,[3] the family lived in the modest circumstances becoming its position, which was half-way between the bourgeoisie and the proletariat. But the writer of the *Livre de mon ami* insists that living at home was in itself a liberal education :

This domestic school was a great advantage to me. The meals *en famille,* so attractive when the napery and carafes are clean and the people reposeful, these daily dinners with their familiar chat give the child a liking for the homely things, the humble and sacred things of life.[4]

Anatole sincerely loved his *foyer*. As a child of eight, 'naturellement câlin et doux,'[5] he celebrated the family anniversaries with gusto, elaborately transcribing greetings to his parents on various festivals.

The Quai Voltaire is a continuation of the short Quai Malaquais, from which it is divided by the Rue des Saints-Pères opposite the Pont du Carrousel. Once called the Quai des Théatins, this street was renamed after Voltaire, since the Apostle of Ferney had died there, at number 27. Other noted residents of the street were such artists as Pradier and Ingres, such a connoisseur as the Baron Denon. But Voltaire's name outshone all the rest. Having moved from the neighbourhood of his statue on the Quai Malaquais, Anatole was nevertheless destined to come ever closer to his shadow and his spirit. But the wheel of Time, appropriately enough, carried him back to the base of that statue, on the day of his funeral.[6]

The environment of the Quai Voltaire is still that of bookstores and curiosity shops; but these establishments have naturally lost something of the old-world flavour which so attracted the growing lad. The main centre of interest for him was his father's book-shop on the first floor—'that hospitable shop on the Quai, redolent of old books, standing wide open to the history of France. . .' In its former locations, it bore the sign 'Librairie historique, spécialité de la Révolution'; but in the new place it was styled, simply if ambiguously: 'Librairie de France.'[7] M. Girard has reconstructed the setting and a typical scene, after the shop was moved to the Quai Voltaire.[8] First, we are to imagine Anatole's father, 'le dernier libraire à chaises,'[9] providing comfortable chairs for his customers and guests. Sitting at ease, these men of letters would chat with one another and with the bookseller. It appears that many Academicians would drop in as neighbours, thus furnishing some rare types for the future novelist. Among the frequenters were to be found such notables as the Goncourt brothers, who mentioned the shop in their *Journal*; Paul de Saint-Victor; the Bibliophile Jacob (for whom a near-by street was named), eagerly detailing his discoveries; poets and dandies and Bohemians, including the half-mad Gérard de Nerval, that belated Romantic; such historians as Barante, famed for his *Histoire des ducs de Bourgogne,* or Chéron de Villiers, the charming conversationalist, and Hennequin, whom Anatole especially esteemed. The octogenarian Barante is described in the *Vie littéraire* as a gentle kindly soul, with a wrinkled face like old ivory. His writings as a historian were less valued by the mature Anatole than his posthumous *Souvenirs.*[10] It is said that Barante supported A.F.'s candidacy for a post in the Senate Library in 1866.[11]

'There came to our shop,' said the Master to his secretary, 'all kinds of doddering old Immortals, released from the near-by Academies. They inspired in me a profound admiration.'[12] (To say nothing of an *emulation* that presently carried him to the doors of the Institute.) Other visitors to the place were the younger Dumas, whom Anatole was later to know well in the circle of Mme. de Caillavet; and Louis de Ronchaud, who imbued the youth with his own love of antiquity.

'How many people have I heard and seen,' exclaimed the ageing Anatole, 'in my father's bookstore! When I think of it, I seem to be walking in a city of the dead, where I am the lone survivor.[13]

A notable document on the book-shop is the article called 'Un Foyer éteint' in the *Chasseur bibliographe.*[14] Although anonymous, this contemporary sketch is probably from the pen of Anatole. We contemplate again the low, dimly lighted shop and its proprietor — and this time the son has more of that 'piété filiale' which he later attributed to himself.[15] He describes the cosiness of the chatty informal gatherings. We have seen how he depicts the grave owner — 'Thibault, *dit* France,' then about to retire. He touches off the clients — bibliomaniacs, novelists, and especially historians. We meet again with most of the names mentioned above — the Goncourts, the Lacroix brothers, as well as the brisk Jules Janin and the Comte de La Bédoyère. The cataloguing of the Count's collection is mentioned. Anatole presently wrote an article on him, in which still other habitués of the book-shop are recalled to mind.[16] Janin, then a sort of 'dieu de la critique,' once received a formal visit from the 'France,' *père et fils;* later, in a well-known 'guide' to the city, he puffed Noël's stock of Revolutionary material.[17]

It is probable that Anatole acquired in the book-shop his taste for learned dialogues and disquisitions of the kind later favoured by Messrs. Coignard and Bergeret. It is likely that the setting and atmosphere of Paillot's book-shop, in the early volumes of the *Histoire contemporaine,* have a connexion with Père France's establishment; there too we find a 'coin des bouquins' and straw-seated chairs. Indeed, as early as *La Rôtisserie* there is a passage that reads like a reminiscence. 'Among the people,' says Jacques Tournebroche, 'who come to turn over my new books and chat among themselves, there are learned historians and sacred orators. . .'[18] In his last years, Anatole Himself would frequently drive from La Béchellerie to lounge and talk in Tridon's book-shop in Tours. In fact, the bookstore theme is a constant one in his life and work.

Back on the Quai Voltaire, we can fancy the lad's 'quaint little figure slipping in and out,' listening with all alertness, brushing past the folios and the catalogues. The Goncourts remembered him as 'a good little boy, who always seemed to have a cold in the head.'[19] As for the catalogues, some of them still survive, bearing the stamp of 'France, Libraire,' and annotated in a careful hand with regard to the prices demanded.[20] When the youth is away in Normandy he pines for the shop and writes his father a letter mentioning various habitués and complimenting the elder France on presiding over such distinguished reunions.[21]

A hostile critic observes that throughout all M. Girard's documentation, Anatole appears as the 'prisoner of his environment':[22] he sees everything, drawings and monuments, life and nature, through a literary medium. His brain became a book-shop. At any rate, as regards bookish tastes, the boy probably 'owed more to his father than to his professors.'[23] At an early date he is aware of the jargon and the technique of the trade. Presently he buys and sells a little both for Father and for himself, learns to cover his books, catalogue them, and give bibliographical indications (doubtless remembering Père Le Beau). A technical knowledge of printing processes was also attained. He learned to correct other people's proof, before correcting his own. Occasionally, when opening his father's packages, he finds a way to commit petty larceny, with his mother as confederate. In many ways, his 'bibliophily' is attested.[24]

In those early days Anatole still had orthodox tendencies. He made his first communion in June, 1856.[25] His orthodoxy was perhaps fostered by certain bookish priests with whom he came in contact either in the store or on the Quais just outside. There was the astronomical Abbé Matalène and later the Chanoine Trévoux, who bore off saints' lives in his cassock. As for the Abbé Blastier, 'grand, grave et solennel,' who often came to chat with Noël France, he served as the model for the severe Abbé Lantaigne in the *Histoire contemporaine*.[26]

The taste most evidently encouraged by the whole atmosphere of the book-shop and its vicinity was A.F.'s abiding love for history. Not only were half the visitors to the place historians. Not only did the boy know them and admire them in the flesh. He read and even bought such works as Guizot's *Civilisation en France,* a history of religion, a *Histoire d'Avranches,* and archæological guides. 'L'histoire . . . il en était tout imprégné.'[27] Frequently afterwards Anatole refers to his fondness for the past, a love which he believes 'innate in man.'[28]

§ 2

He had only to step outdoors to find history and literature 'leaning against the parapets of the Quay.' We have heard already his mature apostrophe to the *bouquinistes,*[29] but one should realize how early the boy became acquainted with his father's colleagues, how he ran commissions to various shops and learned to haunt the 'open-air school' of the stalls along the Seine and in the narrow streets of the Quarter. Another apostrophe, in the *Livre de mon ami,* has been thus rendered:[30]

Ye old rapacious Jews of the Rue du Cherche-Midi, ye artless book venders of the quays, my masters all! How greatly am I beholden to you! To you I owe as much, nay even more, than to school itself, for the training of my intellect. It was you, good folk, who displayed to my enchanted gaze the mysterious tokens of a bygone age and all manner of precious memorials of the pilgrimage of the human mind. Even as I turned over the old tomes in your boxes, or gazed within your dusty stalls laden with the sad relics of our sires and their golden thoughts, I became insensibly imbued with the most wholesome of Philosophies. Yes, my friends, it was when rummaging about among those musty books, those scraps of tarnished metal-work, those fragments of old, worm-eaten carvings which you used to barter for your daily bread, that my childish spirit recognized how frail and fleeting are all the things of this world. I divined that we living beings were but ever-changing figures in the world's great Shadow Show ; and even then my heart inclined to sadness, gentleness, and pity.

Much later he expresses more bitterly this lesson of illusion, declaring that the conversion of great ideas and ambitions into dead bones convinces one that authorship too is vanity and nothingness.[31] But such was not his earlier view. Rather, the first thrills that he experienced in browsing among these tattered volumes persuaded him that he in turn was destined to produce the like and to join the fatal race of authors.[32] Certainly for most readers he became the 'singer' of the book-stalls and the Quais. 'That corner of Paris dates as surely from him as the Boulevard Saint-Germain dates from the Baron Haussmann. Little Pierre and Sylvestre Bonnard gave their peculiar poetry to the Quais. Before 1880, they scarcely counted.'[33] That is, these localities were but slightly known, they awaited the sympathetic eye and the interpreting pen. They were brought into literature and history by Anatole France ; therefore they 'belong to him,' just as the country around Mâcon belongs to Lamartine or the Midi to Mistral.

The theme of the *bouquins* is clearly a major one, for it persists into A.F.'s later years.[34] Throughout the autobiographical volumes we may see this liking for old books originating, developing, blending with the similar taste for old furnishings, trinkets, *bibelots,* which came to be so strong a part of Anatole's equipment. Such were the lasting consequences of his early environment and such was the basis of his omnivorous dilettantism. He reiterates that his sympathy for collectors and his interest in their collections were formed in boyhood.[35] In the *Livre de Pierre* we find him addicted to the grotesque engravings of Callot—exposed in the windows of Mme. Letord[36]—as well as to Chinese idols, and later to the *images d'Epinal.* These have been defined as 'cheaply printed and crudely coloured pictures in broadside form, with brief accompanying letterpress containing fables, legends, or fairy-tales.'[37] Very soon it will be manifest that these were just the subjects best loved by little Pierre, the nectar that long fed his dreamy imaginings. And old engravings of the better type gave him many hints for the stories and descriptions of his maturity.[38]

§ 3

It was not difficult for the boy to pass from the 'city of books' to the 'city of bricks,'[39] for he was also a lover of the sights and sounds in the busy Parisian thoroughfares. He is echoing Molière and still older writers when he ranks himself as among the 'badauds de la grande ville.' The *Livre de Pierre* also declares: 'I was born a spectator, and I think I shall keep all my life that open-mindedness of the street-loafer whom everything amuses.'[40] Almost from infancy he was especially amused by the spectacle of the left bank, the true country of his heart. All that quarter of old Paris along the river then flowered with book-shops, print-shops, and the allurements of the antiquity-dealer's windows:

Even more then than now, this curiosity-mart was abundantly equipped with old furniture, old prints, pictures and books, carved credences, flower-pots, enamels, decorated crockery . . . , tapestry *à personnages,* illustrated books, and first editions morocco-bound.[41]

He summarized these delights: 'We loafed, we bargained, we looked at pictures.' Sometimes he would gaze into the windows on the Quai Voltaire with Etienne Charavay, the son of Jacques, who was equally enamoured of the past.[42] Sometimes Fontanet-Cazeaux was his companion. But Fontanet was less absorbed than Pierre in this window-shopping. The former laughed while the latter adored weird ancestral portraits, sorcery-books, and the kind of medieval armour that is now installed in the Musée Cluny. Pierre once proposed that they should establish a Museum of their own. Failing that, the lad feasted his eyes on the free 'open-air exhibition' and stored his mind with images from the past; when fourteen or fifteen he definitely renounced the gluttonous joys of the pastry-shop for the trinity of books, prints, and bric-à-brac. Responding to their lures, he will presently become a confirmed addict of the Quais and the antiquarians.

Another result: 'All that I saw about the streets, whether men, animals, or things, contributed to make me realize life in its simple and strong forms. There is nothing like the street to make a child understand the social machine.' Walking to and from school, he would see the milkwomen, the water-bearers, the coal-dealers; the shops of butcher, grocer, and wine-seller; the regimental bands. Thus he has kept 'an affectionate curiosity for the trades and trades-people.'

The last two Gospels revive memories of this street-life that are too specific to be untrue. We hear more about Anatole's taste for loafing and a defence thereof ; we are reminded that 'of all the schools that I frequented, *l'école buissonnière* was the most profitable.' Mother would often take him shopping—not into large department stores, which then were non-existent—but into small drygoods establishments, bearing such quaint names as 'Les Deux Magots' or 'Le Petit Saint-Thomas.' The former has long since vanished from the Rue de Seine, but strollers along the Boulevard Saint-Germain will recall a café bearing that name. The latter shop on the Rue du Bac, with its display of sumptuous stuffs, embroideries, and the like, seems to have encouraged in Pierre a strong and abiding taste for the decorative arts. As a good housekeeper, 'Maman' bought her own groceries, each from a special shop-keeper who is named and located by Anatole, sixty years later. It was after one of these expeditions that Pierre made his characteristic inquiry :

'Mother, who gives the money in the shops, the man who sells or the man who buys ?'[43]

Familiar and neighbourly street-names recur in a cozy way throughout the reminiscences—the Rue Bonaparte and the Rue de l'Université and the 'belle rue du Bac,' with its picturesque stores. After school, Pierre and Fontanet, leaving the further reaches of Rue Notre-Dame-des-Champs, would usually come along the old-world Rue du Cherche-Midi, wending to their respective homes on the Rue des Saints-Pères and the Quai Voltaire. On one occasion, looking for a 'poor but worthy' person in order to give him alms, they pursued unlikely specimens from a cabaret on the Rue Vavin, through the Carrefour de la Croix-Rouge, even unto the Street of the Holy Fathers. (There it was discovered that the latest candidate for their charity was decorated and wore a red ribbon in his button-hole.)[44]

Towards the end, the aged Anatole recalls the larks that he and young Etienne shared upon the Quais and smiles at their unextinguishable laughter. . . In *La Vie en fleur* he insists that after three-score years he can hear the rattle of the yellow omnibuses ; he remembers the very first time he saw people watering gardens and milking cows ; he is still persuaded that he learned

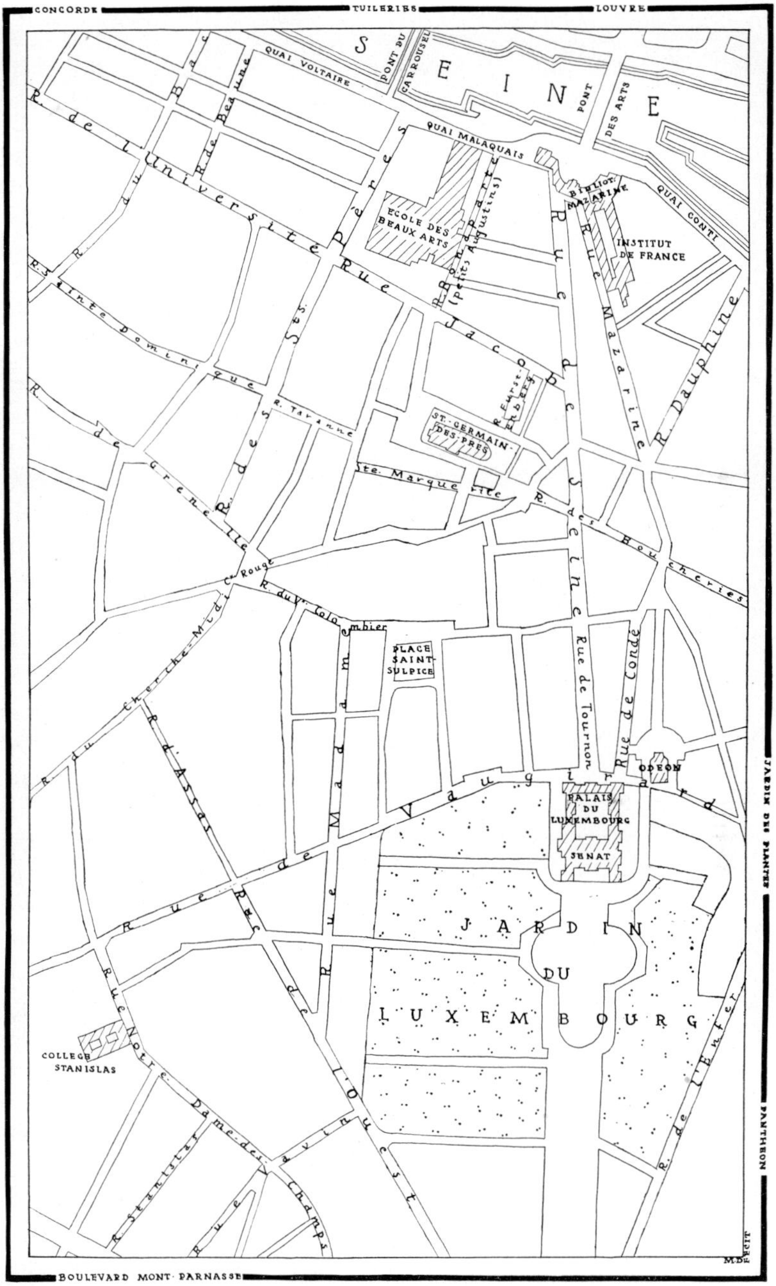

MAP A. PIERRE'S PARIS

more from such sights than from months of school—that day marked the beginning of his respect and liking for manual arts and artisans.[45]

In his own *Book,* Pierre tells us that he would mingle with the street-life the visions of beauty that he found in ancient poets. Reading as he walked, he would suddenly jostle against a dray-horse or a tradesman carrying a basket on his head. Or he would devour the *Antigone* by the flickering light of a chestnut-stall kept by an Auvergnat at the corner of the Rue de l'Université.[46] The reality did not jar with the dream, since both were simple and true, both profoundly interwoven with his youth.

Perhaps the most fascinating spot of all was the Luxembourg garden, across a corner of which he can still see his former self skipping to school. He can evoke this 'petit bonhomme' in Autumn when the skies are ashen and sober, when the Luxembourg is more beautiful in its melancholy, when 'the leaves fall one by one on the white shoulders of the statues.' . . Not until the shadows of evening descend on the avenues does the little phantom of yore fade away.

So in the poem called 'l'Auteur à un ami,' [47] Anatole later speaks of their strolling in the Luxembourg when the 'miserly' November sun is about to set. The cry of the children is heard no more round the great basin, but even in the chilly dusk amorous couples still linger and murmur upon the lovely terraces.

> La bise fait rouler les feuilles du platane
> Au sable de l'allée et fouette également
> Les cheveux tout blanchis au col d'une soutane
> Et le tulle qui presse un visage charmant.*

There are a dozen such vignettes. It was on the terrace of the Luxembourg, by the statue of Queen Margaret of Navarre, that Sylvestre Bonnard was insulted by the self-confident young Gélis. And when Anatole was a young man the Luxembourg became a centre for the gatherings and discussions of his group. It is not surprising, then, that he gives us more than one 'direct vision' of this garden, as well as of the Quais.[48]

Many of his adolescent preoccupations reappear in the inter-

* The cold Norther tosses down the leaves of the plane-trees into the sand of the foot-path, and lashes with equal vehemence the white locks falling on the collar of a cassock and the veil of tulle around a charming young face.

mediate Gospel, *Pierre Nozière*.[49] Here again are objects of art, old books, and little tableaux of Paris. From early childhood Pierre contemplated 'precious armour' and Dresden china in shop-windows, or else he gazed at the blue glasses and medals of M. Hamoche on the Quai. 'Brought up in the dust of books and *bibelots*,' he came to know all kinds of ferret-like collectors and found them a very good sort of people. A certain Leclerc kept ancient armour and was for ever polishing old swords. 'His shop was full of halberds, morions, cuirasses, greaves, and spurs, and I remember seeing a fifteenth-century targe ornamented with gallant devices—a marvellous flower of chivalry.' So marvellous were the suits of Saracen armour, oval helmets, and damasked bucklers, that he still likes to think of Voltaire's Orosmane as thus arrayed. Significant admission ! His imagination deliberately plays round the facts, and the medieval glamour is at this stage the predominant charm of all the antiquity-shops.[50] As for the book-stalls, they make a worthy coronet for the region encompassed by the Seine—'le vrai pays de gloire,' as Anatole, echoing Baudelaire,[51] liked to call it. Not for the last time,[52] he gives a history of the *bouquinistes*, starting in the seventeenth century. 'Even the Elysian Fields offered nothing to the ancient dead that the modern Parisian may not find on the Quais, from the Pont-Royal to the Pont Notre-Dame.'

§ 4

THUS we may watch the germination of the Complete Parisian, 'the most profoundly Parisian of all our writers,' yet with something of the Athenian about him too.[53] The enduring love for his city and her time-honoured institutions came to be more and more central in his work and thought. It inspired many numbers of *l'Univers illustré*.[54] It animates the pictures of old Paris which decorate *La Rôtisserie*. It furnishes occasional *motifs* in most of Anatole's contemporary novels. And it so permeates the memories of the four Gospels that we may well seek to reconstruct that Paris of the 1850's which was the chief impersonal factor in Pierre's formation.

The city was still, says Claude Berton, 'physically and morally Napoleonic,'—until the Baron Haussmann, obeying another Napoleon, upset the topographical apple-cart. But in the early fifties, the main lines were still those drawn by the First Emperor. 'Paris had its large gardens, its old mansions, and its tortuous streets in which people plied a number of curious and vanishing little trades.[55] Glimpses of the little trades are provided by Anatole, while as for the crooked streets he makes it plain that few of the modern great arteries existed on the left bank. The Rue de Rennes, which seems so indispensable today, had not been cut through, the Boulevard Raspail was unheard of, and if there were some long avenues at least one of them soon led (on the famous day when he played hooky) into semi-pastoral neighbourhoods, where the populace was engaged in its primitive occupations. On the way were to be noted many strange customs, a great variety of period architecture, trees 'leaning over old walls,' an abundance of horses and diverse vehicles. Needless to add, 'Paris was then more attractive than it is today.' For then, 'a great prefect was just beginning those large *percées* through which would flow all too freely monotony and mediocrity, ugliness and ennui.'[56] There were no 'vulgar tramways' and few railways, industrialism was not rampant, and as Deschamps puts it, Parisians could still enjoy a 'land of smiling contours and gentle leisure.'[57] All agree that a tranquillity then reigned which this age rarely knows.

The alluring street-life beckoned Pierre first along the marges of the river, when he was held in leading strings by old Nanette. It seemed to the docile child that the bathing-boat of 'La Samaritaine' was certainly Noah's Ark, while 'beyond the bridge of Austerlitz extended the marvellous countries of the Bible'—hence Pierre's original identification of the Jardin des Plantes with the Garden of Eden. (The main difference, under Louis Napoleon, was that the angel with a flaming sword had been replaced by a soldier in red trousers; otherwise the two gardens had pretty much the same fauna and flora.) To the East, the hardy young adventurer dared not go beyond the Pont d'Austerlitz and the Jardin des Plantes, which was then the main 'sight' in Paris.[58] To the West, as he later told Ségur, 'the Universe was bounded by the hill of the Trocadéro,' which, still uncrowned by its grotesque monument, reared its native verdure beyond his domain. 'And it seemed to me an extraordinary world of marvels which I would never finish exploring; it was indeed inexhaustible, since it altered with my changing self.'[59]

So, in the reign of Nanette, the circles of Pierre's metropolitan experiences widened quite slowly; in fact, the universe centred still on the Quai Malaquais, with its pleasant plane-trees and its ancient mansions. But he extends the horizon: 'I joyfully breathed in the air which bathes that region of elegance and glory, the Tuileries, the Louvre, the Palais Mazarin.' On the Quais, he admired the fine façade of the Mint, softened by the myrtles around it; and in after-years he recalled how he and his grandmother often directed their walks toward this 'beau gros bâtiment.'[60]

And the Seine, 'cette belle eau,' was the silver chain that bound these things together. It was his own 'royal river, garlanded with stone.' He adored the natural grace of its ripples, he admired the 'charming miracle' of its ever-new reflections. Yet he loved it so well (we read in *Pierre Nozière*) that he could have wished it to be always the same, a constant chord in his inner harmonies. Its perpetual flow may have helped impress on Pierre the lesson of 'l'écoulement des choses,' the Eternal Flux. At any rate, how often, from the parapet or the windows of his home, he must have watched the diverting spectacle of the passing boats, how often he must have thrilled at the view of the great palaces, new worlds to conquer, just across the bridges![61]

In his early years, the boy knew little of the right bank, but he soon followed the Rue des Petits-Augustins (now Rue Bonaparte, of many bookish associations) 'to the very end, and I thought it was certainly the end of the world.' The fountain of the Place Saint-Sulpice was guarded by four horrific giants—namely, the statues of Bossuet, Fénelon, Fléchier, and Massillon. Crouching under the statue of a Roman cavalier in the Champ-de-Mars, an old woman sold *coco,* probably harnessed in the quaint paraphernalia of her trade.[62] And the 'new Quarters,' round what is now the gay Pont d'Iéna, were then deserted and silent.[63]

With the cook, Mélanie, Pierre would go on long slow walks, by turns monotonous or inspiring. They would wander in the gardens and the open spaces—the Tuileries, the Luxembourg, even as far as the Trocadéro and the Champs-Elysées. 'Country followed country . . . whether blooming or arid, populous or deserted.' But however far they went, there was always another country just beyond, inaccessible and for ever to be desired. . .[64] They pushed even to the Southern boundary, the Barrière d'Enfer; for in those days the more compact city did not reach to the fortifications.[65] The boy did not particularly care for this region, nor for the still more desolate *banlieue* around Billy and Grenelle; yet his keen eyes would take in the characteristic dusty streets, the cabarets, the street venders hawking their wares. He wondered at the great glowing jars in the windows of the pharmacies.

Little by little, the near right bank fell within his province; and here there was much to satisfy the budding artist with an historical sense. The palace of the Tuileries was not yet burned by the mob and razed by certain 'bourgeois malfaisants'; its garden had long been a 'royal and familiar' playground for Pierre;[66] but it was naturally the Louvre which came to be his chief educator in matters artistic. At one period in his adolescence, Anatole visited its galleries 'almost daily,' finding there a spacious centre for all his tastes.[67] He loved the 'Louvre des Valois,' as he usually called it, from its splendid Renaissance façade, through its superb galleries, to the remoter halls, where Assyrian and Babylonian potentates still hold a diminished sway. As for Notre-Dame, he liked it so well that he once missed an important examination, while musing away the time in the towers of the cathedral.[68]

§ 5

In the book of *Pierre Nozière* it is apparent that the youth is already reaching toward a conception of the *ensemble* of Paris. This student could divine sermons in stones, in that *paysage lapidaire* (the phrase is a *motif*)[69] which becomes living history along the quays, uphill and downhill, from the Palais-Bourbon to Notre-Dame. We hear again of the jewel-like Louvre, of the Pont-Neuf, humped-back Atlas of the Parisian world. It had supported three centuries of citizens, who had shouted in their time 'Vive le roi!' as the golden carriages swept by, or who in their time had pushed the Revolutionary cannon that made an end of privilege. 'All the soul of France has passed over those ancient arches whose stone masks, smiling or grimacing, seemed to express the miseries and glories they have witnessed during these ages.'[70] You see the Place Dauphine with its houses of brick just as they have stood for centuries. You see, he enumerates, the Palais de Justice, the restored spire of the Sainte-Chapelle, the Hôtel de Ville, and the towers of Notre-Dame. So we feel the continuity of the generations and of their work ; Pierre's tender admiration for Paris makes him believe that the mission of the capital has been and will always be to enlighten the world ; such is the message of the stones.

That message is confirmed by certain articles in *l'Univers illustré* as well as by the whole tenor of France's address to the *Société historique d'Auteuil et de Passy* (1894).[71] There he insists again that 'the stones speak to those who know how to understand them'; and he evinces a lively interest in local antiquities, the birthplaces of notables, the 'piety' of reminiscences that are attached to small spots — for out of nuggets like these the golden ingots of History are fashioned. Time and again, he protests against the depredations — or restorations — of those who efface from monuments the succession of historical records.[72]

In the later Gospels, frequent are the echoes issuing from charming old streets or reverberating from civic shrines endeared by long associations. There is the church of Saint-Etienne-du-Mont, with its ornate façade ; there is the dome of the Pantheon, with its 'perfect curve'; and intermittently the Bibliothèque Sainte-Geneviève, the haunt of studious hours. . .

> O siècles ! ô souvenirs ! ô monuments augustes des générations ! [73]

Intertwined or inlaid with such Parisian memories are appreciations that seem less characteristic of inartistic boyhood than of the later period when the reminiscences are transcribed.[74]

§ 6

THUS France grew into a wide and comprehensive understanding of the city as a whole : 'I am a Parisian with all my spirit and all my flesh ; I know all the streets of Paris, I adore all its stones.'[75] From Monsieur-le-Prince to Grenelle, from the statue of that lusty vital gallant, Henry of Navarre, to the tiny morgue, that symbol of death, he feasts his keen eyes on this 'landscape in stone,' this *paysage lapidaire*. It does not seem to him possible to have a commonplace mind, 'if one was brought up on the Quais . . . by the glorious stream of the Seine, which glides among the towers, turrets, and spires of old Paris.' The picture thus suggested is completed by the famous panorama enjoyed by Sylvestre Bonnard. Like the Thibault family, the old scholar lived on the

Quai Malaquais. His windows looked out on the river, the bridges, and the Louvre of the Valois kings. He believed that this was 'the most illustrious and most beautiful spot in the world.' Sometimes the view is veiled by frost-crystals on the window-panes. Sometimes the sky is of a delicate gray, the true Parisian sky, 'plus animé, plus bienveillant et plus spirituel' than the brilliant azure enfolding the Bay of Naples. The soft light falls 'on the men and the beasts of the city, who toil at their daily tasks'; on the boats unloading their cargoes; on the cab-horses, each patiently munching his oats from the nose-bag attached to his head. But the heart of the panorama is this:

> All that I discover from my window—to the left the horizon extending to the hills of Chaillot, revealing the Arc-de-Triomphe as a marble thimble; [in the centre] the Seine, *fleuve de gloire* [again!], its bridges, the lindens of the Tuileries Terrace, the Renaissance Louvre, carven like a jewel; to the right, over towards the Pont-Neuf, the old and venerable Paris with its towers and steeples—all that is *my very life, my very self, and I would be nothing without these things* which are reflected by a thousand nuances of my thought, which inspire and animate me. That is why I love Paris with an immense love.[76]

Like his creator, Bonnard as artist and scholar is steeped in the historical beauty of the city and the very spirit of its stones. The Paris which first influenced Anatole and his counterparts was this 'Paris spirituel,' which is the aura of the city, 'which is everywhere and nowhere, the Paris that inspires taste and intelligence.'[77]

CHAPTER IV

Formal Schooling

§ 1

NOW when the Second Empire was in its heyday, when Balzac and the Vicomte de Chateaubriand were dead, when Realism reached its Annus Mirabilis (1857) and Darwin was about to be translated into French—then Anatole France was resisting the processes of formal education and, in the well-known phrase of one of his professors, was often 'occupying himself with matters not pertaining to class-work.' [1] Nevertheless, as it turned out, these half-hearted attempts at schooling were among the most formative of the boy's undertakings.

This statement would hardly apply to his kindergarten days. His first teacher was his mother, who gave him the rudiments of the 'three R's,' but balked at the rules for the agreement of the past participle—a formidable business which the mature Anatole never completely mastered. (This circumstance should endear him to college students of French.) So he was turned over to the mercies of a fair instructress who had violet-coloured eyes and was perfumed with heliotrope. Each day she spent one hour in the Thibault home after lunch; during that time she rarely noticed her pupil; she smiled into vacancy and wrote love-letters. Her blandishments were not without effect, for presently she exchanged her maiden name of Lafont for that of Mme. de Turenne. She had made a noble catch.[2]

In *Le Petit Pierre* the above facts are graciously amplified and this charmer is glorified as 'Mlle. Mérelle.' A very high-class young lady, with an exclusive clientele, she 'consented' to concern herself with the scion of the Nozières. That is, for ten months she set the boy to reading fables and with never a word to him she wrote those love-letters in a state of smiling ecstasy. In the meantime, she 'embalmed the apartment with heliotrope,' which is clearly her *motif,* and what with her eyes, her 'keepsake' curls, and especially her indifference, she was second only to Marcelle as an instructress . . . in the appreciation of beauty.[3]

At the end of the ten months, Mother said: 'Thanks to your excellent teacher, you now know enough French grammar to go to college and learn Latin.' [4]

But according to the legend Pierre went first to another place, of which we hear in the *Livre de mon ami*. We have spoken above of a certain 'dame-school' as if Anatole Thibault actually attended it. This is quite doubtful; yet Pierre's reminiscences of such a school are so definite that we think he may have transferred here incidents really associated with Mlle. Mérelle, with the Institution Sainte-Marie, or possibly with other day-schools.[5] It is true that the 'Institution' was directed by men, while in the *Livre de mon ami* it was Mademoiselle Lefort (cf. Mlle. Lafont), unique of her kind, who attempted to control the minds of Pierre and of his comrade, Fontanet. Unless this personage has been unduly Victorianized in the telling, she seems to have been a fool of the first water. Lost in her own visions, she could maintain no discipline; adorned with 'keepsake' ringlets (Mlle. Lafont again) and a damp blue eye, she was addicted to the composition of excessively tearful poetry. For some time Pierre could not take his eyes off her. That detail, too, is borrowed from his actual experience with the beautiful Mlle. Mérelle. But presently he turned his attention to the other occupants of the room—a score of noisy mischievous children wholly given over to playing tricks on one another and on the schoolmistress. Was it here that the mocking *malin* side of the boy's nature was awakened, the side that later became so conspicuous in word and deed? Young Fontanet abetted him in derision of Mlle. Lefort and all her works, particularly the melancholy lines beginning

> Des vierges du hameau Jeanne était la plus belle.

Many things happened to Jane in that hamlet, and Pierre learned them all from the lips of the melancholy authoress. So far as can be gleaned from the records he learned absolutely nothing else. Mlle. Lefort's volume of verse has recently been identified.[6]

In the matter of primary education, then, the paths of Anatole and of his counterpart seem to diverge; they draw together once more on the threshold of a certain Catholic school,—the Institution Sainte-Marie (called 'Institution Saint-Joseph' in *Petit Pierre*), where Pierre-Anatole (*æt.* 9-11) went through the lower grades.[7] This institution was located in the upper reaches of the Rue Bonaparte and was preparatory to the Collège Stanislas, with which it became amalgamated in 1855. In that year Anatole entered the Collège.

According to the third Gospel, Anatole did not have such a bad time at the Institution.[8] Perhaps the hours were rather long —from eight to four or four-thirty, when Justine took him home again. But he was much better off than the regular boarders were, and he was always grateful to his parents for entering him as a *demi-pensionnaire*. They thought that arrangement would give him a due amount of discipline. They had chosen this school because of its excellent repute : it was 'conducted by priests and frequented by children of good families.' But there was little of that clerico-aristocratic snobbery which Anatole so detested at Stanislas. The teachers were kind and treated everybody alike. The superintendent, whom Pierre calls 'M. l'abbé Meyer,' was a wise and amiable man. The Latin instructor, M. Grépinet, was an able fellow ; he first opened up for Pierre the fascinating vistas of Roman history. But the memory of Richou, who spoiled *Andromaque* in the reading, is 'detested.'[9] The lad did not always make the best of his opportunities, for he sometimes scamped his Latin compositions and disliked routine. There are indications that he already preferred his own way of learning things. In spite of some hazing by his comrades and a consequent early disposition towards inner reveries,[10] there is enough to show that Anatole was not yet unhappy or rebellious as he often became at Stanislas.

§ 2

Presently the youth was promoted from the 'annexe' to the Collège. He attended the latter as a day-pupil for seven years (1855-62) ; and to hear him talk, one would think there never was a worse school than this 'old' Collège Stanislas. It had recently moved into the Hôtel Mailly, at No. 22 Rue Notre-Dame-des-Champs. Anatole later records that although this mansion faced on a deserted street, it had a nice garden, in which one might walk by special privilege ; but he says elsewhere that the building itself was 'ugly, dirty, malodorous.'[11] At that time the school had a staff of thirty professors and about two hundred student boarders.[12] Among these Anatole was, again, not included, since he hated the school refectory and still thought himself fortunate to take most of his meals at home.[13] The lunches at school were enlivened by the reading aloud of devotional works.

Having finished his preparatory grades at the Institution, Pierre was placed 'en sixième' on entering Stanislas ; this would be approximately equivalent to our first year of High School. It may be remembered that French grades, beginning with the eighth and mounting to the first, proceed in the inverse order from the American. For reasons that will appear, Anatole was forced by his mentors to take the grade *en sixième* twice. He was studying Latin intensively in his second grade (*cinquième*), at which period Justine still accompanied him to school ; when he was fourteen he was 'en troisième,' [14] a sort of half-way house ; he was 'en rhétorique' at seventeen ; and this should have been his last year, but he was destined to make several attempts at the baccalaureate before receiving it when he was twenty-one. Occasionally he seems disposed to glide over the fact of his failure and to speak as if he took his 'bachot' along with his regular class-mates.[15]

When Anatole entered the 'troisième' class it was necessary to make a choice between 'majoring' in science or in literature. This is the *bifurcation* spoken of in *La Vie en fleur ;* [16] it was a measure recently (1852) enacted by the minister Fortoul, and was suppressed later (1865) when Duruy's intelligent reforms really established modern French education. As a 'bifurcator,' Anatole naturally chose literature, though not without subsequent qualms. In fact, this whole question considerably upset his youthful mind, and his debates about it offer a good example of his *pro* and *con* method of illuminating (or obscuring) great issues. Consultations with Justine of the Scarlet Cheeks proved of slight avail. Pierre's parents abstained from counsel. The boy naturally leaned toward letters as 'more light and easy' ; but his godfather (and this is a true episode) [17] took him to a lecture on ballooning, with the result that for three days the call of science was the stronger ; ultimately the appeal of the humanities, particularly as expressed in Virgil, won the day.

Let us try to get an idea of the sort of education to which Anatole and his contemporaries were exposed. We should bear in mind that Stanislas was 'a hybrid secondary school, under the control of the Church, yet assimilated with the Government establishments.' [18] It was privately endowed, and many of its pupils became priests ; but the professors were appointed by the Ministry of Education and the scholars were admitted to the general state examinations.[19] The curriculum of such a Collège would roughly correspond to the level of American instruction in the

High School and the Junior College, the break coming 'en troisième' ; but the methods and the contents of the courses are vastly different.

In fact, the kind of secondary instruction then available in France was of a narrow and conventional type. The early Empire had despotically brought education under the control of the government. The Fortoul ministry was responsible for this.[20] An oath of allegiance to Napoleon III was required of all professors —and many of the most celebrated resigned. Naturally, independent thought was not favoured. The programme of the *lycées* was much upset by the *bifurcation,* and certain subjects, notably history and philosophy, were minimized or deprived of significant content. On the other hand, as Maxime du Camp points out, the clerical Collèges were traditionally keen on turning out 'brilliant students,' who by the aid of manuals, books of extracts and good memories, could make a show in society.[21] Such was the case even in the days of Voltaire. Pupils were stuffed mechanically, but they were not usually taught how to work or think. Compositions in Latin were still one of the main resources of the faculty. The reliance upon insipid texts and 'made Latin' seems to have been excessive.

It is not surprising, then, that the seeds of Anatole's social revolt against Church and State, were planted at Stanislas.

§ 3

ENTERING the Collège as a slight lad of eleven, presumably surrounded by larger fragments of boyhood, Anatole soon fell into a sort of awkward age mentally and physically. The 'heaven' which swathed his infancy was no more, and 'shades of the prison-house began to fall.'[22] He represents himself as not particularly ambitious and if not less intelligent than his schoolmates, yet he was more ardent and absorbed by other preoccupations. He still liked long walks and he came to care for unusual readings. In spite of what he had said about being an average or representative boy, he now insists, Rousseauistically, on his apartness from the others, his singularities, his uniqueness.[23] As a sort of maverick, he found the rest of the herd 'brutal,' while the masters seemed dull, indifferent to their pupils, or mechanical in their processes.[24] Therefore he began school with a trepidating heart which continued to annoy him even as an upper classman. 'I was the leanest, the most timid, the most awkward and dreamy of *rhétoriciens.*'[25] To Brousson he insisted upon this timidity and *gaucherie*. The reason was that he really suffered when his professors attempted to draw him from a meditative state into the arena of question and answer; then he became confused, he seemed inert and unresponsive. Yet he read considerably—'my mind was always stirring.' Word for word the above description applies equally well to Honoré de Balzac at the Collège de Vendôme. Both belonged to that class of student which is refractory to ordinary mental discipline, with its fixed periods and its set rules.[26] Both subjected their minds to intensive feeding, but it was their own food, served as they willed it. Hence Anatole particularly was averse to the measuring rod of pedagogues. His ways were not theirs. When he tried to make a speech he was laughed at; then he 'retired into a proud silence.' Nor were the results at home satisfactory: 'Mother did fret and Father did fume.'

But men of talent usually have their revenge on the pedagogues. The elderly Anatole turned the hose of his irony on the Collège Stanislas and considerably damaged that institution. There are three chief counts in his reiterated indictment: he 'learned nothing' at school, or what he did acquire he 'learned alone';[27] the professors were uninspired, often repellent; and favours were awarded either on an aristocratic or on a clerical bias. 'These recompenses were generally bestowed on plump, placid, curly children, who . . . occupied the avenues to their masters' hearts.' They carried off the *couronnes* or prizes. 'I was scarcely listed on the *palmarès* (roll of honour), nor did I win popularity among the masters.' Yet he did win several second prizes (in Latin and French composition and in drawing) as well as a number of *accessits* or honourable mentions.[28] But these were considered trivial successes. It is more significant that once at least Anatole had to take a whole course over again.

However, the awarding of these laurels was an important event in the school-year and furnished a good example of how the Collège 'played politics.' Anatole even declares, a little too emphatically, that through this ceremony there were first revealed to him 'social iniquity and inequality.' To one who has attended the *distribution des prix* at the 'new' Collège Stanislas it appears that Anatole exaggerated; for according to the present writer's recollection, the number of rosy happy faces was only exceeded by the number of *couronnes* and red-bound gift-books ; these were piled heaven-high, it seemed, in a manner to assure a prize for every student.[29] But Anatole goes on maintaining that what the masters wanted in this distribution was 'to give a good opinion of the house, to prove, by reading out sonorous names, that it was truly a nursery-garden for little aristocrats. *Le Palmarès était un armorial* . . . All the nephews of M. de Pourceaugnac and of the Countess of Escarbagnas were there.' It is clear that the son of Noël France felt that a gulf divided him from the self-assured heirs of noble families. But he might have added that many of the true élite were or would be 'there' ; for instance, such writers as Henri de Régnier and Edmond Rostand.

Thus the bitter old man jeers at the aristocratic *préjugé ;* now watch him deride the clerical. He mocks at the stereotyped way in which the children were taught to contrast Corneille with Racine, duty with love. 'Thanks to the excellent education of Stanislas, we triumphed over passion ; we strong-armed it.' And France imitates *ore rotundo* the churchly orator : 'Open the paternal library ! Read Seneca, devour Bourdaloue, savour Pascal, impregnate yourselves with Massillon !'[30]

If it be argued that all this represents the cynicism of age, let us revert to earlier testimony. In *Pierre Nozière* we meet with one of the boy's teachers, styled the 'Abbé Simler,' who combined ecclesiastical with aristocratic snobbery. He did it so well that we wonder whether he was the prototype of the Abbé Guitrel in the *Histoire contemporaine*. Simler had first singled out Pierre 'for the gravity of his thoughts' and had admitted him to a coterie which assembled in order to admire the Abbé's lofty conversation. But Pierre, by donning a grotesque coat, shocked the Abbé's æsthetic Christianity ; and the latter, with Jesuitical politeness, removed himself from the boy's converse. It is with regard to such slights that Anatole remarks with intention : 'I learned to return with usury the blows that I received.' For there can be little doubt that this experience with Simler was authentic and formed, with other such experiences, the nucleus from which France's long animosity against priests would develop. As a student, he began to learn the sweet uses of satire, to turn against the Church, and to recognize social injustice when he saw it. Thus some of the strongest of his later impulses date from his college years.[31]

§ 4

We are now in a position to appreciate judicially the earliest and fullest picture of Stanislas—that given in the *Livre de mon ami*. This Gospel usually is sufficiently rose-coloured ; yet the memories presented there of the boy's school-years, though more humorous, are not essentially very different from the later records. As for the clerical teachers, it seems certain that France, like Voltaire, learned early to scoff at them. Take for instance Pierre's treatment of the episode concerning 'le prestige de M. l'Abbé Jubal.'[32] This Abbé taught impressively the history of France (in verse), he instructed the lads how to receive a minister of God in their homes, and in the chapel he nailed garlands around the niche of the Holy Virgin. Thus he made Anatole realize that priests are 'prodigiously respectable' and that the Abbé's spiritual grandeur was almost immeasurable. Alas ! The day of the distribution of prizes came. The important Abbé was relegated to the rear of the procession, seated on a humble stool off the platform, finally almost smothered under a flag. Was *that* the way people treated a minister of God ? The sharp lad drew his own conclusions.

Here, then, is another circumstance that must have fostered Pierre-Anatole's 'disposition naturelle à l'incrédulité' ; and a German critic is almost warranted in generalizing that 'the worst enemies of the Church are those who have passed through her schools.'[33]

We learn in the next chapter of *Pierre's Book*[34] the silliness of going to confession at an age when one naturally has few sins to confess and no psychological penetration for their discernment. Therefore the boy exaggerated his sin of absent-mindedness, confessed to 'distractions' here and 'distractions' there, like Balthazar Claes in *La Recherche de l'absolu*. The professors took his word for it and made his absence of mind the chief subject of their complaints ; they probably also disliked his presence of body. 'You were one of those pupils, torment or delight of the master,' said Gréard, on receiving France into the Academy, 'who are indolent about their tasks, who evade the ordinary interpretation of a passage, who follow the fancy to which it gives rise, *and construct for themselves another more intimate lesson.*'[35]

Accordingly Pierre was not commended for his day-dreaming

on classical themes ; he was actually told that he 'lacked taste' in French composition ! And whatever grade he was in, whatever school of life he subsequently entered, he would always deserve his master's eternal reproach, 'Je m'occupais de choses étrangères à la classe.' Among such things were pranks with misused ink-bottles and misplaced fire-crackers.[36]

Yet this 'petit bonhomme,' who went leaping with his school-bag through the Luxembourg, had no great harm in him. It is true that he leapt less joyously when returning to school after the holidays. But he looked forward to seeing his comrades, Fontanet and the rest. Also he acquired (though not altogether in the class-room) a lively enthusiasm for classical beauty. He learned, as we shall presently see, something more than he will admit, although he learned it irregularly. In spite of his amused contempt for Dominie This and Abbé That, it is unjust for him to qualify Stanislas as 'the Collège where I learned very little.' Indeed, he later made a kind of retractation, probably too flowery to be sincere, in which he speaks of his gratitude to Stanislas for having formed him and declares that he spent there 'un temps très doux.'[37] While he could not bear the rude *surveillants* or proctors ('black-coated monks,' as he calls the lot), yet he pays tribute to the fine soul and the charming personality of the Abbé Lalanne, who was then director. A later portrait of this worthy represents him as ugly, though attractive, giving the effect of being carved out of soft stone. He had various contrasts in his make-up. 'The good old man was quick, though sturdy, impatient and awkward, eloquent in spite of his stammering. . . He was venerable, yet slightly ludicrous. He had a great and tender heart, a lofty soul, a mind both lively and simple.'[38]

One chapter in a volume commemorative of the centenary of the Collège Stanislas is devoted to the activities of the Abbé Lalanne.[39] The writer, a certain Baron Evian, was fortunate in that he attended the Collège after its reorganization and just after France had left it. The latter is nowhere mentioned in the book, but much is made of the roster of distinguished alumni, especially cardinals and generals, whom Anatole derided in the Gospels. Lalanne is qualified as 'un séducteur . . . un conquérant,' who benevolently guided amateur theatricals among the students. One year the *Philoctetes* of Sophocles was played in the Greek. The director not only loved poetry himself, but encouraged it in others.

All of this is corroborated either in France's souvenirs or in *Les Désirs de Jean Servien,* where Lalanne is quite recognizable under the alias of the 'Abbé Bordier.'[40] Mention is made in Evian's chapter of the Académie Stanislas, a literary society which the students took seriously and which was difficult to enter. We shall see that Anatole achieved some distinction in this 'Académie d'Emulation.' But A.F. would part company from the Baron when the latter declares that the director was surrounded by a professional élite of really inspiring teachers. Examples are given—not those that Anatole would choose. Yet we hear that the senior students could read Latin with some ease. At this later period there seem to have been very few day-scholars.

While Pierre would be averse to this general whitewashing of the faculty of 'Stan.,' he acknowledges in his *Livre* that two of his masters, 'Chotard' and 'Charron,' left with him abiding impressions. Chotard, the incomplete priest,—he did not wear the *soutane*—was undeniably a funny fellow. It was he who gave birth to the immortal page containing 'The Last Words of Decius Mus.'[41] Here the mischievous Anatole makes his professor jumble together his own exhortation to a restless class with the dying speech of the Roman hero:

> Spurring on his impetuous charger, Decius Mus turned for the last time to his companions in arms and said: 'If you don't stop that noise, I shall keep the whole class in during recess. For my country's sake I choose death and immortality. The gulf awaits me. Monsieur Fontanet, you will copy out ten pages of grammar. Thus has decided the wise Jupiter Capitolinus, eternal guardian of the Eternal City. Monsieur Nozière, if you again pass on your work to Monsieur Fontanet for him to copy, I shall write your father. It is just and necessary that a citizen should sacrifice himself for the common good.'

This and more was delivered in a sustained martial tone; for Dominie Chotard had a belligerent nature as well as 'a soul dwelling in antiquity,' all the way from Thermopylae to Pharsala. So Anatole admits that Chotard, aided by Livy, inspired him with heroic dreams.

As for 'M. Charron' (really 'Chéron'),[42] he was respected: morose and limited in mind, he yet had a fine character, as the boys were quick to discern. Anatole's taste (at seventeen) being rather poor, this teacher recommended him to study the hybrid style and rhetorical outpourings of Casimir Delavigne! However heretical in literature, M. Chéron knew how to exemplify the *honnête homme*—'and that knowledge surely has its value.' In short: 'Paul Chéron was so fine a soul,' that Anatole considered himself fortunate to follow his classes. In contrast to him were an evil-minded hunchback, who taught Greek, and an 'unjust' drawing master, 'M. Petit.'

At this stage it may be well to record the actual names of Anatole's principal instructors, i.e., those who appear to have been in charge of the various grades. Pierre's nomenclature, when different, will be indicated by quotation marks. The list follows:

LOWER FORMS

Sixième (the first time): Allain
Sixième (the second time): Monnier
Cinquième: Beaussier (Pierre says 'Brard')
Quatrième: Triaire (the impossible 'Crottu'?)

UPPER FORMS

Troisième: Allain (an unfortunate reunion)
Deuxième: Lerond
Rhétorique: Chéron (also 'Charron')[43]

Other memories of Pierre's rather numerous teachers are found as late as *La Vie en fleur*.[44] A few of the above names and a number of aliases occur here. Thus the director, 'venerable and smiling,' is half-disguised as the 'Abbé Delalobe.' As a rule, neither the teachers nor the memories seem to improve with age. To be sure, Anatole's 'professeur de philosophie' (*sc.* Chéron) was a man of integrity, but he had no conception of poetry. M. Beaussier, who taught the classics, seems to be the original of 'Chotard': he was a 'just man of a severe character,' who found much perversity in Pierre. A similar view was taken by 'M. Brard,' who guided the destinies of the students 'en cinquième.' Minor figures were the immense 'Mésange,' 'Bonhomme,' and Lerond. These are not criticized. The weight of Pierre's displeasure falls rather on a certain 'Crottu' whom he depicts, it has been said, 'with a pen still trembling with rage.'[45] Anatole declares that Crottu was extremely unjust and that he 'span iniquity as a spider spins its web.' Even this might have been pardoned him; but he was also ugly, dirty, an offence to the Muses, a satyr, in fact Marsyas in person. Such crimes are both unforgivable and unforgettable.

Crottu greatly resembles a *cuistre* remembered in the *Vie littéraire,* who stirred a similar vehement hatred. This fellow (probably Triaire, 'mon professeur de quatrième) snatched from Anatole's hands the *Jardin des racines grecques,* because that volume contained a pretty frontispiece. He tore up the picture before the boy's eyes and excited such a feeling of revolt that 'after twenty-five years I take a vengeful joy in delivering his stupid crime to the execration of all people of taste.' [46]

Such diatribes make us understand that if the boy was usually gentle, his was a 'douceur farouche,' which resented interference. He believes that the only thing that saved him from real illness in that 'frightful college' was his sense of humour, so quickly aroused. He insists that 'everything there made study odious and life insupportable.' He enumerates his grievances—the perpetual black marks of the teachers, the erroneous system of rewards and punishments, the dirt of the class-room, 'the horrible mixture of chalk and ink' as an atmospheric blight. At home, when he sought sympathy for his rebellious moods, he found only condemnation for his misbehaviour: Father kept a reproving silence at best, and Mother, wounded in her dearest ambitions, often spoiled the meals by her reproaches.[47] Deep must have been the adolescent dissatisfaction which lasted sixty years and was finally recorded not long before France's death.

§ 5

In the chronicles written for *l'Univers illustré* Anatole harks back a dozen times to his recollections of Stanislas,[48] usually confirming what may be gathered from the Gospels. Thus, in 1884, the name of Chotard occurs, in connexion with practical jokes which the professors had to undergo. A certain proctor who confined the tricky youth in a closet was then severely judged as an 'imbécile'; but now Anatole knows that he was only an idiot. One day he thinks of the poor 'grinds,' who, now as then, are probably doing a sort of three-headed composition—'le thème Cerbère.' What a mixture of things do they swallow! Pneumatic machines and elegant Latinizings, jumbled with proofs of the existence of God!

Happily, the students do not know that most of it is useless. In the autumn, our chronicler's thoughts turn again to the days of the *rentrée des classes.* One pities the galley-slave returning to his labour—'le bagne,' as Anatole sometimes calls it ; yet the schoolboy is by then often bored with his vacation and is ready to come back.

A.F.'s memories of certain teachers are clearly abiding. And he holds that the student remains the best judge of what his professors were really like. Twenty-four years ago (he is writing in 1886), he *knew* that Chéron was equally strong-souled and strong-minded. Then there was a mild little blond from the Jura ; we liked and spared him, for he touched us by his essential nobility and his proud poverty. Like the Abbé Lalanne, he wrote tragedies, but hardly with the same effect. The Abbé himself is appreciated as late as 1891.[49] Our amiable *directeur* could draw moral lessons from the battles of Pharamond or the habits of fishes. He resembled the pictures of Saint-Vincent-de-Paul. 'He had a generous soul and a smiling habit of mind.' The thought of seeing him made the *rentrée* supportable. But the prefects and the mean long-coated monks ! These coarse scolding men still make Anatole feel how unfortunate it was to be surrounded by such creatures during one's most impressionable years.

Other passages from *l'Univers illustré* [50] accord in the main with Pierre's souvenirs—for example, the story of the Tunic and the Two Tailors, which we will shortly hear related. Now he is glad to see that a sensible minister is considering the suppression of the smock worn by schoolboys. That is the next best thing to the suppression of the schools themselves. But one can't have everything. . . The whole trouble is that neither man nor boy was originally created for a life of hard study. Anatole is still against the 'grind' of Stanislas, which made for poor physiques and encouraged 'universal pedantry.' Yet as time passes he is surprised to find that he has not kept too dolorous a memory of this 'tranquil college of the priests.' Some of them—the stoical Chéron and Pélissier, the monitor—were not so bad. Besides, A.F. claims that he never listened to his professors ; owing to that wise precaution, he can still love the Greek poets and the Roman historians. Towards the end of the reminiscences in *l'Univers illustré,* there is a passage in which Anatole repeats some of the above *motifs* and becomes aware of his repetitions. He offers this semi-apology : that he had not intended to speak so often of Stanislas, but certain things are unforgettable, and his habit is always to let the pen follow the thought.

M. Girard's chapter on Anatole at Stanislas is significantly called 'La Prison.' We are here informed that the boy began writing Latin compositions in his twelfth year. Fortunately, the comments of his first professor, M. Allain, have been preserved in a small note-book, and they are illuminating. Except for a few occasions when Anatole did his task, the rest is a series of ill-prepared assignments, neglect of *devoirs,* or hastily written compositions. M. Allain sadly remarked : 'He might have been the first or the second in Latin composition, as he was in history, but for the negligence with which the work was done.' Notes regarding his 'insouciance et légèreté' were entered against him, and his conduct was marked by a 'nonchalance extrême.' This is the famous nonchalance which later in his Parnassian days and even into his old age remains a salient trait in Anatole's personality. He is Mr. Don't-Care. He begins to fashion his panoply of resistance against set ways of doing things, against 'systems,' and especially at present against such a dreary humdrum way of scribbling Latin 'exercises,' when he was disposed to plunge into the heart of Roman history and literature.

§ 6

Fortunately, there was one outlet for this budding talent. First, its fictional (and burlesque) presentment. In *La Vie en fleur* we hear of a school-society, called the 'Académie Blaise Pascal,' which was founded by Fontanet and perished after a brief and turbulent existence. Pierre Nozière was to read the opening oration, but was interrupted by the skylarking of his comrades, and that particular academy never met again.[51] In sober fact, there existed at Stanislas the 'Académie d'Emulation,' more regularly established by the Abbé Lalanne. Here essays were read before one's schoolmates and submitted to the decision of other members.[52] It appears that there were eleven Academicians at the time when Anatole France read his compositions, half a dozen of which were judged acceptable. Fifty years later a private letter recorded that Anatole's *juvenilia* were still treasured among the archives of Stanislas ; and the writer of the letter, M. Calvet, presently indited an article on these 'Enfances.'[53]

They are preserved in a green copy-book,[54] which also includes compositions by Edmond Rostand and others. A.F.'s 'more childish' essays go back to 1859 and 1860, when he was 'en quatrième et troisième.' They are all written with slow scrupulous penmanship. It is significant that three of them contain the word 'légende' in the title. The first of the series is a 'Légende de Gutenberg,' which is simple, short, unremarkable. It concerns a dream of the printer to the effect that his invention would lead on both to civilization and to corruption. And it contains on the margin an old dream of Pierre's — that drawing of his home and of the near-by Académie Française, with a straight line running between them. It is observed that he finally got there by a more zigzag route ; but we see how a boyish ambition may be prophetic. The other 'Légendes' concern Sainte-Radegonde (to be dealt with later) and a certain 'Récluse,' in which one finds as yet no antipathy to the lives of solitaries.

Passing over two insignificant papers, we reach the unusual 'Méditations sur les ruines de Palmyre.' This is the gem of the collection and shows, as Barthou says, remarkable qualities of balance and harmony in the style — especially for a boy of fifteen.[55] While the tone of the final paragraph will remind the English reader of a famous passage in Gibbon, it is more obviously an imitation of a screed in Volney's *Les Ruines* (1791).[56] The schoolboy's peroration presents a traveller who muses upon the past glories of the town and temple of Palmyra ; but like another René he prefers the ruins :

> Salut, opulente Palmyre, royale Babylone, superbe Persépolis ! . . . Dépouillées comme vous l'êtes de vos prêtres et de vos remparts, de vos marchands et de vos trésors, que vous avez d'attraits pour moi ! Ruines de tant de nations puissantes, que je vous sens de vertus ! . . .*

Rhetorical as the phrasing now seems, we have at last the first glimmer of a literary vocation ; the author of *Thaïs* is here in germ. As for his models, together with Volney, France is likewise

* Hail, wealthy Palmyra, Babylon the royal, majestic Persepolis ! . . . Although deprived of your priests and ramparts, your traders and your treasures, you still possess for me a deep fascination. O ruins of so many powerful nations, I still feel the strength of your ancient virtues ! . . .

'decanting' the style and thought of Chateaubriand. The large manner of this master is discernible, as well as the feeling of the flux and of the 'néant' to which René was addicted.[57] Yet the composition shows an individual sense of form and an attentive care which was almost never spent on mere school-exercises.

But such flights were almost as unique as the single occasion on which Pierre stood first in Latin composition and was therefore invited to the 'banquet de Saint-Charlemagne.'[58] These triumphs offered only occasional diversions in the scheme of things, the drab routine of school. Disturbances and pranks in the class-room, tart criticisms of teachers and fellow-students, entries in his diary complaining of unceasing monotony or dreading the *rentrée des classes*—allowing for some literary exaggeration, all this shows that neither in work nor in play did the lad quite express himself at Stanislas. Doubtless he had his moments of fun and his larks, frequently at the expense of others. But it was, as French schooling is likely to be, too confining, too hot-house. The young *flâneur's* 'cuts' were connived at by his mother, who also at times condoned his bad marks; but the school-reports excited the indignation and severity of the elder France, who audibly wondered if his son would ever come to any good end.

Let us conclude with this variety of education, which was 'secondary' in more senses than one. Anatole is persistent in his declarations that as an adult he had to learn over again, less mechanically, what his masters were supposed to have taught him.[59] They drove home, through repeated impositions, certain passages which he learned by rote; they inbred in him the idea of Sophocles' 'grammatical perfection.'[60] But they did not address the 'æsthetic memory,' which was with him the most responsible kind; it functioned slowly but surely, too late for school purposes. In general, the routine and the constant 'odious discipline' weighed upon him, the more heavily as he advanced in his 'teens.[61] In particular: 'I do not like the monks. We have never got along well together.'[62] Thus he confesses the profoundest social result of his experience at Stanislas. It affected his subsequent life, his habits, his whole outlook, and helped to make him the sceptic and scorner that he became. And he tells us so in a parable.

I refer to the episode of Firmin Piédagnel in *l'Orme du Mail*.[63] This youth was like A.F. in his timidity and his sensitive intelligence. Æsthetically attracted to the priestly life, for which he had no real vocation, he was studying in a certain 'grand séminaire.' But his teachers' notes (cf. M. Allain) indicated that Firmin was mainly interested in profane literature and retained from his clerical instructors—as they said—only a taste for 'elegant Latinities, sophistries, and a sentimental mysticism.' The last trait induced in him a kind of exaltation which became conspicuous when he aided the Abbé Lantaigne in serving mass. At the end of the ceremony, he was abruptly dismissed from the institution. The effect of this injustice upon Firmin's nature is worth quoting:

> Suddenly a sentiment was born—a feeling that was to grow within him, to sustain and fortify him. This was the *hatred of the priest,* an imperishable and fruitful hatred, which could fill a whole life. . .

People have found something of Renan in the character of this neophyte; but his counter-conversion is more like that of the man who described not only Piédagnel but the ghoulish Paphnuce and certain unsavoury Italian monks and a number of much-derided fanatics from St. Paul to Evariste Gamelin. Even in the apparent incongruity which led them to cling sensuously to the rites of the Church and imaginatively to its legends, Firmin and Anatole are at one.[64] And it has been pointed out that each was 'the brilliant child of humble parents.'[65]

Were there any more positive assets accruing from this long sojourn at 'Stan.'? We may accept Anatole's belief that much of his 'learning' had to be learned over again. We may agree that the staff was ill-prepared to handle such fundamentals as philosophy and history, and that a knowledge of these subjects had to be acquired under other auspices. We may be amused to hear that A.F. finally quit school with such precipitation that he left behind him all his textbooks.[66] Yet it seems that Pierre read widely whatever was not required of him: moralists like La Rochefoucauld, tomes of historians, together with Greek and Latin poets. And one thing the 'monks' certainly taught the boy, for this had been in the tradition of the clerical Collèges since the Old Régime:[67] they taught him and some other 'rhétoriciens' how to read Latin easily and with a growing pleasure; it seems that at times he could even think in Latin![68] The pupil would not always do his exercises, but he would translate elegantly one of Virgil's *Eclogues* or (to please his mother) compose the life of a saint. Several of these versions have been handed down. They show that in spite of himself Anatole must have become rather well acquainted with the syntactical underpinning to the classics.

It is doubtful whether he imbibed an equal amount of Greek. His own humorous opinion is that 'my professors made me understand the Greek genius, which they did not understand themselves.'[69] His abundant appreciation of the classics will concern us later. But just here we should concede, even if Pierre did not, that one purpose of Stanislas was to impart to its students, *via* the method of Latin and French compositions, a certain traditional culture in the humanities. It was not this formal training of the Collège which chiefly inspired and fostered the 'génie latin' that came to be the essence of Anatole France. Yet his schooling gave him a basis for an increasing absorption in his own particular brand of studies. Let us now see how such interests carried over into the travels and excursions undertaken during his vacations.

§ 7

For in his 'teens the boy's 'circles' extended beyond Paris to various provinces. He had already (*æt.* 9) been placed for a time 'en pension' at Versailles.[70] We hear vaguely of a visit to Auvergne where 'Pierre' rode horseback at some uncommemorated date.[71] We know definitely, through recently published letters to his parents, that Anatole visited Normandy twice, in his sixteenth and again in his eighteenth year.[72] He has his first glimpse of the sea, he takes long 'promenades' to Mont-Saint-Michel, to the Island of Jersey, inspects various Norman houses, and attends the fêtes at Avranches.

Pierre's visits to the 'Avranchin' neighbourhood are connected with an old acquaintance of the Quai Malaquais—'Madame Laroque,' who originally came from the region around Granville. According to the last Gospel, the boy's parents once sent him to stay with Isidore Gonse, a grand-nephew of Madame Laroque and a farmer at Saint-Pierre.[73] This hamlet was only two leagues away from Granville, which the young tourist now visited; the tale of its siege by the Vendéens had already been told him by

Madame Laroque. He roamed the country-side and had an adolescent *crise* of the kind shortly to be narrated as concluding the *Livre de Pierre*.[74] The episode of 'Eglé' (alias Mathilde Gonse) and the raspberries which she smeared on his face is recounted by a Pierre grown elderly.

What, asks M. Huard,[75] is the part of reality in all this? There *was* such an old lady, and her maiden name was Rauline, as Pierre asserted; but her married name was Foulon, not Laroque. As a good neighbour, she sent Anatole to spend his vacation with her relatives, the Fouquets (not the Gonses) at Saint-Pierre-Langers. The girl 'Eglé' was probably her niece, Elise Rauline.[76] It seems that later Anatole—or his mother—asked for the hand of Elise in marriage; but she preferred to become a nun. Do we find here a personal reason for Anatole's rancour against the Church as a devourer of virgins? Two of his poems—'La Prise de voile' and *Les Noces corinthiennes*—display such a feeling.

In any case, his letters point to two sojourns at Saint-Pierre-Langers: August, 1859; August and September, 1861.[77] He describes to his parents the 'Gonse'-Fouquet house, which apparently has altered little since that time. He could get to Avranches almost as easily as to Granville, since the former is only sixteen kilometres from Saint-Pierre.

In writing home about his experiences, what does the young traveller emphasize? M. Girard says: 'What strikes us immediately is the abundance of his literary reminiscences and the diversity of the Latin and French quotations with which he sprinkles his correspondence.' He quotes classical authors apropos of anything from a sleeping family in the train, to a harvest of wheat. He says roundly that people have been too poetic about harvests and 'the peasants are a blot on the beauties of the country-side.' But there is not a great deal about Nature's charms *per se;* usually a natural object calls forth a bookish reminiscence.[78] If he writes of the wind howling across a cemetery, a black sky and 'yew-trees sadly swinging,' he is reminded of Scott's romanticism and declares this would be a proper setting for the figure of Old Mortality. The sea-waves merely recall God's interdiction: 'Thus far and no farther.' If he encounters a church-procession, he does not describe it but simply mentions that it reminds him of a painting in the Luxembourg. This kind of inverted comparison seems to give reason to those critics who aver that Anatole sees nature only through a veil of literary and artistic reminiscences.[79]

Even more apparent is the youth's absorption in the historical and archæological aspect of whatever he observes. Here we recognize a taste acquired at his father's book-shop rather than in college. Does he see a Gothic church ? He has to detail its peculiarities with specific dates. Does he visit Mont-Saint-Michel ? He delights in 'the boldness of its sublime architecture and the poetry of its history,' and he must 'crib' from a guide-book and write home a regular dissertation about the monument from the eighth century down.[80] He also gives us the history of Jersey from early times, dwells on the twelfth-century features of a certain Abbaye, while in Norman houses he discusses the furniture for its archæological value. The former truant seems likely to become a 'joli petit pédant' like Fontenelle ; perhaps, in part, he is showing a good front to Father.

In the *Livre,* 'Pierre's' account of his vacations deals with other matters and is more romanticized. Here the youth of seventeen is fully conscious that he is in the country of Chateaubriand : the scenery, woods and waves and cliffs, is now described and is fused with his emotions and growing pains quite in the manner of 'René' :

> The vague charm of the sea and of the foliage was in harmony with *le vague de mon âme.* I sped my horse into the forest ; I rolled half-naked on the strand, full of desire for something unknown which I divined everywhere and which I found nowhere.[81]

The young man in fact was in love ; but he was slow in discovering what ailed him.

The last chapter in the *Livre de Pierre* tells how the scion of the Nozières is supposed to have visited his ancestral seat in the province of Maine. None of this corresponds to what we know of Anatole and his family ; nor can we tell how much credence may be attached to Pierre's sojourn at Corbeil, on the Seine.[82] There he claims to have lived a monotonous life with a monotonous aunt while he tried to entice a certain M. Planchonnet into publishing a juvenile historical romance called *Clémence Isaure.*

§ 8

Pierre's friends and comrades during these formative years had a considerable influence upon him. Among his school-companions, there was of course Fontanet, always Fontanet, who, 'no larger than a rat, but cleverer than Ulysses, took everywhere the first place.'[83]

Elsewhere, he is described as having the 'profile of a fox' and something of his habits; he was the sort of lad who makes others pull his chestnuts from the fire; and he wore 'an air of superiority which he never laid aside.'[84] Several of the incidents already narrated about the school-life of the two boys would bear out this characterization.

Yet Pierre loved and admired his 'Ulysses,' probably because of the sharp divergences between them. In fact, young Thibault was different from the great majority of his schoolmates, because of his wide-ranging 'speculative mind' and the intensity of his inner life.[85]

Anatole's own diary, selections from which are now published, give the real names and character-sketches of various *camarades*.[86] There is Bridieu, the teaser; there is Cazeaux (read 'Fontanet'), whom he likes best and by whom he would be liked in turn; there are such lesser figures as the estimable Lachesnais, the dandified Martel, the loquacious Homberg, and De Briague, 'très inconstant.' In a day of cold penetration — at seventeen — he thus summed them up: 'Martel, a fool; Lachesnais, empty; Homberg, false; and Cazeaux, an egoist.' Yet the more usual thing is to find the boy putting out tendrils of affection, like Marcel Proust, remaining most sensitive and at times exigent in his demands. 'Even for Cazeaux, the egoist, his soul will have infinite resources of tenderness.'

Of these, only Lachesnais and Fontanet-Cazeaux appear in the Gospels. On the other hand, we find there the names of various playmates or casual acquantances not identified as real persons.[87] Such are the Savoyard chimney-sweep, the coarse Alphonse, the disagreeable Alphonsine, and Hangard with whom one could play at attacking stage-coaches. More community of spirit resulted from a single meeting with the ailing Cyrille; and the 'sweet strange soul' of Clément Sybille alternately attracted and repelled the more mundane Pierre. Both of these frail lads were destined to an early death. This was also the case with Mouron, who attended Stanislas and inspired in Pierre a dislike which changed into an ardent affection, rather excessive in its manifestations. Cyrille, Clément, and Mouron are of the same tender-minded family. They may have sat compositely for the later portrait of Jean Servien. They show at any rate Pierre's fellow-feeling for the more delicate types of boyhood.

Of all these juvenile friends, the closest and the one whom Anatole knew longest was actually Etienne Charavay.[88] The character of Etienne, scholar and Chartiste, will reappear in connexion with Sylvestre Bonnard, of whom he is in part the prototype. We have seen how the families of the two boys were closely linked. Anatole and Etienne had similar tastes and pursuits. They were at Stanislas together, though in different classes, Etienne being the younger by four years. But Anatole lagged behind until the other caught up, and they appear to have taken their baccalaureate together, in 1864.[89] During the process, Anatole wrote these lines to his friend :

> Canards amis qu'un même sort rassemble
> Dans la mare au bachot nous barbottons ensemble.*

Together they haunted the book-stalls on the Quais, since they were both fond of artistic erudition, and together they fell in love and wrote absurd verses on ready-made rimes (*bouts-rimés*). Soon afterwards, their paths separated, young Charavay attending the Ecole des Chartes, where he received in 1869 his diploma as an *archiviste,*[90] and at the same time worked hard to support his family. Yet they often saw each other in their early manhood and shared their projects. We shall find that Etienne stood behind Anatole in his first small ventures as a writer.

In *Pierre Nozière,* there are several pen-pictures of grown people whom the author knew about this time. Rather in the manner of La Bruyère, he sketches these *portraits* indelibly, with firm, fine touches ; and the 'character' is generally key-noted around one outstanding peculiarity. Thus the tailor, M. Grégoire, 'était un artiste,' irreproachable in the matter of making 'tunics' (long coats) for the more aristocratic students at Stanislas. The

* Friendly ducks, whose lot is cast together, we paddle around in the same pool, trying to snap up a B.A. degree.

Nozière family could not afford this distinguished person, so they fell back on a little *tailleur-concierge* called Rabiou.[91] His likeness is done as a pendant to the preceding. His key-note is that he had 'the brow of an apostle on the body of a gnome.' Miserable-looking, poverty-stricken, burdened with a numerous progeny, he was yet 'courageux et mystique.' Did his mystic brow help him in making the tunics ? Gentle reader, it did not. Pierre's garment had a loosely made neck and it 'evaded' downwards, with an ungainly cut. The boy's long head rose above it like that of a stork, and through the open neck Pierre's schoolmates thrust handfuls of pebbles.

We have already heard of 'Leclerc jeune,' who kept a shop full of medieval armour and who has some analogies with Père France. Among the frequenters of the former's shop was a tall old Royalist, who like Anatole's father had served Charles X.[92] Identified as 'M. Gerboise,' this personage, too, is quite a figure in *Pierre Nozière* and tells interesting anecdotes.[93] It is said that Gerboise was modelled on the Comte de La Bédoyère.[94] This does not seem likely, since the latter was a cultivated *grand seigneur,* the former a rough and rustic old soldier. But the amicable relationship between 'Gerboise' and the armourer Leclerc suggests the sort of patronage that La Bédoyère accorded to the Père France. Other reminiscences in *Pierre Nozière,* concerning painters and publicists, have not proved very revealing.[95]

The ladies are not absent from this intermediate Gospel. The reader will recall M. Planchonnet, the journalist at Corbeil who was supposed to publish *Clémence Isaure*. There was a 'Madame Planchonnet';[96] and Pierre (*æt.* 17) found her a pale, *spirituelle,* though ill-made affinity. When they were first thrown together at dinner, the lady and the youth exchanged noble, tender, and perfectly banal sentences. By the time dessert was brought on, Pierre became quickly aware that he greatly admired Mme. Planchonnet, who listened to his expansive remarks with a fatigued smile and (one feels) with preoccupations centring in the kitchen. There followed a good deal of exaltation and—that was all. A party call paid to Mme. Planchonnet resulted only in reserved and commonplace dialogue, and soon afterwards Pierre left Corbeil.

A similar account of the Planchonnet episode is found late in *l'Univers illustré*.[97] The title of Pierre's historical novel is there mentioned as *Clémence Isaure et les Jeux Floraux.* Just after writing it, he felt well-contented with this achievement of his 'teens. 'Planchonnet' was also the name given to the refugee in 'Madame de Luzy.' And the journalist, himself, appears with his 'interesting' wife, under his own name in the *Comte Morin* (which in turn stems from *Marguerite*) before gracing the pages of *Pierre Nozière.*[98]

The boy's interest in Mme. Planchonnet, if it existed at all, was not serious. But if Pierre may be believed, there ensued a full-blown calf-love. More lasting in its effect, and indeed the final crystallizing touch in the adolescent's soul-state, is what happened between him and Another. According to the *Livre de mon ami,* there was among his mother's friends the widow of a pianist, and her name was Alice Gance. Never were there such hair, teeth, eyes; floating, shining, dazzling. . . She drew him with a magnetic force, for beauty, he opines—not for the last time—is a sweet and terrible thing. She was a trifle coquettish, she affected sorrow one evening, she played the piano and, swathed in perfumes, she asked the quivering boy if he liked music. He responded in the well-known words: 'Oui, monsieur.'

After that, he knew a long period of shame, self-reproach, and starless melancholy. Taking his imbecility along, he went on his second visit to the Norman coast, where as we have seen he imitated René. He wept, he stormed, he found his heart too big for his body; he calls on the cliffs and the woods to attest that nothing that happened to him later could equal 'the hurt that I suffered then, nothing equals the first dream of a man. . . The desire for the Unknown makes the whole world lovely.' Sweet—but terrible.[99] It was Virgil's *Aeneid* that revealed the secret of his disturbance: its name of course was 'Love and Alice.' There was nothing to be done about it. He loved the woman before whom he had abased himself—the woman whom he called Monsieur! He could not reappear before her. He indulges in no more romantic gestures. He is only very unhappy. Presently he swallows his despair and, returning to Paris, pursues the path to the baccalaureate.

CHAPTER V

The World Within

§ 1

FRANCE was an inveterately subjective writer. Unlike others, he prided himself upon the constant intrusion of the ego, which he considered unavoidable both in life and letters. Consequently, a study of his formation must include the fabric of that inner world which loomed so large in his consciousness from childhood down. Since external shocks and bruises were always throwing the boy-child back upon himself, it is well to know what visions thronged in his 'inward eye': what dreams and imaginings, what tales of the fairies, what scenes from the Bible and saints' lives, what other legends or reverberations of beauty.

La vida es sueño. Over and over again does Anatole, tired old man or introspective youth, subscribe to this belief. Sylvestre Bonnard has no need to buy a *Clef des Songes,* for he knows that all the dreams of man, joyous or tragic, are summed up in 'le songe de la vie.' And again: 'Everyone accomplishes in his own manner his dream of life. I have had mine in my library.' [1] At the other extreme from the old scholar, we find Little John of *A Travers Champs* (he who naïvely thought of himself as the centre of the world). He too is a dreamer: 'Il songe . . . il rêve.' Likewise, in this story-book we have a defence of dreamers, 'who,' it is maintained, 'can be courageous, just like those who do not dream.' [2] The danger of such castle-building did not impress France, as it impressed Scott in his account of the education of Edward Waverley. Nor did the author of the four Gospels insist with Alfred de Vigny that the substance of the inner life should be a '*forte rêverie*'—something virile and inclining towards action. Many passages show that for Anatole the dream-world was the only livable and 'true' one, the only compensation for the ugliness and monotony of the so-called 'real' one, the only answer to the demi-urge who manufactured the Earth.[3] 'The secret of happiness and of wisdom is to have beautiful dreams.' [4] If they conflict with everyday fact, so much the worse for the latter; they overcome and rise superior to fact. Such are the unsure foundations of Anatole's philosophy of Illusion, which soon becomes a major theme. More Platonically expressed, 'the best thing in life is the idea it gives of something beyond life.' Otherwise, actuality would be intolerable.[5]

The fissure between the two worlds, widening as he travelled on, was scarcely perceptible in France's childhood. That is why, with some exaggeration, he spoke of that period as the only happy one in his existence.[6] That is why the Gospels remain the fullest and the most cheerful record of his reveries. In the first two, 'he is unveiling to us the successive phases of his mental development as an excessively dreamy boy.'[7] In *Le Petit Pierre,* he wishes us to believe that his inner world came into being after he had a room to himself. 'It separated me from the universe—and there I found the universe again.'[8] Perhaps he is still making the phases too distinct, but it seems plausible that his imagination ranged more freely in privacy. Later, he sought to convey to Ségur that the reason any child of his type is content is that he is occupied not with reflections in any sense, but rather with receiving the first impact of forms and figures. Joy and light circulate together, casting an inexpressible sheen upon all objects. The child is carried from one pleasant revelation to another:

> You might call that happy time the *Age of Images.* In silence and meditation—that is, in the only frame of mind which makes life tolerable—one contemplates a delightful fairy-land.[9]

§ 2

FURTHERMORE, the autobiographical volumes contain throughout many references to 'mes rêves.' The author is occupied with showing how Pierre's whole childhood was a kind of joyous dream, full of charming miracles; like his master, Leconte de Lisle, Anatole speaks deliberately of his lost youth as enveloped by the dearest and most tenacious of illusions. One critic would link this day-dreaming with a more definite creative gift: 'Many times he has described the charm of mystery and his power of imagination as a child.'[10]

'As a child'—perhaps the point is there. Perhaps, as Pierre, he did have a genuine, transfiguring, imaginative power, which presently faded 'into the light of common day.' But we may well question whether his ability (in maturity) to revive and render all these personal memories, dreams, and images, is equivalent to a true and abiding creative power. We have heard him disclaim, both for himself and his mother, the possession of the imaginative gift. But Mother had a pretty fancy for embroidering tales 'round the pictures that I had.' And Anatole came to be much the same kind of embroiderer. Consequently, the *motif* 'je n'ai pas d'imagination,'[11] is not a total disclaimer. Both he and his critics speak of his talent as a synthetic rather than a creative faculty.[12] His was an 'emotional imagination' ; an ingrowing thing, it is entangled with his *souvenirs,* while, says Pellissier, it 'prolongs his dreams and colours his inner world' ; his works as a whole, declared his first English reviewer, are less social observations and constructions than the 'subdued and delicate dreams of a soul that has fallen asleep' ; in vain does Pierre at times seek 'ardently to get out of myself . . . to enter fully into the minds of others' ; M. Barthou concludes roundly that France was no Balzac, that he simply did not have the inventive power.[13]

M. Michaut agrees in principle and in accordance with his main thesis ascribes to Anatole the imagination of a 'dilettante.' But in one respect he finds that our author's vision is large and original. This is when he makes a sudden leap from the trivial and concrete to the vast spaces evoked by Pascal, mapped out by modern science, and familiar to the meditations of Anatole France.[14]

But let us return to the boy's more animated visionings, as recorded in *Pierre Nozière*.[15] His childish imagination is at times a potent and uncanny thing. It is stirred by the curiosities and vibrant terrors of a sensitive lad. By what sort of intuition did he know that the falling of a heavy body in the courtyard spelt disaster, and why did he shudder at the knowledge ? Still earlier, when he slept in the small bed near his mother's, 'legions of horrid devils danced their *rondes* about me ; slowly a woman made of black marble passed by, wailing ; and I learned later that these devils danced only in my brain and that the slow, sad, black woman was my own thought.' Even so, Little Pierre ; and she was none the less real for that.

Many were the things he feared : the four stone giants of the Place Saint-Sulpice, the two coffin-like boxes in which M. Hamoche kept his wares ; even the well-known face of Mme. Mathias 'seemed to my childish imagination like a house devoured by an ancient fire.' When he tells of little Jean's delight in his whip and his dream-horses, he declares that children easily imagine they have whatever things they want. This is their particle of the divine fire, for 'when they keep in maturity this marvellous faculty they are called poets and madmen.'[16] The *furor poeticus,* he intimates, can be a dreadful thing, with which he has little personal sympathy.

The later Gospels, especially *Petit Pierre,* are well populated with monsters. Unknown beings, quite different from ordinary men or animals, floated around in the darkness ; and 'marine monsters pursued me in my sleep.' So he was led into a kind of double existence, which became quite supernatural at night-time. Deformed and twisted folk pranced round his couch ; his imagination armed them with such domestic utensils as syringes and brooms. Or shadows and influences rose out of the floor and must have come from an alien world. In those years he invented easily. When he peeped unlawfully into a neighbouring studio, he made up for Mélanie a rigmarole of what he saw — dismembered human limbs, skeletons dancing a *ronde* (again), and seven beautiful wives (evidently Bluebeard's) hanging sepulchrally from the ceiling. . . Thus his tantalizing dream-life was an 'unknown, sombre and silent world, the very notion of which made me experience all the delights of fear.' From the age of five he indulged in the supernatural and had a lively curiosity about *diableries.*[17]

Most of this seems likely enough, if we agree with M. Corday about one particular *hantise* and its source. In connexion with the recurrent dream about the twisted little people, the biographer reminds us that France himself linked this with impressions derived from Callot's drawings —'impressions that were profoundly graved in his memory.'[18]

The same cult of terror for terror's sake is visible in the *Livre de mon ami.* The monsters that here file past his couch, with their bristling moustaches and their strange instruments, arouse in Pierre fascination as well as fear. If he is frightened by the dog who recalls the Children in the Tower, he is rapidly reassured by his mother — for his 'thoughts leapt quickly, as birds leap from branch to branch.' If he looks askance upon a rather tough playmate, his terror is soon mingled with pity in the Aristotelian manner : he contemplated this 'sombre and powerful Cain with all the compunction of a good little Abel.' Even when Pierre's grandmother died and all the neighbourhood round her house seemed affected by that influence, yet his sharp senses discerned chiefly the beauty of the trees, the gentle air, and the shining heaven above.[19]

Some visions are utterly serene. A holy joy descends upon him from the sky that vaulted the Jardin des Plantes, wherein he fancied that God the Father, white-bearded and benevolent, sat enthroned and extended a benediction to Pierre along with the antelope and the gazelle. In short, as a rule: 'I was happy. A thousand things, both familiar and mysterious, occupied my imagination and filled my life.' Such were the dining-room transformed into a village-square, the mahogany side-board converted into the inn of the Cheval-Blanc. He was the cook and the captain bold, or rather the postilion, the horses and the carriage which rushed forth from the little room out to the vast horizons of adventure:

> For then I was a great magician. I evoked for my amusement various obliging creatures and I disposed of nature as I would. Unfortunately, I lost this precious gift later.

We may note the confession.

His father shrugged his shoulders and thought that the boy's *goût de rêverie* would do him no good. 'Solitude exalts his imagination,' said the careful man, 'and I have observed that his head is already full of chimeras.' School was prescribed as a remedy, but the chimeras kept on swarming and making faces. Like the sorcery-books in the shop-windows, everything was more or less mysterious to Pierre. In connexion with the classics, too, he exclaims at the magnificent imaginings that pass through the minds of little rascals. The *images d'Epinal,* already mentioned, certainly excited in him the faculty divine, 'without which nothing is achieved, even in the direction of experimentation and the exact sciences.'[20]

These prints, by stimulating a taste for stories, taught him much finer things than can be learned in textbooks.[21] He may become, to be sure, weary of the 'shadow-shapes that come and go,' he may feel that such images are only part of the universal illusion and the constant flux; yet the very last lines in the *Livre de Pierre* express his gratitude that 'indulgent nature has accorded to men the dearest of her gifts, the gift of dreams.'

§ 3

LIKE father, like daughter. We may anticipate some opinions of his middle years, as recorded in the *Livre de Suzanne*. This portion of the *Livre de mon ami* has been called the 'true jewel-box' of Anatole's heart and it expresses a great solicitude about his child.[22] Pierre Nozière is eager that Suzanne shall be brought up, as he was, under the double influence of old *bibelots* and fanciful reveries :

> I certainly hope that later all these antiquities will give her ideas surrounded by fantasy and develop in her head weird, absurd and charming day-dreams. She will have her visions. She will indulge that pretty imagination connected with detail and style which makes life beautiful. I will tell her foolish stories . . . she will be insane about them.

The kind of imagination described here is clearly the fancy.

Suzanne's mother mocks at her for trying to seize a rooster painted on her plate — and mocks also at her husband who defends Suzanne. In fact, the opposition of common sense to contemplation is as old as Socrates and Xanthippe and foreshadows much in the conjugal antiphony of Monsieur and Madame Bergeret. But Pierre still fondly believes that the Eternal Feminine (when young) may be directed away from practical concerns. Fantasy and magic are said to encircle Suzanne's tender years. The fact that the aforesaid rooster is inanimate exceeds her intelligence. Excellent ! 'That is what makes her so admirable. Small children live in a perpetual enchantment ; everything is a prodigy for them ; and so poetry shines in their eyes. They dwell in other regions than ours.'

'Little fool !' said Mamma.

The father's defence of Suzanne is, characteristically, that her clutch at the rooster means that she 'began seeking the beautiful' at the ripe age of three months and twenty days. This first flight towards beauty, muses Anatole, is 'the natural exercise of noble minds.' His defence recalls the pretty poem of Hugo's about the child who is

> Offrant de toutes parts sa jeune âme à la vie
> Et sa bouche aux baisers.*

* Offering everywhere his young soul to life — and his mouth to kisses.

And Anatole himself wrote a poem in which he surrounds Suzanne with a visionary world similar to the one which Pierre had inhabited:

> Tout dans l'immuable nature
> Est miracle aux petits enfants.*

Their infantile years are passed as under a spell:

> Le reflet de cette magie
> Donne à leur regard un rayon.
> Déjà la belle Illusion
> Excite leur frêle énergie.†

When they are drowned in this 'divine unknown,' people summon them forth in vain, for, most significantly,

> Ils habitent un autre monde.

Their eyes are filled with 'strange dreams,' and thus 'from thrill to thrill, they make the discovery of Life.'[23]

France is best pleased with his daughter when she voices some of his own ideas. But to do him justice, he also loves her pretty ways for their own sake. She is full of charming gestures, as when she points to a star and addresses it in a language beyond our ken. Anatole continues to approve of her devotion to lovely objects. When she was nine, he tells us in the *Jardin d'Epicure,* she was still 'wiser than the sages. She just remarked to me: "Small children ought not to read books. There are so many beautiful things that they haven't yet seen."'[24]

But I question whether the daughter of Anatole was kept away from books for very long. Let us return to her record. The disparate parts of the *Livre de Suzanne* include some sketches of her friends, together with an account of her 'library,' which is really a statement concerning the education of girls; and this is followed by an apparently detached 'Dialogue sur les Contes de fées.' Throughout this miscellany the mature 'Pierre' is insisting—as if answering Mrs. Pierre were still in the back of his mind—on the rights of the imagination, the beauty and desirability of story-

* Everything in changeless Nature is a miracle for small children.

† The reflection of this magic shines in their eyes. Already lovely Illusion beckons on their frail forces.

telling. The tales that he promised his daughter should awaken, he hopes, a 'spark of madness' in her nature ; and her friends are chiefly interesting in so far as they share this propensity. When her playmate, another 'petit Pierre' falls ill, he is solaced by toys that represent an Alpine farm. 'Ce fut une magie' ; the painted blocks recalled to him images of the Swiss farm, and soon, by association of ideas, he is eating and drinking heartily. 'That is what I call having imagination.' It certainly takes a practical turn.

Anatole's views about children's books are contained in an adjacent 'Letter to a Lady.'[25] Children, he holds, are bored by sugar-coated volumes designed especially for them, in which the author makes an effort to come down to their sphere ; they prefer to be transported into a new mysterious world of large interests. They are suited by 'magnanimous works, full of great creations,' clearly composed and strongly written : the *Odyssey, Don Quixote, Robinson Crusoe.* Popular science is anathema—it destroys the sense of beauty. There is much danger that 'in ten years we shall all be electricians.' A certain educator is arguing that the fairy-tales of Perrault should be withdrawn from children and a scientific handbook substituted—because, forsooth, fairies are imaginary beings and the same cannot be said of such products as guano. Well, Pierre would like to tell the Doctor that 'fairies exist precisely because they are imaginary.'[26] It sounds like the sentimental plea in *Peter Pan,* but the author's point is more subtle : whatever exists in the subjective mind is real for the person concerned ; and fairies 'do exist in naïve and fresh imaginations which remain open to the youthful poetry of popular traditions.' The Bretons are right in sharing this 'croyance aimable.'[27] The year before his death Anatole was still affirming that we always need fairy-tales to balance the doses of cold truth which we must swallow.[28]

The transcendental argument above reminds us of the haughty little fairy who appeared to the learned Sylvestre Bonnard with the declaration that learning is nothing and imagination everything : 'I am imaginary ; therefore I exist. People dream about me and I appear. Everything is only a dream, and since nobody dreams about *you,* Sylvestre Bonnard, you have no existence at all.'[29]

Pierre continues his letter to the effect that what children need is not a mechanistic universe but something that stimulates their poetic sense. Hence he desires 'tales for great and small, beautiful tales . . . that make us laugh or weep and convey us into an enchanted realm. . . Faerydom responds to an eternal need of the soul.' Tale-tellers remake the world and give their readers opportunities to do likewise. Nor is the child deceived ; he knows that in actual life dwarfs and fairies do not circulate. So long live noble legends and popular poetry—down with the chemists who fear the imagination ! 'For it is she, with her falsehoods, who scatters the seed of every beauty and every virtue in the world. We are great only through her favour.' Here surely speaks the later France, who has added his philosophy of Illusion to his friendship for glamour and gramarye.

The argument is resumed in the subsequent 'Dialogue on Fairy-Tales.' The typically French form of the dialogue has been handled by such able practitioners as Fontenelle, Diderot, Voltaire, Renan, and Anatole himself in meditative mood.[30] The usual technique, which France follows, is to present several interlocutors, expressing diverse attitudes concerning the matter in debate. In this particular 'Dialogue,' which is quite eighteenth-century in its treatment,[31] the author's mouthpiece repeats and develops what has been said above. It is here that the imagination is decidedly viewed as not really creative, but as simply 'assembling' or curiously collocating material given us by the five senses. Anatole appears as the disciple of Condillac. 'All poetry, all *féerie* consists in these happy associations,' whether found in the legend of Sleeping Beauty or in the *Iliad*. To the objection that such tales are 'absurd and puerile,' the author answers with a *credo quia absurdum ;* when taxed with a strange mingling of Homer's goddesses and Perrault's marvels, he declares that they come from the same natural sources. He is thus launched on a disquisition concerning myth-making, in which Max Müller, Grimm, and others are quoted and some interesting parallels are laid down. Blue-Beard, it seems, was primitively the sun. Mother Goose has been identified with a number of figures, among them 'La Reine Pédauque' or the Web-footed Queen. 'Peau d'Ane' symbolizes the dawn, so does Cinderella. And all stories similar to the Sleeping Beauty legend were first connected with the cult of Adonis, or the awakening of Spring from the bondage of Winter. Several of these names suggest *motifs* that recur in France's later work. He concludes the dialogue in dithyrambic fashion, praising the power and beauty of fairies. They are our destiny, the *marraines* who determine all our actions, for 'liberty is an illusion and faerydom is a truth.'

Truth for him, beauty for him as well. In regard to such legends he willingly allows the 'suspension of disbelief' which Coleridge recommended. He is a true subject of Queen Mab. Elsewhere he declares: 'Blessèd is the child who is brought up on fairy-tales. His riper years should prove rich in wisdom and imagination.'[32] France's devotion to the Folk of Peace, as the Scotch call them, was extraordinary. One critic says that he even restored fairies to the order of nature.[33] They seemed to bear gifts for all periods of his life. When asked in South America what was his 'favourite book' (the tiresome question!), he replied simply, 'the first book of fairy-tales that fell into my hands.'[34]

§ 4

So his works are full of allusions to the Little People. The golden-eyed Marcelle, remember, was a fairy-godmother, acquainted with the future, yet not to be closely questioned, 'for fairies, as I understand them, demand silence and mystery.' The *Blue-Bird,* which the narrator in *Marguerite* calls 'my own favourite story,' is also related by Sylvestre Bonnard to little Sylvestre; and the whole episode of the sprightly fairy who surprised the old scholar is recounted with unusual zest. This intruder is a kinswoman of the salamander who beguiled the leisure of Jacques Tournebroche. There is likewise the story of *Les Sept Femmes de Barbe-Bleue.* There is even a harmless, though naughtily told bit of Hans Andersen, slipped into the alien setting of *l'Ile des Pingouins.* Everywhere France heard the 'slender voices of the fairies.' But his own *pièce de résistance* of this kind is the story of *Abeille.*[35]

Georges de Blanchelande becomes orphaned and is brought up as a foster-brother of Abeille ('Honey-Bee') by the latter's mother. The two children are loving playmates. On adventure bound, each is seized and carried away by a different band of underworld people—she by the dwarfs, he by the nixies.[36] In quaint habitations the young people are long detained, until they yearn to escape and reunite. King Loc [Log] of the dwarfs has fallen in love with Honey-Bee, but he is self-sacrificing enough to restore her to Georges. There is a joyous and fantastic ending.

The sources of the tale are unknown, though folkloristic origins are indicated. The external setting is vaguely medieval, suggesting Brittany. The outstanding thing is that the story is drenched in the supernatural and yet does not lose its feet in such a flood. How does reality keep its foot-hold ? For one thing, the supernatural interferences are delicately and discreetly handled, and well combined with the sentiments and speech of this earth. It is a gift which Anatole France preserved as late as his *Vie de Jeanne d'Arc* and indeed never wholly lost.

We hear of a sunken forest (which may be Broceliande) and of the islands of Avalon and Thule, then not submerged. The Celtic otherworld is in the offing. There are several instances of magic, scattered signs and tokens, an atmosphere of doubt and mystery closing round the lost children. There are many strange *lueurs,* and indeed 'la lumière' is almost the *motif* of the story: floods of light surround the 'Undines' who, like Loreleis, appear and bear the boy away to the depths of the lake. They are the eternal lure ; but the dwarfs who carry off Honey-Bee are industrious and worthy citizens. They are capable, to be sure, of Trilby-like pranks and they are linked with the whole tribe of kobolds, gnomes, and the like. Mime and Alberic are of their kin, although King Loc and his people are better-natured. They have quaint English-seeming names ; but they resemble rather Hendrik Hudson's men in their staid frolics, their costumes, and the great beards surmounting their squat figures. Their constructions underground are described, together with their tastes and habits—even their *bibelots,* dear to the narrator. They admire poetically the beauty of Honey-Bee ; and the magnanimous King Loc transmits her image, by television, to comfort her mother every night ! Less is said about Georges among the Undines. We find him established in a coloured grotto, where he refuses to play Tannhäuser to their queen. In the meantime King Loc suffers from an increasing sadness because of his love for Honey-Bee. The growing pains of the king and of the young people too are depicted circumstantially, while the return to the upperworld is well-motivated.

The author of the tale has been praised by various editors for 'his delightful rendering of child-life and child thought, in which he is unsurpassed in French literature' ; or for writing 'a story overflowing with poetic imagination, wisdom and humour, divine qualities to which the heart of the child is always open.'[37] And yet . . . one knows children who do not like *Abeille,* who remain passive before its brilliance and its light. Perhaps there is not quite enough story; perhaps Anatole disguises insufficiently the subtle appeal to adult minds. We meet with analyses of the growth of love, literary allusions or learned references, a slightly archaic and 'precious' style, hinting of Marivaux and the Musset of *On ne badine pas avec l'amour.* According to some, the brew was flavoured with extracts from Virgil and La Fontaine.[38] Anatole remains Anatolian still, and even in the realm of butterflies he is an 'elderly and erudite butterfly.'[39] The Epicurean philosopher is masked, but it is he who attends and reports the fête. Do we expect this individual to absent himself from any of his stories? After all, in Suzanne's Book, it is Suzanne's father who strings the pearls; it is he who lurks behind the pages of *Filles et Garçons* and other children's stories. In 'Les Etrennes de Mademoiselle de Doucine,' the young girl herself never appears; there are only several old men who wrangle about giving her a present.[40] The tender tale of *Marguerite* (1886) deals less with the child than with the emotions she revives in the narrator through her resemblance to her mother. Again, France himself doubted whether juvenile fiction was his true vein.[41] Apropos of his 'prize-books,' he whispered to his secretary: 'I never speak of them, for I doubt if I pulled it off. It's much easier to write for adults than for children.' Because juvenile readers make no pretence of liking a book when they do not. . . Perhaps there is a kind of *mauvaise honte* in this confession. He must have marvelled that he had ever been 'sweet'; beginning with doses of saccharin, he had ended with a severe case of hyperacidity. In his middle years Anatole may not still 'believe in fairies,' but he still likes to play with them, as he plays with many things.

Thus, *Abeille* is a charming and delightful book (for elders), replete with whimsical humour and spiced with the sly Francian flavour. Anatole's characters are parcels of Anatole. In fact, the line of sages that began with Bonnard is here carried on. One of the author's earliest incarnations is the 'old monk who had escaped from Constantinople' and who gave political advice 'according to a small number of maxims.' A second incarnation, among the dwarfs, might be the old savant, Nur, who is wise because he 'knows how to learn some of the numberless things that he does not know.' At any rate, he knows that the consolations of poetry are more necessary than 'inhuman' science ; he knows too that mankind is ignorant and wicked, and if he esteems the race at all it is because men have the great virtue of pity. How characteristic of the later Anatole is this ! Equally so is the dwelling on the pangs and yet the necessity, the inevitability, of love ; and his mind has not yet been sharpened to the point of abstracting the glow of altruism from a generous passion.[42] King Loc, when he unselfishly bids Georges and Abeille to 'be happy ever after,' thus closes the story : 'A great passion is a fine thing, certainly ; but a beautiful heart-affair is better ; let nothing be lacking in it, neither indulgence nor pity.'

In some respects *Abeille* is not unlike Voltaire's *Candide*. We have the same amused view of humanity's foibles, a like separation of the lovers through fate, similar chapter-titles, which compose a mixture of philosophy and fancy ; and France often employs the swift *coupé* style of his eighteenth-century master.

§ 5

'Religions,' remarks Santayana, 'are the fairy-tales of the conscience.' From childhood down, our author never lost interest in the mythopeic fertility of the various faiths. So in Pierre-Anatole's inner world, two particular obsessions, the Bible and the lives of Saints, figured conspicuously. The volumes of 'souvenirs' contain many allusions to scriptural passages. The great dilapidated family Bible became a sort of measuring-rod which he applied to earthly things. Apparently this 'vieille bible en estampes' consisted as much of illustrations as of text, and one can easily understand the impression left by these solemn engravings. They were executed, it seems, in a 'pompous and hard' fashion.[43] The tome itself is fully described in the opening chapter of *Pierre Nozière*. This work gave the child his 'first idea of the universe,' which was accordingly inhabited mainly by Dutch figures of the seventeenth century—for of that period were the illustrations. In his mind the Terrestrial Paradise was for long a Dutch landscape ; horses (like Elsa) came only from Brabant ; and in the midst of the first menagerie Eve paraded her rotund Flemish charms. (She continued to parade them, even in *La Rôtisserie de la Reine Pédauque*.)[44] Noah's ark was represented as 'a kind of long caravel, topped by a wooden castle with a gabled roof.' Since it strongly resembled a toy ark which Pierre really possessed, that to him was 'a great proof of the truth of Holy Writ.' Another clear memory is that of Samson carrying off the gates of Gaza—a picturesque Flemish Gaza. Observe the deliberate naïveté of the following account:

> So Samson went along, one gate under each arm. I liked him a lot. He was my friend... I still like him. He was very strong, very simple, and had no meanness in him. He was the first Romanticist.[45]

The Philistines and the Amalekites were turbulent people, confusing in their warfare, but distinct in their coiffures.

The New Testament 'had a more intimate charm,' and again the customs and costumes were transposed into seventeenth-century terms. People resembling Anne of Austria, spruce cavaliers and pages approached Christ, seated 'in a garden-close, at the base of a country-house built in the time of Henry IV.'[46] A Renaissance lady delicately offered the Saviour a glass of water.[47] Scarcely need we smile when we remember how the present era seeks to 'rationalize' antiquity, or how the Middle Ages represented the siege of a medieval town, and bestowed the accolade on Lord Hector and Sir Paris and Lord Cupid too.

Every evening the boy looked at these sacred pictures. Naturally he took them to bed with him and into his dreams. Since they formed his earliest conception of the cosmos, small wonder that he recognized, just beyond the Pont d'Austerlitz, the Holy Land, the Dead Sea,—and the eminence from which David surveyed the ablutions of Bathsheba. The lad also found arresting images of God the Father, white-bearded 'in a blue robe,' of Christ walking upon the waters, or of the turbaned Joseph, the darling of his heart. Alas! He laments that the days of simple faith are gone; and now, instead of the Garden of Eden, we can discern only a black abyss at the beginning of creation.[48]

From early times, Pierre was fond of 'maniacs, saints and gods, these first effigies of humanity.'[49] His mother's mind was full of saintly legends. Her room, 'in its familiar and august sanctity, was like the spot on which heaven poured its rays and its favours, as seen in holy pictures.'[50] Pierre listened with delight to her reading of the Saints' Lives. Is it surprising that he was drawn toward a similar vocation? Although his *Imitatio* fell short of the roses of martyrdom, it abounded in fasts and austerity. It was also an imitation of St. Simeon Stylites on his column, of St. Nicholas giving goods to the poor, of the 'Blessed Labre' who preferred muddy apparel, of the Franciscans, whose hair-shirts could be copied, he found, by using the stuffing of an old arm-chair. Sometimes these enthusiastic interpretations offended a mother who was practical as well as pious. The boy would walk with his eyes on the ground, affecting a saintly modesty. The restraints of domestic life irked his sanctity; and he thought of plunging into the desert, the Thébaïde, where doubtless he would have visions like St. Anthony and be buried near St. Mary the Egyptian.[51] Here speaks the future author of *Thaïs*. Evidently, he knew his *Golden Legend* quite early. Presently he describes the attachment of Sylvestre Bonnard to that "vaste et gracieux ouvrage.' Bonnard's desire to have an Old French manuscript of this collection motivates the story of 'La Bûche.' How the scholar rejoices when Mme. Trépof presents it to him, how he clings to this treasure when forced to sell his library! Even Anatole Him-self still narrated, according to his secretary, 'lily-white and edify-ing tales from the *Légende dorée*'—alternating them, it is true, with anecdotes concerning the prowess of Casanova.[52] For, as Doumic remarks, edifying legends and the other kind become mixed in his memory.[53] Another critic observes that if the old saints had their temptations, these holy men offered as a group a continual *tentation* to Anatole. He succumbs to their lure—courteously at first, but with increasing irony as his scepticism matured.[54] The tone of clerical unction is not, with our pseudo-Benedictine, a sign of grace. Probably his 'adolescent religiosity' reveals already a tincture of paganism.[55]

To please his parents, an adaptable child will assume piety as readily as anything else. What of those unique *Christian Thoughts,* written at the age of eight?[56] Fifteen of these maxims are preserved; they embody very orthodox reflections concerning the efficacy of prayer, the view of this life as a passage to eternal reward or punishment, the central belief that God is good and that the devil is to be avoided or confounded. One could not recognize the author of *La Révolte des anges*. The tone is horta-tory, yet simple. And Pierre tells us that he also started for 'Maman' a small theological treatise which began with the in-terrogation: 'What is God?'

§ 6

As we have seen, Anatole's school *cahiers* include transcriptions of three 'legends,' among which is that extremely rare relic, *La Légende de Sainte-Radegonde.*[57] This was also written for the eyes of his mother. The short manuscript (there are but four pages in all) was calligraphed in the fine handwriting of 'Hyacinthe Dufour,' and only eight copies are believed to exist. Anatole himself states, on a privately owned copy of *La Légende,* that it was 'lithographed by my maternal grandfather,' alias Dufour. Various errors about the essay have crept into the newspapers: that it was printed by the elder France; that anywhere between two and ten copies are extant; and that it would occupy *two volumes* in the *Œuvres complètes!* But the facts are given by M. Barthou.[58]

The preface is dated November 29, 1859; it is full of a rather cloying family affection, which rings none too sincerely. The tale relates how Radegonda, a Thuringian princess, was captured by the Franks under King Chloter (*sic*). This monarch had her educated, with a view to marriage. But the Princess hated her conquerors: 'O God, thou alone knowest what this virgin suffered,' when 'Chloter' actually married her. Naturally, she took the veil and became a Christian saint. The good Saint Medardus dissolved her marriage and consecrated her a Diaconesse. The *Légende* also intimates that poetic justice was measured out to Clotaire, in that he too became a monk. But unlike Paphnuce, he seems to have remained a holy man.

As a footnote candidly acknowledges, most of this material is taken from Thierry's *Récits des temps mérovingiens.*[59] Anatole's historical imagination is already at work. Otherwise, the *Légende* offers little intrinsic interest: the 'Méditations sur Palmyre' are far better written. Yet Radegonde henceforth becomes something of a *motif* in the author's mind. There are several minor references to her name; and the substance of her legend is repeated in *l'Orme du Mail,* where the saint reappears—not without miraculous interventions.

France's continuous concern with Radegonde is by no means exceptional. Other saints make their bows in the Gospels and attend Anatole almost to the end of his days. Such was one consequence, he observes in the *Jardin d'Epicure,* of reading at twelve the 'small pious books which reveal the world beyond to simple souls.'[60] *Le Petit Pierre* speaks of a 'gigantic' and unidentified 'Saint of stone.' *Pierre Nozière* contains the lives of several holy men and women—Longis, Onoflette, etc.—whose memories are still fragrant in the Northern provinces. Anatole's favourite trinity of Mary the Egyptian, Margaret, and Catherine crop up in *La Rôtisserie.* Needless to say, the 'voices' of the last two are heard often enough in the *Vie de Jeanne d'Arc.* France has been styled one of the 'great literary patrons' of another trinity composed of St. Francis of Assisi, Santa Clara, St. Bonaventure.[61] The Italian tales (*Le Puits de Sainte Claire,* etc.) echo some of these names; *Thaïs,* of course, abounds in early Christian worthies; while the assembly in Paradise (in *l'Ile des Pingouins*) serves as a gathering-place and a debating-hall for nearly all the saints whom Anatole had most favoured.

Hence we are not surprised when he announces his preference for legend over history; nor do we wonder that his own parchment-bound copy of the *Légende dorée,* still extant at the Villa Saïd, is considered the seed-bed from which germinated—paradoxically—several of the tales in which he opposed a dying paganism to a nascent Christianity.[62] The very word 'légende' is a *motif* in his discourse and comports a liking for dealing with the souls of 'the naïve, the mystics, the credulous.'[63]

If the elderly Anatole loses his pristine faith, yet he keeps, in a manner of speaking, the Works—the Works of many other saints and Fathers. He maintains an interest in all pious things, and he manages to preserve at times the edifying style appropriate to a medieval chronicler or pilgrim. Are not all these things recorded in Brousson, his Book?[64] When France tells a monkish story, he concludes in a snuffling tone: 'And that is how, my friend, the pious wolf of Gubbio devoured the lion of Francis who had become an ill-conducted goat.' He offers this tale as an epilogue to the *Fioretti* of St. Francis. The marvels told concerning this saint, even to the legendary rose-bush, still charm the heart of the old connoisseur. From that bush he brought his secretary a flower, the authenticity of which was guaranteed by the nuns; 'and I have no doubt of it, because the legend is beautiful.' This significant avowal explains his continued interest in the fair and the false. He quotes mockingly, but with a certain sympathy, Jules Soury who cried aloud: 'Give me legends, legends! I am athirst for legends.'

Anatole is then 'steeped in Christian hagiography'[65] and will relate any sort of legend to any sort of listener: the tale of St. Francis' rose-bush, the epilogue thereto which is like a *fabliau,* the ghost-story at the end of the *Livre de Pierre,* sundry tales of terror, allusions galore to hornèd devils, to the cup of the King of Thule, to the story of Blue-Beard, to miraculous deeds as linked with faerydom, to the 'legendary angels that hover round the confines of death.'

When he became a father he still accepted the absurdities of Guignol,[66] just as in his childhood he accepted the myth of the giant Teutobochus, who, like Ibsen's inert Boyg, barred the entrance to the History of France that Pierre and Fontanet had projected. It has been suggested that the 'visionary' side of Anatole may be due to the peasant blood of the Thibault family.[67] Perhaps his apparent gusto for the mythical was partly assumed and became associated with his increasing taste for mystifications, that 'last infirmity' of clever minds.[68]

CHAPTER VI

The Long Thoughts of Youth

§ 1

WHILE Anatole France was learning about love in the country of Chateaubriand, there had been fired, over Fort Sumter, our second 'shot heard round the world.' But it does not appear that Anatole perceived its reverberations. Few indeed are his references to America before the eighties. In 1868 he reproved Alfred de Vigny for recommending a constitutional republic after our pattern.[1] On the other hand, there is little to show that our hero directly participated in that dim carnival which moved through the lingering twilight of the Second Empire in France. What must have been his impressions in surveying from afar, say from his eyrie in Notre-Dame, this cavalcade of Imperialism ?

We know that he saw the palace of the Tuileries in all its splendour. With some distaste he trod the great avenues levelled by that Juggernaut, Baron Haussmann ('Les Comptes Fantastiques d'Haussmann'),— thoroughfares 'beautifully accessible to light, air and infantry.' He probably resented the Baron's notion that in the interest of city-cleaning the outdoor book-stalls should be abolished from the quays.[2] He must have been aware of the industrial expansion, finding its climax in the Exposition of 1867, where everything was exhibited from Herr Krupp's prophetic 'Bertha' to the 'new American rocking-chair.' The *Paris Guide* of those days demonstrated to visitors that by the side of old monuments there were new boulevards and that the quaint booths of yore were yielding place to handsome general stores.[3] It is likely that the visitors responded to this cry of modernity. England was muted and in mourning, while Paris was hailed once more as the authentic centre of civilization. It was the era of the willowy Eugénie and of the billowy crinoline. Gavarni was drawing for posterity his magical silhouettes, suggesting the frou-frou of superb dresses against the background of the Opéra. Constantin Guys, the caricaturist, recorded the types seen at the Exposition, which Anatole attended, as it is written in *Les Désirs de Jean Servien.* It was about then, he also tells us, that Paris became the 'caravansary of the world' ; and little distinction was made between Jew and Gentile.[4] Elsewhere women were donning 'Dolly Varden' dresses and Garibaldi waists (rather prominent waists), but the Parisienne remained *fine,* fragrant, and perilous. To a tune of Offenbach's, preferably the *Orphée aux enfers,* she danced under the flaring gas-light, artfully manipulating her infinite folds and graces, her flounces and furbelows. As a wrap she wore an Indian shawl, a cashmere, or a burnous. Ottomans or *poufs* received her dainty feet. With showers of diamonds bedecking her, she looked like a chandelier ; with wreaths in her hair, she was a flower-garden ; with delicate arched back and sloping shoulders quite *décolletées,* the Parisienne moved like a stately swan in a lordly setting. Did Anatole France see her ? Without doubt. 'In the days of Saint Crinoline,' he mentions later, women lived in a whirl of pleasure.[5]

He also saw, as far as that 'ambiguous creature' could be discerned, the figure of the Emperor in the last days of his still more ambiguous glory. M. Bergeret has commemorated the *regard vague,* the *air de rêve* with which the master of ceremonies floated through the halls of the Tuileries, when the dance was old and cold.[6] We can readily imagine the immense moustache and the pale immobile countenance—what Maupassant called the *enseigne de coiffeur*. Hugo, more savagely, speaks of the Empire as a circus and of the 'imperial spectre beating the big drum.'[7]

A perspicacious youth, in his twenties, looking over from the Latin Quarter, may well have perceived that the tinsel glory was fading out like a mere dream. In fact, Anatole expressed in a periodical of the time his view of the Empire, from a Republican standpoint.[8] He too mocked at Napoleon and his ministers, criticizing the naming of streets after military heroes, as well as the erection of Barye's statue of Napoleon in the costume of a Roman Emperor. 'Public taste and democratic sentiment no longer permit such exhibitions,' said he severely. With a wealth of Latin citations and allusions, the young writer demonstrates the absurdity of these procedures, concluding that the Emperor 'certainly ought to know that the contour of his face has nothing Roman about it.' In his old age he viewed the later Empire more favourably, declaring that there was a good deal of liberty, comparatively speaking, and that journalism was less of a corrupting force then than now.[9]

Historically, it seems clear that the various gestures toward

Liberalism had only made the people eager for more of a voice in the government. The imperial game was nearly up. The elections of 1869 showed an overwhelming Liberal sentiment; it was the same year in which Gladstone headed his first ministry. Once more the Elder Statesmen were condemned. New 'intransigent' figures like Gambetta and Rochefort had emerged, the latter waving like an oriflamme his proscribed *Lanterne*. Discontent—and soon the *débâcle*.

§ 2

To resume the thread of Anatole's life in the sixties, we should first visualize him towards the end of his school-days. There remains a photograph of *c.* 1861, representing a slight pensive lad with something mutinous in the set of the head and the jaw. This was the year of the travels in Normandy and of the first pangs of adolescent love, though the latter experience seems a trifle absurd in connexion with this slim schoolboy. It was in the following year that he failed to take his baccalaureate degree and left Stanislas for good; it seems that he made more than one effort towards the degree before being finally 'received' late in 1864. Indeed, a lady who should know alleges that France never got his *bachot* and once sardonically suggested to an amiable minister that he might repair that breach in the writer's fortress.[10] This appears to be a 'légende.' But what are we to think of Anatole's own reiterated statements to the effect that he duly passed the examination (a mere formality) and was received at seventeen, along with the rest of his class?[11] Is it fact or fiction that in his embarrassment he told a certain examiner (an ex-German named Hase) that the river Rhône emptied into Lake Ontario?[12]

There is no evidence that the youth took his failure seriously to heart. But the Thibault family, again, was not pleased. Anatole's father was naturally discouraged;[13] there was a lack of visible progress and (except for occasional jobs) of visible means of support. This state of affairs lasted a long time. Never has a would-be literary man set about making a career with greater deliberation and 'nonchalance.' In fact, for over a decade, it was not apparent that Anatole expected a career or had any ambitions. 'Sufficient unto the day are the roses thereof': this might have

A.F. IN 1862

been his life-long motto and it was adopted very early. 'I lived many happy years without writing,' he once said complacently.[14] And it is in connexion with this period that we get a plain avowal of his determined Epicureanism : 'I have always believed that the only reasonable thing is to seek for pleasure.'[15]

How did he undertake the search ? Was there, to begin with, much in the way of social life and gaiety ? The last chapters of *La Vie en fleur* show us Pierre Nozière engaged in making contacts with various circles and some interesting individuals. These personages are in part veracious, but more frequently they are fictionized. Among the former is the excellent M. Dubois, whom we shall presently find inducting Pierre into the paths that led to Virgilian myrtles. There were, of course, Godfather Danquin (*alias* Charavay) and the guests whom he entertained.[16] Every Saturday the same company reassembled. Dancing and games were in order among the young people. Pierre-Anatole danced very badly, but he was quite fond of kissing-games and of charades. Under these circumstances, several beautiful girls attracted his innocent attention. Rather overwhelmed by their charms, he felt more comfortable when conversing with Mme. Gobelin the miniaturist and with her daughter, 'Philippine.' The latter, thin, intelligent, endowed with a manifold personality, seemed willing enough to talk about archæology ; but Pierre learned later (to his surprise) that all the time she was dying of love for a bouncing doctor. This circle was formed of bourgeois folk, yet with a flavour of the artistic, the learned, even the medical. An opponent of the Danquin point of view, while Pierre was still a schoolboy, was 'Marc Ribert,' Romanticist and Bohemian. Needless to say, he had the aura and the gestures that fascinated our young friend.

Partly under the impulsions of Fontanet, A.F. presently began to spread his wings. With some reluctance he took riding lessons and appeared in the Bois on a strange tall beast named 'Faust.'[17] ('We never understood each other,' remarks Anatole, parenthetically.) It is of more significance that he penetrated into several salons, where financiers rubbed shoulders with aristocrats. He was dazzled by his first ball, at the home of the blue-stocking, 'Madame Airiau.' Her husband was of another calibre, an engineer on a large scale. 'Airiau was then studying the gigantic enterprise, still not realized, which will change the axis of civilization—the Bagdad railway.'[18] From the context one is led to believe that 'Airiau' is an adumbration of De Lesseps—to whose chair in the Academy France later succeeded—and the Bagdad railway may be the Suez Canal. The idea that Pierre was invited to accompany Airiau on one of his expeditions is pure fiction. But it was through this family that the youth first met a woman who impressed and disturbed him strangely—the Princess Bagration. The description of this mysterious Russian sculptress, who presently killed herself, recalls a real figure in the Paris of the eighties. 'Marie Bagration' is Marie Bashkirtseff; and France himself once wrote for 'La Vie littéraire' an appreciative article about the talented Russian girl.[19]

With reference to the figure that he cut at these parties, Anatole in the retrospect is quite candid. Contrary to Fontanet, who had assurance and easy manners, Pierre lacked boldness. Accordingly, he was not successful with the ladies. Not only did his inferiority as a dancer put him at a disadvantage; his conversation, which skipped alarmingly from the serious to the burlesque, was but little appreciated. His appearance was not very engaging. More ordinary young men got along much better. 'Thus I learned that nature and fortune had not favoured me.'[20] Some of these handicaps will reappear in connexion with the *Désirs de Jean Servien*. But Anatole declares that he salved his wounds by reminding himself of such compensations as a nimble wit and the ability to savour Beauty in all her forms.

Among these forms, painting and kindred arts soon attracted his lasting attention. We have seen that he came to visit the Louvre almost daily; there he learned to admire Assyrian statuary and decorated vases, Etruscan or Greek. He was led on to adore Ingres, so Grecian and voluptuous in his tastes, and to render a lesser homage to Delacroix. Some personal contacts with both of these artists are recorded.[21] With M. Dubois Pierre discoursed about Gérard and his models. One of these, who posed for 'Psyche,' was so beautiful in the picture that she quite bewitched Pierre—until it was discovered that, no longer Psyche nor beautiful, she lived in his own house on the Quai Voltaire. Another neighbour, M. Ménage, was a copyist in the Salon Carré. Through 'Marie Bagration,' Pierre made the acquaintance of Viardot, who as a connoisseur congratulated the youth on his opportunity to collaborate on a 'great work about painters.' In *Pierre Nozière,* we also meet with such types of the 'exclusive artist' as Jean Meusnier, who later sat for a Bohemian figure in *Le Chat maigre.*[22]

§ 3

But none of these experiences could be described as directed towards choosing a profession—unless it be the profession of *flâneur,* to which Anatole was always addicted. Still he did have, in the early sixties, a sort of back-door initiation into the by-ways of literature. This apprenticeship was served partly under Noël France, partly under Etienne Charavay.

Much has already been said in support of M. Huard's view that Father's book-shop 'conditioned France's life and work,'[23] at least to a considerable extent. It was natural that in 1862, when Anatole had no occupation, the book-dealer should use him for various small jobs about the place. It was equally natural that he should be pressed into service when it became a question of a much larger job—namely, cataloguing the Comte de La Bédoyère's library on the French Revolution.[24] This huge collection of well over one hundred thousand items had been slowly amassed by the owner, with the aid of Père France. Anatole had often seen the Count, talking iconography in the book-shop, or installed among his own riches in the Rue Saint-Dominique. When La Bédoyère died and his library came to be catalogued and sold, Noël France, as the 'archiviste de la Révolution,' was designated for the task. The result was a volume of seven hundred pages, called *Description historique et bibliographique de la collection de feu M. le Comte H. de la Bédoyère. . . Sur la Révolution française, l'Empire et la Restauration. Rédigée par France . . .* 1862.[25] Because of its great value, the collection was sold integrally to the Bibliothèque Impériale (now the Nationale) for ninety thousand francs.

Anatole had a share in the preparation of the preface to the Catalogue and a number of *notices;* his own account of the matter makes plain the significance of this contribution to the study of French history.[26] His interest in the Revolution was thereby given an enduring foundation. This predilection takes many shapes, all the way from his youthful 'Project' for getting out an *Encyclopédie de la Révolution* to the final composition of *Les Dieux ont soif* (1912).

But his more personal interest in Father's enterprises seems to have died a natural death after the completion of the Catalogue. He consorted, of course, with various booksellers and actually clerked for one of them a short while; he became friendly with men like Jules Coüet, a bibliophile devoted to the Renaissance.[27] Yet the guiding hand in his destinies at this stage was rather that of his quiet friend, Etienne Charavay.

The intimacy with Etienne had continued. Not only did the two youths finally take their bachelors' degrees at the same time, but it seems that they both admired the same actress, Madeleine Brohan, a celebrated *comédienne* of the period. It will soon appear, however, that France was more deeply caught in the toils of other charmers. There were other links between our juvenile Damon and his Pythias. Since Etienne became an assiduous student at the Ecole des Chartes, where he took his diploma as 'archiviste paléographe' in 1869, the legend has it that Anatole followed the same path.[28] This is now clearly shown to be an error. A.F. himself declared that he never attended the Ecole ('I was too lazy for that'), although he frequently went there to meet his friends.[29] At any rate, Charavay introduced him to the study of autograph manuscripts, and since the former edited a journal called the *Amateur d'autographes,* it was there that Anatole first regularly 'broke into print,' in 1867.

Bibliography with Père France, manuscripts with Charavay—a singular beginning for an imaginative writer! It seems, however, that the collaboration on the *Amateur* was mainly in the direction of book-reviews. Similar articles were written occasionally for the *Chasseur bibliographe,* of which Etienne was also editor, and other such periodicals. So it was really as a reviewer that Anatole began. Having already adopted the pen-name of 'France,' he wrote above this signature dramatic *comptes-rendus* for the *Chasseur,* reserving 'A. Thibault' for book-reviews. We shall later deal *in extenso* with this first published material. Let us now see why Anatole took the easiest way and drifted into the paths indicated by Charavay.

There is little to show that France was at any time a person of decided views and definite character. It is true that when in his maturity he was disturbed in certain cherished penchants and habits, he could strike back. But as a rule he was content to live and let live. As an indolent and procrastinating person even in his twenties, he saw no reason to bestir himself. When somehow he had become known, this attitude did him no disservice: the mountain could come to Mahomet.[30] He admits that as a schoolboy he had no ambition, that his passions were mild where those of his comrades were strong; and that at twenty he could not control the tall horse named 'Faust,' partly because his wits were perpetually wool-gathering.[31] Fernand Calmettes, who knew him well in the Parnassian period, thus sums him up: 'Easy to get along with, disliking violence and not at all aggressive, Anatole France was poorly qualified to take a high or dogmatic tone.' He never posed as a great character, with an idealistic message. He never demanded that man's thought should be lofty, but only that it should be free.[32]

Although we must allow for some 'arrangement,' light is thrown on Pierre's state of indecision by the amusing chapter in the last Gospel called 'Le Choix d'une carrière.'[33] Under the guidance of Fontanet, he visited first the School of Law, then the School of Medicine. Each seemed to have its points, but on reflection their ways were not his ways. How much nicer to be a 'magnanimous and melancholy' officer in the army! Yet perhaps victories and love-affairs were not the whole of military life. . . He considered engineering—and also diplomacy. Advised by 'Mouron-pour-les-petits-oiseaux,' he looked into the question of a bureaucratic position. Alas! Dull examinations stood like lions in the path. For picturesque reasons, farming and even trade attracted him briefly. This multitude of visions left him in a somewhat disorganized state, from which he was rescued by that excellent *littérateur,* Louis de Ronchaud. The rescuer proposed to Pierre a humble but definite task: to help edit a series of painters' lives then under way. Evidently, this was the position on which Viardot congratulated him. He was soon installed in a notable publishing-house and embarked on a succession of clerical 'labours in accordance with my real tastes.'[34]

Other firms provided similar though temporary tasks. The young scholar presently collaborated on a dictionary of antiquities as well as the *Dictionnaire Larousse,* and even prepared a card-catalogue for Nottet's circulating library.[35] It is probable that after he became associated with the publisher Lemerre, he participated in a *Manual of Bibliophily* which the latter got out, partly in order to boost his reprints of the classics. The major interests of bookmen are here dealt with so knowingly that the manual has been attributed to the hand of Anatole himself. (The MS., in fact, is in his handwriting.) The editor alludes to his assistants, E. Charavay and A. France, as 'laborious and erudite men.'[36]

A. France and E. Charavay—so long were those two names coupled that we might look more closely at the bearer of the last appellation. Perhaps not many people know today the quaint old Rue Furstenberg, tucked away in a maze of streets off the Rue de Seine. There the casual visitor may see an unpretending sign: 'Etienne Charavay: Autographes.'[37] For there until almost the present time M. Noël Charavay carried on the business under his elder brother's name. France, too, had a semi-fraternal feeling for the younger Charavay.[38] The career of Etienne was cut short—most unfortunately, but in no way to reflect upon his honour—by disputes over some expert testimony that he gave in the Dreyfus case. From speeches pronounced at his funeral (1899) by Maurice Tourneux and France himself, Charavay's character emerges with some clearness.[39] Not only was he a most knowledgeable person, but his disposition was markedly gentle and unselfish. Anatole evinces his grief at the loss of one who had companioned him for nearly fifty years. (In fact, letters survive showing an intimacy that dates back at least to 1853.)[40] France emphasizes the unobtrusive goodness, the probity, and the even temper of his great friend. In another place,[41] A.F. describes him as a small man with an immense beard, mild and sedentary, but addicted to a military enthusiasm and capable of heroism. He was short-sighted by nature, but had a long vision in historical matters. So together with his brother-in-law, Fernand Calmettes, Charavay was appointed to organize the Exposition de la Révolution Française in 1889.[42] Authorities agree that, through their common association on such journals as the *Revue des documents historiques,* Etienne sustained in Anatole a constant interest in history, particularly in the Revolution.[43] It is a curious fact that the firm of Charavay had brought out a *Catalogue de Documents autographes* on this subject in 1862—the same year when the house of France compiled the *Description historique* of the La Bédoyère collection.[44]

§ 4

We now come to a difficult subject—the part actually played by women in our young man's life. Some of the adventures and admirations attributed to 'Pierre' or to 'Jean Servien' have a foundation in fact; but it is hard to draw the line. Yet several things may be considered as established. Anatole's long preoccupation with the other sex, which has given rise to so many disquisitions,[45] was well under way in his 'teens: his *alter ego* declares: 'Je ramenais tout à l'amour.'[46] Again, his bashful attitude adding to his physical awkwardness, it seems plain that he thought about women more than he consorted with them. He was often upset in their actual presence; he got along best with the old or the ugly—but there was small pleasure in that; he was more at ease when he viewed women as 'fantômes' or as delicate objects of art.[47] Discussions with Fontanet,[48] passages concerning 'Marie Bagration,' indicate that France was familiar with Racine's line:

> Présente, je vous fuis; absente, je vous trouve.

Finally, the transition from the dream to reality was achieved, by no means painlessly, through the medium of actresses.

In his early youth, there was inaugurated on Anatole's part a series of Thespian admirations. Numerous were his contacts, and varied his semi-fictional recollections: from Mme. Rachel in her cashmere shawl, through the actress who offered him his first cigarette,[49] to the heroine of the *Histoire comique;* from Sarah Bernhardt in her golden prime to the lady who beguiled the voyage to South America in 1909. He was pleased by the adaptability which permits such an artist to represent not one woman, but a hundred, thus perpetually 'offering a fresh field to the tender sentiments.'[50] And he greatly esteemed the interpreters of classical and Racinian roles: 'blessings on your heads, Marie Favart and Sarah, Bartet and Weber, and on your divine lips which uttered the honeyed lines of *Esther, Phèdre,* and *Iphigénie.*'[51] Yet except for a few years in his adolescence, when stage-illusion meant the 'passage from one world to another,' France's taste for the actual theatre was not strong.[52] He preferred the spectacle offered by the dressing-rooms, the *coulisses* which the *Histoire comique* presents so realistically.[53]

The names of certain actresses with whom A.F. was more or less on good terms may be mentioned here. His attitude towards Sarah Bernhardt, whose career he followed from the beginning, was half-admiring, half-malicious. He thought Réjane a *bonne fille*. Mlle. Agar and especially Nina de Callias were associated with the recitation or composition of Parnassian verse. As recorded in *La Vie en fleur*,[54] 'Jeanne Lefuel' of the Odéon entered Pierre's life when Victor Pellerin, an ardent amateur, was staging privately the *Lysistrata* of Aristophanes. Pierre-Anatole attended the rehearsals and since he was attracted by the *beaux yeux* of this actress, he 'improved' her part by inserting various speeches in the text. Then he would ride home with her and occasionally be entertained in her apartment on the Rue d'Assas. He liked her lively and picturesque conversation ; and she was associated with the fad for table-tipping, a variety of 'spiritism' that Anatole went in for during this period and subsequently.

This was hardly a love-affair. Nor was France enamoured, as some seem to think, of Madeleine Brohan, who was in the sixties the *amie* of his Pythias, Etienne Charavay.[55] Yet he certainly admired her beauty,[56] which is manifest in the photographs still preserved in the collection of the Comédie-Française. He was also probably drawn by her celebrity and her wit. For no less a person than Théophile Gautier honoured Madeleine Brohan, while Juan Valera fell in love with her.[57] Incidentally, she had the sense to 'give up the role of Célimène when she had reached the age of Arsinoé,' and to retire altogether from the Comédie when she was only fifty-two.

But Anatole was affected by still earlier and deeper impressions. Pierre records several times that on one happy school-day (it may have been in 1859) he came out first in composition ; his pleased parents took him to the Porte-Saint-Martin, where 'at fourteen' he fell romantically in love with the very first actress whom he had seen.[58] This was Isabelle Constant, a young *protégée* of the elder Dumas. She was playing the role of Marguerite d'Ecosse in a melodrama by Jules Lacroix called *La Jeunesse de Louis XI*. She was a slim blonde and therefore not the 'dark ladye' whom Anatole celebrates in his love-poems. Yet he was overcome by a 'trouble extraordinaire' and sobbed in his seat ; of course he identified her with her noble role in the play. But inquiry being made, it was discovered that Isabelle was the daughter of a barber who used to take her to the Luxembourg to dry her hair ![59] Anatole never saw her again. We shall see later how this situation was developed fictionally.

Although stage-illusion glorified Isabelle for a brief while, the charm was still more potent in the case of another actress who dominated his heart for several years. Even as a schoolboy, he tells us, he had bought cheap seats at the Théâtre-Français and listened to the plays of Racine and Corneille as part of his education.[60] Presently he heard there a 'belle et honnête tragédienne,' who, without understanding them, declaimed well the lines of Pauline and of Emilie. 'If I had that opportunity at present,' says the maturer Anatole, 'I wouldn't talk to her about Corneille.'[61]

Now for some time after 1859 these and similar parts at the Français were taken by a *tragédienne,* about six years A.F.'s senior, named Elise Devoyod. Noted for her beauty, she had won honours at the Conservatoire and had been connected with the Odéon. By some she was considered the successor of Rachel, whether in classical or Romantic plays.[62] France celebrates *his* lady as associated with most of the parts actually taken by Elise Devoyod; she wore (in his verse) the 'bandeau de Rachel,' and she was tall and thin, which was also the case with Elise. On particular dates in 1865 the Devoyod played in the roles of Emilie and Phèdre; and Anatole on the same dates commemorated the success of his inamorata in these roles. A further projection of this actress will be found in the *Désirs de Jean Servien.*

§ 5

As already hinted, we can learn a good deal about the state of Anatole's mind and heart, at twenty-one, by considering a certain collection of poems. These have never been printed in full, but M. Girard's volume contains interesting and revealing selections.[63]

Anatole France, a Romanticist—Anatole inditing respectfully adoring love-lyrics! Such is the unexpected revelation offered by this manuscript volume of thirty-eight poems all written in 1865, dated and arranged for a possible publication that never materialized. There survives also an unfinished Romantic drama of the same epoch.

The lyrics, which are quite short and undistinguished, sigh in vain for an *inamorata innominata*—to wit, Elise Devoyod. On occasion, she could wear an 'antique mask' and act in *Œdipus Rex* as well as in French tragedy. The lyrics in her honour express Romantic despair, the fatality of passion, and a humble prostration before her image. Since the original is not for him, Anatole will have to be content with that image, which has already dwelt in his heart for four years.[64] But he still invokes blessings upon her head and speaks in a vein of abnegation and of idealistic ardour which is more like Sully Prudhomme than what we know of Anatole. Through various allusions, and particularly in their form, the poems reflect the influences of Hugo, Byron, Gautier, and perhaps Walter Scott. Gautier and Byron are mirrored in the verses called 'Les Propos de Don Juan.' Hugo is Anatole's chief master, especially with regard to the handling of historical themes, Romantic bravado or *panache,* the use of rhythm and of antithesis. Certain verses also bear an antique or a Parnassian stamp.

There is nothing Parnassian about the *drame* of *Sir Punch,* written during the same period—perhaps in the hope that Elise would accept the heroine's role.[65] In its setting, its plot and its fantastic title, this production invokes the shades of Shakespeare, Hugo and Musset. Only three scenes were written, but the verse is more finished and effective than that of the preceding lyrics, and the sketch has a certain dramatic dash and brilliancy. The hero is a kind of Falstaff crossed with Don César de Bazan :

> Je suis le rire énorme, éternel, triomphant,
> Je suis grand moraliste et je suis bon enfant.*

He carries his buoyancy to the point of relating his amorous adventures to an appreciative wife called 'Kat' ; and she, in the next scene, is ready to provide a tit for tat by flirting with Don Juan.

These were youth's violets, 'forward, not permanent,' but they seem to indicate that France, like many adolescents, went through a ferment of Romanticism which his critics are disposed to neglect.[66] The Gospels, particularly *La Vie en fleur,* contain evidences of such growing-pains.—

'I can hardly recognize Pierre,' said Maman, 'his disposition has become so changeable and queer.'

So he fled into Normandy, the solitude and the woods, where he sobbed and yearned.[67] We recall, from the *Livre de mon ami,* similar pangs in the country of Chateaubriand, and in fact he declares that he was always made melancholy by the northern

* I am outrageous and eternal Laughter,
By turns a preacher and a giddy brat.

woods. In *Petit Pierre,* too, we find the youth in a state of exaltation, leaping to meet the embrace of Nature.[68] But this was no lasting *liaison ;* he came to distrust his temporary mistress. More symptomatic of abiding trends are the pæans in praise of unsatisfied Desire, the heart of all beauty, the spark within the clod ; 'vivre, c'est désirer' ; and one type of Romanticism has been defined as 'infinite indeterminate desire.'[69]

France's juvenile verses evince a similar Romantic upheaval. In his poetic idealism, his early conception of love, his literary admirations, the trail of 1830 is clearly visible. It is a long trail by the time Anatole treads it — a great deal of literary rubbish has been tossed upon it, and the traditions of the 'Quarter' have camped there. So it is a bookish and would-be sophisticated rather than a spontaneous Romanticism that our hero experiences. Undeniably, his personal development soon combined with the creed of the Parnassians to promote in him a violent reaction against the gods of his youth : Hugo, Chateaubriand, Michelet. But as in other affairs of the heart the strength of the early affection may be measured by the vehemence of the recoil.

§ 6

AMONG other juvenile attempts should be mentioned a project shared with Louis-Xavier de Ricard, who has left an account of the enterprise.[70] Ricard and France had been among the collaborators on the Larousse Dictionary ; later, in 1868, they conceived a plan for an Encyclopedia of the French Revolution. Thus, for the third time during this decade, Anatole's interest in the Revolution was stirred by his immediate associates : by his father, *via* the book-shop and the La Bédoyère collection ; by Charavay in numerous ways ; and now by Ricard and this proposed 'Encyclopédie.'[71] When the project was advanced, Anatole and his friend wrote a prospectus which impressed readers with the extent of their knowledge on the subject ;[72] and the editors were promised the collaboration of such men as Michelet, Quinet, and Louis Blanc. Ricard continues his account : 'We drew up our plan. [The work] should comprise not only events, institutions, biographies, but also analyses of literary and artistic masterpieces, and *all the details* of public and private life. It was to take up about twenty volumes.'

One is reminded of the History of France, in fifty volumes, 'avec tous les détails,' which Pierre and Fontanet dreamed of in their tender youth.

In spite of some financial backing, this project came to nothing. Its interest is in showing what preoccupations were then in the mind of France and what were his politics. On the whole he was a Liberal and even a revolutionary, in that he then thoroughly believed in the 'principles of 1789'[73]—more thoroughly than when he wrote *Les Dieux ont soif* in his final disillusionment. In the late sixties, Anatole was especially drawn to the Girondists, to the 'belle nonchalance d'artiste' of Vergniaud. Along these lines, the prospectus of the proposed Encyclopedia declares for the 'spirit of the Revolution,' for the 'ideas of liberty,' and comes out strongly against the deterministic or necessitarian theory of history. 'Our modern conscience is now active in the historical field, and absolute doctrinaire systems are no longer permitted to contest the validity of its judgments of human affairs.' Like Voltaire, France always hated systems. In protesting against the school of Guizot, he also offers his earliest plea for relativity and intellectual freedom—what Bayle called 'la conscience errante.'

In further collaboration with the friendly Ricard, Anatole wrote during that same year (1868) a one-act 'philosophic' comedy in prose. This was *Le Valet de Madame la Duchesse,* in which egalitarian opinions were advocated. The manuscript was rediscovered in 1902, when France had forgotten all about it; it appears that the play was submitted to the company of the Odéon, but it was buried in the archives of that theatre and never performed.[74] After its rediscovery, the comedy was published in *La Revue,*[75] where the curious may take note of its sentiments. It is a question of an aspiring valet, a mixture of Figaro and the amorous Chérubin, who seeks for himself alone the favours of his employer, 'la Duchesse.' To this end, he rejects the attentions of a mere ladies' maid and contrives to bring about a rupture between the Duchess and her noble lover, 'le Marquis.' The clash between the two men, aristocrat and plebeian, is again reminiscent of Beaumarchais. But Frontin is a rather cowardly rebel against the social structure of the Old Régime. Also the tone of the comedy is light and not very propagandist. The moral, if any, might be found in this maxim, uttered by the *soubrette:* 'All men, whether marquises or valets, are equally stupid and equally gallant.' Another one-act play, called *Les Métamorphoses de Pierrot,* is of the 'genre burlesque et funambulesque,' which was much in fashion round 1870.[76]

This is not the place to discuss France's early journalistic endeavours ; but it might be remarked in passing that, for example in the *Amateur d'autographes,* his taste for history is again the salient thing. With regard to definite periods, his life-long preferences — for antiquity at one end and for the French eighteenth century at the other — are beginning to emerge. But it is noteworthy that at this stage particularly, when Anatole was a Republican after the order of Michelet, he expresses himself severely regarding the seventeenth century, the Golden Age of Louis XIV.[77]

To the growing consternation of Noël France, this Republicanism, abetted by such friends as Charavay and Edouard Pelletan, resulted in certain overt acts. Anatole followed lecture-courses, wherein the Second Empire was likened to that of Rome at the beginning of its decay, with gratuitous allusions to the orgies of Tiberius, Caligula, and even Messalina.[78] Under this inspiration, Anatole published in the *Gazette rimée*[79] two poems charged with the virus of anti-imperialism. These were 'Les Légions de Varus' and 'Denys, tyran de Syracuse.' According to Ricard, they were the most violent poems ever published by the *Gazette rimée* and had much to do with its immediate suppression ; it is not unlikely that Ricard, who was an ardent progressive, influenced A.F.'s radicalism of this period.[80] 'Les Légions de Varus' does not disturb the ashes of Tiberius or Caligula, but exploits the more despotic side of Augustus, as heralding the third Napoleon. Furthermore, the poem at once suggests a parallel between the destruction of Varus in Germany and the Archduke Maximilian whom Napoleon III sent on the ill-fated expedition into Mexico.[81] In either case it was an unnecessary 'war for exercise' ; in either case the difficulties of the climate and the battles with the enemy had proved disastrous to the imperial legions. Anatole causes 'La Patrie' to apostrophize nominally Augustus, but really the French Emperor :

> César, rends-moi mes fils, lui dit-elle, assassin !

Napoleon III is represented as the violator of his country, and as 'infâme' ; such epithets are quite in the vein of Hugo's contemporary invective in *Les Châtiments*.[82] Finally, the Emperor is haunted and menaced by the shades of those soldiers whom he has virtually slain.

It is not surprising that the imperial censorship turned a threatening eye on the *Gazette rimée* and the author of this poem. And 'Denys, tyran de Syracuse' had already, less powerfully and more covertly, indicted the insolence and megalomania characteristic of despots.

But Calmettes[83] and others do not wholly agree with Ricard's account of his comrade as a thorough-going revolutionary. Like the hero of *The Princess Casamassima,* France was too susceptible to the charms of luxury, the beauties accessible to and through the rich, to hurl the bomb that would abolish them. This became a lasting ambiguity in his mind and character—if indeed he had a character, which some people were disposed to doubt.

CHAPTER VII

The Heights of Parnassus

§ 1

IN the meantime the budding critic had brought out his first printed volume. This was a tiny monograph on *Alfred de Vigny* (1868), undertaken by Bachelin-Deflorenne, a publisher of the Quai Voltaire who also sponsored some of A.F.'s bibliographical labours.[1]

It need not surprise us that France's concern is now chiefly with poetry. At that time he was, in a double sense, climbing Parnassus on his own account ; and indeed, questions of poetic form and sentiment continue to be a major interest well into his third period.[2] His attachment to the Muse was a long-enduring if not a single-minded devotion. Again, this *Vigny* was not only the first book that Anatole wrote : it was the last that he corrected, in the year before his death ; and for various reasons it solicits our attention.

As a youth, Pierre had admired the 'magnanimous' Vigny, whom he had once glimpsed as a serene heavy-featured old man in M. Nottet's circulating library.[3] As a critic, France has a more respectful sympathy for the author of *Eloa* than for any other Romanticist. It is said that later he qualified this as a rather naïve respect, accorded to the aristocrat as much as to the poet ;[4] but although his final revisions tone down somewhat his early fervour, yet among France's *juvenilia* the *Alfred de Vigny* is lacking neither in discernment nor in taste. Probably the booklet was written partly with the intention of naming an ancestor for the Parnassian group of poets with whom Anatole had recently become associated.[5] Certainly he attributed to Vigny some of his own fetishes—mother-worship, the passion for the past and for the stones of Paris. There is, however, evidence that the idealism and the meditations of the man who wrote *Chatterton* were then quite congenial to the biographer, who admires Vigny's 'consciousness of the priestly eminence which the intellect occupies.' In his preface he insists that the poet should live ideally and that Vigny thus offered an example of *une belle vie*. True poetry is not merely a skilful game ; it demands self-respect and lofty ambitions.

The book is structurally a plain biography, with anecdotes and conversations interspersed, and the manner of it is a little naïve and bare. No one could say severer things about the juvenile complexion of this essay than did its author when he finally (1923) made his extensive revisions.[6] Yet here and there we find phrases characteristic of the Anatole of 1868. For example, Vigny's Ivory Tower, his disdain of the multitude, and his serenity are emphasized. These traits may serve as a lesson to the Parnassians and they imply a corrective to the other Romanticists, with their excesses and violences. Such, unfortunately, is the bent of most modern poetry:

> Its strength displays itself in effort and not, as the Greeks desired, in serenity and repose. Alfred de Vigny knew and loved that tranquil beauty of ancient Hellas.[7]

Therefore *Eloa* is the purest flower of Romanticism and *Chatterton* contains 'one of the most marvellous types of women created since Racine.' But Vigny is disposed to make too elaborate preparations in affairs of the heart. He might have learned that one can 'simplifier quelque peu ces apprêts.' This is decidedly in the manner of the later Anatole; so is his approval of Vigny's 'profound and gentle scepticism,' his horror of a noisy and vain activity in the market-place. And the epigram, 'irony is the last phase of disillusionment' is quite prophetic.

Characteristic also is the idea that genius begins by imitating and borrowing; at first the 'membres épars' which it takes from others bear clear traces of their origin; but presently the writer learns to organize these fragments into a harmonious whole. Therein resides all artistic talent. This is identical with France's views, already cited, on the creative imagination.

In 1922 Anatole was prevailed upon, contrary to his habit, to undertake a thorough-going revision of his first work. After the customary delays and dawdling, the results were visible in a 'magnificent and imposing volume'—the last to appear during his life-time.[8] As the author intimates in his new preface, a *péché de jeunesse* thus became the final tribulation of an octogenarian.

With all that had occurred between, France found himself unable to integrate the revision in terms of either youth or age.

But he did make numerous retouches, whehter in style and treatment or in the actual content, by means of added notes.[9] In the former direction, we find the experienced author working from pedantry and grandiloquence towards simplicity, from vagueness towards the real right word. In the notes, various errors are amended, including an amusing instance where originally France had copied out the wrong extract from an Academy *Discours;* and some intimate material is added, concerning the rupture between Vigny and Marie Dorval, the actress—material that reflects credit on neither party. But aside from this unsavoury stuff, there is little to indicate that France's opinion of Vigny, as poet and as man, had depreciated during the long interval.

Since the writing of verses was then Anatole's chief delectation, it is natural that he should provide in this volume both an historical sketch and a theory of poetry. In primitive times, he declares, verse was national and popular, 'made by all and understood by all.' The poet might have another occupation, war for example, and he was involved in the common weal. But now (read, 'after Romanticism'), the poet is only an individual, his language and thought are so peculiarly personal that his work necessarily incurs the risk of being ill-understood. Hence he becomes sad, and his sickly Muse can only decorate herself with personal sorrows, 'or seek, among ancient memories, the joy and the serenity of vanished ages.'[10]—*De te fabula.*

§ 2

THE statement of this theory was probably due to France's association with the group of poets known as the Parnassians.

There was once a suave and enterprising publisher, Alphonse Lemerre his name, whose headquarters were in the Passage Choiseul, near the Rue de Richelieu and just off the Boulevards. He was a literary horticulturist who brought out in small Elzevirian form the Spring displays of aspiring poets, whether the 'earlier leaf of pleasure' or the 'latter flower of pain.' Appropriately enough, orange-merchants hawked their wares round the modest shop. Above this, in a square room, would gather an intense and at times a turbulent band of neophytes, the embryonic Parnassians. So close was the connexion between upstairs and down that 'you might well ask whether "le Parnasse" was a literary school or a book-shop.'[11] The canny publisher would also occasionally entertain his young friends at his home.

The acknowledged master of the group, although it is not clear that he frequented their noisier gatherings, was Leconte de Lisle. This haughty, hieratic and impoverished leader had already achieved a discreet fame through the metallic magnificence of his *Poèmes antiques* and his *Poèmes barbares*. Foremost among his admirers and adherents were soon to be numbered such future celebrities as the sonorous Heredia, the lascivious Catulle Mendès—and Anatole France. When the last-named became assiduous *chez* Lemerre, he found there an inner circle composed in part of his familiar friends, Xavier de Ricard and François Coppée; of the eccentric Villiers de l'Isle-Adam; of the semi-mystic, Léon Dierx, and Paul Verlaine, whom he was not so sure about.[12] It is probable that Louis Ménard, the Hellenist, also frequented these gatherings as well as the more formal salon of Leconte de Lisle; but Anatole is quite silent regarding Ménard, who presently exercised a decided influence upon *Thaïs*.[13] On the fringes of the group were librarians like Lacaussade and Louis Ratisbonne, who was helpful to Anatole on more than one occasion. Léon Cladel, a robust poet-peasant, would sometimes wander in. France declares that in 1868 'we had a respect for our masters and a love of art,' which was most sincere.[14]

In fact, this devotion was the chief link between rather disparate souls. It is curious to note that men as different as Bourget, Verlaine, Coppée, Sully Prudhomme, and France himself each wrote a first volume in the Parnassian style. For they soon deviated widely from that standard and from one another. The fact is that no literary school can long remain a coherent and unified body: in each member the fresh sap stirs and fresh departures are in order. The Parnassians, in particular, were agreed on only two points: the cult for form, the dislike of expressing personal emotion. Their Muse should be an impeccable, impassive, and patrician lady, lifting her skirts from the mire of democracy, thoroughly aware of science and of antiquity, but shaking a minatory finger whenever a shred of personal feeling began to emerge from the hinterland of consciousness. Eloquent 'reconstitutions' of the historical past were a fetish of the school—and this would appeal strongly to the future author of *Thaïs*.[15]

The Parnassian movement evolved slowly from a nexus of literary periodicals. Mendès and Ricard founded two of these—*La Revue fantaisiste* and the *Revue du progrès moral, littéraire et artistique*. Their tendencies were rather dissimilar; yet it is held that from a fusion of these trends there emerged the famous anthologies which gave body to the doctrines of the school.[16] Altogether, Lemerre published (in 1866, 1871, 1876) three volumes of this *Parnasse contemporain, recueil de vers nouveaux*. As a series, they included practically all the names that became associated with the movement. Verses by Anatole France appeared in the second and the third volumes; he was also a member of the jury that decided what poems should be selected for the final volume.[17] By his enterprise in this publication, Lemerre paved the way for the reception of his beautiful little Elzevirs containing the works of various individual poets—for example, the *Poèmes dorés* of our author.

Before joining the group in the upper room, France served an apprenticeship downstairs. Although the son of the publisher mentions an earlier date, it was probably in 1867 that Anatole first appeared in the Passage Choiseul and became reader to the house.[18] This may well have been soon after the suppression of the *Gazette rimée,* which Lemerre published. A.F.'s official title was 'scoliaste éditorial des classiques,' in connexion with a 'Petite Bibliothèque littéraire.' This meant that he wrote short 'notices' or prefaces for Lemerre's reprints of famous authors. We shall find that the most elaborate of these ultimately grew into a volume. Thus, while still sheltered by the wings of Charavay and of Bachelin-Deflorenne, Anatole was picking crumbs from the table of Lemerre. They were not very large crumbs. His total emoluments for exercising the editorial function, writing prefaces, and passing on manuscripts, were one hundred francs monthly. It is not surprising, as Roujon says, that his relations with his employer presently became 'orageux.'[19]

But Anatole soon fitted still another string to his bow. If he had first presented himself at Lemerre's establishment 'as the son of his father,' he wore his erudition with a difference in the *cénacle* upstairs. He had been trained as an expert bibliographer and professed in the *Livre du Bibliophile* that he was wholly consecrated to that art;[20] but he appealed to the comrades of Parnassus rather as 'un lettré très fin,' not only well-informed but in possession of an 'open, inquiring, and quite contemporary mind.' It was also a well-filled mind, as his comrades were shortly to discover, for as he tells us, he had in those days little to do but read and think.[21] That he thought to some purpose is evidenced by the growth of his influence in the circle; one partial witness even declares that France was 'the first, after the Master,' and that Paul Bourget was then his 'disciple.'[22] There are other tributes to the impression made by his learning, the brilliancy of his conversation (when he felt at ease), and the gradual increase of his authority, especially after 1870.[23]

Preceding that time, the youth still had the bump of veneration. He took his poetic calling with due earnestness, for he later wrote of waging arms 'obscurely and bravely' among the Parnassians.[24] Many are the passages in which as a mature critic he recalls the personalities and gifts of his brother-poets. In one of them,[25] he mentions the joint admiration that they shared for such veterans as Gautier, Baudelaire, and of course Leconte de Lisle. He goes on to emphasize the particular contributions of Sully Prudhomme, of Coppée, Dierx, Heredia, Verlaine, and Ricard. But of them all, he thinks that Catulle Mendès was the liveliest and most striking embodiment of the "Parnasse contemporain."

Although Hugo is listed above as among the elder masters, whose virtuosity our poet imitated, yet France found the camp divided into Hugonians and anti-Hugonians; he presently cast in his lot with the latter. He also found antiquity honoured with a good deal of word-worship; knowing his ancients better than most, he was probably closer to them in spirit than, for example, that somewhat chilly pagan, Leconte de Lisle. For this gentleman mingled with his Hellenism a sort of 'primitive barbarity,' as well as a Hindoo strain.[26]

§ 3

Anatole's relations with his nominal 'Master' form a curious chapter in literary anecdotage. First of all, there is no doubt concerning the power and prestige within his circle of this 'Jupiter in a black frock-coat.' Erect on his hearthstone, 'beau comme un dieu,' he would receive the young poets and their productions.[27] Greatly respected and jealous of his authority, he would pass judgment upon all the poems — and they were many — submitted to his inexorable eye.[28] Not only did his disciples pause with bated breath until the supreme decision was rendered; several of them, e.g., Coppée, Dierx, and Heredia, dedicated their precious first volumes to the awe-inspiring Leconte de Lisle. In thus inscribing the *Poèmes dorés,* France was observing a well-established ritual; and the 'lively and constant admiration' which he there professes was, for some years at least, no less than the truth.

There are numerous early passages bearing witness to this admiration. France would tell a mutual acquaintance (the daughter of Jules Breton) that Leconte de Lisle was 'charming' and one of the 'most amiable of men'—surely an excessive statement; or in one of his earliest critical utterances he would pay tribute to the latter's knowledge of Greek — an opinion later revised; or he would highly commend the *Poèmes barbares,* for their thought, form and suavity; or he would be thrilled to the bone when invited to read a poem in the Master's salon.[29]

But Leconte de Lisle was an Olympian with a menacing monocle, an Æolus commanding blasts of irony. The man who could dismiss Hugo with the label 'bête comme l'Himalaya' was not the sort to put his guests at their ease. Overcome by the honour of being invited to these rather formal 'at homes' in the Boulevard des Invalides, young Anatole sat wordless, on the edge of his chair, quite in the background. He would listen with all his might; then he would rush forward and congratulate almost too emphatically the speaker of the evening; after which he would retire in confusion. He was still an unformed youth, a timid *séminariste* stamped with the stamp of Stanislas. He was by turns too backward and too forward, exhibiting a smiling complaisance that bordered on obsequiousness. This trait made it difficult to ascertain his true self and his real opinions—whether, for instance, he was wholly a Liberal or in part a Conservative. Actually he was not fond of ceremony, yet he affected for some time a 'parade cérémonieuse.' He endeavoured to unite, apparently, the results of a clerical education with the salaams of a dancing-master; and the combination was for a time coldly received.[30]

There are other descriptions by eye-witnesses of France's personal appearance and demeanour on such occasions. His conversation, says Bourget, was marked by a sort of hesitation, as if he were seeking for the right word. He was at twenty-five awkward and gawky, with a recently grown and ill-shapen full beard. Apparently, he had also a 'fine moustache brune' and large dreamy eyes. A lady who as a young girl often saw him among the Parnassians has drawn this telling portrait:

> He was tall and thin, with sloping shoulders, a long pale face, close-set black eyes, chestnut-coloured beard, and very short hair cut *en brosse*. . . He expressed his convictions clearly enough, but in an elaborate style, emphasizing important words by gesturing with his right hand. . .
>
> He rarely sat down, but walked from one group to another, and his walk was like that of certain stilted birds.

At times he would discuss verbal usage with the handsome Bourget or listen, hawk-like, to the reading of others, while waiting for an opportunity to read his own verse. Among such habitués as Bourget, Heredia, and Jules Breton, he may have been at a disadvantage physically, if not mentally. Altogether, what with his 'disagreeable' head, his inharmonious features, his addiction to fulsome compliments, and his uncertain political views, he inspired at this stage some distrust.[31]

But in this *milieu* as in other things, Anatole and his 'long thoughts' could afford to wait. Presently his intellectual power and his native charm emerged. An early poem on the Thaïs legend must have attracted some attention. He obtained consideration through 'La Part de Magdeleine,' which was recited by the actress Agar and appeared in the second series of the *Parnasse contemporain*. Later he read a paper setting forth the objective theory of the school. Contrary to his subsequent 'impressionistic' attitude, but in harmony with the tendencies of the *Poèmes dorés*, France here maintained that verse should limit itself to a scientific description of natural phenomena. The paper, much discussed in the salon of the Master, seems to have given Anatole a position of some authority.[32] This rise in power and his subsequent relations with Leconte de Lisle belong to the period after the Franco-Prussian War.

§ 4

THERE were, on the slopes of Parnassus, still other stamping-grounds and seed-beds productive of far-flung associations.[33]

Tidings of the New Youth movement reached as far as Guernsey: Victor Hugo was requested to furnish a letter-preface for a volume of the *Parnasse contemporain*. The lion shook his mane and responded in his most apocalyptic manner; four pages of startling antitheses contrasted his past with their present.[34] Another respected member of the elder generation was Théodore de Banville, in whose salon France and others occasionally met. On Thursday evenings, half a dozen of the group would find themselves at the home of Heredia, whose perfect sonnets Anatole always admired.[35] They were as splendid as his neckties! It is pleasant to know that Heredia returned this admiration and for a time enlisted Anatole's services in connexion with a translation from the Spanish.[36]

But France's familiars were rather Catulle Mendès and François Coppée, together with the oft-quoted Calmettes and Xavier de Ricard—and for a time the Bohemian actress Nina de Callias.

He frequently visited Mendès in the Rue des Martyrs, where the Bohemian's beautiful wife, Judith Gautier, presided over poetic reunions. The modern 'Catullus'—an even greater scapegrace than his namesake—seems to have participated in some escapades with Anatole. We learn of a long day spent together, in the course of which, what with dining, wining and discussion, the whole of a monthly salary from Bachelin-Deflorenne evaporated. However, this modest stipend did not greatly exceed what was paid to France by Alphonse Lemerre. Much later A.F. still considered Mendès as 'le Parnassien par excellence'; and Henri de Régnier agrees with this judgment.[37]

In behalf of François Coppée, Anatole wrote an article which is a defence both of poetry and of friendship.[38] The occasion was the *première* of Coppée's *Le Passant,* a charming little fantasy, which made the reputation of the author as well as that of Sarah Bernhardt in her golden youth. France attended and applauded the play, as he admired subsequent works by the same writer.[39] Some critical snob remarked on the fact that Coppée spent most of his time as an employee in the Ministry. Could he, then, be a true poet? The defence gives us our first glimpse of Anatolian irony, still a little too obvious in its innuendoes. Poetry has become so abnormal, he says, so unique a thing that it throws criticism badly out of joint. 'But console yourself, Monsieur le critique, and learn that a man can earn an honest living and at the same time write comedies.' There follows a general tribute to his brothers-at-arms. The dwellers on Parnassus, so much scorned by the critic in question, have a rough road to travel in their daily lives ; yet it is their effort which has caused poetry to be born again in France.

These two votaries of the Muse had first met about 1866 and soon found that they had much in common—their humble origins, their understanding of *le peuple* and of Parisian street-scenes. France came to know Coppée in his family life and greatly esteemed his character as well as his verses. A.F.'s later tributes are numerous. In one of them he declares that in order to understand this 'enfant de Paris,' one must have had a similar childhood, must have grown up (*sc.* like 'Petit Pierre') 'a thin and pallid child, in an ancient street.' Thus only could one fully appreciate the exquisite pictures in *Les Humbles* and *Les Intimités*.[40]

In fact, Coppée wrote several prose volumes analogous to *Le Livre de mon ami*. Such were his *Souvenirs d'un Parisien* and *Toute une jeunesse,* an autobiographical novel. François clung to the people, while Anatole became a mandarin ; yet the two men continued to be warm friends, at least until the period of the Dreyfus affair.

The *cénacle,* especially Coppée, France, and Mendès, would occasionally assemble at the home of the Marquise de Ricard, Louis-Xavier's mother. Here friendly discussions were waged on politics, poetry and the art of cooking. But if this influential salon was the 'temple' of Parnassus, quite another place was the 'boudoir'—namely the establishment of the witty, musical, and slightly hysterical actress, 'Nina de Villard.'[41] This lady was also known as Nina de Callias, since she had married and divorced a drunken journalist of that name. She then became the good fairy of the Parnassians, and in successive dwelling-places she persistently threw wide her doors to all and sundry. Hers was no select salon. Most of the poets already mentioned, together with a number of Bohemians, attended her turbulent *soirées*. Noisy declamations or performances of some Romantic *drame* were frequent. Nina herself styled her home a 'Charenton' or Bedlam.[42]

She was hand in glove with Paul Verlaine and others and at one time she seems to have been fairly intimate with Anatole France, who along with Dierx and Coppée haunted her establishment. It is quite possible that France aided her in the composition of two sonnets which appeared over her name in the second series of the *Parnasse contemporain*. It is likely that he collaborated with her on an 'acte en vers,' supposed to be found among the archives of the Comédie-Française. Fragments of this play, called *La Dompteuse,* have been printed by Pierre Calmettes. His acceptance by Nina and her circle may be taken as another sign of Anatole's increasing sophistication.[43]

§ 5

In the meantime the Franco-Prussian war had intervened. It does not appear that Anatole was very much involved in the events of 1870-71.[44] He belonged to the National Guard, but was officially declared unfit for active military service shortly after Sedan. Yet during the war and the siege, he went through experiences that were soon afterwards partly recorded in *Jean Servien.*

For example, we learn from various sources that France and Calmettes, although mobilized in the Guard, wore no uniforms and were mostly concerned with patrol and sentry duty. 'We were soldiers of a special kind.' Anatole remembers their 'brave' Captain Chalamel and how on December 2, 1870, the regiment was stationed on reserve near the fort of La Faisanderie. Our hero and Fernand watched the cannon-smoke from the Prussian attack roll away among the hills. The young men read their Virgil and made bets as to how many shells would fall into the Marne. . . There is also an anecdote about a sally, a halt due to the death of an officer, a confused retreat, and the pillaging of a bakery when back in Paris.[45]

Save for memories of confusion and hunger, the war made little impression upon A.F. But its aftermath was another thing. When the Commune became dominant, he objected (May, 1871) to being enrolled in its ranks. Evidently his anti-Imperialism did not extend that far. Fortified with a Belgian passport and a false name, he slipped out of Paris and visited for a month the Calmettes family at Ville-d'Avray, near St. Cloud. On May 4 he wrote to Charles Asselineau, explaining his flight on the grounds that 'the Commune threatened to disturb my serenity.'[46] It appears that during this respite he and Fernand Calmettes once ran over to Versailles, where the two Parnassians made the acquaintance of the 'venerated' Théophile Gautier.[47] . . Ville-d'Avray seemed for a time an ideal retreat, but the government troops had invested Paris and were advancing; Anatole became alarmed about the safety of his parents during the 'Bloody Week.' In fact, the elder France had kept during that sanguinary struggle a *Journal de la Commune,* which has recently come to light.[48]

Installed with his wife in the Rue de Tournon, the former guardsman was alarmed not only by the bullets which occasionally struck his home, but by the civil warfare which threatened almost to destroy the city. In the Rue de Seine, barricades were swept away by the advancing troops. The Thibaults 'saw with grief' flames emerging from the Palais du Luxembourg. Musket-fire raging in the Place Saint-Michel . . . the Pantheon taken . . . firing-squads in the gardens and a ruthless incendiarism in many quarters . . . there was enough to strike consternation to the heart of the old Parisian and of his absent son. Anatole tells us that Charles Asselineau, that devotee of belles-lettres, heroically faced the insurgent mob in the Bibliothèque Mazarine and persuaded them to relinquish their incendiary designs.[49]

Yet enough damage had been done, in all conscience. On May 31, Anatole wrote his mother, very characteristically:

> I will not think of the ruins, as long as you and Father are safe and sound. The Louvre, the (National) Library and the *Muséum* have been preserved; so the intellectual life is not yet made impossible in Paris.[50]

But his double anxiety led him to return to the city a few days later. And what did he actually find? The Tuileries had been swept away; a number of other historic buildings, including portions of the Luxembourg and the Louvre, had been badly damaged; and the ravages of the Communards were visible everywhere. These events effected a profound change in A.F.'s political attitude. The would-be Radical had seen radicalism at work. He remained a rather tepid Republican. But for many years he thought and wrote with loathing of what the mob, that 'government of madness and crime,' had done in 1871—and even in 1793, for his reaction against the Commune extended back to the Revolution itself. Evidences of the two reactions can be found all the way from *Les Désirs de Jean Servien* to *Les Dieux ont soif* (1912).

Anatole had another grievance—the late events had left him penniless and practically without employment. He writes Charavay, who was still off soldiering, that the book-dealers are financially decrepit. Only small commissions are procurable from Lemerre; and temporarily Anatole, conjoined with Leconte de Lisle, has hitched his star to a Dictionary of Cooking![51]

§ 6

WHERE did France settle down for the six years preceding his marriage? And if with his parents, what are the relations now obtaining between the two generations? There is some conflict of opinion on these points.

In July, 1866, the elder Thibault having sold his stock of books, the family moved from the Quai Voltaire to No. 15 Rue de Tournon, near the Jardin du Luxembourg.[52] They were all modestly installed *au quatrième,* and apparently the tiny salon was reserved for the labours of the young man of the house, who was evidently beginning to find himself. But either at this period or after the war Anatole lived alone for a year or so. He found bachelor quarters in a place not far from the Pantheon. On the whole, it seems likely that this was some time after the war; the separation could not have lasted long, for just after 1871 Anatole returned to his family in the Rue de Tournon. From there he must have moved with them to the Rue de Rennes, in 1875. A letter of the following year is dated from that locality.[53]

Yet around 1868 domestic relations were decidedly strained. Despite the fact that Père France had done much to pave the way toward his son's first clerico-literary positions, and despite Anatole's flowery tributes to the retiring book-dealer in 'Un Foyer éteint' (of 1867), it is certain that the two men were not well agreed, especially under the same roof. In the following year Noël wrote gloomily to a friend regarding Anatole's present and future:[54] 'He has no position. He writes, or rather he scribbles. What I feared since his childhood has happened—*par une fatalité.* . . . I am weary of struggling with him.' The old man declares it very doubtful whether Anatole had talent enough to earn his own living, but he fears that severity may 'alienate him from the domestic hearth.' This seems to mean that the son had not yet left home.

Anatole Himself gave Brousson a rather different account of the whole matter.[55] His father cast him off, 'because I wrote verses.' On the part of a bookseller this dread of literature seems rather inconsistent, especially since he too was occasionally guilty of verse-making.[56] Anyhow, the young poet found a garret near by, and there he wrote, mostly in bed and in a happy poverty. There were, however, consolations. Various friends, such as Coppée, were within easy reach. Pretty and accommodating neighbours would visit the *mansarde,* and Anatole, contemplating the cupola of Sainte-Geneviève, doubtless found it very pleasant, as Alan Seeger wrote later:

To wake between Our Lady and our love.

He suggests elsewhere that his moving was partly on account of his mother's objection to his *modiques amours,* and especially was it due to her terrible habit of sitting up late at night for the prodigal's return. In these days, Devoyod had been replaced by more concrete and venal loves. He went in for quantity rather than quality; he preferred shop-girls; and in his old age he still licked his lips over certain erotic reminiscences.[57]

Presently France must have resumed his modest position with Lemerre, for several of his longer 'Notices' (subsequently collected in *Le Génie latin*) date from the early seventies. But he did not achieve an independent position before 1876. Except for the year of freedom, it is probable that after the war he still lived with his parents until his marriage. As *Le Livre de mon ami* attests, A.F. was never a rebel against the conception of 'home'; it has even been maintained that, like Dickens, he owed the unfolding of his talent (in the eighties) to the 'warmth of the *foyer*.' Again, it seems likely that father and son got along better as the former mellowed and the latter matured. They actually did some travelling together in 1874. M. Carias has remarked on the curious fact that it was only after Noël had retired that Anatole began really to produce. Had he waited, in his leisurely way, for the torch of Literature to be handed down?[58]

§ 7

He was still climbing the Sacred Mount. After 1870, his position as a leader among the Parnassians became more assured. At this point, the recollections of Fernand Calmettes and of Robert de Bonnières become particularly useful. The former was linked to Anatole through the Charavays—he married Etienne's sister—and being a savant rather than a poet, he could view the Parnassian group with a semi-detachment. However, France was an intimate of his household. He probably exaggerates in estimating A.F.'s prestige as second only to that of Leconte de Lisle. Yet others declare either that our hero stood absolutely first with regard to the appreciation and revival of Hellenism; or that he ranked as 'among the best poets of Parnassus.'[59]

There are indications that after the war the circle had rather changed its character. Certainly the group had grown more extensive. Leconte de Lisle was now officially Librarian of the Senate; he was established in an 'annex' to the Palais du Luxembourg, at 64 Boulevard St. Michel. For many years, all varieties of poetry-lovers came to this modest but illustrious home.[60] Also Calmettes believes that the former 'salon mâle' had become more feminized; frou-frous and cigarettes made a new atmosphere; there were likewise new adherents less stalwart than the old brothers-at-arms.[61] In the home of Nina too, now located in the Batignolles quarter and as noisy as ever, there was a difference: the older habitués had become respectable and most of them were not among those present.[62] As for Anatole, he was still on terms with the Master, but he was acquiring satellites of his own. Calmettes bears witness that 'at the age of twenty-seven or twenty-eight he dragged along in his orbit Bourget, Robert de Bonnières, and Frédéric Plessis,' a scholarly Petronius. There is related an amusing incident concerning A.F., a family group—including a baby and perambulator—and M. Paul Bourget. This caravan was progressing toward the Rue de Rennes, and the discussion of poetic theory was complicated by the movements of the baby-carriage. Bourget, already a man of many elegances, was disconcerted when the eagerly gesturing hands of Anatole allowed the pram to glide towards the gutter.[63]

Several of France's critical articles think back to his early associations with Paul Bourget.[64] The two poets, who were to become much more noted for their prose, first knew each other shortly after the war. In those times, 'since we had nothing better to do, we remade the world.' Five or six kindred spirits would stroll and chat almost daily along the Avenue de l'Observatoire or nightly among the misty statues of the Luxembourg. Wind or mist or sun—all was welcome then, all quickened their zest for living. . . Bourget was younger than the others, but seemed wise in philosophical lore and in subtle analysis. He already showed the psychological acumen which was to distinguish him. A.F. mentions him frequently and with deference in *La Vie littéraire*.

Although partly formed by Parnassus, the two men later followed very different roads. After the death of France the author of *Le Disciple* wrote an account of their earlier friendship. The picture given of Anatole at thirty represents a rather sedate and 'nonchalant' person, sufficiently sure of himself to be in no hurry about anything, least of all about arriving. He passed his time in reading and ample meditation, in careful chiseling of verses and essays.[65] M. Carias observes that from the time the family was installed in the Rue de Tournon, Anatole became something of an anchorite and accumulated, to the amazement of his comrades, an 'immense culture.[66] This sojourn constituted a sort of turning-point in his life. He also produced, on Bourget and others, the effect of a man of firm judgment. 'We came to realize, through hearing and reading him, that even his first efforts were based on a certainty of method that had little in common with our hazy ideas and plans.' He practised an 'intellectual discipline.' Bourget, too, recalls pleasantly their discussions on the famous terrace of the Luxembourg.

This garden was in fact a main gathering-place for the coterie. In one of the reminiscent articles just cited France invoked the shades of his companions in order to recapture the mysterious charm that enveloped their happy youth. He appealed to Bonnières, to the musician Benoît, to Frédéric Plessis, who was possibly the 'dedicatee' of a poem ('L'Auteur à un ami') that strove to bring back the spell of those open-air reunions. Others link this poem with the name of François Coppée, who also loved the Luxembourg.[67] The painter, Jules Breton, would sometimes join the comrades there.[68] And perhaps from an earlier avatar the astral bodies of Little Pierre and of Fontanet would still linger. For who better than they were acquainted with the shrubbery of the Luxembourg and with the vanished statue of Velléda ?[69]

Another associate of the same period, Robert de Bonnières, has left 'memoirs' partly concerning Anatole. Here we learn that a widening circle of Parnassians and others, including the younger

A.F. IN 1873

Coquelin, would meet by night in the Bonnières mansion, Rue de Condé, or during the day-time under the familiar plane-trees of the garden. By now Anatole, at least among intimates, had become a sprightly and entertaining conversationalist. Bonnières' portrait of France (*c.* 1874) has been thus aptly translated:[70]

> Never have I known a man less fitted for action than Anatole France; never have I known a man with a greater gift for the regular exercise of his intellectual faculties, or one endowed with so marked a disposition to grasp things and to understand them. Thus his friends found in him a good and useful counsellor. His constitutional unselfishness was portrayed upon his long and placid features, in his rather dreamy physiognomy, and in the languor of his expression, which was kindly, visionary and gentle; it was even evident in his mode of speech.

As a good friend himself, Bonnières probably exaggerates the friendliness of France.

Frédéric Plessis looked up to Anatole as a wise adviser and intellectual guide. This feeling was commemorated in two poems.[71] In 'A Anatole France,' Plessis recalls how his counsellor advised him to seek relief from a disappointment in love through labour and through conning the pages of such masters as Virgil and Euripides. In 'Soirs Evanouis' there are memories of how the older man would listen to his disciple's verses in the stillness of his study or, once more, among the lilacs of the Luxembourg. Like Bourget and others, Plessis evidently admired the sagacity of France.

Corresponding to the boyish sketches of his schoolmates, Anatole has left short *caractères* of various comrades, in which good-fellowship is less conspicuous than psychological penetration.[72] Bourget is hit off as a 'fashionable Normalien . . . a lover of the intellectual type'; Heredia is 'a Spanish grandee—high sounding and heroic'; Armand Silvestre is 'an angelic Priapus'; Sully Prudhomme 'solves problems of passion by means of equations.' France is again key-noting his subjects in the manner of La Bruyère.

§ 8

In these last years of his bachelorhood Anatole travelled a little in the provinces with various intimates. It was a habit that grew upon him in the eighties and nineties, when we often find him spending the late summers in the country or by the sea-shore.

One plain-living vacation was spent in a small town near Grandville, with the Calmettes. Already in 1873 he is once more invading Normandy, this time with Etienne Charavay. He revisits the Mont-Saint-Michel and Avranches. Records of this tripping are found in four articles which appeared in the *Amateur d'autographes* that autumn.[73] In the following year he helps Father, who has now developed into an excellent travelling-companion, make an inventory of a library at Montluçon, in Allier (central France). And he spent the greater part of August, 1875, with Frédéric Plessis and his family at Royat, in Puy-de-Dôme, near Clermont-Ferrand. Here plain living was enhanced by recitations of poetry, in which Anatole willingly participated.[74] But on one occasion quite a banquet was offered by a political personage to the brother bards. The mayor of Clermont-Ferrand was present and is represented as being 'lost in ecstasy'; it is not clear whether his rapture was gastronomic or poetic.[75]

Behind all such junketing there was still the question of winning an independent livelihood.

As early as 1866 France had been an applicant for a post in the Library of the Senate, situated in the Luxembourg Palace.[76] Ten years later—another case of slow but sure manœuvring—he obtained this position. His original application, although backed by various librarians and by such old friends of the family as Barante the historian and the 'Bibliophile Jacob,' had been shelved. Finally, according to Girard, in August, 1876, our 'papillon de bibliothèque' (as Henry Becque once called him) was appointed to a subordinate post in the Bibliothèque du Sénat. His appointment was partly due to the influence of Leconte de Lisle; yet the result was to prove disastrous with regard to the amicable relations of the two men.[77]

Even on the summit of Parnassus there had been something of a schism, and Anatole did not remain merely a docile pupil. In opposition to the hieratic pose of Leconte de Lisle, A.F. resented any dogma and held only to perfect freedom of thought; even in their joint admiration of antiquity it has been seen that the two men reveal very different tastes. When Anatole read his notable paper on poetic theory, Leconte de Lisle was restless, discerning that the trend of the essay was to indicate Heredia rather than himself as the leader of the school.[78] No such usurpation occurred; but henceforth the Master was distrustful.

The ultimate rupture took place later than our present period, but it was prepared for by the train of events at the Senate Library, where already two other poets had fought a duel, with umbrellas, at the entrance to the Palace. The fact is, what with Leconte de Lisle, Lacaussade, Ratisbonne, and France, there were too many librarians around—and they had too little real work.[79] The results of Anatole's labours were presently summarized by the head-librarian (Charles-Edmond) in the emphatic word, *'Néant';* and relations with his superiors became somewhat strained. With reference to the Head-Parnassian in particular, was France to become merely a refractory pupil, or was he to display the 'black ingratitude' of which he has been accused ? [80] Time will tell.

At all events, Anatole at thirty appears as a quite different person from the awkward collegian who stumbled on the threshold of Parnassus. M. Bourget possesses a photograph of him—presumably the one shown above—that dates from 1873. This reveals, says the owner, 'a face both sharp and simple, open and subtle, not yet too-experienced.' [81] Experienced enough, however, the psychologist admits, to have assumed some authority and to have formed a characteristic literary technique. His devotion to style was already manifest. In conversation he would halt and hesitate until the magic word was found ; but there was no hesitation in the fluent enthusiasm with which, then as always, he would quote from memory passages of his favourite authors. Already his comrades appreciated the amiability of his converse, the urbane nature of his wit, not yet steeped in the acid of irony. Evidently he was the kind of figure of whom one's associates predict, 'il ira loin.'

In 1873 had appeared France's first collected volume of verse—*Les Poèmes dorés,* containing, as we shall see, lyrics of mingled inspiration, but mainly Parnassian in their molding. Three years later, Lemerre further obliged by publishing the neo-classical drama of *Les Noces corinthiennes.* In order to understand these works, we must understand first the author's conception of the 'two antiquities.'

CHAPTER VIII

Ancient Sorceries

§ 1

OF all the elements that composed France's 'education,' the influence of classical antiquity seems to have been the deepest and the most enduring. His passion for the past, his speculative reach into the future, made him view contemporary life *sub specie æternitatis*: therein lies a great portion of his charm. But the eternity that he saw dated from the Greeks and the Romans, for there he thought that authentic history began. His devotion to the humanities was lifelong, sincere, and at times exclusive. No modern was better fitted to be their defender; no one occupied a more privileged position as an ambassador from the ancient world to the nineteenth century.[1] True, it may be argued that here too he was an echo, that he soon found himself in the midst of a Neo-Hellenic cult. But of this cult he became the most shining example and devotee. With some exaggeration he would confide to his intimates that at bottom he loved 'only antiquity'; or he would repeatedly regret that civilization has wandered from that simple and natural way of life indicated by the pagan sages.[2]

If we seek by what sinuous paths France was led into the groves of ancient Arcady, several pictures rise before our vision. They are all painted by his own master-hand and they carry us back to the days of boyhood and adolescence.

The first, from *La Vie en fleur,* is the picture of a tall old gentleman, severe-seeming in a long green frock-coat.[3] This is M. Dubois, a survivor of the *ancien régime*: he thoroughly impersonated the eighteenth century, both in philosophic attitude and in his love for the classics. An occasional visitor to the house on the Quai Voltaire, he was not above puzzling Father and teasing Mother with his critical clairvoyance.[4] His voice must have been most persuasive—Anatole at seventy-nine could still hear its gentle penetrating timbre. 'He applied himself to making me love the ancient art and poetry which he loved so well.' Leaning over the boy's shoulder, he would read with him a time-battered text; and the group recalled to Anatole Himself a Satyr teaching a faun to play the flute. Or else the old man would translate aloud from

Euripides, philosophizing as he went. How much better, declares his devoted pupil, was the wise guidance, the pure and lofty taste of M. Dubois than anything offered by the professors at Stanislas! Not only poetry but the researches of Winckelmann, the knowledge of archæology and statuary, were within M. Dubois' province and were communicated, by classic examples, to 'Petit Pierre.' In short, the old sage taught the young one (*æt.* fourteen) his credo:

> In poetry, art and philosophy, we must go back to the ancients. Why? Because since their time nothing so beautiful has been achieved, nothing so good and wise. It was given to the Greeks to carry art to its perfection. Such was the privilege of this talented race, with their lovely climate, their clear sky, their harmonious surroundings on land and sea—and their cult for liberty.

M. Dubois evidently inspired in Pierre a taste for plastic beauty. Apprehending antiquity in the eighteenth-century manner, he wanted to make a clean sweep of the moderns and rejected everything later than Virgil—a doctrine to which Pierre listened 'with respect and awe.' In fact, the old stoic attached only a moderate value to life and to books; and he thus promoted in the lad a certain disillusionment. But he stood out as 'the greatest intelligence I have ever known,' and his renderings of ancient beauty and wisdom remained unforgettable. He was probably the prototype of various 'sages vieillards' in France's writings, notably of the Abbé Coignard.[5]

The second picture is thoroughly Grecian in its inspiration.[6] It includes the figures of Alkestis and Antigone, who gave Pierre, the schoolboy, 'the noblest dreams that a child ever had.' Burying his head in his dictionary, he saw floating above the ink-stained desk, 'divine figures, ivory arms falling on snowy tunics,' and he heard 'lamenting voices, more melodious than the finest music.' The vision was extended: he beheld Thetis uprising from the waves, Nausicaa and the 'palm-tree of Delos,' Ulysses voyaging on the Mother of Seas. For Homer and Sophocles were revealed to him in the second year that he studied Greek, and immediately his mind was 'flooded with joy and light.'[7] He neglected everything for Sophocles. His enthusiasm survived the amateurish attempt made by himself and his schoolmates to play the *Philoctetes* in the original. In one of his earliest articles he conjures up the shades of Electra and of Antigone ; they seem still to float near a high-placed temple, surrounded by sacred olive-groves and the murmuring of waters.[8]

All of this at Stanislas ? Yes, in spite of Pierre's cavillings at his masters and their manners. Even M. Chotard, slightly ridiculous as he was about Decius Mus, loved his antiquity, heart and soul. He undoubtedly helped to give the boy his taste for good Latin. So the third picture is Roman, conveyed through the medium of Chotard.[9] When the teacher's heavy voice slowly pronounced, 'the remainder of the Roman army reached Canusium under cover of the darkness,' then the lad's imagination evoked the passage of that army, in the silent moonlight, over the bare *campagna:* —'haggard faces, soiled with blood and dust, dinted helmets, tarnished breast-plates, broken swords. And this dim vision, slowly disappearing, was so sombre, grave and proud, that my heart leapt in my breast with sorrow and admiration.' Not otherwise did the words *Consul Romanus* stir in De Quincey the pulse and swing of impassioned rhetoric and cause the pomp of Rome to sweep with its gorgeous train through his spacious imaginings. So M. Chotard—when, perchance, he did not move to Homeric laughter—called from the vasty deep of a boy's consciousness great dreams and images. Pierre became, in his way, 'a good little humanist,' feeling powerfully whatever was splendid in ancient literature. He believed that this is the best way, as the old masters well knew, to form the mind of a child. The 'humanities,' he said, are rightly so called, because they set up the highest ideal in the making of a man. The pagan strain in our hero is already manifest. Little Pierre felt in his boyish fashion the power that was Rome and the magnificence of ancient poetry. He even became 'as Attic and as Ciceronian' as was possible under the circumstances.

Therefore he raised, early enough in all conscience, the flag of Classicism in the fullest sense of the term. '*Je suis resté un classique.* They can call me an aristocrat and a mandarin, but I believe that six or seven years of literary culture give to the mind . . . a nobility, a strength, a beauty, which are not obtained otherwise.' Anatole would also have others instructed in the beauties of the ancients. In the 'Bibliothèque de Suzanne' he would include 'great-souled works, whose composition makes a luminous whole.' Such a work is the *Odyssey.*[10]

§ 2

THUS far the *Livre de mon ami.* The other autobiographical volumes contain similar professions of faith.

Among the scattered material in *Pierre Nozière* is found a tribute to that harmonious Hellenic art which 'knew a kind of truth surpassing scientific truth and revealed only by poets and artists.' For all his intermittent admiration of 'la science,' Anatole was well aware that great literature goes deeper than scientific accumulations and cannot long be shuffled away amid that valley of dry bones miscalled philology. The same volume again extols the *Odyssey,* especially for its eleventh Book ; the compiler of this knew how to express 'harmonious sorrow,' and had the genuine Grecian feeling for beauty. One section of *Pierre Nozière* is labelled 'Notes Written on the Margin of Plutarch,' but the annotations have little to do with their point of departure. Yet there are classical allusions derivable from this worthy ; and to say of M. Debas that 'he lived like a man from Plutarch' is no small praise.[11]

Apart from incidental allusions to antiquity, *Le Petit Pierre* contains another finely glowing page, again evocative of Roman grandeur. This time it was M. Grépinet at Stanislas who read selections that summoned up for Pierre fascinating glimpses of Romulus and the wolf, the plight of Rhea Silvia, Egeria and her favoured king, other 'adventures' suggested by the organ-roll of heroic names. It was too bad that a medley of Etruscans and Volscians had to tumble into the story and dismay the boy's ardour. As he says in another connexion : 'Art should be left in its noble nudity.'[12]

But it is naturally in *La Vie en fleur,* under the tutelage of M. Dubois, that Pierre expands most visibly in the direction of antiquity. 'In what,' demanded the preceptor, 'are we really superior to the Greeks ? . . . Do we make finer statues or more serene temples ? . . . Will our plays ever equal in beauty a trilogy by Sophocles ?' Where is this Progress they talk about ? Has not the world been the prey of barbarians since the fall of Rome ?[13]

To such admonitions did Pierre seriously incline. He agrees that the most excellent trait of the Greeks was to take 'man as the measure of all things' . . . however unscientifically anthropomorphic this may later appear. He visits the halls of the Louvre, to see paintings and sculpture with the eyes of M. Dubois. But he grants too that Stanislas had done its bit to open his own eyes: in those 'sordid halls' there first appeared to him 'Greece, which taught men knowledge and beauty, and Rome who pacified the world.'—Incidentally, *La Vie en fleur* records the fact of France's more mature contributions to a Dictionary of Antiquities.[14] And his habit of offering *pastiches* from Greek or Roman writers—imitations 'strewn with mythological flowers'—still asserts itself in this final volume.[15]

There is ample evidence to show that this cult of Anatole's was sustained throughout his life. Whether in the form of 'allusions, images, reproductions, or tales, he needed antiquity to the very end.'[16] Such volumes as *Thaïs* and *Sur la Pierre blanche* owe their aroma largely to his love for the ancient world. We cull from various periods certain illustrative passages.

Sylvestre Bonnard, the savant, leaves his medievalism when he grows quite old and keeps ancient masterpieces within arm's reach. In its leanings toward what France considered the only philosophic 'Way,' the *Jardin d'Epicure* obviously contains many echoes from ancient heroes or sages—Cadmus, Socrates, or Ulysses.[17] In the thick of the Socialism abounding in *Vers les Temps meilleurs,* the convert pauses to uphold an older tenet: 'There is only one art which still combines both craftsmanship and beauty.'[18] The very title of *Le Génie latin*—a phrase which France often repeats[19]—is a perfect tribute; and the Preface to that collection of essays (1913) concludes with a notable passage:

> This is an act of faith and of love for the Greek and Latin tradition; it is a tradition wholly compact of wisdom and of beauty; apart from it there is nothing but error and confusion. Whether in philosophy and art, or in science and jurisprudence, we owe everything to Greece and to her conquerors, whom she has conquered. The ancients, still alive, are still teaching us.

France's last work of fiction, *La Révolte des anges,* contains the 'récit de Nectaire,' that marvellous hymn to creation from the antique point of view. It contains also this measured appreciation of the Greeks: 'They carried beauty and wisdom [once more] to a point that no other people reached before them and that no later people has approached.' Why did this double flower grow on the soil of Attica? Because the Greeks recognized no dogmatic priesthood and no jealous God. The god of Hellenism, its ideal of beauty, emanated from its own *génie*. And that was composed of 'grace, harmony, moderation and wisdom'—of all that was most worthy of the Immortals.[20] It is curious to note in this connexion that France preferred the form 'les dieux' to 'Dieu' in the singular. And he held that the most interesting gods were 'those of antiquity because they symbolized the forces of Nature.'[21] He once praised a monograph by Michel Psichari, his future son-in-law, because it showed what the Romans, through their poets, really thought of their gods.[22]

Two years before his death, France pensively averred that he had loved many things, but now his shortening days compelled him to cling to three supreme things—Greek sculpture, the poetry of Racine, and the work of Goethe.[23] Need we add that he admired the classical foundation of all three?

§ 3

It is not surprising that the critics of his own period were almost unanimous in recognizing either the Atticism or the Latinism of Anatole France. Jules Lemaître long ago set the pace when in a famous sentence he called his fellow-critic 'the ultimate flower of the Latin genius.'[24] The classics gave him, says another, 'a discipline to which his whole work testifies.' His familiarity with the ancient and especially the Greek tradition is attested by numerous critics and scholars.[25] Not only did several professors of Greek amiably bear witness to Anatole's competence,[26] but the great Hellenist, Alfred Croiset, saluted him as the 'genius of Greece made French,' and as 'the most Attic of our writers,' whether for subtlety of thought, smiling irony or winged words—all these gifts being permeated by a 'luminous reason.'[27] These courteous remarks probably need some discounting, since France himself was present on the occasion when they were delivered. But there is much other evidence. It is interesting to observe, for example, that in his writings, forming a link with the Grecian Nemesis, are many allusions to 'implacable destiny,' 'inexorable fatality' and the like.[28] We are told that he found again the radiance of a pagan world, not ours to be sure, but properly his because he thoroughly belonged to it; also, he was deemed an 'Atticiste' in his style, thought of as containing qualities very similar to those which M. Croiset had emphasized.[29]

The fact is, as Lemaître showed in an interesting article, that there was a whole movement towards Neo-Hellenism in the seventies and eighties. Such women as Madame Adam (Juliette Lamber), regular Parnassians like France and Leconte de Lisle, a scholarly withdrawn poet like Louis Ménard (who influenced the composition of *Thaïs*), all 'loved the Greek gods'—and their own visions of Greek civilization. Such works as Ménard's *Rêveries d'un Païen mystique* (1876) chimed in with the mood prevalent amid the Parnassians.[30] Among this group, Anatole was 'one of the most fervent. That enthusiastic adoration of Hellenic life, religion, and beauty was one of the most remarkable traits of the last poetic generation.'[31] A later critic would place France, whether for his enthusiasm or its effects upon his style, among the foremost of these devotees. He put 'his whole temperament into his Neo-Hellenism. . . The last of the pagans of Paris is perhaps the most elusive of them all.'[32] But he was not really the last, for such writers as Frédéric Plessis and even Charles Maurras were in this respect his acknowledged disciples.[33]

Anatole's love of the Græco-Latin tradition is evident as early as the reviews written for the *Amateur d'autographes*. 'He came to us,' says Ricard, 'as a Latin child,' already accustomed to draw the honey from the classical masterpieces, 'not as a scholar, but as an artist.' The same witness accords him in Parnassian days a full quota of that classical serenity which inclines toward a measured strength and *pondération* even in passion.[34] M. Paul Claudel objects that the Greeks, especially in tragedy, were not so serene as all that and protests that A.F. has promulgated a false legend concerning their harmony and moderation.[35] But we suspect that M. Claudel is a special pleader.

At the time of Anatole's death, the chorus swells again, although with some dissident voices. Various articles[36] emphasize 'his perfection of form and how he prolongs a tradition frequently called "Attic."' It is pointed out that his style usually forms an effective blend of Grecian harmony and Latin precision. Paul Ginisty declares that Anatole seemed nourished on the ambrosia of the Classic Muses and thence derived, by virtue of an immense but always elegant erudition, 'the perfection with which he handled the purest, clearest and most substantial French.'[37]

Practically the same view of France as almost the last complete representative of Græco-Roman culture is upheld by a number of recent critics. He is a 'humanistic æsthete'; or (rewording Lemaître) he is 'la suprême fleur des humanités'; or his favourite 'enterprise' was that 'of making the ancient poets and thinkers live again for the modern imagination'; or he has 'never ceased' to draw measure and power from his oldest forebears.[38] Consequently, his readers are chiefly those who have been formed in the same tradition. His appreciations are usually from a neo-classical standpoint and they 'date' because they rarely descend later than the eighteenth century.[39] He does not then exaggerate so very much when he insists, 'je n'aime que l'antique'—including its prolongations. A recent admirer [40] has written poetically of the fine appearance of Anatole as an 'august old man'—

> Où tout, comme en son nom, n'était que Grèce et France.

In fact, when it comes to discriminating, the weight of opinion seems at first to incline the balance more toward Greece than Rome, as the preponderant factor in France's culture. He was virtually a 'contemporary of Pericles'; like an Athenian, he relied only on the light of reason, the power of reflection ; regarding contemporary matters he took the positions that one would expect from 'an intelligent, cultivated and eclectic Greek thinker.' [41]

In his striking study on *Le Génie du paganisme,* M. Clerc further differentiates and outlines the sort of ancestor-worship that affected, he believes, a number of France's works :

> He evokes neither the antiquity of myths, nor that of ruins, nor that of Utopian sculpture. . . His antiquity is rich in *ideas* that struggle amicably and in refined *sensations*. It is the end of a banquet [cf. *Thaïs*] where spirit and flesh settle down to amiable converse. Preferably, the scene is laid at Corinth, in the complex Age of the Antonines. . .

In short, it is 'Hellenism on the decline'—a point that will soon demand scrutiny. But however much Alexandria may have tempered Attica, it is still 'the Attic spirit, the finest of human things that lives again in him' ; it inspires his poetry with an 'ancient perfume' and his prose with a delicate nobility.[42]

But there is something to be said on the other side of the medal, and it is perhaps M. Amiot who says it best. He maintains that Anatole is not really a Hellenist and not primarily a thinker. Else why should he make so little of Plato and of Aristotle ? Furthermore, he ignores Thucydides and Demosthenes. Even among dramatists, he appears to have been stirred only by Sophocles and that not frequently. At bottom, he was swayed principally by the sophists and their disillusioned philosophy. That is not a very large part of Greek civilization, which consequently affected France only to a limited degree, just as Greek style affected him only at a third or fourth remove. It is a style, which for all its taste and its 'tempered' Atticism, is composite rather than natural and aims often at *pastiches* from antiquity. In brief, Anatole should be classed with the tertiary order of Hellenes.[43]

This view, though doubtless extreme, offers a useful counterpoise to the more numerous commentators who would completely Hellenize Anatole. And we are led to raise the question, Why do they nearly all, even Croiset, persist in relating him to Greece rather than to Rome? France was more familiar with Latin literature than with Greek; he held, too, that his own civilization was closer to the Romans. Whether or not Amiot is right in calling A.F. a 'pseudo-Hellène,' there is little doubt that he more fully 'felt and understood the Latins.'[44] The Roman world was his hearthside, his natural habitat, to which he returned more and more constantly; Greece was a 'fair outsider,' whose charms dazzled the youth and with whom he conducted an intermittent flirtation.[45]

This 'devotee' of Hellenism did not learn Greek until rather late in his school-life (*c.* 1860-61). We may partly retrace our steps, to see how this particular revelation affected him, then and later.

§ 4

THE passage already quoted in part from the *Livre de Pierre* is the *locus classicus* in a double sense. It is where the boy awakens to the sense of Grecian loveliness. 'In approaching Greece, he saw Beauty in her magnificent simplicity.' He cared little for Æsop. But Homer opened his eyes, and for six months he could not leave the *Odyssey*. It was then that he visioned 'Thetis, Nausicaa and her companions.' Nothing is said of the *Iliad;* from the first he turned strongly to the poetry of emotion and passion. Æschylus he hardly understood; 'but Sophocles, but Euripides opened to me the enchanted world of heroes and heroines and introduced me to the poetry of misfortune.' Every tragedy that he read brought fresh tears and sighs in its train.[46]

The dreamy student thus incurred the celebrated reproach of not sticking to his class-work. Even into the dark winter streets he would carry 'that light and that harmony' which dwelt within the soul of Greece. He would read his tragedies under the lamp-post and he long associated a great line in the *Antigone* with the odor of roasted chestnuts.[47] In a letter to Mme. de Caillavet he writes, in 1888, of lingering near the Auvergnat and his chestnut-stove, because of the memories of childhood thus powerfully recalled. As for the *Odyssey* again, he started, in 1891, something of a controversy regarding the proper translation of a certain Homeric passage.[48] Homer and Sophocles . . . he rings the changes on these names, and these are the two Grecians that aided most in establishing his taste. In the full tide of his third period, he turned, naturally, to the more personal Euripides and he had by then familiarized himself with the Greek Anthology.

In his youth Anatole 'learned by heart many lines.' This was his private method of absorbing masterpieces, and it produced notable results, for the habit of memorizing the classics is what makes him quote so frequently, almost unconsciously, from Virgil and Lucretius and Racine.[49] This habit was doubtless inaugurated on the benches of Stanislas, where the scholars used such compendiums as the *Selectae* of Jean Heuzet, which was full of heroic 'traits,' together with the well-known *Jardin des racines grecques*.[50] And even into his old age France would recite, for his own satisfaction or by way of 'showing off,' poetic *morceaux* in various languages. Especially he had 'an ear sensitively attuned to the music that sounds eternally' in ancient tongues.[51]

In the *Livre de Suzanne,* the simplicity and the imagination of the ancients are put on a par with fairy-tales, whether for their charm or their cultural value. Both Homeric poems are now praised for their simple beauty. The poetry in the speech of Thetis, like the poetry of fairy-tales, is said to consist entirely in the 'happy intermingling' of natural elements. Clearly, the Greek mythology fascinated him more than any other.

In *Pierre Nozière* there is little or no reference to the golden age of Greece, but in *Sylvestre Bonnard* we find additional allusions to Sophocles and the *Antigone,* together with an apostrophe to 'Invincible Eros.' The old scholar declares, in connexion with the fairy's visit, that he 'received in childhood a taste for allegory from the Greeks.' He compares himself now to the old men in Homer, the retired veterans seated on the ramparts, mere spectators of the combat. He pays tribute to Sicily as a 'land of glory' still guarding her antique beauties. A very early poem shows us Anatole reading *Œdipus Rex*.[52] We have seen that the *Alfred de Vigny* contributes its praise of an Olympian serenity. *Le Génie latin* contains an article (of 1878) on 'Daphnis et Chloé' ; here we begin to suspect that Anatole's taste included the Neo-Hellenic decadence as well as the Age of Pericles. Becoming reckless with his dates, he confuses the *Daphnis* with the preceding Milesian tales. To account for the popularity of the latter, he alleges that they were recited to the wealthy voluptuous Ionians, while they reclined 'under airy porticoes, shaded by groves of myrtles.' Offering natural scenes for jaded palates, there came Longus' *Daphnis and Chloë,* the product of a retarded season. Longus saves himself by the abundant imitation of his greater predecessors. It is very Anatolian, very much like his own method, to approve of literary pillaging in such terms as these:

> There was always, in the best ancient literature, a taste for free imitation. This was keenly felt by the latest writers. It maintained the purity of their language, it carried them back to the truly beautiful.[53]

He probably exaggerates the 'purity' of Longus ; but the interesting thing is the apparent willingness to put up with half-gods when the gods are gone. That is the leaning that makes Lanson declare that France was less susceptible to the grandeur of Greece, whether in oratory or philosophy, than to the 'picturesque and witty art of the decadence.'[54]

This raises again the question whether Anatole was a pure Atticist, or whether he was more of an Alexandrian, a 'pseudo-Hellène.' It is a hard question to resolve, but the following considerations may incline us toward a temperate position. In the first place, as Lemaître points out in connexion with the Neo-Hellenic revival, who can be a pure Grecian these days ? Did not each of the revivalists put his or her own dream into the vision that they called Greece ?[55] This is the sort of argument that France himself would be among the first to admit. That much being granted, then, the whole movement has been appropriately termed a 'renaissance alexandrine,'[56] in much the same sense in which Tennyson's art has been called Alexandrian or composite. But more specifically it is argued that Anatole's syncretic paganism reflects chiefly and by his own preference that last phase of the long Hellenizing period when the remote deities of the old Olympus became more humanized as they clashed with the new Christianity.[57] Certain poems to be considered in the next chapter, as well as the whole of *Thaïs,* would support this view. And in line with it we are told that what France particularly cherished in the Greeks was the subtlety and agility of their minds; or that he was less a child of lucid logical Athens than of the 'soft Ionian towns of Asia Minor'; or that he lacked the integration, the oneness characteristic of the 'best classic types.'[58] Messrs. Michaut and Giraud tend to confirm this Alexandrianism, although they seem to attach it rather to the Roman than to the strictly Greek decadence.[59]

In this double significance, we may admit the indictment for what, after all, is not a major offence. France was an 'Alexandrian,' just as he was many other things, because of his cerebral involutions, because of his fondness for epochs of controversy, because of his addiction to literary *pastiches.* For of one cognate truth I am convinced, although the demonstration of it cannot be fully made here: except in the Gospels and a few other places where simplicity is desirable, Anatole's *style* is not simple or classical in the sense that it is unvarnished or devoid of undertones. It is more usually composite, like the man himself. It is patterned loosely upon the thought, like the many devious folds of Greek drapery. It has, as Sainte-Beuve said less truly of Balzac's style, the wonderful adaptability, the subtle broken body of an ancient mime. And when this manifold style matches the sinuous thought, as in *Thaïs,* we get a 'last flower' of something that is very Hellenistic, but also very late.[60]

We may well conclude, then, that whatever France's liking for ancient Greece, he was equally responsive to the complexities of an Alexandrian age, since he lived in one himself and had a most adjustable and Protean outlook. The penchant that he certainly had for the Hellenizing period will soon recur in connexion with his poems. Here we may note that the Invocation preceding *Les Noces corinthiennes* crystallizes his early love for Greece as a whole:[61]

Hellas, ô jeune fille, ô joueuse de lyre,
Toi dont la bouche aimait les baisers et le miel . . .

O fille de la mer, assise aux plages blondes !
Ton sein a contenu la belle volupté,
Et la sainte harmonie a de ses grandes ondes
Empli ton chant d'amour abondamment jeté.
Moi, cet enfant latin qui te trouva si belle . . .*

—Yes, even I, though I do not sing your untroubled youth, yet have I placed pale violets on your breast and depicted you at the time when new gods plucked from your brow the holy fillet.—

Dans le monde assombri s'effaça ton sourire ;
La grâce et la beauté périrent avec toi ;
Nul au rocher désert ne recueillit ta lyre,
Et la terre roula dans un obscur effroi.†

This is strongly reminiscent of Leconte de Lisle's apostrophe to Beauty (in 'Hypatie') :

Et les mondes encor roulent sous ses pieds blancs.‡

It is already evident that Anatole France owes much to Leconte de Lisle, especially as regards the full harmonious flow of the strophe. The two men were also akin in their adoration of *la lumière* and in associating an intensity of white light with the old Greek civilization. For Leconte de Lisle, Venus is the 'white mother of the gods' and the idyll of 'Kléarista' is full of the beauty of dawn, whose radiance is blended with the beauty of the Sicilian girl. We have heard Anatole too speak of Grecian poetry as one intoxicated with 'cette lumière et ce chant.' His own volume of *Poèmes dorés* begins with an introductory ode, 'À la Lumière.' He invokes light as the 'white mother of visions' and shows how

* Hellas, O Maiden, thou player on the lyre,
Whose mouth adored both kisses and honey from the bees,

O daughter of the Ocean, seated on golden strands !
Thy breast has known the sting of Voluptas,
And holy Harmony has with its urgent billows
Filled thy song with love abundantly thrown abroad.
I, that Latin child, who always found thee fair . . .

† Then in the darkened world thy smile grew dim ;
Beauty and queenly charm were lost with thee ;
None in the barren desert sang thy hymn,
While piteous Earth forgot thy minstrelsy.

‡ And still the worlds roll on beneath her dazzling feet.

the sunshine affects various natural objects. Anatole is exceedingly fond of the classical apostrophe or invocation, whose use with him generally indicates a mounting tide of emotion, of sensitiveness to lyric beauty. This threshold-poem continues to associate the light and harmony of antiquity, which he would prolong in his own measures:

Sois ma force, ô Lumière ! et puissent mes pensées,
Belles et simples comme toi,
Dans la grâce et la paix, dérouler sous ta foi
Leurs formes toujours cadencées.*

—A prayer that in this case was answered.[62]

In this connexion, we are reminded[63] how Anatole was lastingly impressed by 'the lines in the *Antigone,* in which the chorus of Theban elders addressed the rising sun.' This is probably the invocation ('O sainte lumière') that inspired France's threshold-poem and that is referred to in an article in *Le Temps;*[64] there Anatole also mentions the charming effects of light upon the Ægean sea and the mountains of Greece. There are still other passages where this association is made;[65] and 'la lumière' is a constant *motif* in *Abeille.*

§ 5

We conclude that France, until complete manhood at least, was well-acquainted with comparatively few Grecian masterpieces, though he loved and preferred these artistically above almost all others. He had a much wider range in Latin. Mr. Stewart points out that 'it was Roman poets rather than Greek satirists that he loved to quote, and among these, though he quotes him but seldom, it is the spirit of Lucretius that he most frequently recalls.'[66] It is true that the Lucretian view of Nature animates some of our author's most eloquent passages, from an early poetic fragment called 'Genèse' (see below, Ch. XIII) to the 'Récit' of Nectaire mentioned above. Whenever France was 'anthropologically' minded, he was likely to draw upon the author of *De Rerum natura* or upon his master, Epicurus, whose Garden became Anatole's 'second fatherland.' The Darwinism conspicuous in the

* Be my strength, O Light! And let my thoughts, fair and simple as thou art, display in allegiance to thee their cadenced forms, gracefully and peacefully.

Poèmes dorés contains, in solution, traces of Lucretian doctrine, which came to him as a 'revelation.'[67] But this influence is more manifest in the works of France's later periods.[68]

There are other Romans whom Anatole knew early and well. His general view was that he could learn more from the Latins than from his contemporaries, 'more from Petronius than from Mendès.'[69] In the *Livre de Pierre,* we find allusions to Horace and memories of Livy. The latter furnished the famous picture of the Roman retreat to Canusium, after the battle of Cannæ. When Pierre was twelve years old, 'the tales of Livy moved him to generous tears.' Alas! The generosity presently evaporated, and youth had gone before. In his final phase, Anatole called 'Tite-Live' a liar and considered that by his 'hollow rhetoric' he had upheld the spirit of militarism.[70] But Horace continued long to be a favourite. In *Sylvestre Bonnard* the Roman Epicurean is approved for wisely counselling Leuconoë, 'the beautiful rebel, who wanted to know the secrets of the future. . . Your friend [Horace] showed himeslf a man of sense in advising you rather to filter the Grecian wines.'[71] Before that, Anatole himself had written a poem to this 'Leuconoé' ; and in connexion with the poem he had reprinted an earlier essay on 'Les Femmes d'Horace.'[72] The Horatian philosophy is usually commended as the only one that accords with real life. Anatole Himself still speaks of 'that charming Horace, that Voltaire of Augustus' court'[73]— a comparison in which there is about as much truth as in most historical parallels.

France showed another and less *mondain* attitude towards the poets of love. He tells us that the Roman elegists, especially Propertius, caused him as an adolescent *en rhétorique* to 'mingle love and death in the poetry of my dreams.' The shade of Cynthia, beloved by the Roman writer, was dear to Anatole too. On her funeral couch she appeared to him in the dusty schoolroom, and evoked images half-sensual, half-pious. This remained a characteristic mood.[74]

In spite of his dreaminess, Anatole did not always object to militarism.[75] In fact, the Latinity first inspired in him by M. Chotard was of a bellicose nature ; this martial professor rejoiced in the heroic stand of Brutus at Philippi and of Pompey at Pharsalia. The rout at Cannæ, the corpse of Varus in the Hyrcanian forest—all fired the soul of Chotard and of little Pierre. Anatole's juvenile travel-diary and his early articles as well are strewn with references to the Romans. One is amused by the candid pedantry—which later he learned to conceal with adornments—in the allusions to and quotations from Horace, Virgil, and others. He grows weary of the Norman country-side and would like to return to Paris and Tacitus. Suetonius provided most of the background for the poem called 'Les Légions de Varus.'[76] It was somewhat later that he came to know and appreciate Ovid, whose *Ars Amatoria* would naturally appeal to France. There was nothing unusual then about this array of Latinity; two years before *Le Livre de mon ami,* Mr. Gladstone could still quote Lucretius in the House of Commons.[77] We shall see presently how A.F. came to the defence of Latin when around 1887 it was threatened in the schools.

§ 6

BUT when and how did Anatole conceive his deep passion for the

wielder of the stateliest measure
Ever moulded by the lips of man?

How did he fully discover Virgil? Here again France uses the language of revelation and summons up for us yet another picture—the fourth in the gallery of his youthful literary infatuations. We learn in the *Livre de Pierre*[78] that in Normandy he carried about a pocket-edition of the Roman poet, which still contains pressed flowers from the wood of Saint-Patrice. This was the time when at seventeen he wandered in the forest oppressed by recent memories and a prey to a vague uneasiness. He imitated and participated in the world-weariness of Chateaubriand. But a mightier than Chateaubriand was destined to disclose what really ailed the lad:

Through force of habit I opened my Virgil and read:
Hic, quos durus Amor . . .
'Here those whom a pitiless love has slain with cruel languor are found concealed in mysterious glades, and round about the groves of myrtles cast their shade.'

The groves of myrtles cast their shade around! Ah, well I knew that myrtle-grove; it was all within my consciousness. But I did not know its name, which now Virgil disclosed to me. Thanks to him I knew that I was in love.

Long ago Godmother Marcelle had revealed the soul of Beauty; Dubois had revealed antiquity; but it was left to Virgil, the tender Pandarus, to forge the golden link between. The passage quoted is the prelude to the injured Dido's appearance before her recreant lover in that region of Hades which the poet calls the 'Fields of Sorrow.' No wonder that Virgil and his myrtles are constantly found henceforward, and that Anatole, very characteristically, sees Virgil as the singer of fatality and sentiment rather than of Roman grandeur. There is no other classical writer who exercises such an ascendency over France. It is a signal case. Consequently, we shall try to show how this major 'theme' reappears throughout Anatole's entire life.

The lad Pierre even before going to Normandy, 'adored and understood Virgil almost as well as if my professors had not explained him to me.' There are allusions, in *Petit Pierre,* to M. Triaire's efforts along this line — and in general to Virgil's fondness for 'delightful fabrications.' Still a schoolboy, Anatole translates for his mother part of the first Eclogue, with a tiny introduction and notes, all in apple-pie order. No myrtles yet, but beeches, lambs, and shepherds. Tags from the *Aeneid* and the *Georgics* figure in the youthful letters written home from the country of Chateaubriand. In an early article from *Le Globe,* France admires Virgil's rusticity, as well as his modesty. Lines from the fourth and the tenth Eclogues are quoted by the sapient Sylvestre Bonnard.[79]

M. Dubois had set the pace in learning Virgil by heart.[80] He believed that the author of the *Aeneid* was the 'most profound' of Latin writers. He impressed on Anatole the thought that Nature alone could explain to him the Mantuan poet and thus teach him the laws of harmony. Probably the old man meant (like J. C. Scaliger and other devotees) that Virgil was a second nature. It was during the siege of Paris that Anatole read the sixth Eclogue and found himself in thorough agreement with Silenus as to the origin and destiny of the globe. He points out the Lucretian and the evolutionary aspects of Virgil's treatment. This is the same eclogue that Jean Servien read and praised, under the German guns. It has been thought by friendly judges that France's own verses have at times a Virgilian sonority.[81]

By his middle period, France had become well-nigh a 'complete' Virgilian. As he significantly declares in *l'Univers illustré,*

'If I began speaking here of Virgil and Tacitus, I would never stop.'[82] The series of the *Histoire contemporaine* offers a conspicuous example. M. Bergeret, when preparing his lectures on the eighth and the tenth Books of the *Aeneid,* is rather depressing about Virgil. Like 'M. Jal' (who gave France the idea), Bergeret is preparing a learned monograph on 'Virgilius nauticus,' or the marine terms in the *Aeneid.*[83] When he is in a low frame of mind, he underrates this philological labour and reflects that the European reputation of Virgil rests on certain misunderstandings. But when Bergeret's fortunes improve, he thinks better of his task and of his master.[84]

Anatole Himself spoke willingly of the 'pleasant age of Virgil';[85] and we shall see in a moment the critical role he plays in *l'Ile des Pingouins.* Here the Roman poet, after acting as cicerone to Ulysses and Dante, is represented as guiding still another personage into the eternal shades.

But the forest of myrtles in particular furnishes, like the insistence on *la lumière,* one of the minor *motifs* that serve as recurrent threads in the Anatolian pattern. Since the myrtle was the tree sacred to Venus,[86] it has formed a suitable background for the unhappy Dido's shade; and it rises darkly in our author's mind whenever he

longs to talk with some old lover's ghost.

The passage is referred to again in *l'Etui de nacre* and is hinted at in other volumes; it is fully developed in an early essay where Chateaubriand is represented as succumbing to Virgil's power.[87] Is it really Chateaubriand who succumbs? There is in the *Mémoires d'Outre-Tombe* but slight reference to Virgil.[88] Anatole is rather attributing his own sentiments to another, through association of ideas. For it was originally under Chateaubriand's influence that our author at seventeen, had, as he says, 'rolled on the strand, full of desire for something unknown which I divined everywhere and which I found nowhere.' Then followed the revelation of love through Virgil, already quoted from *Le Livre de Pierre.* Now it is Chateaubriand who is credited with Anatole's own experience, with lying in the long grass and summoning up 'that figure whose immortal ardour enchants across the ages all imaginative youth.' And the passage of the myrtles is again quoted to the very last line of the Latin:

Aut videt aut vidisse putat per nubila lunam.

Nor in his old age was Dido forgotten. In *La Vie en fleur*[89] France tells us that when at Stanislas he had to choose, as major elective, either science or literature, he at first chose science—but 'on the fourth day the Virgilian myrtles and the hidden pathway of the forest of shades renewed their old temptation.' Finally, a few months before his death, in receiving a sympathetic English visitor, Anatole quoted the *Aeneid* at length.[90] Plucking a flower, he laid it once more between the pages of a pocket-Virgil, in close proximity to the immemorial myrtles. Thus Eighty reached back to Seventeen—the Eternal Return of old age.

As he had read his own Virgil-worship into Chateaubriand, so he ascribes a similar Maronolatry to Racine. When Saint-Cyran, the head of the Jansenists, told Racine 'that Virgil was damned for having written these beautiful lines,' the sensitive schoolboy must have felt (writes Anatole)[91] a melancholy and delicious charm surround the shade of Dido. Religion offers to voluptuous souls an added *volupté*: *'la volupté de se perdre'*—a phrase that he liked well enough to repeat several times in later works.[92]

In *l'Ile des Pingouins* France takes up and develops a theory regarding Virgil laid down years before by M. Dubois. That pagan had maintained the superiority of the hexameter over the modern fashion of riming. When Marbode pays his visit to Hades, he, like Dante, finds Virgil in Limbo—and the Roman poet, preferring hexameters, is critical of the *terza rima* of the Florentine.[93]

In fact, as May suggests, the cadences of Anatole's prose often recall 'that haunting Virgilian music.'[94] The same writer emphasizes how Anatole made Virgil a part of himself by a process of transfusion or, as we might say, by a kind of literary metabolism. The two authors show a similar indulgence and compassion towards humanity, a sense of man's 'doubtful doom.'[95] And this emphasis on destiny is clearly one element in the transfusion. It has been pointed out that there are some forty references to Fate in the first three books of the *Aeneid* alone.[96] France, too, particularly in connexion with the passion of love, has expressed frequently his conception of this

Fortuna omnipotens et ineluctabile fatum.

In Virgil, Fate is most frequently identified with the will of Jove, to which Aeneas must dumbly bow his head.[97] But it is characteristic that France should rather treat Fate as a power coeval with Amor, and that Dido, victim of the two forces, should occupy in his memory a place disproportionate to her role in the *Aeneid*. He was probably thinking of her when he wrote the poem, 'Le Bûcher de santal,' where the incident of the funeral pyre is repeated.[98]

The Frenchman has still other affinities with the Roman.[99] A certain *pietas,* in the double sense of compassion and respect for venerable things ; the *religio loci,* whether of Rome or of Paris ; an addiction to meditation, to 'moderation of tone' ; these are the most obvious similarities in the natures of the two men. With regard to the art of writing, the resemblances are more distinct : Virgil is said by Mr. Sellar to be 'deficient in spontaneous invention,' and Anatole doubts whether such a thing exists ; both are essentially bookish in their view of the cosmos ; neither could write without indulging in numerous literary reminiscences ; but each 'possessed a remarkable power of giving new life to the creations of earlier times.' Consequently, just as the *Aeneid* seems a mosaic of allusions and imitations, so does the whole work of Anatole France seem a palimpsest of buried meanings and faint allusions. This tendency would account for such traits, in both writers, as 'imitative imagery' and the *curiosa felicitas* of phrase. There is a tale that Virgil ordered the destruction of the unfinished *Aeneid*—to such an extent did the passion for perfection rule his mind. What else has controlled the pen of Anatole down to his last years and his latest editions ? Both have ranked among the 'most cultivated' men of their respective periods, both offer a singular compound of artist and scholar, and both believed in style as 'the fruit of long reflection'—and reflections from earlier masters.[100]

Such were the classical models admired in Anatole's adolescence. There was every reason why a youth, turning from the Christian tradition, should seek wisdom and beauty in the ancient sages. And enough illustrations have been given to indicate why France, the iconoclast, was conservative in his poetic theory and in his literary admirations. The question now arises how these and other matters find expression in his poetry.

CHAPTER IX

Esoteric Verse

§ 1

FRANCE'S interest in the sunset of antiquity, especially when placed in opposition to the rising moon of the Christian faith, finds expression in some of his earliest verse. The poem called *La Légende de Sainte Thaïs, Comédienne* is, in fact, his first direct manifesto against Christianity. Published in 1867,[1] before the Parnassian leaven was fully working in Anatole's brain, it may well be considered here. These verses are interesting not only as a 'document,' but because they represent the initial stage of what presently became a famous novel.

The story of the *Légende* represents Thaïs (of Alexandria) as an actress and courtesan of compelling beauty. The grave Galileans who brought Christianity 'au pays des Egyptiens' suspected her as one animated by the demon of lust. But the Gentiles flocked to the theatre, to see her dance and sing. She had two lovers—a fat Syrian governor, who celebrated her charms at banquets, and a handsome centurion, who was really her *amant de cœur*. The former had the latter imprisoned and induced him to commit suicide. After this event, Thaïs and the governor parted company.

One day the courtesan passes by an unsavoury group of Christians and is presently reminded that her mother had brought her up in that faith. But this group (which Anatole acrimoniously describes as very unclean) makes an outcry against Thaïs and prepares to stone her. Whereupon a tall and wild-looking old man sardonically reminds the rabble of the Scriptural saying about him who casts the first stone. The rescuer of Thaïs is depicted as saintly and tolerant; but he too distrusts her beauty, especially when she throws herself at his feet, offering to serve and love him. She is ashamed and repents of her past. After the conversion-scene, the saintly *vieillard* will take her to a nunnery; but first she must go home and burn her worldly possessions, including her mirror and other luxurious furnishings.

The old man takes Thaïs on a wearisome march through the desert. He shuts her up for twenty months in a kind of coffin-like cell. At length he unseals this retreat and finding that she has become transfigured by holiness, the monk bows his head and demands her blessing. Here the poem proper ends. But there is an unfamiliar and somewhat obscure after-piece. This narrates how Thaïs is now guided by a guardian angel. Following a star through the desert, she meets and is attracted by a strange celestial woman. Their Lesbian loves are sheltered by the angel.

The composition of the poem is marred by this after-piece. Otherwise it adumbrates the "hour-glass" type of construction for which the novel is notable—i.e., the spiritual rise of Thaïs, set off by the humiliation of Paphnuce. In style, the verses are crude, uneven, and at times awkwardly turned. The language often has that deliberate and semi-Biblical naïveté which came to be characteristic of France's treatment of legendary material. But the choice of words and the tone also impress one as derivable from Vigny's treatment of Biblical themes. The line which concludes the poem proper—

> Le verbe est dans ton sein, car le verbe est SOUFFRANCE—

is quite in the manner of Vigny. Other touches recall Hugo. But the chief poetic influence, once more, is that of Leconte de Lisle. This appears in the emphasis on 'lumière' and 'flamme,' in the close description of persons and things (e.g., the belongings of Thaïs), as well as in the objurgations against the early Christians. Furthermore, the actual wording sometimes betrays the Parnassian neophyte. For instance, these lines refer to the governor's delight in his mistress:

> Déliant de Thaïs les ceintures glissantes,
> Il fit jaillir ses seins en strophes frémissantes;
> Et calme, triomphant, ce corps *harmonieux,*
> Pareil au marbre où rit Kypris, mère des dieux,
> Comme *aux beaux jours d'Hellas* et sur *le mode antique*
> Chantait *l'hymne sacré de la beauté plastique.*[2] *

The high priest of Parnassus often spoke in this tone. The incident of the bleeding feet of Thaïs as she went through the desert is probably another reminiscence from Leconte de Lisle.[3]

The general and much-vexed question of the sources of the

* He stripped the actress of her gliding robes;
Like trembling verses, he revealed her breasts;
And then that perfect body, calm, triumphant,
Most like the Cyprian Venus, cast in marble,
With high Hellenic pomp, in ancient measures,
Chanted the hymn of plastic loveliness.

legend may be reserved for our treatment of the novel.[4] Suffice it to say here that neither the *Légende dorée* nor the *Vies des Pères des déserts,* which give the general outline of the story, will account for all the *motifs* that France has wrought into the poem. In particular, touches describing the courtesan's life together with the vaguely Sapphic conclusion seem to derive, piecemeal, from a work by a 'bibliophile' with whom Anatole was well acquainted. This was a *Histoire de la Prostitution chez tous les peuples du monde* by Paul Lacroix.[5] Emphasis is here laid on certain homosexual practices permitted within the sect of the Cainites.

The points of contact between poem and story have been thus elucidated :[6]

> The following elements of the poem were retained in the novel : the beauty of Thaïs, her wickedness, her fear when confronted by the monk, her offer of herself to him, the discovery that she has been baptized, the burning of her treasure, the journey to the monastery when she passes over the sands of the desert with bleeding feet, her unworthiness to raise her hands in prayer or to lift her eyes to heaven, the place and manner of her penance.
>
> The principal differences are these : the love affairs of Thaïs in the novel, while like those of the poem in a general way, differ in actual details ; the same is true of the list of treasures that she burns ; the manner of her meeting with the monk is entirely changed ; Paphnutius seems to be an older man, as he asserts that he has prayed and fasted for sixty years ; he is not the lover of Thaïs ; the end of the novel bears no resemblance to that of the poem.

One may add that while the character of the monk deteriorates in the novel, that of Thaïs, as a credulous and sensuous *gamine,* remains much the same throughout poem and story. The conversion-scene, which ultimately became part of the grotto-scene, is not at all worked up in the *Légende*. The novel, of course, evinces a greater mastery of form, more delicacy and maturity of mind. And certain crudities disappear. On the other hand, Anatole's dislike and distrust of early Christian asceticism are already conspicuous in the poem. This surely is one of France's major themes. That fact and the fact that the tale of Thaïs lingered in his mind for over twenty years, have led us into a full account of his little-known *Légende*.[7]

§ 2

This was not the only poem to find a separate publication. The verses called 'Genèse' have been mentioned and will be studied later. We have seen that two pieces, attacking Napoleon III, had appeared in the *Gazette rimée*. None of the above were ever collected in volume form. But the *Parnasse contemporain* printed in its second series (1871) two titles subsequently included in *Les Poèmes dorés*—namely, 'La Danse des Morts' and 'La Part de Madeleine'; and in its third series (1876) appeared the first Part or act of *Les Noces corinthiennes,* shortly before this play was published as a whole.[8] A quantity of intimate or fugitive pieces were never printed at all. Such were the *juvenilia* dealt with above (Chapter VI); such was, according to Souriau, a miscellany called *Statues et Bas-Reliefs,* which Anatole committed to the flames. Certain individual poems were also 'scrapped,' although in two cases—'À Théophile Gautier' and 'Diane de Noirlys'—the careful author saved some fragments for still other verses.[9]

Altogether, six of the poems collected in the *Poèmes dorés* had figured previously in periodicals or anthologies; six others were added in later editions; and several important titles, originally appearing in *Les Noces corinthiennes,* were presently transferred to these later editions of the *Poèmes dorés.*[10] We accept the 'definitive' text of this volume (including *Les Noces*) as our standard.

The sub-title *Idylles et Légendes* was already used in the first edition to head a certain group of poems. But it did not appear on the title-page until the collective edition of 1896; and it was never employed as the title for a separate volume.[11]

All told there are thirty-nine poems in the 'canon' today. As for the dates of composition, the *Poèmes dorés* had been written at any time from 1864 to 1873; and a number of them precede the Franco-Prussian war.[12]

§ 3

It must be evident that in his twenties France wrote a considerable amount of poetry. Two questions arise in this connexion. What was his opinion of the form? And did his liking for verse continue beyond the period of actual productiveness?

As became such an artist in language, Anatole recognized

poetry as the most consummate form of human expression. 'A single beautiful line,' he once declared, 'does more good in the world than all the masterpieces of metallurgy.' [13] Like other things, poetic modes shift and date and pass ; so the poet who lives is the poet who sings naturally above all else ; he it is who may distill 'a few drops of elixir' ; an incomparable elixir that may well become immortal just because the singer has not aimed at immortality.[14] Several thoughtful critics appreciate this supremacy that France accorded to the Muse. Mr. Schaffer points out that he

> considered poetry not merely one of the finest of the fine arts and, as such, a highly desirable ornament to any civilization, but one of the very indispensables of life, as necessary as bread and meat. And the great poets of history assume in his eyes the guise of giants of wisdom, of master-performers on the keys of the human emotions, and of makers of music that is second in beauty only to the music of the spheres.[15]

Furthermore, this major interest endured far beyond the period of actual poetic achievement. France's lasting obsession with Racine and with Virgil are cases in point. It has been calculated that over one-fourth of the articles in the collected *Vie littéraire* deal entirely or in large part with poetry.[16] Anatole never ceased to memorize and recite verses from his best beloved authors. As late as 1911 he composed an edition and commentary on the famous *Poèmes du Souvenir*. Well into his old age, as the reminiscential volumes show, poetry remained one of his paramount themes, whether in thought or conversation.

It is with great interest, then, that we turn to the content of the *Poèmes dorés*—remembering Leconte de Lisle's prophecy that his pupil would some day be a 'grand prosateur,' because of his careful attention to the harmonies of verse.[17] But first let us emphasize certain positions taken in the aforementioned article on poetic theory which caused something of a stir in Parnassian circles.

The objective attitude which this article upheld had little to do with questions of sentiment ; but it was much concerned with the positivistic philosophy then current. Taine and Darwin were the true preceptors of the Parnassians. Like the chief of his school, Anatole decides for a descriptive poetry, which shall avoid the vague and 'l'idéal,' which shall prefer the concrete, and which as a pendant to natural science shall instill a kind of Lucretian philosophy, intermingled with *tableaux* of flora and fauna. Alike in observation and in expression, verse should approximate a scientific exactitude. Add to this France's belief that 'tout est dit' and that invention or creation of new matter is an illusion. It follows that the poet can really innovate only in matters of form. Concentrating, then, on prosody, he elaborated (to Bourget) his conception of the fullness and resonance of the best Parnassian verse. Here too it is a question of concreteness : the epithets chosen should avoid generality ; they should be specific, they should fuse closely and harmoniously with the thought. Thus the poetic sensation will be prolonged.[18]

It is to be expected, then, that France's poems will treat mainly of Antiquity, of history at large, or of natural history, whether from the philosophic or the descriptive standpoint.

§ 4

As a matter of fact, the *Poèmes dorés,* including the *Idylles et Légendes,* fall readily into five main divisions. Of these, the group reflecting some variety of ancient inspiration would number seven or eight pieces. We have already spoken of the 'Ode to Light'—

ô Lumière,
Blanche mère des visions.

This well-knit and 'durable' classical Invocation maintains that light animates the beauty of women, of primordial Nature, and of the poet's handiwork. Another piece, 'Vénus, Etoile du Soir,' hails Venus as the twin-star of Earth, with a similar destiny, probably with similar forms of life ; and the poet imagines that the fertility of her women together with the aspirations of her savants may demonstrate that

Connaître pour aimer, telle est la loi de l'être.*

The verses called 'Théra,' depict that island-volcano in a semi-Lucretian fashion : she is represented as a powerful Bacchante adorning her flanks with vineyards. 'Le Captif' is quite in the manner of Gautier, describing dexterously a satyr and an Eros,

* To know in order to live, such is the law of being.

one confined in a marble sheath, the other erect on his 'Pentelican pedestal.' Here as in other titles, antique light and ancient myrtles still border the blue waves of the Mediterranean.

More of a philosophic trend is to be found in those poems, stretching over a decade in actual composition, which, like the verses on Thaïs, express the conflict between paganism and Christianity and exalt the dominion of the older gods. 'La Part de Madeleine,' we have seen, was recited with effect by the actress Agar. This poem demands particular attention, for it appears that Mary Magdalen was a *motif* in the author's thought. As early as 1868 he had written an article on her, which contrasts her disturbing 'Christian' type with the calmer beauty of Helen of Troy.[19] In 'La Part de Madeleine'—and not for the last time—France for his own purposes confused this Mary with Mary of Bethany and represented that the 'lot' of this composite heroine, namely the pursuit of love, was preferable to the domesticity of Martha.[20] Like a later heroine (Leuconoë), Mary has known the *amari aliquid* which is after-passion:

> L'enfant de Magdala, la fleur de Béthanie,
> Gémissait dans la pourpre et l'azur des coussins.*

She thinks of bathing and purifying herself in Lake Gennesaret. She ends by bathing the feet of Jesus—

> Et la terre connut la tendresse infinie.†

The poem called 'L'Adieu' (of 1866) also tells how a woman passes from profane to sacred love and how the Galilean carries off 'all our Magdalens.' The mystery of feminine penitence, the confusion of its impulses, often attracted France's somewhat bitter attention.[21] As in Swinburne's protest, there is a touch of almost personal rancour in the lover's indignation at his loss:

> Toute femme qui pleure est déjà ton épouse,‡

he says to Christ, and he resents the sublimation of passion into mysticism. This evidently anticipates the still more personal feeling animating 'La Prise de Voile,' even as 'La Part de Madeleine' burgeons into 'Leuconoé.'[22]

* The child of Magdala, the flower of Bethany,
Sighed amid the soft blue and scarlet of her cushions.
† And Earth then knew an infinite tenderness.
‡ Every wailing woman is ready to become your Spouse.

That notable poem, although not published until 1876, clearly belongs in this group. In 'Leuconoé,' too, the period is that 'époque de vertiges' when Christianity was seeping at the traditions of the ancient world. Here again it is a woman who represents the yearning of her sex for the new Gods from the Orient. It may be that Renan and Louis Ménard had first drawn France's attention to this phenomenon; he himself alleges a page of Michelet as a partial source for the development of this notion in the poem.[23] At any rate, it is clear that both the conception and the symbol of Leuconoë herself remained with him a long time. In *Sur la Pierre blanche* the Syrian courtesans are still associated with 'adolescent gods.' The lovely Roman became the incarnation of this semi-mystical longing, of this 'religiosité troublante.'[24]

The name 'Leukonoë' occurs in the *Odyssey* and also in the Odes of Horace, where she is recognized as the poet's mistress; considerably later, she occupies a page in the *Crime de Sylvestre Bonnard,* where we have seen her apostrophized as a 'fair rebel, who would know the secrets of the future.' In the present poem she is depicted as having followed in the paths of the Pompeian Venus. Now she is meditative and vaguely sad because—

> Le mal des jours nouveaux s'allume dans ses veines.
> Le monde a désappris ce sourire ingénu
> Que reflétaient si clair les antiques fontaines;
> Un âge de langueur et de fièvre est venu.*

She now seeks, among the fair strange gods, to which one she shall tender

> L'ardente et lourde fleur de son dernier amour.†

Of all the shining adolescent deities, it is the wounded body of Adonis that is favoured,

> Et Leuconoé goûte éperdument les charmes
> D'adorer un enfant et de pleurer un Dieu.‡

As in the *Noces corinthiennes,* Adonaï serves as a middle term

* The malady of our latter days is kindled in her veins.
The world has lost that frank young smile
Once clearly reflected by ancient fountains.
A languorous and fevered age has come upon Earth.

† The final, heavy, ardent flower of her love.

‡ And Leuconoë wildly tastes the delights
Of adoring a youth and of lamenting a god.

between Adonis and Christ. It is Christ, then, whom Leuconoë is vaguely seeking, and it is prophesied that other sin-weary and yearning women will bring on the reign of 'this mysterious king who weeps and who consoles.' The Notes to the poem carry on the theme by reprinting in part that interesting essay of Anatole's on 'Les Femmes d'Horace.'[25] He insists that they were all Eastern women, destined to 'troubler *le génie latin,*' by their morbid ennui and their 'sensual piety.' Such a one was this mistress whom Horace met during his retreat at Baiae and whom he reproached with her addiction to astrology. Her type will not long be satisfied with the deities 'hidden in the impure darkness of the Suburrus,' nor with the rigid gods of Egypt. These women will demand a gentler faith and a more human god, to whom they may submit themselves in a sort of voluptuous martyrdom. 'When Horace constructed his science of the Pleasures, he failed to point out the most essential one—the pleasure of tears.' Nor could Horace quite realize that these ailing women 'would shatter the great Roman edifice, change the world, and become the first Christians.'

In several respects, notably in its glorification of physical love, this poem anticipates *Les Noces corinthiennes;* but here the hostility to Christianity is more veiled, more insinuating. In form, 'Leuconoé,' from the first line* to the last, is Parnassian in *plastique* and colouring. The quatrain cited above is in Leconte de Lisle's manner. The heavy march of the stanzas and the parade of religious beliefs are equally characteristic of the Parnassian master. Anatole thought well enough of this poem to inscribe it to Jules Breton. It was admired by George Sand and by Taine. The latter even preferred it to *Les Noces corinthiennes,* for he held that France spoke better in his own person than when he tried to indulge in dramatic dialogue. Maurras warmly commends 'Leuconoé,' esteeming it 'one of the purest pages in all our verse.'[26] Others would extend A.F.'s poetic and philosophic competence, so evident here, to include the whole group of subjects in which he handles the early clashes between paganism and Christianity.[27]

Among similar poems, we find that 'La Prise de Voile' is a *débat* between body and soul. The latter seems triumphant in the

* First line:
La mer voluptueuse où chantaient les Sirènes.
Cf. Heredia's
La mer qui se lamente en pleurant les Sirènes.

lines describing how a well-born maiden takes the veil, as well as in the exhortation of the priest, who welcomes this sacrifice to the Most High. But the voice of Nature soon speaks, declaring to the neophyte that she has known other maidens consumed by the ardours of a less ambiguous desire.

C'est cette volupté, cette Vénus, c'est elle
Qui consume tes sens de toi-même ignorés,
Et dans l'enchantement des mystères sacrés
Revêt pour toi ton Dieu d'une beauté mortelle.*

Still the maiden may cling to her illusion if she can. Here we perceive the doctrine of Maya, dear to Leconte de Lisle : 'If you keep your faith, what matter that it be false ? The beauty of the lover dwells only in the heart of his mistress, and the whole universe is merely a vision.' Yet in the long run we who abide with the clay will have the better of you who seek to transcend it and are left with—nothing.

The personal accent found here has been attributed to an early disappointment that Anatole experienced.[28] For that matter, the same feeling may underlie certain portions of 'L'Adieu' and of 'Leuconoé.'

§ 5

One section of the *Poèmes dorés* is more heterogeneous. There is a considerable group which deals, broadly speaking, with tales and legends from the past, outside of classical antiquity. Some of these develop exotic or prehistoric themes of the kind favoured by the Romanticists as well as by the Parnassians. So the subject of 'La Fille de Caïn' recalls Vigny's 'Le Déluge' and transposes his 'Eloa' : the pure angel of God is tempted by the 'daughter of men' and falls. But in treatment this poem, like 'Homaï' with its voluptuous Persian atmosphere, is very close to Leconte de Lisle. 'Homaï' offers a variant of the Judith story, while other subjects are taken from the Middle Ages and the Renaissance. Certain medieval details in 'La Veuve' or in 'La Sagesse des Griffins' are carven in a fashion suggesting Heredia. In poems casting back to medieval faith and 'fixity' (e.g., 'La Danse des

* It is Voluptas, it is Venus, who, all unknown to you, inflames your senses ; and who by weaving the spell of holy mysteries clothes your God with a mortal beauty.

morts'), Anatole again assumes that air of deliberate naïveté, as when he asserts of the Wicked Workman—

Car il aime d'amour le démon Aspasie.*

Another section contains poems descriptive of trees and animals: saplings and oaks; the deer, the monkey, the partridge. Natural history was also the domain of Leconte de Lisle, who, however, usually celebrated, with more colour and allure, beasts of a larger calibre. In each author the animal is depicted without anthropocentrism and is made subject to jungle-law. In France, the voice of Darwin is clearly heard. Of the two deer, fighting for a doe, one is 'armed too feebly for the future struggle, and he perishes *selon de bonnes lois.*' His animal soul becomes dispersed in the forest; he gives back to earth and trees and flowers all that he had taken from them. This theme contains more than an intimation of France's later doctrine that Hunger and Love are the driving forces of all life. And the poem ends with another hymn to creative Voluptas:

L'Amour, l'Amour puissant, la Volupté féconde,
Voilà le dieu qui crée incessamment le monde,
Le père de la vie et des destins futurs!
C'est par l'Amour fatal, par ses luttes cruelles,
Que l'univers s'anime en des formes plus belles,
S'achève et se connaît en des esprits plus purs.† 29

So too the partridge dies, having accomplished its labour of love. The monkey, in his last moments, is seized by the nostalgia of the jungle; and the dragon-fly, who has been impaled by a collector, wins free and returns to his marsh to perish. Even the 'Abandoned Oak-Tree' is described in terms of inevitable and progressive decay. For a similar naturalistic treatment of life and death, one may compare Maupassant's contemporary poem on the 'Vénus rustique.'

Repeatedly and in varying terms the 'laws' of existence are stated—that 'la Volupté' exhales her sweet breath upon the trees as upon the rest of Nature; that she sends her sap, fruitful both

* 'Tis said he madly loves the witch Aspasia.

† Powerful Amor, fertile Voluptas—that is the god who constantly creates and renews the world, that is the origin of life and its future destinies. It is by fatal Amor and the cruel strife that he provokes that the universe unrolls its quickened forms, becomes more beautiful, more purely intellectual, and finally completes itself.

of joy and sorrow, into the sturdy limbs that battle against the winter's rages; that insects and parasites do well to abandon the crumbling oak; that death is the absolute end of all. Still Parnassian in his vocabulary, Anatole is definitely Darwinian in his outlook.

A final group of reflective poems reiterates the above messages. 'Le Désir,' a 'brief, sombre and splendid evocation,'[30] debates the problem of pleasure as opposed to idealism in love-affairs. The author begins by yielding a point to his adversary. To our surprise he seems to admit the 'vanity of all profane desire,' so perishable, so fragile are the luring charms of a mistress. Yet why do they give the illusion of eternal things? The answer is that such aspiration and idealism serve as camouflage to veil the purposes of Nature. In woman 'universal life bursts forth, and every man totters, drunk with beauty, round her form.' She passes—but Life goes on. And her 'perfume and light' are given her in order that she may bring forth life to go on. So in a Lucretian poem beginning, 'Les choses de l'amour ont de profonds secrets,' we are told that the 'primordial instinct disturbs the chaste bride in her rich adornments'—

> Et, savante en pudeur, attentive à nos lois,
> Elle garde le sang de l'Eve des grands bois.*

(Anatole was never disposed to make much difference between the Colonel's lady and Judy O'Grady). Again, a sonnet on 'La Mort' maintains that if love spurs us on, it is because Death is spurring after. This moral recurs in one of the Tales of Jacques Tournebroche, 'La Leçon bien apprise.' But the preoccupation with death and love in the present volume, the mingling of these two *motifs,* may be due to the influence of Gautier, who was similarly obsessed. 'Au Poète,' by the way, is a masterly tribute to Gautier and shows an understanding of his processes revealed likewise in not a few of Anatole's own quatrains.[31] This panegyric has a curious history, lately revealed by M. Jasinski.[32] Anatole wrote first, for a memorial volume to Gautier, some verses descriptive of the dead poet's sensuous appeal and his power to evoke past loveliness. But on reflection A.F. decided to substitute for these lines a eulogy ('Au Poète') containing more of his own reac-

* Though obedient to our code of modesty,
She inherits the blood of sylvan Eve.

tions and beliefs. Yet he retained two stanzas, which are still found in 'Au Poète,' while a third was saved to make the quatrain now called 'A Théophile Gautier, Sur sa nouvelle d'*Arria Marcella*.' Thus not everything was lost.

Finally, we may recall certain poems of sentiment, like 'La Dernière Image' and 'L'Auteur à un ami.' [33] These are rather in the manner of Sully Prudhomme, for France was not wholly wedded to the metallic Parnassian creed and considered its high priest too hieratic and absolute.[34] The author of 'La Dernière Image' is capable of supple shifts and of a tender grace ; he can use *suggestion* rather than direct descriptive processes.

§ 6

THE first and most apparent thing about the *Poèmes dorés* as a whole is that the collection lacks originality. Besides the general influences already mentioned, and to which we shall presently return, it would not be difficult to quote additional lines reminiscent of particular masters. Anatole seems to be exemplifying his own denial of the possibility of genuine literary creation. In part, it is much learning that has made him so versatile an echo. Otherwise expressed, the divine fire with him was a stifled flame, and imagination was, as Larroumet puts it, 'subordinated to erudition' : spontaneity yields to 'la poésie savante.' [35] There is little or no lyrical afflatus—for he is less of a bard than a technician and a lapidary. Hence the implications of the title itself. 'Les Poèmes dorés' is on a par with Gautier's 'Emaux et Camées,' or with Coppée's 'Le Reliquaire.' The suggestion is of something carven or graven and of something gilded as well. France borrowed from his brother-Parnassians 'their lines chiseled like precious stones, adorned with festoons and arabesques—*leurs vers dorés*.' [36] Again, about half the poems are simply deliberate exercises in the art of riming—calisthenics in *terza rima* or in descriptive effects or in quaint archaic diction. This goldsmith can gild the lily or the rose ; his later retouches still show his happy craftsmanship.[37]

All this being true, it is difficult to agree with those who consider his poetry as possessing a high individual value.[38] Such friendly critics are more friends than critics. Maurras would put several of Anatole's poems among the best ever written in France; and he even regrets that their author, supremely gifted for the distillation of high moments into verse, unfortunately abandoned poetry for prose!

Yet certain formal qualities will appear on analysis. Although the *Poèmes dorés* made little stir at the time of their appearance, they have been much debated since France became famous. Regarding their artistic value, many and diverse opinions have been expressed. For some connoisseurs,[39] there emanate from the collection golden vapours and voluptuous perfumes, redolent of a rarefied and modernized antiquity; or a caressing light, an 'exquisite delicacy' is shed over the descriptions; or the chiseling and the 'gilding' of the verses suggest a supreme Parnassian dexterity. For other evaluators, less amorous of complexities and miscellaneous mosaics, there nevertheless emerge such masterpieces as 'Leuconoé' and 'La Prise de Voile.' But one writer objects on principle to 'all the rest of these verses about Oriental vases, old bindings and prayer-books'—which is incidentally not a very accurate description of the content of the volume.[40] And even a lenient critic reminds us that though France's poems may 'sparkle like gems,' yet from gems there radiates no heat. But Lanson emphasizes the 'lumière heureuse,' the supple prosody, as well as the 'tranquil disenchantment' characteristic of the school.[41]

Still others find in this harmonious measured verse a traditional artistry, a combination of thought and rhythm that would seat France among the neo-classical masters.[42] Of these, Chénier is his most direct model.[43] Yet several of A.F.'s admirers acknowledge that the best thing about his poetry in general is that it fathered his mellifluous and 'marvellous' prose.[44] France himself admitted to Gsell that he was not a poet, since he thought first in prose; and he told Maurras, in 1890, that he had quite lost the sense of rhythm and had definitely abandoned the Muse.[45] By then, it is true, he had lost other things as well.

One may grant most of the qualities mentioned above as general features of the Francian art; one may appreciate the thoughtfulness, the contemporaneity of the conflicts that he presents;[46] one may add the grace and suavity of his tone, the technical virtuosity, the 'proud full sail' of the Parnassian prosody, even the keen analysis of certain soul-states; yet the fact remains that there is no 'one clear tone' to his harp and too many diverse strings. As

Giraud puts it,[47] the numerous chords in the Anatolian symphony are not resolved 'into the vibrant intensity of a deep individual accent.' He did not feel enough ; he had no deep convictions to express. The nearest thing to a message is the recurrent hymn in praise of Voluptas. But *Les Poèmes dorés* remain a very informing psychological document.

§ 7

JUST the contrary is true of *Les Noces corinthiennes* (1876)—it is greater poetry and, save in one direction, it reveals less of the author's inner life. The kernel of the drama derives from Goethe's *Bride of Corinth:* both versions go back to an apocryphal letter recorded by a late Grecian historian.[48] France's debt to Goethe has been fully studied and need not, in all its detail, be considered here.[49] Suffice it to say that the two moderns agree in adding to their Greek sources the conception of a warfare between Christian asceticism and a natural life according to the ancient ideal. But the Frenchman alters Goethe's gruesome device of having the lover 'woo a dead maiden'—his Daphne is still alive.

Anatole's play is laid near Corinth, in the time of the early Cæsars ; it is divided into three Parts, as follows :

Hippias, a young trader, comes to say farewell to his sweetheart Daphne, before going on a long voyage. They are betrothed ; but after his departure the girl's Christian mother (as in *Atala*) makes her take a vow renouncing the world.

After a time, Hippias returns as the guest of the house. Daphne, who has been long immured and who is wasting away, accidentally meets her former lover. This night-scene is the only important thing taken from the Greek source, and even this is treated differently. In the original, it was really the dead maiden who paid suit to the guest of her parents ; here it is a lover who woos the maiden ; and she is dead only in the sense that religion has made her cold to the appeals of love and life. But she finally melts and agrees to meet Hippias by an ancient tomb.

The scene there recalls the catastrophe in *Romeo and Juliet.* First, a sorceress brings poison to Daphne, who takes it before giving herself to Hippias. A bishop, Theognis, has learned of her plight and comes to release her from her vow. But it is too late.

Hippias declares that in death they will be reunited among the pagan gods. For the lovers are symbols and fated 'victims of divine strife' [50] — even as Goethe had understood them.

Evidently, we are again in the atmosphere of 'Leuconoé,' and again we anticipate the clash of creeds in *Thaïs*. 'I have dreamed,' Anatole says in his Preface, 'the dream of the ages of faith. I have given myself the illusion of living beliefs.' He goes on to repeat his hackneyed creed that only the dream matters, even though it lies, and that mankind will always live (and presumably lie) in and for the cherished illusion. He claims that in this play he has written of 'holy things with a sincere respect' ; and besides, artistic harmony required a 'pious' treatment in tone with the subject.

None the less, and in spite of the admission of a broad-minded bishop to the scene, there can be no doubt as to the direction in which Anatole's sympathies are turned.[51] They are now expressed more emphatically than anywhere heretofore. Let us be deceived neither by his professions of impartiality nor by the classical balance observed in the grouping of the characters. Hermas and Hippias, i.e., the father of the girl and her lover, are pagan, Daphne and her bigoted mother are Christian, the bishop is a moderator, but what then ? The force of love, the forces of life itself are found on the pagan side of the balance, and in spite of the tragic issue, the ultimate, the ideal Victory, again as in *Romeo and Juliet,* is on the side of these forces. If the Galilean has conquered, he triumphs mainly in the natures of morbid and fanatical women who have again confused the cult of Adonis with that of Christ, and who would don the veil because they are not capable of love's delights. Here Anatole first definitely develops what later became one of his guiding principles — that asceticism and abstinence are opposed to Nature herself. The healthy simple soul of Hermas, the hardly-won joys of the lovers, the vineyard scene with its Bacchic songs, the constant touches of local colour, and allusions to the power and beauty of the ancient gods, are all on one side. On the other are the severity and coldness of the mother, her conception of Christ as a 'gloomy god to whom suffering is congenial,' and the author's fresh insistence on the sickliness and sensuality of women who have merely transferred their affections from Adonis. The girl admits that her Christ is a 'deity of the dead,' and her frustrated lover inveighs against him as the hater of life and humanity.

Nevertheless, neither here nor in *Thaïs* does France appear as an absolute pagan. He might have said with Musset:

Je ne puis. Malgré moi, l'infini me tourmente.*

He is a pagan, says Rod,[52] 'haunted by the preoccupation with Christ,' belonging not to the age of Pericles, but to that of Julian the Apostate. This is in harmony with what has been developed concerning Anatole's Alexandrianism. At times he seems to have thought that *à la* Chateaubriand he held an even balance between Polytheism and Christianity.[53] Yet let us not suppose that this calm and amiable heathen—who actually gave a copy of *Les Noces* to a clerical friend, calling his attention to the portrait of the bishop Theognis—was for all that any less of a heretic. It was not quite just to call the work a 'cri de rage contre le Christianisme'; but it was fair enough to place it on the *Index,* where from 1922 all of France's works were listed.[54] If the remonstrances of Hippias and Hermas should hardly be styled 'blasphemies,' yet it is true that France adopts these reproaches as his own.[55] At this point in our discussion, there arises a two-fold general question that, at the cost of a digression, we should make some attempt to answer. Why did France become increasingly and more bitterly anti-Christian with the years; and yet why is he never able to leave Christianity alone?

In part this hostility may be ascribed to the naturally sceptical bent of his mind, reacting even in the youth of 'Pierre' against the orthodox teachings of his parents and the formal clericalism of Stanislas. When he reached manhood, his pleasure-seeking temperament led him into a long-enduring opposition to all forms of asceticism and abnegation.[56] On the intellectual side, the influences of Renan, Leconte de Lisle, and others induced him to consider all religions as at best striking but ephemeral manifestations of past modes of thought among particular races. Also, as already hinted, a private grudge may underlie the attitude found in *Les Noces* and in several other poems.[57] As Stuart Sherman puts it: 'Especially has he haunted the steps of the Brides of Christ, irresistibly drawn by the allurement of their celestial roses . . .'[58] France wanted their perfumes to linger on this planet.

* I cannot [wholly disbelieve]. In spite of myself the Infinite disturbs me.

But instead of making a clear break with the Church, its creed, its records, and its rites, Anatole throughout his life is much concerned with just these things.[59] Thus, in dealing with medieval faith and 'fixity,' he is not unsympathetic like Leconte de Lisle.[60] How can we explain the seeming paradox? It is difficult for those in Protestant countries to realize to what extent, even apart from matters of belief, the Church remains an integral force in Latin civilizations. The Rock of St. Peter is still a cultural monument; and such an exponent of culture as Anatole France found the Rock at every step in his route. As archæologist, historian, dialectician, and traditionalist at large, he could not fail to be 'enveloped' during all of his eighty years by the mightiest tradition on the face of the earth. And this in spite of frequent girdings, revolt, and irony. The last quality, so abundant from the nineties on, hardly appears in *Les Noces corinthiennes.*

So much for the thought of this closet-drama. In pure form, it has nearly everything to recommend it.[61] For example, symbolizing the twilight of the old gods, the play contains an interlude, a choral debate between Artemis and Aphrodite, which is a lovely Grecian thing:

Non, jamais plus la nuit divine,
Sous l'astre pâle au front changeant
Ne verra dans les fleurs d'épine
Etinceler mes pieds d'argent.*

As a whole, the drama is vigorously and beautifully written, thoroughly classical in its restraint and vocabulary. In an unpublished letter, George Sand declares, 'c'est beau et frais comme l'antique.'[62] Although its formal beauty remains unimpaired, it now seems less 'fresh,' since it reflects the Neo-Hellenism of its own era. Some contend that this type of Hellenism was sufficiently universal to live for ever; but one is rather inclined to agree with those who maintain that in this 'tragic eclogue' we have another pleasant blending of the ancient inspiration with the Parnassian technique.[63] Although *Les Noces* seems to be almost the only thoroughly Parnassian play, its values are on the whole more

* Nevermore the Night divine,
Beneath a moon of changing brow,
Shall watch 'mid fields of thorn or pine
My bright feet glitter then as now.

poetic than dramatic. Maurras goes so far as to say that the lyric strophes and the tirades where Anatole himself speaks for the personages are far more effective than the rest.[64] But noteworthy, too, are the passages where Hippias invokes Eros or where he describes Daphne bending over her flowers, 'more marvellous to see than even her image in my closed eyes'; and the sacred myrtles, which surround the temple of the new god, adorn her brow when she steals forth to the night-meeting with her lover. The scene is full of eloquence and passion.

On the whole Anatole is more his own master, more virile, in *Les Noces corinthiennes* than in the *Poèmes dorés*. The form remains pure and objective, the composition excellent.[65]

Since it is essentially 'closet-drama,' and not for the multitude, *Les Noces* has not been represented very often. It was played once by amateurs, in an adaptation by Francisque Sarcey, during January, 1884.[66] Although the representation was in a private salon and the way had been smoothed for a favourable reception, the action was interrupted by the protests of the orthodox.[67] It was probably on this occasion that a certain Louveau took the part of Hippias.[68] The play did not reach the legitimate stage until the present century, when two 'revivals' were given. The first was undertaken by M. Ginisty at the Odéon, January 30, 1902. Mlle. Piérat played Daphne. France and Mme. de Caillavet attended the rehearsals and made themselves agreeable. But according to the producer it was necessary to have two kinds of 'répétitions': one for real business and another in order that the players might listen to the charming conversation of Anatole.[69]

Another and more notable interpretation was given at the Comédie-Française, in a series beginning on February 9, 1918. A distinguished cast took the leading parts. On one occasion (probably about March 11), Anatole came up from Tours in order to attend the performance. Unfortunately, German bombs were falling not far away, and there were intermittent alarms throughout the evening. The author remained in his box, while the audience insisted that the play should go on. Although it impressed people as belonging to another era, *Les Noces* was courteously received by the Parisians.[70]

§ 8

SINCE after these two volumes France parted company from the Parnassians, we may consider a few additional points wherein he resembled the school, as well as some features that differentiate his talent from theirs.

As for resemblances, it has been stated that *Les Noces* in particular 'offers all the characteristics of Parnassian poetry: the antique setting, the qualities of restraint, purity, and a certain neo-classical tinge.'[71] Who are the contemporary dwellers on Parnassus most frequently mentioned in connexion with France's work? They seem to be Leconte de Lisle, Gautier, Coppée, Sully Prudhomme, Heredia, and Louis Ménard.[72] The last-named, it has recently been demonstrated by Professor Peyre, although standing a little aloof from the school, exercised among them something of a general pervasive influence; and his type of Hellenism has been thought quite close to the kind exemplified by Anatole.[73] This view seems more nearly correct than that of certain admiring critics who would set France apart, not only from Ménard but from the leaders of the Parnassian school.[74]

It is true that the vein of personal sentiment discernible in four or five of the *Poèmes dorés* is more akin to the *Vaines Tendresses* of Sully Prudhomme than to the impassive doctrines of the regular Parnassians.[75] Yet to the analogies with Heredia already indicated may be added the fact that both poets were skilled workers in mosaics of the past; and that France occasionally uses ancient epitaphs in a manner definitely recalling the scholarly author of *Les Trophées*.[76]

Before the chain was broken altogether, there were forged still other intellectual links connecting Anatole, by affinity or imitation, with that old Inveterate, Leconte de Lisle. Not only should we recall their similar methods in the resurrection of the past, their treatment of natural history, their attitudes toward the pagan world, but particular poems and turns of speech show that A.F. was an assiduous reader of the *Poèmes antiques* and the *Poèmes barbares*.[77] Some find this influence at its height in *Les Noces,* especially in its 'Invocation'; others point to those individual poems which in Barrès' beautiful figure, are 'found kneeling on the marble of races dead and gone.' For example, Leconte de Lisle celebrated Cain, while France glorified 'Cain's Daughter.'[78] 'Homaï' is derivative from the Master not only in its kind of exoticism but in the cruelty of the theme and its philosophic Nihilism:[79]

> Je sais que vivre est vain, et que la mort est bonne,
> Qu'elle a des charmes doux et de profonds secrets.*

Mongrédien concludes that France 'assimilated his Master's tastes and thoughts and feelings'; that much of the younger writer's virtuosity in versification was similarly inspired; and that enumerations of adjectives in descriptive passages are found only in Anatole's Parnassian days. One might add that the two poets had a common preference for such terms as 'glauque' and 'blafard,' an addiction to 'nénuphars' and 'le Néant,' a partiality for 'vibrant' light and 'sheaves' of radiance—though Anatole liked his light to be more tempered.

While under the spell, A.F. seemed more of a mimic than he really was. In fact, the two men were quite different in several important respects. Leconte de Lisle was the more 'tough-minded' of the two, the more implacable and forthright. He should have written 'Homaï'; but he could not have written 'La Dernière Image.' Occasionally, sentiment will break through the Parnassian enamel with which France provided himself. And then he writes with a delicacy and a 'fluidity' which belong to quite another manner.

There are, indeed, several respects in which Anatole wears his Parnassian mantle with a difference. For one thing, he is not devoted to description for description's sake. For another, he was too fond of life to contemplate 'le Néant' with gloomy rapture. It is beyond our scope and our powers to distinguish, as M. Desonay endeavours to do, between the several varieties of Hellenism that are illustrated by these 'new pagans.'[80] But it seems that within the French tradition itself France was better grounded than most of the group and at times used modern resources which the majority of them preferred to leave alone. He admired Baudelaire and echoes him occasionally.[81] In 'Le Vénusberg' and in 'Les Cerfs,' a Hugonian influence has been traced[82]—but Hugo was anathema to Leconte de Lisle. *Les Noces corinthiennes* owes part of its plot to *Atala*[83]—and Chateaubriand was not

* I know that Life is vain and Death is fair—
Full of sweet secrets she, and hidden charms.

usually liked by the Parnassians nor indeed by Anatole himself at a previous stage. In several poems, e.g., 'Les Arbres' and 'Le Désir,' as well as *Les Noces,* the old classical strain has been filtered through Chénier.[84] One critic goes so far as to say that Anatole's chief literary admirations, for Virgil, Racine and Chénier, were not shared by his brother-Parnassians.[85] At any rate, these tastes were not so fundamental with the others as they were with France. The extent to which he accepted the cultural landmarks of his own country, in poetry as in other matters, will partly appear in our next chapter.

CHAPTER X

Anatole and the Old Régime

§ 1

WHEN on Christmas Eve, 1896, Octave Gréard formally welcomed France into the Academy, he spoke of the newcomer's literary *liaison* with Cleopatra. He recalled how the schoolboy, in the dull refectory at Stanislas, heard the name of the Egyptian queen and how she appeared to him in all her splendour, across the pages of Plutarch and of Rollin :

> Then a delicious vision filled my eyes ; the blood pulsed in my temples with the great throbbing that announces the presence of glory or of beauty. I fell into a profound ecstasy. . .

Still another picture from antiquity, the reader may say. But Gréard derived from his reminiscence a broader lesson concerning Anatole's tastes. He would always see 'troops of beauties' arise from the grave pages of history ; and he would always love the twilight legends of the past, the crannies which the lamp of Clio has imperfectly illuminated.[1]

In fact, through all his long commerce with the Muse, Anatole regarded her less as a taskmistress than as an amusing companion. Like the Salamander in *La Rôtisserie,* she perched archly among the volumes in Father's shop. When M. de Barante spoke to the coterie, she was there, and she doubtless approved when Pierre pilfered volumes of Guizot and other learned votaries.[2] She brightened the dusty stalls along the Quais and informed dead monuments with a living breath. This sprightly Clio cheered France on the footpath way when he began writing historical reviews for Charavay's journals. She inspired little-known prefaces — charming structures that mingle art and imagination, towering over basic 'documents.' She remained stoutly by his side during the long years of 'La Vie littéraire' and *l'Univers illustré.* And though her charms were slightly soiled and crumpled by time, she staggered along with him through the dour days of *l'Ile des Pingouins.*

Historians have declared that A.F. had a profound 'sense of the past,' that he was a 'magician, extracting rare perfumes from its roses' ;[3] we have seen that his love for it has been often professed and evidenced. Let us consider a few of the less familiar passages that support this *credo*. In an article of 1882 he not only reiterated his belief that the present is rooted in the past but gave expression to his own reactions before the monuments of Alsace:[4]

> All ruins, trivial or important, induce in me a pious revery; all forms of the past have a soul which seeks my soul. In whatever fashion they have accomplished their *dream of life,* the dead always inspire in me a sentiment of *affectionate curiosity.*

Elsewhere he mentions the 'puissante douceur' with which he feels former ages coming to life again within his consciousness; and in the heyday of his career, he thus addressed a body of local antiquarians:[5]

> The past, gentlemen! Life would be a pretty short affair if we did not prolong it into the past and into the future. Those are the two essential leaves that lengthen and give dignity to the table of life.

It has been well said that for Anatole and others of his generation the world in space seemed less significant than the world in duration, the *longum illud tempus* of yore; and he loved that storied past more than the little present. Again (according to Edmund Wilson), this preoccupation permeates 'the bulk of his writing. . . Even his [fictional] studies of contemporary France he labels "Contemporary History."'[6]

But it is not always nor chiefly the dignified aspect of history that attracts Anatole. He prefers Clio in undress. His articles for *l'Univers illustré* frequently terminate with an anecdote from the Old Régime. The 'curiosity' which he constantly evinces may penetrate through all eras of history but attaches itself more particularly to those ages when Legend flourished, or her half-sister, Gossip.[7] His devotion to the Muse comprehends both her general allure and the smallest items of her négligée. Like Sainte-Beuve, he combines with the zeal of the 'researcher' the inquisitiveness of a Paul Pry. Not only does he go after quaint psychological twists in notable personages; he is busy storing and recording *ana, petits faits,* side-lights, and a myriad details of the kind that vivifies *Les Dieux ont soif*.

It is in part this view of the past that leads Anatole to affirm and reaffirm his conviction that history is an art rather than a science. His theory and his line of argument are very similar to those which Lytton Strachey later professed.[8] What, insists France, can we really *know* about the causes and sequences of past events ? Their very existence is often subject to dispute. 'There are few genuine truths in the histories, and the only facts on which we agree are those which we derive from a single source.'[9] Still, A.F. must have been aware that the singleness of a source constitutes no argument for its reliability. There may once have been a cloud of witnesses against its veracity. As a rule, in the tangled web of testimonies, we do not know where to turn. Consequently a certain intuition must come into play, a certain 'divination' must aid the competent historians to penetrate into the darker ages. Is it mere coincidence that France places highest on his roll such men as Michelet and Thierry, who have freely called on imagination in their reconstructions ?[10] If history, like philosophy and criticism, is only a 'kind of novel,' if it offers us only a 'succession of images,' what are we to conclude ? That 'la vieille histoire est un art' ; although inexact, it can be made beautiful ; it charms us through its power of portraiture and resuscitation ; it has its own domain and should not be too 'scientific.'[11]

Nor for him does history connect definitely with any ethic or philosophy. Its 'lessons' are particular rather than universal. It may be that while Taine held sway over Anatole's mind, the deterministic attitude is apparent ; but Voltairian Pyrrhonism is the more lasting influence, and this view challenges our insight into causes. With reference to the idea of Progress, that question hardly arises until France's fourth period, and even then his opinions vary too much to establish conviction. During most of his life he believed that human beings do not alter for the better down the ages ; they are always subject to the same passions and failings (cf. Roujon). Therefore he could declare in agreement with such masters as Gibbon and Voltaire : 'The life of a nation, like that of an individual, is a perpetual decline, a series of crumblings, an endless array of wretchedness and crimes.'[12] For all that, it can offer a thousand fascinating traits to the psychologist and the artist.

One thoughtful critic accepts the above points, in so far as subjectivity and relativity are concerned, and emphasizes one consequence of France's 'nihilistic' view. In his own writings he will definitely and maliciously subject historical events and personages to a certain lowering treatment. After all, they were not historical *at the time:* they were on an everyday level of life. So in 'Le Procurateur de Judée' as in *Les Dieux ont soif,* the author's endeavour is to restore that everyday level and sometimes to go below it. Thus he takes the stilts away from history and becomes one of the earliest 'debunkers.' [13]

§ 2

If it is something of an exaggeration to say that nothing historical was alien to Anatole's interest, yet the reminiscential volumes alone would offer ample proof of the breadth and variety of his information. And this was often of a kind that specialists in a given field could respect. M. Hovelaque bears witness: [14]

> He spoke with an equal abundance and originality of the ancients and the moderns, of Jeanne d'Arc and of Napoleon, of the greatest as of the smallest historical personages, of all the periods in France, from Gregory of Tours to the Third Republic. . . The remarkable extent and penetration of his knowledge, the great ease with which he moved among ideas and centuries, gave substance to his ironical disquisitions and added a philosophic background to all that he wrote.

The last point, indeed, is what gives a 'Francian' flavour to many of his glimpses into the past.

But there are evident limitations to his scope. I cannot find that he was very solicitous about anything outside of 'la vieille Europe,' nor that he often went east of the Rhine, nor that he bothered with the British Empire. He thought of America as exemplifying a very mechanistic civilization together with much simplicity of mind. For him the three high points on the chart of all the ages were Greece, Italy, and France. His two favourite periods were epochs of strife, of subtlety—and of masterpieces: [15] the decline of the Roman Empire, the flowering and the decadence of the Old Régime. And usually, of course, his own country came first in his interest. He once pointed out that in spite of the Revolution there is no definite break in her history, and that 'the new France has issued from the old'; he thought that this lesson of continuity could be enforced particularly well in such a storied place as Fontainebleau.[16] It has already been illustrated how local piety sustained his sense of tradition. Perhaps these considerations helped launch him on an enterprise about which little has been said by biographers. In his thirties Anatole conceived and wrote for Lemerre a two-volume *Histoire de France* from the beginnings down to the Revolution. For reasons that will concern us later, this work has remained unpublished. But the fact that he did complete the task (though with his usual dilatoriness) further convinces us of his knowledge and his love of the subject.

With reference to medieval France, it is clear that Anatole was no Pierre Champion, nor yet was he a Gaston Paris. His article on the latter in *La Vie littéraire* is a sufficient demonstration. On the other hand, his interest in the Middle Ages, as an amateur and as a picker-up of not quite 'unconsidered trifles,' is apparent in some of the early *Notices;* it connects with his taste for saints' lives and soon clusters round the figure of Joan of Arc. A number of his articles about her date from the eighties. Some think that his penchant for the whole period was of a ferret-like and 'gossiping' quality; others that in his desire to stress the principle of continuity he dwelt willingly upon the achievements of feudalism; certain others that as he became more anti-Christian he loses his benignity toward the saints and emphasizes rather the darkness and intolerance of the medieval outlook.[17] This would be the impression derived from such a late work as *l'Ile des Pingouins*. But in his earlier stages his opinion about this prevailing darkness is less assured—it appears to vary inversely with his opinion of Leconte de Lisle.

Mlle. Antoniu has shown how, in his Parnassian phase, the pupil echoed some of the master's anti-medieval diatribes.[18] We recall that this was also the time of Anatole's *republican* phase (*c.* 1867-1870), a state of mind which would incline him away from intolerant despotisms, whether temporal or spiritual. Certain passages in the *Amateur d'autographes* and the *Bibliophile français* are almost as violent in tone as 'Les Légions de Varus,' and for similar reasons. At twenty-five, our neophyte disliked the brutality of the feudal wars, the ignorance and coarseness of the warriors, the phobias that they aroused. He hated the fanaticism of the Church, the ugly 'Byzantine' art that it inspired, the warping of human nature that it caused. He has not yet elaborated his appreciation of orthodox naïveté—he thinks it merely stupid and cowed by fear. He is hostile to nearly all the 'terrible and hideous manifestations of the old Catholic spirit.'[19] Medieval literature, e.g. the *Chanson de Roland,* seems to him monotonous and barbarous; but we find that even then he made some exceptions to this judgment. For example, the romances of chivalry, in so far as they were *courtois* and idealized, conformed more nearly to the young man's rather intransigent standards. When he joined *Le Temps,* he worked himself into a more broadly tolerant frame of mind. Yet it is probably true that A.F. could never be styled 'a fervent adorer of the Middle Ages.'

There exists a monograph on *Le Moyen-Age dans l'œuvre d'Anatole France.*[20] The work scarcely does justice to the extent and variety of Anatole's medieval readings, nor does it sufficiently stress the changing nature of his views at different periods. Also it overplays his not very profound sympathies with the epoch. It does, however, make the following points, most of which seem to be justifiable, if we rise to a bird's-eye view of his whole career. — While he never ceased to deprecate cruelty and war, persecution and the Inquisition, he gradually saw that these were not the most abiding elements in the social picture and he reproached the leader of the Parnassians for assuming too grim an attitude toward the 'Siècles Maudits.' While recognizing that his own interest was founded on the romantico-historical approach (Chateaubriand, Thierry, Michelet, Hugo), France's prevailing treatment is not quite romanticized in the usual picturesque fashion — a fashion which he ultimately derided. In one way or another, the element of *religion,* receding to be sure into a sort of mild crepuscular glow, comes to be central in his rendering of medieval thought and manners. This element is a main ingredient in such volumes as the *Contes de Jacques Tournebroche* and the *Vie de Jeanne d'Arc;* but it is diffused through several others. The fact is that when France came to sense the artistic possibilities of a faith-*cum*-legend atmosphere, he suspended direct hostilities against the Church. Candid credulity, Gothic monuments, dozens of Saints' lives, miracles of the Virgin, the *Imitatio Christi,* Gregory of Tours and St. Francis, Joan of Arc and the fifteenth century as the culmination of the whole era — all these themes or *motifs* appeared to serve their turn. Occasionally he indulged himself in a literary *Imitatio* which is as nearly perfect as such a thing can be.[21] At times he may have envied the followers of a faith which he could not possess. Anatole undertook Joan probably because Renan had shown him the way. But he worked up a genuine interest not only in her patriotic and unifying role but also because his task evolved into a typical study of the environment of belief; and France was never averse to observing sympathetically the folkways of the humble and the simple-minded. As a relaxation, he could consort with the more learned figures of the period and follow the streams of pagan culture that were still filtering down a rather alien soil. If the two cultures happened to collide or merge, all the better for their nonchalant interpreter. . . Although he occasionally turns his gaze toward the more varied aspects of medieval life and institutions, literature and feudalism, yet through its very remoteness his vision becomes in part poetized, abstract, a compact and simplified picture.[22]

Glimpses of these facets of the epoch appear as early as the second phase in A.F.'s education. Such are half a dozen descriptions of medieval monuments, a number of saints' lives (especially in the travels of Pierre Nozière), and such a poem as the 'Danse des Morts' or 'Le Mauvais Ouvrier.' Deliberately mingling the legendary with the actual, the historical attitude with the artistic, he is beginning to create a *moyen-âge* which he presently learns to address in a special tone—something like a parent condescending to a child who is not overly bright. True that he once made a habit of collecting things medieval. But the fact that the child temporarily lent A.F. his toys did not constitute a very vital bond between the two.

§ 3

Anatole does not fail to celebrate the 'dawn' that came with the Renaissance nor, on several occasions, to contrast it with the shadows of the preceding age. It was an 'adorably hesitant moment' of transition, a sort of April of the mind, when the fair land of France began to smile again.[23] But these are only isolated passages. His chief tribute to this period, the *Vie de Rabelais,* lies beyond our limitations. The work offers an interesting picture of sixteenth-century France and we know that the author had dwelt with the subject many years. He was one of the first to join the *Société des Etudes Rabelaisiennes,* and for a time he presided over their banquets. He won the suffrages of competent scholars like Abel Lefranc and Pierre Villey.[24] The latter considers him essentially a Renaissance figure. So we are not surprised at France's personal admiration for such typical Renaissance figures as

Bernard Palissy and Henry of Navarre, the 'lusty gallant.'[25] Yet he thought there was too sharp an opposition between the aristocrats and the people. His opinions regarding individual authors of the era will emerge later in our discussion. But relatively speaking one does not find very much about the sixteenth century in A.F.'s writings before 1890.[26]

The fact is that Anatole had already cast in his lot primarily with the Age of Louis XIV and his successors. To the tumultuous conquests of the Renaissance he preferred the ordered brilliance of a civilization that had reached its peak. As the companion of a life-time, Racine proved more congenial than Rabelais. There were several general reasons why our hero should appreciate the Old Régime above all other periods in French history. It is nearer to us than the Renaissance and therefore more comprehensible. It was marked by an increasing refinement and charm in manners—French politeness attained its acme in the dungeons of the Conciergerie.[27] It was honoured by notable writers, several of whom, it will appear, became Anatole's chosen intimates and counsellors. Its roster of fascinating and (one might almost say) 'reappearing' characters included people whom our author loved and gladly revisited. If he did not quite follow Victor Cousin's example and conceive violent passions for *grandes dames* of the Old Régime, at least he frequented the society of Mme. de la Sablière and Mme. de La Fayette, of the Baron Vivant-Denon and the Duc de Penthièvre, whom he finally converted into a figure in *l'Anneau d'améthyste*.[28] Above all, France was aware of certain stabilizing virtues of the period, virtues which he adapted to his own creed as a writer and never forswore. Such were the classical traits of measure and moderation, the graces of insight and of learning lightly borne, sensibility tempered by reserve,—in short, the ideal of the well-rounded *honnête homme*. Yet Anatole was well aware of the turbulent emotions that seethed under the surface in the age of the Grand Monarque ; he knew that cruelty and horror sometimes found their way out, as in the Affair of the Poisons ; he would even attack, occasionally, the abuses and oppression that stained the whole era.[29] He made much of these during his 'republican' phase, when he found Louis XIV an 'odious' person.[30] But nevertheless he presently looked backward with an affectionate regard. Some differences are discernible in his attitudes toward the seventeenth and the eighteenth centuries.

He honoured the former, as a son; he adored the latter, like a sister.

On the whole, it seems that Anatole's conception of the seventeenth century was founded rather on a literary than a strictly historical basis. We shall discuss his early opinions of French classical writers in connexion with *Le Génie latin.* Just here it may be remarked that he apparently approved a *mot* of Jules Lemaître to the effect that nobody had written in good French since the seventeenth century. Roujon points out that this age was the only one that he *respected*—even in the devastating satire of *l'Ile des Pingouins.*[31] This appears to be true, with the parenthetical exception of such 'revolutionary' remarks as those found in the *Amateur d'autographes,* where the period is condemned as 'féroce et malpropre.'[32]

§ 4

ALTHOUGH the furnishings in both of Anatole's final homes testify that his collecting mania invaded the Middle Ages, yet he spoke as if he were forced into this habit by Mme. de Caillavet, who claimed the eighteenth century as her domain. Thus they established a 'concordat archéologique,' as Brousson styled it; and the terms of the agreement are elsewhere developed by the secretary:[33]

> I don't much care [said A.F.] for all those quaint objects with which I am surrounded. My taste, you know, would incline me rather toward the eighteenth century and the Consulate. But Madame has reserved those two periods. For the sake of peace, I have fallen back on the Middle Ages. . . To me are allotted, on our shopping expeditions, the saints, the virgins, medieval reliquaries. . . I don't wish any harm to Madame, but I am beginning to be fed up with that ecclesiastical bric-à-brac.

The language of this plaint is probably a little arranged, as usual; but its general tenor is supported elsewhere, and it is a fact that after the death of his mistress, France sought consolation among the *bibelots* of his favourite modern epoch.[34]

There can be no doubt that the eighteenth was the century in which A.F. delighted most. *La Rôtisserie de la Reine Pédauque* and a dozen other tales would amply prove the point. Indeed, he spent much of his third and fourth phases under the shadow of Voltaire. Besides, there are the confidences recorded in the reminiscential volumes. For example, he told Ségur that whenever he wanted repose, he withdrew to 'le dix-huitième' as to a country seat. There he found ease with dignity, without haste, without noise, without vulgarity. Everything was better ordered then : there was a 'beautiful equilibrium.' The art of conversation was cherished, and as always good talking was the ante-chamber to good writing.[35] As early as 1869, France observed (in the vein of Heine) that after Christianity had overplayed the other world, 'the eighteenth century in its fair impiety brought life back to its legitimate abode on this planet.'[36] That insistence on life for its own sake is a recurrent moral in his work. Again, we are not surprised to hear him declare that he and the companions of his twenties thought that a new era of 'universal rationalism' dated from the age of the great sceptics. 'And I still think so,' he asserted in 1890.[37]

General recognition has been accorded to the predominant role of this period, side by side with antiquity, in the education of Anatole. The majority of his youthful aggressive articles have 'le dix-huitième' in the background or the foreground. For him this was always truly the 'grand siècle.' Or it is said that, after the order of Voltaire and Diderot, he was 'a man of the best eighteenth-century type,' whether in virtues or defects. Or we find him 'constantly praising' the period in all its works. Or it is held that he loved it alike for its 'ancient culture and its paganism' — since A.F.'s own infidelity evolved in good part from his early readings among the sceptical *philosophes*. Or it was Lemaître who once remarked that Brunetière, in his controversy with France, forced him to 'bring into action all the eighteenth century that he had in his blood.'[38]

The fact is there are two sets of reasons why a person of France's Protean outlook should be drawn *par excellence* to the period. The first set would cluster around the charm exercised by its abundant if waning culture. How much still survives in its fading records to stimulate or soothe the avowed Epicurean ! How gladly does he draw portraits of its frail delicious heroines — 'Mme. de Parabère, Mlle. Aïssé, . . . la du Barry !'[39] In that age gaiety and gallantry, *la volupté* and the arts of pleasing were still paramount, as Anatole ever wished them to be. Like the Goncourt brothers, he saw and proclaimed that 'woman, beauty made incarnate, was the ideal of the eighteenth century. All its artistic efforts pursue this ideal.'[40] His own efforts often pursue the pursuers.

Yet he could vibrate from this nostalgia for an over-ripe civilization to an appreciation of its more forward-looking element. He could commend, as we may sufficiently see, the liberalism of Voltaire and the Encyclopedists; but he did not therefore associate them always or necessarily with the overthrow of the Old Régime, a *débâcle* which he never quite condoned. Stewart tells us that A.F. liked in his final years to point out how, if it were a question of tolerance, the *philosophes* under the Bourbons were granted more of it than they had a right to expect. And such characters as M. Dubois or Brotteaux des Ilettes (in *Les Dieux ont soif*) showed that forceful and stoical types could emerge from the midst of pleasures encouraged by royalty itself.[41]

But even while contributing to the *Amateur d'autographes,* France was aware that the cult of liberty was a 'constant preoccupation' with eighteenth-century thinkers; that Voltaire, the most integral representative of the age, added to this cult the virtue of humanitarianism; and that such influences were visible in the first and the more ideal stages of the Revolution.[42] (A curious though symptomatic feature of these early articles is that Anatole is already showing his interest in the occult and finding it frequently under the surface rationalism of the Old Régime.) He knew, then, that the general development of the spirit of inquiry and criticism must perforce extend from Church to State. 'New social conceptions were born: tolerance, love of justice, respect for the trades, and especially the view that the value of each man depends on the services that he renders to others. . .'[43] Such ideals were destined to carry far.

For all that, and increasingly as his knowledge deepened, Anatole looked upon the actual manifestations of the Revolution with scepticism and distaste. There were several phases in his attitude. In his youth the subject offered a strong intellectual appeal; it became a mental predilection, sharpened by curiosity and his usual liking for anecdotage. We have seen how his knowledge was in part hereditary, acquired through the medium of Noël France's book-shop and publications, no less than by their joint labours on the La Bédoyère Catalogue.[44] The whole period, in fact, overflowed the Quarter and 'came home to him through the frequenters of his father's shop.'[45] During 'Pierre's' acquaintance with collectors, with historians of the epoch, with eye-witnesses who had seen the Gironde and the Terror, he absorbed the background for the vivid incidents portrayed in the *Livre de mon ami* and *l'Etui de nacre*. In the *Notices* written for Charavay's journals and others of an esoteric type, it appears that this interest was sustained and was occasionally benevolent. Incidents connected with the Revolution prelude the plot both in *Jocaste* and in *Le Crime de Sylvestre Bonnard*. We shall find that Anatole's interest was whetted by the 'Exposition de la Révolution Française,' which occurred in 1889. Thus the foundations are laid for a preoccupation that increases throughout his heyday and finds its climax in *Les Dieux ont soif*. Gradually he made good his claim of having an extensive knowledge of the whole turbulent era.[46]

But did he really accept and believe in the Revolution ? Only for a few years, during the above-mentioned 'republican' phase. This was the time when he was reacting against Father's Royalism and Napoleon III's Imperialism ; the time when he penned his two poems of revolt ; the time when he projected with Ricard the 'Prospectus' that upheld the Revolutionary spirit.[47] This favourable attitude was dissolved by the Commune, as *Jean Servien* will show. Numerous writings henceforward will testify that the early glow could not be recaptured. Several major works will later speak for themselves ; we may cull, here and there, isolated passages. For example, we learn from Giraud that Paul Verlaine, in his own person, had witnessed A.F.'s stage of Revolutionary fervour ; but when Verlaine appears as Choulette in *Le Lys rouge,* he fulminates against the imbecilities and false 'égalité' of the era. Can we doubt that Choulette is speaking for the author ?[48] Similar criticisms of the Revolution are found in *l'Univers illustré* and in the *Opinions de Jérôme Coignard*. Again, in 1903, Anatole told a friend that 'life was much happier before the Revolution. The historians have magnified an event which was in itself both useless and harmful.' He insisted that it opened the age of great national conflicts and made it impossible for a Frenchman to remain the 'good European' that he could still be in the eighteenth century.[49] To another intimate, he spoke in scorn of the masquerading and fol-de-rol aspects of the Revolution.[50] He had no use for its fanatical and bloodstained leaders.

In short, if he was willing to admit the existence of generous illusions in the Constituent Assembly, he held persistently that the subsequent divisions and bloodshed spoiled everything.[51]

§ 5

It remains to be shown how, in the matter of literary preferences and tastes, Anatole set the productions of the Old Régime above all others written by Frenchmen. He tells us in *Le Petit Pierre* that quite early he 'began to love the well-adorned reasonings and the beautiful symmetry of classical art,' [52] as practised in the seventeenth century. Gradually he formed a *beau idéal* compounded of ancient and of French classicism. He was once asked to account for the fact that all his characters spoke a uniform language. He answered, 'c'est la tradition classique,' and asserted that he was willing to bear a criticism equally applicable to Racine and Corneille.[53] It is not surprising that he came to have a great admiration for certain French masters of the Golden Age and of the subsequent period ; while few writers of the nineteenth century have expressed so wholesale a condemnation for the literary tendencies of that era.

Even in the days of his apprenticeship, after some adolescent flirtations with Romanticism, we find A.F. making a thorough acquaintance with French classical culture. The 'passion of the past' included in Anatole's case a reverence for 'our fathers and their beautiful thoughts.' The chief source for his attitude in the seventies and early eighties is the volume of essays now called *Le Génie latin.** In spite of the author's warning that the contents have but little direct connexion with antiquity,[54] the very title of the work indicates the welding of two traditions.

France's 'Avertissement' deprecated the rather jejune and inexperienced quality of *Le Génie latin*. In fact, those who are accustomed to the subtleties and savours of the later Anatole, who come to this volume after reading the very different essays in *La Vie littéraire,* are likely to be disappointed. These fifteen articles were written in nearly all cases as prefaces to Lemerre's editions of standard authors ; and save in scattered passages they do not usually rise above the level of respectable hack-work.[55]

* Published 1913, but containing critiques dating from 1874ff. For particulars, see Bibliography and *O.C.*, XXI, 367-85.

They are in essence old-fashioned biographical *Notices,* nine-tenths narrative, with a small amount of literary criticism toward the end of each article. As a rule the style is curt, matter-of-fact, not individual. It has little colouring or humour or flexibility of contour. In several of the essays there is a noticeable lack of flow or undertones. Irony, too, is lacking, save as it plays a little around the innocent head of Bernardin de Saint-Pierre. Yet as unadorned biographies, the sketches have a good deal of narrative interest; they frequently offer affiliations with France's journal-articles;[56] they show, as we might expect, much antiquarian and historical knowledge; and such a study as that on 'Paul Scarron' not only provides an excellent social background but sets the character well upon his feet. France liked such labours and took unusual pains with them. In this connexion he told Lemerre one day:

'Your publications do honour to my prefaces, and my prefaces do honour to your books.'[57]

Opinions vary as to the amount of personal revelation to be found in the *Génie latin*. I find less of this than some other critics do.[58] One may grant that there are occasional glimpses of the satyr that was in Anatole. But when it comes to dwelling on his general observations and *maximes* as a personal contribution, I believe that this is rather part of the classical heritage, from Corneille to Voltaire. Perhaps, too, A.F.'s constant concern with what is 'vrai' and what is 'beau' is as classical as anything else in his procedure. Generally, as stated in the preface: 'Things are treated without any erudite fuss (*sans apparat*), in the good old fashion, and this defect is doubtless the single merit of these essays.'

We may follow the text of 1913, since save in two cases the original prefaces and articles were but slightly retouched for this edition.[59] Let us consider the essays chronologically, according to their content. The brief notice on 'Daphnis et Chloé' has been sufficiently dealt with, and several others will yield for our purposes only incidental material. Thus, in the Renaissance period, the notice on 'La Reine de Navarre' (1879) interests us only through its learned allusiveness, and a gallant compliment or two to Marguerite, whom Anatole had also admired elsewhere.[60] 'Paul Scarron' (1880) expresses some characteristic Epicureanism; the little hunchback is approved for seeking 'all the treasures that he could enjoy.' Any follower of France will hear the well-known ring in this passage.

To make other people's lives pleasant, it is not necessary to be hard on one's self ; have a care of these ascetics (*bourreaux de soi*) ; they will mistreat you too, unintentionally.

One would expect a disciple of the Mantuan to dislike Scarron for his burlesque on Virgil. Not at all. Anatole considers it 'very funny' and notes that it was secretly relished by Racine and by Boileau.

In the seventeenth century, it seems significant that none of the great prose masters, whether *moralistes* or churchmen, ever deeply affected Anatole. His admiration goes rather to the semi-pagans of the period. In this volume, Molière, La Fontaine, and Racine are studied individually and all are well placed in the setting of their times. But the late article on Molière (1906), while bearing witness to Anatole's continued esteem for the 'good-hearted and great-minded' dramatist, is purely biographical and is already out of date. More to the point are passages in France's earlier writings. In the *Amateur d'autographes,* he had classed Molière for his robust gaiety with Rabelais and Régnier ; and he could not understand how the Romanticists 'found sobs and tears in the frank laughter of Molière.' Later, he reprehends the Naturalists likewise for viewing Molière as a 'sad thinker, dealing with melancholy subjects.'[61]

We are impressed by the article called 'Remarques sur la langue de La Fontaine' (1883).[62] This is valuable as showing how Anatole was already interested in questions of style. Like other French children, he must have been acquainted with the *Fables* almost from his cradle. He commends the old masters, who, like La Fontaine, draw their vocabulary 'from the popular source, but dispose with genius of the rich common stock.' When the fabulist finds a good old expressive word, he picks it up and is likely to use it soon afterwards. Such gleanings are often met with among the people ; Malherbe was then right in referring to the haymarket as a standard of good use. Furthermore, Anatole does not wish that the imaginative writer should employ vague and general terms. On this point he differs from the usual practice of the French classicists and recommends rather the specific term (*mot propre*). La Fontaine, in this respect, is better than Buffon, who was too 'noble.' The critic quotes Racine approvingly for restoring to words their antique splendour and significance. On the other hand, he does not believe that the great writers used neologisms; they were satisfied with manipulating the 'common stock.' In conclusion, Anatole seems to echo Du Bellay by saying that he has written these remarks in order to increase Frenchmen's love for their native tongue. 'It has often changed, but the alteration has been from one kind of beauty to another.' It has come down to us enriched by the experience and thoughts of many generations and is therefore a 'patriotic heritage,' to be cherished by all. Critics have plausibly argued that Anatole in his youth was equally attracted by the pure, if rich, style of La Fontaine and by his light way of taking life.[63] Both authors were more addicted to chastity in language than in behaviour.

The sturdy Boileau also receives, in diverse connexions, his meed of praise.[64]

§ 6

But all of these admirations dwindle when compared with Anatole's life-long devotion to Racine. Here is another major theme to whose repetitions and variations we may hearken during the whole of France's career. As in the case of Virgil, let us follow the involutions of the long-drawn music, remembering that the two classical writers are often thought of as sharing a 'moral affinity.'[65] Indeed, A.F. himself declared that the noble harmony of Racine's verse was only equaled by that of Virgil's art, and that the former's 'magnificent and true creations represent one of the rarest moments in the human mind.'[66] In both poets Anatole prized especially the artistic and the sentimental values. 'I have heard him,' recalls one critic, 'quoting *tenderly* the corrections of Racine'; and the same writer asserts that 'what made the author of *Andromaque* so dear to him was his taste for the psychology of sentiment.' To another friend France confided that there were three mental journeys that he often undertook; and that he went to the country of Racine whenever he needed to hear such perfect music as is found in *Phèdre*.[67]

These interests, these delights give to the article on 'Jean Racine' (1873, 1874)[68] in the *Génie latin* a different flavour and a more personal appeal than those previously considered. It is singular that in the 'Avertissement' to the volume Anatole should speak of this article as 'the oldest and the weakest of these little works,' for in no other do we find such an intimate and sympathetic tone. He begins by treating the effect of Jansenistic seclusion upon Racine's upbringing: 'These solitaires had an additional beauty in their lives: they were unfortunate.' Such was the result of the persecutions directed against them. It is rare that Anatole, with his Epicurean twist, can find any beauty in suffering and asceticism. Yet here he has a particular point to make, a particular soul-state to depict, that of Racine in the woods of Port-Royal . . . to say nothing of Little Pierre dreaming on the tower of Notre-Dame or of Jean Servien affected by the *mal de René*. No one without a similar experience could write thus of those sensitive souls who contract in the cloister 'a strange disease which is not without its delights: the malady of chasing chimeras, the dangerous gift of mixing in with the brew of life reveries, phantoms, and beautiful images, and of becoming absorbed in their blessed nothingness.' This indicates that Anatole himself had learned the dangers of day-dreaming, to which formerly he had been unreservedly addicted. Follows the passage, already quoted, about how Virgil showed Racine the forbidden charms of Dido and taught the young mystic 'une volupté de plus; la volupté de se perdre.'[69]

This much by way of 'pious' education; then came for Racine the *éducation sentimentale*. The high tone of the women whose society he frequented developed the best of his genius, to wit, 'cette souplesse harmonieuse, cette sensibilité fine'—qualities transferable to Anatole. The latter shares also in the semi-reproach which he addresses to the dramatist: 'the gift of reacting quickly to all sorts of impressions leads to inconstancy and a kind of perfidy.' One may say at least that France often seems prone to a semi-perfidious juggling with contrary opinions. Perhaps the reason and the defence too may be found in this further statement about Racine:

> Men of a wide intelligence become involved in infinite complexities, they hesitate, they lose the way and find it again: *they have learned how to doubt.*[70]

Such men are well guided if they find a simple strong nature in whom they can confide, as Racine did in Boileau. Anatole's fictional counterpart, Jean Servien, formed a similar relationship with the robust Garneret.

So the essay proceeds, with frequent suggestions of the writer's own views and feelings. He refuses to consider Racine's affair with La Champmeslé as a great passion ; the actress loved too widely to love well. Nor is it certain that the inconstancy was all on one side. With regard to Racine's later 'detachment' from his mistress, the critic significantly generalizes to the effect that what we love in others is less themselves than the bonds that link them to our own personalities. When these links are altered, our sentiments alter to correspond. There speaks the Epicurean in emotions and æsthetic reactions.

The career of Racine is traced in its greatness, its loves, its disillusionments, its final resignation to the will of God. Anatole does not take very seriously the cabal formed against the dramatist. We are rather to believe that Racine withdrew because he was weary of the struggle :

> He felt that bitterness, that great nausea, that disgust of things which comes to the best of us, to those who work with the most ardour. The men who have written works by no means vain or empty yet recognize best the vanity of everything. Desolation and sadness overtake them and cause them to pay dearly for the pride of intellect.

How often afterwards does he tell us that thought is an abnormality in the race, a dangerous disease !

Finally, Racine, being born in the Golden Age of the Bourbons, having attached himself early to the tradition of the ancients, 'toute de raison et de beauté,' having known later the springs of terror and pity, the surges and recessionals of passion, was in every way qualified to be what he became, 'the most perfect of French tragic poets, and the greatest through the continuity of his greatness.' In the 'Avertissement' (1913) to the volume, Anatole finds that he has praised Racine insufficiently ; abjuring all former 'severities' and reserves, which he maliciously attributes to the influence of the Romanticists, he now declares that he will no longer refrain from 'adoring in his every line the most perfect of poets.' This article, then, is only one evidence of a cult which increased in fervour until France's death. Even in the years before *La Vie littéraire* there are a number of references to Racine. We learn how as a child 'Pierre' imagined that Esther and Athalie were two real people—a shepherdess and a little girl whom she cared for.[71] His real acquaintance with these and other Racinian characters must have come in the days of his adolescence when he frequented the theatre and heard the stately Alexandrines moulded by the lips of Elise Devoyod and others. We have seen how France was credited with restoring Racine to favour among the Parnassians. In the Vigny volume a comparison is instituted between Monime in *Mithridate* and Kitty Bell in Vigny's *Chatterton*: 'I do not know which of the two has a more exquisite purity or a more delightful modesty.' In *Abeille* there are allusions to *Andromaque,* whose author is admired as 'le plus délicieux des poètes.' [72]

In his third period Anatole drew much of his nourishment from Racine. Reserving the material found in his critical essays, we may note some characteristic traits ascribed to his old age. It is said that the rift between Jules Lemaître and France (they had been separated by the Dreyfus affair) was healed because of our hero's admiration for Lemaître's volume on *Jean Racine* (1908); not long after this France declared to Sándor Kéméri that Racine was a capital example of how a genuine artist could wed learning with poetry.[73] Private letters of the same period show him comparing the French dramatist with Euripides, to the detriment of neither; if the latter has the greater naturalness and freedom, the former holds his own in the treatment of passion and in nearly perfect expression.[74] ('Nearly perfect,' because Anatole would not use the word in an absolute sense and maintains elsewhere that even his idol is 'perfect' only when compared with such an inferior rival as Pradon.) [75] For all that, this Racinolatry became an increasing devotion; and it is most manifest in the fact, abundantly attested, that Anatole Himself was much addicted to quoting from memory, or copying out for lady-friends, long passages from his favourite dramatist. Before his death he must have known, literally by heart, the greater portion of his master's lines. Finally, in *Petit Pierre,*[76] Racine too, like others among France's darlings, receives the tribute of a well-rounded apostrophe:

> O great and tender Racine, best and dearest of poets! Such was my first meeting with you, who are now at long last my delight and my love. . . I have learned to know and to adore you, O sovereign Master, in whom are found all truth and all beauty! In my youth, spoiled by

the precepts of those barbarous Romantics, I could not at once understand that you are the purest and the most profound of tragic writers; my eyes lacked the strength to contemplate your splendour. . . What are the women of Sophocles and Shakespeare by the side of those whom *you* have animated? Only your creations truly love and desire. . .

Yet it speaks well for France's catholicity that he could pass strictures on Racine's medium: he was by no means wedded to the classical Alexandrine *per se,* nor even to the set form of classical tragedy. In the Vigny volume he called it a 'worn-out mold,' whose narrowness and inadequacy neither Corneille nor Racine was able to conceal; and elsewhere he did not deny a certain monotony in the beat of the unending hexameters.[77] Of the two dramatists, Corneille appealed least to Anatole, partly (one may infer) because he was too heroic and tremendous, partly because of his 'queerness' and uneven style. But A.F.'s constant admiration for Racine's style is shown not only through general tributes but through his detailed discussion of certain epithets.[78]

We now approach the question of the direct Racinian influence. A sizable volume has been written, by M. Gabriel des Hons, on *Anatole France et Racine.* The author demonstrates first that Anatole experienced what Charles Maurras calls 'une perpétuelle possession Racinienne.' M. des Hons thus indicates the steps in the development of this obsession: it was 'an instinctive and precocious admiration, which was restrained at first by an environment unfavourable to Racine, but which increased to the point of becoming a veritable adoration, and was presently almost exclusive in its fervour.' The adoration reaches its height from 1888-95. In each of the works of that period, M. des Hons finds an average of no fewer than fifteen quotations, 'echoes,' or allusions to Racine. In France's whole work the critic finds as many as three hundred and thirty such echoes; but in view of the general nature of the parallel passages cited, it would probably be better to reduce this total by at least a third; Des Hons sometimes confuses reminiscences of Racine with France's classical 'baggage' at large.[79] Of the plays, *Phèdre* leads with twice as many echoes as any other. Then come, practically on the same level, *Esther, Athalie,* and *Britannicus.* Further details do not concern us here. The most obvious results of his great familiarity with the tragedies appear in France's description of the psychology and the effects of love, as well as in the simplicity, rhythm, and imagery of his style. His middle-class heroines chant their woes or desires in a full harmonious manner—the manner of Phèdre or of Hermione.[80] The conclusion is that the manifold resemblances do not raise the question of plagiarism, but rather of 'parentage': they are the consequences of a true 'impregnation' between two authors belonging to the same family of minds and interested alike in the passion falsely called tender. It is on this basis that France, in *La Vie littéraire,* could label Racine 'the boldest, the most terrible, and the truest of the *naturalists.*'[81]

Anatole was then an *enfant latin* who diluted his Racine with Chénier and would intermingle much Art with his imitation of Nature. This makes him really a Neo-Classicist; hence his easy comprehension of eighteenth-century writers.[82]

§ 7

CERTAIN permanent bents in France's mind are surely due to his long acquaintance with the *philosophes.* They formed part of his self-education from the days of his early marauding on the Quays: it has been pointed out that these book-stalls abound in eighteenth-century sceptics, side by side with theological works.[83] Among his associates there were probably friends both young and old (e.g., Charavay and M. Dubois) who encouraged his readings in liberal directions. There are definite traces of this habit in *Le Génie latin* and in cognate articles. In the first place, it is clear that France approves the moderation in tone, the aversion to extremes, the good sense flavoured with gaiety, which, with some exaggeration, he thought of as associated with the *philosophe* spirit; M. de Malesherbes might have taught Chateaubriand (had 'René' been a teachable person) his own equability, his largeness of mind and simplicity, in short:

> all the natural humane qualities that Malesherbes shared with the philosophic talents of his time. . . He thought, with Raynal and Diderot, that a man really counts socially only by virtue of the services which he renders.[84]

Elsewhere Anatole spoke of the *philosophes* generally as 'those religious men, those saints of the human Bible.'[85] But what writers would be included in this praise? Evidently not Rousseau, but rather those who ran counter to Rousseauistic doctrines: Voltaire, of course; Diderot and the Encyclopedists; to a lesser degree, materialists like d'Holbach and Helvétius; the sensationalists, especially Condillac, who is styled 'mon vieux maître.'[86] With all of these Anatole familiarized himself in his second period, and in the main he was always faithful to their standards. But in one respect he wavered in his allegiance and contradicted himself—he was never quite sure of the viability of the idea of progress.[87]

We cannot attempt at this stage to reckon fully with the 'shadow of Voltaire' as it fell ever more portentously across our hero's footpath. As a boy he played around the philosopher's statue on the Quai Malaquais; after his death the funeral rites were held close to that statue. Actually as well as symbolically, France never went too far from this smiling effigy. In an early tribute, he spoke of Voltaire as a 'good and great' laughing philosopher, the best among that 'divine' society; it was he who overturned the old witches' caldron of intolerance, wherein so much human flesh had been consumed.[88] M. Gaffiot emphasizes how much the Abbé Coignard resembles Voltaire and how numerous are the Anatolian reminiscences of *Candide*.

The same authority points out that the *Grande Encyclopédie* was not only an arsenal from which France drew many of his conceptions of the eighteenth century; it was, in his estimation, a landmark defining a new era in civilization, mainly because of its emphasis on manual labour and industrial production. All honour, then, to Diderot, the 'precursor of Lamarck and of Darwin.'[89] Anatole had already insisted, in *Le Génie,* on the more terrene and utilitarian aspects of the undertaking of the Encyclopedists.

Our volume also includes articles (of 1878) on Lesage and on the Abbé Prévost, who may be viewed as eighteenth-century classicists, particularly from the standpoint of form. This Anatole himself makes clear. The *Diable boiteux,* he says, may be taken from Spain, 'but it is quite French in the only thing that counts, which is style.' *Gil Blas* is epitomized as a 'true and simple book which faithfully depicts mankind.' Similarly, *Manon Lescaut* is appreciated for its naturalness and truth.

Before leaving the period, we may glance at some opinions regarding the varieties of influence which these writers exercised upon France. In his *Discours de réception,* Gréard put his finger on the spot by telling A.F.: 'You are a disillusioned Encyclopedist.'[90] Others indicate how he was a disciple both of the Encyclopedists and of Voltaire in his image-breaking and in his passion for ideas; how his 'positive Voltairianism' included 'intellectual courage, love for freedom and justice, humanitarian sympathies'; or how his somewhat restricted view of the imagination derives from Condillac.[91] His comprehensive liking for the epoch could also, we have hinted, be reflected in more artistic ways. The numerous and characteristic little touches that embellish for instance *La Rôtisserie de la Reine Pédauque* are somewhat in the manner of the eighteenth-century story-tellers, and still more in the manner of eighteenth-century engravings. France once indicated his liking for 'le conte gros comme le doigt,'[92] and occasionally he imitates the licence of this form. It has already been suggested how much of his word-painting derives from the pictorial representations of the Old Régime. He assimilates, says M. Lanson, not only the 'literary spirit of the era, but the very technique of the engravings and the little *tableaux de genre*. To Voltaire and to Rétif de la Bretonne he adds Baudouin, Saint-Aubin, Cochin, Fragonard or Pater.'[93]

Hence too, *à la* Boucher, the recurrence of small erotic scenes, in 'boudoir or grove'; for clearly his whole conception of amour, like that of his eighteenth-century masters, is voluptuous and gallant rather than sentimental or really passionate.[94] These masters, I might point out, continue to exert their power to the very end. The *Dernières Pages inédites* are still redolent of the age that on the whole affected Anatole more strongly than any other in history.

Finally in this connexion the article and the *plaquette* on 'Lucile de Chateaubriand' contain a number of passages either depicting or deriding the Revolution. The depiction outlines *motifs* that Anatole will develop later in *l'Etui de nacre* and other volumes. There are breadlines in the streets; there are also pikes bearing human heads. Courageous women frequently hide the *ci-devants*. Illiterate patriots seek for them, diving into sewers or chimneys and (this recurs repeatedly) thrusting their bayonets into mattresses. There are constant denunciations, street-quarrels, and neighbourly chats about it all. The derision—at times it seems mere detachment—usually takes the form of opposing 'immortal principles' to human nature's daily food. The revolutionaries might shout ideals—but they needed bread. Fits of ferocity alternated with expansive moods of pre-Utopian content. A scullion, by denouncing his former master, could fancy himself a genuine Brutus. Even that hardy old Encyclopedist, M. de Malesherbes, was deceived. He 'saw with joy the death of fanaticism and saluted the new reign of tolerance, humanity and universal brotherhood.' But in his revised text of the essay, Anatole pointedly adds: 'When the Revolution appeared (in its true colours), those who had predicted it could not recognize the phenomenon.'[95]

§ 8

In a discussion of Sainte-Beuve A.F. wrote that it was the Revolution which had 'inoculated' the critic and his contemporaries with the *maladie du siècle*. This mother of woes had left the inheritance of 'a sublime discontent, the yearning for an undefined beauty, the dis-ease of unassuaged appetites.' For since 1789 there were no limits to what might happen.[96] A distrust of what *did* happen in the way of literary upheavals is strongly suggested. In fact, several articles in *Le Génie* offer tentative attitudes toward Romanticism. These should be compared with the considerable influence, briefly signalized above, of the Romantic school upon France's *juvenilia*.[97] It will be recalled that his *inédits* include a fragmentary drama and a number of love-poems. Now M. Girard has characterized *Sir Punch* as:

> Shakespeare crossed with Byron, a great deal of Hugo with a dash of Banville, a truculent lyricism mingled with fantasy: such is the fabric of this *drame* which reeks with Romanticism.

Historical colouring, enumerations, *panache,* the grotesque juxtaposition of antitheses—all this is very Hugonian. The uncollected *Poèmes* are more Lamartinian, for idealistic love-dreamings together with Romantic despair make their brief sojourn in the heart of the poet. Perhaps that is why he suppressed these verses, as too revealing and too uncharacteristic.

There are also, in these productions, some direct allusions to Romantic leaders. France tells his mistress that he discovered her through reading Byron—

Vois si ce n'est pas toi que Byron a rêvée—*

and he translates the poet's lovely description of Haidée. Byron's Don Juan, everybody's Don Juan, and everybody's Elvire haunt these early pages. The other insistent presence is that of Hugo, whose name, says Anatole, 'shone in the midst of less illustrious signatures' upon a black wall—a reminiscence, perhaps, of the Wall of the Ages in the *Légende des siècles*. In the *Amateur d'autographes* France spoke of Hugo as a universal genius. In the Vigny volume he maintains that *Hernani* is 'almost classical in its *fond*,' but he is already aware of the exaggerations of Hugo: 'with his magnifying eye he interrogated the gnomes and demons of Notre Dame... The blood boils too loudly in his head to allow his ears to perceive the gentle footfalls of the past.'[98]

Among these 'gentler footfalls' there echoed occasionally in Anatole's ear the steps of Quentin Durward and of Old Mortality. It appears, too, that he was addicted in his first youth to the 'frantic' school of Romanticists, exemplified by Nodier and Gérard de Nerval. But his more lasting admirations were for Musset and, to a lesser degree, for Lamartine. They are praised, in later passages, for their naturalness, simplicity and true feeling. It was still the classical virtues that he sought.

The essays that now concern us from *Le Génie* mostly date from the years 1877-79 and they show little of the preceding juvenile enthusiasm. The article on 'Sainte-Beuve Poète' (1879) gives a brief sketch of the Romantic movement, together with a clear indication of whither Anatole (*æt.* 35) is now turning. From Lamartine on, it was a 'magnifique éclosion'; the reception accorded the *Premières Méditations* cleared the way for abundant floods of lyricism; yet perhaps it was less poetry than eloquence. For 'since the revolution the Frenchman has become terribly prone to exaggeration. He is moved by sonorous words rather than by profound sentiments. The poetry of things escapes him; he must have a *drame*.' Not much admiration of Hugo about that, nor of the 'sincerely spleenful' Joseph Delorme; rather is Anatole interested in the attempt of Sainte-Beuve to renovate the *élégie* and in the curious convolutions of a mind that greatly resembled his own. He is closely critical of Sainte-Beuve's language, remarks drily that he did not die of his poetic melancholy, and indulges in

* See if 'tis not thyself whom Byron has depicted.

some sarcasm about the contemporary penchant for skulls and ruins. In similar vein, France speaks of the fantastic visions that haunted the brain of Albert de Glatigny, that 'Don Quixote of romantic poetry.' [99]

An earlier article on 'Bernardin de Saint-Pierre' (1875, 1877) [100] contains some ironies about the naïve natural religion of this writer and his mania for inventing final causes; as a Pre-Romantic, to be sure, Bernardin is credited with a true power of feeling nature and of making it felt. But by the side of his fair creations, he left many 'empty pages.' Later on, France was to prove less kind to the transports of Paul and the prudery of Virginie. This essay was praised by Taine for its sober compact style and its discreet irony.[101]

Bernardin is not the only transitional figure who leads Anatole to suggest unfavourable comparisons of the new order with the old. Certain fancies of Xavier de Maistre—the author of the *Voyage autour de ma chambre*—seem to our critic rather colourless 'after the better seasoned jests of the eighteenth-century philosophers.' [102] And a late article (1889) on 'Benjamin Constant' is more sympathetic toward this writer than toward his mistress, Ellénore. Why? Precisely because Ellénore, i.e., Mme. de Staël, is too romantic in her moods and make-up, whereas Constant with all his faults had more of the Old Régime in his system.[103]

But it is naturally in the articles on Chateaubriand and his sister that Anatole chiefly stresses the opposition between the two eras. The delicate and charming essay on 'Lucile' (1877, 1879) was first published in book-form as an introduction to Charavay's edition of her works. It was thus the only one of these *Notices* not written for Lemerre. It was thoroughly overhauled, condensed, and rewritten before appearing in *Le Génie*. In its original form the *plaquette* was based largely on the first Book of the *Mémoires d'Outre-Tombe* and certain documents regarding the poet, Chênedollé; [104] and it is by no means an unsympathetic portrayal of the wistful sister of 'René.' The strange, solitary, and Gothic upbringing of brother and sister, the effect of that rearing upon Lucile's imagination and her melancholia, the way her affections concentrated on the only lovable being whom she knew—all this is faithfully rendered.[105] But we have already seen how the Revolution further upset this unstable nature; and we have gathered that Anatole preferred the good sense of M. de

Malesherbes to the 'immoderate' sensibility of Lucile. René himself confessed that his sister was an unreasonable creature.

A more decided antagonism underlies the article on 'La Jeunesse de Chateaubriand.' It will be recalled that Père France's fervour for the Vicomte early turned Little Pierre in the opposite direction. In spite of occasional tributes in later years, mingled with recollections of what the *Livre de mon ami* owed to the *Mémoires d'Outre-Tombe,*[106] Anatole's attitude remains fairly consistent. On the whole he disapproves; but he recognizes that the 'Sachem of Romanticism' stirred deep chords in many adolescents, including himself.

It has been told how Pierre at seventeen suffered his growing pains under the spiritual patronage of Chateaubriand and of Virgil. These two writers are again linked in the present essay. The Vicomte's life in the ancestral Château of Combourg, his romantic melancholy, his travels, and even the *Génie du Christianisme,* are capably though briefly dealt with. It is mentioned that the last-named work marches with pomp and parade. It is argued that the famous *Mémoires* show a good deal of 'affectation and arrangement.' Narcissus is depicting Narcissus. Yet we are reminded how he brought in the taste for the Gothic, how he stimulated the 'natural regret for things past.' All the dreaming youth of the period wept and believed with Chateaubriand. But *Atala* is treated with more than a hint of distaste:

> He captivated all by the magic of a marvellous style, by his brilliant and heady imagination. He evinced from the beginning that unbalanced beauty, those dazzling defects, those powerful errors that attract flocks of admirers and disciples.

In very similar terms had Sainte-Beuve judged Chateaubriand. The famous *mal de René* is summed up as consisting of a perpetual demand for love on the part of a personality which was 'too cold to bestow love on anything.' He showed from the beginning his haughty talent, his sombre imagination, his 'brilliant faults' that drew to him so many admirers. And he wanted these to come in crowds even to the 'desert' which he professed to love: his yearning for solitude was surpassed by his avidity for glory. So he stands forth for France, as for many another, in all his melancholy and illusory radiance.

It may be that the portrait of Chateaubriand's intimidating

father caused Anatole to remember his own. At any rate, it is definitely to his own parent that he attributes the reason for his surfeit of Chateaubriand.[107] Romantic despair in general, he tells us in *Le Livre,* was 'exhausted by our fathers'—the generation that wore their hair *en coup de vent.* Romantic splurges in style also cause him to depreciate Michelet, the historian whom otherwise he much admired.[108] Presently Anatole reached the point of calling the whole movement the 'liquefaction of the French mind.' His leaning in that direction was only a brief stage in his general experience. The Romantic vapours were quickly dispelled by a more rigid discipline and were hardly discernible from the heights of the *Parnasse contemporain.* To the end of his life France scarcely ceases to inveigh against the main faults of the school, which he characteristically signalizes as unstable equilibrium, excess, lack of taste, ungoverned feeling, and too much imagination—'la folle du logis.'[109]

CHAPTER XI

Private Life : 1876–1886

§ 1

SOME time ago (Chapter VII), we left Anatole, *æt.* thirty, maturing as a scholar and poet, while occupying his modest post as a subordinate in the Senate Library. He held this position, not wholly to the satisfaction of himself or his superiors, until 1890. For a while after his appointment he continued to live with his parents in the Rue de Tournon, then at No. 90, Rue de Rennes, whither the family had moved in April, 1875.[1] But the next dozen years were to witness profound changes in Anatole's private life. He was married in 1877; several years later he lost his mother, whom he sincerely mourned.[2] Relations with his father, as we have seen, had grown more amicable in the latter's declining years. The old gentleman not only expressed pride in his son's articles for *Le Temps,* but even had some intention of writing for that journal himself. Without bringing that hope to fruition, the elder France retired to Neuilly in 1887, and died there in 1890, at the advanced age of eighty-five. In the 'Post-face' to *La Vie en fleur,* Anatole referred to the 'mossy stone' which sheltered the tomb of his parents—in the cemetery where he would ultimately join them.[3]

Before Mother relinquished her role, she had helped arrange something definitive (as she thought) for her offspring. It may be recalled that once before she had abetted his fancy for Elise Rauline, the niece of 'Madame Laroque.' But the young lady had preferred the cloister. Now at Neuilly the Thibaults apparently discovered a charming young girl, to whom Anatole, as early as 1876, became attached. That was very satisfactory. Also the young lady brought with her a dowry of 3,000 *écus* or nearly 10,000 francs; and she came of a distinguished family. Her name was Valérie Guérin (de Sauville). It was pretty clearly a *mariage de convenance.*

Details concerning the courtship are quite lacking. We know only that on April 28, 1877, a marriage service was performed—at the *mairie* of the sixth arrondissement—between Anatole François Thibault and Valérie, daughter of Jules Guérin (de Sauville), connected with the Ministry of Finance. The groom's witnesses were M. Charles-Edmond, his 'chief' at the Senate Library, and his publisher, Alphonse Lemerre; with both of these men Anatole was destined to have ructions before long. After the usual honeymoon, the married couple lived with the Thibaults for a time, then moved to Neuilly, where they shared a house (No. 3, Rue Louis-Philippe) with M. Guérin.[4] A home of their own was in the offing, so was a child, so was a well-rounded ménage. Mother Thibault may have seemed justified, before she passed away, in folding her hands in peace. But perhaps there were some factors in the situation with which she was not well acquainted.

§ 2

THE distinction of the bride's family was readily admitted by all the interested parties. There appeared in the *Revue des documents historiques* a series of articles on 'Les Guérin,' written in all probability by the careful hand of Etienne Charavay.[5] In October, 1885, Anatole himself published in the *Revue alsacienne* an article based on the same material that Charavay had used, namely certain archives treasured by Jules Guérin. It is true that A.F. added some supplementary data gleaned during his trip into Alsace, which was undertaken partly with that objective. But it is characteristic that even in this rather personal matter he should lean heavily on Etienne's researches. The two writers take up the same four outstanding 'Guérins,' and in much the same way.

For a century, says Charavay, this Alsatian family, first in Strasbourg and then in Paris, have been notable practitioners of the arts of engraving, painting, and drawing. Anatole adds that the same fine moral strain has persisted down three generations, and that he feels it 'an honour to be allied to such a clan.' The founder, Jean Guérin, remained in Strasbourg, where he had two sons, Christophe and Jean-Urbain. Both of these became well-known: Christophe—the great-grandfather of Valérie—for his connexion with the Strasbourg Mint and the establishment of a Museum in that city; and particularly Jean-Urbain (1761-1835), for historical portraits and skilful miniatures executed under the Revolution and Empire—to say nothing of his prestige as the great-granduncle of Valérie. Since one infers that his talents and achievements were often mentioned in A.F.'s household, they may be briefly recapitulated here. This Jean-Urbain settled in

Paris in 1785 and soon became the miniaturist *à la mode*. Anatole discourses on the great vogue and variety of miniatures at the time and cites freely from the painter's own unpublished journal.[6] Not only did the enterprising young man from Strasbourg paint Louis XVI and his wife and many of the great nobles ; he came safely through the Revolution, when, although he stood by the royal Family, he did portraits on both sides ; and he got along swimmingly under Napoleon. He painted Bonaparte himself (in 1797) and Josephine, together with Kléber and other notables. The fourth important Guérin and the father of Jules was Gabriel-Christophe, who turned out historical paintings both in Strasbourg and Paris, although rather, says A.F., in the 'manière strasbourgeoise.' Charavay illustrated his articles with numerous fine reproductions from the works of all the Guérins. Anatole piously concludes his contribution with the hope that the Alsatians will remember this excellent family, who loved Alsace and honoured it by their labours. Whatever these Alsatians may have done, there is no doubt that Valérie Guérin frequently remembered. For M. Bergeret later remarked about his wife : 'She had a dynastic pride . . . encouraged by her father.'[7]

§ 3

Valérie should at this point be contrasted with her husband. It must be evident by now that Anatole, at thirty-three, was a fairly mature person. A photograph of him, taken in 1873,[8] represents him with bushy trailing side-whiskers and an expression of sardonic shrewdness. Throughout all this period, in fact, his face-value was not large. Another likeness, taken in his fortieth year, with a full ragged beard and a precipitous collar, gives him a severe and scholarly aspect. On the other hand, Valérie (b.1857) was young and lovely. We hear that she was frequently taken for the daughter of Anatole. She is described by Mme. de Martel as a rare type of blonde, with 'marvellous' hands and feet ; when Jules Breton declared she had Grecian lines and compared her to the Venus of Milo, Anatole responded : 'True—but her arms are much better !' Breton's daughter adds that A.F. told the painter he was endeavouring to overcome Valérie's timidity and (paternally) to form her mind. His task, he thought, would be lightened by the fact that, as a Guérin, she had art 'in her blood' and particularly appreciated painting. But it seems that presently the tastes of these twain (in the matter of house-furnishings) diverged considerably.[9]

A few years after their marriage, husband and wife possessed their own home. It was purchased with the wife's dowry, as contributed by Jules Guérin, who also provided most of the furniture and occasionally 'staked' the still indigent Anatole. Under the circumstances, it was natural that 'Papa Jules' should continue to live in his daughter's household. He seems to have been an amiable person, 'quite affectionate and simple,' according to a letter that A.F. once wrote to Charavay.[10] The small but attractive house was situated on the Rue Chalgrin, just north of the Avenue du Bois de Boulogne, near the Arc de Triomphe. At that time, this location was decidedly suburban, almost rustic. It has been described by Jacques Roujon as a 'village corner,' with no pavements and few vehicles. Modestly installed on the top floor, Anatole and his wife picked their furniture with care, descended into a diminutive garden (also used as a workshop), and occasionally entertained visitors. Henry Roujon, an art-connoisseur who lived near-by, together with Charles Grandjean, who was under France at the Senate Library, gradually became intimates of the household. Mme. Demont-Breton tells us that she and her father dropped in, to find the slippered Anatole happily boasting of his garden, his bees, and his better half. There was also an 'enigmatic' manservant aptly called Virgil and a cat named Pascal. The latter was the model for 'Hamilcar' in *Sylvestre Bonnard,* but was of a less bookish and more foraging disposition. Is it characteristic that France, like Baudelaire, usually preferred cats to dogs?[11]

Altogether, there was little at this stage to indicate that this house was fated to be the scene of *Le Mannequin d'Osier,* as is attested in several places.[12] But there was perhaps enough to make the inhabitants understand the double significance of a home, which Anatole in his old age thus generalized:

I came to know the ancient Nemesis pretty well. I even personified it in my house on the Rue Chalgrin. For it is our roof-tree that encloses our destiny. And in a sense there is nothing truer than the old superstition about haunted houses. They are haunted by happiness or unhappiness, they prepare our joys and sorrows. They keep in store for us on the one hand death, dishonour, treason, disillusionment; or on the other, love, festival seasons, health, the marvellous orgies of literary creation, the satisfactions of intellectual joys. . .[13]

This domestic interior was, for many years, the setting of a normal and cheerful existence. It was, said one friend, a 'calm and reasonable' life; others testify that this was the era when Anatole came closest to true happiness.[14] France himself, believing in his 'star,' not only rejoiced in a prolongation of his honeymoon; he celebrated, perhaps with some exaggeration, the bliss of his domestic atmosphere in the prologue to *Le Livre de mon ami,* where to the refrain of 'Sleep, my dear ones, sleep,' the author represents himself as hovering in spirit over the slumber of the mother and her two children. As a matter of fact, there was but one child. But the cosiness of the home and the solicitude of the student-father's night-watch are delightfully rendered.[15]

All this in spite of the fact that even in *Le Livre* there are tokens of incompatibility: France was 'born old,' as one friend puts it, and an elderly Bonnard is not the best company for a young Guérin. Also there are signs that Valérie's somewhat domineering tendencies ultimately prevailed over her husband's timidity and his unaggressive nature;[16] thus she came to rule over the house, which she may have thought of as originally her property. (As a matter of fact, the couple were married under the system of joint property holdings, or *communauté des biens.*) But during most of the eighties, conditions were calm enough. There were two chief influences making for a fairly contented ménage. One was the advent of the beloved daughter, Suzanne. The other was that Anatole achieved a sounder integration of his personality—a fact which added to his literary power and furthered his wider recognition. In various ways, this period may be considered as an era of peace and prosperity.

§ 4

The 'Suzanne' whose pretty ways have been partly described above (Ch.V), in connexion with the *Livre de mon ami,* was actually born in the Rue Chalgrin in 1881. Even in her babyhood, she was a great pleasure to her father. The family's journey into Alsace was undertaken in August, 1882, ostensibly to get material on the Guérins; but the record of that trip contains still more

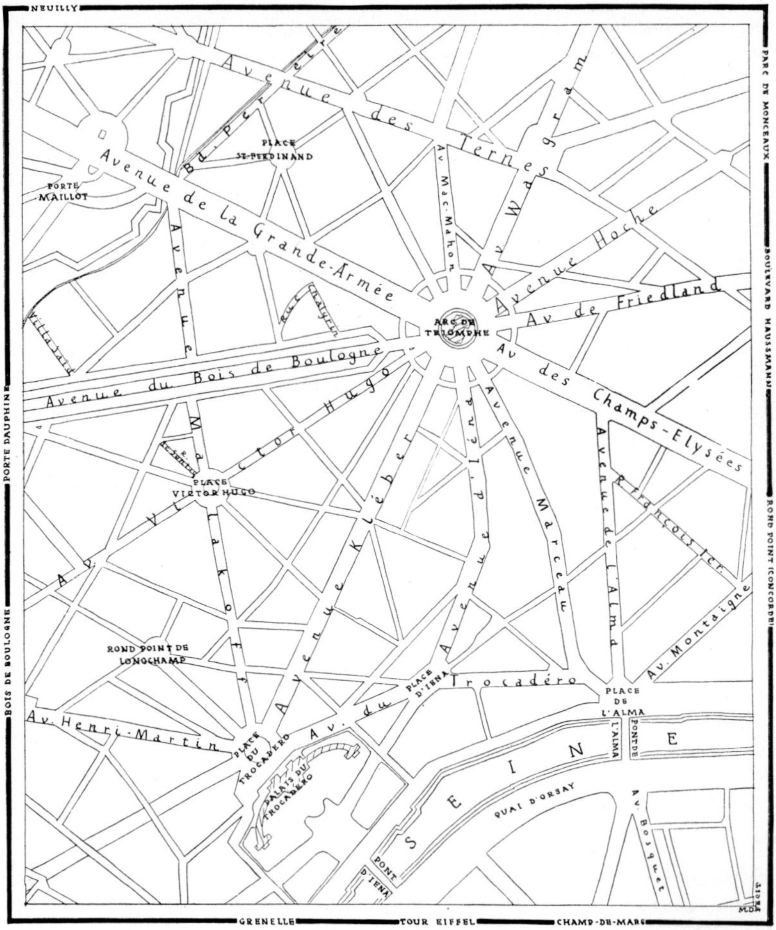

MAP B. ANATOLE'S PARIS

about Suzanne. The very title of the article—*Vacances sentimentales*[17]—suggests in what direction Anatole inclined in the early eighties. The tone throughout is tender and delicate. The father is absorbed in his daughter, who was then eighteen months old. He describes fondly the way she is dressed, how she reacts to older children, her impressions of cathedrals, her first acquaintance with flowers. She discovers them very much as she discovered the star in the *Livre de Suzanne*. 'The true name of the Hochwald for her,' says Anatole, 'is the Revelation of the Flower.' The article concludes with the remark that he has jotted down these notes so that his daughter may read them some day and understand that her presence was what made the trip so pleasurable. Similar preoccupations with Suzanne are found in letters home to Henry Roujon.[18]

During her childhood in Paris, Suzanne's name is frequently on her father's pen. One of their favourite diversions was to take walks together. Just as Madame Mathias once guided Little Pierre, so now the tall shambling form of Anatole subdued its pace to keep step with the little girl. But instead of haunting the Latin Quarter, these two rambled along the Champs-Elysées or pushed as far as the Tuileries, especially if a good Punch-and-Judy show were available. Anatole told Ségur that when he passed by one of these Guignols in later years, his mind became softened by recollections. He was absorbed in Suzanne; he watched keenly the growth of her intelligence, not unlike his own. One who knew them both says that she came to resemble him—the same features, the same eyes, together with 'his insouciance, his fancy, his ironic and compassionate understanding, not devoid of the necessary dash of folly . . .'[19]

In one of Gyp's novels we hear of a certain 'Suzon Gaule,' who is evidently Suzanne France, since her father is called 'the first writer of our time, after Barrès.' The child is described, at the age of eight, as thin and delicate; but she has fine eyes and a mass of blond hair. Gyp adds that she seems 'very intelligent.'[20]

About this time, Suzanne begins to have a point of view of her own. We have cited her conviction (*æt.* nine) that children should concern themselves less with books than with the fascinating outside world. In fact, she has begun in a small way to dip into the 'world' proper, for she was invited to various children's parties. She went to a private 'Guignol' at Madame Welschinger's and attended festivities given by other members of the Jewish élite. Her father's social chronicles have complacently recorded these triumphs. When she was ten, she thought nothing of breaking into Anatole's study and demanding attention in spite of the presence of a visitor. The visitor was M. Huret of the *Echo de Paris;* and he has left his impression of a sweet long-haired child, playfully despotic with her indulgent father.[21]

There is little doubt that the *Livre de Suzanne,* already examined in part, contains various parental reminiscences suitably embellished. It has been hinted in this connexion that the parents of the semi-fictional 'Suzanne' were rather humorously at odds with reference to her upbringing, and this from her tenderest years. The differences between them consisted mainly in the opposition of the pure and the practical reason. If Suzanne ransacks a drawer, Father finds her 'pleine de poésie'—to the amusement of Mrs. Pierre, who says that their daughter thinks only of eating. If he accompanies her to a Punch-and-Judy show, they leave Mother at home, for they take their diversion seriously. When they watch the performance, they are both pleased with the simplicity of the passions represented. This outing is described in one of the most charming chapters in the book.[22]

But they are not always on the street; the *Livre de Suzanne* also contains 'interiors' done by the same subtle brush. At times, the mature Pierre likes to read his former self into the experiences of his daughter. For her, too, 'the world is a toy, cut out and painted.' And Father must moralize that playing games is the principle of all the arts. At other times, Mother is right in the centre of the picture—practical Mother, who will not boast of Suzanne, but who is immensely proud of her, nurses her conscientiously, takes her on her knees and lulls her. 'And then all three of us were perfectly happy, because we thought of nothing.' The parents had been discussing the colour of the girl's eyes, but they cease the discussion to laugh with her, for Suzanne is full of gaiety. It is true that when disappointed, she can bawl like a gendarme. And Mother is at her wits' end between a crying baby and a husband who philosophically insists that strong passions are excellent driving forces. . . Peace is restored. 'Happiness comes back to the dwelling. Hush! Let us make no noise.' For Nemesis may be hovering over the unconscious household.

Thus, as with many men, France's affections were moving

down the family scale. First he loved his mother, then his wife, then his daughter, ultimately his grandson. But there were variations in intensity, 'intermittences of the heart,' as Proust calls them, associated presently with interruptions from outside the charmed circle.

§ 5

There are already certain tokens and prophecies of the insatiable traveller that France was later to become. During this period, he was too fond of his home to leave it frequently. But evidently (to lay the foundations of his 'geographical dilettantism'),[23] there were some excursions besides the trip to Alsace. There was, first of all, the question of where a small family could go for summer vacations. Two towns of very similar names and in adjoining departments are involved ; and some confusion has resulted. First, the fishing-village of Saint-Valery-en-Caux, 'chef-lieu de canton' in the department of the Seine-Inférieure (Normandy). This is a coast-town on the Channel and has little importance today. But it was much more of a place and had a busier life in the middle eighties. Anatole was there in the summer of 1885, and allusions in one of his articles suggest that he had visited the town in a previous summer.[24] He gives us his recollections of an old clock-maker whom he had known when both were younger. And he mentions excursions to Dieppe and other sea-side resorts, where he found that the visitors were usually rather bored.

It was in the following summer (1886) that Anatole, accompanied by his family, first spent his vacation at Saint-Valery-sur-Somme. This second incarnation of the saint (in urban form) is in the ancient province of Picardy, not far from Abbeville. It is also a 'chef-lieu' and is situated on the bay of the Somme, where the river widens into the Channel. The town is noted for the fact that William the Conqueror once put in there with his fleet ; it was still a considerable place under the Old Régime ; but in modern times it has become less accessible for large ships than the coast-towns proper.

Thither the little family of the 'Frances' repaired early in August, 1886. They were accompanied by Gilbert-Augustin Thierry, nephew of the historian, with his wife and children. This Thierry wrote during his sojourn there a novel called *Marfa* which A.F. subsequently reviewed for *Le Temps*.[25] And subsequently to that, he seems to have quarrelled with the novelist. But in 1886, the two families amicably shared a small house (Rue de la Ferté, No.110), which today bears a memorial tablet.[26] Anatole witnesses that from the windows of his study he could see the whole bay or estuary, while a salty wind blowing in from the Channel whirled about the papers on his table. This was the very place and atmosphere in which Victor Hugo composed his 'Oceano Nox.' Regarding the village and its surroundings A.F. wrote for *Le Temps* five articles, portions of which were reprinted in the 'Promenades de Pierre Nozière en France.' [27]

In wandering about the old ramparted town, with its turrets and its fifteenth-century church, its antique façades and gables, Anatole found much to charm his mind. He would pause to spell out blurred escutcheons or inscriptions. He would drop into the town-library and find a sixteenth-century manuscript of antiquarian interest. He would watch the fisher-folk, their customs and diversions. With Suzanne or with Fernand Calmettes as his companion, he would stroll along the sands when the tide was low. Perhaps with Thierry or with a visitor named Adolphe Racot, he would undertake, as several of the articles testify, excursions into the pleasant wooded country around or into such neighbouring villages as Eu or Cayeux.

On these various 'promenades,' France's reactions are very characteristic. His descriptions of landscapes or monuments are brief but vivid. His meditations are those of the archæologist, the historian, and occasionally of the philosopher and the patriot. He lingers among the votive offerings placed in the little Chapel of the Mariners. At Eu he piously formulates the silent message of the stone houses, with their secular traditions ; he objects to the methods of Viollet-le-Duc and his school, whose restorations (in medieval terms) do away with the deposits of successive ages and the architectural harmonies which Father Time has created among them. On the historical side, A.F. is aware that Joan of Arc, as prisoner of the English, once passed through Saint-Valery ; and he elaborates on the fact that William the Conqueror was forced by contrary winds to wait there before his invasion of England. As we have seen (Ch.V), Anatole mingles legends of the saints, especially the patron saint of the village,[28] with his chronicles. And he dwells upon such scenes as a death by drowning, the departure of the torpedo-boats, or the festivities connected with merry-go-rounds and races. Altogether, he drew much from his visit of two months to Saint-Valery-sur-Somme. It is indicated that he returned there in later years.[29]

Other excursions of this decade have likewise left traces in France's work. When a trip to Rouen or Pierrefonds or Chartres was on the docket, friends recall that there were temperamental obstacles in the way of catching the proper train. A.F.'s refusal to bestir himself would cause him to postpone leaving his house, or even rising from bed, until the last possible minute. 'Everything had to be done for him,' including getting him into his clothes, hurrying him to the station and actually purchasing his railway ticket—for, like royalty, Anatole seldom carried ready money upon his person. Under these conditions, he visited Chartres certainly before 1887.[30] As for Pierrefonds, it is attested by a local newspaper that he spent two months there, perhaps on the trail of Joan of Arc, in August and September, 1884; and he must have paid the town a flying visit before that. His gleanings round the château and its art-treasures are recorded briefly in *l'Univers illustré,* more fully in *Pierre Nozière*.[31] The castle is situated in a 'gentle' country-side, the heart of storied France, so he loves it both as patriot and as antiquarian. If the beech-trees and the wild flowers claim his attention for a moment, he is more concerned with that 'enormous plaything,' the castle itself. The towers are capped by statues of eight worthies who represent distant and very different ages. Yet they all wear the same costumes, a fact which leads A.F. to comment on medieval naïveté. He wonders, however, whether his own most historical century will not seem equally naïve to scholars of the future. And he again complains of Viollet-le-Duc for too much medieval standardizing in his restorations of Pierrefonds.

As we have seen, the regular resorts on the Norman coast, such as Trouville or Dives, did not interest France profoundly. He remarks of one place, probably Dieppe, that the casinos with their fevered gambling have made most tourists oblivious to the beautiful scenery.[32] He is better pleased with the little town of Vernon, on the borders of Normandy, where he visited the Plessis family in August, 1887. This is a tiny tranquil spot, but it has souvenirs of a stormier past; and he likes to turn its 'pages of stone,' as if they were pages of vellum. So he touches on its history (from the thirteenth century), its armorials, its notables, and the saints who honoured it with their presence. This colourful picture of the town's destiny includes a discussion of its motto—*Ver non semper viret*—which is inevitably and gracefully linked with Diana Vernon in *Rob Roy*.—According to letters written to Madame de Caillavet, A.F. recalled from this neighbourhood his older acquaintance with Avranches and the Mont-Saint-Michel.[33] He also spent one or more vacations at Brolles, near Fontainebleau.

§ 6

IN Paris itself, Anatole could enjoy more than ever the sights and sounds of the metropolis. Since he no longer lived on the left bank, the circles of Pierre's knowledge now embraced the whole city. The 'chronicles' which he wrote about Parisian institutions and events will concern us directly in connexion with his post on the staff of *l'Univers illustré*; but be it noted that this appointment (from March, 1883), together with his increasing royalties and modest stipend at the Senate Library, made active financial worries unnecessary. When he had joined *Le Temps* (1886), the family could henceforth live in comfort and comparative ease.

We may now attempt to reconstruct, largely from the reminiscences of his intimates, the sort of person A.F. was and the sort of life that he led during this flowering-period. The *home* was the all-important factor. For some years, France and his wife went but little into general society. But in the small house on the Rue Chalgrin there were assembled from time to time a group of Anatole's friends who, says the son of one of them:

loved the smiling profundity of his mind, while they admired the breadth of his culture and his grasp. The essential part of the *Vie littéraire*, of the *Opinions de Jérôme Coignard*, and of the *Jardin d'Epicure* was expounded, some years previously to the appearance of these books, before Maurice Barrès . . . or before Robert de Bonnières, Fernand Calmettes, Etienne Charavay, Charles Grandjean, Henry Roujon, Gilbert-Augustin Thierry, the sculptor Soldi, and Camille Benoît.[34]

Most of these names have already become familiar. Of the Library's five officials and employees, only Grandjean and Louis Ratisbonne were found congenial. The latter is amiably mentioned in France's correspondence and articles. Frequently at the house were Charles Grandjean, who ultimately became Inspector-General of Historical Monuments, and Henry Roujon, who was later to review *Sur la Pierre blanche* and recall Anatole's 'adorable story-telling.' [35] This Roujon started his career under Jules Ferry; he was presently made Director of Fine Arts and was 'boosted' by Anatole in *l'Univers illustré* as an agreeable, tactful person and an excellent administrator.[36] As for Camille Benoist, he once got amusingly entangled with a bicycle; and he did a translation of *Faust* which A.F. commended highly.

It appears that in the gatherings of this group our middle-aged *littérateur* outshone the rest by the brilliancy and depth of his conversation. It is even held that in these intimate *causeries* the man shone superior to his works. Thus Anatole, in his own set, was a 'causeur incomparable'; the statement that the substance of these chats often underlay his contemporary articles and books, seems quite likely; and so we are led to believe that the repartee of larger and more worldly salons could provide much material for the *Lys rouge,* the *Histoire contemporaine,* and subsequent works. A particularly good separator, to wit, the mind of France, divided the nuggets from the dross. And would not his liking for conversation help account for the frequency of the dialogue-form (so thoroughly in the French tradition) in many of his best passages?

Physically, he might be inept, inert, indolent. He was clearly averse to business or any kind of practical activity, before which he stood uncertain and hesitant. He even hesitated in his manner of speech, which exhibited a kind of stammering or an aimless repetition of the 'b-b-b' sound. Also, he avoided responsibilities and was not very adequate as the head of a family. He was extremely vague; he could never lay his hand on anything he wanted; he had a sort of social timidity in larger circles; it was excessively difficult to get him to work; he preferred to fob off his publishers with oddments revamped in order to fill out any particular volume.[37]

On the other hand, although he naturally looked out for his interests as a rising author, he had then no marked literary vanity and never considered that the race of writers was a race apart. He was a pleasant and witty companion, throwing off *obiter dicta* about the ordinary accompaniments of life: e.g., 'If the theater isn't excellent, it's execrable.' He could chat easily about politics and current events, the new books or 'vieux Paris,' often adopting the light tone of *la blague* which your boulevardier uses to season his discourse. He was not yet a monologuist and never claimed to be an authority.

But when it came to the domain of ideas proper, a change pervaded his spirit and his expression. Both became more translucent and compelling. He would make a remark that would cause people to exclaim : 'France, you are a marvellous thinker !' [38] He would reveal, even in familiar converse, the *habit* of the superior mental range. He is credited with an 'unbelievable penetration' and clairvoyance — a doubtful gift that may have lighted the way to his later nihilism. But in the eighties it seemed simply a belief, an absorption in 'la pensée' as the first of human blessings.

All in all, these were his happiest days since childhood. He was more nearly integrated, morally speaking, than either before or after. He had his position, his friends, his daughter, his books. His wife impressed people as still a 'brave femme,' who manifested in her daily walk an Alsatian calm, and who accepted if she did not appreciate A.F.'s literary labours. He would usually write or read aloud from his manuscript in the evening. His friends were sure that in those evening sessions around the lamp they were listening to 'the true Anatole France.' In those days, no one doubted that he had a heart.

Thus, the period of the eighties was what we may call his sentimental period. He could at that time feel and respond to his experiences more fully, more normally than at any other epoch in his career. He had passed through the stresses and strains of young manhood. He was kind and gentle ; the corrosions of his scepticism had not yet affected what Mme. Demont-Breton calls the 'élans de son cœur vers le Beau, le Bon et le Bien'; even a Catholic writer found in him a 'charming and obliging friend,' still respectful of the Church.[39] Altogether, Anatole's age, environment and circumstances made for him then a stratum of relative serenity. Above all, he realized that, as Stevenson says, the artist 'lives for a frame of mind.' And his frame of mind, by his acceptances no less than by his rejections, had grown harmonious. This sentiment and this harmony are conspicuous in such books as *Le Crime de Sylvestre Bonnard* and *Le Livre de mon ami*.

§ 7

YET we cannot say that France's life was a perfect bed of roses, nor that the prevailing serenity was unmarred by ructions. Some of these may be more fitly dealt with later on. The relationship with Leconte de Lisle was an increasingly sore spot, which had not yet come to a head. Affairs at the Senate Library did not cause a rupture until 1890, but there were some circumstances connected with this position that obtained through all the eighties. In the first place, the job was practically a sinecure. As *commis-surveillant*—a kind of superior clerk—France was in attendance only a few hours a week.[40] His salary was 2,200 francs a year. For this he was supposed to keep the card-catalogue up to date and to oversee certain governmental publications. But it appears that neither he nor any one else could be relied upon to open these documents. Senators or visitors who asked for *Le Journal officiel* were likely to be disappointed.

The fact is that, whether because of the low remuneration or the lack of steady employment, no one on the staff took his duties very seriously. Lured by the 'silence imagé des vieux livres,' Anatole once wrote a friend that he became a 'pretty good librarian.'[41] Probably he deceived himself, for a time. It is amusing to hear France defending elsewhere the honour and dignity of such a position. As examples of librarians who had done distinguished service, he cites the names of Sainte-Beuve and of Leconte de Lisle. The Master of all Parnassus had replaced François Coppée at the Luxembourg, on the latter's urging. Coppée generously felt that the old age of the rather indigent Master should be provided for—and withdrew in good order to a similar post at the Comédie-Française.[42] At the time of Anatole's advent, Leconte de Lisle was not the only poet already on the staff. There were also Auguste Lacaussade and Louis Ratisbonne who 'enjoyed a precarious existence in anthologies.' Four bards altogether. . . No wonder that A.F. later declared to Brousson that the Palace of the Senate, where writers so abounded, was the gloomy work-shop or school-room and the adjoining Jardin du Luxembourg was—once again—his playground during recesses.[43]

Among these colleagues, France seems to have had only one subordinate and only one lively companion—Charles Grandjean. The official head of the whole staff was a Pole by birth and an imposing personage—M. Charles-Edmond. This 'chief' thought it best to exempt Anatole from a certain routine—'in view of the small zeal which he displays.' The Luxembourg Palace was no more loved than Stanislas had been by the refractory 'Pierre.' M. Barthou, well-acquainted with this period in France's life, gives a vivacious account of his continual resistance to discipline and order.

During most of the year 1881, France was on uneasy terms with his old friend and publisher, Alphonse Lemerre. It is probable that some of the circumstances, particularly the legal moves involved, have not yet been fully revealed. Enough is known, however, to set forth a very interesting case of author *vs.* publisher—or the other way around. On the one hand, we find a writer who was, to say the least, indolent in fulfilling his express obligations. On the other, there is a publisher who had, as he thought, patronized budding talent (at a low figure) for a number of years and consequently had the right to profit by his position, and to remonstrate when France did not keep his word. It is true that the publisher was slow to recognize the author as anything but a diligent compiler of prefaces for standard editions. At any rate, a long association was presently ended, and Anatole appeared no more in the Passage Choiseul.[44] Calmann-Lévy became his regular publisher.

Although the first differences of opinion between France and Lemerre belong to the present period, the whole matter did not come to a head until 1911, when a notable lawsuit resulted. The proceedings were recorded *in extenso* in an official *Revue* of important legal cases, and this is the account that we shall mainly follow.[45]

Lemerre, the plaintiff, engaged as his lawyer a certain Maître Dreyfous, while France was defended by no less a person than M. Raymond Poincaré, not long before he was elected President of the Republic. From the *plaidoirie* of Dreyfous we get first the impression that Lemerre had 'discovered' Anatole, employed him as reader, printed his verse, and generally acted as his benefactor for some ten years (1869-79). At the end of this period, Lemerre wished to bind France to the delivery of certain works *in esse* and *in posse*. Anatole (indiscreetly) signed a contract to give Lemerre various MSS., presumably *Jocaste,* etc., for which he already stood committed to Calmann-Lévy; and furthermore—

which is the crux of the matter—Lemerre should have the MS. of A.F.'s 'Histoire de France,' of which the first volume was completed, while the second should be delivered by the end of 1879. For this work France was to receive the sum of 3,000 francs, a stipulation that was duly observed.

We may pause here to reflect upon the fact—which seems to have escaped general notice—that Anatole did indeed write a sizable chronicle of his country. This will help to explain his recurrent emphasis on such an historical approach in his other productions of almost every period. As he wrote, between jest and earnest, in the Preface to *l'Ile des Pingouins:* 'My life . . . is wholly bent upon the accomplishment of one great scheme. I am writing the history of the Penguins.'

But the second volume of this *Histoire de France* came down only to the Revolution and apparently was somewhat loosely strung together in its final sections. Furthermore, the contract was violated, inasmuch as this volume was handed over to Lemerre only in 1882, after repeated adjurations. These took the form of legal summonses during 1881. France was ordered to stand and deliver the *Histoire,* the *Désirs de Jean Servien,* and *Pierre Nozière.* The first two titles were appropriated by Lemerre, who published *Jean Servien* (1882); but *Pierre Nozière* was brought out long afterwards by Calmann-Lévy, who had in the meantime (1879) published, according to his previous contract, *Jocaste, et le Chat maigre.*

Thus Anatole had done about half of what he agreed to do for Lemerre. Since the latter also claimed the *Crime de Sylvestre Bonnard,* the contract seems to have been some form of 'blanket' agreement. (A dangerous weapon, it may be said, addicted to recoiling on the user.) By way of response to Anatole's delays, Lemerre took a magnificent revenge: he held up the MS. of the *Histoire de France* until 1909! Then he threatened to publish it—and this law-suit was the consequence. Twenty-seven years had rolled by. The fame of the writer was world-wide. It had been particularly promoted, in the historical line, by the appearance in the previous year of his notable *Vie de Jeanne d'Arc.* In 1906, there had been some preliminary skirmishing between the parties involved; and the firm of Calmann-Lévy had, curiously enough, appeared in the role of peace-maker and secured a partial abrogation of the old contract. But it was not until 1909 that

Lemerre, biding his time, decided to strike—to the astonishment and embarrassment of Anatole Himself.[46]

Most of the above representations by M. Dreyfous seem substantially correct in point of fact; some pressure is naturally exerted to display Lemerre as the injured party; it is interesting to observe that Dreyfous anticipates the rebuttals of Anatole and his lawyer. These will take the form that not only is Anatole a very different Anatole, but that France is a quite different country from what it was in 1882, and that the science of history is quite a different science. Consequently, the whole basis of the *Histoire* is out of date and, its author maintains, the work is 'unpublishable.'

First, however, M. Poincaré wishes to clear up some correlated matters. He does this, as he conducts the main argument, with the acumen that one would expect and with all the care which he customarily gave to civil cases. The skirmishings of 1906 (he maintains) resulted in the *total* abrogation of the old contract of 1878, including the *Histoire de France*—a debatable point. Moreover, it was plainly the original intention of both parties that the *Histoire* should be published shortly after it was completed.

Now will the court please, urges Poincaré, look upon this picture and on that. On the one hand, a shrewd publisher, a keen business man, accustomed to pushing young authors, it is true, but also to drawing whenever possible his profit from them. For some years previously to 1878, Lemerre had paid Anatole a paltry 150 francs monthly for his editorial labours and his *notices*. The dreamily incompetent poet (it is intimated) allowed himself to be 'bound to all eternity' by that blanket contract. That there might be delays in completing the *Histoire* was understood by both parties. Yet Anatole, poor driven hack, was harried about his delay, as later he was harried about a certain 'Notice sur Molière,' (which it is said that Poincaré had to force him to write).[47] On every occasion, including A.F.'s election to the Academy and during the vogue resulting from his *Jeanne d'Arc,* Lemerre has shown himself alert to bring up forgotten issues, in order to profit by the rise in the author's stock.

The most interesting part of the argument is where M. Poincaré reviews, as one speaking with authority, the considerable shifts in historical attitude during the preceding quarter of a century. In many cases, fresh documentation in the field has come to light. The public has recently been shown the extent of M. France's conscientiousness regarding Joan of Arc. Now if we turn to the old *Histoire,* what do we find? This manuscript is positively *weak* on Joan of Arc. The writer was then by no means so much concerned with social and economic environment as he would be today. The whole (disproportionate) treatment of the Middle Ages would have to be brought up to date. Actual errors of fact would have to be corrected. In 1882, France accepted as true certain 'legends' which he would now be the first to reject. Passing to the final chapter of the work, it may be demonstrated that M. France was again weak on the 'préludes de la Révolution. One great inevitable omission was that in 1882 the indispensable *Cahiers de doléances* of the Third Estate were not known to the historian. And M. Poincaré shows, on principles of general equity, how unfair such a publication would be in 1912.

His arguments won the day. The court decided, rightly enough it would seem, that Lemerre should return the MS. to its author and pay the costs of the trial. France should return him the 3000 francs—for value *not* received. Whereas the defendant was wrong in supposing that the *Histoire* was included in the contractual abrogations of 1906, yet it was the author's privilege to maintain that the work should have been published shortly after its reception. The publication today would be an 'impossible' thing.

The fate of the MS. is not definitely known to the present writer. It is altogether likely that Anatole destroyed it. He once reminisced about the whole affair, recalling the main circumstances quite clearly. He gives us the additional point that Lemerre's publication of *Le Génie latin,* after the conclusion of the law-suit, was in the nature of an *amende* or a compromise. And he does not seem wholly satisfied with Poincaré's conduct of the trial. Perhaps, after all, the masterful lawyer had found too many weaknesses in Anatole's *Histoire de France.*

§ 8

A CERTAIN care for one's literary reputation is visible in the above manœuvres. Even in the eighties, this became a matter of some concern to France. After his marriage he learned gradually to consolidate his position and to anticipate a career. Gone are the days when he wavered this way and that, returned on his steps, went in for the most diverse things. For fifteen years before 1880, says M. Vandérem, at an age when most writers are nesting their eggs, 'we see him scattering over a thousand interests, a thousand "jobs," without any well-determined vocation, and seeming rather a dilettante than a person carried away by the wind of inspiration.'[48] But now—if this be a sign of a 'vocation'—he manifests a certain *aigreur,* a spirit of rivalry and harshness toward other writers. Not only is he annoyed by the triumphs of Naturalism, but before that he shows severity toward such brother-poets as Verlaine and Mallarmé.[49] He now feels the need to concentrate; and he grows more fully aware of himself as a not unworthy practitioner of the literary art. Although he may later make light of his fame, there is evidence that he made arrangements to 'arrive' as an author. For one thing, he endeavoured to get favourable notices and even furnished a few himself. For another, he presently wrote (as we shall see) a peremptory letter to the authorities at the Senate Library, insisting on his literary prestige, just as he had, through fellow-feeling, insisted on that of François Coppée.[50] Both writers maintained that their respective sinecures were no less than they deserved.

Although Anatole's legendary *paresse* has been exaggerated by himself and by others, it is true that he did not qualify as a regular man of letters until about his fortieth year. When *Sylvestre Bonnard* was crowned by the Academy (1881) and when, two years later, its author took his post on *l'Univers illustré,* the ground-work of his career was laid. But it was not until 1886 that the edifice began to rise in the sight of the general public.[51]

After his fame had attained international proportions, France could afford to look back on its earlier stages with modesty and even with an apparent indifference. In his daily life and walk he often gave evidence of a genuine humility. It is naturally the most intelligent men who are the most modest. For they are constantly aware of the abyss that separates our efforts from our achievements, as well as the tiny place that each of us occupies in the total scheme of things. Anatole usually attributed his phenomenal fortune to the caprices of chance or to the good offices of friends—in particular, Coppée, Mendès, and Lemaître. The first two helped him to place his 'copy'; Lemaître and Barrès wrote articles in his praise.[52]

The tribute of Maurice Barrès has some curious features.[53] This young Lorrainer—he was only twenty—had recently come to

Paris; he was still a literary neophyte, but with a 'most knowing eye.' His article expresses reserves about *Jocaste* and *Jean Servien* but commends *Sylvestre Bonnard* as a masterpiece of charm and originality. Its author does not seek a wide public, although he should appeal to all intelligent people for his qualities of head and heart. Similar admiring phrases are found in private letters from Barrès to France. The writer has not yet evolved into the subtle exponent of the *Moi,* nor into the ardent Nationalist that he still later became. In these avatars he cared less for Anatole (save in so far as Anatole was the expression of his country—a gentle Ile-de-France garden, full of a 'dangerous softness')—and even maintained that he was a man without character. Of his talent the stark Lorrainer later opined: 'Certaine beauté est un dissolvant.'[54] But in 1883 Barrès was not averse to a smiling dilettantism.

The 'article de lancement' by Lemaître (1886) served as a more effective step-ladder for Anatole.[55] It was written at a time when the two 'impressionists' were fairly intimate, with social as well as literary consequences. While the article mostly concerns *Le Livre de mon ami,* it also deals with France's other volumes to date—his poetry, his novelettes, *Le Crime de Sylvestre Bonnard.* Lemaître expressed himself warmly in praise of *Le Livre* and undoubtedly aided its success.

There were other tokens of admiration abroad and at home. Shanks tells us that during the trip into Alsace, Mme. France observed that Swiss and Russian readers were 'spoiling' her husband. The *haute juiverie* was taking him up in Paris. No less a person than Taine lauded *Sylvestre Bonnard;* the distinguished Melchior de Vogüé complimented its author and invited him to lunch; and certain devotees of the Caillavet circle (e.g. Loti) were in the offing.[56] France was decorated with the ribbon and cross of the Légion d'Honneur early in 1885; his name figured, as *chevalier,* among the New Year honours.[57] He had already formed an important journalistic connexion. The *Nouvelle Revue* was in its heyday from 1875-90, first as an organ of 'la Revanche' against Prussia, then as a medium for the oncoming generation of writers. Bourget, Loti, and others were among its notable contributors. Its editor was Mme. Juliette Adam, well-known as novelist and Hellenist. France had made her acquaintance in 1879, at a garden-party given by Edmond About. The two writers already had a common bond in their Hellenistic tastes. Partly in consequence, no doubt, the *Nouvelle Revue* first published serially *Le Crime de Sylvestre Bonnard* (1880-81) and later (1883) fragments of the *Livre de Pierre* under the title of *Le Petit Bonhomme*.[58] It is clear that by the middle eighties France's originally 'small reputation' was widening out. And the salons were almost ready to take a hand in the game.

§ 9

WHAT sort of social 'front' could A.F. present to the world? What was his initial equipment as a lion and a drawing-card? Here we need to distinguish. Physically at least he was less akin to the lion than to the horse. A number of people have commented upon the equine shape of his head. Now although Balzac once declared that there is 'something of the horse in the heads of all great men,' yet this anatomical feature may not prove a strong attraction in the parlours of the rich. M. Emile Hovelaque, who first knew France round 1887, mentions this peculiarity among others. Anatole offered, to the gaze of this beholder,

> A long, heavy, equine face, slightly twisted and asymmetrical, the jaw askew under a rough imperial; stiff hair worn *en brosse,* a large nose, a coarsely grained complexion. But his black brilliant eyes were magnificent. . . He spoke, and spoke badly. His voice was solemn and unctuous; but it hesitated and had a nasal quality at times. His tongue would become water-logged—he would stop in the middle of an anecdote, as if intimidated. His conversation of that period, full of repetitions and reconsiderations, was by no means what it became later.[59]

Is this in contradiction to what has been said above regarding France's conversational charm, or does it refute Barthou's description of him as a 'causeur merveilleux'?[60] By no means. We must distinguish, again, between Anatole's various audiences, as well as between the different grades of his conversation. It was one thing when he was forced into ordinary chit-chat; it was another when he warmed up to a subject that really enthralled him. Then, as M. Hovelaque admits, the charm began to operate, the magnetic eyes, like those of the Ancient Mariner, gripped their prey; and the harmonious voice (no longer stammering) 'held and will always hold' the listener.[61]

As for audiences, something evidently depends on whether a man is talking quietly to friends or whether he is appearing in a formal salon. It may be granted that France's inherent timidity long impeded his flow in such gatherings. Under those circumstances, he preferred to keep quiet; he was not at ease and he may have felt that he lacked social distinction; the lion had to be trained before he could roar, if ever so gently.[62] The insinuating, semi-clerical manners which he had learned at Stanislas were no more prepossessing *dans le monde* than they had been among the old coteries of Parnassus. The Comtesse de Martel wrote of him as unknown, socially speaking, in 1882, and declares that he would have stayed unknown but for a benevolent Egeria. 'His awkwardness, his timidity, his entire ignorance of social usages, everything destined him to be an outsider, whatever might be his talents. It was Mme. de Caillavet who educated him from head to foot. We observed, with surprise, his relatively rapid transformation.'[63]

We shall hope to be present at one or two of these transformation-scenes. Let us note that so complete was the ultimate alteration that later listeners to France's monologues sat enraptured. One of them declares that at his best he wielded 'the miraculous powers of a magician.' His conversation became 'a dazzling series of fireworks, wherein all the centuries were illuminated, all intellectual categories, all artistic talismans had their turn—but always with subtlety.' Victor du Bled asserts that in his talk, 'he stirs more ideas than anybody else, they rise before him like flocks of game.'[64] Among these 'categories' was one—perhaps the most useful one in society—of which little has hitherto been said. I mean Anatole's growing interest in contemporary politics. A brief digression will allow us to reckon with a field which soon became paramount in France's mind—in his talk no less than in his work.[65]

In this field, too, according to M. Régnier, A.F.'s 'mania for talking politics' reveals the stamp of his social origins and habits.[66] It is not at all the stamp of the man of the world ('il se moquait des gens du monde'), but rather that of a descendant of the lower bourgeoisie. These shop-keepers are the people who talk politics incessantly and they are the people, the aristocratic Régnier adds with some disdain, whom France always most willingly frequented. I do not think, however, that this view will quite account for his political attitude during his middle years; his position was that of the 'bonne' rather than of the 'petite bourgeoisie.' That is to say, it was Left Centrist and for some time definitely Conservative. To such a compromise has our wild Republican of the late sixties, having revolted against the Commune, now been driven. He supports the army, he is not directly hostile to the Church. As for the Republic—that depends. These were the years, after 1879, when the 'Republican republic,' under the powerful leadership of Gambetta and tutored by Jules Ferry, was settling into its stride. The policy of a speedy 'revenge' upon Germany was abandoned by the former. There was less to fear from the Legitimists or from any of the parties who desired a monarchical or imperial restoration. Anatole on the whole accepted, if he did not exactly 'venerate' the forces in control; yet he declared, in 1920, that 'even in those far-off days . . . I was no great lover of the Third Republic, with its pinchbeck virtues, its militarist imperialism, its love of money, its contempt for the handicrafts, its unswerving predilection for the unlovely.' He avowed even then a distrust of democracies (i.e., demagogueries), of politicians and parliaments, which reached the climax of at least one curious manifestation.[67]

General Boulanger, the hero on the black horse, attracted in the late eighties the interest of many people who disliked the vulgarity and mediocrity of the actual régime. France was among this number. He met and for a time he admired the General, who fomented hopes of a more brilliant *patrie*. At dinners and at gala receptions, organized in behalf of the new movement, Anatole seems to have been actively present. He even wore the pink carnation which, like Disraeli's primrose, became the emblem of the reactionary party—i.e., 'les boulangistes.' But before the General's star had set, our sceptic perceived that it was waning. His enthusiasm slackened and presently ceased altogether. This flurry has been considered as just one episode of Anatole's 'courte vie mondaine.'[68]

§ 10

WAS it, then, so short? And first, how did it begin and along what lines did it continue?

There were two main avenues of attack, or rather of peaceful penetration. One was *via* Jewish society, the other was through the salon of Mme. Aubernon. Both these avenues converged in that *rond-point* which was Mme. de Caillavet. We shall see later how as a chronicler for *l'Univers illustré* France, nothing averse, came into contact with the Jewish élite and how, before that, he was allowed to read extracts from *Sylvestre Bonnard* in Mme. Aubernon's drawing-room. It was probably in 1886 that he was presented to this obese, imposing, and dictatorial lady. France and others describe her extraordinary way of regulating conversation among her guests. When she thought a given subject had been sufficiently discussed, she would ring a bell to command a change of topics—say from 'Adultery' to 'Incest.' If she had eleven guests, at dinner, she would ask each one in turn for his opinion on the fresh topic—duologues being forbidden until after the meal was over. This system was not highly regarded by free-lances like Anatole France or Victor Cherbuliez. But others, e.g. Dumas *fils,* succumbed and even presented the lady of the house with silver bells to ring out the changes.[69]

Yet Mme. Aubernon was a kind-hearted exuberant person, and the conversation in her house was for long esteemed as the best in Paris. Like her eighteenth-century predecessors, the hostess knew how to play up the ability of each guest and to compose a group of 'superior men, intelligent, witty and elegant women.' The mistress of the salon was sometimes styled 'la précieuse *radicale.*' She had plenty of *esprit,* as for example when she improvised a brilliant ten-minute parallel between the talent of Jules Lemaître—and that of Anatole France. It was here that A.F. came to know—as far as one *could* know—the ageing, dreamy, unctuous, but still fascinating Renan, and acquired for him a reverence which time did little to diminish. Perhaps, too, from Renan, or from the general atmosphere, Anatole imbibed something of that 'characteristic inconsequence' which is attributed to these *conversazioni.* At any rate, he must have caught their tone and made his impression, for soon, as if he were a Fontenelle or a Montesquieu, three of the salons were contending for the honour of his presence.[70]

Strictly speaking, he had come to know Mme. Arman de Caillavet before he frequented the house of Mme. Aubernon. The facts regarding his relationship with the former lady are not at present wholly available. Their correspondence is as yet uncollected and for the most part unprinted. The letters that have appeared in our chief source, *Le Salon de Madame de Caillavet*—

by her daughter-in-law, Mme. Jeanne Pouquet—are usually undated.[71] The numerous treatments of the subject are often prejudiced, for or against. In what immediately follows regarding the beginnings of the friendship between 'Mme. de C.' and France, as well as in subsequent chapters, we shall aim at the unbiased truth.

§ II

Léontine Lippmann (*née* 1847) was the daughter of a wealthy Jew, but had no decidedly Hebraic strain in her character. Her brother, Maurice, is represented as a man of much charm ; he had married a daughter of the younger Dumas, which may account for the fact that the playwright was at home in the Caillavet salon. Léontine herself married, in 1868, a M. Albert Arman, whose father had made his money in vineyards and added the 'de Caillavet' to enhance the family name. The Armans were of essentially bourgeois stock. Léontine's husband was something of a sportsman (he wrote the yachting news for *Le Figaro*), and seems, in spite of his startling cravats and equally loud voice, to have been still more of a nullity.[72]

But there was nothing null about Léontine. When in 1878 she bought the mansion at No. 12 Avenue Hoche,[73] in the Etoile quarter, it is likely that she had her plans. She had been trained, by Mme. Aubernon, in the art of receiving and drawing out her guests. For all that, feminine charm was not her chief asset. She was more like a man, and furthermore like an *honnête homme,* in her hard intelligence, her judgment, her lack of deviousness. She had a sort of calm arrogance and she could be perfectly regardless of other people and their standards. Her independent and combative nature could not put up with the witless. She is credited with 'an iron will, very few scruples, and an immense energy.' What she wanted, she went after directly and unsentimentally,—and that is how she presently went after France.[74]

Yet on their first meeting and for some time subsequently, she was not favourably impressed. It may or may not have been at Victor Hugo's house, but it was pretty certainly in 1883 that she first fixed Anatole with her penetrating blue eye. It was, says Robert de Flers, 'a most direct gaze, without indulgence and without meanness.' According to the same lyrical admirer, it was charged with all the 'lucidity, vigour and radiance' of her splendid

MADAME DE CAILLAVET

mind. When this formidable engine was turned upon Anatole, what did it discover? A poor thing—and not yet her own. She found in him something vague, shiftless, stammering, uncouth—something with which one had to deal in a peremptory manner. She almost turned away. For a time she treated him cavalierly; she preferred Jules Lemaître. But Lemaître loyally pressed the good qualities of his friend. Could she not overlook France's awkwardness and the obsequious contortions of the *séminariste?* Could she not gaze at the soul within? But it was precisely the soul within, 'animula, vagula, blandula,' that she found so uncertain. What she finally succumbed to was France's intelligence; and even so the process was gradual. Once more, Anatole's nonchalant persistence won the day; it won him much the same sort of comrade-mistress, in character, mind, and general role, that Voltaire had known in Madame du Châtelet.[75]

But for a long time things moved very slowly. It took months, even years, for Mme. de C. to get over her dislike of France's appearance and manners. After all, his social experience had been largely limited to his own kind. His persistence, thought Barrès, was due mainly to a desire for a wider recognition; and perhaps there was a touch of snobbery in his make-up. But he was undoubtedly attracted to this dynamic personality, so different from his own. 'Les France' were invited to the Avenue Hoche and even to the Caillavet estate, at Capian, near Bordeaux. It became evident that Mme. de C. took pleasure in Anatole's company, if only from the fact that she took much less in the presence of his wife. Valérie, she thought, needed badly to be mastered, and Léontine had little use for the writer's abjectness before his imperious spouse. The hostess was relieved when the couple departed. But later she frequently invited France (alone) to Capian, she saw more of him in Paris, and their correspondence increased between times. Anatole admires her letters for the sharp sense that they display; he complains that she does not write more frequently and fully. Presently the pair admit that they are bored when they cannot see each other; and Anatole goes so far as to say, 'there is nothing I fear so much as displeasing you, and there is nothing I desire so much as seeing you again.' Evidently, the affair is progressing.[76]

We shall consider later the various people with whom A.F. became acquainted through the Caillavet salon; but we may as well consider now (since some of the testimony dates from far back) the thorny problem of Mme. de C.'s influence on his character and his career. France's own view, *if* correctly reported, is fairly definite. He is said to have told Brousson that he was only a miserable librarian and scholar when 'Madame' singled him out. She gave him a home and habits of luxury, both of which as a 'delicate' writer, he had badly missed. (The last sentence is mostly bosh and agrees with nothing that has been said above regarding his domestic 'interior.') Is it true that he was only a hack-writer when 'discovered'—or that, as he says, in a certain flowery inscription to Mme. de C., he would have produced no books without her encouragement ? Such statements are great exaggerations. He had already written *Bonnard, Jean Servien,* and much of the *Livre de mon ami* before knowing Mme. de C., and he had taken his post on *Le Temps* before they became intimate. His powers of productiveness and his general happiness were maintained for some years by his *home.*[77]

On the other hand, it is true that he might well, but for this extraneous influence, have remained at the scholarly stage represented by Bonnard. He might never have ranked as a real novelist, nor become widely known. His Egeria connected him with important people, the masters of opinion. As an *éducatrice,* she was easily the first in her class. It is held that she brought him out, as Madame de Loynes brought out Lemaître, and that she even brought him to the doors of the Academy.[78] If this proves to be correct, it would be a triumph for Mme. de C. and for Anatole as well. The direct way led from Father's book-shop to the cupola of the Institute. That is a very short distance and easily traversed on foot. Is it characteristic of Anatole's indirect methods that he should go all the way round by the Etoile quarter ? But sometimes the longest way round is the shortest way there.

We should accept the view that in the way of worldly success, Mme. de C. did an 'immense' deal for France.[79] She liked to do things for those whom she befriended, and it must be admitted that she spared herself no pains. For one thing, it will appear that she fashioned for him an imposing mask which he could wear to advantage in society. For another, she helped make him harder, though this change (visible in the last two volumes of *La Vie littéraire*) [80] was primarily due to the rupture in his marital relations. But Mme. de C. was, to an unknown extent, responsible for this rupture. Before that, she had claimed him for her own, both as man and as 'lion.' The bargain was not too one-sided. She needed a great man for her salon, just as her rivals needed a centre for theirs. 'Elle affichait France.'

§ 12

ONE reason why Léontine capitulated, with gratitude, to Anatole was that for her sake he had deserted the drawing-room of one of those rivals, to wit, Mme. de Loynes. Even before this, both A.F. and Mme. de C. had deserted (the term is a bit strong) Mme. Aubernon. These triangular or polygonal intrigues take us into characteristically French complexities.

It was in the crucial year of 1886 that the old friendship, which was really a discipleship, between Mme. Aubernon and Mme. de Caillavet cooled off. The dominant spirit of the former lady and the independence of the latter form a sufficient explanation. Mme. de C. simply wanted her own galaxy, her own bright particular star. The alienation between Mme. du Deffand and Julie de Lespinasse has been cited as a parallel case, and there is a certain resemblance. In both instances, the more agreeable hostess carried off the *convives* of the other, who complained of ingratitude. But in the modern instance, the younger woman had not been brought up in the household of the other, nor did she exactly show disloyalty in leaving it. She simply grew bored with Mme. Aubernon—and so did Anatole. In *l'Univers illustré* he gives a gossiping account of a well-known salon-leader, who was, he says, depicted in Pailleron's *Le Monde où l'on s'ennuie*. She is very fat, and being the 'amie' of Academicians, she wears a violet dress to receptions at the Institute. This portrait, in the main, sufficiently resembles Mme. Aubernon, although it is rather Mme. de Loynes who stalks lions and Academicians in *Le Monde où l'on s'ennuie*.[81]

The last-named lady represented the third side of this feminine triangle. Mme. de Loynes was quite a different type from Mme. de Caillavet—of an older *souche,* probably more aristocratic, if less audacious. Léon Daudet, who belonged to the same political camp, credited her with directing the most important of the Nationalist salons, in the pre-war years. At any rate, she fostered two generations of writers and politicians, drew them out and won their confidence. More self-effacing than her rivals, she was yet capable of *bons mots,* no less witty than profound. The portrait by Amaury Duval (now in the Louvre) accentuates her delicate, wide-eyed and melancholy beauty. Her more formal dinners —we are told that hers was the 'best table in Paris'—took place on Friday and Sunday evenings at No. 152, Avenue des Champs-Elysées.[82]

Some say that it was Lemaître (the ubiquitous) who presented France to Mme. de Loynes, in 1885 ; others (notably Meyer) name Renan as the introducer. At any rate, it appears that the drowsy author of the *Vie de Jésus* could bestir himself sufficiently after dinner to applaud the rounded periods of Anatole in this salon. Under the wing of A.F. came the young Barrès, 'for to admire and to behold.' For a time it seems that France outshone Lemaître, to the latter's discomfiture, but soon the tangle was straightened out : Mme. de Caillavet took Anatole, and Mme. de Loynes, gracefully resigned, became the *amie* of Lemaître. Anatole ceased attending the Friday dinners of Mme. de Loynes, while Lemaître was rarely seen at the Wednesday receptions on the Avenue Hoche. The break between the two groups was destined to widen at the time of the Dreyfus affair.[83]

We have anticipated some events in our subject's 'private life.' Let us, in the next few chapters, retrace our steps to discover (partly through little-known channels), what France was revolving in his head and what issued from his pen during these momentous years.

CHAPTER XII

Productions of This Period

§ 1

ANATOLE'S literary labours, great and small, became rather complicated during this same decade. There were various periodicals that claimed his intermittent pen. As editor, historian, and writer of prefaces, he was not idle. Neither in this nor in the following period can we judge of his activity purely from his well-known works. Of these, there are half a dozen, representing three or four diverse strains. *Les Désirs de Jean Servien* (1882, but written earlier) recedes into another epoch ; it reflects the storm and stress of the early seventies and even of the author's adolescence. *Jocaste ; et le Chat maigre* (1879) are two novelettes which have touches of what a German critic calls the "humoristic-human" side of A.F.'s talent.[1] Again, both *Jean Servien* and *Jocaste* show him struggling with the more deterministic concepts of science. The sentimental vein, which we have found prevalent in his personal life, was the last to reveal itself in his work. It flows abundantly, of course, in *Le Crime de Sylvestre Bonnard* (1881) and in *Le Livre de mon ami* (1885). And in another form it appears in the children's stories of *Abeille* (already analyzed) and of *Nos enfants, scènes de la ville et des champs* (1887). On these two, M. Carias comments : 'The adventures of *Honey-Bee* form a royal cortège to the more rustic scenes of town and field.'[2]

This remark suggests that Anatole will be at his old game of dovetailing or morticing his themes. Moreover, none of the three strains mentioned above will be absolutely dominant in any given work. As usual, there will be admixtures and alternations of various kinds, to say nothing of counter-currents and *repentirs.*

§ 2

Subordinate only to the personal infiltrations into these writings would come France's maturing interest in *la science*—in the broadest sense of the word. This has already been mentioned and will require later development in connexion with his periodical articles.[3] Here we are concerned with the first outbreak of his enthusiasm for the scientific disciplines, under the guiding hands of Taine and Darwin.

His whole generation, Anatole significantly tells us, 'learned to read in the books of Darwin, Spencer, Taine.'[4] But for this kind of learning some preparation was necessary. In Pierre Nozière's youth, the time soon came when he regretted that the famous 'bifurcation' at college had impelled him away from science; he became aware that showy knowledge is one thing and the mind-building operations of the exact sciences are quite another; so he went to his father for help, and Dr. Nozière guided his steps in the directions of mathematics, chemistry, and natural history.[5] Probably this is applicable only in the most general way to Anatole. It is true that he describes himself as a 'young ass' for neglecting the sciences at Stanislas. But as for later guidance, it was certainly not Père France who furnished that—it was rather the *Zeitgeist.*

The reader will recall the scientific trend in Anatole's Parnassian creed and the extent to which Darwinism is developed in the *Poèmes dorés.* Yet it is difficult for us to realize how this 'revolutionary gospel,' when it was fresh and compelling, affected a whole generation. The very foundations of life and knowledge appeared to be shifted and settled for ever on a firmer basis. In French thought, 'transformism' had been running as a muddy 'underground current,' which Darwin clarified and canalized. The *Origin of Species* (1859, transl. 1862) was contemporary with the *Poèmes barbares* and similar manifestations. Leconte de Lisle was not exactly an enthusiast, but Anatole and others speak of the new revelation in apostolic terms. 'Darwin,' says Professor Stewart, 'had been his Bible and the Zoological Museum [in the Jardin des Plantes] a place to frequent as the devout frequent a sanctuary.' In the *Vie littéraire,* France himself declares that there had appeared, like a new Saviour, 'a man who liberated all mankind from needless terrors.' Discussions in the Luxembourg, gatherings at the Café Procope, centred round this new conception of the world, nay of the universe. For, as Ségur puts it, the 'marvellous spectacles provided by Darwin' brought us a light that penetrated into every corner of the cosmos. Furthermore: 'I could not be content with my morning until I had explained the universe itself.'[6]

Even in the retrospect, France recalls how this new hope dazzled his youth and how the vision of this blissful dawn led to a sort of mental delirium. From Darwinism was born not only a fresh conception of life, but fresh attitudes in poetry and the arts. 'Transformism' transformed everything.

> Then an intoxicating ferment filled the atmosphere which we breathed. The human imagination itself was renewed. Although predicted by others, the doctrine of Darwin had burst like a revelation. ... Charavay was humbled by the certainty of our descent from monkeys, but as for me, I was proud to think that in climbing up this spiral we might ultimately surpass the present status of mankind.[7]

Thus, in a sense, Anatole stood paradoxically 'on the side of the angels.' Evolution affected him first as a joyful deliverance, rather than as a materialized prison, shutting out celestial hopes. But, alas ! 'To these mornings of ardent illusions succeeded dull and disappointed evenings.' Not even Evolution could completely answer the riddle of existence. Around 1890, the 'bankruptcy' of science was proclaimed, and Symbolism appeared as an irrational refuge for those who were sick and satiated with unfulfilled promises. Once more, says Sherman, the millennium had been postponed.[8] Anatole never went so far as to accept the 'bankruptcy' idea and in the nineties he said some very wise things about what Science may yet give us, if we do not ask too much.[9] But a certain impatience with her votaries is evident in the *Livre de mon ami*. At present we are rather concerned with previous writings, where A.F. appears as still a devout disciple. In several periodical articles of the early eighties he expounds lengthily the theories of Lyell and Laplace, while in others he goes so far as to attribute a scientific *fonds* to the novels of George Sand and even to the nature-worship of the Rousseauists.[10] These were the days when Evolution was still his religion. Portions of the creed become articulate in two of his first three tales [11] — but the enthusiasm of the neophyte is replaced by the more sombre and restricting view which he assigns to Charavay. Anatole no longer consorts with the angels : he hobnobs with the surgeons.

It was natural for a mind steeped in the eighteenth century, in Voltaire, Diderot, and the Sensationalists, to accept the doctrines of Darwin and Spencer. It was equally natural for Anatole, surveying in the Zoological Museum the succession of the species, to hail Venus Genetrix as the sole creative force. It appears, too, that he became interested in physiology about this time and attended a medical clinic. To France, as to Renan before him, Science appeared for a time as a better support than anything else. It was not very long before this faith, as an Absolute, was shaken; the precepts of Laplace and of Darwin came to rest in the hinterland of his consciousness. Of *la Science,* in the French sense of exact and extensive knowledge, he continued to be a faithful adherent. He 'wanted to know everything' in his youth, and this *libido sciendi* was always unappeasable. In 1889, he wrote:

> I have practiced as much as anybody the cult of science. . . I have consecrated long, lovely hours to the study of the physical world. No theory of the universe, no new experiment concerning the constitution of matter or the laws of organic life has found me indifferent.

Michaut, in citing this passage, makes it clear that Anatole was less interested in the pure sciences than in those associated with man's destiny; while he may express notions about physiology or archæology, astronomy and physics, 'it is especially the history of mankind that attracts him.' France himself candidly told Gsell that his scientific 'baggage' was light enough, but that the essential thing was the impact of all the new discoveries upon the trained sensibility of a humanist.[12]

After Darwin, one should also reckon with the more immediate influence of Taine's determinism. France corresponded a little with this philosopher, read his works, and perhaps attended his lectures.[13] His system inspired among the young Parnassian group, as Anatole has recorded in an autobiographical leaf:

> . . . an ardent enthusiasm, a kind of religion, what I may call the dynamic cult of life. It brought us method and observation . . . science, in short. It delivered us from the abominable Victor Cousin and his abominable school. . . At that time we had in the Latin Quarter a strong feeling for the natural forces; and the books of Taine contributed much to put us into that state of mind. His theory of *milieux* made us marvel; and I was right in thinking it very fine and logical. . .

But then follows a characteristic *repentir.* Later he learned that several other theories are just as good (if not better); that nothing can lead us to the Absolute; that Taine's system, like all others, simply provides convenient categories for arranging data. With his inveterate habit of making his experiences climactic, Anatole qualifies this discovery as 'my second or third disillusionment in the matter of knowledge.'[14] One would think that a good many similar let-downs must have intervened between the death of old M. Hamoche and the 'debunking' of Taine.

The hard tension of the latter's outlook and manner doubtless affected the 'âcre et dur' tone of *Jean Servien,* which also expresses the theory of environment; more generally, the theory of Vitalism, outlined above, encouraged what Flaubert once called the supreme temptation—the Temptation of Matter.

§ 3

Of the productions nominally belonging to the eighties, there is one that reflects an earlier and quite different attitude. *Les Désirs de Jean Servien* was originally composed about 1872 and was subsequently much revised before publication.[15] There are thus few traces of the tone and feeling that characterize the *Livre de mon ami. Jean Servien* belongs to a more bitter and unsettled stage in France's development; and it depicts that stage with considerable fidelity. In fact, it is largely because of its strong autobiographical element that this unpopular first tale by A.F. is notable. For in fictional values proper, the book is mostly lacking—the hand of the tyro is evident.

As stated in a curious preface which France later suppressed, he turned to the contemporary scene because he had despaired of faithfully representing antiquity; and he indicates that the story has a modern psychological as well as a partially realistic trend. On the former basis, it was compared by Barrès to Flaubert's *l'Education sentimentale,* and even to *Madame Bovary;* the analogies with Bourget's *Le Disciple* are more apparent, for each novel deals with the perilous stuff in the head of its hero (as determining his fate), and each is impregnated with Taine's influence.[16]

But these distinguished comparisons are out of place, if they suggest that *Jean Servien* is a masterpiece. It is a thin, colourless, humourless tale, with few intrinsic virtues. The fact that it is slightly built, that the dramatic interest is meagre, is both characteristic and pardonable. But the chief personages, even the poor fate-ridden hero, are not stood on their feet, and the style is unformed and drab. Perhaps the latter feature is in accordance with the novel's realistic pretensions ; but it is none the less unpleasing. The book is written in what Giraud calls France's 'first' prose manner—even less individual than the *Notices* in *Le Génie latin*. There is no true creative fire. Consequently, this tale and *Jocaste* too have been fairly rated by Pellissier as 'incoherent and *baroque* narratives.'[17]

On the other hand, and this is what mainly concerns us here, *Les Désirs de Jean Servien* constitutes an Anatolian document of the highest significance. For straight information, it is to be preferred even to *Le Livre de mon ami*. 'Jean' is surely Pierre's *alter ego*—Pierre in difficulties and surrounded by dullness. Memories of Anatole's actual home environment, of Stanislas, and especially of his infatuation for Elise Devoyod, lend to the story what substance it may possess. Again, *Jean Servien* is the only novel in which the author reveals a recurrent disgust with his early surroundings and a desire to rise in a material society. During this phase, France reacted like a Balzacian 'climber,' and Bourget is right in speaking of his twenty-year-old imbroglios as including a 'crise de tentation balzacienne.' Furthermore, Taine's theory of *milieux,* combined with Anatole's own fatalism, causes Jean Servien's life and love to be quite conditioned by his narrow circumstances, together with the impacts of fortuitous encounters.[18]

It is not enough to speak of *Jean Servien* as semi-autobiographical. The book is definitely confessional, and Carias goes so far as to consider it the most personal of France's novels. According to others, divergent currents of a timid sensuality, or of proletarian sympathies, flow from the struggling author to the maladjusted hero.[19] Let us trace certain parallels between the two.

§ 4

DEPICTING as it does, 'the humble and scanty romance of his life,' the story tells simply how Jean Servien was brought up among the privations of the working-class ; how his schooling (especially in Latin) filled his head with dreams ; how an Italian scapegrace, Tudesco, turned up casually at each crisis, to misdirect Jean's life ; how the youth fell in love with the first actress he saw and how this love became a monomania, absorbing his every thought and impulse; how finally he was shot, almost by accident, among the horrors of the Commune.

Like Anatole Thibault, Jean was reared in a small shop. His father, a book-binder, was 'serious and meditative' like the elder France; although he could not understand his progeny, he was a more indulgent parent than Thibault:[20] he followed and encouraged his son's scholastic labours. Yet he too was worried because the youth would not adopt a profession. Later he opined that 'all those speeches and stories from the old Roman books have made my son's head-piece boil over.' Thus thought François Thibault also. And Bourget agrees with both fathers when he says that this novel reveals how Anatole's early readings had turned his head—'considerably disturbed his young sensibility.'[21]

The mother of Jean Servien died early; she resembled Anatole's mother in her gaiety, her affection for her child, and especially in the ambitions which she formed for him. It was owing to her dying wish that Jean learned Latin. There was also an aunt, who is 'visibly inspired by Madame Mathias'[22]—for she takes her charge out walking and chats with people of the neighbourhood. The realistic intention of the novel is exemplified partly by *tableautins* from the humble life of Paris. A street-dancing scene, the portrait of an old woman who sells gingerbread and gossips about incidents in the Quarter, a passage on the herd-instinct of the crowded thoroughfare, and the view from Belleville of the whole 'enormous and smoky city which had kindled the desires of Servien at the footlights of its theatres and nourished his fever in the dust of its traffic'—such are the details of the Parisian picture. At times Servien revolts against the restrictions of poverty, at times he appreciates and commiserates the laborious life of his father.[23] As a counterpart to his own dreaming nature, the lad's staunchest friend is a workman, Garneret, who has sensible views and a stout courage.

Familiar memories reappear: the plane-trees of the Luxembourg, the statues of the stately women 'like white phantoms' on the terrace, the chestnuts in the Tuileries. But the Paris of the Commune disgusts Jean as it disgusted Anatole. For a while the plebeian youth, through his hatred of the rich, desired and accepted the Commune; but soon he is revolted by its excesses. Like his hero, France himself was hustled by the seething crowd on a night of mob-violence.[24] The ironical nemesis of the story is that Servien is ultimately killed by the Communards, through the misinformation of a woman of the people.

It is in a narrow and cramping environment that Jean leads his small, stunted, haphazard life. Thus, the irony of maladjustment and the irony of misconception are both in evidence, and both have analogies with Flaubert. Again, among the ridiculous aberrations of the Commune is the idea of giving a position of leadership to the burlesque figure of the Marquis Tudesco. This old Bohemian and parasite is, unconsciously, a master-ironist. He is the first of a long line of semi-learned, semi-rapscallion cicerones and *raisonneurs;* the Abbé Coignard is his direct successor. I have suggested that Tudesco may stem from the Dufour-Victor genealogy; but M. Michaut is more probably right in relating him, first, to a crazy acquaintance of France's who wore bed-ticking in actual life and, secondly, to a demonstrative Italian whom Anatole had known in 1866.[25] At any rate, he is an inept vagabond, who manages at the same time to be the evil genius of the hero, through his habit of bobbing up as an absurd *deus ex machina.* His flow of verbiage, *à la* Micawber, impresses the bookbinder, who engages the Marquis as tutor for Jean. He is full of learned allusions and strong *liqueurs.* Replete, he is a perfect Silenus, and perhaps on that model he confers on Jean a 'lesson in transcendental philosophy,' to the effect that we are fools to pay attention to the views of others or to sacrifice a single one of our desires for 'l'opinion, cette maîtresse du monde.' This is one of the few places where Tudesco speaks in the vein of Bergeret.

It is under these auspices that Jean begins the study of Latin. Soon, like 'Pierre,' he adapts his learning to his temperament. He fails in a state-examination because he spells badly; but he dreams in the wake of Euripides and of Shakespeare; he too has visions of Cleopatra sailing the Cydnus on her gold and scarlet barge, and he reads Sophocles as an escape from the classroom. The actual event of Anatole's reading Virgil on the ramparts is closely reproduced. Jean and Garneret are listening to the thunder of the Prussian guns, while Jean translates the 'delicious' chant of Silenus and remarks how well the passage illustrates the 'serious and tender soul of Virgil.' Garneret, the scientific workman, observes rather how the eclogue anticipates Laplace and Lyell on the formation of the globe. Anatole's accounts of the real incident show that Fernand Calmettes was the original of Garneret, at least as far as this episode is concerned.[26]

Jean Servien also had his Stanislas, or rather two of them. After a brief training in a primary school near the Luxembourg, he was promoted to a *Lycée* where his Latin themes were occasionally praised. 'His versions were less remarkable for exactness than for elegance.' He too had an early *crise* of æsthetic religiosity, accompanied by a taste for edifying legends and saints' lives. This *motif* was paralleled later by the experience of Firmin Piédagnel, already recorded. Jean took his baccalaureate at the age of eighteen, which is approximately what Anatole should have done. Presently, he became a *pion* or usher in a certain 'aristocratic and religious institution,' which bears many of the earmarks of Stanislas. The director was the elderly 'Abbé Bordier,' who was chiefly occupied with composing sacred tragedies—very like the real Abbé Lalanne, on whom he was probably modelled. Both 'Pierre' and Jean hated the discipline of the school and the odours of the refectory ; both sought refuge in dreams from the routine ; both were humiliated and angered by the attention paid to aristocratic pupils.

But the book is primarily a depiction of Anatole's Romantic phase. The adolescent Jean is also abundantly endowed with

> desires and adorations,
> Wingèd Persuasions and veiled Destinies.

He was superior to his comrades through his imagination. He entered early the world of Illusion, the 'perpetual miracle' which transformed his surroundings and his toys into marvellous things. This dream-world was wonderfully enlarged by an excursion to the fair of Saint-Cloud, in the company of a schoolmate and his mother. The description of the fair anticipates Anatole's frequent descriptions of the 'fête de Neuilly,' in *l'Univers illustré*.[27] But amid the riot of these popular pleasures, Jean 'saw only his dreams, full of elegant, absurd and noble images.' Later, the memory of a lovely face combined with the reading of Corneille 'were sufficient to keep him in a state of beautiful illusion. An image and a few sounds—that was his world.' Still later he had visions of all the seductive and sorrowful heroines of literature : Ophelia and Marguerite, Phèdre and Manon became visible, then vanished all too soon. He mused upon magnificent and voluptuous tragedies, or (like Rousseau) upon a châtelaine wandering under crenelated towers. He indulged in reveries and began to cultivate luxurious tastes. As Anatole said on another occasion, there might be a rude awakening from such visions. These 'imaginative adolescents,' who dreamily mingle sensuousness and emotion, are subject to unusual perils. And it's a cruel thing, when one has caressed the shade of Cleopatra, to be turned down by a scatter-brained *midinette*.[28]

But of all these elements the most significant are naturally the 'désirs de Jean Servien.' The word is used as a *leit-motif*. Not one of our yearnings should be sacrificed, Tudesco prologizes, and presently Jean tells him tumultuously of all his 'dreams and desires.' They emanate alike from the vision of his lady-love or from the lady in person. The key-note of the book seems to be the bitter query hurled at Fate : 'What inept and brutal god had immured in poverty his soul so rich in desires ?' For actually none of them can be consummated, and the seamy side of Romanticism is the 'bitter something' that comes from unfulfilled longings no less than from their achievement.

A similar emphasis on Desire, the word and the thing, is found in Anatole's other writings and naturally in his personal life. The more rosy, as well as the darker side, is contemplated. On the one hand, 'le désir est triste' ; and that view would seem to be borne out by the analogies which Lemaître traces between Anatole's youth and that of Jean Servien. Each underwent :

a hard and poverty-stricken youth, with absurd loves, with *disproportionate desires,* with wild aspirations towards a brilliant and noble life . . . disillusionment . . . bitterness.[29]

But the author of *La Vie en fleur* maintains that this very poverty caused him to keep intact the one priceless gift, which resides at the heart of beauty and constitutes the charm of nature— 'le Désir.' Pierre's innocent passion for Mlle. Mérelle taught him that infinite unconscious desire brings with it a perfect joy, for this yearning is its own fulfillment. Pierre must have learned better later on . . . Yet the youth stoutly maintains that 'living is desiring,' even if one only craves a drum ; and, speaking for Anatole, he declares that this force has ruled his whole life : 'I can say that my existence has been but one long desire ; I love both the joys and the sufferings which it brings. To want anything earnestly is almost to possess that thing.' France himself doubts retrospectively whether he had worked out that philosophy at the age of ten. But few have been found to doubt that it ultimately became a corporate part of him. Michaut demonstrates this at length; the final sentence in his critical study concludes that France's work as a whole 'est vouée au Désir et à la Volupté.' So the very title of our story serves as a prelude to a complete orchestral development.[30]

The entrance of the actress into Jean's life is prepared for, as with Pierre-Anatole, by a certain amount of minor *Schwärmerei.* 'A woman passes'—and she leaves with the lad of seven the memory of a perfume sweet as a caress. This resembles Pierre's experiences with the lady in white and with Marcelle. Like his awakening by Mme. Gance is Jean's expedition to Saint-Cloud with Madame Ewans, whose coiffure seemed to him mysterious and beautiful, who first revealed to him the delight of a woman's nearness, but who, alas! was displeased by his awkwardness as a dancer and turned the sweetness into gall. Thus she awakened within him class-hatred and disgust with the chill penury that froze his noble rage.

It will be recalled how Anatole was once rewarded by his parents with his first theatre-party and how he immediately fell in love with Isabelle Constant. He generalized the experience by saying later that for him actresses were a sublimation of living beauty and that 'as a youth I could never distinguish the real person from her ideal roles.'[31] Much the same thing happened to Jean Servien, who celebrated his baccalaureate by seeing 'Gabrielle T—' playing Emilie in Corneille's *Cinna.* Avidly his eyes devoured her classic costume, her beautiful bare arms, her lips . . . here was living loveliness offered as a spectacle, and he wanted immensely to seize Gabrielle and carry her away, intact in her role.

Thus, in each case it was 'love at first sight' for a heroine of the stage. And several of the details correspond, both in fact and in fiction. But we have seen that Anatole felt still more strongly about another actress, who dominated his youth and his love-poems. Elise Devoyod has already been described as a *tragédienne,* the successor of Rachel; she played with dignity the parts of Phèdre and of Agrippine.[32] Both in Anatole's poems and in *Jean*

Servien the part of Emilie is also assigned to the inamorata ; and in both the lover deposits an awkward kiss on the thin arm of the actress. The Devoyod had thin arms ; her biographers have shown that she played in nearly all the roles in which Anatole glorified her fictional counterpart. Both women were tall, perhaps a little ungainly ; both rode horseback astride, 'en amazone.'[33] Soon after the appearance of his confessional novel, the author alluded casually, in a journal article, to a Racinian heroine as rendered, he 'believes,' by Mme. Devoyod.[34] As if he wouldn't know ! It is evident, from various sources, that Anatole's passion for Elise underlies the love-story in *Jean Servien.*

The vision of 'Gabrielle' produced in Jean, of course, endless dreams which he prolonged with *volupté.* The obsession is gradually developed, in a fashion recalling Stendhal's theory of crystallization, by associating her form with everything that is beautiful or interesting: he links her with 'all the representations of art and luxury' in the Exposition of 1867 ; and the poets are unconsciously filled with allusions to her charms. He sees her in many roles, of whose splendour she is the incarnation, he reads great plays, 'and in all these creations he saw only one image' ;[35] if he throws himself with surprising zest into amateur theatricals, it is because that seems to bring him nearer to Gabrielle and her profession ; she is mingled with the mutter of the mass, with the softening effect of incensed religiosity—once more, 'la religion a donné aux amants une volupté de plus . . .'

Yet in all this there is only frustration, only the passion of a schoolboy, excluded, awkward, unhappy. He has watched Gabrielle on the stage many times, he has confessed to Tudesco his *grande passion,* before he attempts at all to seek out and know the actual woman. To bring him to that point, there is required the stimulus of hearing ordinary gossip about her from an old family friend—even as Anatole heard the plain truth about Isabelle Constant. Note that Jean is not discouraged or disgusted when he learns that Gabrielle has a lover. The theory of fatality comes in : 'We love because we love and in spite of everything.' In similar vein, Anatole remarked concerning his first theatrical night, 'there happened what was bound to happen—no one escapes his destiny.' So he insists in his later years that in love-affairs every one wins salvation as best he can.[36] When the stout Garneret presently tries to persuade Jean that a woman is only a woman, he is yet forced to admit the uniqueness of each woman's charm for one particular person. It is like Paganini and his special Stradivarius. A similar analogy is used in *l'Ile des Pingouins.*

But poor Jean is no Paganini. When he desperately waylays Gabrielle at her gate, he has no convincing manner of approach ; he bruises her hand, and the barrier is closed in his face. In his humiliation he begins to hate her violently, realistically—the *amari aliquid* again. When he actually sees that impossible person called Bargemont and learns that he is now the 'protector' of Gabrielle, Jean falls fainting on his sweetheart's staircase. Excessive emotion and disillusion bring on a grave illness, after which she becomes a dear phantom, a *pâle souvenir,* just as his own life seems about to fade away.

That is how the youth was affected by love—the 'dim little monosyllable.' In proportion to the frustration was the deep searing of desire and memory. We may judge that Anatole himself was similarly seared and probably frustrated ; for of all his books this comes nearest to depicting his soul-state as a young man. Truly the poignant farewell to Jean Servien and 'his fair locks that a mother had kissed with so much love' is also the farewell to Anatole's own Romantic ego. Incidentally, it is possible that the 'strange' fair-haired figure of Clément Sibille, Pierre's old schoolmate, sat for the physical portrait of Jean.[37]

§ 5

THE three tales written in the seventies (*Jean Servien, Jocaste,* and *Le Chat maigre*) all bear witness to another tendency which accompanied the scientific revival of this period—I mean the drift toward Realism in fiction. Flaubert's last works, Maupassant's first *contes,* the oncoming of the Goncourts and of Zola would help account for France's rather sudden and uncharacteristic interest in *tableaux* of low life or depictions of the shabby-genteel, as well as certain pathological preoccupations. (Specific parallels between *Jean Servien* and Daudet's *Le Petit Chose* are also suggested by M. Michaut.) Anatole's method of treatment in this early fiction is still objective, however autobiographical the material may be. In this respect he remains Parnassian, although he has temporarily abandoned antiquity and turned to the contemporary spectacle. There is still almost no hint of the personal and engaging manner of the eighties. The descriptions are treated in the minute and enumerative fashion inaugurated by Balzac.[38]

If *Jean Servien* is the first-written of France's novels, *Jocaste* is his first *nouvelle,* or long short-story. It was published together with *Le Chat maigre* in 1879. The two tales are certainly linked, not only because of their realistic and semi-scientific features, but because they are both small chronicles of their day. In fact, there are those (e.g., Wyzewa) who hold that all the stories of this period are more or less chronicles. From the beginning, the author shows his dislike for large enterprises and his preference for limited objectives. Another characteristic of these inventions, it is held by Pellissier, is that they are not *raisonnables*: they all lean to the depiction of the fantastic and the half-mad. In 1902, Anatole wrote unsparingly of *Jocaste—et le Chat maigre* as 'ill-inspired, awkward, truncated and altogether damned. The first is even more execrable than the second, unless it be the other way around.' [39] Let us see.

As the title implies, *Jocaste* is the story of a woman who becomes involved in the death of her husband. In fact, there are several murders in this gruesome little yarn, which also lugs in complications about missing heirs and is therefore more conventionally melodramatic than is usual with its author. Hélène Fellaire has come to love, almost unwittingly, René de Longuemare, a young surgeon. But he leaves for China, and she is persuaded by a fussy though affectionate father to marry the banker Haviland, an eccentric Englishman. This husband grows more singular and more obsessed by his manias; he also becomes feebler in health, since he is gradually poisoned by a servant named Groult. Longuemare returns; he and Hélène realize that they are profoundly in love. The gruesome Groult is dismissed from service, but Hélène allows her husband to continue taking the dangerous medicine. After his death, she grows remorseful and finally hangs herself in a bathing-establishment.[40] The melodrama and crimes of this action might have 'waked to ecstasy Gaboriau.'

As usual in Anatole's fiction we rise through an ascending scale of values, with the plot on the ground-level. In the entresol are the characters. On the *piano nobile* are graciously installed the fair forms of his general and personal ideas.

The characters here are not without interest, if we except the old cold Englishman, who is interesting only to himself. M. Michaut is right in remarking that this 'conventional islander' seems worthy of the pen of a caricaturist rather than of Anatole France.[41] It may be noted that like some of A.F.'s other creations, to say nothing of their creator, Haviland has a mania for collecting ; select vials in which repose, carefully stoppered, choice specimens from the waters and rivers of all the earth, seem to meet his mental needs. (Chateaubriand, in his *Itinéraire,* had mentioned his practice of drinking from all the famous rivers that he had crossed, from the Mississippi to the Tagus.) Otherwise the 'islander' is precise, silent, and inept even in his own affairs. Across from him at table sits a lady, his exact opposite. She is indolent and voluptuous and has been marked by these traits from childhood. Naturally, she drifted into a rich marriage, having been brought up with a precocious taste for luxury and sensual sloth. Yet, like her creator, she has a kind of imaginative sensitiveness. Consequently, she is very suggestible. This appears in the scene where an oral translation of Sophocles causes her to see herself as a modern Jocasta and leads to her suicide. The title of the story refers us back to the *Œdipus Rex;* but it has been pointed out that 'biological fate' has replaced the ancient Erinyes.[42]

Hélène's father, the best realized character in the novel, is a broker of expansive nature and loose habits. Like Tudesco, he has the gift of infinite verbosity, which spills in the direction of bourgeois claptrap and sentimentalities. Verbose about his food and wine, about his affections and family troubles, he calls himself 'romantic at bottom.' He offers a neat contrast to his strange son-in-law, who presently closes the door against him. That does not prevent M. Fellaire from attending Haviland's funeral and alluding to him reminiscently as a perfect son and gentleman.

René Longuemare is a scientific surgeon who accepts Darwin and quotes Bichat. Anatole himself had recently been following the physiological clinic of a certain Dr. Péan ; and Longuemare is the author's mouthpiece as regards materialistic philosophy.[43] We are prepared for this from the beginning of the book, where the violent young medico discourses largely on frogs, on his 'experimental theory of suffering,' on the silliness of the Stoics who denied sensation. (Yet René, too, seeks protection in a kind of ironical Stoicism.) Later he launches a fleet of epigrams, of which the first is adapted from Taine :

Virtue is a product, like phosphorus and vitriol.
Heroism and holiness result from a congestion of the brain.
Only general paralysis can make great men.
The gods are adjectives.

René's deterministic view of the cosmos is that 'nature is the scene of eternal carnage, and nothing lives except by slaughter and rapine.'

'You go entirely too far,' said M. Fellaire.

Yet several of these *maximes* became part of Anatole's stock in trade.

After the loss of Hélène, the surgeon remains glum and brutish on his father's farm. Presently he returns to experimenting with frogs; and ultimately he discovers that he has a liver-complaint and notes his symptoms with satisfaction. This is an example of the kind of realism that dips readily and curiously into pathological details. Instances may be recalled from Balzac, Zola, and especially the Goncourts. In *Jocaste,* pathology is further displayed in connexion with the illness and death of Haviland, the nervous condition of Hélène, and her hanging, as well as her love-symptoms. Toward her husband, she goes through singular alternations between hatred and tenderness.

But Anatole's talent does not lend itself easily to clinical realism. Nor is he convincing in exhibiting another brand, that which deals with the small and ugly detail, although this pursuit left results on his future work. Examples of such details are to be found scattered through *Jocaste* and they predominate in the opening pages of *Le Chat maigre.* (They may be typified by the evil-smelling much-bitten cigar which M. Fellaire leaves on the edge of a table.) Let us grant, however, a certain effectiveness in the author's way of 'isolating' a small fact, in order to make it stand out.[44] Still more characteristic and acceptable are the frequent little pictures of Paris, whose 'light,' whether falling on the dome of the Invalides or picking out with dazzling clearness various objects in the street, is again lovingly described. There is a vivid presentation of that famous Parisian scene done by so many novelists, namely the drive to the Bois de Boulogne. There is the funeral of Haviland, a depiction well-focussed around M. Fellaire. In another vein, there is the gracious gesture of Hélène, when she raises her arms like the handle of an amphora—a simile repeated in the *Histoire contemporaine.* There is also a brief reminiscence of the Collège Stanislas, whither young Georges Haviland is sent and where he learns to mimic his professors and do rapid versions from the classics, with his tongue in his cheek—all very Anatolian.

Several of the personages and descriptions cannot fail to recall Dickens, whom France then considered 'one of the most powerful creative writers of the century.' M. Michaut points out that A.F. strives for the 'colour and humour' of Dickens; that his heroine's father is a kind of Micawber, while Groult has traits in common with Jeremy Flintwich. The same critic finds other analogies with *Little Dorrit,* as well as with *Our Mutual Friend.* The suicide of Mr. Merdle or of Ralph Nickleby—not to mention that of Monpavon in Daudet's *Le Nabab*—may have suggested the similar end of Hélène.[45]

It is true that A.F. pays tribute to the author of *David Copperfield,* not only in the preface to this volume, but in passages from other works.[46] Whether or not one accepts all the resemblances suggested by Michaut, Anatole was then evidently 'under the spell' of the English magician. In *Sylvestre Bonnard,* no less than in our two novelettes, the peculiar mingling of sentiment and humour recalls Dickens as well as Sterne. Some think that the delicate whimsicality of the latter is the more conspicuous influence.[47]

However that may be, it is clear that A.F. occasionally breaks out with 'l'humour anglais'—which the French, as curious aliens, love to analyse.[48] They point out that he will surprise you by juxtaposing dissonances: the comic elbowing the beautiful; a heavy weight of erudition surrounding a triviality. But Stapfer holds that even in such a juxtaposition, France will maintain his sense of classical harmony and measure. These are qualities that his English counterparts disregard. Perhaps, then, *l'humour* is on the whole less pronounced in Anatole than the more Gallic quality of irony. For how does Mr. Chevalier define this Irony? It is 'the perception of incongruities on an extensive scale'—not merely verbal, but implicit in the situation, in the material, in life itself. The addiction to ironic undertones is a growing habit with France. In some tales (*Jocaste*) it is well balanced by sympathy; in others (*Le Chat maigre*) irony predominates.[49]

§ 6

Le *Chat maigre,* a slight and inconsequent little tale, yet offers some points of interest. Although the scene is laid nominally around Montmartre,[50] where the 'escapades' usually occur, yet the reminiscences are more clearly associated with the left bank. The realistic descriptions of ugliness are still found: e.g., the picture of the 'hill' of Montmartre on a rainy, muddy evening, or that of the mulatto's dingy room—even the famous Parisian *lumière* is soiled before reaching this abode. The story is concerned largely with the people and the affairs of Haiti, on which the author had 'documented' himself, as a good realist should. We wonder why Anatole should introduce various personages from Port-au-Prince into the story and cause the plot to revolve around them. To understand this choice we must drift back to Father's book-shop and perceive how Son applied the law of least effort. When he tells us in *Le Globe* that he read nearly everything written on Haiti, we get the impression that a considerable energy was expended. But as a matter of fact, Anatole hardly needed to leave his father's (or rather now Honoré Champion's) domain. For Père France had not only dealt in works on the Revolution: he had acquired as well a fairly complete collection of publications dealing with the colonies; and old catalogues show that Haiti was not neglected. It was probably this circumstance that originally suggested to A.F. the background for *Le Chat maigre.*[51]

One purpose served thereby is that we have a satiric account of the founding of the Haitian 'Empire,' a visible parody on that of Napoleon III. Another result is that the divagations of the Quarter are approached partly from the standpoint of a fresh young foreigner, indolently 'studying' in Paris, and are seen through his eyes. This recalls Montesquieu's *Lettres persanes* with its countless imitations. The picture of life *à la* Murger is apparently faithful and certainly amusing—the Bohemian side of Anatole has full play. The inevitable group of 'artists' foregathers at the *brasserie* which is called 'Le Chat maigre.' This use of a sign-board as a book-title is paralleled by Balzac's *La Maison du Chat-qui-pelote* and by France's own *Rôtisserie de la Reine Pédauque.* That he was interested in such names is evidenced by articles in *l'Univers illustré,* where he mentions a number of them in Montmartre, including *Le Chat noir,* where Caran d'Ache held sway.[52]

The frequenters of the place, according to the avowal of the author and the consensus of opinion, are mostly madmen. They indulge in the wildest pranks and burlesques. A mystification of Baudelaire's is imitated ; Villiers de l'Isle-Adam is parodied ; there is even what Schaffer calls a 'take-off on the Parnassian cliques and their ephemeral periodicals.' Doubtless France had known many similar incidents and personages.[53]

The actual types include a sculptor who never gets down to work, because he always feels the need of vast preliminary readings ; also a deliquescent poet and a philosopher who evolves the most fantastic myths from his inner consciousness. We sniff again the smoke-laden atmosphere of the *brasserie,* we lounge across the bridges and into the Bal Bullier. When one of these impractical creatures receives a legacy of 300 francs, the group plans to found a journal, which reminds us of the author's Project for an Encyclopedia of the Revolution. It has been pointed out that these Bohemians are like the *ratés* in Daudet's *Jack*.[54] They are full of the usual slogans and paradoxes : they talk of the 'miserable epoch' in which we live, a modern Diderot declares that creative art must be brutal, while one industrious painter, bored by the intruding sun, calls it 'ce sacré bibelot.' It is part of the *Vie de bohème* that the young Haitian should fall in love with his neighbour across the way—a typical window-sill flirtation.

He presently pursues her to Avranches, where we have recollections of Anatole's previous visits—the festivals, and the archæology of Mont-Saint-Michel. But before this, the student has been confided to a fellow-countryman, a very casual tutor, who, although the portrait is humorous rather than satiric, recalls the irresponsible Tudesco ; he also anticipates the genial Abbé Coignard.[55] M. Godet-Laterrasse talks about the 'fundamental classics,' but he rarely frequents their company. After taking his pupil to a book-shop on the Quai Voltaire—again, it might have been the 'Père France' book-shop—he is careful to leave the youth to his own devices.

Apart from such reminiscences and the setting, the story seems rather pointless, though it has amusing touches of fantasy. One of these is the dog, Miragoane, who as an intelligent listener foreshadows M. Bergeret's Riquet. The dog, in fact, seems more intelligent than the humans. That is probably part of the sardonic intention of the author, who, in his preface, called the story a 'petite chronique . . . où il n'y a que des fous.' He pays his mocking compliments to all theorizers, whether 'philosophic, æsthetic or political.'[56] On the whole it is not surprising that the volume containing *Jocaste et Le Chat maigre* had but a limited success with the reading public.

§ 7

The remaining works of this period usually exploit the sentimental vein which Anatole developed some time after his marriage. Several of the tales in later volumes (*Balthasar* and *l'Etui de nacre*) also hark back to this second manner—a manner, be it remembered, naturally linked with the temporary conservatism of his thought. For France's 'virility,' as M. Seillière has pointed out,[57] 'marched on the paths of traditional morality and social conformity.'

The incomparable *Crime de Sylvestre Bonnard* was his first real success. The story of this is too well known to require a lengthy analysis, but one may dwell on the more characteristic features. *Bonnard* includes two parts, of which the first, *La Bûche,* was published serially in 1880,[58] thus following close upon *Le Chat maigre*. But what a different inspiration! An old savant does a deed of kindness to a young mother and is rewarded, years afterwards, when as a Lady Bountiful she presents him with a coveted manuscript of Voragine's *Golden Legend*. As for the second part, *Jeanne Alexandre,* this was originally called *La Fille de Clémentine;* for in the first version it was the daughter and not the grand-daughter of his old sweetheart whom the scholar rescued from a hateful *pension* and finally betrothed to Gélis, the promising student. Such is the 'crime' of Sylvestre Bonnard, whose figure is the only link between the two stories. Consequently they 'do not hang together,' as Taine was one of the first to perceive. The linking was even less evident in the first edition; for a revision of 1902 the author made many thoroughgoing changes,[59] enhancing thereby the style and the general treatment.

But even in 1881 Taine had praised the 'vieux philosophe' both for his soul and for his style. As a character, Bonnard is in part derivable from the *Abbé Daniel* of Theuriet, which has a very similar plot.[60] To a greater degree, he is modelled, as a philologist and a product of the Ecole des Chartes, upon Etienne Charavay. The author 'reveals a perfect knowledge of whatever concerns that learned establishment.'[61] Conversations with Charavay and Camille Pelletan gave France the groundwork not only for the similar discourses of Gélis and his comrades, but for much of the technical erudition displayed. It seems that the personality of Charavay also served to some extent as the 'prototype' of Bonnard. But more evidently the old scholar is a projection of Anatole himself into the future. And not necessarily into the far future; not too 'vieilli,' says Lemaître; Anatole at thirty-seven, having spent all his young manhood in reading, loitering, and flirting with literature, might readily, 'to fame unknown,' have sunk into the slippered ease of Bonnard; it was the success of 'Bonnard' that in part prevented this consummation. Now that the author and his type are alike ageless, they seem more and more to merge into one person.

One of the most fully rounded of Anatole's characters, the eccentric Sylvestre sits bemused in his 'Cité des livres,' to wit, his library. (The phrase, which was formerly applied to the rich collections of the Mont-Saint-Michel and other abbeys, is found in a certain *Itinéraire* which France probably knew.)[62] The scholar's name may derive from that of Sylvestre Boulard, a bibliographer and mayor of the sixth *arrondissement* under the Empire. In that same quarter our Sylvestre leads his sedentary life. He is served by the grumbling, devoted, and despotic Thérèse, a sort of female Caleb Balderstone; he is attended by the lordly and 'voluptuous' Hamilcar, whom he apostrophizes as the cat of all cats, assuming his intelligence as M. Bergeret does that of his dog. Erudite is the Cité des livres in its contents and traditions. Are not elderly savants reckoned by such critics as Larroumet and Barrès as being among Anatole's favourite characters? Is not Sylvestre a partial sketch of France himself, 'reduced to the limits of his library'?[63] An ardent philologist, of the school of Paulin Paris, M. Bonnard is not too old-fashioned to appreciate the incisive manner of *les jeunes*—such as M. Paul Meyer! But he has dwelt with words, words, words, until he perceives everything across a verbal veil. Among words piled into cherished volumes he has dreamed his life away. Pathetically he enumerates his treasures when he is selling them to provide Jeanne with a dowry. Though a medievalist, Bonnard's culture has covered many epochs. Anatole's favourites reappear by allusion or quotation: among them are Homer, the Antigone myth ('O sainte lumière!'), Virgil and Horace (the Leuconoë poem). At one period, Bonnard 'had commerce only with the ancients.' But in the course of the narrative he revels also in saints' lives and legends, the glory of a *princeps,* echoes of Racine and Renan. The last name leads us further into the question of the book's sources.

It has been demonstrated that the description of Sicily, probably the names of Gellias and Polizzi, even the Virgilian quotation with which the old savant embarks on his journey, derive from Renan's *Vingt Jours en Sicile.*[64] It would be natural for Bonnard to remember his Renan; they are of the same stock. Yet an Italian thinks that the wine-merchant 'Michelangelo Polizzi,' is less closely connected with Renan's guide of that surname than with a certain distinguished archæologist, Raffaello Politi. The latter's works (among others) may have helped to give Anatole the knowledge of the two Sicilies with which he is credited.[65] However that may be, it seems that the choice of 'Mlle. Préfère' as the name of the schoolmistress was very simple. A.F. suggested several possibilities to his wife, who hesitated and said, 'Je préfère. . .' Whereupon Anatole took her up and 'Préfère' it was. In an elaborate article, M. Huard indicates, along with other 'influences livresques,' where Anatole got his description of the manuscript given to the scholar.[66]

Apart from such erudite matters, there is the fictional development. We may bear in mind that the plot interest is but slight: *La Bûche* is an anecdote, and *Jeanne Alexandre* a sentimental episode. Now certain touches in either one may be taken from Daudet. Furthermore, M. Vandérem considers that both *Bonnard* and *Le Livre de mon ami* show decided traces of such English humorists as Fielding, Sterne and (once more) Dickens.[67] Of the last-named, France imitates 'the humoristic details, the comic stresses, the *fun.*' It seems probable, indeed, that the wooing of M. Bonnard by Mlle. Préfère has analogies with the famous case of Bardell *vs.* Pickwick. There is the same sentimental insistence on the lady's part, while the gentleman experiences the terrors of the threatened male; and the smug shyster called in by the plaintiff is much alike in both stories. Indeed, one critic declares that the whole book is 'impregnated with the spirit of Dickens,' which is going rather too far.[68]

What of the small fairy whom Sylvestre sees in his drunken dream? The description of her may proceed from certain eighteenth-century reminiscences, of the kind that later produced the sylph in *La Rôtisserie de la Reine Pédauque;* M. Mornet thinks of *La Poupée* by Bibiena; M. Michaut recalls rather About's *Le Roi des Montagnes.* Doubtless other echoes could be found, for Anatole, as M. Potez points out, is like a marauding bee; 'the flowers have grown pretty much everywhere; but the honey is M. France's own.'[69]

The type of learning thus refracted has now become an 'érudition souriante et ailée.' We find no more the rather heavy hand of the schoolboy and the youthful traveller. The author moves about easily in his scholar's livery. The quality of this learning is not strained. That is, fine points and minute accuracy are not Anatole's forte. Let Charavay attend to such matters and go after the documents. Then A.F. will arrange the results artistically, relying upon his general information and penetration.[70] Perhaps that is better than being a pure *érudit.* But, as Bonnard proves, France was well acquainted with specimens of that type and stood close enough to it personally to depict it at more length than any one else had done.[71]

What sort of figure does Sylvestre cut and wherein does he reflect his creator? In his essential philosophy, this quaint original is primarily wise and serene. 'René Longuemare,' says Lemaître, 'has become calmer with age.' Gentle irony, tolerant scepticism, impracticality, and a dilettantism which approaches the range of France himself—such are the chief traits of our modest and contemplative scholar.[72] Very appropriately, Bonnard lives on the Quai Malaquais, he enjoys and delineates the view of the river and the right bank so familiar to Anatole—and, parenthetically, he is a member of the Institute. But there are serious drawbacks, he perceives, in a studious life. The race of savants is infirm, bald, and subject to colds. Like A.F. himself, they are also subject to 'distractions' which are not appreciated in social circles. And are their learned labours really worth while? On the one hand, the effort that scholars make to preserve the memory of dead things is a 'vain and painful effort.' The fairy who treats the old gentleman lightly and tickles his nose—she was the kind of *mutine* fairy beloved from boyhood—declares that 'M. Sylvestre Bonnard is just a little pedant.' Nevertheless he knows that he really has contributed to 'that renaissance of historical labours which will remain the honour of this uneasy age.' But the downright young Gélis (France's other self) holds that history is readable only when it is false, that it is impossible as a science and mendacious as an art. His indictment of Michelet, together with Bonnard's own view, may be compared with Anatole's other utterances regarding the Romantic historian.[73] Although scholarship evinces a 'noble curiosity' (an echo of Montesquieu), the philologist becomes disillusioned about research after his illness and demonstrates how 'the very progress of the sciences renders useless the works that have contributed most to that progress.' In a word, Anatole is at his old game of *pro* and *con*. The fact that there is more *con* than *pro* would perhaps suggest that he has penetrated to the inmost recesses of the student's heart. . . Like both the Thibaults, Sylvestre finds that there is no more attractive and gentle reading than that of catalogues. He too is a *badaud,* a *bouquiniste* in love with the quays and the monuments of old Paris. Finally, like Michelet, Bonnard turns amorously to flowers and insects in his last stage—a proof, as Mornet suggests, that sentiment may at times be mingled with science. But Huard tells us that this veering, or semi-retreat, on the part of the old savant was again suggested by Renan.[74]

There are other things than learning in the book: there are interwoven philosophies, with beauty-worship paramount; there are souvenirs and sentiment, relieved by a delicious humour.

When the old gentleman goes off to the Two Sicilies in search of his precious manuscript (which all the time was for sale in the Rue Lafitte), the spectacle of Neapolitan pleasure-making convinces him, rather belatedly, that such Horatian pursuits as wine and songs, Leuconoë and love, form the only philosophy suitable to the realities of life. The beauty of Sicily, the lure of its myrtles and marbles, awakens in him memories of Ceres and of Arethusa. In other places and seasons, he is moved, in passing, by the high-sounding verses of the Pléiade, or by a pastel of a lady of long ago, or by a baby with dimples laughing in the rosy flesh. When the baby's mother sends him the manuscript of the

Golden Legend, a shower of violets falls out of the book, and that was a 'belle et rare folie.' The indulgent philosopher is convinced that education, too, should be largely a matter of beauty and delight, thus recalling Fénelon and anticipating *Le Livre de mon ami.* 'We are on this earth,' the Platonist tells the methodical notary, 'to take pleasure in the beautiful and the good. . .' So he would bring up Jeanne to learn joyfully and to be responsive to all fine and fair things, whether in poetry or landscape or human experience. M. Carias thinks that with France the æsthetic sense was more spontaneous than with Bonnard.[75]

Especially is his sense of beauty stirred in connexion with the memory of Clémentine whom Sylvestre loved as a youth. Since he has become old—and this is good psychology—it is a calm, untroubled memory, even when he stands by her tomb. But he brings back the fresh and tender vision of the girl in her red hood, with her violet eyes; he apostrophizes her as Anatole always addresses the objects of his deepest interest. Along with Clémentine, souvenirs of 'Pierre's' own boyhood come crowding back. Her father, a survival of the eighteenth century in his Voltairian royalism; replicas of Anatole's parents, the gracious happy mother, the aloof father; the episode of Uncle Victor, Napoleon's sturdy captain, who disdained dolls; another maniacal collector, and Thérèse, the domestic tyrant, agglutinated from various figures in Pierre's tetralogy. *Bonnard* is indeed rich in types.

Altogether, a wise and charming book,—certainly one of the few, Mme. Lahy-Hollebecque tells us, 'in which emotion takes the upper hand of *esprit.*' Little irony, plenty of humour, and no lack of grave reflection. Work and meditation and pleasant dreams, shot through with light.[76] Little plot, a sort of *dégagé* treatment of personal events. A kind of musing tenderness, the mood commonly aroused by the author's own memories and nothing else.[77] The 'noble' humour and what irony there may be are made incorporate with a tender brooding over human destinies. That is why Lemaître could not read the last pages of the book without experiencing a strong impulse toward tears. That is why Pellissier declares that in those days France put his trust in sentiment and that he still believed it is 'more necessary to feel than to understand.' The pessimistic days have not yet come.[78] Bonnard, the idealist, has no hate or harshness in him.

The Academy report, which crowned the book, spoke of it as a 'delicate and distinguished work. . . If at times the style tends toward preciosity, the composition (*facture*) is generally elegant and correct.' The occasional preciosity is not annoying and is usually felicitous. On the whole, France is at ease in this second manner; he moves with a natural if stately stride. Hence echoes of the great classics, say of the *Odyssey,* impressed one critical reader, while another (Barrès) noted that the style 'falls like a robe around the thought, falls in folds that are clear-cut and charming.'[79]

One agrees, then, with those who associate *Bonnard* with the four books on Pierre as 'the most human of all his works, the most living, the least burdened with metaphysical or sociological digressions.'[80] All of which need not imply that this vein is the most characteristic of the author throughout his career. Did not the elderly Anatole grow weary of hearing the constant hymn of praise proffered to his early masterpiece? 'Always *Sylvestre Bonnard!*' he is said to have exclaimed to some visiting Etonians. 'Why, of all my books it is the most *fade,* the most tiresome. I wrote it just to win an Academy prize.'[81] . . One wonders if he really did.

§ 8

So much has already been written about *Le Livre de mon ami,* so much of our material has been taken from this volume, that we need consider here only certain supplementary facts. Published in 1885, the *Livre* was written *nel mezzo del cammin di nostra vita,* if we may credit the author's preface in which he dedicates the book to his family. Its 'early publication,' under the title of *Les Aventures de Pierre Nozière,* was announced in *l'Univers illustré* for November 1, 1884; and the same journal published certain extracts with favourable comment.[82] In the *Vie en fleur,* France indicates, not quite accurately, this middle term of his own life as his thirty-seventh year (1881); about that time he told Cuvillier-Fleury that he was bringing out 'a little book of reminiscences.'[83] He would, perhaps, seek to antedate the composition in order to reject the alleged influence of Renan's *Souvenirs* (1883). Yet a considerable likeness is apparent. Whether in the dialogues or in the dilettantism, the Master's voice is audible; proof of the disciple's admiration will presently be accumulated.[84] The basic appeal of Renan's volume and of the *Livre de Pierre* is much the same; it emanates in each case from the author's wistful return to his unforgotten youth. Anatole's pensive preface speaks of illusions that have vanished, the diminished confidence in life and in the future; but there remain the pleasures of memory and of recording these memories while he is surrounded by a beloved family. We have seen that France insists on the essential, the 'psychological' verity of the recollections.[85]

Nevertheless there has descended, between the author and his boyish ego, a thick 'curtain of literature.' Consequently the art is less spontaneous, a thought more mannered than in *Sylvestre Bonnard*. This is visible, as already suggested, in the over-emphasis attached to certain experiences as great revelations. The reminiscences do not constitute an orderly progression, but the unity of tone, like that of an ancient, burnished pastel, is remarkable in the first Part. The *Livre de Suzanne* has no such unity; its haphazard construction includes three or four quite disparate *morceaux*. Many 'echoes' or anticipations in *Le Livre* have already been mentioned. Here is one which, as far as I know, has not been recorded. When Anatole objectifies Pierre as an *alter ego,* a 'petit bonhomme' who tripped through the Luxembourg on his way to school, he strongly recalls a passage in *David Copperfield:*[86]

> That little fellow seems to be no part of me; I remember him as something left behind upon the road of life . . . and almost think of him as of some one else.

The description in *Le Livre* is also an anticipation of a similar passage in *Marguerite*.[87] Such themes as the author's trend toward Epicureanism, his distrust of science, his tolerant indulgence toward humanity, and his desire to maintain classical traditions, have been in part indicated and will be further developed in their proper connexions.

No later judgment on *Le Livre* can surpass Lemaître's early appreciation. He said, concerning the book's wide appeal, that its delicacy will charm women, its fancy will delight poets, while philosophers will find there much meditation and psychologists a keen analysis of a child's soul. For humanists (he continues), there is the lure of its cultural background; the tender-minded will find sentiment, but there is enough moderate scepticism to please the 'tough-minded' likewise.[88]

The volume of children's stories called *Nos Enfants, Scènes de la ville et des champs,* dated '1887,' really appeared in December, 1886. It contains nineteen tales, of which five were presently republished in *Pierre Nozière*. It was charmingly illustrated by Boutet de Monvel, and these illustrations were kept when (in 1900) the stories were distributed into two separate volumes, *Nos Enfants* and *Filles et Garçons*.[89]

Some of the tales told here were first related by 'Maman' to Anatole. Some of the children are analogous to Suzanne's playmates, 'André' or 'Pierre.' The book as a whole evidently belongs to the epoch and shares the inspiration of the *Livre de Suzanne*. There are writers who affirm that apart from the Gospels, children scarcely appear in France's work.[90] But when we group the above titles together with *Abeille* and other more incidental appearances (e.g., that of young Haviland in *Jocaste*), one certainly finds enough to discredit these critics. More important is the question of how the children are treated. In *Nos Enfants,* at least, the small figures are for the most part faithfully portrayed from their own standpoints—the egocentric 'petit Jean,' Marie, who naughtily wished to eat the flowers, and the big boys in 'Les Fautes des grands' who walked too fast for the little ones. We are edified by the good girl, Lucie, who takes care of her sick sister; we recognize Michel, the artist; we meet Jacqueline, who is of the same 'monde' as her big dog; and another 'Suzanne,' who explains to some puzzled savants that a certain bas-relief in the Louvre represented two girls exchanging flowers on their birthdays. Thus Anatole comments on the text, 'A little child shall lead them.'[91]

In various tales, children are placed in familiar domestic settings. Sometimes they play soldiers or are absorbed with other toys at home; a beloved hobby-horse is prophetic of maturer manias. Sometimes they proceed, irregularly, on their way to school; or they are convalescing from illness; or they scamper, as the sub-title promises, 'in the fields'; or they strive to learn the language of animals, suggesting an atmosphere of fairydom. Familiar *motifs* are also found. There are the small boys who admire a miscellany of pedler's wares, including the oft-mentioned *images d'Epinal*. There is Rose Benoît, the pupil who was weak on subtraction, but surpassed all others in describing the Terrestrial Paradise and Noah's Ark. There is a certain Catherine, who makes her dolls carry on a polite conversation ; some day she will run a salon, 'where the traditional French politeness will flourish.' Could it be Catherine who grew up into Mme. Aubernon or Mme. de Caillavet ?

High praise has been accorded by good judges to France's understanding and rendering of child-life ; it is held that he admires and reflects excellently the simplicity of the growing mind.[92] Without denying this, I suspect that as in *Abeille* (although to a lesser extent) the adult mind is hovering around. But who would object to that ? Hans Andersen once confessed that although he told his stories as if addressing children, yet he always reminded himself that one or two elders might be listening in.

As another witness to France's benignant frame of mind during this period, we may pause upon the short tale of *Marguerite*.[93] Fictionally, it is a pendant at once to *Jeanne Alexandre* and to the *Livre de mon ami*. To the former, because it narrates again how a mature man finds in his path the daughter of a former sweetheart and how he saves her — not from Mademoiselle Préfère this time, but from a dangerous malady. Even as Bonnard had harked back to the vision of Clémentine, so the narrator in *Marguerite* retells the love of his youth, recalling its religious emotion, its ideal vagueness, so perfectly expressed 'in Virgil, in Racine and Lamartine.' As the image of Clémentine was associated with her *capote rose,* so the old love here is remembered by her bright golden hair. And when the politician who relates the story meets the child Marguerite, he knows her for her mother's daughter by her hair of 'liquid light.' It was this mother, he says, who had 'first awakened in me the sense of beauty,' — which Marcelle had done for Pierre.

The childhood of Pierre and that of Suzanne are recalled by various analogies. When the politician resuscitates his 'ego' (which has been throttled by red tape), he is walking near the Pont de la Concorde and takes immediately an interest in street-life, in the shops and their wares. Particularly is he fascinated by an apothecary's glowing bowl, which, just as the chestnut-stall affected Pierre, sent him precipitately back into the mirages of his childhood. The same shop contained the soldier-toys in which he once revelled, together with the *images d'Epinal* (again !)

from which, 'I learned things finer and more useful than anything I ever got from the little grammars and history-books that my schoolmasters gave me.' Follows a paragraph in praise of fairy-tales—blessèd is the child who is brought up on them. It is the theory of education characteristic of Suzanne's father. And the ailing girl, Marguerite, is won back to health by a dexterous admixture of amusement and imagination. The whole tone of the story, in fact, classes it with *Bonnard* and *Le Livre.*

§ 9

But one story-group of this same period partakes of a very different inspiration. In March, 1884, there appeared in the *Journal des Débats* a *roman-feuilleton* which Anatole, following an article by Chénier, called *Les Autels de la peur.*[94] France is again evincing that interest in the Revolution which recurs in all of his principal stages. *Les Autels,* a novelette in eleven chapters (which have merely dates as titles), was loosely strung together round a series of Revolutionary episodes and characters. Presently A.F. decided to detach the chapters and to use about half of them, with modifications, as short stories, first in diverse periodicals, finally in *l'Etui de nacre.* The process is the reverse of that used by Balzac in amalgamating half a dozen distinct stories into *La Femme de trente ans.* Here France dissociates what had originally been consecutive chapters, renames his characters in each episode, and uses other such devices.

Although we shall find some similarities between *Les Autels* and *Les Dieux ont soif,* the former tale is not, as some have thought, an earlier version of the latter.[95] But the Revolutionary material in *l'Etui de nacre*—five tales in all—derives, to a greater or less extent, from *Les Autels.* These stories will be considered below (Ch. XVI) ; but we may pause here on some of the general features of *Les Autels,* together with those episodes which were never properly republished. For a limited *édition factice* was got up, nominally in '1885,' though really in 1926, as a mild literary hoax.[96]

In spite of our frequent allusions in other chapters, it has been impossible to indicate in any detail how often France shows a minute knowledge of Revolutionary *ana.* The elder Thibault's book-shop, the La Bédoyère catalogue, Etienne Charavay's researches—all contributed their quotas. More particularly, about 1870 Anatole became interested in a work by Charles-Aimé Dauban, called *Les Prisons de Paris sous la Révolution, d'après les relations des contemporains,* which he reviewed twice.[97] Dauban's book, together with the *Souvenirs de M. Berryer, doyen des avocats de Paris, de* 1774 *à* 1838 and Prudhomme's *Histoire générale des crimes commis pendant la Révolution,* were all contributory sources to *Les Autels.*[98] The story also uses contemporary documents. We may understand, then, the author's original announcement: 'I have invented nothing in this whole narrative. Its episodes have been taken from writings of the period, and I have even introduced conversations which actually took place.'[99]

Four chapters in *Les Autels* (Chs. II, IV, X, XI) were not reworked for *l'Etui de nacre,* although the first of these furnished material for the 'Mémoires d'un volontaire' in that volume.[100] An examination of these four will corroborate some of the points made above regarding A.F.'s approach to the Revolution and will offer occasional hints of matters discussed in *Les Dieux ont soif* (1912) and elsewhere. As a rule, the general tone and historical background in Anatole's great Revolutionary novel are foreshadowed, rather than particular incidents.[101] Yet certain chapters in *Les Dieux* seem to recall events in the earlier story. For example, the episode called '9 juillet 1790' describes the preparations for the Fête de la Féderation with touches in the *genre* manner of *Les Dieux,* which definitely refers back to this festival.[102]

In the original scene, an old man is bringing earth in a wheelbarrow, in order to build up the altar for the celebration. Again, there is an easy-going lass who is free with her kisses like Elodie and others of Anatole's later heroines. A subsequent chapter in *Les Autels* ('12 Brumaire An II') represents first a scene on France's favourite Pont-Neuf, from which the statue of his lusty gallant, Henri IV, has been dismounted by the mob.[103] Following this, we have the deed of a noble heroine, who tries to testify before the Revolutionary tribunal in behalf of a person falsely accused. Similar prejudiced denunciations, sometimes connected with supposed plots, illustrated by frequent court-scenes, are found in *Les Dieux* as well as in other places.[104] The final chapters of *Les Autels* depict the absurd trial and condemnation of the principal figures. They pass on to the place of execution, noting the beauty of the Seine and the sky as the tumbrils advance. They exchange solemn farewells, and the hero dies with 'Vive la Révolution !' upon his lips.[105]

There is also a general similarity with *Les Dieux* in the author's attitude towards the Terror and what led up to it. Like a true scion of 'Grand'Maman Nozière,' Anatole's sympathies are less with the vengeful mob than with the persecuted aristocrats and with those who tried to preserve a spirit of moderation. Many-headed fanaticism is for A.F., here as elsewhere, a thing to be detested and ridiculed. The Revolution, on the whole, does not win his attachment ; and this attitude he preserves later. As in *Les Dieux,* finally, he depicts, with sardonic relish, the enactment of violent events against a background of normal and even trivial happenings. The street-life of the period is often described, with similar touches, in both novels, and the refrain of *ça ira* is heard throughout.[106]

In his old age, France spoke rather slightingly of *Les Autels de la peur* as 'fragments of a revolutionary novel which I did not succeed in finishing.' When Ségur directed his attention to a certain story in *l'Etui de nacre* where the heroine is called by different names, France regretted that he had not been more careful about assembling his 'fragments.' To another confidant he mentioned that Evariste Gamelin, the fanatical hero of *Les Dieux ont soif,* was first adumbrated in these early tales of the Terror.[107]

A.F. IN 1883

CHAPTER XIII

The Higher Journalism

§ 1

TO understand France's flowering as an 'intellectual,' one must cast back into the previous decade. We usually picture him as composing 'well-bound books that speak of love.' [1] Yet for years he composed chiefly articles that spoke of literature. We think of the well-bound volumes as containing the bulk of his writings. But at least one-half of what he wrote has never been collected in volume form. This half consists of numerous notices as well as full-bodied articles, which appeared in a dozen or more periodicals from the late sixties to the early nineties. About then he developed the habit of repeating himself copiously, so these later echoes are not very important. But from 1867-93 he wrote for the most diverse journals contributions which are often revealing in content. In mere quantity they are sufficient to disprove the frequent assertion that France was an indolent and sparsely productive writer. Indolent enough in the body, yes, and much averse to practical doings; yet it seems that his pen was never still.

Why have these miscellaneous articles been neglected, not only by the larger reading public, but also by professed Anatolians? Here we need to distinguish. A good part of this material has real value of one sort or another and should properly be included in a truly 'definitive edition' of France's works. On the other hand, the earlier contributions to the more technical journals are ephemeral or specialistic in character and need not be revived. Yet even these will be dealt with briefly in the present chapter, because of the light that they throw on the mind and talent of Anatole. We see him beginning with the preoccupations of bookman and scholar, but constantly broadening his culture. We observe him, dogmatic and even angular at first, gradually losing 'his juvenile asperity to reach that tolerant smile, that elderly disillusioned indulgence which we find so pleasing in the author of *La Vie littéraire*.' [2] Nor are we to think that journalistic writing as a whole was a bad thing for his development. It taught him something about punctuality, limbered up his style, and broadened his range of interests.[3]

The connexion with Lemerre resulted in the rather uncharacteristic type of criticism found in *Le Génie latin*. The persistent association with Etienne Charavay not only stimulated France's taste for documentary scholarship and his interest in the Revolution ; Charavay also directed two of the journals to which Anatole soon became a contributor. Later labours undoubtedly refined his style and broadened his appeal. Else why should Hébrard have chosen him for *Le Temps* as the best *chroniqueur* in Paris ?

So let us no longer think of France as beginning his career of journalism on *Le Temps,* in 1886. He was an accomplished journalist, both as critic and as chronicler, some years before that. He had become acquainted both with literary bondage and vagabondage. The articles written under the rubric of 'La Vie littéraire' represent the culmination of a talent which began to bloom in *Le Globe* (1879) and which is certainly manifest in the series of fortnightly gossips with the readers of *l'Univers illustré* (1883-96). Likewise, the earlier notices and reviews, with which we are immediately concerned, often give us interesting glimpses of Anatole's personality. And their more particular merit is this : that several of his life-long preoccupations appear early and recur frequently. Among such themes would be his concern with bibliophily and old books ; his constant historical curiosity ; and his interest in art, both painting and architecture, on which he wrote more during this period than in any other.[4] In what follows, I shall as usual seek for these and other abiding trends in France's mental make-up.

§ 2

THE record begins with his contributions to *Le Chasseur bibliographe* (of which he was literary editor), when the contributor was only twenty-two years old. These are among the very first things that Anatole had printed. They show the youth as still haunting his father's book-shop, as occupied with catalogues, sales, and general bookman's lore. This obscure and short-lived 'little review' (there were only seven numbers) also published articles by Noël France and by Etienne Charavay ; so it was almost a family affair. Is it significant that, like the *Gazette rimée,* the journal suddenly perished while Anatole was on its staff ? At any rate, he wrote seven 'pieces for the paper' during the first three months of 1867. And there were probably other brief articles by his hand, for he used various pseudonyms.[5] Let us glance at some of these short and scattered notices.

That he should still praise Leconte de Lisle and his knowledge of Greek is not surprising, for these are Parnassian days ; that he should revel in a bibliographical miscellany[6] as a succession of 'glorious panoplies' is very characteristic. Less so, perhaps, is his appreciation of Baudelaire's harmonies and of Verlaine's poetic richness, for, as editor of *Le Parnasse contemporain,* France rejected poems by these two men.[7] His theatrical notes show approval of the realistic traits in the Goncourts and in Augier. But no play can compass such magnificent realism coupled with such 'hidden poetry' as we have in *Madame Bovary*. Surely these are very mature judgments for a lad of twenty-two.

The most notable document in the *Chasseur* is France's first poetic treatment of the Thaïs story ; this has already been discussed. Next in interest is that anonymous article, 'An Extinguished Hearth-stone,' which commemorates the closing of Noël France's bookstore.[8] We view again with Anatole the place and its proprietor — and this time the son's eyes have become more tender. He describes the comfort of the chatty shop, the demeanour of its grave proprietor, then about to retire. He touches off the clients and customers, as we have already seen.

Passing over a rather didactic article on nature-poets, contributed to *Le Rappel* in 1869,[9] we continue with the periodicals addressed mainly to a public of specialists. The *Gazette bibliographique* was brought out by Lemerre. It contains by France, during 1868-69, three descriptions of important libraries ; the writer either concerns himself with sales or, in one case, provides the kind of itemized catalogue that his father had trained him to prepare. His usual enthusiasm for rare volumes is evinced. For other obscure labours of a bookman accomplished in these years, let us be content with the ground covered in the treatise by Mlle. Antoniu.[10] There is much here to throw light on France's beginnings as a critic and to disprove, as applicable to this period, his later remark : 'I lived through some happy years without writing at all.'[11] On the contrary, a quantity of short articles were composed, e.g., for such journals as *La Vogue parisienne* (on prisons under the Revolution) or the *Musée des deux mondes ;* and more particularly for the *Amateur d'autographes* and the *Bibliophile français.*

Collectors today are well acquainted with the *Amateur d'autographes,* until recently brought out by the house of Charavay. For many years (1867-92) Etienne was the editor-in-chief of this fortnightly review ;[12] and he persuaded Anatole to join its staff. The collaboration undoubtedly ripened France's knowledge of historical as well as literary by-paths. Just as in later articles, Etienne could be relied on to furnish the actual documents and to aid in their interpretation. France was still picking the brains of this excellent 'Chartiste' and almost seemed to become one himself.

For ten years (1867-77) Anatole wrote under various headings the book-reviews for this journal. He contributed to about thirty-six numbers. Many of the articles are from the special standpoint of the connoisseur, but others treat critically of such later preoccupations as street-names, engravings, the supernatural, Voltaire, Rabelais, and Racine. We note particularly a friendly article on Jules Breton, the poet-painter whom A.F. knew well in the seventies.

The *Bibliophile français* was an illustrated monthly, something of a successor to the *Chasseur bibliographe.* Twenty years later France alluded to it as a 'sumptuous review addressed to bibliomaniacs, dealing with incunabula, Renaissance bindings, and the like . . . I cared little about any of it.'[13] Yet the *Bibliophile français* lived for six years (1868-73), and for four of those years Anatole contributed with some regularity to its 'almanach' or chronicle. Early in its career he wrote for it a significant article on the Comte de La Bédoyère, connecting him again with the elder France's book-shop and linking both men with the Revolution and its history. Subsequently, France wrote regularly for the *Bibliophile* a section on 'Books of the Month.' Here his views on literary criticism begin to be formed. Under the influence of Taine, he declares that a critic should explain rather than judge an author and should explain him with close reference to the environment and circumstances which determine his talent.[14] Fortunately, this severely deterministic theory is modified by Anatole's personal preference for a more fluid and æsthetic type of *causerie.* The two tendencies in him produce some queer clashes for a time, but ultimately the systematic method loses ground and

Impressionism triumphs in the *Vie littéraire*. Even in the *Bibliophile,* his manner is usually chatty and elastic.

Conspicuous here is the reviewer's interest in the fine arts. He announces that in an age when writers and artists freely exchange techniques, the critics must adopt similar habits, 'passing from museums to libraries.' Hence we find frequent notices of books on art. In all, Anatole reviews about thirty titles, in ten articles, some of which were also published elsewhere. There is a noticeable duplication of subjects and material between the *Bibliophile* and the *Amateur,* and in fact it has been sufficiently demonstrated that the author thought nothing of using the same 'copy' again and again for various journals.[15] Already France, in his easy-going way, seems to believe, as the proverb has it, that 'repetition is the soul of instruction.'

§ 3

WHAT general trends are to be discovered in his opinions as expressed in these two journals ? In the background we have noted the drift towards Taine and the scientific Reign of Law. This will find confirmation elsewhere. Let us remember, too, that France was not yet emancipated from Parnassian habits of thought and the domination of Leconte de Lisle. And in politics he was liberal before 1870, but decidedly conservative after the Commune—a tendency which lasted on the whole for two decades. These predispositions will help account for some striking views regarding literature, in the two periodicals under consideration.

It need not surprise us that the juvenile critic is already a firm believer in literary tradition. 'This is the only way to keep in the right path,' he roundly declares. Any break in the chain leads to decadence ; and among great links in the chain are of course Virgil and, more unexpectedly, Richard Wagner—who goes back to Æschylus ! France himself gladly goes back to all Greece, with the usual arguments in behalf of her measured beauty. He favours, too, the Alexandrian period, with its Milesian tales and its 'lascivious charm.' He disliked the Middle Ages, as we have seen, yet about the Gothic *per se,* he seems uncertain : there may be a 'beau gothique,' fascinating in its repulsiveness. But in general the cathedrals were 'gigantic maladies,' and the Catholic soul of the age was a sick and ugly soul.

We recall that France was wont to 'adore' transition periods, for the interesting medley of standards which they offer. The full Renaissance, because of its resurrection of the antique, wins his admiration ; so do such masters of mirth as Rabelais and Molière. But with the exception of the last-named and of Racine, the Age of Louis XIV, like the great monarch himself, seems to our critic superficially pompous with a shabby and cruel background. (This is the opinion of the unregenerate Republican who wrote 'Les Légions de Varus.')

In the name of 'La Volupté,' Anatole again accepts the eighteenth century and all its lighter works : gallantry, learned ladies, feminized art, and piquant anecdotes. He also approves that cult of human liberty which finds its symbol in the undying smile of Voltaire—a figure who was much more 'human' than malicious. . . The majority of France's early articles concern this favourite period. Very characteristically, he discovers in it a considerable taste for the supernatural and mystical. Cagliostro is the counterpoise of Diderot.

As for the moderns and their poetry, France has taken the attitude which he long maintains : that of 'an Epicurean, with classical and Parnassian predilections.'[16] True that his early astonishment at Hugo has not quite vanished. Also he clings to his Musset and, as we have seen, savours the original essence of a Baudelaire. Otherwise he bows the knee to the high priest among the Parnassians. He values Leconte de Lisle for his serene power, for his enduring types of beauty, for his sense of historical relativity. The Master is scientific in his rendering of the natural world, while his voices from the past speak in harmony with their proper environments.[17] Was not this the chief effort of the author of *Thaïs* and *Les Noces corinthiennes,* of *The Gods Are Athirst* and 'The Procurator of Judea' ?

Thus Anatole, like a matchmaker of old comedy, is always trying to wed the Muse with Knowledge. The groom should bear himself like a Roman senator, with laurels on his brow. But the Muse too, though a supple lady, should assume a proud carriage. She must be calm, she must proceed with measured paces. 'The true goddess is revealed by her footstep.' So France remembers his Virgil, in order to caution Verlaine.

§ 4

Equally alert during the seventies are the historical interests and curiosities which our author shared with Sylvestre Bonnard. We recognize the young scholar who hesitated to return to Paris after the Commune, lest the libraries and galleries should be laid waste. Indeed, before that he had collaborated on an *Almanach de la Révolution française pour* 1870, contributing brief notices to this calendar of Revolutionary days. More significant was his connexion, already mentioned, with *La Revue des documents historiques*. This journal was a sort of younger brother to the *Amateur d'autographes,* and according to Ségur it seems to have been printed in a stable. 'You directed it all alone, my dear Etienne,' France later tells his friend, 'and this review had everything in its favour : learned contents, admirable facsimiles, fine printing—and even some subscribers. I wonder why it ceased to appear ?'[18]

On the covers of the magazine are found book-notices, some of them signed 'A.F.,' extending from 1873-76. These confirm France's interest in such classics as Molière and Montaigne, republished by Lemerre. He shows himself as already well-grounded in Rabelais. He reviews a tale by the Baron Vivant-Denon, that old charmer who long ago had fascinated Little Pierre. There is a short account of Renan's *l'Antéchrist*—apparently Anatole's first printed utterance concerning the master who subsequently dominated his thought.

Much more elaborate are two long articles based on manuscript material, entitled respectively 'La Fauconnerie au Moyen-Age' and 'La Dernière Maladie de Louis XV, mort et funérailles.'[19] The first of these, wherein the art of falconry is discussed historically, is unfortunately dull and contains little of a personal or philosophic nature. The death of Louis XV is more vividly set forth, with the support of medical bulletins and the account of an eye-witness. We are reminded of Carlyle when we read of how the viaticum was administered to the king, of the delay caused by court-intrigues, the defection of the Du Barry, the excitement and terror around the death-chamber. It was long before the disease was recognized as smallpox, and the king's awful end is described with no abatement of the pathological details.

Another historical article on 'Louis XIV et Henriette d'Angleterre' contains little that is not better told by France elsewhere.[20]

The documentary material for such essays was furnished and doubtless interpreted by Charavay. Etienne also probably wrote for this *Revue* the account of 'Les Guérin,'[21] which France later used as a basis for his article in the *Revue alsacienne*.

Long before Anatole joined the staff of *Le Temps* he had composed for that journal (where *Jocaste* also appeared) half a dozen essays of some weight. These extend from 1875-78 and are mostly concerned with contemporary novelists—if George Sand may be so termed, along with the Goncourts, Turguenief, and Zola.

France always had a considerable respect for the authoress of *Le Meunier d'Angibault*. Here[22] he declares that her imagination is as fresh as ever, while she remains most feminine in her emotions, particularly in her feeling for Nature. The love of the soil, the taste for animal and peasant life, have increased in her with the years ; and this critic, like others, believes that her rural novels are her very best things. Her descriptions are simpler and stronger than heretofore, her landscapes are more closely connected with the characters and their emotions. In the ensemble of Nature she discerns a beauty which the Naturalists do not perceive.

This passing dig at Naturalism is in line with France's fundamental views, although at this time he was himself dabbling with the realistic method. Other articles in the present series show that he is quite familiar with the theories and the works of the Goncourts and Zola, for whom he has small native sympathy. He expresses himself here peremptorily and fully, with a slow getting under way which continues through the *Vie littéraire* and a sophomoric didactic tone which is later discarded.

What ails the Goncourt brothers . . . in spite of their assiduity round Father's book-shop ?—Let us go back, in order to see. Genuine people were first created by Stendhal, genuine *milieux* by Balzac, while Flaubert mingles small details with the ability to give the illusion of life. Were the Goncourts sent us in their turn to make us expiate the 'fine dreams of our fathers'? As ultramoderns, they throw tradition overboard : a believer in tradition rises up and calls them distinctly not blessèd. For instance, he objects, these Siamese twins of literature show life brutally, *via* photography and physiology. Always observing, they amass detailed notes, leaving their novels uncomposed. For pictorial purposes they have invented their would-be 'écriture artiste,' which France can't stand at any price. It says what they want to say ;

but why do they want to say such dreary things? It is highly dangerous to break with our past, and 'violent novelties are against nature.' Here speaks the true Anatole, and he speaks well.[23]

What ails Monsieur Zola?—France's favourite sport as a critic is the baiting of this heavy figure, whom he derides in a dozen places. The long article in *Le Temps*[24] admits that Zola is a 'robust artisan,' who deserves to be taken seriously. It is a pity that he can worship only brute force and the body, making what he considers 'overwhelming' physiological discoveries. Hostile to much of the Rougon-Macquart series, Anatole is forced to acknowledge the observation shown in various novels, together with the power and reality of *l'Assommoir* in particular. Hostile, too, to the man's crude style, France yet perceives how he energizes objects and the lower orders of people. But for Zola *homo* is never *sapiens,* while Nature for him is always a welter or a riot. Cannot he understand that Nature is fundamentally orderly and that art should be the same? Let him look at the great classics! . . . France is by no means through with Zola; this article sets the pace for a number of later attacks.[25]

§ 5

In the late summer of 1879, the members of the Thibault family took their outing, as they often did, at Saint-Valery-en-Caux. Here were written, for *Le Globe,* some of the descriptive articles already mentioned. But that dignified newspaper also printed during the summer and autumn of this year fifteen rather long book-reviews.[26] These too are pitched in a serious tone, without much suavity. The author speaks his mind concerning literary notables of the day. About half of the articles deal with ephemeral topics, while the others offer material of more interest. For example, Anatole states his present—and prophetic—view of criticism. He dislikes the tendency to put a writer on a pedestal and thinks the critic should, on the other hand, give us characteristic details and anecdotes about his subject. We discern here the disciple of Sainte-Beuve, the future gossip of *Le Temps.* We find other idiosyncrasies and recurring traits. There is a 'puff' for a booklet by Charavay and a glorification of Coppée's dramas. There is fresh admiration for the virile Henri IV as well as for the delightful Alphonse Daudet. Regarding Constant and his

Adolphe, Anatole is less favourably disposed here than later in *Le Génie latin.*

As we might expect, there are passing allusions to Virgil, always in an admiring vein. Especially good is a biographical essay on André Chénier and his poetic revival of the antique.[27] Chénier's very name summons up images of graceful Grecian figures, the real tangled with the ideal in a long and charming procession. But should we not distinguish at least between the ancient epochs, between the orchard-close of Antinoüs and the *bocage* of Theocritus ? In such a grove is Chénier's true Elysium to be found—on a voluptuous Ægean island, where Hellenic purity mingles with Asiatic softness. (Here France himself is making a familiar confusion.) The poet, in fact, creates a new antiquity after his kind, very eighteenth-century in tone, particularly with regard to the heroines of these amorous elegies.

Anatole's concern with the marvellous, so 'natural to man' as he insists, appears partly in a fine tribute to Edgar Allan Poe[28] —partly in his questioning of mesmerism and in his guarded satire of spiritualistic séances. Along these lines he assumes critical attitudes that will be developed later. As for philosophy, he respects Positivism, while sceptical about metaphysics. Let us glance at his review of Lange's *History of Materialism,*[29] for his language here supports his claim that he was by no means a dilettante or an indifferent with regard to speculative thought. Seldom indifferent but usually sceptical . . . Anatole strikes that favourite pose when he faces Herr Lange and his abstruseness. This thinker has tried to reconcile 'two hostile sisters,' metaphysics and science. Yet as philosophies both materialism and idealism are pure speculations. We cannot *know* that matter exists, since we possess only the testimony of our senses, relative and subjective witnesses. Idealism is in no better case : it has never explained the relation of movement to sensation ; it presupposes the existence of the soul, which is 'asking a great deal.' In short, France like Voltaire opposes the 'chimeras' of the Platonists. Aristotle, too, seems to him a word-worshipper. Philosophy did not really mature until Descartes and Gassendi came along. To all these Anatole really prefers latter-day Positivism, rather the French than the English variety. A subsequent article confirms this preference : the Positivists headed by Littré are a worthy regiment, although personally our irregular sharp-shooter objects to joining definitively any brigade whatsoever. For all that, he was more nearly a Positivist than anything else, however much later he may have gibed at Comte and Lafitte.[30]

We now reach the more mature articles and tales written for *La Jeune France* from 1878 to 1884. Anatole—another kind of 'jeune France'—was for a time enrolled on the staff of this magazine. The photograph of him reproduced above (opposite p. 128) dates from 1873; he is bearded like an Assyrian king and wears an expression of mingled slyness and benevolence. This picture later appeared in a frontispiece to *La Jeune France*,[31] among a galaxy of other contributors—the inevitable Leconte de Lisle as the central sun, surrounded by such juvenile planets as France, Coppée, Sully Prudhomme, Paul Arène, and Daudet—a fairly homogeneous array. It was also a mutual admiration society, whose members wrote up one another as 'Les Hommes de la *Jeune France*.' Under this rubric Anatole discussed Sully Prudhomme and was himself discussed by Maurice Barrès—the first critical article of importance dealing with our author and among the first written by the young Barrès.[32]

As a journal of the left bank, *La Jeune France* (1878-88) professed a lively liberal creed.[33] To some extent it reflected the dominant views of Hugo—ageing but still masterful—and of his circle. Alphonse Daudet and Jules Claretie helped to make it an organ of democratic sentiment. Although 'republican' and rather insurgent in political affairs, *La Jeune France* remained conservative in literary theory; it indicted the school of Zola as the scavengers of fiction. Despite the fact that he sympathized with this attitude, there is no evidence that our hero was at that period aggressive in politics.

In the course of six years we find eighteen contributions to this journal by Anatole France, the majority of which are signed in full. Five are short stories or episodes, later reprinted with some changes. One tale, called 'Une Cure du Docteur Hardel,'[34] has not been republished; it is a provincial story, rather in the sardonic style of Maupassant, and represents a notary's clerk sighing for a doctor's wife, much as 'Pierre' sighed for Madame Planchonnet. The substance of this tale was later reworked into 'La Signora Chiara' (*Crainquebille*), where again the husband-doctor gets rid of a young rival by pulling out his tooth.[35] Browsing among the other contributions, we observe that historical and philosophical matter is still more abundant than literary criticism proper. As for the manner, the genuine velvet touch of Anatole is already perceptible; his previous angularity has largely vanished, while a familiar and sprightly vein begins to emerge.

There are two articles on great ladies of yesteryear:[36] 'Madame de la Sablière,' as the friend of La Fontaine; and 'Madame de Montespan, Poisoner?', as illustrating the lax standards of the Old Régime. To the first heroine our author was uncommonly faithful. He went back to her at least four times, the treatment varying from the dignified to the gossiping, according to the type of journal in which each article appeared.[37] In *Le Temps* later on, the love-life of Madame de la Sablière is subordinated to her religious conversion. Here it is the gossiping tendency that predominates, the article being based on the lady's unpublished correspondence with her confessor. A good deal of the material, especially the part concerning La Fontaine, is used afresh in *Le Génie latin*.

France's review of a book on Madame de Montespan and the famous 'affair of the poisons' leads him to conclude again that the seventeenth century was not so well-behaved as is often represented. His characteristic leaning towards historical doubt or Pyrrhonism is thus manifested. Closely scrutinized, the great era 'loses something of its classical beauty.' As he had already said in the *Amateur d'autographes,* manners were not on a par with the arts; and lovers were less lovely than a reading of Racine's *Bérénice* would make us think. Evidence plainly shows an almost unbelievable badness in this 'racket' of the poisons, black mass, and the like. Anatole would almost agree with the historian who wrote of the Age of Louis XIV as so foul that the investigator has to hold his nose when descending into that sewer.[38] Yet our indulgent cynic holds that the period was probably no worse than another. Sad to see how slowly humanity leaves its brutal heritage, how it maintains almost an algebraic constant in its evil!

The same magazine contains by our author several other historical articles: on an Egyptian papyrus, on Heredia's 'brilliant and poetic' translation of a *conquistador* chronicle, on the funeral apotheosis of Mirabeau, perhaps (though this is not authenticated) on Michelet's historical method, and—very Francian this last—on 'Autres Prétendants. Les Faux Louis XVII.' As for the false Dauphins, Anatole is perpetually on their trail in *l'Univers il-*

lustré. This preoccupation runs parallel to his interest in still 'other pretenders,' such as the spurious Jeanne d'Arc. The brief article on Michelet is signed simply 'La Jeune France'; its tone is scarcely Anatolian, but some of the criticisms of Michelet are like those expressed in *Sylvestre Bonnard* just about this time.

We turn to the heart of the matter, as preserved in a series of philosophical articles, a poem on the cosmos, and a critical study of Sully Prudhomme. All these bear on philosophical topics, particularly on Evolution. Here is farther proof of France's prolonged concern with scientific explanations of the universe. This concern went deeper than we might suppose, to judge merely from the quite audible anti-scientific explosions in the *Livre de mon ami*. But are not these the injured reactions of a former lover, of an ardent devotee who, like Renan, had hoped for more than his stern mistress could give? At any rate, we find in *La Jeune France* frequent links with the Darwinism already sketched in *Les Poèmes dorés*. The three articles bear the general title of 'Les Origines humaines' and deal successively with 'The Earth,' 'The Earth and Man : Transformism,' and finally with 'Man,' considered by himself.[39]

Much of the first article is an adaptation of a study of geological origins by Sir Charles Lyell, for whom France had a considerable respect. Anatole thinks that the history of the earth, including the nebular hypothesis of Laplace and the procession of geological ages, has a scientific certainty. He did not always hold to that belief, but at this period the scroll of latter-day science was just being unrolled before an earnest élite. France is duly impressed by the 'inconceivable immensities' of Time before the human record begins. He is critical of the 'Days' and of the Deluge in Genesis. Ultimately, after sea-life has spawned, after the great carnivora, the advent of man is thus hailed : 'So Man is born, endowed with delicate senses and an anxious soul, destined to love, to know and to suffer so much.' (This is rather a *fin-de-siècle* Man, made in the image of Anatole.)

The second article, quite characteristically, cites and approves in part the cosmogony of the ancients, who held science high. Therein they showed their intelligence, for 'One wearies of everything except the art of understanding.' This oft-repeated saying is here attributed to Virgil. Its wisdom is esteemed worthy of that 'serious and tender soul which was wrought upon by a great curiosity'—another link between the Roman poet and the French Epicurean. The sixth eclogue, the fragment containing Silenus's chant of Creation is used once more and is now quoted in full. It is equally significant that France should again use Venus as the symbol of generation. He alludes specifically to a well-known Museum—probably that of the Jardin des Plantes—which exhibits all organic forms from the polyp down and which appropriately displays a marble Venus as the be-all and the end-all of the 'chain of being.'

While accepting biological evolution, Anatole refuses to make one swallow of Darwin, then at the height of his fame, and patriotically reminds us that Lamarck was a genuine precursor. He repeats his adherence, manifest as early as the *Poèmes dorés,* to the main principles of natural selection and the struggle for life, but injects cautious reservations as to 'indefinitely modifiable forms.'

The third and last article develops the idea of a slow social evolution, corresponding to the biological. Later in his life, France had no sincere convictions regarding human progress, but here at least he avers: 'From the blind slow labour of many generations emerges finally for the race a happy and beautiful existence.' He accepts Lyell's divisions of the epochs, together with the results of prehistoric archæology. A sketchy purview of primitive man contains notions found later in *l'Ile des Pingouins* and other places. Naked and stupid, urged on by hunger, men of the tertiary period had powers of elementary adaptation. Hairy and deformed, the immediate descendants of a Probably Arboreal ancestor 'had no language but a cry.' Presently they named things, they distributed adjectives, they acquired gods and fetishes. Their flints, their gradual use of the genius of fire, have resulted through secular efforts in our inventions and luxuries. 'Our delicate and powerful arts' also stem back to their crude conquests of nature. France concludes in sentimental vein that this survey has moved him to a deep sympathy with his progenitors, and like Sully Prudhomme he may truly say:

Et depuis ce temps-là je les ai tous aimés.

The lines called 'Genèse : Fragments d'un poème cosmogonique en préparation'[40] represent France's single brief attempt to rival the greater philosophic fragments of a Lucretius or a Chénier. These verses on the 'Genesis' of things are awkward but revealing. The nebular hypothesis is again to the fore, and there are evident links with the *Poèmes dorés,* especially with its prefatory 'Ode à la lumière.' In both places France hails light as the fertilizing power, the mother of life on a large scale ; and the supremacy of 'le Désir' is curiously connected with the mutual attraction of the stars.

Thus, certain features in the article on Sully Prudhomme as a philosophic poet had been variously anticipated. In fact, as early as 1878 in *Le Temps* France had raised the main question about his friend. Deeply as this fellow-poet may plunge into the sciences, thoroughly as we other seekers may approve his thought, yet Anatole cannot but regret personally the passing of the more intimate and elegiac note which marked his earliest volumes. His lyrics are superior to his wholly philosophic poetry, although that is the path (since 'we weary of everything but understanding') which he will probably follow to the end.

He was still following it when Anatole wrote this second article for *La Jeune France*.[41] First we hear echoes of haunting themes, such as Venus Genetrix, the Museum of organic forms, foreshadowings of our knowledge by the ancients. A.F. now attempts a fresh survey of the sciences ; and he turns it into a detailed eulogy of these fields : astronomy, whose infinite vistas always fascinated our author ; geology and world-changes (much as above) ; physiology and natural history ; archæology, which illuminates the epochs in the life of the race ; comparative philology ; and 'ethics . . . as scientifically constituted by the English Positivists.' These domains are closely bound together and make up the 'magnificent spectacle' which has recently been revealed to mankind — including Sully Prudhomme.

All this certainly seems splendid material to write about. And yet — and yet. . . May he speak frankly, as one who greatly admires his friend, but disagrees with his æsthetics ? Sully Prudhomme has been a fine exponent of doubt, of melancholy, and of unsatisfied love. He has even tried to widen his emotion and to make his sweetheart a symbol of cosmic urges. In such recent volumes as *La Justice,* however, the speculative tendency has become supreme ; and this on the whole is a 'dangerous path' for a lyrist ; for how can one solve the problems of metaphysics in verse or solve, within poetry, the problem of how to make such matters concrete and humanly appealing?

Does not the argument indicate that while Anatole might praise and pursue science, he was still aware of more individual forces and of less logical delights?

§ 6

In 1886, just before he joined the staff of *Le Temps,* France was nominally director, for six months, of a handsomely illustrated monthly, *Les Lettres et les arts,* whose editorship he took rather casually. He later recognized his unfitness for this task.[42] The assembling of articles and illustrations he would often nonchalantly leave to others. But he seems to have gathered round him, as contributors, several of his old Parnassian associates. His own contributions include a number of brief book-notices,[43] together with a single article and two stories. These last ('Le Manuscrit d'un médecin de village' and 'Marguerite') were subsequently reprinted elsewhere.

Among the book-reviews we may pause on the longer and more characteristic. We meet with France's old friend, Henriette-Anne d'Angleterre, who has just been made the subject of a biography.[44] Referring back to his previous Introduction to Madame de La Fayette's life of the princess (see below), Anatole now admits that this book probably did more harm than good to the reputation of Henriette-Anne. The present biographer brings to light her political role as negotiator and correspondent with Charles II of England.

In the same number there is a significant notice of the study on 'La Parabole des trois anneaux' by Gaston Paris—significant because France presently found room for this parable in *Le Lys rouge.* Here he dwells on the keenness of method displayed by Gaston Paris in analysing the variants of the tale. Such researches, with all the skill and knowledge they imply, interest not only the learned, but 'all those who are concerned with the intellectual history of humanity.'

Another notice discusses Siméon Luce's book on *Jeanne d'Arc à Domrémy.*[45] Anatole was destined to use this volume considerably in his own life of Joan. Already he is well-versed in the field and has decided personal views. Generally he approves of

Luce, particularly where the biographer has placed Jeanne in her proper setting of deed and creed—exactly his own intention as manifested later in a famous preface.

Other reviews briefly mention Renan's translation of the *Song of Songs,* with emphasis on the illustrations ; an essay on Bernard Palissy, incomparable craftsman ; a study of the artist Prud'hon, of whose paintings France became in his old age a diligent collector.

These various notices suggest that the policy of *Les Lettres et les arts* was to stress the latter half of its title, and such was indeed the case. France falls in line when he devotes an article to the annual Salon [46]—an institution which elsewhere he usually left to his collaborators—for example, to the facile pen of 'Gyp.' The exhibits of this year (1886) seem to him up to the average standard. He is particularly keen on portraits—'the proper study of mankind.' His observations are not very technical but lean more, as we might expect, towards the humanistic or the historical approach. He warns us that he will ramble where he likes, among the fine decorative dreams of Puvis de Chavannes, or the peasant-studies of Jules Breton. He even accepts Bouguereau without blinking and smacks his lips over certain luscious nudes. Altogether, a random literary *causerie,* in the manner inaugurated by Diderot. But it is interesting to note that A.F. stresses, as in his poetry, certain pictorial effects of radiance and light.

More widely read magazines also welcomed material from France's pen in the eighties. We have seen how Madame Adam enlisted his services for the celebrated *Nouvelle Revue.* In fact, a number of his best-known works during this and the following period appeared first serially in standard periodicals, such as the *Echo de Paris,* the *Revue des deux mondes,* etc.[47] Presently his contributions reached as far as the *Neue Freie Presse* of Vienna. The *Echo de Paris,* in particular, also printed during the nineties many single articles and stories. For six years Anatole favoured this journal with an abundant if erratic collaboration. But most of these 'feuilletons' came out presently in the regular editions. We are not usually concerned here with what was published later in book-form ; but incidentally we find a single story—'Le Comte Morin, député'—in the *Revue indépendante ;* [48] also in the *Revue bleue* a series of children's tales (1882) and a study of *Faust* (1889) which later became a preface.

In this same *Revue bleue* and never anywhere else France published, likewise in 1882, a very significant article. We have alluded to this under the title of 'Les Vacances sentimentales.' It was the record of his journey to Strasbourg and the adjacent country. The tour impressed him so much that he remembered, eleven years later, what a guide had told him about the University of Strasbourg.[49] But he never cared to republish the article, perhaps because of the subsequent estrangement from his family, or because of the amount of tender feeling, especially toward Suzanne, contained in the 'Vacances sentimentales.' We have already touched (Ch. XI) on these personal aspects; here we may consider some of the other topics treated. These are fairly numerous, since the article, like one of 'Gérôme's' in *l'Univers illustré,* skips lightly from subject to subject and in form resembles notes from a diary. Most of the reflections are written in a high good humour.

Anatole is interested in the art of cooking as well as the art of sight-seeing, when guides are not too clamorous. He still ponders upon quaint engravings and ancient houses; he still uses his gift of historical perspective and still insists, apropos of the Maréchal de Saxe, that small causes may bring about great events. In semi-Germanized Alsace he remains patriotically French. He turns from the spectacle of soldiers drilling—he feels that certain impressions are 'too painful.' Admitting the excellent education and the governing ability of the Germans, it seems to him that the true Alsatians, especially the women, don't want them there. Because there is no reason stronger, no reason purer than the 'raison de sentiment.' If Alsace regrets her weaning from France, this is proof that she loves us still—and therefore we may keep our hopes.

The Strasbourg cathedral with its dreaming spire impresses him more than the famous mechanical clock. He describes well the valley of the Andlau and an ascent made to the old church of Saint Odile, whose legend he of course relates. In connexion with the convent church and its chapels, we find once more the *motif* of 'old stones.' These do not tell the same story to Anatole and to archæologists: the latter, with all their pretensions, guess too much, whereas the former frankly listens to the horns of elfland amid the ruins. He cares only for fairy-tales and their imaginative suggestions. Imagination, anyhow, makes all that is worthwhile in the world. Thus he addresses an apostrophe to a certain stone figure as arousing in him a sense of the contrast between the ever-gracious eighteenth century and the 'sombre asceticism of the great Christian ages,' when Odile, the virgin abbess, founded her nunnery. For 'toutes les formes du passé ont une âme qui cherche mon âme. . .'[50]

§ 7

In addition to the fourteen prefaces written for Lemerre, France during his long career tossed off a great many others — about sixty in all. Of these, some two dozen belong to this and the subsequent period (through 1896), and the chief of them may as well be considered here.[51] As a group, they are not the least interesting and valuable, for they are comparatively free from the taint of perfunctoriness which often steal into the *notices* of a later date. These two dozen prefaces were written for diverse publishers (notably Charavay and Ferroud), and no complete collection of them exists.[52]

The reprint of an article on Jules Breton indicates that France still desires to befriend the painter-poet. An historical notice on the work, especially the *verrerie,* of Bernard Palissy (1880) also recalls a former interest; A.F. characteristically denounces the 'haughty scorn' which the Renaissance nobles were too ready to feel for plebeian workmen. A discussion of a comparatively innocent tale (*Dorci*) by the Marquis de Sade contains an almost clinical study of his case and shows how his more 'abominable novels,' in their mingling of suffering and pleasure, anticipate a tendency of Baudelaire's. France's theoretical fondness for animals is illustrated by his preface to the tale of *Jocko* by another eighteenth-century figure, the Comte de Pougens. This Count brought home from the wilds a tiny female monkey, whom he proceeded to train in the arts and graces of the period.

These are all rather slight compositions, but the eighty pages of the original 'Introduction' to Madame de La Fayette's *Histoire d'Henriette d'Angleterre* (1882) takes Anatole into the heart of a subject where he felt particularly at home. In spite of certain errors acknowledged later,[53] his treatment is scholarly and prevailingly historical. He points out the gaps in Mme. de La Fayette's account of the Princess, while quoting liberally from the letters and portraits which the authoress provides. In discussing the latter, he evinces psychological discernment, e.g., regarding the alleged 'gallantries' of the Princess and her connexion with Racine's *Bérénice,* that touching 'elegy.' France dwells on the shadings of the language under Louis XIV, and his general purpose is to interpret Mme. de La Fayette's use of that language, as well as to fill out her characterization and the historical background. The style, not yet fully mellowed, is nearer to that of *Le Génie latin* than to the urbanity of *La Vie littéraire*. This essay was supplemented a few years later by a preface to the *Princesse de Clèves*. It is claimed that Mme. de Caillavet wrote an 'admirable page' of that introduction.[54] But it is Anatole who skilfully replaces the novel in its setting, with regard to the circumstances of its composition and publication ; who shows an easy acquaintance with the strong-minded and mysterious authoress, as well as with the circles that surrounded her and the period at large ; who attaches the *Princesse de Clèves,* by virtue of its natural and penetrating psychology, to the other great classics of the era. It is equally characteristic that he should not warm to the heroic idealism which Mme. de La Fayette carries over from the age of Corneille : our critic would prefer, on the part of the heroine, less resistance to passion, less preoccupation with severe social taboos.[55] Within a few years, he wrote three articles on the novel and its authoress.

One variety of Anatoles' concern with the past is evidenced by those prefaces in which he links architectural monuments with their former glories. In 1888 he was employed to furnish the descriptive text for a *de luxe* volume on *Le Château de Vaux-le-Vicomte,* illustrated by Rudolph Pfnor. This edifice was built by Louis XIV's minister, Fouquet, at a cost of 18,000,000 livres, and in magnificence it outdistanced most of the royal palaces. In modern times (*c.* 1875) Vaux was purchased and sumptuously restored by a M. Sommier. Apparently Anatole and his illustrator were accompanied over the château, which is near Melun, by its restorer ; and the last part of France's Introduction describes the building and its erection in order to entertain Louis XIV. But our humanist, as usual, is more fascinated by the career and personality of Fouquet himself—his 'âme démesurée,' his lavish expenditures, his associations with the artists and writers of his period, his rivalry with Colbert, his resounding fall. The study appears to be well-documented (with numerous quotations from letters and the like) and it is certainly well-written. A sort of pendant to this came out in the following year, when Anatole prefaced another volume by Pfnor—the illustrated *Guide . . . au palais de Fontainebleau.* Here our picturesque historian can attain to a larger panoramic view. At Fontainebleau, he declares, the 'stones' chant the glories of a long line of rulers. These halls preserve ancient and undying echoes: the royal loves of the Valois, the state-craft of Henri Quatre, Madame de Maintenon's intrigues, finally the 'heroic farewell' of the Emperor.

A philosophical lesson is appended. We should learn at Fontainebleau to respect the old France, from which the new derives. Once more, it is a gross error to hold that our country dates from the Revolution. Our visit to this historic palace must show us the 'continuity of the French spirit reincarnated through the various régimes.' The philosopher goes so far as to say that it is an 'illusion' to conceive of these régimes as opposed to one another. Rather, they proceed naturally from one another—more naturally and less violently than he is disposed to grant elsewhere.

As will soon be seen, 1889 was a banner-year for the trumpetings associated with the name of General Boulanger, then at the height of his popularity. This fact may help account for the more militant patriotism found in another preface by A.F. which appeared during that year as an article called 'Le Faust de Goethe, à propos d'une traduction nouvelle.'[56] In book-form, it was reprinted in 1891, prefacing the two-volume translation of *Faust* by Camille Benoît. Anatole's remarks take the shape of a letter to this translator. There are several noteworthy passages. In one of them we find a defence of war as conducing to splendid, immemorial virtues—a tribute paralleled in *l'Univers illustré* about this time.[57] Another defence, that of the Latin spirit as peculiar to French culture, is warmly maintained. This is a familiar echo; but it is singular that in a eulogy of *Faust* (including the second Part), France should peremptorily declare: 'The Germans have no business with Helen and with her beauty.' The chauvinism and the intense conservatism of this preface have been emphasized by several critics.[58]

Accordingly, A.F. develops here a theme stated in the *Vie littéraire,* to wit, that Goethe can never be 'a classic for us'; but elsewhere we are given to understand that this same Goethe was, *after* the classics, the foreign author most esteemed by Anatole.[59]

We remember, too, certain tributes, including the 'sincerest form of flattery,' that were connected with *Les Noces corinthiennes.* So we are not surprised when scattered points in the preface bear witness to a divided mind. Though A.F. cannot feel music, yet he believes it superior to poetry. Though he does not understand *Faust,* yet he senses that it contains a great poetic richness. That is because he impressionistically makes the poem a part of him, personally adopts it, as he had done with Racine. 'Quand je lis le *Faust,* c'est mon *Faust.*' So he does not mind a certain amount of vagueness, of suggestiveness in the effect attained. (It was about this time that Anatole was becoming more receptive towards the French Symbolists.) The hero is clearly apprehended as a 'microcosm,' whose real hell is not in any *diablerie,* but implicit in the eternal warfare between heart and head ; Mephistopheles is merely the *active* side of Faust—his sinning, struggling embodiment. This portion of the critique has led a Goethe scholar to praise the whole article as 'a subtle, searching introduction,' revealing 'deep sympathetic insight' into both parts of *Faust.*[60]

The Baron Vivant-Denon, who received attention in the *Revue des documents historiques,* was honoured by a 'Notice historique' to his tale, *Point de lendemain.*[61] Paul de Musset was appreciated for his sketch of *Le Dernier Abbé,*[62] as well as for his general knowledge of the Old Régime, and for his lack of jealousy toward his more famous brother. What is supposed to be a prelude to Paul Ginisty's *l'Année littéraire, 1891,* turns into a characteristic monody on the evanescence of books and the vanity of fame. What will posterity care for our little yellow volumes, already crumbling into dust ? Yet—and this is even more characteristic—France promptly opposes his own argument. There is no reason to think that an increasing proletariat will scorn letters : it is better qualified than the bourgeoisie to appreciate them. However, you cannot expect too much of a semi-socialized brute, caught in the universal flow of things.

Passing over some minor matters, we reach a group of Introductions to notable fictional resuscitations of the ancient world. As might be expected from the author of *Thaïs,* these are done with amorous care and in a choice style. The first is a preface to Flaubert's *Hérodias.* Our critic had admired the sturdy Norman ever since he visited him on his estate in the early seventies.[63] The chief fault that he found with the realist was ever his excessive devotion to documentation and archæology. But in the case of *Hérodias* these objections are not raised ; and France himself leans considerably in that direction. In fact, the greater part of this long preface is given over to a brilliant account, rather *à la* Renan, of the Herodias—and the Herods—of history.[64] This is followed by some remarks on Flaubert's sources and his painstaking erudition. The real wonder is that he has turned the pale Josephus into a substance of colour and light and magic. Salome's dance is the finest description of a dance ever written. Flaubert (or France) knows how to work up myriads of scattered details into a unified picture. Total result : 'his tale is a marvellous poem.' And the Introduction to it is an act of homage from one master-mosaïst to another.

Gautier, as a poet, was also admired by France, and it is not surprising that we find the latter embroidering prefaces (1893-94) for two of 'Théo's' prose fantasies.[65] They were both prepared or reshaped for *de luxe* reprints by Ferroud. The introduction to *Le Roi Candaule* is not the best of this group. It is jerkily composed of long quotations and *disjecta membra.* Since Herodotus was Gautier's principal source, the passage used is quoted in full. But again, it is a question of *how* the slight material is retouched by a master. After all, the tale of Gyges is mostly legendary stuff, and none the worse for that. So Gautier imaginatively transforms the story and animates it with 'a sentiment of plastic beauty quite unknown to the Greek historian.' Anatole hints that this is not exactly his own variety of 'goût antique,' that he wears his Hellenism with a difference.[66]

Several times in his essays France recurs to the *motif* and the 'vision' of Cleopatra. When he writes that he composed in a day or two the elaborate preface to Gautier's *Une Nuit de Cléopâtre,* we are at first surprised. But the surprise vanishes when the preface is compared with a couple of articles written for *Le Temps* about four years previously.[67] The essential matter and even the wording of the two productions are almost identical. The fact that the articles had recently been reprinted in book-form did not deter France from using them again in this preface. Certain alterations are made in view of the different occasions for which the two versions were written. Since the *Temps* articles dealt ostensibly with a play by Sardou and with a book by Houssaye, the material on these men is deleted for the preface. Some allusions to Shakespeare, the quotation of Heredia's sonnet, and the development about Little Pierre's vision of Cleopatra also disappear. There are added a few allusions to Gautier, but no criticism or analysis of the actual story in question. It is a typical specimen of a warmed-over dish.

But the dish in itself is excellently served and spiced ; it will not hurt us to taste of the chef's handiwork. He manipulates with ease his raw material, i.e., the Roman historians, orators, poets. He dismisses categorically certain legends : Cleopatra was no 'monster' and as far as we know she did not love promiscuously. But she loved dangerously, she loved beautifully, and that is perhaps the main reason why her figure is immortal. We do not know what she really looked like. But we know that she was sufficiently fascinating to stir both Cæsar and Antony. The affair with the latter Roman was beautiful, if you like, but it was also 'terrible,' in its effects, its madness, its disproportion, its challenge to Nemesis, who took prompt revenge. Cleopatra herself was not without political perspicacity and had some idea of measure and harmony ; but she was forced beyond herself by her position and her passion. As for Antony, 'ce Grec démesuré' was doubtless a good soldier, yet he had in him less of classic balance than of Oriental disorder and a certain 'romantic eloquence.' . . Most of the treatment is from this rather curious, over-literary standpoint. The saving grace is that Anatole himself semi-romanticizes his classical example and writes about it in sentences that are as beautifully carved and as richly laden as the barge that swam the Cydnus.

A few miscellaneous prefaces of France's middle period may be briefly summarized. In the course of some perfunctory compliments to Di Rienzi's *Profils contemporains,*[68] Anatole expresses scepticism about the judgment of posterity as providing a test of literary excellence. He also wrote an 'Epigramme' in the Neo-Hellenic manner to Maurras' *Le Chemin de Paradis,* thus obtaining the effusive and lasting gratitude of the latter.[69] In introducing a poem called *Mentis,* by Léon Hély, A.F. sadly confides his horror before the 'universal flow of things,' the emptiness of the skies, the hollowness of modern science which reveals these facts. We shall find that this was a frequent mood in the later series of *La Vie littéraire.*

Marcel Proust, then a youthful *précieux,* knew and admired

France—who may be in part the 'Bergotte' of *A la Recherche du Temps perdu*—and was well received in the Caillavet circle. It is stated that through the influence of Mme. de Caillavet, Anatole was reluctantly persuaded to write a preface to *Les Plaisirs et les Jours* (1896).[70] This is probably nearer the truth than unauthenticated suggestions that above France's name Mme. de C. herself wrote the introduction and that the former had no use for Proust.[71] As for Brousson's fiction that the preface was written after he became Anatole's secretary (1904), that absurdity has been quite discredited.[72]

In several respects the said preface bears the hallmarks of A.F.'s style and thought. The manner of it is graceful, enveloping, *fin-de-siècle*. In the youthful decadent's reveries and sketches, the master unerringly discerns his future psychological prowess. Already his portraits show 'a marvellous power of observation, an intelligence that is subtle, delicate and penetrating.' The hot-house atmosphere, the analyses of snobbery, the addiction to 'invented and artistic sorrows,' are all perceived and commented upon. Proust is a mixture of a 'depraved Bernardin de Saint-Pierre and an ingenuous Petronius.' Were further proof of the authorship needed, it could be found in a reference to the grave Hesiod, his *Travaux et les Jours*.

Finally, in that same year Anatole, again following Renan, wrote from Palermo a 'Lettre de Sicile,'[73] to serve as a preface to Bellessort's translation of the *Oaristys,* an idyll attributed to Theocritus. Once more France endeavours, not in vain, to recapture the beauty of ancient rustic life and the monuments that preserve its memory. We hear of the gardens of myrtles, the fountain of Arethusa, the song of the pine tree piercing the blue empyrean. We watch the modern successors of the amorous Daphnis and the flushed Amaryllis. Cenotaphs and steles in honour of Theocritus show that the Syracusans have not forgotten their bard. But did he really write this idyll? Anatole mentions arguments on either side and characteristically fails to conclude. 'Truth is a Biblis that slips between our fingers.'

From these specimens, what are we to think of A.F.'s 'eternal introductions'? Grouping them with those found in *Le Génie latin,* it appears, first, that France really liked doing this sort of work, when the subject was well within the compass of his interests. Brevity and ennui mark the notices where this is not the case. But it is worth observing that the best of them were to have been combined in a volume of 'Récits historiques'; for the historical penchant combined with the biographical is the most pronounced leaning in many of the pages analysed above. We cannot agree, with M. Giraud, that *all* the prefaces are 'finely written and extremely living,' nor that a complete edition of them would be as 'interesting' as it would surely be extensive.[74] But we are glad to have the volumes of selections that have severally appeared. A final point: Anatole's literary parsimony is again illustrated by the fact that he uses more than once the greater part of the material found in these prefaces.

§ 8

NONE of the above writings are so important as the articles resulting from France's long association with *l'Univers illustré*. This was a weekly, something like our old *Harper's Bazaar* and still more like *l'Illustration* of today. Designed for general and family consumption, it offered Conservatism with a spice and addressed its readers in a familiar and chatty tone. It ran sections devoted to current news, politics, the theatre, and occasional book-reviews, the whole illustrated in the taste of the times. Here as in American magazines of the period we may see the last beautiful days of the old woodcuts and the passage to photogravure. One section called 'Courrier de Paris' was written in alternation by several collaborators, who signed themselves collectively 'Gérôme.' Anatole was 'Gérôme' every other week from March 3, 1883, through August 23, 1890.[75]

Above his own signature, he continued his fortnightly contributions for six years more. But these later articles do not seem so authentic. Genuine as 'Gérôme,' he became adulterated as 'Anatole France,' thus scoring on the editor who had insisted on the full signature. Secretarial aid was invoked for many articles of the nineties. It is believed that Madame de Caillavet sustained his pen even to the extent of appropriating that graceful object—so closely could she imitate his style and thought.[76] It is certain that the alleged 'Anatole,' with plentiful paste and scissors, began about 1893 to repeat voluminously in *l'Univers illustré* what he had previously said there or elsewhere.[77] We simply do not know as a rule which of the later articles are wholly Francian ; until the canon is established we confine ourselves, with some important exceptions, to the utterances of 'Gérôme.' Corroborative additions from the later material may, however, be found in Appendix A.

There is enough, in all conscience, before the end of August, 1890. By that time this half of 'Papa' Gérôme had written about two hundred articles, each of them running to several columns.[78] Nearly one hundred were composed when France joined *Le Temps,* after which we find a curious contrast in tone between the two sets of contributions. The *Vie littéraire* is naturally the more dignified, as well as more 'literary' in content. The 'Courrier de Paris' continues to be easy and familiar. Although the author was modest about his achievements as 'Gérôme,' others maintain that these chronicles should certainly be preserved.[79] The results of France's morganatic marriage with *l'Univers illustré* are often fresh and lovely creatures, and it is a pity that they have vanished from the world's knowledge. Let us try to rehabilitate them.

What subjects were of interest to casual French readers fifty years ago ? Apparently the most diverse topics (thought our author), beginning with Anatole himself. For the personal note is by now strongly audible, and we learn first of all a good deal about his private life, most of which has already been embedded in these pages. We participate in his diversions and avocations, his relations with a number of people, and we hark back with him to the moods and memories of college days. We hear, of course, something about *bibelots* and still more about his literary principles, admirations, dislikes. Nor is this all of it. The chronicler for a 'Courrier de Paris' must show himself as a fully equipped Parisian. The monuments, the street-life, the expositions of the capital are woven into the ample pattern and are embroidered with many a sly quirk of humour and many a dig at the municipal authorities. In politics, the Anatole of this period remains a 'good' Conservative, an attitude compatible with much criticism of the Republic, while in religion he is respectful towards the Church, as regards both her belief and her practice. This does not prevent a distinct taste for the supernatural and the occult. Occasionally a tale of that nature, like 'Leslie Wood,' will be woven in.[80] His enduring concern with historical matters, his objections to the Revolution and the Commune are reinforced.

His interest in women, particularly in actresses, remains unabated. In general, we come closer to the man, to his ways of thinking and feeling.

Let us sketch first his attitude as a *chroniqueur,* together with his views on the art of writing.

A.F. realizes that a journalist is primarily an entertainer. Ever-bored humanity is apt to demand its bedtime stories in the daytime. So Gérôme's task is to beguile his readers and to hold them in confidential chats. He usually takes light subjects, or he takes serious subjects lightly ; he will not grieve with the judicious ; he would rather flock with the populace. Hence the prominence of tales and anecdotes in the 'Courrier.' Sketches of such people as Hugo and Balzac consist largely of stories about them. An anecdote or a joke is frequently used as a concluding touch to a *chronique.* But in addition to entertainment the reader and Gérôme also want savour, elegance, charm. Such qualities, thank Heaven, can still be found in Paris : 'Do you know what I am looking for ? *Je cherche des élégances.* I should like to show you something delicate, subtle, exquisite. . .' Often there is more of this in the past than in the present, and Anatole confesses to his passion for the past, again admits how he loves to 'make the stones talk.' Ever since little Pierre ran round the Quai Malaquais, the stones have been speaking to our attentive author.

Literary criticism, Anatole emphasizes, is not primarily the chronicler's concern, although we shall disinter a fair amount of the informal variety. His attitude in this field is personal and already half-Impressionistic. Our divergent theories of art can accord only with our individual qualities and defects. No painter can contemplate with real satisfaction any painting but his own. Whoever interprets 'my Racine' must be very careful. More broadly, the good critic must be in love with his subject and with beauty at large. Anticipating a well-known later passage, France declares that such truly appreciative criticism is an admirable invention of the nineteenth century : 'it presupposes a marvellous culture of the mind.'

The individual trend suggested here represents Anatole's vagabondage, the thrust of his personality against authority. Yet there was one kind of bondage that held even him in thrall : he was, as we know, a devotee of reason and of the traditional virtues of French classicism. Thereby he finds himself in temporary agreement with the dogmatic Brunetière, whom in a few years he would attack so vehemently. At present, he is glad to link himself with the future editor of the *Revue des deux mondes* as having an equal comprehension of Molière, an equal detestation of Zola. He is pleased to be in the company of such a rational critic, acquainted with the abiding laws of the human mind. Indeed, our vagabond always headed toward the more stable shrines of beauty and taste. Here as in the *Livre de mon ami,* he protests against teaching science to children; talk to them rather 'of the beautiful and the good, which are soul-elevating.' Like all the Epicureans, he would have us cling to the fleeting beauty of the Rose; but for him she is a symbol less of nature than of whatever civilized man may have snatched from the wild waste of creation. Let each person hold to his vision of supernal beauty, let him adore this with the adoration of the Magi. Let us all recognize—once more—that Illusion is essential. Science may deal with *tacenda:*

> But Art, whose single aim is to please and console us, should tell us only, through delicious falsehoods, that life is good and that the earth is beautiful.[81]

The true preservative of beauty is taste, and French taste, he thinks, has done as much for the world as Christianity did. Later, he thought it had done more. It is evident that taste is pretty well extinct today,[82] in an age of parvenus and profiteers; all the more reason, he intimates, why the children of light should protect their inner radiance. Nor should their light shine in eccentric fashion. *Naïveté* is the best sign of originality, and simplicity is more blessèd than decadence.

Thus Anatole held fast to the classical virtues, whether they be drawn from antiquity or from the age of Louis XIV. The ancients, to be sure, find little place in this journalistic record, for Gérôme knew what his public would stand. A few references to Sophocles and to Virgil's Dido, along familiar lines, are considered quite sufficient. The French classical period receives brief but earnest tribute. If Anatole has any purity in his style or any nobility in his thought, it is because he was steeped as a youth in seventeenth-century drama. Racine, he avers, is still his idol, while Molière, he insists, is all compact of gaiety. The latter is a social conservative rather than a pessimist or sceptic; the former may be a 'Christian psychologist,' but happily he mixes unguarded emotions with his Jansenistic formalism. We learn, incidentally, that France had already seen *Phèdre* no less than eight times and had decided views as to the proper stage-setting for this play.

§ 9

In spite of our critic's love for the Old Régime, eighteenth-century literature, for obvious reasons, can receive but little attention in *l'Univers illustré*. Rousseau, that compound of rascal and angel, had a master-gift of eloquence and the power to make a whole generation feel as he felt. But Anatole does not want to feel like that. Since tradition is his mainstay, we cannot expect to find him very cordial towards nineteenth-century men and movements. We shall not here particularize his opinions on very many individual writers, for that would involve much repetition. He sets his face for the most part against such movements as Romanticism, Naturalism, and Symbolism. Faded entirely is his former cult of the Romantics. Chateaubriand, whom the elder France had unduly admired, is great only in the *Mémoires d'Outre-Tombe* and only because (anticipating Anatole), he there indulges in wistful recollections of his youth. The high priest, Hugo, now seems to our critic a lubberly wight—a remarkable poet, if you like, but lubberly. His extraordinary drawings, in which pale heroines gibber at the moon, reel with a terribly romantic attitudinizing. And the poems ? Well, if Hugo had been a properly balanced person, he would never have invented that theory of the grotesque, which is suitable to his own queer genius but not to a mannered world.

Were his contemporaries much better ? The elder Dumas, at any rate, created more living characters, while George Sand (as before) seems to France wholly admirable in her understanding both of nature and of human passions. He is enthusiastic about her correspondence with Flaubert, the 'giant' whom he sketches from personal knowledge. This reminds us of Anatole's visit to Flaubert in Normandy and of that subsequent superb preface to *Hérodias*. Gérôme's opinion of Balzac, as the greatest creator of a dream-world since Shakespeare, is appreciative and well-founded. And he is still fond of Daudet, especially of the *Tartarin* series.

In contrast to such praise is the attitude taken toward Zola, whose name, after that of Renan, looms largest in these pages.

We have seen above that Anatole stood strongly against the doctrine of Naturalism; if it takes us back to nature, as people say, what a 'shameless and violent Nature' she must be! What a ridiculous interpreter has she chosen in M. Zola! Again, France waxes ironic (for irony is one of Gérôme's best weapons) anent Zola the redoubtable—whether as a possible Academician, or as a user of low language, or as a self-appointed prophet. Granted the power of certain novels, one must also grant the filthiness of others. These peasants, these kitchen-maids, this pseudo-science, this belief that the novel should become 'naturalistic, documentary, physiological, pathological, natalogical, scatological . . .' anything but Art! I want Beauty not the Beast. But that ugly vogue is passing. We weary of everything even (housewives please copy) of the kitchen sink.

With regard to poetic movements, we note first that France has now cooled toward the Parnassians and says little about them. Relations with Leconte de Lisle have become strained; there is only a perfunctory notice of the Master's elevation to the Academy. Baudelaire is now adjudged too gruesome. As for later movements, the 'Décadents' or Symbolists demand ironic treatment. 'Among the Decadents, atrocious nonsense is a signal mark of talent.' Their manifesto, issued by Prophet Moréas, is riddled by much the same protests that we shall find subsequently in 'La Vie littéraire.' But let us not advertise all this 'deliquescent literature' with its typical neuroses. Verlaine, the 'humble, innocent and naïve' child of Bohemia, is partially excepted from this indictment; his verses may not mean much, but they are exquisitely musical.

Certain tributes to other contemporaries do not call for development here. Such are the remarks on the brilliance of Barrès, whom France treats gingerly, or on the excellence of Augier and the younger Dumas. Several authors are lauded for reasons partly personal. Thus Pailleron, Anatole's charming old neighbour, is hailed, rather too amiably, as a 'true French classic'; thus the budding talents of Hervieu and of Loti are encouraged—perhaps because they too were protégés of Madame de Caillavet.

The writer most frequently honoured in the 'Courrier' is Ernest Renan, whose death in 1892 moved Anatole more deeply than any other literary event of the time. In general, as we shall maintain later, there is reason for believing that no author, not even Voltaire, more profoundly affected the mind and talent of France. His eulogies of Renan, frequent in these pages,[83] increase in volume and emphasis during the next two decades and culminate in the sincere flattery of the *Vie de Jeanne d'Arc,* whose method imitates that of the *Vie de Jésus.* 'Gérôme,' however, is less concerned with Renan the thinker than with the 'enchanter,' the Merlin of our age.

We find first a tribute to the 'fine mystical language' in which the ex-cleric celebrates the delights of renunciation. Then an entire article is given over to a review of the *Souvenirs d'enfance et de jeunesse* (1883), that 'most lovable' book—which surely was not without its effect on the *Livre de mon ami,* then in process of composition. 'The youth of distinguished men,' says Anatole, 'narrated by themselves, has a certain charm which moves us powerfully.' For by their appealing youth these writers resemble us. So with Rousseau, Sand, Chateaubriand, Dickens, Renan—a list that sounds familiarly on our ears.[84] The last-named best links feeling with high intellect. We are surprised to find him cavilling at friendship, for without such affections how could he have written those pages of living dreams and delights ? [85] It is not strange that women in particular adore his idealizations, for the hall-mark of his mind is its 'gentle nobility.'

In his last years Renan wrote some closet-dramas which scandalized certain rigorists. France defends the pagan legend of *Le Prêtre de Némi* and the illicit passion depicted in *l'Abbesse de Jouarre.* Why should not the historian write of love, taken on a high level ? That is how Renan takes everything (France speaks from personal knowledge), and altogether the Master awakens in him 'an infinite admiration and a profound attachment.' Amiability, candour and simplicity are among his salient attributes. When Renan died, Anatole wrote an open letter to the editor of *l'Univers illustré,*[86] in which he declares that though grief-stricken he wishes to bear testimony to the Master's courage and greatness. This very morning for the twentieth time he reopened that peerless volume of *Souvenirs.* Repeating what he had said before about the charm attaching to childhood recollections, France insists that Renan's secret and his chief literary lesson is that 'we should write only of what we love.' Evidently Anatole is doing that. He sketches sympathetically the life and works of the dead man, who was the first to give us a true understanding of the Orient, whose style had always the perfect naturalness of conversation, who while he thought mere literature frivolous yet became one of the great literary artists of his age. Of no other modern does France speak in such exalted terms.

One peculiar variety of criticism found in these columns would include some anonymous self-praise, together with 'puffs' for the works of Anatole's friends and collaborators. Through discreet references to 'M. Anatole France,' [87] we are informed that he is high on the road to Parnassus ; we learn excellent things about *Les Noces corinthiennes* and *Le Crime de Sylvestre Bonnard,* that work of a master-hand. Gérôme unblushingly calls Anatole an 'exquisite writer,' a 'brother of the bees,' and points out that George Sand returned his hearty admiration. Copious fragments of *Le Livre de mon ami* are quoted before book-publication, much as they were read by A.F. in the salon of Mme. Aubernon ; and it is interesting to know that the author of these delicious morsels has just been decorated (New Year, 1885) as a Chevalier de la Légion d'Honneur.

Still as Gérôme, France is equally bountiful of space for the benefit of his friends and co-workers. Similar tributes, especially in behalf of Coppée and Sully Prudhomme, had already been insinuated in the columns of the obscurer journals dealt with above ; so Anatole already knew how the press could extend a helping hand. Its 'power' is here turned to account—first, on behalf of Etienne Charavay, that skilful Chartiste, whose business as a dealer in autographs is cleverly boosted. One puff gives us an early pen-portrait of Etienne as 'a small, gentle figure,' but valorous withal, as was shown in the campaigns of 1870-71. The article that glorifies the Café Procope [88] also pays tribute to Etienne's varied erudition, shown in organizing the Exposition of the French Revolution. His brother-in-law, the robust Fernand Calmettes, together with other Parnassian comrades, are likewise awarded free advertising.

For example, François Coppée has just been made an Academician. He is admired by all for the charm and truth of his poetry. If he has kept his fine simplicity, that is because (like A.F.) he grew up in a humble and healthy environment. Again like France, he has recorded with insight his early impressions and he loves Paris as his fatherland. Incidentally, the two men were also fellow-spirits in that both resigned with dignity from their onerous sinecures as librarians; Coppée's letter of resignation is quoted, and its terms are strikingly like those in which France insisted, before the library board of the Senate, on the merits and due emoluments of the author's calling.

Who were the collaborators of France on *l'Univers illustré,* and particularly who were the other components of 'Gérôme,' that multiple personality? It seems to be established that Ludovic Halévy occasionally and 'Richard O'Monroy' usually wrote the alternate numbers of the 'Courrier de Paris,' when France took his week off. Since it was a feature of the 'Courrier' to treat several different topics in the same issue, it may be that there was more criss-crossing of contributions than we can now satisfactorily disentangle. At any rate, when France was clearly 'Gérôme,' he naturally wrote some puffs for his collaborators, even as they did in turn for him. It seems likely that the pseudonym 'Richard O'Monroy' is an insidious pun on that song of the Old Régime: *O Richard, ô mon roi,* which harks back to the days of Blondel and the lionhearted king. The journalist's real name was the Vicomte de Geniès. As a man about town, he apparently took charge in these columns of sporting events and the like. Regarding the division of labour, France once confided that he and O'Monroy were the Castor and Pollux of the journal. Pollux, as the more dazzling twin, is better fitted to wear heroic helmets and to write on subjects of a worldly and elegant interest, while I am restricted to such matters as the Black Mass. . . For his part, O'Monroy once declared that on alternate weeks 'Gérôme' changed his spots—and that he could lay no claim to the ideas of his 'witty colleague.' Several of the Vicomte's lively volumes of stories are here commended by Anatole. The latter's journalistic complaisance extended even to the point of boosting to the skies his predecessor in the chair of 'Gérôme,' a certain Armand de Pontmartin, who is exalted as one of the foremost critic-historians of his time. France is guilty of the same exaggeration, though with the further excuse of gallantry, when he lauds so frequently the sprightly pen of 'Gyp,' alias the Comtesse de Martel. An occasional contributor to *l'Univers illustré,* this lady was also a friend of the France household and has left, as we shall see, important testimony concerning its dissolution. To call the authoress of the witty *Autour du mariage* a charming writer is doubtless correct; to speak of her as a serious *moraliste* is quite another matter. One must admit that France's personal relations with authors frequently caused deviations of his critical needle.

Anatole's solicitude for the French language is always apparent. We have seen that he admired Renan, as he admired the 'grands classiques,' partly because of their mastery of the mother-tongue. None better than Pascal and Racine incorporate the pure genius of the language. Such a stylist as the author of *Thaïs* would naturally savour and insist upon perfection in the writing of French. Yet its niceties, he maintains, cannot be learned from schoolmasters; grammarians are mostly geese, and grammars are mausoleums for the defunct imperfect subjunctive. And France still dislikes the tortuous dislocated style of the Goncourts. As for a universal language, we are all becoming standardized fast enough. Why not use numbers? Why not say, '3278' instead of 'Mademoiselle, je vous aime'? . . . It is curious to reflect that when Anatole joined the Academy he participated in a movement for simplified spelling.[89]

§ 10

So much for his literary views, in general and in particular. What about his philosophy of life during this important period?

The France of the later eighties is no longer so keen on science (to which he never quite returns) and definitely opposes humanism to the natural world. In the latter realm it may be necessary for species to devour one another—a wide-spread habit which he had emphasized in his poems—but this no longer seems a proper law for mankind. Do we progress? As to this he is by no means certain; he even contravenes Renan by doubting whether the good ultimately emerges. It might, if the world were well-guided, but decidedly it is not an orderly world. It whirls eccentrically on an inclined axis, and every leaf in it chooses to differ from its neighbour.[90] 'My friend, nature does not like symmetry.' But man, you will say, is defined as a reasoning animal. Really? Perhaps reason is the ability to decide between two follies. Man is in a state of perpetual uncertainty about himself, and knowing nothing whatever about his latter end, he is yet harried by Death, ever riding nearer.

Hence a brief apologue, pointing the usual Epicurean moral. The other day, in the Louvre, he saw a lovely lady contemplating the massive architecture of Persia. But 'the wisest are those who do not forget the value of the passing hour.' She proved her wisdom, as well as her loveliness, by merely glancing at the Persian remains and hastening out into the warm sunshine, doubtless to a rendezvous. Love, however, is a most variable affair, differing enormously according to climates. Generally, it is fluctuating 'opinion,' as the Marquis Tudesco had insisted, that makes and unmakes standards. Anatole speaks like Montaigne in calling this opinion an 'uncertain and changeful thing.' And the old lesson of relativity is reinforced by an appeal to the great race of sceptics: 'That strong race indigenous to our soil, which reaches the heights of genius with Rabelais, Montaigne and Voltaire.'[91] These were three among his own forbears. 'All the masters of French thought,' he avers elsewhere, 'were sceptics, and I am their humble pupil.'[92] He continues that tribute by naming again the three writers abovementioned, together with Molière and Renan.

How indeed, inquires Gérôme, could we get through our earthly journey without strong doses of scepticism? Sweet are the uses of relativity, which teaches us abundant tolerance. Indulgent, humane and slightly ironic withal, Gérôme still applauds, understands, or commiserates his fellow-men. At this stage, he is all for sympathy and kindness. He hates cruelty to man or beast, whether on the part of the hunter or of the vivisectionist. What sort of a doctor do we most admire? Not the rigorous specialist, but the old-fashioned family practitioner, who is not drained dry of pity and human feeling. Our philosopher still esteems the charity of the New Testament as a major virtue. It is better than justice, for how are we to be 'just' and in whose name? In that of Brutus, perhaps? Nonsense! 'The world is founded not on justice which slays, but on love which multiplies.' Christianity is right in enforcing divine grace as the true law of human nature. Racine and Renan, his two demigods, realize the power of this grace as well as that of kindly affection. France's own domestic happiness probably leads him benevolently to associate the Christmas season with good cheer and the rejoicings of children.

But clouds began to gather in the late eighties; their sombre reflection is cast upon the pages of this 'Courrier' soon afterwards. Indeed, traces of pessimism are found throughout the record. The spectacle of human affairs and the condition of men, we read, are gloomy and wretched. This is partly because we are easily bored, and 'boredom is the worst of evils.' France now reverses the lesson of imminent death : dust we are very soon, we make lamentable endings, and so the foretaste of death is in our delights. Youth and Spring may lure us on—but they are only lures. Even knowledge may prove a curse, since man was not made to know. How can a being full of contradictions extract clear ideas from life's confusions ? Why should the spirit of mortal be proud ? We are all feeble and corrupted by Satan.

Much of the above was written in the Spring of 1890, which decidedly was a bad time for Anatole. Before that date, radical pessimism is not fundamental in his nature. He became a radical after his intimate happiness was destroyed ; while that flourished, he seemed in many ways a conservative—in literature, in political and social matters, even in his attitude towards religion. Probably the standards of *l'Univers illustré* inclined him still more in the conservative direction. At any rate, for a time he allowed the Yea side of him full scope. Soon enough it will be the turn of the Everlasting Nay.

In general, declares Gérôme, true progress issues from a respect for tradition, and all revolutionaries are abominable. The continuity of the French tradition in letters and its value in matters of art and taste are repeatedly emphasized. The effect of such conservatism on France's historical and political views will concern us shortly. It is noteworthy that he supports the Church against municipal reformers who sought to laicize the Pantheon and remove the names of saints from the city streets. A decade later, M. Bergeret would gladly laicize the Pantheon, together with everything else.

§ II

As an observer of men and things, Anatole often weaves in 'impressions' from his travels. During this period we note the beginnings of that taste for travelling and adventuring which became so marked in his later years. Not yet, as far as we know, has he visited his favourite Italy ; but it appears that he has already been in London and has viewed with favour the 'jeunes misses' of Pre-Raphaelite tendencies. This penchant will reappear in *Le Lys rouge*. He is less pleased with the streetwalkers and sniffs at the hypocrisy of the English authorities in affecting to ignore them. Surely they manage such things better in France.

Occasionally in these later years he would spend his vacation at Saint-Valery-sur-Somme, where he composed that part of *Pierre Nozière* which deals with the young man's 'Promenades en France.' Such outings, we have seen, were enjoyable enough for a few weeks. He came to know Brittany, too, in the eighties; his remarks on Breton folklore attracted the favourable attention of Renan, who presently invited France to visit him in the country of the 'pardons.'[93] There were, of course, excursions to such places as Fontainebleau and Compiègne, while some descriptions of the country surrounding Bougival and Malmaison suggest a sojourn there. Yet Anatole is not particularly good at descriptions of scenery. He lacked the appreciative eye as well as the feeling for Nature.

But his own metropolis still remained his abiding love, as one writer has sufficiently shown. Says Mr. Stewart:

> Anatole France was first and foremost a child of Paris . . . it was his immediate surroundings which not only constituted his material but in great measure formed his temperament.[94]

Another critic says that Paris would be less Paris, 'if M. France had not described it.'[95] He willingly called himself a 'vieux Parisien,' full of experience; and he never forgot that he was officially conducting a 'Courrier de Paris,' which often turned into a tour of the metropolis. So his columns contain more information and comment about the city than about any other single topic. Leaving his own Quarter, Little Pierre has evolved into an accomplished boulevardier, who glorifies the joys of strolling along and taking in the sights. For the true Parisian, he maintains, is by nature, a loafer, 'flâneur et badaud.' Let us accompany 'Papa Gérôme' on his evening strolls.

He will ramble down the Rue Sainte-Beuve and congratulate himself that the city fathers have not yet abolished *that* saint from their sign-posts. He will return to the Boulevards and pleasantly greet his friends under the flaring gas-lights. He leans on his cane and studies the theatrical placards on the Morris columns.

'Shall we go to the theatre this evening?' offers Henry Roujon or Charles Grandjean.

'No, I don't think so,' answers Anatole with a sigh. 'I don't find any Racine, and the modern stage is ruined by the vulgarity of the cafés-concerts.'

A tirade (oft-repeated) against the loudness and coarseness of these institutions, which offend against the sacred mysteries of *la Volupté*. Let us go to a brasserie! At the Chat Noir, Caran d'Ache is showing his superb silhouettes. That will remind us of the atmosphere of *Le Chat maigre,* perhaps. It will be an engaging pastime to watch the artists and the women there; and *en route,* to observe 'that gentle gaiety which the Parisian naturally exhibits in the street.' Another night, he will call for Charavay—passing, of course, by the old haunts on the Quai Malaquais, where unfortunately some of the best antiquity-shops are closing down. For old times' sake, these twain proceed to the Café Procope, soon to be abolished, and drink their beer at the red marble table, where Voltaire once sat, and where Gambetta held forth in his youth. Those were truly the salad days, declared Anatole Himself to Ségur, when thought soared freely, as on wings.[96]

On other occasions, we may approve with him the Punch-and-Judy shows, especially if Suzanne comes along; or the wooden stalls and the itinerant venders on the Boulevards—provided they do not sell those ugly *articles de Paris*. He is fonder than Jean Servien was of street-scenes on the fourteenth of July and he loves the street fairs, especially the 'gingerbread fair,' to which he goes every year. . . One afternoon, we will climb with other pilgrims up to the Sacré-Cœur and contemplate the great city lying in a golden haze below. Another day, leaving the big smelly vital thoroughfares, we will wander in the intricate sidepaths of the Bois. Or we rediscover a 'magic corner' of the Luxembourg . . . the white queens . . . old memories . . . water, trees, and flowers combining in sunny landscapes, where no traffic impedes our loitering. 'Never say that Paris is deserted in September, or if it is deserted, say that it is never more lovable to a devotee.'

Let us saunter in the working quarters, where the girls are like Tanagra figurines. Let us take a couple of pretty *midinettes* out to lunch—always a favourite pastime. Or on a balmy Spring evening, let us catch the fragrance from the carts of the flower-merchants (Anatole ever adores flowers), let us be charmed by a Parisienne throwing open her coat to reveal an exquisite corsage. 'How I love *my* city! I cherish her less for her rare beauty than for all I have gained and learned, reposing on her brightly armoured breast. I love her beyond reason, through sentiment, and especially for the multiple sensations which she gives me.'[97]

Festivals and expositions solicit his attention. The church festivals over and over: New Year's, Epiphany, Easter, Ascension, Christmas. And expositions: books, paintings, memorials of the Revolution. As for the 'fête de Neuilly,' he celebrates it every June, he repeatedly declares that it is a national institution. What a pity if it became instructive and 'Americanized'—the latter term already suggesting mechanized living! What a shame if Paris should be converted into a mere hive, a huge railway station!

His concern for the 'stones of Paris' again shows how the child was father to the man. He laments the passing of many antiquities and approves the founding of a society to guard the city's monuments. Why should the ministry neglect that civic treasure, the Arènes de Lutèce? It is fortunate that they are putting memorial plaques on the former homes of the famous dead. To come across such a tablet in a desolate quarter makes one dream of the past and revive half-forgotten images.

Our boulevardier nourishes his own memories. Though he now lives near the Etoile and frequents sales in the Hôtel Drouot, he can still hear the Boul' Mich' from afar; he keeps his fondness for the brasseries, the Musée de Cluny, the Jardin des Plantes, so wisely arranged and administered. But he follows the eternal fashion in grieving that the Quarter is no longer what it used to be. Let us cling fast to our gay recollections, let us look with sympathy upon the habits and the pranks of the students. If they wage war with grocers' assistants, may Heaven protect their bérets! If they, including Little Pierre, judge severely their professors . . . well, they are the best judges. And we view again, every September, the old picture of the Return of the Classes, and we hear again the old refrain: 'College is a prison.'

To get back to the monuments, it is clear that Anatole frequented the galleries of the Louvre. The near-by Place du Carrousel comes in for some tart criticism. In fact, there are two 'sights' in Paris that our chronicler cannot stand at any price. The Place du Carrousel, with that monstrous frock-coated Gambetta, is the shame of civilization; the Eiffel Tower is a 'terrible machine,' an 'immoderate caldron' erected to the God of Bigness. Many shared that opinion round 1889.

The *bouquins,* of course, with their aroma of the past, are not forgotten, and every now and then Gérôme remembers his earliest training as a bibliophile, e.g., when he speaks amorously of great libraries. *Bibelots,* engravings and the like become a veritable passion ; thus the future magnificence of the Villa Saïd is adumbrated. Anatole admits that he has always had a 'vast sympathy for collectors.' [98] He recognizes that this kindly feeling dates back to his childhood and was a product of his environment on the Quais. Whether in connexion with Oriental art, or with the treasures amassed by Thiers, he is constantly 'rummaging in old drawers' after historical bric-à-brac. We often find him pausing before shop-windows, taking in their contents with the eye, or the nose, of a *fureteur.*[99] This antiquarianism would naturally include engravings and costumes. The former can teach us many things—for example, that the Palais-Royal used to have grace in its gallantry.

Decorative art has always charmed him, as is shown by his remarks on the 'noble and fragile ornaments' which bedeck the dwellings of the Old Régime. Roses interwoven in the lofty marble suggest to him a light gay world tripping across a perfumed garden. But in one respect Anatole's artistic education is still incomplete. He confesses that he does not know how to look expertly at pictures. In fact, his rare comments on the Salon, or on Manet, Monet, and Bouguereau, contain little that is personal or profound. The first two painters are applauded for their modernism, while 'Bouguereau-Perfection,' it is decided, had as well keep on manufacturing sleek faultless nudes for American consumption. At any rate, France has now risen above Bouguereau. The Salon, as an institution, reminds him at once of Diderot, and characteristically he relates its history from Colbert down.

§ 12

We reach the question of France's political opinions in the earnest eighties. They form a rather surprising creed, in view of his past liberalism and his future iconoclasm. But they accord with what we know regarding his free, frequent, and often *frondeur* conversations with his intimates about the government at this time.

First of all, he wishes politics to be taken seriously. This is his 'dada,' his mania. People say that it's a tiresome subject. Not so :

it is confessedly not 'jovial,' but it is vital to all, especially under present exasperating conditions. For now, 'we are a prey to the greatest evil which can afflict a country ; we have no government at all.' Anything positive were better than this nothingness. From the Third Empire to the World War, Anatole really admired no French régime, except briefly the radical ministry of Combes. Otherwise, he was temperamentally 'agin the Government,' for a variety of reasons.[100] These formed a temporal rather than a logical sequence. Since he stands in the eighties for an efficient administration, the future image-breaker now styles himself 'very tepidly liberal' and thinks he would accept a portfolio only under a benevolent despot. He even dreams back to the graces of the old order, when the Parisienne rained influence from beyond the hurly-burly. Today the Chamber is an unholy brew, compounded from the 'vile passions of an ignorant mob'—the creature whom he later called Pecus. The elections are absurd and debasing affairs. He hates all this fuss in the streets, he is surfeited with lying placards, with meetings and speeches. He is distrustful of the ministries, particularly that of education.

Therefore Gérôme waxes ironic about liberalism, which is all too tolerant of benighted opinions ; and about the voice of the people, which is far from being the voice of God. They are so enlightened, so generous ! Was not that perfectly demonstrated in the massacres of September, 1792 ? Gérôme is privately for a strong central control, while openly and sincerely he is an ardent patriot. 'Chauvinism is one of our most precious virtues.' And though he may soften such fanfares by declaring for international reciprocities in Art, yet otherwise 'internationalism horrifies me.' What a far cry it is to the old Communist, who befriended the misunderstood nations, from Russia to Armenia ! Now as with most Frenchmen of that era, 'la Patrie' is supreme. 'Our' patriotism (meaning that of *l'Univers illustré*) is not suspect, since the Germans forbid 'us' to circulate in Alsace-Lorraine. It may be that France was warped somewhat, though probably not unwillingly, by the policy of his paper.

Nor is this all. The future pacifist is now a convinced militarist. Shades of Uncle Victor, applaud ! 'Gérôme's respect for the army is well known.' He admires a flag-waving work called *Victoires de l'armée française ;* and like many another Frenchman he cocks a sullen eye towards Berlin. He wants the permanent army maintained at its standard for security's sake; he scoffs at the idea of making the weapons of warfare less lethal. Besides, if we may believe him, he is personally fond of the 'fine and gallant' military, perhaps in memory of Pierre's belovèd toys.

Some of this thorough conservatism may be explained by France's genuine anti-Prussian patriotism; some is due to his distrust of the functioning power of the Republic. But probably a deeper cause underlies this hostile attitude.

The Commune of 1870 had destroyed democratic illusions both in Jean Servien and in his creator. The latter's recollections are still active and angry. He goes so far as to aver that the young criminals now swarming in Paris were products of that Commune, 'so often stained with crime.' Jean Servien, like another Christ, suffered for the people, and the people betrayed him. How could Anatole really believe in Pecus after that?

The working creed of Gérôme, taken by and large, seems to be something like the following:

'I believe in the true, the good and the beautiful. But the sovereign people invariably destroy whatever is true and corrupt whatever is delicate. Hence I cannot wholly believe in the "Republican" republic, or government by grocers. I believe (at times) in education; but I do not believe that universal education will bring back the Golden Age. Accursèd be the democratic ideologues who hold ye should seek salvation through loud speaking and oceans of print!

'Yet, because one must believe in something, I have a pragmatic belief in the conservative ideas of the Left Centre; but I do not believe in their representatives. To these demagogues, I prefer General Boulanger.

'I do not believe in any of the assemblies of Pecus, neither in the League against Tobacco, nor in the League for the Protection of Women, nor even in the League against Vivisection. May all such Gatherings be anathema! Shall Alca, which is Paris, then become Americanized? I believe that the crowd (which is Pecus) is besotted in its folly. Yet because the people have been misguided since the beginnings of time, I will in my infinite mercy take compassion upon them; and I will stand by the side of the meek, the humble, the disinterested; and I will say, "Blessèd are the poor, provided they are not poor fools."'

The fools, it seems, were particularly abundant among the members of the Municipal Council. These 'édiles,' as Gérôme calls them with mock-respect, were not only unintelligent about civic monuments; they also promoted an ineffective fire-department and certain abortions known as Municipal Grammars. They actively planted trees on the site of the Tuileries, where they should rather have sown salt.

This is all part of the Parisian's usual levity concerning officialdom, which includes municipalities, ministries, and census-takers. Individual politicians, statesmen by courtesy, are sharply analysed. Duruy, who had shaken up the old educational system, was admittedly a good minister. But Jules Ferry, prominent for secularizing education, is here simply characterized as a Bonapartist devil. We gather elsewhere that Gambetta in the flesh was hardly better than his statue. He was 'a great talker, before the Lord.'[101] Gérôme gives a keen description of Clemenceau in his early days. He has 'hollow brilliant eyes, salient cheek-bones, and a lively manner.' Fallières, not yet President, is astute, which is more than can be said for Rouvier. In view of his fatal end, Anatole takes almost a prophetic tone about the frail black-bearded Sadi Carnot.

But the political comet of those times and the idol of the populace was the troublesome General Boulanger. This meteor swam into the ken and sometimes the approval even of the intelligentsia. The latter were displeased, as France was, with the loud-mouthed leaders of the Republican republic. To these Left-Centrists, Boulanger seemed to stand for the recovery of his country's prestige, for 'glory,' and possibly for 'la Revanche.' So Anatole in these columns is not so hard on 'Chatillon' as he became later in *l'Ile des Pingouins*. Military heroes do not now offend Gérôme, who finds in the General some excellent traits: for example, a good memory and a willingness to serve people. As the central personage of holiday street-scenes, he is a fine upstanding figure—though perhaps too cunning and too conscious of himself in a Napoleonic role. But later, in 1889, when Boulanger became more prominent, Gérôme appears to have lost this shadow of distrust. He declares that the General is at any rate not a professional politician and he is admired in all camps. He is a symbol and an ideal. Hail to the 'hero,' on his magnificent black charger! . . . We have seen that Anatole's disillusionment swiftly followed.—He had apparently become interested in the

General through the influence of Mme. de Loynes' aristocratic salon.[102]

Politics are after all an extension of history; and some of Anatole's views on contemporary affairs are grounded in the remote past. Archæology, to be sure, strikes him as an inexact and useless science . . . and consequently rather amusing. Are there some 'braves gens' who concern themselves with flints and reindeer? Well, well! Does a Portuguese think he has discovered Tertiary Man? Ah, but this Tertiary Man is for ever eluding us and has to be discovered all over again.

Although the author of *La Rôtisserie de la Reine Pédauque* naturally loves to piece together mosaics of the past, yet he knows that it is impossible to create a genuine historical reconstruction. Fragmentary voices come to us, from the Assyrian wing of the Louvre, or from the lips of Madame Custine, cleverly restored to life and sighing for her faithless Chateaubriand. Pleasing are the voices, sweet are the wandering odours from the perfumed alleys of the long ago. When Gérôme visits a mellow old town, such as Avranches, he steeps himself in its secular history. When he attends the Exposition of the Revolution and finds the quarter of Saint-Antoine built up again in terms of 1789, he revels in the enchantment of the scene. Thus he savours the poetry of the past and crowds the street with fantastic figures; we shiver at the thought that their bones are long since dust.

Anatole's curiosity keeps him alert in the search for historical detail. He knows when the art of cooking was established in France. He knows that his favourite eighteenth century was unhygienic. He keeps up his excellent habit of carrying back an institution, say New Year's presents or the prison of Saint-Lazare, to its earliest foundations.

There is not a great deal here about the Middle Ages—the era which Madame de Caillavet later insisted on his cultivating. At present he considers the fifteenth century as the 'saddest epoch in our history.' There are, however, several significant passages referring to Joan of Arc. In one he mentions a manuscript chronicle which singularly vivifies 'la brave Jeanne.' In another, he again assumes the tone of an authority and recapitulates what has been learned about Joan in the last sixty years. Evidently his interest in her and his knowledge of the period are still increasing. He is maturing his final conception of her as undeniably a heroic figure, who was at the same time a product of natural and environmental forces.

But as a whole it is the eighteenth century, Old Régime and Revolution, that interests him most; and especially does the Old Régime still retain its seductive power. It may be, he now admits, that the lords and ladies of the time slapped paint and powder on their unwashed surfaces; but in comparison with what followed, they were charming surfaces. The reign of Louis XVI was at least 'amiable.' The vogue for amateur theatricals throughout the whole period allures France, as it had once allured Voltaire. Casual remarks show Anatole as already poring over engravings of the epoch—the engravings which he later used as sources.

Incidentally, there is much in these columns about Naundorff, the false Louis XVII.[103] The phrase, 'la fauxdauphinomanie,' was coined to denote this obsession. Furthermore, France evinces his constant interest in impostors and pretenders of various kinds. This appears also in connexion with the Maid of Orleans' imitators. Could Renan have awakened this concern for false Messiahs and the psychology of the credulous?

Anatole may dwell upon the pictorial side of Saint-Antoine, but he cannot love it otherwise. He knows it too well. He may endure and pity, but he will not embrace. Just as he objected to the Commune, so he still objects to the Terror, with its new tyranny and coarseness. The ugliness of the Revolution, above all, is what he cannot forgive. Though sometimes sublime, it was often horrible and always tasteless, as the Exposition abundantly shows. There were no truly great men among its leaders (elsewhere he excepts Mirabeau). The portraits of Danton reveal him as common and ignoble, for all his power of speech and decision. Marat was a toad-like neurasthenic, Robespierre a vain fool, Saint-Just a 'horrible and virginal rascal,' while Camille Desmoulins—one of whose speeches furnished France with the title of 'Les Dieux ont soif'—was simply 'un drôle.' What is the sense in naming new streets after a crew like that? In short, the Revolution was made by madmen, and Anatole, deriding both the taking of the Bastille and the misnamed Festival of Reason, shakes loose impatiently from the tentacles of such a monster... How infinitely preferable is folk-lore! How pleasing to dip into this 'charming science,' to cull fireside tales that beguiled our ancestors! 'All this retraces the history of those who have no history.' Thus France, the mandarin of taste, shows benevolence towards his humble progenitors.

The conservative attitude in religious matters is also apparent, though less thorough-going and probably less whole-hearted. True that Gérôme gibes at the confessional and proposes casuistical questions to priests. But the mocking tones of the sceptical Anatole are here considerably muted. For the most part he stands, willy-nilly, as a defender of clerical institutions, if not of the faith. He pointedly dislikes anti-clericals and those free-thinkers who make a nuisance of themselves by constantly strutting in funeral processions. Not really nice people, he thinks. He heartily attacks the laicizing of hospitals: why banish the Sisters, 'those irreproachable nurses, whose only fault was to believe in God and pray to him?' The Pantheon should remain consecrated. The saints are still in high favour, as associated with his earliest recollections.[104]

Yet Anatole's general scepticism flashes out in an occasional dig at miracles, as well as in frequent remarks on the supernatural, on occultism, spiritualism and the like. For a time he tries to suspend judgment on these phenomena, as when, in familiar vein, he gives us the *pro* and *con* about levitation. Mediums, séances, typtology, Houdin, William Crookes[105] and his 'Katie,' the whole question of communications with the dead—all such things occupy what seems a disproportionate amount of space in the chronicles from 1883 to 1896. Why this prolonged concern, and why does A.F. alternately blow hot and cold with regard to the possibilities of spiritualism? Here we touch the secret springs of France's mind. For one thing, he prefers to think by antinomies, he is a lover of contradictions. For another—if the sceptic thinks he doubts, or the renegade seeks to believe,

They know not well the subtle ways
I keep, and pass, and turn again.

Anatole could never leave the supernatural alone. It may be altogether lies; but it is eternally fascinating. The spiritualists, like the Magi, like the miracles, like the saints, will always appeal to that twisted side of the man which says: 'Help thou mine unbelief.' Do the true believers quarrel among themselves? Would I could share that burning and fanatical faith! A talking table is surely more vital than the one on which I am writing this chronicle. Yes, the conversation of the spirits is stupid and queer; yet telepathy and television are almost as credible as animal magnetism, which is practically proved. A.F. claims to be among the first to note down the scientific progress of hypnotism. As a social diversion, 'magnetizing' parties are not wholly a success. But his general conclusion is that the contemporary rage for 'magic, sorcery and occultism' is one of the curious signs of an epoch falsely called incredulous.

§ 13

THESE were the years of France's slow development from a studious writer into the social lion formed by Madame de Caillavet. His physical man underwent corresponding changes, as will be seen from a comparison of the three photographs of 1883, 1887, and *c.*1894.* The first is that of a dreamer and scholar, an intimate of Sylvestre Bonnard, who maintains his Latin Quarter air, together with a certain ruggedness and reserve. The second (from *La Revue illustrée*) is the alert chronicler, the essential Parisian, with an appropriate gastronomical curve. The last, majestic but mummified, penetrating yet *poseur,* is a Mask. Oiled and curled and conscious of posterity, the Mask seems a cross between a professional author (rights reserved in Sweden and all points south) and a barber's exhibit. Such were the strides taken towards Parnassus, *via* the Champs-Elysées, hand in hand with Society and *l'amour*. So what Gérôme has to confide about Society, women and love is of uncommon interest.

He tells us that French society is one of the marvels of the world, especially when the sexes keep up a certain standard of smartness. Let the Parisienne be always brilliant and lustrous, let the Frenchman be a well-curried soldier-type. Social life, in the châteaux particularly, is still a kind of parade. Perhaps the painter had better stick to Bohemia; but Gérôme is no painter, and his early aversion to society becomes gradually mitigated. He returns from the country, looking forward to some pleasant dinners and musicales. We hear of certain soirées at Madame Adam's, the private *guignol* at Madame Welschinger's, a ball at the Koenigswarters', a reunion *chez* Madame Sacki-Kann, including 'the

* These will be found respectively opposite pages 262, 316, and 514.

élite of the Israelite world.' Was France pushed in this direction by Madame de Caillavet, whose mother was a Koenigswarter and who was therefore of Jewish descent? If so, he was nothing loth, since he always had a penchant for intelligent and artistic Jews.

Most of this was in the season of 1887-88, but before that, as already mentioned, Anatole had come into touch with some of the great salons. In the role of Gérôme, he could interview Madame Adam; he could attend Madame Aubernon's receptions. Still under that pseudonym, he could even mention that Anatole France read there some charming extracts from *Le Crime de Sylvestre Bonnard,* 'a marvel of grace and kindness, of subtlety and sentiment.' As for this salon itself, it is 'one of the last where people really converse.' But later we find a more sardonic account of another soirée *chez* Madame Aubernon, when presumably Anatole did *not* read; he reports the rather acid compliments and the 'catty' remarks exchanged in the various groups.

As for feminine chiffons, Gérôme lingers with the corset, viewed as an engine of warfare and a primary source of sex-appeal. There are two major tendencies in France's attitude towards women, here and elsewhere: with regard to their emancipation he is extremely conservative, some would say benighted; and perhaps as a consequence he insists on the fundamental opposition and attraction of the sexes.

The ornamental half of the species may go in for healing, since this is a suitable function; but they should not be educated very much and they should certainly not attempt politics. The idea of their perorating in public meetings and marching in processions! What nonsense! Banal as it may seem, their place *is* the home, from boudoir to back porch. And their elementary purpose, their Final Cause, is quite manifest: 'They give love; they brood over the generations; what better thing would you have them do?' To obtain conjugal delights we do not need gawky misses with diplomas.

This semi-Oriental attitude will account for France's distrust of the sex when it is not functioning in terms of amiability or physiology. Women can become dangerous creatures, as the Church and Renan recognize. The weaker sex has a power of its own; so France is ironic about its needing protection from gentlemen. Are the ladies so soft and downtrodden as to require this

League of Protection ? Is lovely Woman a poor disregarded object ? She certainly attracted a good deal of attention from Gérôme in the year 1888, when the chronicler was flitting from the domestic hearth and trying his wings abroad. Then he loquaciously declares that the final work of Nature is *La Femme.* Her 'perfidious and charming beauty' stands at the peak of all the ages. Shall we curse the hour when this disturbing loveliness stole upon our senses ? No, for through beauty alone do we suffer and truly live. Only through such experience can the arts and genuine poetry be born.

Here echoes the familiar note of France the sensualist, the pagan, almost the mystic in his apprehension of 'fatal' love and beauty. From that point of view, a 'useful' education naturally seems futile ; the important thing is that a woman should have a lively mind.[106] Why stupefy it with pedantry, why inflict orthography upon that typical 'Parisienne all compact of taste and delicacy' ?

Among fascinating women, the most fascinating are actresses — because each one in her time plays many parts and 'makes us dream of many things.' Various and mutable is still . . . our Anatole. Foreshadowing the *Histoire comique,* his columns contain much about the acting profession in the way of appreciation and anecdotes ; but rather to our surprise it is not so much the actress's art that primarily concerns France. In his maturity he rarely visited the theatre and even admitted in these columns, 'I understand nothing about the drama.' Yet this must not be taken too literally. He debates, for instance, with Sarah Bernhardt, Diderot's old 'Paradoxe' as to whether the actor should play from inspiration or from studied calculation of effect. Needless to specify which side was upheld by each debater.

Reminiscences of Pierre and of Jean Servien appear in this passage concerning the pleasures conferred by such manifold women :

> I love actresses because they furnished the poetry of my juvenile dreams. As a youth I could not distinguish the real person from the role which she represented. I attributed to them all beautiful virtues and even more lovely weaknesses.[107]

Gérôme no longer indulges in that particular brand of admiration, but he still insists that the *comédiennes* palpably incarnate the soul of beauty. Thus they cause him to enjoy a sweet mixture of contemplation and desire. It is, of course, folly to suppose that these Circes are long on virginal candour. They are rather chartered libertines, and it's all over with the credulous youth who happens to marry one.

As for individual players, we have already dealt with the material found here on such actresses as Constant and Devoyod, who charmed the adolescence of 'Pierre Nozière.' There is also a passing reference to Rachel, as wearing the diadem of Phèdre—Rachel, who once gave her blessing to Little Pierre on a stairway of the Hôtel Chimay. But as might be expected Sarah Bernhardt is from the beginning most frequently discussed by Gérôme. He has with her a rather silly interview, in which the cat and her son Maurice are unduly featured. She has, A.F. admits, foolish ideas about staging *Andromaque* with the settings and costumes of the Stone Age—a feathered and tattooed Orestes slaying Pyrrhus with a flint knife ! Yet she deserves her remarkable vogue, because she really embodies *le beau*. To him then she gives this old delight, to which her more bourgeois auditors are not responsive.

And *l'amour ?* Surely it is to be exalted above all else. Even those who sell it, like those who sell money, remain the masters of the world. France is for much liberty, of course, both of speech and action. The standpoint is usually that of the boulevardier. Only once does he take a quite serious view, in associating love with marriage. It seems to him a law that 'all enduring loves can last only through being transformed.' He may well be thinking along personal lines.

It has been noted that in 1888 a certain restlessness about women creeps into these pages. Within that same year we find a series of piquant observations about love. Renan truly says (Gérôme reminds us) that young and old are subject to its flames, but that philosopher is wrong in holding that we moderns have exhausted its possibilities as a topic. How can that be ? France implies that there is nothing of more importance to write about. And later, returning to the influence of fashions, he shows how unconsciously lovers are bewitched by ephemeral costumes. Does that matter ? Not at all, for in what concerns love, 'illusion is as good as truth, if not better.' France is still clinging to the skirts of Maya, goddess of illusion. Thus the chronicles of Gérôme, who had seen and recorded a thousand things, swing round full circle to the point from which Little Pierre had departed so long ago.[108]

§ 14

ONE special preoccupation may be considered apart. Many things show that round 1890 Joan of Arc, the true or the false, was a constant interest of Anatole's. In one journal of this period his contributions are entirely devoted to that interest. From 1889-92, France wrote, for the *Revue de famille,* a series of eight articles on such subjects as 'Les Voix de Jeanne d'Arc,' 'Jeanne d'Arc et Saint Remi,' 'Jeanne d'Arc, a-t-elle été brûlée à Rouen,' etc. These titles are suggestive of certain chapters in the later *Vie de Jeanne d'Arc* (1908), and indeed there is little doubt that the articles in question (after being partly reprinted in the *Echo de Paris*) provided much of the scaffolding for the biography. This may be illustrated by an examination of the first four studies in the series.

They appeared from August 1, 1889 to November 15, 1890.[109] Several of the series are digressions in the sense that they are concerned less with Joan than with her associates and environment; but similar digressions are found in the biography itself. Thus 'Frère Richard' contains material not only about this militant friar, who was won over to Jeanne's cause, but also about two of her rivals, the saintly La Pierronne and the impostor, Catherine de la Rochelle. In France's *Vie,* this material is scattered round in several different places, in order to fit into his new organization. But an astonishing amount of the old article is kept, whether in substance or in form. Some twenty passages of varying length are almost identical with the previous version, while others repeat the gist of what Anatole had already said. These echoes deal with such matters as Brother Richard's career, his sermons (textually reproduced) to the Parisians and the inhabitants of Troyes, his championship of Joan as well as of the other two prophetesses; also with Joan's antagonism to Catherine and how it was forcibly expressed. The fact that a number of speeches are virtually the same in the two versions is due partly to France's addiction to dialogue, of which he found a goodly amount in his chief sources —the two *Procès* regarding Jeanne. Certain changes from article to volume-form show that he had made a closer study of these *Procès* in the interval.

The second article, on 'Le Petit Berger,' contains fewer textual resemblances to the *Vie;* but it begins with an interesting revelation of A.F.'s general intention :

> This narrative forms part of a series of biographies in which I propose to make known various people who had visions, who prophesied, who thought they had a divine mission at the time when Jeanne achieved her great deeds. My object is to make [humanly] intelligible the story of the Maid. . . She has nothing to fear from such comparisons.

This intention did not vary during the twenty years that elapsed before the appearance of his monumental volumes on Joan. In either case, the procedure is like that of Renan, who brought in 'false' Messiahs, as Anatole played up the predecessors and imitators of the Maid. The 'little shepherd' of Gevaudan belonged in the latter category : he too had visions, heard voices, thought he had a patriotic mission, and was taken along as a mascot by the military leaders. The substance of this article is repeated in two widely separated passages of the *Vie*. The first of these is considerably abbreviated from the article, the last contains close similarities, especially regarding the military uses of the shepherd, the display of his stigmata, and his final inglorious exit. As in the other reworkings, France's aim is to concatenate certain *données* provided by the individual article with the larger picture of affairs given in the definitive biography.

The third article, on 'Jeanne d'Arc et les Fées,' is naturally a subject after Anatole's own heart. And in expatiating on old folklore and survivals of Druidic cults, he is eager, as usual, to show criss-crossing between pagan rites and those of the Church. The implication is that Jeanne and the other inhabitants of Domrémy were pagans *sans le savoir*. What ancient fires were stirring in their blood, when they celebrated, round fountain and beech-tree, the return of Spring-tide ? What sort of a blend is suggested by the fountain called 'aux Bonnes-Fées-Notre-Seigneur' ? Why, when the country-side was full of fairy-lore, did Jeanne preserve at her trial a perfect silence about *this* aspect of her inspiration ? The curés and the saints themselves were in no doubt as to what went on round the numerous natural objects associated with the fairies. But no exorcisms or excommunications could eradicate for the people the voices and influences, good or maleficent, that emanated from the Tree of Dames or the Fontaine des Grenouilles. For these things were linked, as in the case of the knight, Granier, with an imperious fairy-mistress, or with a dark sense of the fatality of destiny. Old as the fairies were, they were descended from the still older Fates.

Such are the passages, written in Anatole's best vein, that are transferred abundantly to the very first chapter of his *Vie de Jeanne d'Arc.* Scattered through those volumes appear echoes from the last article that we shall consider — on 'Merlin l'Enchanteur et la vocation de Jeanne d'Arc.' Much the same approach is used as in the previous article. Again France insists that the old French villager (*paganus* by rights) stuck to 'his ancient beliefs with a naïve obstinacy.' Driven from their temples, the divinities of yore sought refuge in wood and field, where they intermingled with fairies and magicians. Merlin, 'enchanter' and prophet, predicted that from such a haunted wood — 'le Bois-Chenu' — there would come forth a virgin who would conquer the English and rescue the fair realm of France. The belief in this prophecy was what set Joan on her way and what sustained her through all difficulties. And she won over to this belief peasants and captains, the king's confessor and even the poetess, Christine de Pisan.

While the *Vie* keeps most of the above material, it subordinates the prophecy of the Bois-Chenu and plays up other presages regarding the role of Jeanne as a deliverer. But the background of popular credulity is still emphasized.

Similar anticipations of the *Vie* could be found in the four articles not analysed here. It might be noticed that material from the first two articles examined above is reworked into a short story, 'Frère Joconde' (*Contes de Jacques Tournebroche*), which is contemporary with the life of Jeanne d'Arc. The biography ultimately absorbed also a quantity of stuff from *l'Univers illustré* and *Le Temps,* together with the *Revue de Paris* and other journals reaching beyond our period. But as a whole this matter of the *Revue de famille,* etc., furnishes a major illustration of the theory set forth elsewhere in these pages : that the ground work for Anatole's later productions was often laid before his domestic situation became intolerable and before he had risen to general fame.

ANATOLE ON 'LE TEMPS'

§ 15

WHILE still on the staff of *l'Univers illustré* and *Le Temps,* the versatile Anatole undertook a series of seven short articles for yet another periodical.[110] This was *La Revue illustrée,* a general weekly, adorned with what were then the new-process photogravures. (The fair tall ladies abounding here are of the period of Du Maurier.) The articles ran fortnightly from December, 1889, to March, 1890. They are chatty and discursive book-reviews, of much the same type as those written for 'La Vie littéraire,' where indeed, according to the author's custom, some of this material is revamped. A.F. is still interested in such matters as the inevitable Jeanne d'Arc, in popular magic and Emile Zola. In the very first of the series, he falls into his favourite vice: he repeats in similar terms his former arguments against the folly of giving scientific manuals to children. They should read uplifting literature—like *The Fair Maid of Perth.* But France is careful here to safeguard himself as a devotee of true science. He is probably thinking of his previous scientific curiosities in the passage, already quoted, about his concern with cosmic problems. For all that, it is better to go back to the legends, to the two-cent book-boxes, to old Debas. . .

A fresh topic for Anatole's pen appears in his review of *Impressions de théâtre* by Jules Lemaître. This fellow-critic and comrade of pre-Dreyfus days had deserved well from the author of *Bonnard* and *Le Livre de mon ami.* So we find France in an expansive and appreciative vein. As in the 'Vie littéraire,' he mentions Lemaître's light touch and his praiseworthy scepticism. His 'aerial and Puck-like' soul is an authentic off-shoot of 'cette noble Touraine,' where all good things grow. Perhaps his sensibility is keen rather than deep, but as an impressionistic critic—and this is the tribute of a brother-artist in that line—he is endowed with subtlety, wit, and a laudable naturalness. He too has been reproached with literary vagabondage; yet surely one should have the right to wander where a curious mind may lead him. There's a philosophy beneath all the fluttering.

This is followed by a significant page in general defence of impressionistic criticism—a manifesto very similar to those awaiting us in 'La Vie littéraire.' France had elsewhere declared that criticism at its best presupposes a universal culture; he now claims that it 'embraces everything, absorbs everything.' It has passed from the hands of dogmatists and pedants (a dig at M. Brunetière). Its breath is the breath of life itself, and it expounds all that is current in the world. Perhaps even by virtue of its divining and epitomizing faculties, criticism offers 'the definitive supreme formula for all our uncertainties,' together with 'a Lethe of indulgence' ; and it constitutes an enviable post for observation of the mundane spectacle. Surely, Anatole sees himself as occupying that post and exercising that indulgence. He adds that the well-rounded critic must be at once an artist, a philosopher, a poet. . .

It might be argued that from these various angles 'Gérôme' or the author of 'La Vie littéraire' was more fully equipped for his business than was the author of *Le Lys rouge* or even of *Thaïs ;* and that in spite of the more imposing fame of these masterpieces, Anatole was by nature a contemplator rather than a creator ; less of a novelist than a critic both of life and of literature. The latter function, to be sure, is not salient in *La Revue illustrée.* But as we look back on the long array of articles considered in this chapter and look forward to the still longer series published in *Le Temps,* we may find a justification for our prolixity not only in the inherent merits of the material and its fresh revelations — we also remember that France for a dozen years took pride in his continuous performances both as chronicler and as critic.

CHAPTER XIV

Le Temps: 'La Vie Littéraire'

§ 1

WE now turn to the subject of Anatole's long association with *Le Temps,* in the double capacity just mentioned. Early in 1886 Adrien Hébrard, as managing editor, called upon France to join the staff of the leading French daily. In a dedicatory preface to the first volume of *La Vie littéraire* [1] (in book-form) A.F. expresses his astonishment that the active Hébrard should have engaged such a languid and meditative person, together with his gratitude towards an editor who 'triumphed over my idleness' and actually turned a 'sly Benedictine' (such was Hébrard's phrase) into a productive and regular writer.[2] The position of critic on *Le Temps* had previously been occupied by the moralistic and severe Edmond Scherer; the editor and his readers were probably glad enough to encourage a change in tone.[3]

There is no doubt that France's audience and his appeal now became much wider. The ascent to Parnassus could henceforth be trodden on a broader and higher road-bed. Anatole could now address his observations to leisurely people of Epicurean tastes. His thought was unhampered, save by the dignified traditions of *Le Temps;* he could float with the tide, keeping his head well up. Almost as in the case of Sainte-Beuve, the column or two of 'La Vie littéraire,' appearing every Saturday, was a weekly event, and A.F.'s new enterprise was from the beginning an amiable success which increased with the years. 'Of a judge's seat he made a comfortable armchair.' [4]

It seems clear that his association with *Le Temps* helped to make France one of the leaders of contemporary letters. Some go so far as to say that he presently succeeded Renan in that position, 'on the throne of Latin culture.' [5] He evinces a graceful faculty for assimilating and presenting ideas. He conducts a sort of literary bakery, in which flour of all grades is converted into rolls, *croissants, flûtes,* and edible walking-sticks—everything but solid brown bread. Since very soon the critic supersedes the chronicler, you might expect him to have a narrower scope than that of 'Gérôme'; yet little in his country's intellectual life is foreign to him, while he observes it all from a higher conning-tower. The smooth easy sinuous style is perfectly adapted to the standards of a great paper. Unlike others, France considered journalism not a bad school for the professional *littérateur*.

§ 2

Anatole served on *Le Temps* a little over seven years, from March, 1886, to May, 1893. Apart from occasional stories and isolated contributions,[6] his newspaper work fell into two distinct series. The first, headed 'La Vie à Paris' and 'La Vie hors Paris,' consisted of chronicles appearing from March 21–December 26, 1886. The second—'La Vie littéraire' proper—ran from January 16, 1887–April 30, 1893; this forms a total of some two hundred and ninety articles. Of all these, only one hundred and thirty, or *less than half*, have been republished (with few changes) in France's collected volumes of criticism.[7] The remainder must be studied in *Le Temps* itself.

To dispose first of the chronicle-series of 1886: the five articles entitled 'La Vie hors Paris' are mostly concerned with doings at Saint-Valery-sur-Somme, which have already been recorded.[8] Before and after these appeared the much more numerous articles on Parisian life.[9] Many of them are in the vein of 'Gérôme's' contemporary 'Courrier' and repeat familiar themes. They start without any trumpeting and adopt a chatty tone, while often covering several topics within the same article. As in 'La Vie littéraire,' all France's contributions are signed in full, but they do not all convey his characteristic flavour. Some of the chronicles are quite perfunctory space-fillers, others have a genuine interest. We mention briefly (and chronologically, for a change) those of the latter kind. It may be noted that Anatole's fondness for dialogue, as an animated form of discussion, is already apparent.

France begins [10] modestly by remarking that he has dined with M. Aulard, whose work on the Revolution he much admired; he extends his admiration even to the 'bold eloquence' of Danton, whom elsewhere he scarcely favoured. Presently we find him in the thick of Easter Week and regarding the Church celebrations with an indulgent eye. A little later in the Spring, he shows his fondness for rambling in the garden of the Tuileries: approval of the merry-go-rounds and reminiscences of the marionette shows—

especially the Temptation of Saint Anthony—seen in his boyhood. Renan is praised; Hugo is criticized; A.F. talks about bibliophiles and the dangers of books. Very favourable to Jeanne d'Arc, the 'sweet creature' who gave us back our France; how the way was prepared for her by similar legends. Less favourable to spiritualism (Home and Crookes), which for all its dealing with miracles cannot explain the miracle of genius. On Lamartine: his memory is fading out, because each generation wants its own poet to show it how to love. The fête at Neuilly in July. The great scientific vision and audacity of Diderot, followed by a strong defence of war and war-like virtues (cf. *l'Univers illustré*). A milder reaction than usual towards the Collège Stanislas: 'It brought me up, and I am deeply grateful'; he even preserves 'delicious recollections' of the pleasant times spent there. (The recollections may be pleasant, but Stanislas was hardly that; we recall that France readily sentimentalizes in this period.) He insists that this training gave true culture to the few who wanted it. Lalanne was a charming and idealistic director, like an old statue softened by age and moss. Of course he was too far gone on poetry to be a capable administrator (cf. *Désirs de Jean Servien*). 'Chéron' (i.e. Charron) was honest and wise, but the proctors were a set of graceless loons. Hence, he again concludes, 'I don't like monks.'

There is a good deal throughout this series concerning popular amusements, expositions, and paintings. After returning from the holidays, France sees at the Musée Grévin the bath-tub of Marat; hence comment on that savage character and his popularity with the mob.—A defence of Voltaire's philosophic tragedies, as expressing the heart of his century.—Disquisitions about gambling; a Prince who killed himself because of losses at play was ignorant of the law of labour; of all earthly blessings, work is the most blessèd and bringeth its own reward.—As usual, the Schoolboy's Return in October, and as usual the question of Latin: 'I tremble for our humanities.'—Soon Winter is coming in, with almanacs and chestnuts; the Quai Malaquais is wind-swept, and we cannot linger around the precious book-stalls.—What Rome sends to an exhibit at the Ecole des Beaux-Arts; France tells a furious modernist that tradition and schooling do not really harm original talent. —He pokes fun at an exposition of Incoherent Arts and rambles along about Pierrot.—He speaks respectfully of the Sisters of various orders that succour the unfortunate. Since Revolutionary times, the State has had them 'in aversion' ; but Anatole in these days is rather on the side of the Church. Though still repelled by needless asceticism, he understands what makes a vocation.—The protection of animals and vivisection *pro* and *con ;* progress versus pity ; the former wins.—A dialogue, rather in Fontenelle's manner, on the Academy, and much about Octave Gréard, who will presently receive France into that institution.—At the Academy, one may find a debatable virtue rewarded by prizes, while in the Senate madness is much discussed : paradoxical praise of folly as a sort of 'sick reason.' He visits the asylum at Bicêtre and discovers that even idiots, cretins, and epileptics have their points ; they enjoy a negative happiness, and if they dream their lives away, why so do the rest of us.—Thus old threads are woven with new into the Anatolian pattern.

§ 3

If all the articles originally written for 'La Vie littéraire' had been reprinted, they would run to ten duodecimo volumes instead of the four that are usually found. This gives an idea of the extent and importance of the original series. Furthermore, none of the articles written during the eighteen months subsequent to September, 1891, have been included in France's volumes of criticism. It follows that the books now entitled *La Vie littéraire* do not adequately represent his activities on *Le Temps*. The omissions have grieved those [11] who care to know their Anatole thoroughly. For it does not appear, on due consideration, that the omitted articles are any less worthy or any more ephemeral than those reprinted in volume form. In either category, we find hasty-puddings that are 'timely' and little more ; and we find carefully studied essays that are timeless and a good deal more. They are all clearly stamped with the personal hall-mark of Anatole. As he says in a preface,[12] the public encouraged him to republish (in part), because it believed in his sincerity and naturalness ; and in view of these virtues, people forgave him his faults.

Those who seek for a definite method, like that of Taine, will, he knows, be disappointed. France has a horror of systems.[13] He is a butterfly, a vagabond, wandering where the truant spirit leads him. He acknowledges a certain indolence, an objection to pen and ink if imposed as a duty; he is still occupied with things not pertaining to class-work. Indeed, he confesses in one place that he is 'not a critic' at all.

What does A.F. mean by such an abjuration? Apparently, that he will offer us less in the way of solid analyses than inspirational *causeries* or 'literary fairy-tales.' He will take us on winding promenades, full of delays and divagations. He is roaming in the woods and will rest on sylvan benches. But the worst of lingering in fairy-haunted forests is that we may expect to be late for supper. Beginning with a slow general introduction, halting at every side-track, Anatole is yet surprised to find that it will sometimes take him several weeks to get over his ground. What was promised as an article develops into a series. This happens when he is writing on Joan of Arc, on Lamartine's 'Elvire,' on the letters of Madame de la Sablière, and so forth. There are also cases where (they say) he wandered all night and never got home at all. Oft-cited instances are the review of Renan's *Histoire d'Israël* in terms of the Noah's Ark of Pierre's boyhood; and a woodland dream over Gaston Paris's *Littérature française au moyen-âge*. But be it noted that the dream contains a plausible vision of the Middle Ages, and that France had already reviewed, not without occasional power and profundity, the first volume of Renan's work.

Yet Anatole definitely disclaims any intention of doing 'heavy' notices of serious books. He avoids giving résumés. He shuns *longueurs*. How much better to begin with an anecdote or unexpectedly to insert a quaint digression! There are dozens of such tidbits that Gossip Gérôme whispered into the ear of Anatole, the curiosity-seeker. For he is after the individual quirk or the citation that shows off his man. Voltairian irony occasionally appears, or more frequently the *pro* and *con* type of dialogue, with an amused and benign critic holding the scales of the argument. You cannot tell which way he leans, except that he really seems to lean both ways at once. This anatomical peculiarity may be discussed when we arrive at the contradictions in his thought.

The personal side of things was always the prime interest with Anatole, so we are never surprised to find him cajoling his audience with his confiding manner. Fortunately, the listener 'indulges my mania for yarning about my memories and impressions.'[14] Probably, he thinks, the reader recognizes himself in the confessions of another average person. The two will poke the fire together or drop into a church or look over the old family Bible once more. They will part regretfully, and Anatole will wonder whether he has done his hospitable best by this week-end visitor. At any rate the two have communed with simplicity and candour. The whole duty of the critic, as entertainer, is thus summed up at the end of an argument with Brunetière :[15]

To keep the familiar tone of the *causerie* and the alert step of the promenader ; to stop where one pleases and share confidences ; to follow one's own tastes, fancies, and even caprices, provided one remains always true, sincere, and well-meaning ; *not* to know everything and to explain everything ; to uphold the inevitable diversity of opinions and feelings, and to speak, by preference, of what should be loved by all.

Whether in mild debate or radical disagreement, France usually remains within the limits set by a strict politeness. He is courteous in his controversies with the Jesuit Brucker, the mad Moréas, the intransigent Brunetière. Again, he is deferent about what others have thought and discovered on a given subject. Sometimes this is linked with his way of surrounding himself, every now and then, with clippings and 'finds,' in order to build up a really thorough article on a basis of genuine data and sound opinions.

For in spite of France's declaration that he will not use notes, the fact remains that some of the best articles (or series) are 'documented.' The curious volume which we call 'Anatole's Scrap-Book' testifies to his occasional zeal in assembling not only notes from appropriate volumes, but also newspaper articles by distinguished contemporaries on the subject at hand. That fine meditation, 'Rêveries astronomiques,' is based on an amalgam of a certain Schmoll, Camille Flammarion, lists of the stars, and jottings as to astronomical distances and the like. This type of article atones for the more flimsy and ephemeral kind. The Scrap-Book discloses other vistas of such a hinterland when, for instance, France is priming himself to write on Feuillet, Rosny, or Dumas *fils*. The four 'Elvire' articles rest similarly on a batch of fresh letters and investigations. The case of Madame de la Sablière, the great lady whom Anatole would never desert, is interesting.[16] He had written on her three or four times before joining *Le Temps,* where she is again considered 'd'après des documents inédits.' These consist mainly, as the Lion Collection proves, of letters written to her confessor. Ninety pages of this correspondence were painstakingly copied out by France from manuscripts communicated by Charavay. Furthermore, there exist 'chemises' covering assembled newspaper clippings, general notes, and even Anatole's sketch-maps of seventeenth-century Paris, to restore the setting of his heroine. Naturally she emerges from this mass of evidence as a three-dimensional person ; for France knew well how to assort and enliven the inert documents.

§ 4

But I am not primarily concerned at present with his luminous treatments of individuals. These have been capably summarized elsewhere.[17] We should reckon rather with Anatole's conception of his craft. Invariably personal in his point of view, he ranked, with Jules Lemaître, as an outstanding defender of Impressionism. Let us see, mainly in his own language, what this term then conveyed.

As later in *La Revue illustrée,* so here France fully states the case in connexion with Lemaître's *Impressions de théâtre*.[18] Since variety is the spice of criticism, he congratulates Lemaître on showing a various countenance. The good critic is a romancer, an autobiographer : 'he who relates the adventures of his soul in contact with masterpieces.'[19] Needless to say, France was ever faithful to this celebrated slogan. And he is on familiar ground when he avers that criticism, the last of literary types, now embraces them all through its ample culture. It is the truest form of history. It is well-suited to a long-civilized and intellectually curious society. Yet the would-be impartial recorders, such as Flaubert, are deceived in thinking that they are absent from their work. Truly objective art, objective criticism, cannot exist, because we can never get out of ourselves.

Every book tells us only of its creator, the subject of most interest to writer and reader alike. Hence the great success of confessional literature, from Saint Augustine, through Rousseau, down to present-day intimate journals. France is moved by a volume of stories because the writer has become personal and thus made an 'indefinable and deep *impression*.' The word is often at the point of his pen. Usually it is an emotional impression, 'un éclair de sentiment,' that is thus awakened in the critic. With a delicious shudder, he recognizes the authentic touch.

The judgments and appreciations expressed above are as lucid as can be expected from the intermittent defender of so vague a thing as Impressionism. Indeed, Anatole did not wholly adhere to the school, which had affiliations with the superæsthetes of the nineties in Paris and with *The Yellow Book* in London. In addition to personal whimsicality, the versatile critic should certainly, he believes, cultivate other literary qualities, such as open-mindedness, adaptability, charm and beauty. In the main, France's attitudes towards other practitioners of the art accord with the above trends. Sainte-Beuve, 'from whom we all proceed,' is respected as the St. Thomas Aquinas of criticism. Cuvillier-Fleury, Taine, Bourget, excel respectively in portraiture, the study of environment, or psychological analysis. Faguet, whom A.F. personally disliked, is depreciated, while Lemaître is honoured in several connexions.

The last-named provides a text for one of Anatole's favourite sermons. By virtue of his keen sense of relativity and mutability, Lemaître offers living proof that criticism has left behind the dogmatic phase. France also told Brunetière that the age of great principles has departed and that we dwell now among the shifting sands. Relativity is king. Yet 'it is better to speak with some uncertainty of fine things than to keep wholly silent about them.' Their secrets may be delicately discerned by a humanistic criticism—which is 'a science mingled with art, intuitive, uneasy and never complete.'

Beauty may be shifting and evasive. It is none the less the chief constituent of art, of poetry, of France's critical creed. The feeling for beauty lures him along on the foot-path way. 'Is any one sure of having a better guide ?' Whatever is ugly, like Naturalism, is thereby proved false. George Sand sees Nature more truly than Zola. The humble in heart are nearer than the dogmatists to the 'secret of the Beautiful.' But since *le vrai* often escapes us where *le beau* is palpable, why not, dream for dream, 'seek and savour preferably images of grace, of beauty, of love' ? The whole effort of civilizations, and here the Greeks offer a capital example, is towards the embellishment of real life. When France asserts that beauty is one of the virtues of this world, he is not uttering a glib commonplace : he sincerely means that for him it is *the* virtue.

Critics generally recognize that this was his central preoccupation in *Le Temps* as elsewhere. Nicolas Ségur [20] points out that his attitude is like that of some Renaissance figure, primarily plastic in his conceptions, largely receptive and responsive to diverse forms of loveliness.

But how infinite are the approaches to *le beau!* How absurd to nail our banners to any particular battlements! 'The forms of art change like the forms of life itself.' Therefore France shows a gentle but pervasive scepticism regarding time-worn æsthetic standards. In criticism as in philosophy, *pro* and *con* are the rulers of thought. Nothing is sure but the fact that nothing is sure.

So France will not style himself an æsthete or a critic, if anything absolute is indicated by these terms. Having no taste for disputes about the nature of *le beau,* he has small confidence in metaphysical formulæ. Yet for all his scepticism, he is not without underlying principles, or touchstones, in his apprehension of what is fair and lovely.[21] Ideal rather than factual Truth may to some extent prevail; Simplicity ('my Racine') is a most worshipful goddess; Sentiment is precious for poets; but Taste is the flower of life itself. For all these virtues mentioned should be governed by taste, that 'nothing which is everything,' that dominant in Anatole's harmonies. 'All his thought,' says an English critic,[22] 'is based on the acceptances and rejections of his taste.' France esteems it a priceless jewel; if anything surpasses it in value (which seems doubtful), he can name only intelligence and probity. But taste combines a just understanding with an exquisite feeling; and therein lies its strength and its perpetuity.

As for the domains of Art, one is surprised to find so little in *Le Temps* about paintings and the like. It seems that this penchant developed later, in connexion with the Villa Saïd. Now he simply likes old prints and *images,* he dwells on the 'terrible' caricatures of Gavarni, and he depicts Judith Gautier as surrounded by *bibelots* and sculpture.

We are glad to find this unusual brevity supplemented by a dialogue (apropos of Balzac) concerning the supposed dangers of viewing artistic objects. A fantastic and bookish personage objected to France's 'adoration of images' as encouraging diabolical inventions and tending toward lascivious delights. Anatole mildly answered that the contemplation of Art might just as well elevate and educate. . . Many men of many minds—some of them being slightly cracked. No wonder that France distrusted systems and found opinion so unstable. In the welter, he clings to two other personal beliefs : that literature, to say nothing of art, 'has a quarrel with ethics' and need not be edifying ; and that a good style is always essential. Here only may originality be found, manifest either in ordering and nuancing the thought or in the choice of detail, the characteristic turn. Renan illustrates one process, Lesage the other. All the rest is mere grimacing or mere profusion. Facility is particularly to be dreaded, and concision to be applauded. Michelet touches us by his sensuous style alone, but the pleasure may be too long drawn out, for even 'la volupté' must be paid for in this exacting world.

If poetry, in especial, is not easy to write, it should be quite easy to read, since all art is by its nature pleasurable, 'useless and charming.' Its higher and its more unsettling functions do not normally appeal to France. In his appreciations, then, we may expect him to be impelled mainly by personal taste, by a genuine sense of beauty and of style, and by an analytical capacity for sifting ideas. As he has hinted, there might be worse guides.

§ 5

THE series of 'La Vie littéraire' is probably more sophisticated in tone and naturally inclines more to the discussion of books and ideas than did the chronicles in *l'Univers illustré*. With this exception, we shall find a rather similar content and some inevitable repetitions.

The predominant interests are philosophy, religion, history, and certain literary forms ; to these divisions we shall return in a moment. But no definite categories can limit a curiosity that ranges from the criminology of Lombroso to the statesmanship of a Bismarck or a Carrel, from the medieval sermons of Olivier Maillard to the *jeunes filles* described by Octave Feuillet. In one issue Anatole cheerfully excavates in ancient Eolis, while in another he digs into the new Grande Encyclopédie. With Stanley, he discovers in darkest Africa strange subjects for meditation, nor does he forget the hermits of the Egyptian desert. Of course he loves to regale his vision with fair pictures — of dainty marionettes, of 'dear dead women,' of such a lovely ghost as Madame de

Sabran, or of an eighteenth-century fabulist whose image the critic polishes like an old pastel. The *chansonniers* of the Chat Noir solicit his attention; and on another occasion he goes lengthily into the matter of popular songs and legends, emanating from the four corners of France.

As before, we may perceive that the brisk and dapper boulevardier has not forgotten the days of his youth. He mentions certain figures at Stanislas. He is eager to preserve the student outlook, when he talks with the young men of the nineties.[23] And he takes every opportunity for doing this. The rising generation arouses in him concern and sympathy; he participates in their inner struggles toward a fresh faith. With reference to this faith too, Anatole has his doubts. In fact, 'honest doubt' is the greater part of his own faith.

Mankind, indeed, seems to him in a perilous state, precisely because, having eaten of the tree of knowledge, we have lost our old certainties. Having learned that we are but little flecks on the surface of the globe, how can we ever return to the naïve eras of belief? And anyhow, would that be desirable? They were likewise eras of persecution—witness the Middle Ages. For himself, he much prefers a mildly tolerant and *philosophic* period, like the Age of the Antonines.

Anatole is still speculative; philosophy (*pro* and *con*) receives much of his attention. On the one hand:[24]

> The noblest use that man can make of his intelligence is to form images of the cosmos; and these images, which are the only realities that we can reach, give life all its assurance and beauty.

Some belief, some kind of morality, is essential to every generation. At times it seems that in spite of all, we must cling to science and the philosophy founded thereon. Even if we can never fundamentally *know,* yet it is something to oppose the Unknowable with the keen rapier of our thought. But there are other times when the blanket of mystery seems to smother all our efforts to win clear. Then Anatole, having read Schopenhauer, wonders whether a great philosophical system is not as admirable and as empty of human content as a game of chess.

Perhaps France's most characteristic view of the cosmos is found in the afore-mentioned 'Rêveries astronomiques,'[25] so carefully prepared, taken in conjunction with a preceding article on which this one was remodelled. It is interesting to know, too, that among his last efforts was a 'Dialogue sur l'astronomie,' which remained his favourite science until the end.[26]

He begins the article in question by declaring that we can scarcely recreate today the state of mind of a Thomas Aquinas, who believed that the earth was the centre of everything, with the smoke of hell below and the home of God above. Now the fixed firmament has been broken through by our penetrating thought. We know that Earth, as compared to Sirius, is a grain of dust. And this conception is the greatest, the most far-reaching in the history of the human mind.

The heavens, no longer 'incorruptible,' share in universal change. Mars is habitable; forms that we cannot imagine are probably multiplying there and elsewhere. From the most distant point of view, our galaxy may be only a globule or a mite. True that the universe, thus considered, is 'desperately monotonous'; whether in moons or meteors, there appear always the same chemical combinations. True that change and decay infect every atom and every planet. Aghast at this and limited to our tiny area, we may yet remember that the surrounding Vastness is a discovery of Homo Sapiens: if we had not named the farthest fixed star, that heavenly Thule would not exist; and 'the only grandeur which should astound us is that of the human spirit.' [27]

Thus France is a latter-day 'humanist' and much resembles his favourite Vigny in his attitude towards Nature. She is an indifferent mother; her children, who surpass her standards, do well to leave her and set up on their own. She taught us badly at the beginning—the primitive struggle for life, the crimes of the cavemen. She still allots us many miseries. But on the whole, mankind has risen gloriously to a higher level of justice and peace.[28] Anatole will not side with those who hold that the 'state of nature' was a blessèd state. Surely the savages were more savage than we.

At least . . . so it seems on one Saturday. On another, France is painfully aware that civilized life, too, involves struggle and sacrifice and death. On still another day, 'Nature, red in tooth and claw' (as Tennyson called her) is viewed as seducing men even now. But taking him by and large, we must recognize (cf. *l'Univers illustré*) that Anatole is a humanist in the full sense of the word, rather than a naturalist in any sense. Nor is he thoroughly a determinist, either. Although fairly rigorous while under the influence of Taine (cf. *Jean Servien*), A.F. is not in this period so sure about the Reign of Law. The 'apparent incoherence' of the universe became more and more manifest. This view did not prevent his acceptance of Lyell's theory of 'actual causes' as operating slowly in the physical world.[29]

It has been seen how the France of this period lost his early enthusiasm for a scientifically ordered universe. The author of *Jocaste* and of 'Les Origines humaines' had yielded place to a milder sort of person. Neither Sylvestre Bonnard nor 'Gérôme' could be styled a devotee of science. Few men could keep the fervour of the seventies, when Evolution and the like were comparatively new ideas.[30] The pupil of Darwin can now smile at his former fatalism and the pupil of Renan has abated his faith in the future of *la science* (i.e., organized knowledge); although, unlike Brunetière, he never came to accept its 'bankruptcy' as a working creed. This was a moot point while 'La Vie littéraire' was being written, and France recapitulates, not too unsympathetically, the case against science. It cannot give us ultimate explanations of the Universe. It is neither moral nor human. It would strip man of his spiritual side, which was his especial glory. Yet is there any adequate substitute for this probing Knowledge?

One phase of the debate is concerned with the possible moral consequences of scientific researches. Anatole considers the question in connexion with a play by Daudet and with Bourget's famous novel, *Le Disciple*. Here the 'Master' was a cold determinist, a travesty on Taine. But he should not be additionally laden with the misdemeanours of his disciple, who perished through pride, rather than through determinism. (Bourget was duly grateful for this defence.) France continues that in no case are the savants responsible for the crimes that wretches commit in their names. But evidently in the conduct of life, a good heart is worth more than the gymnastics of philosophers. There is another side to the medal. We weary of everything except the desire to know ; and that longing can now be gratified on an encyclopedic scale.[31] Science as an Absolute may be discredited, but never the particular fields of knowledge. What, after all, is more stirring than the recent developments and interrelations of the sciences? When France appreciates them, he does so, naturally, as a philosophic layman. Thus he admires the larger achievements of astronomy and mathematical physics, of chemistry and physiology, of archæology and comparative philology.

Among the exact sciences, astronomy is 'the noblest' and appealed most to Anatole. It satisfied his love for the cosmic sweep, it presented the lure of the metaphysical 'abyss,' over which he and Pascal hung fascinated. And both thinkers—so different otherwise—were obsessed by the contrast between the infinitely great, which is Vastness, and the infinitely small, which is Man. Among our chilly travelling companions, Mars seems the most neighbourly. Sirius (to which Renan was always pointing) is a million times greater than Earth in his almost immeasurable distance. Hardly can we ever know what lies beyond *him* or what galaxy he floods with light. Yes, astronomy has shown us this larger vision and has taught us likewise definite facts about the movements in our own system, which Anatole enthusiastically describes. Much of this information he drew from the popular works of Camille Flammarion,[32] whom he knew and interviewed.

It is in relation to another field that France gives us further observations on the comparative value of science. He is writing an open letter to a physiologist, who in some respects reminds us of René de Longuemare in *Jocaste*.[33] You and I (Anatole tells this correspondent) both agree and differ. We agree that religious myths and all 'fetishes' are out of the picture. We agree that experimental results, carefully proved, must be accepted. Yet I would point out that the 'truths' of today are often the fallacies of tomorrow, 'for Science wears a mutable countenance and her speech is uncertain.' How many of your old masters and methods have fallen from repute! Furthermore, your Science can never scale the heights of metaphysics, nor support in any way our feelings about beauty and virtue. You yourself fall back on instinct as regards the question of immortality. Why not admit there are 'truths in the realms of imagination and sentiment, just as there are truths attained by observation'? . . . The rejoinder of the correspondent has not been recorded.

§ 6

As for definite philosophical creeds, we have seen that France elsewhere leans towards Positivism, but does not want to be bound to the sect fathered by Comte. Here the doctrine impresses him (cf. later M. Bergeret) as rather ridiculous in its 'adoration of the Great Fetish, which is Earth.' Comtism is particularly valuable for its co-ordination of the sciences. But the mystical side of the creed prevents France from becoming a 'white-robed neophyte.' Why should our fancies not continue to toy with metaphysics and the 'delicious follies' of astronomy? Surely there is too much 'organizing' about these Positivists.

And they are too optimistic—a fault which Anatole will rarely commit. How can they cherish the hope of ameliorating our sojourn on 'this little ball, carrying us like vermin on its rotting surface'? We are still barely adolescent, and by the time we grow up, the Sun will have grown cold. Those who create Utopias depict a future mechanized society, whose unfortunate members will have no passions, hence no art or poetry. Such a State can never be well-founded. For man does not change at bottom; he is always 'âpre, égoïste, jaloux, sensuel, féroce.' The 'royal tiger' of the Renaissance has now become a domestic cat—that is all. Not much Progress there!

Persistent are the passions which make the glory of life and art; paramount always are love and hunger, which is a kind of love. Are we better or worse than other worlds? There is a vein of recurrent pessimism in certain articles, more especially in those written from a cosmic standpoint.[34] I do not believe, however, as some insist, that this is a prevailing attitude in the last two published volumes.[35] As articles, they were written before the big upset of 1892. Later, in a week of despair (during the Spring of 1893), France gloomily supposes that evil and suffering are universal. What do we know about the whole phantasmagory? 'Our view of the universe is purely the result of a nightmare in this troubled slumber that we call life.' A dream—a nightmare—an illusion . . . On his philosophy of Illusion, on the inevitable flux, on change and relativity, France advances in *Le Temps* little that we have not heard before. He stresses his old belief that we should cling to the fairer images, the more sustaining illusions. There is much about the processes of thought, to which we shall ultimately return.

The vein of absolute Nihilism, soon to appear conspicuously in his works, is scarcely visible in *Le Temps* before 1893. An obsession with the *cui bono* would not please his readers, nor would it harmonize with his greater inclination towards Epicureanism.

Take for instance our philosopher's indulgent view of current ethics. Nothing could be plainer than his relativistic opinion that morality shifts with the sands of time and clime. Nevertheless, for practical living, man must always have some definite standards. The general message of the 'Vie littéraire' seems to be : Let us keep up good works for the sake of our country and of our young people ; courage and kindness are always desirable qualities ; indulgence should be fostered, crime should be condemned. Anatole is normally for all the 'simple' duties like patriotism and a neighbourly solidarity. Justice is a more complicated affair and less spontaneously human. 'Gérôme' had thought that the world is better governed by a Biblical charity than by a severe justice. With Anatole, as with many Frenchmen, 'La Justice' comes presently to be a true ideal, throughout the Dreyfus Affair and down to the days of *Crainquebille*. But here, if we find him selecting this virtue as peculiar to man, he nevertheless doubts if it is at all in the order of things. It is a *triste* sort of virtue—nobody wants it. Divine grace on the one hand, loving-kindness on the other, are much more appealing. Also Anatole prefers to dwell on those more active virtues lauded in his article, 'La Vertu en France.'[36] Honour, courage, effort, and forbearance are part of the French record. Again, the gentle creed of Buddhism may offer speculatively the best of moralities. But, alas, Europeans want action rather than contemplation—and they never cease wanting !

The stoical strains found in these two articles were doubtless sincere at the time ; but they are not characteristic of Anatole. How uncharacteristic they are may be judged from his remarks on Blaise Pascal, whose asceticism was most repugnant to our author. This fanatic hated beauty and was suspicious of the most natural affections. We are not surprised that Pascal, the arch-Christian, displeased such anti-Christians as Voltaire and Anatole France. These opponents dwell on the darker and more negative side of one of the few great metaphysicians in French literature. Anatole's Pascal, in particular, was cut after the same pattern as the monk Paphnuce and the fanatical Gamelin in *Les Dieux ont soif* . . . Peace to all such !

Our critic's 'code of ethics,' says Guérard, was based on 'freedom, sympathy, pity ; also a growing hostility against . . . supernaturalism, asceticism, dogmatism.'[37] It is plain that rather than linger with the sterner virtues, France prefers to steal away into his Epicurean garden and from there to urge upon his fellow-men his favourite panaceas of Irony and Pity. We shall watch the development of that philosophy in the *Jardin* itself. Here Anatole simply suggests how these two complementary principles may operate beneficially. Irony can make life pleasant, while pity makes it sacred. The former is 'not cruel' but gently stimulating: it mocks neither at true love nor at beauty, but only at the fools and the wicked. The medicament of pity, cordial rather than astringent, goes straight to the heart and is a mighty specific against moral and physical evil. Aided by such tonics, the Epicurean foresees himself and his friends 'peacefully conversing under the last of the elm-trees that border the pathway of life.' Is there anything to disrupt the placid vision ?

Reader, there are the terrible and essential passions, there is above all the sting of *la Volupté !* We know that France himself was often disturbed by this gadfly, this prepossession. Though not a deeply passionate man, he was recurrently titillated by Eros ; and here he insists on the preponderant sway of the passions in general. They have their eternal rights, for they 'constitute the very soul of human affairs,' and mortals would indeed be dull without these enticements of Mother Nature, lawless and shameless. Among all passions, the 'sweet and cruel' impulsion of love lords it over the others, with which it is frequently mingled. Only through this major and elemental experience can a man find himself entirely. Love can destroy all philosophies—even that of Epicurus. It can elevate two ordinary beings to the point where they 'put the infinite into an hour.' It can dim reason into a glow-worm and make the will a mush.

Eros was the oldest of the gods. Before him there was 'neither justice nor intelligence in the world' ; and they have never followed in his train. Blindly he created us, and blind we remain while under his dominion. Perhaps the ladies are less blind and more practical. Let us not be surprised that the sexes conceive of love differently. The one seeks always the high moment of possession, the other expects an eternal gratitude for her gift. Let us not wonder that misunderstandings and adulteries ensue. In the latter event, France (not M. Bergeret) is for the 'theory of pardon.' For is it not clear that passion contains its own sufficient penalties ?

Eros takes unto himself the most contrary emotions and instincts. A 'divine indulgence' should be there, if only to counterbalance an inevitable cruelty. A mad and complicated jealousy—witness most of Anatole's novels—is the seamy side of desire. This arises from our refinements upon Nature, who with her less exclusive views was for once more sensible than man. *L'Amour-passion* has been exalted into a civilized shrine, round which are grouped all the treasures of art and imagination. But it may be too dearly paid for at the price. Between Nature and Modesty, Anatole picks the former to win. Here as elsewhere he dwells with amorous delight on terra cotta figurines, on luring adolescent forms that attain a kind of 'sublimity' in sensuality. For the sense of *la volupté* is a delicately balanced thing which should not be jarred by vulgar tastelessness. An offence against this feeling is almost as bad as an offence against virtue itself. Coarseness for France is an æsthetic rather than a moral lapse.

Of course Anatole has much to say about women, especially round 1890. They are the real experts in love, their chief preoccupation and prerogative. How quickly do the *mondaines* of Bourget lose interest in all other matters! The great lovers of the past, the Dames of Yesteryear, splendidly illustrate this specialization. From Cleopatra, through certain favourites of the Old Régime, down to Madame de Staël and Madame Récamier, all loved highly if not holily. In this connexion Anatole recurs to his old refrain of how love was unconsciously glorified by the Church Fathers and by the saints. Through their warnings against it, they made it precious and disastrous. Thus Tertullian created modern passion. Thus the Church revamped Aspasia and Cleopatra as 'ladies from hell.' Pagan nymphs had been but casually desired; Christianized women became a luring mystery mingled with remorse. When the dread of damnation was added to the force of desire, then love became indeed a madness. And the visions of anchorites increased tenfold the seductions of sex.

To all this A.F. exclaims: 'Quelle gloire!' You are now truly invincible, my sisters, for civilization has given you veils and religion has crowned you with scruples. Therefore, seek not to rival men in their own everyday fields, hold fast to your mystery, for Illusion still lends her rosy gauzes to *l'amour*. Fear not lest we penetrate your ultimate secret; for all that we learn of your souls, we had as well possess an automaton as a much desired mistress.

So Anatole keeps it up—a singular blend of the Neo-Romanticist and the Grand Turk.

On occasion, he will develop an attitude regarding the 'rights' of women, similar to that found in *l'Univers illustré,* although superficially more enlightened.[38] Emancipation, 'Americanization' are in the air—but A.F. is no Great Emancipator. Women may become journalists or lawyers, but it is questionable whether they will become more lovable in such professions. Were it not better for them to retain their charm, their powers of conversation, above all, their amiability? Home-makers and nurses may do this. As for the Female Deputy, we gather that Anatole is likely to pass by on the other side. On feminism, as on other matters, he is prone to hedge or compromise.

§ 7

LOVE and the knowledge of nature, art and the core of religion—they are all founded on half-truths or fair falsehoods. What does this attitude suggest as to the ultimate stand of our philosopher? Rejecting Positivism, not yet ready for Nihilism, where can our Epicurean find a foothold in matters of belief? Evidently with the Pyrrhonists, on the extreme brink of scepticism.

But he will not take the plunge, for the perfect sceptic is at times a doubter of the doubt. This occurs especially when, after communing with Barrès, he feels disposed to brush away the cobwebs of analysis, to cultivate one's garden in the name of action; or when, in order to bewilder Brunetière, he admits the 'formidable sterility' of *Je doute*—an affirmation which would condemn one to a consistent silence. Rather than doubt, he prefers to *believe* . . . 'in the relativity of things and the succession of phenomena'—if that can be called believing.

The habit of sceptical irony is by now so strong in France that he impregnates us with this feeling even when he seeks to be serious. He approves the habit and, as before, he sings the praises of certain illustrious sceptics. Their saving grace of a gentle sarcasm adds 'gaiety to thought and joy to wisdom.' A man of keen and wide intelligence is necessarily ironical. Personally, A.F. is sceptical about a great many things, including the judgment of posterity and the validity of such a criterion as universal consent. Yet he is not certain about protesting against whatever laws and customs may be current; what better ones can be found? He is sure of the excellence of no 'system,' however plausible it may seem. He is not sure of the quality of poetry. He is not even sure of his own existence, any more than Prospero could be sure that Setebos was not the true god. In short:

No man so sure as Omar once was sure.

Touching great sceptics, Anatole lingers with the Greeks. This is in his review of Victor Brochard's book,[39] so freely used for the banquet-scene in *Thaïs*. Here France employs as mouthpiece a fictional Abbé who has much to say about the sect of Pyrrho: 'If one has the misfortune not to be a Christian, the better part of wisdom is to be a Pyrrhonian sceptic.' Among contemporary Pyrrhonists, Lemaître's 'happy perversity' consists in doubting for evermore. And there is always M. Renan. His case is not so clear. They call him a sceptic, while at bottom he is an indulgent dogmatist, who believes in working for the kingdom of God on earth, and in some sort of Judgment Day, and in spreading knowledge abroad.

But this was the earlier Renan, and on the whole France seems to touch his case with tongs. He clings to this instrument when dealing here with religious scepticism. Is that because *Le Temps,* like *l'Univers illustré,* was a journal 'bien pensant'? Or did Anatole prefer to save his more shattering artillery for *Thaïs* and subsequent volumes?

We cull, however, a few remarks, not wholly orthodox.—A vague religiosity is to be distrusted; intelligent youth is right in demanding something both definite and credible. Yet it is doubtful whether the intellectuals can ever forge a religion, which proceeds rather from the obscure masses, unthinking and prone to sentiment.—Intolerance belongs to all religious periods. Men dare not scrutinize too closely the origins of their beliefs, lest they vanish into thin air.—The creeds should soften and broaden down, seeking their greatest common denominator. This *entente* could be much facilitated by the elimination of priests—a Voltairian precept.

Viewed historically, Christianity was entangled from the beginning with certain pagan elements. For instance, the custom of Easter eggs goes back to primitive peoples. The resurrection of Christ, we are reminded, was associated with that of the 'eternal

Adonis' and with the procreative powers of Spring. The personality of Jesus, that 'exquisite spirit,' is not displeasing to our sceptic. He accepts several of the Beatitudes, while disputing with certain Reverends about other matters in the New Testament record. France's interest in the Apostolic Era is evinced by several reviews and stories. With regard to medieval Christianity, he is capable of appreciating the consoling precepts of the *Imitatio,* together with the majesty of the *Dies Irae*. He has a surprising evaluation of Dante's *Vita Nuova,* which exemplifies (he thinks) how Christianity blended with chivalry to idealize woman. Throughout, the names of favourite saints recur and their legends are told again. We hear the tale of St. Hubert and his stag. We meet again with Saints Catherine and Margaret, so closely associated with Joan of Arc. We spy St. Simeon Stylites on his pillar, where we shall still find him in *Thaïs*. As in that novel, 'le grand Saint Antoine' wins the particular admiration of France, because he was joyous and robust and had little nonsense about him.

But some of the saints' lives were not so edifying. They were subject to 'deviations.' They nursed smouldering fires. Choice impurities were elaborated by the solitaries of the Thébaïde. Even St. Catherine of Siena offended, even St. Francis of Sales wrote a mixture of pietism and sensuality. Having dipped considerably into the mystics, France is ready to swear that they abound in a suave eroticism. He is keen neither on the monks of the Desert, nor on any other monks whatsoever. He cannot penetrate their souls. Their asceticism, their mania for solitude, seem very 'singular.' Among the orders, he rates the Franciscans highly and greatly admires their Founder. Various other saintly lives and stories are related, usually according to the *Golden Legend* of Jacques Voragine. This version, it will be remembered, was the special treasure of Sylvestre Bonnard. It will appear again.

Anatole's general attitude towards the Church is, as he claims, respectful and even at times sympathetic. 'I cannot be accused of an excess of faith'—but he dislikes anti-clerical intolerance and is indulgently aware that neither religion nor love can prosper without a certain 'fetichism.' Rarely and lightly does France touch upon matters of doctrinal faith. The Garden of Eden is no longer so credible as it was in his boyhood; immortality seems unlikely; miracles, in the ordinary sense, are absurd and puerile affairs. If a miracle were ever established by valid testimony, it would no longer be a miracle : it would be a natural fact and should be investigated as such. The return of the dead is possible only in the sense that we hesitate to ascribe any impossibilities to Nature, since many of her laws are doubtless still unknown.

His whole approach to the supernatural becomes perplexed, because of his shifting standpoint. From the artistic and imaginative point of view, he maintains an undying interest in the occult, just as he does in saints' lives and miracles. That is why he appreciates fantastic tales by Poe or Hervieu and pays occasional tributes to such 'magi' as Péladan or Papus. Though we cannot believe in the supernatural, yet we 'love it desperately.' The doctrine of Illusion enters into this—'fair falsehoods' are essential to the imaginative.

So in his article, 'l'Hypnotisme dans la littérature,' 40 France prologuizes : 'Vainly do we strive to be reasonable and to love only the truth ; there are seasons when common reality no longer satisfies us and we want to transcend nature' as well as our everyday selves. Hence our thirst for the beyond. Hence M. France (of *Le Temps*) shares with 'Gérôme' a certain preoccupation with mediums and the like. Can the supernatural, then, be credited in religion ? Ah, that is another matter ! Here we shift back to the ground of the reasonable and the verifiable. On that basis, I do not at all believe in the supernatural ; I do not admit the miraculous ; I merely concede its possibility. For our knowledge of nature is still limited and some day, after all, metaphysics may be comprised within the domain of physics proper. Even so, scientific and historical evidence will always serve as the supreme tests.

§ 8

WITH regard to the historical field, our critic (if that is the proper term) evinces his usual interest in particular periods, events and personages. Bearing lightly on ancient history, he dips into the Middle Ages and lingers willingly in the heart of the Old Régime. But his range also includes many outlying provinces. One week he is busy with his fine 'restoration' of the figure of Cleopatra ; another time he exhibits, fairly enough, the personality of Bismarck ; again, he depicts housing conditions in the sixteenth century and later. In a detached, semi-indulgent tone he recounts the crimes of Cæsar Borgia, the tiger of the Renaissance ; presently Bonaparte, that more modern *condottiere,* claims his attention. This was a new interest for Anatole and one which he kept up even in his last years. He is capable of large generalizations, as when he maintains that the old monarchies of France at least strove persistently to unify the kingdom.

So-and-so, remarks our author, may surely be considered a historian, for 'he brings forth uncertainties.' This suggests that the ghost of scepticism cannot be laid—it is too lively a ghost. One article, 'Les Torts de l'histoire,' shows awareness of the 'mendacity' and the conventions of much historical writing. Anatole quotes with approval from his own *Sylvestre Bonnard*—as well as from M. Renan—passages on the difficulty of establishing facts. Should this frailty and falseness of the historical Muse drive us into the arms of statistical science? Heaven forbid! It is foolish to replace a rose by a potato. Let others cultivate the science, Anatole will ever cling to 'the charming and magnificent *art* of Thierry and Thucydides.' The argument is developed along familiar lines.

The whole duty of historians is expounded in two 'heavy' articles, on Taine and on Thiers respectively.[41] The former has one of the strongest minds of his time. Perpetually constructing systems, 'he manœuvres facts as Napoleon manœuvred men.' And *re* Napoleon Taine too 'manœuvred' the data to the detriment of true historical judgment.[42] Thus, far from being stubborn things, facts offer themselves to the choice of the systematizer. The notability of events, their authenticity, are judged arbitrarily, according to one's scheme or predisposition. Furthermore, as already hinted, the links of *causality* between them cannot be predicated by the modern reader. Now he who chooses and arranges his material is essentially an artist.[43]

Thiers, however, is rather 'a politician who happens to write history.' The later volumes of the *History of the French Revolution* are the more authoritative because their author had become a public man and was better informed on various political matters. There are some excellent chapters on conditions under the Terror: Anatole should know, since he freely used these chapters in *Les Dieux ont soif*. . . In general, our latter-day urge towards specialization will never supplant comprehensive histories. Thiers wrote with an engaging facility, not ill-suited to his long task. (The latent criticism here recalls Carlyle's remark on Macaulay: 'Flow on, O shining river!') In his old age, our critic changed his opinion and called Thiers 'the worst writer in the French language.'[44]

From casual remarks in the above essays, it is clear that Anatole had savoured a great many styles and read thoughtfully many historians. He is by no means opposed to adequate documentation, if not too obtrusive. We have gained thereby, he considers, a better understanding of the real past. The men of preceding periods, notably the Middle Ages, depicted any past whatsoever in their own contemporary terms. Even a Racine assumed immutability in manners and customs. Well, the doctrine of relativity has helped the moderns just this much : we are enabled to create (illusion aiding) something like a comparative history of the race. Undoubtedly, such 'young sciences' as philosophy, ethnology and archæology have contributed their quotas to such partial reconstructions. All of which seems well and wisely argued.

As for particular epochs, France once more makes plain, though not along strictly historical lines, his love for antiquity. He develops his previous arguments on behalf of the ancient languages. The 'question of Latin' was then as now agitating educational—and political—circles ;[45] and the humanist must view with concern its loss of prestige. He declares that 'our' bachelors of arts never knew Greek and now they can scarcely read a page of Latin without undue toil. The language may gradually disappear from the curricula. Inevitable as this may seem, it would be most regrettable. How can such 'pushing' substitutes as the sciences and modern languages bestow the feeling for traditional values that accompanies Latin studies ? The ancients, he repeats, impart to our minds a grace, a force, a discipline not to be found elsewhere. What are facts and still more facts as compared with this perennial culture, the foundation of Gallic civilization ? What else can so form men and teach them to think ? When A.F. 'trembles for the humanities,' he is really trembling for the *génie français* as much as for the *génie latin*. Thus, in his long review of Latin studies down the ages, he is occupied with the continuous associations between France and Rome. Yet in the 'Vie littéraire,' Anatole does not linger with Latin authors.

Our beauty-loving critic pauses preferably on the radiant hours that saw the birth of 'the fairest of all things,' the Attic spirit. Once more the Greek masterpieces swim into his vision. The wily Ulysses pursues his adventures, innumerable as the waves of the

Mediterranean. On those perfidious waters, the sirens sing again their enchanting song. Tiresias, after a draught of blood, projects his prophecies beyond the *Odyssey*. Thus Homer stamped his genius upon an amalgam of folk-lore. Alas ! The golden and harmonious days of Greece's prime pass by. There follow the uneasy times represented by the anxious and melancholy figure of Euripides. The fates and the passions ravage the work of this all-too-human master. Did serenity ever revisit the Hellenic folk ? Yes—in their graves. Epitaphs in the *Anthology* communicate the peace of the tombs and the endless slumber that they give. For the Greeks embellished even the simulacra of Death and they feared him less than many Christians have feared him.

All this is written in the harmonious and semi-lyrical style that France reserves for his genuine admirations.

When we come once again to the periods of French history, we find that the Middle Ages are more fully and favourably treated than in the chronicles of 'Gérôme.' The two prominent articles were written respectively in praise of *La Littérature française au moyen âge* by Gaston Paris and in disapproval of Leconte de Lisle's attitude in the poem, 'Les Siècles maudits.' The former essay, very Impressionistic, sets forth a day-dream which came to France while seated under an oak-tree, musing over the learned volume. There is little learning in the review : it is mainly a simplified 'miniature' of medieval life. The details are clear and pointed, as in a fairy-web. He sees a landscape of winding roads, sprinkled with cathedrals and *manoirs,* with peasants and pilgrims. He finds that the vernacular literature of the age was compressed within the spheres of feudalism and faith.

As already hinted, Anatole changes front here and reproves Leconte de Lisle for 'pursuing the Middle Ages with his hatred.' A.F. now esteems it a purblind view of history to find in medieval times only ignorance and famine and persecutions. Surely there existed also high heroisms, some excellent laws, a feudal structure that made for good as well as evil, a chivalric spirit that is the greatest achievement of our race. And he has another 'vision,' in which he summons up 'a thousand terrible and charming images' of the past : the unknown, devoted artisans, the studious clerks, the shepherd-maid who restored a kingdom, the busy hive of common civic life. He concludes again by honouring the fathers who left him such images and such traditions.

That medieval luminary, Joan of Arc, is by now considered as a star of the first magnitude. There are some ten passages,[46] mostly full-bodied articles, paralleling in part those written for the *Revue de famille*. To begin with, Anatole deals with imaginative renderings of the Maid of Orleans' story. Modern versions either lack the essential naïveté, or else they attribute too much magic to Joan. She was a marvel rather than a miracle. Heaven was in her soul, and therefore she did great things on the human level. That is why such medieval interpretations as the *Mystère du siège d'Orléans* represent her as coming close to the hearts of the common people. Joseph Fabre's work[47] has clarified her continuous role in popular legend, as well as the political and theological atmosphere surrounding the lawsuit for her rehabilitation. The simple folk were indeed near to the truth of her personality and mission, though of course they were too ready to accept the miraculous both in Jeanne and the 'false Pucelles' who followed her. For the times were 'singularly favourable to impostures.'

As in his imposing later biography, France says he has sought to establish a human and credible setting for his heroine ; he 'has lived the life of fifteenth-century men and tried to share their sentiments and beliefs.' He insists, as in the articles dealt with above (Ch. XIII), that this jewel of a woman shines out from a matrix of folk-lore and prophecies, saints' lives and sermons, as well as from the native poetry of the woods and fields. These old beliefs and traditions, commingled with a fresh virgin-worship, were crystallized in the vocation of Joan, and brought forth a fascinating but wholly natural prodigy. For long her haloed figure continued to reign over the minds of her compatriots.

That reign suffered an interregnum (he might have added) under the protectorate of Voltaire ; the eighteenth century was addicted neither to simple faith nor to English blood. But this era remains the familiar stamping-ground of Anatole France. As the penetrating Herr Curtius phrases it : 'Our sage plunged all his roots into the period which he celebrated as the most magnificent in history—the age of *lumières*.'[48] What he valued most in the thought of his own time really sprang from the eighteenth century. When others berated the epoch, Anatole leapt to its defence. Confirming previous appreciations, he honours 'our fathers,' the *philosophes,* who left us liberal minds as the best of all possible legacies. At its climacteric, it was an era of manifold culture : it was at once 'Neo-Hellenic, didactic, encyclopædic, erotic, romanesque, sentimental, tolerant, atheistic, curious.' It was blest by the presence of such great souls as Madame de Sabran and other gifted ladies, whose prime virtue was to be endowed with proud hearts and free minds. If they had lost their faith, they had kept what is even more precious—the spirit of enlightened and benevolent tolerance. Their daughters were brought up in a hardier fashion than now and were better taught domestically.

Ranging far back into the Old Régime, Anatole draws a telling picture of the daily activities of the *honnête homme* or gentleman. Coming down to Revolutionary times, he still dwells on the delights of the salons together with the growing importance of the families belonging to the upper bourgeoisie. He agrees with Talleyrand as to the charm and savour of those 'incomparable years' when French society paused for a little while on the edge of the abyss. How he would have loved to hear the conversations, too faintly recorded, of such wits and philosophers ! Failing that, he reconstructs an imaginary dialogue, in the manner of Fontenelle, between a philosophic economist and a *grande dame* in her proper setting ; and he evidences by many discreet touches his close knowledge of the period.

The Revolution is still prominent in the thoughts of Noël France's son and heir. As he says, this event is linked with the earliest recollections of Pierre's youth—when he saw the last survivors of the Terror pass like shadows down the street. Unwittingly, these wraiths taught him something of the secret springs of history. Anecdotes, picturesque incidents, still attract the interest of our connoisseur. He devotes two articles to the composition of the 'Marseillaise,' first called the 'War Hymn of the Army of the Rhine.' He reconstructs the scene when Robespierre led the procession at the Festival of the Supreme Being. Looking like a 'mystical cat,' this cruel idealist held garlands in his hand, the while he perorated in behalf of State Deism. A pool of blood was the source of *his* religion, and in a pool of blood he was shortly to end. Anatole emphasizes that we should distinguish between the various phases of the movement and between their leaders.

As manifest in other writings of this period, our critic is at heart a political Conservative. He holds that, whatever the temptation, 'la belle France' has never torn up her roots. The patriotic motive is still strong in him, encouraged no doubt by the 'bien pensant' tone of *Le Temps*. But the scoldings and girdings at the actual government, frequent in *l'Univers illustré,* are usually absent from this journal. What abides is a reverence for his country. Like an exquisite peach, France has long lain in the centre of the European fruit-basket. She has been well styled the 'light of the world,' she stands foremost in upholding the causes of humanity and justice and beauty. Let us keep all that is best in her past and in her provincial life as well.

The provinces, indeed, cling to their distinctive traits. Political unity need not remove a desirable diversity in customs, a welcome variety in landscapes and local products ; for these things add to the charm of France as a whole. Declaring that the country is none the worse for 1870-71, Anatole goes so far as to praise the quality of pure and delicate patriotism which was born with the Third Republic. I cannot think that this sort of blatant chauvinism was quite sincere, nor does it correspond with what we have seen above. He is more truly himself when he inspires his Talking Oak (in the review of Gaston Paris) to address a typical Frenchman : 'Know thy ancestors, prolong thus thy ephemeral life, be "pious" toward their shades, and venerate thy native land, whose soil is sacred.'

Even the French army is 'sacred.' It should be discussed only with the greatest respect. Abel Hermant's coarse picture of garrison life, *Le Cavalier Miserey,* is severely reproved.[49] Evidently, the militaristic spirit is still that of Gérôme.' Strange to think that as the defender of Dreyfus our author would one day scorn the 'shakers of the sabre' along with the 'holy water sprinklers' ! But his critical spirit is now muted, as a rule, before reasons of State.

§ 9

As for Anatole's journeyings and his descriptions of France, we shall presently see that the chief 'junket' here recorded was an extensive trip into the Midi (1890).[50] This was to attend certain festivals of Provençal poets. In another direction, he remembers the summer days spent under 'the pines of the Hochwald,' in Alsace. There are also allusions to various expeditions into Normandy and Brittany. Adolescent trippings around Avranches are not forgotten. The admiring article given over to Octave Feuillet recalls that Anatole had made this novelist's acquaintance as early as 1881, at the ancient town of Saint-Lô. The chronicler still remembers the aspect of the steep and tortuous streets dominated by the twin spires of Sainte-Croix.[51] Another passage revives the memory of a drear winter's night passed in the half-dead village of Valognes. Brief have been his flights into Brittany; but when he reads poems of the soil he sees again the desolate strands and the granite, the dark greenery around the rivers, the tall reeds, and the 'peasant-women grave as nuns.'

In 1888 France visited the cathedral in 'ce riant et riche Bordeaux.' Through his summerings at Madame Arman de Caillavet's estate, 'Capian,' Anatole had come to know the near-by capital of La Gironde, as well as the country-side and vineyards roundabout.[52] He watched the tanned labourers fanning wheat and wondered if his day's work was equal to theirs. He is keen, naturally, on survivals of old customs. Just as he had stressed elsewhere the provincial 'Noëls' or Christmas carols, so here he shows a liking for popular songs, whether they deal with love or soldiering. Also he is much impressed, throughout the country, by the diversity of landscapes: wet meadows here, clear blue horizons there, each suitably reproduced by poet or romancer. 'One might make a fine study of the literary geography of France.'

One might . . . Anatole has only sketched it. Sometimes his literary pilgrimages are undertaken merely by the fireside, book in hand, pictorial reminiscences in mind. Altogether, there is ample confirmation of what we have already noticed: that our critic views all scenery primarily from the angle of literary or artistic associations.

Paris, of course, remains his chief love. He repeats the sentiments of Gérôme and of Sylvestre Bonnard as to the 'miracle' of the jewelled Seine, the charms of the quays, the lessons of the stones. They teach (once more) the continuity of the French tradition; but the perpetual flow of the river and the glimpses of old books remind one rather of the melancholy passing of all things. Parisian in his 'soul and flesh,' he will cling whenever possible to memories of early days in the Quarter. In Coppée's volume of recollections, certain passages about old streets can make him shiver with delight; he sees again the books and the stalls, he sniffs the atmosphere of the Quai Malaquais, which condenses the aroma of the whole city. Paris is like an immense cup with a flowered rim ; it is a cornucopia heaped with luxuries and with the products of the manifold arts.

Let us ramble through ancient by-ways in the dusk, even though our promenades be enveloped in wistful sadness. We shall pass by the home of Sainte-Beuve or that of Octave Feuillet. We shall notice 'that dark little Rue Hautefeuille,' where Baudelaire once perched, though Anatole remembers it rather as connected with a lady novelist. He likes its jutting balconies and its turrets. When we drift towards the Rue Rousselet, off the Rue de Sèvres, France is moved to a lyric apostrophe. That street is 'dear to the hearts of all true Parisians,' for it is replete with memories. There Madame de la Sablière spent her saintly old age. There the gallant Barbey d'Aurevilly lived thirty years in a noble poverty, not without consolations. There Anatole France once visited him, and inhaled the precious scent and savour of long ago . . . O blessèd Rue Rousselet !

What is our critic's attitude toward French society ? He is aware that the salons, as in former days, can still produce wonderful conversationalists and make literary reputations. He has watched M. Caro and M. Brochard shining in such roles. These remarks seem prophetic of his own development at the hands of Madame de Caillavet, especially when he adds, concerning feminine trainers : 'There are seductions which it is very difficult to resist.' Women of the world are the chief educators of the creature Man. They teach him how to charm an audience and deepen his sentimental understanding.

Has society gained or lost through the democratic trend ? If one considers the matter of bringing up children, there we have clearly lost in 'force and firmness.' Education (in the widest sense) used to flourish vigorously when it produced 'la plus belle société du monde.' Yet it is useless to lament the passing of the old order—we *had* to build a new régime for our habitation. The edifice is a monotonous and unhandsome structure, but it is at least livable.

If Anatole is more lenient to the existing order in *Le Temps* than in *l'Univers illustré,* we may recall that the former journal is and was a semi-official organ. Perhaps too in these palmy days the critic is more disposed to occupy his pleasant corner without shaking a stick at the Republic. This need not mean that he has wholly accepted democracy. Pecus still has his gross faults. The machine age, already beginning to triumph even then, makes for automatism and mediocrity whether in ideas or emotions. Thus we pay dearly for our material progress. Anatole doubts if there is any help for this state of affairs. Renan has realized that the future belongs to the herd, that the power is Caliban's. His stupidity constitutes his strength: where the delicate Ariel would perish, Caliban pushes on by brute force and by instinct.

And certain things about the modern world are not so bad. Never was there 'such pleasant living and such easy thinking.' (!) People use the term 'fin de siècle' as if we were really on the brink of destruction. But France holds that far from being decadent, his age has not even reached the peak of civilization. Consider how slowly man emerges from the womb of the past. As for the future, who knows, who knows? It may be significant that our Conservative manifests a dawning interest in the doctrines of Socialism.[53]

Not the least feature of French culture is the beautiful language which helps hold it together The mother-tongue is spoken of as an obliging handmaiden, 'so sweet and fresh, so alert and gay.' Among its prime merits are its naturalness and its clearness—let none seek to confound it by mere verbal gymnastics. Give it time and elbow-room and it will say nicely whatever need be said. And let none think that good French is the property of the élite, whether social or literary. On the contrary, Anatole argues that it comes from the soil and belongs to the folk. We should beware of exposing this natural growth to learned graftings or tortuous dislocations. To the deuce with the pundits and their spelling-reforms! Like the Latin, the French tongue is basically rustic. As in dealing with the language of La Fontaine, so here Anatole lingers on certain savoury terms connected with farming or hunting. His insistence on 'popular' French recalls to us his democratic origins and the pride that he took in learning to speak aright at his mother's knee. In connexion with lexicography, he wants us to think of all the life that lies embedded in the countless columns of a modern dictionary, to remember how these represent 'the birth-pangs, the blood and the soul of the fatherland and of humanity.' Each word brings to us visions of long ancestral labours or experiences. Thus, France the stylist would cling to past usage and preserve the traditions of his native tongue.[54]

§ 10

Before continuing with literature proper, we may pause on various matters connected with book-learning, book-loving, book-collecting. As already hinted in these pages, the author of *Sylvestre Bonnard* maintained a varied interest in the kind of scholarship that is cultural rather than pedantic. He still likes fine points in historical or literary research, where genuine human interest is involved. His esteem for savants—of the right kind—is sincere and abundant; he knows that a vigorous method is essential to their enterprises; he realizes the value of harking back to original sources and applauds the scholars who can do this and yet keep their readability. As for himself . . . but his whole attitude here is so frank and sensible that I shall quote a paragraph from his review of Reinach's *History of Mithridates*:[55]

> Works of pure erudition do not fall within my range and cannot provide the substance for one of these literary chats which demand easy and varied subjects. Specialistic and particular points are not our business. Fortunately, the true scholar is often led by his researches into generalizations from which curious minds can draw both pleasure and profit.

Illustrations of this procedure can be found in his chats about volumes by a Maspéro or a Darmesteter, a Renan or a Reinach.

It is on this basis that France prefers the humanities to the sciences. The latter give rise to a comparatively limited number of general views, most of which he had already exploited—for instance, in the articles on 'Les Origines humaines.' Evidently, his curiosity will hover on the border-line between scholarship and belles-lettres. He admires the brief biographies of the 'Grands Ecrivains' series. He appreciates, apropos of Chénier, the equipment needed to make a critical edition of a poet. He values philology, is keen on folkloristic origins, and likes nice questions of attribution and authenticity. He cares for small choice editions, particularly Elzevirs, of which he says: 'I have loved these little books from the days of my inquisitive youth when—if whimsicality and knowledge could have hit it off together—I might well have become a scholar.'[56]

Indeed he might. But if he had actually become Sylvestre Bonnard, then *Le Crime de Sylvestre Bonnard* could hardly have been written.

Occasionally France waxes humorous about scholars, especially if they elevate their noses too high or sink their eyes too low. Certain archæologists are found to be perniciously 'stuffy,' certain writers of fat five-hundred-page tomes had as well perish with their works. He points out mockingly that you must never ask a scholar about anything alien to his specialty — each is proud of his own show-case, while turning his back on the others. More favourably put, savants 'are resigned to knowing little, in order to know it well.' This gives them mental peace ; and as a race they are now much more amiable than they used to be, say in the Renaissance.

In the educational field, Anatole pays tribute not only to the excellent methods of the Ecole des Chartes, which he knew through Charavay, but to other institutions of the higher learning, particularly the Ecole Normale and the old Collège de France. How welcome are such oases in the monotonous deserts of our ignorance ! Secondary education, on the other hand, has become largely standardized memory-work, especially since the virtual abandonment of the humanities. The Collège Stanislas, for example, has fallen into a rut, even more so than in his own school-days. At least then they could not quite spoil Homer and Virgil for 'Pierre' and his kind. Our semi-scholar expresses himself not only about the French but about German and American universities as well. The German type has a vast intellectual influence, modified now by an unfortunate utilitarian trend. An emphasis on practical and physical tendencies is also characteristic (he is informed) of American universities. He is impressed, as far back as 1890, by the number and extent of our private foundations. We lack for him the charm and the traditions of Oxford ; but he is open-minded and tolerant about athletics, 'student-life,' and other features that the French, he believes, would do well to imitate.

Opinions already delivered regarding feminine education are here reinforced : a distrust of high specialization and a conviction that women should learn the essential things in the world about them as well as in the world of culture. For them, education is properly 'a gentle and discreet solicitation,' which is much what

Fénelon thought. Indeed, why should any of us become proud and pedantic about the fragile links (miscalled Knowledge) that we have established with Nature?

Some general remarks about books and authors.—Since our Hedonist maintains that there is 'no true love without sensuality,' we find him caressing the polished backs of his best-beloved books and approving the priests who show concupiscence toward calf-skin bindings. The association of ideas causes Anatole to demand primarily 'well-bound books that speak of love'—a Shakespearean echo and a slogan that has become famous. It is clear, too, that for the true lover volumes should not be very voluminous. Small Lemerres (in compliment to his publisher),[57] small Elzevirs, small perfect tales like the *Princesse de Clèves* and *Candide,* are infinitely preferable on this basis to the great tomes of Balzac.

Yet as to whether books are in the long run friends or enemies, Anatole is not so sure. What is the essential value of these little black signs which I and others scatter helter-skelter over white pages? At times books seem to be the opiates of the Western world—we are drugged, we are deadened, I am oppressed in brain and heart by several thousand of these creatures. I fear they are my masters. . . And we remember Bonnard befogged in his 'cité des livres.' After all, are there not other things in the world than ink and paper? A book is a 'work of sorcery, which releases disturbing visions.' Hence the hashish-eaters, the dream-readers, the devourers of sweet poison:

> Let us love books, as those smitten by Eros love their malady. Let us love them, for they cost us dearly. Let us love them, for we are dying of them! Yes, books are slaying all of us. Take my word for it, since I too adore them, since long ago I surrendered to them absolutely. . . They slay us by force of numbers.

As for the weavers of these spells, too much devotion to his calling can make a monster out of an 'artist.' It was thus that Flaubert erred. A young writer, especially, who shuts himself up in his Art is running into a blind wall. Why live to write, when having lived is the only excuse for writing? The everlasting *pro* and *con* of it are further illustrated. *Pro* utters a hymn in praise of the Muse of Letters, in behalf of those devotees who beguile life by the love of books, living in an enchanting and 'beneficent illusion.' But *Con* tells us, apropos of Loti, that this writer is wise in preferring nature to books, for the latter can give us only imperfect images of the former. So let us detest with Loti 'that vanity of vanities, the literary mind.'

Whether or not Anatole meant all this, there abides his taste for that concrete thing, the Book. 'Love comes back to his ancient dwelling,' namely the Quai Malaquais with its mellow aroma. He touches up faded portraits of the past. Old Debas, more bent over with age, still poor but independent, holds a little longer his place in the sun. Enter the two good priests whose secret sin it was to linger round the parapets and occasionally stick tattered volumes in their cassocks. Peace to all these, who pass innocently through this transitory life! And peace to more famous bibliophiles—a class of people who seldom read. Such was Asselineau, whom it was a pleasure to find surrounded by his 'firsts' of the wilder and woollier Romanticists.[58] Such was Charles Monselet, of blessèd memory, whom one used to encounter near the two-cent book-stalls. Where are the other 'fine ferrets' who could sniff out the precious essence latent in old paper? Where is the dust of yester-year?

O crooked and venerable Rue Saint-Jacques, whose narrow pavements were crowded with the flotsam of the ancients! O my *Antigone,* redolent still of roasted chestnuts! . . . Nowadays one barely has time to pause in the galleries of the Odéon. One envies the studious folk standing there, fingering uncut volumes. These sparrows pick up tidbits, more appetizing perhaps than entire meals. I have done too much of that wholesale consumption. An excellent book-dealer used to bring me basketfuls. I swallowed them all. And I am humble, for I realize that my whole body contains little that is not book-knowledge. If the Game of Letters leads to anything, surely I am an old hand at that.

But this 'vie littéraire' which Anatole led so long was not uneventful, nor did it always meander peacefully through favourite haunts. There were incidents, controversies, passages at arms. In fact, many of France's sallies into current literary discussion are directed towards three main battle-fields: the war waged upon Zola and Naturalism; his skirmishes with Moréas and the Symbolists; his fight with Brunetière about impressionistic criticism. The first two of these contests also involved certain minor feuds, while the last topic will lead us back to that agora where critics discuss the literary art. A good deal of human interest emerges from these combats. Let us consider them in order.

§ II

In 1891, a journalist called Jules Huret conducted for *l'Echo de Paris* a series of interviews later published in volume form. The very first of the series contains opinions of the 'maître critique,' Anatole France, who subsequently resented what Huret had made him say about Symbolism. But on Naturalism he seems to have been fairly well reported, for the utterances here agree with those found in his periodical articles. He told Huret that the Naturalistic movement was dead and buried ; that it died partly because it was excessive and ugly, partly because it could not furnish a topic for conversation with ladies ; and that while Zola's bestial peasants are revolting, the novelist had done good work in *l'Assommoir* and *Germinal*. France defends himself from the charge of being an enemy to realism in general and declares that he admires the method so well inaugurated by Flaubert and the Goncourts.

When we turn to the pages of *Le Temps,* we encounter early the most famous and rabid article,[59] which deals directly with *La Terre*. This diatribe against Zola's filth, his gratuitous bestiality, his falsifying of peasant life, is notorious, partly because it is rare for France to write in such a harsh vein ; but it contains little that is new for those who recall his previous indictments, especially in *l'Univers illustré*. More unusual is the tone of stern indignation with which he asserts that this man is 'among those unfortunates who should never have been born,' and that one can accord him at best only a 'profound pity.' Almost coinciding in time with a protest by five of Zola's disciples [60] who now deserted his standard, Anatole's well-timed onslaught had its share in defeating excessive Naturalism.

Subsequent critiques of the movement and its leader number about a dozen and include four full-length articles.[61] After the excellence of *Madame Bovary,* France laments, was it not a pity that the leadership fell to the man from Médan, with his coarse and narrow talent, so lacking in proportion and beauty ? His methods are as crude as his scientific pretensions are laughable. The 'experimental' idea is inapplicable to literature. A little thought will demonstrate that, but the Naturalist never thinks and is therefore incapable even of experimenting according to his own false formula. An honest realism is one fundamental need of every reader. But the sort of lopsided 'Naturalism' that we have now is a horror, a mental malady. Boileau would think us all crazy. To absorb *La Terre* presupposes a perversion of the senses; to appreciate *Le Rêve* requires a general state of coma.

France's article on the last-mentioned novel bears the sardonic title, 'La Pureté de M. Zola.' This much advertised and over-edifying chastity seems to leave *Le Rêve* a complete blank. Zola on all fours is preferable to this nebulous and ethereal Zola. He has soared up to some stained-glass heaven where he has even forgotten what concrete religious practices are like. . . Yes, the whole school and its detailed methods are now (1889) just about through. We have had a sufficiency of small facts and low sensations. Presently France goes so far as to say that there is no such thing as Naturalistic art. Let us clear the way for more idealistic or more psychological approaches to the proper study of mankind.

In the clearance we had as well include *La Bête humaine* and all that is symbolized by that title. For the discussion of this novel, Anatole stages an amusing dialogue between professional people. Each of these characters handsomely admits that Zola is excellent in dealing with anything but the speaker's specialty. A mechanical engineer thinks him learned in the law, but a magistrate infinitely prefers him on railroads, while a Naturalistic novelist declares that Zola is anything but a Naturalist. Among the diners is a critic who presumably states Anatole's attitude: Zola is an informative and glorified Jules Verne on the one hand, a pornographer and a pessimist on the other.

The victory having been won, our champion can afford to be kinder in subsequent articles. Since the 'Naturalistic terror' is well over, let us (after 1890) be generous and acknowledge that under its reign were erected such imposing monuments as *Germinal, l'Argent,* and *La Débâcle*. Now that the idealistic novelists are carrying it with a pretty high hand, Anatole reacts to the point of surveying the wreckage of Naturalism with an eye to salvage. The Rougon-Macquart series is, then, an impressive if clumsy mass of architecture, marred by various obsessions (heredity and obscenity), but giving a powerful expression to the life of the instincts. The depiction of classes in *l'Argent* is solid and true; *La Débâcle* is really fine and marks Zola's growth in intelligence and 'a large humanity.' (Later A.F. added *l'Assommoir* to the list.) Finally, France becomes semi-apologetic regarding his previous severity. 'I regret somewhat my wrath.' As an apocalyptic prophet, Zola need not condescend to good taste and measure; he has up his sleeve great muscular power and an indispensable kind of flesh and blood reality.

But this calmer and more contemplative tone hardly justifies certain critics [62] in holding that France, taking him by and large, was favourable toward the leader of Naturalism. On the contrary, if humanity was Zola's *bête par excellence,* Zola was for long Anatole's *bête noire.* (It might be mentioned that Zola had once written slightingly of our author as a critic who knew almost nothing about contemporary literature—a reproach which others have repeated.) [63] Still MM. Carias and Kahn seem right in maintaining that, when the Dreyfus affair brought the two men into closer relations, France's more admiring attitude then did not constitute a betrayal of his previous convictions: that attitude had been prepared for by the articles of 1891-92. By the time he delivered his funeral oration on Zola (1902), he could objectively praise the man's work and message. But he never really liked the sort of writing characteristic of *Les Rougon-Macquart.*[64]

As a pendant to these diatribes, one may notice again France's assault on another Naturalistic work, *Le Cavalier Miserey,* which is itself an assault on the French army. Anatole finds Abel Hermant's tale of garrison life both tiresome and untrue. For perpetual descriptions and hosts of details do not constitute general verity or *vraisemblance.* In *Le Cavalier Miserey,* the author shows only the 'small sides of great things.' The critic approves a military order directing that every copy of the work found in barracks should be burnt. Anatole declares there is more sense and patriotism in this order than in the four hundred pages of the book. We shall presently see how Hermant took his revenge.

It is clear, then, that the Naturalistic novel, as a whole, was not among France's preferences. The sort of fiction that he liked was what he considered well-balanced and with no excesses—by request. Hence he could admire either the classically psychological or the soberly realistic. A digression here will permit us to summarize his views on the fictional form and its chief practitioners.

Like any other work of art, a novel must be well-composed and not consist of mere 'slices of life.' So-called 'documents,' seasoned with scientific or neo-psychological verbiage, are unpalatable. Once more, literature derives from human nature and instincts rather than from science. *Manon Lescaut* and *Madame Bovary* tell us more of actual life than all the sages can. The same conditions apply to historical fiction, which must deal with people rather than with costumes and local colour. The tale, the *nouvelle,* of which France gives quite a sketch is often superior to the mediocre and too-abundant yellow-backs. Who would not admire the short stories of Daudet and of Maupassant ? Who would not contemn the platitudinous Ohnet, 'outside of literature' as he surely is ?

Anatole is fond of the heartier kind of English novels—Fielding, Scott, Dickens. At home, Rabelais, of course, and Lesage have the same large human quality, together with distinctive merits of style. Madame de La Fayette's naturalness and truth installed her *Princesse de Clèves* in the harmonious 'concert of the classics.' Later and in its own way, *Candide* showed a similar profound knowledge of the human heart. Still later, we may admire the joyous yarns of the elder Dumas ; or Mérimée's delineation of strong passions ; or George Sand, as 'a great artisan of the Ideal' ; or Balzac, as 'the greatest historian of modern France.'

Under the ægis of Mme. de Caillavet, France had come to know Paul Hervieu and Pierre Loti, both of whom he praises rather intemperately. The latter, through his exposures of sensibility, brought back the confessional note into literature ; and this fact naturally pleases Anatole, who proceeds to discourse in the same article[65] on his beloved genre of confessions. Loti's name is now added to the list of those who have written in the most appealing form of direct personal memoirs.

On the whole, France cared more for the novel than for the drama.[66] It has already been hinted that he did not go to the theatre often and when he did (he explained) he was more interested in the audience than in the play. Also, because Sarcey was dramatic critic for *Le Temps,* Anatole politely makes way for his colleague and has little comment on the new productions. Personally, he prefers marionettes ! These puppet-shows correspond to his private conception of the theatre as a cross between a Noah's Ark and a box of Nuremberg toys. Thus the soul of little 'Pierre' goes marching on. For in the hands of a magician like Sophocles or Shakespeare, plays become 'enchanted toys.' As the greatest of poets, Shakespeare makes us feel rather than think — a view which is worth considering. If we respond warmly to Hamlet, it is because the 'sweet prince' touches individual chords in each of us. This paragon of plays ranks along with *Faust* for the confused and cloudy wealth of its 'Northern' images. In Goethe (whose name is 'frequently invoked') we find particularly depth of thought,[67] while in Shakespeare's magic Arden, we find everything ; for the latter conducts us on the 'most magnificent promenade that genius ever undertook through the dreams of man.' Half a dozen other dramas are touched upon, with insistence on the vastness, the universal quality, and often the 'sacred horror' that envelops us in the Shakespearean world. Certainly, for a classically-minded person, France shows an uncommon appreciation of this world, an appreciation that Voltaire, for instance, could not command. Racine, of course, is still A.F.'s favourite, still linked with Virgil among the myrtles, still considered the incomparable analyst of women and of the diverse forms of love. He cannot cease to adore his 'own' Racine, adore him with 'flesh and blood, heart and soul,' as of yore. And he stands ready to pick a quarrel with any one who adores him otherwise.

Although the tradition of 'l'aimable et robuste comédie' wins Anatole's respect, yet very few contemporary dramatists are esteemed. Among them are Augier, for his good sense and his great heart ; and the younger Dumas, for his splendid moral and mental force, despite the danger of over-sermonizing ; and Pailleron, for observation as well as Racinian penetration, a blending of 'exquisite art' with perfect naturalness. France is constant in his admiration for these three and almost none besides.

§ 12

But neither fiction nor drama was the genre that France favoured most. He is still faithful to the poetic Muse — so faithful that he instinctively resents any attempts upon her virgin integrity. This leads him into his second mellay with contemporary schools : he has a confused bout, which turns into a reconciliation drama, with certain leaders among the Symbolists. But first we should define his general attitude toward poetry and note what developments or changes appear in his views about preceding poets.

Not only does France write more frequent and more notable articles within this field than in any other; it is clear that his long pervasive interest in poetry causes him here to shine at his critical best. Inevitably, his Parnassian experiences had left abiding furrows in his mind. And others[68] have pointed out that it was his life-long habit to read and ponder over verse, which was a favourite topic of discussion among his intimates.

He held that the chief requisite for poetry, as for art in general, was neither rime nor reason, but genuine sentiment. 'Elle est dans je ne sais quoi qui nous gonfle le cœur.' Hence his fondness for spontaneous folk-poetry. Indeed, all true verse, like trees and flowers, should spring from the germinating forces of life itself. The poet endears himself to us by helping us to love and by bringing to light what we feel darkly. Anatole is aware, too, that poetic forms are constantly changing and therefore offer nothing absolute or final. 'Beautiful shapes count above all through the spirit which animates them.' Like lovers, he declares, poets are often happily ignorant of their technique and sing best when they proceed by instinct. We should take our poets fresh, like fruit. But does this imply that we can no longer savour a Racine or a Chénier? By no means! And does it imply that France would discount artistic effects in verse? How could he do that? On the contrary, he particularly esteems 'les vers bien faits.' There is no poetry without art, no art without a training. In the judgments that follow, the apparently rival claims of technique and sentiment represent less a conflict than a shift in emphasis.

Much later,[69] France wrote a *Tableau de la poésie française* which gives a good general sketch of the earlier movements. In *Le Temps* he rarely goes back of André Chénier and the eighteenth century. The plastic beauty and neo-classical grace of Chénier caused him to be one of the poets whom A.F. most admired. His thorough acquaintance with the verse of this master was shown by an amusing 'mystification' perpetrated as early as 1864. At that time France startled the readers of *l'Intermédiaire*[70] by printing as hitherto unpublished and with erudite comment 'ten lines of André Chénier.' They were smooth harmonious verses, concerned with the myths of Proserpine and Dido. This 'discovery' attracted some attention, and presently the lines were incorporated in the critical edition of Chénier by Becq de Fouquières. But it was a complete hoax. Anatole himself at the age of twenty had composed these verses and had slyly played the sedulous ape well enough to impose them upon the world of letters. In the *Vie littéraire,* France lightly alludes to the mystification, pays his compliments to the learned editor, discusses the sources of Chénier's poetry, and dwells on his 'masculine virtues.'

A series of articles[71] is devoted to a leisurely review of a publication by Lemerre—the *Anthologie des poètes français du XIXe siècle.* The publisher himself, that old patron who was shortly to become a business enemy, is 'puffed' as the only man capable of assembling such a rich collection. With regard to the Romantic poets, France seems more tolerant than we have found him heretofore, when he wore the cloak of Gérôme ; he credits the men of 1830 with their picturesque power ; yet he remains less responsive to the flamboyant leaders (e.g., Hugo) than to the sentimental Lamartine and the intellectual Vigny. The latter was endowed with a noble intelligence as well as with a compassionate heart. We are reminded that Little Pierre, as a child, had seen and admired this peaceful gentleman, whose name became the Alpha (1868) and the Omega (1923) of his literary life. Here he praises the *Maison du berger* and is glad that they are honouring with a tablet the house where Vigny died. Who better than he imposed respect through 'a benevolent pride, a pensive wisdom . . . a great and sensitive soul' ? Lamartine also was appreciated, for quite different reasons, by Anatole. Four consecutive articles[72] were devoted to the shade of 'Elvire,' who had inspired the best *Méditations.* This is one of France's deliberate and well-documented performances, based on material furnished by Noël Charavay, Lemaître, and others.[73] The writer retraces the portraits not only of Mme. Charles but of her husband and rectifies properly the position held by Lamartine in the triangle. Anatole has not changed his conception of Lamartine as a lyrist. An improviser rather than an artist, he preserves the power to touch our personal memories. His vibrant bow awakens our inmost feelings, his loves are metamorphosed into ours, and we remold him still nearer to the heart's desire.

But Anatole hears his former comrades calling. What is his present view of the Parnassians, among whom he achieved, as he says, 'obscurely and bravely my first feats of arms' ? Evidently, that early ardour has cooled. The breach with Leconte de Lisle, we shall see, was widened by France's veering about Symbolism ;

but it is a mistake to hold that he has squarely turned his back on his old colleagues and their doctrines. He declares that some 'twenty fine years of poetry and study' were initiated by the Parnassians of the sixties. He is proud to have formed a part of that generation which earnestly cultivated art and sought for truth:

> We never declaimed. . . We tried our best to learn. We reverenced the masters. Probably we lacked high inspiration and audacity; but we did possess a sense of what is exquisite and finished. I dare to make this proclamation: O my birth-mates and work-mates, you have deserved well of Literature, and your volumes of nineteen years ago form today a part of the proud heritage of your native land![74]

Elsewhere he asserts that 'we' led a modest and laborious existence, devoted to our high calling and desiring only a discreet glory.

It has been sufficiently demonstrated[75] that on the whole France remained loyal to the band whose principles of prosody he never discarded. To this group is dedicated a good half of those articles in the *Vie littéraire* which bear on poetry. Thus, Léon Dierx, that semi-Parnassian, is loved for his harmony and beauty, to which he adds a Symbolistic power of suggestiveness. Mendès and Plessis are still admired by their old friend. Heredia, the bright particular star of the Parnassian firmament, is honoured for his many adornments, from his splendid neckties to the final lines of his sonnets. His work will surely endure; for he wrote, or rather painted, the best sonnets since Petrarch. It is true that he was rather too impassive, but all of 'us,' including Ricard, had that affectation.[76]

It was, then, only with regard to Leconte de Lisle that France really changed his tune, and that partly at least for personal reasons. As early as 1887 a rather cool article appeared in *Le Temps* when Anatole's former chieftain became an Academician. After defending the Middle Ages from the attacks of the elder poet, our critic roundly declares that this Old Inveterate is by no means infallible. For all his vaunted impersonality, what we mainly perceive in his verses is the presentment of—Leconte de Lisle. Certainly (he admits later) they are marvellous verses, well-turned and luminous; and far be it from A.F. to reject the stoical scepticism that emanates from the doctrine of illusion. Also be it admitted (what still later, according to Brousson,[77] was denied) that in his modellings after the antique, the poet-scholar went directly to Greek sources and that his other translations from the Greek are well done. Altogether, a dexterous and *fin-de-siècle* way of damning with faint praise. It was the dogmatist, the high priest in Leconte de Lisle, that France came to dislike.

With regard to the Symbolistic or 'Decadent' movement (the terms were once used interchangeably) Anatole, although hostile at first, presently achieved more of a real *volte-face* than he did in the case of Zola. The aims and practice of the school were originally confused and obscure. Anatole was not a partisan of that absurd cult of the unintelligible which has progressed so far since his day. Consequently, when in 1886 Jean Moréas and Gustave Kahn brought forth a strange compound dubbed *le Symbolisme* and when the former issued a 'Manifesto' to explain his intentions, the chief critic of *Le Temps* could not hold his peace.

In this 'Manifesto,'[78] Moréas, a Greek by birth, declares first that a more vital and modern poetry is needed after the Parnassian attempts. Does not Symbolism, with its new vocabulary, its disorderly syntax and its striking metaphors, offer tokens of another Renaissance ? Its precursors are Banville and Baudelaire. Its main object is 'to clothe the (Platonic) Idea in a concrete form,' to subordinate the latter, while adumbrating and decking out the former with analogies and 'esoteric affinities.' If we are obscure, why so much the worse ; Shakespeare and Goethe have borne the same reproach. Furthermore, we are through with the impersonal declamations and descriptions of the Parnassians ; subjectivity is king.

These rambling phrases afford ample elbow-room for France's irony ; and his first attack,[79] in contrast to his foes, is written with a deliberate clarity. He perfectly understands dressing up the 'Idea' in sumptuous apparel — most poets do that — but he is not certain of the 'secret affinities of primordial concepts.' This habit of never calling things by their right names, this perpetual 'adumbration' leads to much obscurity. Every now and then appears a new and intolerant apostle, who fails to convert us Gentiles. Such was Zola with his dogmatic Naturalism ; such is Moréas, with his inability to see anything but Symbolism. 'That is the danger of systems.' The Renaissance writers to whom you appeal — especially Rabelais — had a wealth of words but believed in a rich simplicity.

If Banville was really your ancestor, he was a plain-spoken old gentleman. Like Balzac's painter, you will turn your canvas into a daub by over-elaboration. Let me advise that you put away esoteric words and tin-foil wrappings.

Moréas politely answered that France as a 'fin lettré' has written one of the few 'reasonable' rejoinders to his manifesto. Of course he cannot accept these arguments as to the necessary failure of the Symbolistic enterprise. Banville is certainly on 'our' side, particularly with regard to projected reforms in prosody. Moréas adds : 'You admire Lamartine, while still esteeming Baudelaire ; I admire Baudelaire, while (distantly) esteeming Lamartine.' Such is the essential difference between the two debaters.

France stuck to his guns by maintaining, in another connexion, that unintelligibility destroyed whatever virtues the Decadents might otherwise possess. Presently he wrote a letter to Charles Morice, reiterating his difficulty in knowing what the Symbolists are driving at and his belief that they are afflicted with a genuine malady, even as Zola was. Morice attempted a rejoinder,[80] which asserted that novelty, intuition, *youth,* have their values as well as traditionalism. This provoked even more downright statements from France. He who 'loves the light' can never be pleased by enigmas ; the accomplished writer tries to make things easy for his readers. As for the power of 'suggestion,' what is new about that ? Perhaps only the fact that the Symbolists suggest, not ideas, heaven forbid !—but merely emotions and sensations. Mallarmé's sonnet on Poe is cited as a case in point. These men insist that the crowd, who cannot understand them, must be disdained ; and France points out the dangers of scorning one's audience.

The truth is, as Gustave Kahn amiably said later, that Anatole was 'disturbed' by Symbolism and disliked its peculiar style.[81] Finding it difficult to get used to Mallarmé and the rest, he thought it better to follow Sainte-Beuve's advice and read an old book whenever a too new one appeared. He remains on the firing-line in other articles that poke fun at a 'Glossary' issued by the Symbolists and that speak of the movement as a growing madness beset with empty hallucinations. The preface to the second volume of *La Vie littéraire* maintains that the sense-transferences recommended in Rimbaud's 'Sonnet of the Vowels' constitute a genuine neurosis. But France steadily excepts Verlaine, a true poet, the Wandering Jew of melody and dreams, from this blanket condemnation of the school. With all his divagations, 'Poor Lelian' knows where the winds of inspiration are still blowing.

By the end of 1890, France is ready to admit that other Symbolists, too, share worthily in the new revelation. He has, as M. Barthou puts it, 'changed his altars.'[82] Yet it must have come as a surprise to the orthodox when Anatole wrote a favourable review of a recent volume by Moréas, *Le Pèlerin passionné*. Former objections are now minimized : one must accept the *relative* obscurity of this 'Ronsard of Symbolism' ; one must concede that his poetic innovations are mostly sanctioned by Banville ; and generally (since all things shift and veer) the new prosody contains little that is really offensive or inartistic.

Should this change of heart be ascribed to a sense of fairness or a process of erosion ? Perhaps more than anything else France hated being classed as an old fogy by *les jeunes*. At any rate, he continued to lower the barriers. Late in 1890 he wrote a friendly letter to Moréas, inviting him to call at the Rue Chalgrin and talk things over. When A.F. attended a banquet for the poet early in 1891, he had a 'good digestion' and deigned to smile at the insurgents. He had previously (though ambiguously) acknowledged that he had made errors and confusions[83] in sizing up the Symbolists, the Decadents, and the Impressionists . . . because after all they *are* equally hard to comprehend and sort out. But just as the Romanticists once revolted against the 'rules,' why not the Decadents now ? By 1893 France goes so far as to confess that he can often enjoy what he cannot quite understand. Mystery may at times 'conspire' with poetry. He was in error when he strove for a rational conception of modern verse, instead of sticking to the truer touchstone of sentiment.

These and similar tergiversations did not pass unnoticed. Some declare[84] that he was generally blamed in 1891 for supporting Moréas. Remy de Gourmont spoke of his 'formidable aplomb' in the practice of hypocrisy ; Bergerat considered his move 'incomprehensible' ; Huysmans actually opined that 'the Symbolistic movement was a 'game got up by Anatole France to annoy the Parnassians' ; and Leconte de Lisle peevishly agreed with this surprising judgment, adding that A.F. would presently be ashamed of himself.[85] Mendès, more charitably, attributed the article to France's desire to reconcile the opposing camps.[86] Much of this was calculated to sting ; but what stung most was that in the afore-mentioned interview by Huret [87] Anatole was apparently misrepresented to a considerable degree. He is in fact *quoted* as praising the Symbolistic revolt in contrast to the 'impassivity and the aridity of the Parnassians' and as approving the efforts of the innovators to make the Alexandrine line 'more free and elastic.' Leconte de Lisle and the rest are styled backward-looking old men, while Jean Moréas is a 'charming artist.'

The latter suitably acknowledged France's tribute. But there followed an acrid correspondence with Leconte de Lisle, conducted through the intermediary of Huret and the *Echo de Paris*. In the course of this regrettable incident, the senior poet expressed himself as 'odiously insulted' and as having a poor opinion of Anatole's character. France promptly replied that the elderly gentleman is offended because the critic has not praised his poetry of late—and inquired whether his private character was indicated. His former Master said : 'No ; I am not interested in that. But I am not too old to offer him a duel. Two witnesses of mine will await him at my home.' Such was the wrath in celestial souls ! For a week the Passage Choiseul heard the echoes of civil war. But Anatole pooh-poohed the idea of sending witnesses in such a cause. He must reiterate that Leconte de Lisle is quite a veteran and is therefore 'untouchable.' Furthermore, he has removed the slur on A.F.'s private life—and is one of the 'glories' of our age.

But this whole episode left its mark, and France gave vent to some irritation and resentment in 'La Vie littéraire.' [88] Not only has his attitude toward the new schools been badly misinterpreted ; for several months he has been 'shaken by various insults and condemnations.' He has merely striven to be sympathetic toward every important movement, whether old or new. He still differs from the Symbolists on certain technical points of prosody. . . But after all, why bother about people who speak falsely of me without knowing me ? If I am silent about them, they read malice into silence itself. M. de Gourmont believes that I have a mediocre mind which is afloat on a sea of errors. Then why should he object that he doesn't occupy much place in this mediocre mind ? And why should I concern myself with all that, when everything passes along and Sirius still holds coldly aloof ? *Pax vobiscum !*

Yet there remained in some circles a belief that Anatole, to the dismay of his former comrades, favoured and even 'launched' the

Symbolistic enterprise. One result (cf. Barthou) was that the break with Leconte de Lisle—overdue for a long time, because of the exacting nature of the Master and the irreverence of the 'refractory' disciple—became definite and final. An additional consequence, possibly, was that the unfought duel, taken in connexion with another such incident, may have caused the whisper to circulate: 'Anatole n'est pas brave.' But, according to Le Brun, his rebellion against the Parnassian yoke seems to have brought him into the limelight.[89]

§ 13

The third controversy was likewise a lively affair. If ever two men were made to misunderstand each other, they were Anatole France and Ferdinand Brunetière, the grim, dogmatic, and forceful upholder of what he thought a sound critical tradition. As successor to Taine, Brunetière was then strong for the 'scientific' approach to criticism, a view which he later modified. As the chief opponent of Naturalism, he had found Anatole on his side. But as assistant editor of the *Revue des deux mondes,* he had, to the latter's great displeasure, trimmed *Thaïs* of twenty-six pages before sanctioning its appearance in that periodical. It has even been said that he developed a 'contemptuous hate' for A.F.; and the warfare between the two men has been characterized as a latter-day counterpart to the quarrel of ancients and moderns.[90] It is worth noting that while the Impressionists accepted Sainte-Beuve as their ancestor, Brunetière inveighed against him as the chief source of their regrettable emphasis on the subjective.

Preliminary skirmishes to the break occurred as early as 1889, in connexion with those articles on *Le Disciple* which several authorities consider a definite turning-point in France's creed.[91] It was here that he remonstrated against Brunetière's view that the effort for artistic representation and even the exercise of 'pure thought' might well be limited by moral and social considerations. The dispute waxed warm, but the particular matter of debate here was not Impressionism.

In 1891, the high priest of dogmatism wrote an article for *La Grande Encyclopédie*[92] in which he laid down his principles of literary criticism. This important form thrives on combat and 'ne se pose qu'en s'opposant.' Whatever they may say, an objective criticism does exist; there is an ascertainable 'literary truth'; and there are definite hierarchies. The threefold purpose of serious criticism is then 'to judge, to classify, and to explain literary works.' One is aware of 'ingenious' and sophistical attempts to get away from this obligation, but criticism of its nature is bound to be judicial. Also we must overcome the tendency to intrude our personal reactions (and impressions) into our analyses. This detachment, he repeats, is possible to a greater degree than some people will admit. The function of the critic is to maintain the 'identity of the national conscience' and to promote good ideas among authors themselves as well as among the general public.

If this leaves doubt as to its application, that doubt may be removed by consulting a previous article of the same year on 'La Critique impressioniste.'[93] Preluding that it may be a bold thing to teach other people their business, Brunetière yet dares assert that the role of criticism must rise 'superior or exterior to the conception of it formed by M. Anatole France of *Le Temps,* M. Lemaître of the *Revue bleue* and M. Paul Desjardins of the *Journal des Débats.'* He appreciates to the full the learned friskings of Lemaître, the amiable irony of France, together with the subtle elegance of his thought. But much as he loves them all, he loves Criticism better. France's argument that we can never get out of ourselves, that subjectivity rules everywhere is clearly overdone and is 'fallacious.' A theory of relativity thus misdirected leads to all sorts of confusions and contradictions in the critic's utterances. It may even cause him to dispense with a real study of the book nominally under review: witness the intrusion of Little Pierre's Noah's Ark into Renan's *History!* Are we not human chiefly through our ability to get out of ourselves and consider ideal values? As for the hierarchies, the three critics named practically admit their validity when they give Zola a low grade. Like the rest of us, these Impressionists are occupied with clear-sighted judging and classifying. At their best, they are 'mandarins' who *know* and use their knowledge under all these provoking disguises. This is the greatest concession that Brunetière makes. It seems especially applicable to France with his wide culture and his stock of abiding principles, as already outlined in these pages. But his adversary practically withdraws the compliment when he condescendingly remarks that the Impressionists are at heart poets and romancers who find a temporary lodging in the statelier halls of Criticism; and he concludes by insisting on firm criteria, by warning his colleagues once more against the unimportance of manifesting personal tastes and prejudices.

The effect of all this upon Lemaître was to make him exclaim characteristically: 'Juger, toujours juger, quelle horreur!' In another place, he gives over an article to exhibiting the faults and merits that he discerns in Brunetière's doctrinaire system; and he outlines the virtues that he finds in a more appreciative and elastic approach.[94] Lemaître had already turned a defence of Impressionism into a general eulogy of Anatole.[95] Since tastes and standards vary, since even tradition is a conventional approach, a keen appreciation is more to the point than the *ex cathedra* attitude. After all, we are good judges only of what we like. Now France's mind is 'rich with all the intellectual travail of the century' and alive to most of its curiosities. That is sufficient to make him interesting. He is then justified in defending against his opponent the 'limitless rights of free speculation.'

And what of A.F. himself in the mellay? He had already evinced, as above recorded, his ample admiration for Lemaître, with whom he was then in full agreement. He had spoken of those exquisite *Impressions,* which made him love the drama infinitely more. His respect for Brunetière had cooled off, even before this controversy. Promptly after the appearance of 'La Critique impressioniste,' France took up the cudgels for himself and his friends.[96] The first of his two articles mildly discusses Brunetière's general system of applying 'Evolution' to the literary types, particularly to criticism. Doubtless, the scheme has its attractive aspects. The disadvantage is that criticism can never be properly scientific: its subject-matter (*belles-lettres*) is designed primarily to *move* us. Now what moves us is likely to be a secret between us and the author. Yet there is no harm in discussing such delicate contacts—suggestively and artistically rather than dogmatically—and the discussion may resolve itself into 'philosophy, ethics, history, criticism, in short whatever constitutes the romance of humanity.'

He has (once more) lingered over his prologue and allowed himself the 'pleasure' of praising his adversary. His own defence appears partly in the form of an attack on Brunetière's degrees and hierarchies of literary excellence: it is by no means clear that there are 'incontestable' superiorities, that everybody, for instance, would put Balzac above Flaubert ; Anatole also takes occasion to develop his notions of relativity and personality in the art of writing,—notions that are crystallized in the *Préface* to the third volume of *La Vie littéraire*. This famous preface begins by declaring A.F.'s willingness to join issue with such a distinguished warrior as Brunetière. They disagree as to the merits of Lemaître, but at least they have a common ancestor in Boileau. While my learned friend finds my criticism 'annoying,' I find his excellent—at least in its constructive power. If this power seems at times to leave the earth and to become a sort of theoretical acrobatics, M. Brunetière will and does retort that my subjectivity is still more dangerous. For subjectivity corrupts all things, makes all things illusory or merely sensual. For it is abominable to take pleasure in literature, for reason is our only guide, for reason leads us directly to instruction of the mind, for instruction demands formidable mental edifices, for objective criticism is the only real thing.[97]

Anatole's defence of Impressionistic subjectivity follows lines already made familiar.[98] Always we get only images of things ; we are confined by our senses within individual caverns ; universal consent in matters of taste is a myth—disproved by Brunetière's own examples, e.g., Shakespeare. Critics have agreed neither as to what authors 'exist,' nor as to how they should be graded. Principles are lacking—all is uncertain—let him 'judge'—let me wander.

This has been characterized as a rather evasive reply,[99] containing only truisms not all of which are relevant. The fact is that since the two leaders of divergent critical schools no longer spoke the same language, their mutual rejoinders cannot follow a strictly logical sequence. Anatole also takes a few later flings at his opponent, emphasizing his dislike of contemporary literature, his theological dourness, the folly of setting up rigid genres. Look what *Hernani* did to these ! Let these 'Kinds' go their own way and for heaven's sake let authors go theirs ! And leave us alone to take some pleasure in what we individually feel.

But Brunetière had the last word. In a preface[100] of 1896 he spoke severely of those critics who 'mock at doctrines' because they are unaware of possessing any. Yet our much-vaunted tastes, our 'impressions' are not so exclusively personal after all ; they are products of group-feeling, heredity, and the like. So we can and do 'get out of ourselves,' and all this talk about relativity is, once more, out of place. He hopes that M. Ricardou's book will do its share in the rout of Impressionism and dilettantism. The latter term is significantly coming to be a centre of disturbance.

§ 14

THE debate was carried on by other critics, who take sides according to the nature of their tastes and talents. Some emphasize the 'dogmatism' of Brunetière and his lack of sympathy for modern literature; others point out the insufficiencies, the 'dilettantism' of the Francian method—or lack of method. It is evident that the controversy made a considerable stir in literary circles. The following names are salient among those who then or later expressed themselves definitely about France's standing as a critic.

First, there is Lemaître, whose animadversions on Brunetière have already been recorded. In favour of France,[101] Lemaître was again prompt with his admiration for the wit, the wisdom, and the engaging style displayed in the very first volume of *La Vie littéraire*. Suppose its author does digress, what of it? At least he digresses like a gentleman; and like a philosopher, he 'marvellously elucidates' his subject while talking about something else. He is characterized by his friendly rival as 'an amused and curious Buddhist, a tender sceptic, endowed with a sort of voluptuous detachment.' And Lemaître averred later that if A.F.'s scepticism has grown less tender and more combative, much of the change is due to the severe M. Brunetière, who took Anatole to task and 'forced him to exude all the eighteenth century which he had in him.'[102] These phrases are memorable.

Then there is Georges Renard, who in 1890 amiably expressed both fascination and disapproval.[103] France for him is the successor of Renan, or an anarchical leader of a bombing-squad 'under the flag of dilettantism.' But for all his insistence on subjectivity and illusion, he keeps as a preservative a fine sense of beauty. So he is more of an artist than a critic; his comments on books are superficial though charming.

Then there is Georges Pellissier, who strives to keep the balance between the two schools and to reach a higher synthesis.[104] Since Boileau, critical doctrine has on the whole evolved from dogmatism towards Impressionism. The latter is distinguished by three fundamental trends, all hostile to the classical spirit—namely, 'modernism,' relativity of outlook, and the subordination of reason to imagination and individual sensibility. Perhaps a reconciliation is possible, not between the temperaments but between the underlying principles and tastes of the adversaries. Both camps, as Brunetière himself once contended, are bound to classify and judge, the one less truculently (and less frequently) than the other ; both have a group-consciousness as regards tradition and values ; France and Lemaître possess a breadth of culture which usually guarantees the sureness of their tastes. Thus, one school may take the shortest way there, while the other goes the longest way round.

Still during the nineties, other pundits expressed themselves more briefly regarding A.F.'s place in criticism. When Gaston Deschamps replaced him on *Le Temps* (October, 1893) he spoke politely of how readers would miss the 'exquisite fancy,' the learning, the style, and the sensibility of his predecessor. (But he did not mention, says M. Carias, how this predecessor had made himself and his weekly column almost world-famous.)[105] Around the date of Anatole's retirement, the question of the value of this very personal criticism was much debated. Admitting his subjective penchant, Maurice Spronck pointed out that not only was this the manner that thoroughly suited France himself—since most of his works are really personal essays—but that it suited his cultivated Alexandrian audience as well. Yet Edouard Rod, holding a brief for the impartial type of criticism, objected that a portrait-painter endeavours usually to portray another person, not to achieve a *Selbstbildniss ;* this intrusion of the ego, this *fantaisie,* was the only thing that kept France from being a Universal Doctor in his own right.[106] More censorious journalists raised the question whether Anatole was just to his contemporaries, and one of them accused him of being 'criminally silent' about the books that really merited his appreciation.[107] An Italian writer, Vittorio Pica, suggested that because of A.F.'s ambiguities of expression, it is often hard to tell whether he praises or blames. . . If these reproaches are occasionally warranted, we may recall that Sainte-Beuve often employed similar tactics.

Later on, especially after France's death, such passing remarks while not necessarily favourable, naturally reveal a longer 'inverted' perspective. Anatole the critic is now more definitely placed within his genre and in his tradition.[108] We are informed that his mind offers a happy blend of Racinian and Voltairian elements, and that the *Vie littéraire* presents first of all 'the dazzling *conversations* of a great intellect.' Or we hear that it was a fine thing to have one clear mind functioning in an era when Zola plus the politicians were muddling everything. Or it seems to Charles Maurras, consistent private admirer and public enemy of A.F., that the latter and Barrès were equally efficacious in throttling Naturalism and in restoring to the intelligence its primary rights. Or André Beaunier, while holding that France's primary endeavour was still to foster *le génie latin,* asserts also that he made no 'Moloch' out of his critical throne and stressed the enjoyment of literature as part of his general Epicureanism. Or Michaut sums up and reinforces the arguments that these volumes contain too much about Anatole and too little about the authors whom he is nominally reviewing. Or it is the thesis of M. Seillière (always on the adverse side) that France's controversial articles usually advocate 'immoralism.' Or Jacques Roujon emphasizes his penetrating 'diagnosis' and his power of detachment. Or Vandérem, whom we have heard on the success of the *Vie littéraire,* attributes to its author the gifts that make the ideal critic: 'prodigious culture, approved skill, refined taste and delicious style.' Yet even the ideal critic may grow weary; perhaps that is why A.F. in his answers to Brunetiére was either evasive or truistic; and on the whole Vandérem thinks that Brunetière was better answered by the rather more substantial productions of Jules Lemaître.[109] Others agree with this view or at least hold that France as a critic is not to be measured with his contemporary rivals.

In fact, one present-day authority deals particularly with this question. M. Belis[110] holds that if France offers less substance than Lemaître, he attains a more consistent and more thoroughly sceptical attitude. Both insist on the variability of all things, on the intuitive approach, on Impressionism as a 'critique voluptueuse.' Both are justified in their opposition to the encroachments of science, in their championship of humanism and human liberty. Both have left behind productions consisting of assorted mosaics, edifices which seem frail and fantastic when contrasted with the more shapely and solid *ensembles* of the dogmatists. Preferring the latter type, M. Belis yet recognizes that the master-Impressionists are capable of sensible views under their surface flippancy. What they lack in continuity they gain in charm.

Mlle. Antoniu concludes her work by savouring the artistic aroma of the *Vie littéraire*. In criticism, too, she contends, sentiment and fancy are needed. *A priori,* Impressionism may seem a 'weak form,' but when the personality of a France is poured into it, the mould fills out and becomes firmer. If he maintained a sound traditional standard in belles-lettres, yet more importantly he illustrated the same by the sheer power of his creative pen. Consequently, while the critical value of the *Vie littéraire* fades with the years, the authentic, whimsical, spontaneous inwardness [111] of it will long appeal to the élite. If the critic dies because of his Impressionism, the artist thereby lives.[112]

Finally, Victor Giraud harks back to an early declaration of France's critical principles, dating from the time of his association with the *Bibliophile français*.[113] There Anatole had already indicated his preference for the free and discursive type of *causerie* addressed to cultivated people : this should be based on no 'system,' least of all in æsthetics. Giraud demonstrates how this sort of literary costume exactly fitted our 'fantaisiste' and his idiosyncrasies ; and how his individual charm adorns especially his articles on the poets. The discursive method is evidently less appropriate in relation to historical and philosophical works. Giraud agrees with Brunetière that subjectivity is there out of place ; but he emphasizes how much personal revelation is to be found in all these 'chronicles.' And he anticipates Mlle. Antoniu by viewing the *Vie littéraire* as essentially a form of artistic self-expression.

The view of one American critic, probably the most influenced by France, may also be cited. Gamaliel Bradford is frequent in his admiration for the broad sympathies, the 'delicious perfection of sceptical Epicureanism' characteristic of the *Vie littéraire*. Although recognizing the desolation of our author's ultimate outlook, Bradford declares that for years he considered this work as his own literary model. He might despair of attaining to the delicate grace of its manner, that 'quintessence of exquisiteness' ; yet during the formative period, it 'was closer to me than any other book and probably influenced my thought and style . . . more than almost any.' [114]

There were two phrases currently employed by French reviewers and essayists in dealing with the Anatole of this and the following period.[115] One was the term 'mandarin,' implying a certain aristocracy of taste. Another, as already seen, was 'dilettante,' often used in a pejorative sense. In the latter connexion, France's name is frequently linked with that of Renan. For example, one writer remarked that in the *Vie littéraire* we find its author 'metamorphosed, *renanizing* for the first time and in possession of a new manner.' Not equipped with Renan's historical knowledge, Anatole has tried to ape his genial ways—and his dilettantism. Giraud holds rather that France's taste and moderation class him with Sainte-Beuve; and apparently does not object to his amiable and 'universal dilettantism.' This quality in him is denied by very few; but it is defended or at least indulgently allowed by such writers as Truc and Shanks. A more virulent attack is contained in a pamphlet called *Autour du dilettantisme,* by the Abbé Klein. This cleric is convinced that there are too many people around like Renan and France, or like Lemaître and Barrès. The *Jardin d'Epicure,* for instance, is replete with scepticism, dilettantism, and immorality—all pretty much the same thing. In fact, from *Thaïs* down Anatole France (for the Abbé Klein) has been too violently anti-Christian to be a 'good' dilettante; while trying to keep the tone of one, he lacks the light touch, the *bonhomie,* and he runs into rampant egotism. Could anything be more diabolical?

Calmer and more measured in tone is the investigation by M. Michaut.[116] At the time of his death, Renan was the playboy of the world of ideas. By unanimous suffrage, France as the 'prince of dilettantes' succeeded Renan in this domain. Anatole's whole training and his persistent Epicureanism brought him early to this pass. Michaut, at least, defines his terms. For him, dilettantism is 'an attitude of mind which in the presence of things refuses to examine their advantages or disadvantages in order to consider their beauty alone.' The truth of ideas and the morality of men must bow to Beauty. Such a view is anarchical, self-contradictory, and only an attitude after all. But by holding the pose Anatole has made it seem almost upright. In him, 'intelligence, imagination, æsthetic sense and sensibility, all converge towards' . . . dilettantism. And M. Michaut's book constitutes a formidable development of this indictment.

Various others have glanced at the question, but perhaps Souday, in his review of Michaut's book, best provides us with tools for making some discriminations.[117] He declares that if Michaut means by dilettantism merely a frivolous sipping at the cup of knowledge and a capricious way of touching the surface of many subjects, that charge is not true either for Renan or France. Souday himself would rather define the term as 'a comprehension of the various forms of culture and of thought, thus becoming the highest and the most complete expression of the critical spirit.' Why expect scientific systematizing from a *littérateur,* who is emphatically an artist? Furthermore, Michaut confuses metaphysical subjectivism (Anatole's kind) with the excessive egotism that contemplates only its own navel. France, in spite of Brunetière, never abandoned his wide and high intellectual curiosity . . . which is the right kind of 'dilettantism.' M. Lanson leaned in the same direction when he once remarked that A.F.'s supposed failing was 'more apparent than real.' It is true that the great scholar elsewhere qualified this view.[118]

§ 15

AND what conclusions are possible from all this array of evidence? Evidently, the point of view is the important thing. That of the present writer, regarding France's critical activities, is something like this.—If we would understand his approach to any given *causerie,* let us bear in mind both his previous training and his conception of the article-type which he illustrates. His long 'bondage' to *l'Univers illustré* had made of him an accomplished *chroniqueur;* and it was in this role that he was first attached to *Le Temps.* Now it is true that he writes much more about literature in the latter journal than in the former—and more than is evident in the preceding sections of this chapter, since analysis of individual writers has been for the most part neglected. At the same time, in all these discussions, Anatole remains true to the canons of his trade, which is that of the literary journalist. 'My task here is only to brush the surface of things.' No more than Gérôme does he set up to be a professional critic. 'I am chatting, and a chat has its sudden turns and adventures.' In fact, it has been said that his *causeries* are more 'chatty' than those of Sainte-Beuve, who in his last years spaciously filled the chair on *Le Temps* that Anatole was to accept.

Not only does France refuse the judicial and ponderous robe

of the critic: he usually declines to do impersonal and informational book-reviews. His articles are designed less as reviews than as essays. They are subordinated to no extraneous consideration, they constitute a little genre of their own. For if he is not a professional critic, he is more and more conscious (with his widening fame) of being a professional *author*—which is a very different thing. It is true that there are a good many cases (touched upon above) where A.F.'s knowledge of a particular subject is more basic and better documented than is frequently supposed. But always with him it is less a question of the factual knowledge than of how that knowledge is directed; in other words, he is primarily concerned with the artistic treatment. He positively refuses to stuff his article with what another person (e.g., Gaston Paris) has said about the matter in hand. Is he not an author himself? Does not an author possess authority? Should not my vision of the Middle Ages serve better for literary purposes than an attempt to assemble the dry bones laid out by Gaston Paris? Thus, I fancy, would run his argument. It may be noted in passing that something of the same process appears to underlie the practice of contemporary reviewers in our weekly journals. Those who have or assume authority in a given field go directly into that field, whether it be Byzantine painting or duck-hunting, with only a passing bow to the writer whose work is nominally under contemplation. In fact, the conscientious review-article, which deals extensively with what the particular book contains, is a fairly recent and 'scientific' product. Older by far is the tradition of the essay, whether in England or in France. Macaulay and Lytton Strachey exemplified the type. In the writings of either one unscholarly and uncritical errors occur—and yet the writings of either one endure. Both adopt the leisurely general introduction, both indulge in the digressions which are also dear to the heart of Anatole. Of course, his own tradition proceeds rather from Sainte-Beuve, who assumes authority without the mantle and digresses when he feels like it. Similarly, we have observed that whenever Anatole goes wandering in the woods, he is likely to make a night of it.

With the light touch, with apparent nonchalance, France grazes the deepest problems. He will not let corrosive analysis penetrate such problems in these articles—for he must 'ménager' as well as awaken his bourgeois readers.[119] Yet it is unwise to think that at this stage he is fundamentally sceptical. There are plenty of affirmations, e.g., regarding the relationship of art and ethics, the more sympathetic virtues, the hatred of ugliness, the horror of suffering, the value of the higher Hedonism, the convictions of the Conservative, the essential freedom of the critical spirit. It is unfair to say that, for all his impatience with systems, he has no literary principles or criteria. A man may possess standards without waving them. When it comes to their application, he does not yield even to Brunetière in insisting upon the fundamental and abiding features of the French standards. Perhaps it is not so strange that Pellissier proposed, on that basis, a 'reconciliation' between the two critics. They agreed not only as to Molière and Zola, but also in their belittling of various contemporary phenomena. No less than Ferdinand, Anatole maintains the value of tradition as a winnowing force, reiterates the permanent qualities in literature, emphasizes the choices of a discriminating taste. Like Sainte-Beuve again, he holds that in the last analysis it is taste that, almost instinctively, receives or rejects. His own taste was as refined, if not quite so catholic, as that of his master. In this (relative) catholicity and tolerance, he is glad that old forms and barriers have been broken down, that the gentle reader may now roam freely in the wide, wide world, without undue restraint. This he surely does — and gathers roses where he may.

Nevertheless, it is quite possible to hold that France does not tell us enough about the books under discussion. On the other hand, he tells us, as he professes, a great deal about himself. As in the case of Montaigne, this microcosm reflects a considerable part of the universe. Perhaps we should be content with the man — and his mind. These volumes are, as Barthou said, 'peopled with the shadows and phantoms of his memories.'[120] For our own part, we are glad to hear familiar strains, with some new flourishes. Major and minor chords are struck again; old *motifs* vibrate through the swimming air. The fascinations of history are again unfolded, the well-known figures — Cleopatra or Joan of Arc or Elvire — arise with their enchantments unstaled by usage. Poetry and the classics, the Old Régime, the city of Paris, its stones and its *bouquins,* with enough of contemporary issues to give salt and savour — these and their like constitute the fabric of *La Vie littéraire,* which remains exactly that : it is literature made alive, whether or not it is formal criticism. Antoniu and the other defendants are right. The *causerie* becomes an art-form, when it is thus strained through a manifold yet coherent personality. The dilettante justifies his existence: as the word originally indicated, he apprehends and communicates delight.—

> This is that Lady Beauty, in whose praise
> Thy voice and hand shake still,—long known to thee
> By flying hair and fluttering hem. . .

The pleased reader is grateful for all that he receives and becomes aware of a further fact—that by the time the many-sided revelation draws to its close, the development of Anatole is nearly completed.

CHAPTER XV

Life : 1886–1896

§ 1

OTHER than bookish influences had contributed to this slow development. We may now take up the thread of France's active life where we left it, in Chapter XI. The decade on which we are about to enter contains the most triumphant years of his career. In fact, that career proper, as already hinted, was inaugurated in the late eighties, *bonae sub regno Cynarae*. But before this particular Cynara, to wit Mme. de Caillavet, could openly assume the throne, Anatole had to rid himself of certain ancient customs, including his wife and family; he had to enlarge his being in terms of a new domicile, more travelling, a wider amatory and social experience; his character and his 'front' are subtly altered to fit these changed conditions and harmonize with his increasing fame. Such are the events that we shall now discuss.

A.F.'s connexion with the Senate Library was one of the first links with the past that he severed. After twelve years of intermittent service, he came into direct conflict with Charles-Edmond, his official chief. In August, 1888, this Director, who had grown weary of prodding Anatole, promoted a much younger man over his head. Indignation on the part of A.F.—a letter breathing injured innocence was dispatched to the trustees. Not only, he urges, was this promotion unjust, not only did it 'violate rights' of seniority hitherto held sacred in French administration; but also (and here he uses the tremolo stop): 'You have cut short the career of a father of a family,' who at forty-five and leading an exemplary life cannot lower his dignity by taking orders from a mere youth. Had he not obtained the cross of the Legion of Honour? Had he not, he later inquires, served French literature with some *éclat*? [1]

The crux of the matter was there. When it came to the point of reprimanding the author of *Le Crime de Sylvestre Bonnard,* the trustees were embarrassed. In spite of Anatole's vanishing tactics, they attempted a conciliatory policy. But in October, 1888, Charles-Edmond made a long report concerning France and his 'customary negligence'; and the latter, summoned and admonished, promised to reform and did not reform; he was, indeed, little fitted to be a placeman or a regular worker; he preferred the near-by Luxembourg to dancing attendance on the 'conscript fathers' of the Senate; month by month his attendance and his assiduity grew less noticeable. In 1890, he finally resigned, under pressure, or euphemistically he 'left an administration which has poorly recognized my services.' He had held the position fourteen years. Was it by way of revenge, suggests M. Barthou, that he wrote *Thaïs* on the official paper of the Senate Library? But this first draft was so written two years before his resignation, and I suspect that Anatole simply wanted to save stationery.

He retained most of his friends on the Library staff, notably Charles Grandjean and Louis Ratisbonne.[2] But shortly afterwards, as we have seen, his personal quarrel with Leconte de Lisle came to a head. The critical controversy with Brunetière also dates from 1891. Decidedly, our hero is becoming more combative during this period. The rupture with his old Master was never mended, and France's later allusions to the elder poet are extremely hostile and at times not warranted by the facts.[3] But a greater breach than any other was the increasing disparity of purpose between Anatole and his wife.

§ 2

'It is our roof-tree,' said Anatole Himself, 'that encloses our destiny.' Under her own roof-tree, Valérie Thibault was domineering and deadly practical. She scolded her timid husband. She had no great appreciation of his talent. She asserted her conjugal rights in the matter of house-furnishings—a question of taste that led to a violent quarrel. Also, like Tennyson's conception of Freedom, her figure 'slowly broadened down' with the weight of the years. And 'tis said the poor thing had lost almost all her teeth! This hardly excused the exhibition of her tempers when, according to one report, she would declare to all and sundry that her husband had no talent and would never earn a livelihood. The same witness represents her as unappeased when France fell heir to 100,000 francs on the death of his father. Her own father had given her more than that—and she alleged further that Anatole had probably secreted part of the inheritance in order to buy *bibelots*.[4] She had a habit of being unpleasant about money.

On the other hand, what with his elderly ways and his inability to look out for himself, A.F. must have been an irritating housemate for the 'petite bourgeoise.' Whether at home or in company, they were inharmonious. It came to be what onlookers called a 'detestable' ménage ; Anatole himself called it simply 'hell.'[5]

Mme. de Caillavet, sharply eying 'les France,' came to her own conclusions. For some time she had thought that the awkward, retiring Anatole would not serve as her 'lion.' Then she changed her mind. With proper shaping, *he* might do, but the narrow-minded Valérie, never ! The rift between husband and wife might serve her ends. Could it not be allowed to widen ? Could not one wait and see ?

Even in 1888, it was noticed that Anatole sometimes neglected his roof-tree. Soon he set up a bachelor establishment in the Rue de Sontay (near the Place Victor Hugo), where he entertained Mme. de Caillavet. He became the great man of her salon ; he became her lover ; their open *liaison* wounded the susceptibilities of Valérie, who now rarely went out with her husband. As for what may have happened on the Rue Chalgrin—who today knows the whole story ? There are a few hints from bystanders and there are the suggestions, factual or fictional, emanating from Anatole's own pen. For one thing, extracts from *l'Univers illustré* would show that as early as 1884 thoughts about incompatibility and possible readjustments were running through his mind.[6] Apropos of the Naquet divorce law, then before the Senate, we find France meditating about the crisis in most marriages—a crisis in which 'one's sentiments must be transmuted, if they are to endure.'

Furthermore, the account, in the earlier volumes of the *Histoire contemporaine,* regarding the relationship between the Bergeret couple, has doubtless some personal foundation. A few years later, when out walking with his secretary, Anatole is said to have paused before the house on the Rue Chalgrin and to have remarked, 'That is an historical mansion : it was the scene of the *Mannequin d'Osier.*'[7] What are the similarities between the story and the actual domestic situation ? There really was a dressmaker's model, a 'wicker-work woman,' which in each case drove the master of the house to the point of exasperation. That state of mind was in each case prolonged by the fact that the spouse, whether a Guérin or a 'Pouilly,' often boasted of her superior family.

Whether as Thibault or as 'Bergeret,' the husband, after the rupture, took his revenge by a policy of continued silence. There are other minor resemblances, but amid them we discern one difference: no evidence exists pointing to an infidelity on the part of Valérie France. She did not have much faith in her husband, says M. Carias, but she had 'no other faults.' Yet she scolded him, nagged him, and accused him of general worthlessness. And there are those who believe that Valérie was unfaithful, partly because of other close analogies with the situation in *Le Mannequin,* because of France's undying rancour, or because his wife's 'language' is said to have contained the most opprobrious terms.[8] Where the testimony is uncertain, it is better to reserve judgment.

Here are the stages of the break, as nearly as they can now be discovered.[9] On one occasion, Anatole is said to have torn the wicker-work woman to pieces, in a transport of rage. On another day, probably in 1891, France and his wife had a difference of opinion about the hanging of some Genoese velvet, unfortunately presented by Mme. de Caillavet. Valérie locked her husband and the upholsterer in the study, not without vituperative reproaches. During this temporary imprisonment, Anatole peacefully continued his writing. But another time, about a year later, the language became such that he walked out of the house in his dressing-gown, carrying a half-written article in his hands. This was in June, 1892. He soon repaired to the Rue de Sontay; and he never returned home. He wrote his wife an extremely bitter letter, breaking off relations. For some months he was in an unsettled and depressed frame of mind. With the aid of a friendly intermediary a preliminary 'séparation de fait' was contrived;[10] but soon steps were taken to make this final. The whole affair came before the Tribunal of the Seine in July-August, 1893, with momentous results.

The present writer believes that what now follows is entirely fresh information; it is also authentic. That so little has hitherto been known on this subject is partly due to the fact that, in France, newspaper publicity about marital disagreements is frowned upon. There was no mention of the lawsuit in the *Gazette des Tribunaux.*

Much uncertainty has been evinced concerning which party sought the decree for absolute divorce.[11] On this point doubt is no longer possible. It was sought by Madame Thibault ('*dite* Anatole France'), and it was pronounced in her favour, on August 3, 1893. The grounds were her husband's abandonment of the domicile and his refusal to return there when duly summonsed. This in French law constitutes an 'injure grave.' Whatever may have actually occurred, no other grounds of complaint were officially recognized. Neither incompatibility nor adultery was alleged. Whereas (the decree reads) the defendant began straying from home in 1888, after which date his absences multiplied; whereas he refused explanations to his wife and communicated with her only through the medium of a servant (this corresponds to the conjugal silence of the Bergerets); whereas he definitely abandoned the hearth-stone in June, 1892, and sent an offensive letter, breaking off all communications; whereas being summonsed, he refused to return home and added further 'wounding appreciations' of his wife: now therefore the Tribunal gives judgment against 'Thibault, *dit* Anatole France, and against Gieules, his lawyer.'

Thus the marriage was dissolved, and along with it the régime of joint property holdings under which system the Thibaults had been married. A notary at Neuilly was appointed to liquidate the separate interests involved. Valérie naturally kept the house on the Rue Chalgrin. To the ex-wife was also awarded the child, Suzanne, together with a small allowance (350 francs monthly) for maintenance; Anatole had to pay certain costs. It is reported that he was not always prompt in the payments.

We shall consider a little later the more general and profound effect of the ruptured marriage upon France's character. Just here we may note that during the years 1892-93, as witnessed both by his letters and certain articles in *Le Temps,* his state of mind was full of weariness and disgust. 'His dearest habits were broken,' says M. Carias, and though he might be homeless, he was never made for an independent existence. In his later years, he became chary of allusions to his first marriage; it may be that he had said all he wanted to say in *Le Mannequin d'Osier;* yet he once admitted to a friend: 'I behaved very badly.' His old circle of intimates could not approve his conduct.[12]

§ 3

After the divorce, Valérie resumed her maiden name, of which she was so proud. Presently she married M. René Dussaud, curator of antiquities at the Louvre, who also helped to care for Suzanne. Apparently Valérie never forgave Anatole; she is said to have uttered threats against his estate at the time of his second marriage.[13] Mme. Dussaud died in 1921, three years before the death of Anatole.

For the most part, Suzanne lived with her mother, although there was an arrangement by which her father saw her occasionally, some say weekly.[14] Their meetings were either at the Villa Saïd or at 'Gyp's' home, in Neuilly. The slim child whom various callers had glimpsed on the Rue Chalgrin was growing into an equally slim young woman. Later visitors to Anatole at the Villa Saïd observed that she had 'her father's big eyes, his brow, his long face'—and something of his intelligence.[15] Something of his ill-luck in matrimony seems also to have been her portion. On December 10, 1901, she married a Captain Mollin, who was attached to the staff of General André, minister of war. Of this son-in-law Anatole approved to the extent of issuing invitations to the civil wedding, which, however, he did not attend.[16] (It is characteristic that he preserved a goodly number of invitations and used their blank spaces later for note-taking.) Captain Mollin was a convert to the cause of Dreyfus and that naturally pleased France. In 1904 Suzanne was still to be seen at her father's house, and for a time all parties appeared reasonably happy.[17]

But there ensued a rift in this marriage, when Suzanne became more interested in Michel Psichari, also a soldier and a member of a notable family. Her divorce from Mollin followed, and in April, 1908, she was married to Psichari. Certain circumstances in this relationship displeased Anatole; his final rupture with his child dates from about this period. He went no more to Neuilly, whether to visit 'Gyp' or his daughter. Under the eye of the Dussauds, Suzanne lived on with her new husband and their son, until Psichari was killed at the front. Shortly afterwards Suzanne herself fell a victim to the epidemic of influenza in 1918.[18]

France travelled up from Tours in time to attend his daughter's funeral. He suffered acutely for a while, regretting his past severity and recalling the faraway days when he enjoyed Suzanne's childhood and wrote the 'Vacances sentimentales' in her praise. He was presently persuaded, by his second wife, to acknowledge and adopt as his grandson young Lucien Psichari—who was also the great-grandson of Ernest Renan.[19]

For not only were the Psicharis a notable family : through their alliances they formed a shadowy bond between the dead Renan and the living France, who were already such close kindred in their minds.

Jean Psichari or Psicharis, born of Greek parents in Odessa, had settled in Paris and through his scholarly attainments had become professor of Byzantine philology and modern Greek at the Ecole des Hautes Etudes. He married Noémi, the favourite daughter of Renan, and seemed destined to a brilliant career. But throughout these imbroglios the distinction of the various parties concerned does not seem to have closed the doors on the vagaries of passion. Jean Psichari became involved with a young girl and, in order to marry her, divorced Noémi, who in turn resumed her father's name. The illustrious Renan seems to have provoked a certain jealousy or pique in the bosom of Psichari, who once wrote : 'My two sons are peculiar in that they have no father ; they have only a grandfather—on the maternal side.'[20]

Whether as writer or polemist, Jean Psichari became noted as the Du Bellay of Neo-Hellenism. That is, he stood for the literary capabilities of the modern Greek language and 'illustrated' them in his own work. But one infers it was rather his classical heritage that interested Anatole France, who gives him favourable mention in *l'Univers illustré*.[21] In return, Psichari had much to say about Anatole, although he feels that he must say it cautiously because of the family bond. Not only have they a grandson in common, but Suzanne is represented as having been a 'devoted daughter' to both of them. His personal debt to Anatole is large. It seems that A.F. was one of Psichari's oldest friends and counsellors and aided him considerably in getting his poetry written and published. Since these things are so, it is rather ungrateful of the beneficiary to question the merits of his master's style and to doubt whether his works will last.[22]

This Greco-Parisian, who died in 1929, had three children : a daughter, Henriette ; and two sons, Ernest and Michel. The elder son far outshone the other members of the family, and this is visible in the volume of recollections which his sister has consecrated to his memory. A hero of the Great War, in which he fell, his name is attached to such semi-mystical works as *l'Appel des armes* and especially *La Veillée du Centurion.* But he had little to do with the France family. That was rather the concern of Michel, the younger brother, who gratified his father by his addiction to classical philology and even won the passing interest of Anatole by a dry scholarly monograph on Horace, for which the latter deigned to write a preface in 1904.[23] France also proffered a graceful compliment to the Psichari family as a whole. But it is probable that Suzanne, to the displeasure of her father, found other than scholarly qualities in Michel. Their son, M. Lucien Psichari, became in time the residuary legatee of his grandfather and is today the owner of the France estate, whether in Paris or near Tours.

Most of these events go beyond the limits of our present study. Let us return to the nineties and to Mme. de Caillavet.

§ 4

EARLY in the New Year of 1910, a white-haired woman who found some difficulty in breathing gave to her daughter-in-law a sealed package with the adjuration that the contents should be published after her death. That event occurred a few days later. When the package was opened, it was found to contain a number of letters that Anatole France had written to Mme. de Caillavet, during the long course of their *liaison.* Accordingly Mme. Pouquet published, in the work we have cited so often, many of these letters—particularly those that best displayed the 'incomparable' devotion of Mme. de C. to Anatole.

But Mme. Pouquet, who was then Mme. Gaston de Caillavet, did not print everything in the package. Her husband, the playwright, thought it best to destroy the greater part of the correspondence. This was done immediately after his mother's death and in partial disregard of her wishes.[24] One can only surmise his reasons, which were probably prudential. However, there was a precious remnant of seventy-two autograph letters (exclusive of those addressed to other correspondents), of which considerable portions have since been printed.[25] It is unfortunate that the originals of Anatole's letters and of a number of his MSS. should have been scattered among various collectors (at the Caillavet-

Pouquet sale in 1932), instead of being acquired by the Republic and housed among its treasures. It is the more unfortunate, since Mme. de C. had already left in her will to the Bibliothèque Nationale a quantity of autograph copies of France's works[26]—fair copies which A.F. had made himself at her behest—together with a collection of congratulatory missives received at the time of his election to the Academy.

From the truncated 'confession of France's soul-states' which this correspondence offers and from other sources we may try to reconstruct the relationship of this unusual couple during these critical years. Slow as their friendship was in its formation, things began to move rapidly round 1890. The definitive break with Mme. Aubernon had been followed by the virtual adoption of Anatole as the chief luminary of the mansion on the Avenue Hoche. Says one writer:

> Madame de Caillavet became, from 1891 on, what his mother had been till he was thirty-six and what his wife had been thereafter: the organizer of his life and the champion of his literary fortune. She was a coach and a publicity manager rolled into one.[27]

Neither his wife nor his mother had been quite all that. Furthermore, whether on the Avenue Hoche or the Rue de Sontay, it is pretty clear that the pair had already become intimate. Not only in Paris did she care for him, but also at her much-embowered 'Château Caillavet,' among the vineyards of the Gironde, where he spent a month almost every summer. In 1892, he was for a brief time a guest on the yacht of Monsieur de Caillavet; in the Spring of 1893, before the divorce was obtained, Anatole went off with his *amie* and others on a visit to Florence which will concern us later.

In these two years particularly he needed all the comfort and distraction that he could get. Separated from his family, living alone as a bachelor, and perhaps harassed by his conscience, he was in a low state of mind. This has already been exemplified in connexion with certain of his works and will shortly appear in others. His correspondence, too, shows that he needed help. And to whom should he turn save to the woman who was destined in good part first to break and then to remake him? When she is away, he is infinitely weary and melancholy. 'Je suis très en peine de vous.' He works like one in a torpor, and the work is not satisfactory. His little apartment is like a rudderless boat on a sea of sadness. Later on, it is evident that both his health and his morale are suffering. Similar phrases, indeed, are found throughout his letters. When visiting 'Gyp' in 1892 he complained consistently that though he worked eight hours a day he could really accomplish little in the absence of 'Madame Arman.' He felt both bored and stupid ; he was aware of a great emptiness round him. His correspondence is full of tributes and compliments to her excellent qualities and helpfulness. Some of this may be gallant lip-service, but it is evident that Mme. Arman answers a constant need. When she is absent from Paris, A.F. takes pains to relay to her the gossip about their mutual friends.

By 1893 France is almost entirely under the influence and the discipline of Mme. de C. Daily he repairs to her house for lunch and for labour after lunch. During the following year she assisted him with his installation at the Villa Saïd ; but neither the attractions of a new home nor a widening circle of friends caused him to abate his habitual frequentation of the Avenue Hoche.

If onlookers and certain later critics agree as to Mme. de C.'s 'admirable rôle auprès de lui,' it is yet suggested, what the decorous and discreet remnant of the correspondence would seem to bear out,—namely, that theirs was a 'liaison plus littéraire que scandaleuse.'[28] Yet there are many things of which we know little or nothing. We are unacquainted with the suppressed letters, with the extent to which *Le Lys rouge* may reflect the height of their passion, with any full record of their relations previous to the era of 'all passion spent.' One thing only seems certain : her love was more deep and abiding than his.

Indeed, Anatole, according to his own confession, 'never knew a great love,' although much prone to lesser ones ; his feeling for Mme. Arman had in it less of greatness than of selfishness, peevishness, and helplessness. These traits increased with age. If France was much broken up at the time of her death (as the *Carnets intimes* bear witness) that might be due in part to his realization that he had treated her badly during the last years of her life.

It has been hinted that Mme. de C. was not without experience in these affairs ; among others the name of a certain Gassou, a sporting type from Bordeaux, who was portrayed under an alias in *Le Lys rouge,* has been mentioned.[29] However this may be, there is no doubt regarding the intense and possessive devotion which she accorded to France. It was jealous—because she was suspicious of his minor *amourettes* and she could not bear him really to admire another woman, whether Marcelle Tinayre or the actress who accompanied him to the Argentine in 1909.[30] It was masterful—because she would hardly allow him out of her sight and often ordered him around. Yet it was unselfish, because she made herself subservient to his fame, his work, his monologues, even to the point of taking notes of his conversations for his future writings. It was, all in all, the kind of self-consecration that Mme. Récamier bestowed upon Chateaubriand in his later years. In short, it was so abundant and diverse that Anatole, to no one's surprise, became restive under all these ministrations. Mme. Arman was, says M. Carias, 'his professor, his secretary, his translator, his adviser, his judge.' We should add: his mistress, his constant companion, his overseer, his taskmaster. And she held her position as Egeria-in-chief for no less than twenty years! The same authority points out that Anatole ultimately confided to his notebooks a curious sort of balance-sheet, in which his foibles were set over against (and linked with) the excess of her qualities. He writes of 'her character—my weakness'; 'her errors—my faults'; 'her strong will—my deplorable frivolity.'[31]

There are indications that A.F. fared better with the ladies of Mme. Arman's establishment than with the men. The rather blatant master of the house could hardly have appreciated Anatole's presence there, and various verbal skirmishes between husband and lover have been recorded. Gaston de Caillavet took at first a definite stand against his mother's protégé; although she scolded him for his attitude, and although Gaston then tolerated France and even collaborated on a play drawn from *Le Lys rouge,* the two men seem to have become estranged again later. It was not until Mme. de C.'s last days that a better understanding was reached between them. With Gaston's wife (later Mme. Pouquet) and with their young daughter, Simone, Anatole seems to have been consistently on pleasant terms.[32]

§ 5

One of the most interesting features of the partially revealed correspondence is the light that it throws on France's productivity and how Mme. de Caillavet kept him at it. Anatole's polite exaggeration that he 'would have done nothing without her,' has been played up considerably by those who seek to make of her a veritable *collaboratrice* in his labours.[33] This problem will concern us a little later. Just here it is well to admit that by an infusion of her will-power no less than by the constant and detailed interest which she professed in all his writings, Mme. Arman was truly his Minerva. As was also the case with Balzac and his lady-friends, this correspondence shows A.F. giving her an almost weekly report, 'un compte-rendu exact de son travail.' On one typical occasion he adds up what he has done in a fortnight: material for the *Opinions de Jérome Coignard ;* an article on Joan of Arc, already a major preoccupation ; another article and a preface. 'After that,' he says with pardonable pride, 'you may still judge that I am doing little or nothing. For there is a great diversity in human opinions.' The last is a characteristic touch.

This *compte-rendu* is of such great documentary value that we may well follow it for a few years.[34] As early as 1888, France reports on the favourable reception of articles for *Le Temps* and *l'Univers illustré,* with which Mme. de C. had helped him. He is already beginning the composition of *Thaïs* and he confides that the robe of Paphnuce fits him better than that of Gérôme. In 1890, his trip through the Midi is written up, in terms recalling the travel-sketches that he composed for *Le Temps.* In the following year he describes his documentation for the articles on Mithridates and Mme. de la Sablière—but his inspiration drags when he is parted from Egeria, and his readers are sensible of the difference. Presently he elaborates what he is doing for the *Revue de famille* on Joan of Arc, for *Le Temps* on 'Elvire,' for himself on *La Rôtisserie :* it would all be much easier if Mme. Arman were there to counsel him. In 1893, they have a dispute regarding the tale of 'Guido Cavalcanti,' and France dwells upon the difficulties he finds in rounding out the volume on the *Opinions de Jérôme Coignard.* We shall see how Mme. de C. tried to come to his aid in this matter.

Curiously enough, it is in this connexion that we hear the first protests muttered by Anatole under the yoke of his driver. He has been working, in a rather discouraged fashion, from eight to twelve hours daily and therefore insists that his friend is wrong 'in believing that I am not trying to get ahead. . . I am rather to be pitied than blamed.' His correspondent must have kept on urging him (apparently she felt at a loss without his proofs to correct), for a little later we find him setting up a definite defence by tabulating his labours in the passage cited above, ending with the dry remark about the 'diversity of opinions.' This is emphasized as his first revolt against the iron hand, the entering wedge for those 'dissensions which were to darken their relations.' These rifts grew large after our period ; but already there are signs of Anatole's willingness to evade in rather puerile ways those laborious sessions after lunch ; hints of his distaste for spending hours in making those fair copies of his MSS. for Mme. de C.; echoes of his resentment at being questioned and commanded like a child.[35] It must be allowed that Egeria did not always play her trump cards with subtlety.

There are those who declare further that Mme. Arman exercised such a pervasive influence on France's writings, notably on the masterpieces of this period, that she was practically his collaborator ; and she herself is reported (incorrectly, I believe) as asserting that she actually wrote at least a third of his total work.[36] Although there are a few cases in point, such sweeping statements are far from proved and they give a false impression of her role. Those who should know best, e.g. Mme. Pouquet, are careful not to go too far in this direction. If occasionally Mme. Arman provided an article or slipped a few phrases into a story, the part assigned her was usually 'more humble and more vast.' We should realize that she *subordinated* herself to France's talent, for which she had a great respect, and to his thought, which was in no degree hers, and to his worldly fame, which was largely her creation. As Charavay and others had done before, she energetically provided materials which the less energetic Anatole—and only he—could properly use. She 'gleaned' for him, right and left, in the libraries and in social converse, she made translations, particularly of the Italian *novelle,* she jotted down his own table-talk. All of this was done devotedly, for his greater glory. Her partnership was like that attributed to Auguste Maquet, in the Dumas 'factory': the head of the firm was the story-teller ; the sleeping partner 'had the gifts of a librarian.'[37] And she undoubtedly harried him into doing certain things which might otherwise have remained undone. When Hovelaque complained of an unfulfilled promise about a preface, Mme. de C. suggested : 'Come to me next time. It is I who fulfill his promises.'[38]

Yet we have met with some instances and we shall meet with still more where her pen became an active asset. Some of these may here be considered. Although she inspired *Le Lys rouge* in conception and treatment and actually wrote the tale of 'Mademoiselle Roxane' (with the intention of padding the *Coignard* volume), her services were more normally required for minor journalistic articles that had to be furnished on time.[39] We have mentioned the probability that she did a good deal of hack-work for *l'Univers illustré,* especially in the nineties ; the extent of this work is unknown, but it is more than likely that it consisted mainly in copying out France's previous utterances or his quotations from somebody else. Here and there single articles, e.g., on Loti and Lemaître, have been attributed to her. We have seen that she wrote the preface to Constant's *Adolphe,* which ultimately appeared in *Le Génie latin.* We recall less reasonable attributions, such as Anatole's preface to Proust's volume. Much has been made of this and of the part she is supposed to have had in the Introduction to Mme. de La Fayette's *Henriette d'Angleterre :* on examination the latter 'collaboration' is reduced to one short page, *quoted* by A.F. himself as expressing the view of a feminine friend. I conclude that with regard to the share that Mme. de C. had in the penning of France's masterpieces, much ado has been made concerning a minor participation.

On the other hand, although we hear little about it, Mme. Arman was a writer on her own account.[40] She produced two novels, one of which, *Le Roman d'une Demoiselle de modes,* was published under a pseudonym in 1908. She avoided publicity, on account of France's aversion to her appearance as a woman-novelist. But she confided the manuscript to several of her intimates and finally arranged for its publication. The story was discussed on the Avenue Hoche and the 'secret' was preserved by a plausible fib. Mme. de C. claimed to have made the acquaintance of the young provincial author. She even arranged a luncheon in honour of this 'Philippe Lautrey' and passed round a telegram alleging his regret at not being present !

This *Tale of a Shop-Girl* (who is a rather superior person) contains but few traces of Anatole's influence and reflects little of the social life of the authoress. It is a quite independent account, plainly and realistically handled, of the heroine's career and amours. The only respect in which it could be considered Anatolian is that sensual love, usually followed by disillusionment, is made the main element in conduct. But Mme. Arman was quite capable of thinking that out for herself. France disliked the story; he deemed that his Egeria might be better occupied, whether with writing correspondence or with himself. The fact that he demanded the sacrifice of her own talent is another thing that may have clouded their later relations.

§ 6

But all this was in the far future when in the brilliant nineties the house on the Avenue Hoche became one of the busiest centres of Parisian life and talk. It has been said that the history of that life, literary and political, for two decades, could not be written without frequent reference to Mme. de Caillavet's influence.[41] If not absolutely the 'last salon,' hers was certainly one of the most prominent during the pre-war period. Many of the visitors came for pleasure, others for profit, of one kind or another. The hostess, shrewd and poised, presided with the technique that Mme. Aubernon had taught her. We picture her as imperiously arraying her guests, with her auburn hair, henna-dyed and soon to be flecked with gray, flashing under the chandeliers. She dominated both the large receptions on Sunday afternoons and her more intimate dinners on Wednesdays. Numerous allusions to these affairs occur in the reminiscential volumes and elsewhere.[42] In what follows we shall not usually try to discriminate between the years that preceded and those that followed the Dreyfus upheaval, since Anatole gave, so to speak, a continuous performance.

The mistress of the house exerted for long an almost magnetic power. People recognized that beneath her overbearing manner, beneath the energetic tenacity which was perhaps part of her Jewish heritage, lay a rich nature, generous and loyal to her friends, with acute sensibilities under a worldly crust. She is described by 'J.-H. Rosny' as 'une petite femme rousse,' rather chubby and quite brisk, with prominent blue eyes. She endeavoured to impart her briskness to France, to whom probably she had been lecturing upstairs beforehand. She must have recognized that they were indispensable to each other, that she had no salon without him and he no pedestal without her. The pedestal was her hearthplace, decorated, as was the whole drawing-room, in the best eighteenth-century manner. The atmosphere was that of a pleasant conservatory, a forcing-house where admiration was in the ambience and the blossoms of *l'esprit* might fitly flourish. The stage was set for the entrance of the affable Master.[43]

Correctly garbed, then, appreciative of the luxury with which he was surrounded, smiling and suave, A.F. was on these occasions as witty and as winning as the best of his books, which were freely strewn about to gladden the eye of the beholder. In every sense, the way was cleared for him by the mistress of the mansion. He was encouraged to take his stand in a prominent position before the mantelpiece. It was like 'a railway-station,' with Anatole as *chef de gare*.[44] People were brought up, presented, and remained eddying around. If the Master desired to loiter in a window-seat with a pretty woman, he was quickly haled back to his semi-official duty. Having arranged the setting, Mme. Arman also arranged for the delivery of the 'conversations d'apparat,' France's prepared monologues. She would unfailingly give him his cue directly or indirectly, usually by calling for this anecdote or that recitation from Racine. And Anatole, having grasped his subject, was loath to drop it ; just as with Mme. Aubernon, the audience was required to stay with that topic until a shift was ordered. All this, of course, was managed with deftness and charm, with true social artistry. Occasionally France, especially in the smaller gatherings on Wednesdays, would read from his own best prose. Occasionally he would step down, in order to allow a play of his to be acted, or to listen to a Russian singer. But more usually a courteous silence surrounded his voice, talking on of love and illusion, 'of politics and art, of literature and history, crowning everything with anecdotes and sallies and paradoxes.' It is fortunate that so many of his utterances have been recorded, even though in free form, and that they still survive for our delectation.

But the entertainer-in-chief was not always affable. Sometimes he would appear, as Mme. Scheikévitch represents him, when his expressive eyes would emit a 'malicious, mocking light, amidst a yellow, chaotic and sullen face.' The famous monologues (in which he assumed that the hearers knew all about the subject) were not always so successful. They would degenerate into the hesitating kind of talk that was more habitual with him when among intimates. Then he seemed shy, bored, not at his best.

He indulged in bewildering digressions and stopped frequently to correct himself. 'When I speak,' he said of such occasions, 'you can hear me crossing words out.' But most people would rather hear him putting them in.

Who were, then, the privileged frequenters of these *conversazioni?* They ranged from the bouncing master of the house to the latest thing in æsthetes, from the elderly Renan to Marcel Proust. Sometimes even Leconte de Lisle would come, severely silent, and René Dussaud, the second husband of Valérie Guérin, who must be separated by at least the width of the living-room from her first.[45] Clearly there was enough variety among the guests to keep a hostess on her mettle. Let us glance at them, more or less in the order of seniority.

Mme. Arman's own family and connexions, together with her old friends, some of them transferred from the rival court of Mme. Aubernon, were naturally present. Not all of these were favourable to France, whom they might well consider an intruder. For example, M. Arman de Caillavet, he who wrote for the yachting columns of the *Figaro,* under the sobriquet of 'Djeb Topsail.' According to one witness, this 'hilarious Penguin' would introduce himself at the receptions by exclaiming : 'Permettez ! . . . *Je ne suis pas Anatole France.'* Or he would style himself, somewhat unconvincingly, 'the master of the house.' He wore curious white cravats and was conspicuous for a booming voice which he hurled in Anatole's direction ; for they were opposing types who became reconciled only when they were planning dinner menus together.[46] Mme. de C. had trouble in keeping the peace, and on occasion she would call her husband down quite sharply for annoying or twitting her lover. She was less successful in bringing her son to heel : although Anatole admired young Gaston de Caillavet, the son of the house did not really care for France. There were others in her circle who must have resented her exclusive devotion to the coming writer. Gassou, the Bordelais sportsman already mentioned, must have had good reason to think that he was superseded in her affections. And if another old admirer took the matter more philosophically, that was doubtless because he was a philosopher, and a 'gallant' one, by trade. I refer to Victor Brochard, then attached to the Ecole Normale, and author of *Les Sceptiques grecs,* a work to which France was considerably indebted ; he was likewise indebted to Brochard personally for the graceful way in which the former favourite yielded his position.

Among the 'oldsters,' the shade of Renan survived Renan himself, and through him one seemed to reach back to emanations from the age of Voltaire and Mme. du Deffand. The attendance of Lemaître was becoming less frequent, since he had cast in his lot with Mme. de Loynes ; but he did not break with France and Mme. Arman until the time of the Dreyfus Affair. Dumas *fils,* as a connexion by marriage, was almost a member of the household ; the dramatist's relations with Anatole seem to have been cordial enough. We do not know to what extent Mme. de C. entertained Jewish society, against which France had no prejudice ; he may have met here some of the types depicted in the *Histoire contemporaine*.[47] Calmann-Lévy appeared for a time, and that other publisher, Adrien Hébrard, who egged A.F. on to do his articles for *Le Temps*. Other people whom Anatole came to know were the dramatists, Pierre Véber and Robert de Flers (presently a collaborator with Gaston de Caillavet); the journalist, Arsène Houssaye ; Réjane and Sardou ; the exotic Pierre Mille ; and ultimately certain distinguished foreigners, like D'Annunzio or George Brandes, who usually called on Mme. Arman when in Paris. It seems to be quite true that without her aid France could scarcely have formed so many contacts with makers of opinion.[48]

There was also a sort of intermediate group, politicians or men of the world, who sooner or later came into his ken. Aristide Briand 'slipped silently' into the drawing-room ; or Raymond Poincaré would occasionally appear : or such embattled figures as Jaurès and even Clemenceau. One would find an old worldling like Ludovic Halévy, gossiping gently of former grandeurs ; or a polished linguist like Michel Bréal ; or the historian, Ferrero, holding forth on Roman antiquity.[49]

But it was of course the writers among whom France felt most at home and with whom he increased his fame by the personal touch. Some of these, like Barrès and Maurras, he brought with him ; Sully Prudhomme, too, had already shown himself a faithful comrade. Among Anatole's newer friends, Pierre Loti and Marcel Proust were pronounced in their allegiance to the lady of the house. Once when Loti made one of his 'hieratic' appearances in the salon, he thanked France warmly for an article written in his behalf, only to learn that it was probably Mme. Arman who had written it.[50] This does not seem to have affected the excellent relations among the trio.

It has been said that Mme. de C. had almost a school in the group of promising and ultra-æsthetic youngsters—so many supple and diverse talents—by whom she was surrounded.[51] Prominent in the lot were the Comte Robert de Montesquiou, a bard of fanfares and arabesques, who became the model for the Peacock in Rostand's *Chantecler*. No less than forty-five letters, from Montesquiou to France, survive. They are written in the prolix and tortuous style, and in the ornate chirography habitual with this æsthete. There came also the Comtesse de Noailles, beautiful in her person as in her poetry ; Charles Maurras and a talented but unfortunate writer named Coulangheon ; as inspirers to these, the lovely women called the 'three Magdalens'; and always effervescent, Marcel Proust in his juvenile phase. Of them all, Proust seems to have been the most faithful in his double cult—he actually inscribed one of his books to Mme. Arman in sentences put together from France's *Vie littéraire*. A number of letters from Proust reveal him in all the elaborateness and courtesy of his wit ; and he is already occupied with social observances and ritual. He praises France for appealing in his works alike to the humble and to the wise. Proust thus furnishes the best example of a strong but delicate link between the two generations.

But not all of the younger writers were dazzled by France's prestige. Abel Hermant, author of *Le Cavalier Miserey,* had a bone to pick with Anatole because of his slating of that novel in the *Vie littéraire*. Hermant took his revenge partly in the *Souvenirs du Vicomte de Coupières,* which contains some veiled satire on salon-life, but more especially in *Les Renards* of 1912. In this novel we find a portrait of a certain lady, Mme. Durand de Lectoure, who 'would have preferred Renan' as her chief attraction. Failing that, she fell back on 'Olivier Maudru,' who is characterized as a 'bizarre combination—a bull who had a flair for beauty.' (The more brutal side of the portrait is said to depict Octave Mirbeau, then very friendly with France.) Mme. Durand applied herself to the forming of Maudru :

She got a false Renan, whose intellectual fire-works were intermittent, a juggler with ideas, a first-class stylistic artisan. She disguised his atrocious irony as *esprit*. She made of him a sort of domestic cat who became tigerish only in time of extremity.[52]

Hermant continues to the effect that the salon-leader turned Maudru-France into a Dreyfusard, which is an exaggeration. Other traits of his hero are very much like those of Anatole. He would arrive late at dinners and receptions. He was rudely treated by the husband of Mme. Durand. He became somewhat restless under the domination of that lady and since he was quite fond of actresses he presently espoused one secretly, in order to hurt nobody's feelings. He was also fond of theology and church history, which he liked to talk about at all times. But he was fondest of old books, *bibelots* and beauty in the concrete. . . No informed person would fail to get the implications of this portrait. Later utterances of Hermant make, somewhat grudgingly, amends to A.F. as artist.

§ 7

SOMETHING has already been suggested about the extent to which Mme. de C. actually 'made' or remade France. Perhaps we are now in a position to sum up the findings with regard to this important matter. We have seen that she did not form him as a writer ; but she did furnish him with a wider audience and turn him into a social personage. Let us embroider a little on this theme.

If she did not guide his pen, she certainly guided his footsteps, and for the most part into pleasant paths. Furthermore, she aided considerably in the deepening of old interests, such as his taste for objects of art and the eighteenth century, and in the scanning of new horizons—Italy, travel in general, the political outlook. Since her influence upon him really endured the rest of France's life, we should note the various spheres of its activity.

On the personal side, she encompassed him with the attentions both of a mistress and of a mother. There are strong indications that hers was the more affectionate nature. As she aged and her attractions waned, we know that Anatole's eye often wandered ; instances of her jealousy, whether directed against his *amours d'épiderme* or the more lovely visitors to her own salon are on record.[53] The heyday of their association as lovers was probably at the time of *Le Lys rouge ;* the revelations of this novel will concern us later. Her maternal solicitude was frequently in evidence. She was worried about his health, which at times, because of liver-trouble, was none too good. She would take him for walks, whether in the morning or the afternoon. When he reached the Avenue Hoche, she would give him lunch, make him work afterwards, and sometimes detain him for the afternoon reception ; she would allow him barely time to go out and purchase a bouquet, which, we are told, he would present with the air of one having just arrived at the establishment :

'Madame, since I happened to be passing near your house, I could not refrain from stepping in to offer you these flowers together with my respectful homage.'

Apparently Mme. de C. listened benignly to this phrase every Sunday. It has been stated that she watched over his coats, his collars, and his cravats and busied herself with his investments. If there was any part of his wardrobe which she could not attend to directly, she entrusted it to Joséphine, the capable female factotum of the Villa Saïd.[54]

But these material cares were merely the groundwork of the higher ambition which she entertained for him. Her role as bear-leader has been likened to that of Juliette Adam in connexion with Gambetta, for in each case the hostess transformed her awkward 'bear' into a presentable being.[55] Quite early in the game she began to bring him out and to sing his praises in her circle ; bystanders began to follow with interest the 'exteriorization' of his talent, which according to some of them had been latent until this period.[56] We should now know better than that. There are numerous arguments, which I will not repeat, to show that Mme. de C. did not truly 'discover' France, did not exactly take an immature Anatole from his chrysalis and help him to spread his wings for the first time.[57] But worldly people are apt to think that theirs is the only recognition that matters : not to know 'society' would argue oneself to be unknown. I wonder where Shakespeare and Keats and Alfred de Vigny would have arrived on such conditions ?

The question can, however, be argued from another angle. 'It is to Mme. de Caillavet,' declares M. Hovelaque, with some apparent reason, 'that we owe our France of the great years.' We shall not anticipate the evaluation of these 'great years'; but it is a tenable hypothesis that Mme. Arman had much to do with the volumes then turned out. If she did not give him his talent, she did to a considerable extent direct it — towards contemporary subjects, towards life, love and action. In these respects, she exerted an influence, which we may elaborate later, upon *Le Lys rouge,* upon *Thaïs* and even upon sections of the *Histoire contemporaine.* It is noteworthy that she never thought much of Anatole's researches about Joan of Are. She wanted actuality, because she knew that was what the great public wanted. She wished to bring her bear from the recesses of the menagerie into the market-place and make him dance, sometimes to the political drum. Thus he began capering with Boulanger and presently nearly did a break-down with Dreyfus — not at all to his discredit, be it said. But there are certain doubts that may be hinted, even at this stage. Is a man of scholarly tastes at his best in the market-place ? Is the whip of fashionable success the best instrument to urge him on ? And did A.F. never feel rancorous about the transformation of Sylvestre Bonnard into the salon-heroes of *Le Lys rouge ?* [58]

§ 8

AFTER Anatole had become a well-trained celebrity, there were naturally other mansions which welcomed so distinguished a guest. According to the social columns of *Le Figaro,* he was increasingly in demand during the period 1890-96, and on all sorts of occasions.[59] Sometimes it would be a banquet in honour of such poets as Maurice Bouchor or Jean Moréas ; sometimes a lunch for Jules Lemaître, or a dinner and reception at the home of Munkacsy, the Hungarian painter who was then much in vogue. The marriage of Maurice Barrès would require Anatole's presence, so would several funerals, and inevitably he would attend a 'fête artistique chez le comte Robert de Montesquiou-Fezensac.' A.F.'s name figured on various committees, to honour such creative artists as Baudelaire, Puvis de Chavannes, and Constantin Guys ; probably the name was all that our absent-minded friend contributed. We pick up again the thread of his Jewish relations when we find him, in 1895, among the guests at the wedding of Mlle. Hélène Koenigswarter to Gaston Calmann-Lévy of the famous publishing firm.

Twice at least he is reported as dining at the home of Mme. Hugo Finaly, and we have other testimony as to the impression that he made there. He was 'élégamment simple' and a charming *causeur*. He had then reached (1894-95) his full physical maturity, 'a phase which found him at his best, transforming the awkward collegian into a sort of accomplished *mondain*, very correct in dress and deportment.' He was by now perfectly sure of himself. He wore his hair carefully arranged, his imperial was becoming gray, his moustache was waxed and heavy-winged. His eyes, still 'truly magnificent, seemed to embrace life at large.' Yet the same witness noticed that in his expression a deep mockery prevailed and that when he attended her own receptions he seemed like a man whose power of feeling had been exhausted.[60]

Thus he became a diner-out, but because of his nonchalance, there were two safeguards that would-be hostesses had to apply. Although A.F. readily accepted invitations, he forgot them even more readily ; therefore he had to be frequently reminded of his obligations, if only in order to forget them once more. Again, it was considered *de rigueur* to ask Mme. Arman for any occasion on which France was to be present. It is likely that Anatole would not have come without the expectation of finding Egeria there. She would watch over his table-talk, follow closely his every word and gesture, and occasionally toss in a word of her own, to serve as 'kindling to his flame.'[61]

Yet A.F. was quite capable of forming or maintaining relations outside the charmed circle of Mme. Arman's salon. For instance, his rise in the world did not mean that he turned his back on such old friends as Etienne Charavay and Honoré Champion—quite the contrary. But he appears to have seen the Calmettes less often. As for Mme. de Loynes, to whom Mme. de C. became the avowed rival, Anatole showed no haste in ceasing to attend her Fridays. This did not happen until 1898, when the Dreyfus Affair was at its height.[62] There were also certain people whose friendship was apparently shared between France and Egeria. Such was the elder Calmann-Lévy, whose death in 1891 called forth quite a tribute from 'Gérôme' : 'He was kind to me in my obscurity, he bore with me and tried a thousand times to overcome my laziness and timidity.'[63] Such was the Comtesse de Martel, the amiable

'Gyp,' who not only had been a fellow-journalist with Gérôme, but had tried to maintain an impartial though sympathetic attitude when dissensions arose in the Thibault-France household. We have given her account of the final break. With regard to her position as a writer, we have seen how Anatole affably placed her far too high, in the columns of *l'Univers illustré*. Yet in her day she was widely known as the sprightly authoress of *Le Mariage de Chiffon* and *Petit Bob*. France, who considered her an 'excellent creature,' visited her often at her country home at Lion-sur-Mer, near Caen. And for nearly twenty years he was a familiar guest in her town house at Neuilly.[64]

A.F.'s catholicity of taste is shown by the fact that he could get on with such a professed Naturalist as Octave Mirbeau (who addressed him as a 'pure and strong genius') and such an æsthete as Marcel Schwob, with whom he held absorbing conversations about the ancients. Both Schwob and Maurras are supposed to have been France's secretaries for a while. But the only person who actually held that post in our period was a certain Mlle. Cantel. Maurras has declared that he was merely a disciple and devotee of the author of *Thaïs,* who as patron and guide did much to ripen his sense of style. The two men first met in 1890, when they were companions on a 'junket' to the Midi; it was in the same year that A.F. presented his young admirer to Mme. de C., who came to esteem him greatly. Thus was formed a relationship which did honour to both parties. For, as these pages bear ample witness, M. Maurras, reactionary and Royalist, has never allowed political differences to diminish his reverence for France as a writer.[65]

Finally in this group, we may return to the case of Maurice Barrès. Here we find the contrary of what happened between France and Maurras—namely, a discipleship that was presently broken for personal and political reasons. It will be recalled how attentive the youthful Barrès was to the 'Master' and how the latter presented him to Mme. Arman; thither he still went during the nineties, 'to pay his devotions to France,' considering him apparently an 'archbishop of the Church of Renan.'[66] But Barrès was capable of a consecutive loyalty neither to Renan nor to Anatole. Critical animadversions and retorts were exchanged; and after 1900, though the younger writer was still constrained to visit the elder one, friendly relations existed no more. The partisans of Anatole declared that the critic, Henri Massis, had 'passed over to the enemy,' merely because he called on Maurice Barrès ! [67]

One consequence of France's participation in the social whirl was that he was called on more frequently to propose or respond to toasts at banquets and the like. This happened at the notable banquet to Moréas, when A.F. was thought by some to have deserted the Parnassian cause, while in 1895 he gave an inkling of his cosmopolitan sympathies (which later became pronounced in behalf of Armenians, Bolshevists, etc.) by proposing the health of certain Hungarian journalists.[68] As time went on, he was even called upon to make set speeches—which he usually read from manuscript, with less of an oratorical than a literary effect. A certain number of these have been printed and will receive attention in our last chapter. For the sake of the biographical record there may be mentioned here a speech before the Institut Polytechnique des Jeunes Filles in 1894 and the notable *Conférence* of the same year before the antiquarian Society of Auteuil and Passy. In June, 1894, he spoke at the Fêtes de Sceaux before the society of Félibres ; he recalled pleasantly his excursions to the Midi and to Pierrefonds.[69] In 1896, as we shall find, he was much in demand on various occasions ; for example, he delivered a speech at Douai, where a monument was inaugurated to the poetess, Marceline Desbordes-Valmore.[70]

§ 9

DANTE once said that it was not an agreeable business to be forever ascending 'other people's stairs.' Perhaps France was of the same opinion, for in 1894 he decided to have a domicile that would be entirely his own. And it would be a handsome home, such as he and his visitors could alike enjoy.

Through the increasing sales of his books and well-placed investments he laid the foundations of what came to be quite a tidy fortune. This was not, as in the case of Voltaire, due to any financial acumen on A.F.'s part. All such matters he left absolutely in the hands of his devoted and capable publishers, on whom he could draw at will. When he had passed his fiftieth birthday, he must have felt that in several ways the Calmann-Lévy firm had treated him royally.

The apartment that he had rented at No. 13, Rue de Sontay, had but a few rooms and he had taken with him but a few personal belongings. It was evidently time to expand. The Avenue du Bois de Boulogne was then as now one of the most fashionable regions in Paris—and however much one might regret the Latin Quarter, it was necessary to remain near Madame. In the summer of 1894, France was induced to pay 70,000 francs for a house and grounds in this vicinity. Some say the price was 60,000, but Anatole himself laments that he did not offer the lower figure; as usual he was helpless in commercial transactions, and Mme. Arman was out of town. He busied himself with notary and architect, and in September of that year the purchase was completed. Carpenters and decorators could take up their tasks.

The 'Villa Saïd' was France's residence for twenty years, from the time he left his 'English and æsthetic' apartment on the Rue de Sontay until he went down to La Béchellerie shortly after the outbreak of the Great War. Because of his long sojourn there and because he made the place peculiarly his own habitat, one is eager to repicture the setting and the sort of life that he gradually came to lead. The reconstruction is not always easy, since the house was thoroughly remodelled, inside and out, after the death of Mme. de Caillavet. Those who inspect the mansion today, viewing it as a sort of shrine to the Master, must use a faculty that he frequently used—to wit, the historical imagination. To help us think back to the nineties, we have the records of a number of people who knew the Villa then or shortly afterwards.[71] And we have especially the monograph by Pierre Calmettes, *La Grande Passion d'Anatole France*. The latter work contains a quantity of information, together with illustrations from paintings which the writer made of the rooms in the 'old' Villa. In spite of occasional chronological uncertainties, this book is invaluable. It was composed by the son of Fernand Calmettes, Anatole's great friend of former days; the younger Calmettes was constantly at the Villa, whose owner he knew intimately.

The term 'Villa' is not limited in meaning to a single mansion, but may apply to a congeries of houses, of which France's was Number 5. This little community, which possesses its own private gate and road, is set back from the Avenue du Bois de Boulogne, on the North side, not far from the Bois itself. Entering the driveway, grass-grown and tranquil, the visitor—Henry Massis or

Paul Gsell or any one of a hundred others — soon found himself opposite Number 5, a tall, narrow, three-storied house, whose green door immediately attracted one's attention. Along with an ornate mail-box, it offered a knocker wrought in Florentine bronze, while near-by was a door-bell of the same material. Both of these represented human heads, which 'greeted you with a smiling grace.' Not so the Cerberus who answered the bell, when it happened to ring. This was the formidable Joséphine, the housekeeper who owed her allegiance, it seems, as much to the Avenue Hoche as to the Villa Saïd and who admitted you grudgingly if at all. But once in the vestibule you succumbed to the particular atmosphere of the place, an aura that ministered to several senses : a dim filtered light stole in to linger on marbles and paintings, an odour of long ago arose from the furniture and *bibelots*. But let us be more precise.

Every one who has written about the Villa Saïd has used the term 'Museum' to describe it, and Pierre Calmettes, who spent two years in delineating its treasures, has elaborated France's intentions in assembling such a medley, pictorial, statuesque, antiquarian.[72] Since the place was absolutely his own, he could fill it with objects reflecting 'his tastes, his habits, his desires and intimate sentiments.' Since he loved the past almost *in toto,* there would emanate from the thousand relics with which these halls were strewn something like a vivid contact with his own 'subtle mind.' There was also a partial kinship between the works which that mind threw off and the abode where many of them were conceived — partial, because when he came to decorate and furnish the rooms according to the procession of his favourite periods, he found that there were enforced omissions. In their treasure-hunting, Mme. de Caillavet claimed for herself the better part of the Old Régime, and Anatole must stop with Louis XIII. We shall see later how he took his revenge. The emphasis, then, was on the Middle Ages and the Renaissance, with certain outlying provinces ; and the model for a good part of the collection was the old Musée Cluny, which Anatole had haunted in his younger days. Although the tendency was toward period-furnishings, yet there was some overflowing and crowding of objects into odd corners. The reason was lack of space — the house had only two rooms on each tall story. So when Ségur paid his first visit to A.F., he was surprised by that interior which seemed at one and the same time a cloister, a museum, and a Florentine chapel. Paintings after Cimabuë, doubtful Madonnas of the Sienese school adjoined medieval shrines, Gothic statues . . . and a thousand other things from palaces, cells or sacristies, wherein appeared the rather stiff allure of the early Renaissance as well as the rough vitality of the Dark Ages.[73]

If the total effect in a given instance was not displeasing, that is because France was an artistic collector and arranger, and could produce results from unusual juxtapositions.

We are in the presence not only of a 'grande passion,' but of the manifestations of a whole life and a harmonizing personality. He infused this into disparate objects and thus aligned them. In spite of confusions and a disorder which seemed to increase as one went further upstairs, Anatole gradually attained to an integration of this cross between a palace of the Muses and the *Cité des livres*.

One unifying effect was that the whole place was bathed in a half-light produced either by candles or by a wan sun stealing through stained-glass windows. These *vitraux* were everywhere and must have helped to make the mock-religious impression that is still apparent at La Béchellerie. Anatole in his youth adored the joyous Parisian sun ; but as he aged, he preferred more subdued tones, though still rich and sumptuous. One visitor admired particularly 'the statuettes vivified by the warm light from the old *vitraux*.' The Calmettes paintings, those 'symphonies des obscurités fauves,' are said to render well the original crepuscular settings. It appears, too, that Anatole composed a room as he would compose one of his volumes, by assorting and combining many pieces into a personalized ensemble. Numerous objects, of course, were 'association' items, souvenirs whose stories he was never weary of relating.

But how are we to orientate ourselves in this miniature Cluny, where fine sixteenth-century 'speaking' portraits alternate with Greek torsos, where the chimney-pieces range from Venice to Bruges, where the Orient jostles the Middle Ages, where pure Pre-Raphaelite virgins cannot make us forget the portfolios containing the seductive nudes of Prud'hon ?

Let us return to our synthetic visitor who has been standing all this time in the tiny vestibule. When his eyes had grown accustomed to the semi-darkness, they were doubtless startled by the walls which revealed a jumble of Persian pottery and niches where stood worthy saints and virgins. Tanagra figurines, then as now, were strewn about. Some of the virgins also climbed the stair-case immediately facing the visitor. As he mounted with them, he probably noticed likewise bas-reliefs of marble and panels of carven wood. When he reached the top, he was rewarded by meeting an old friend of France's. An image of the Magus, Balthasar, no less, stood guard on this landing, accompanied by reliquaries and glass-cases, which indeed abounded everywhere.

But perhaps we have been in too great a hurry to go upstairs. There were two less pleasant alternatives for the visitor. After sending up his name he might wait in the entry, surrounded by crockery, virgins, other visitors' hats and coats, until Joséphine returned and grumpily told him that the Master was not receiving; in this case one bade farewell to the Madonna leaning against the newel-post and retired in confusion. Or if it were a Wednesday, the day of the more formal receptions, one might be directed to the left, into the rather large drawing-room. Here the Renaissance was mingled with the seventeenth century, whether in the old wooden chests and Venetian embroideries, or in the serried array of paintings, which extended from Henry IV to Louis XIV. On the ceiling was a large map of Paris in the time of Turgot—a striking feature on which Anatole loved to dwell. A *rétable* or altar-back, brought from Venice, was turned into a chimney-piece, and is now found in the Collection Lion. As usual, hundreds of *bibelots,* large and small, were scattered about: rare laces and sumptuous chasubles, a lacquered Buhl clock, reproductions of angels, virgins, and voluptuous Italian beauties.

At the rear of the salon was a glass gallery, called the 'chapel,' because it housed a fine fifteenth-century Madonna of painted wood, standing in her niche. . . It was in this *décor* that Anatole was at home on the afternoon of his daughter's wedding (1901), and callers still remember how the omnipresent candle-light caressed and blended the tones from innumerable 'articles of virtue.'

On the other side of the vestibule was the dining-room, done entirely in late Gothic or early Renaissance and in terms which appealed to at least two among the seven deadly sins, namely, Greed and Luxury. The Abbé Coignard would have been at ease in this *milieu,* where appetizing kitchen-ware alternated with woodwork on which the figures of naked nymphs abounded.[74] The outstanding piece was a huge fourteenth-century chimney, with sculptured decorations. Both dining-room and kitchen displayed everywhere a quantity of old pottery and porcelain from many countries.

But Anatole frequented the ground-floor much less than the *premier étage ;* so let us return upstairs.

After passing Balthasar, the visitor walked directly into the library, which was the show-place of the house and its master's favourite room. From our frontispiece the reader may surmise something of its splendour. Entering through the carven Renaissance door, one might notice first on the left a four-hundred-year old printing-press, an adequate symbol for the *Cité des livres ;* then a large much-littered work-table ; then a great marble fireplace, chiselled in the Italian manner ; then, between chimney and window, the precious glass-case of Tanagra statuettes, whose delicate forms France loved to handle ; then the bookshelves crowded with almost innumerable volumes. On a pedestal, the torso of a tutelary Venus, voluptuous and lovely, presided over all.

And again the slanting golden light stole in through the stained casements of the sixteenth century, to enhance the beauty of the statuettes, to linger on the ivory bindings made out of ancient antiphonaries, to impart a lustre to old bronzes and Etruscan vases, to animate the tapestry recording the deeds of Joan of Arc. On the bookshelves, the rare bindings glowed, the earliest Elzevirs beckoned, the classics exercised their pristine appeal. Behind the work-chair, Bayle and Littré stood ready to hand. Racine and Rabelais were honoured in edition after edition. At its height, the library contained some eight thousand volumes, now alas !, widely scattered between the new Villa and La Béchellerie and the Musée Carnavalet. In the early stages of its growth, the intention was to choose volumes in accord with the prevailing medieval or early Renaissance tone — old missals and folios and the oft-mentioned Bible of Nuremberg. Later these gave place to the works of the High Renaissance, and finally to the French classics of the seventeenth and eighteenth centuries — but always in choice editions and with varied rich bindings.

Before leaving the second floor, our respectful visitor might be allowed to tiptoe into the bedroom. It was mainly sixteenth cen-

VILLA SAÏD: 'LA CITÉ DES LIVRES'

tury, Italian or French, reflecting the age of Medicean domination and blending purple with gold. The great columned bed, of the time of Henri II, stood on a dais and was surrounded with velvet canopy and curtains. Silken festoons and embroideries enriched this monument, which was covered with a Venetian bedspread of crimson satin. On the wall was painted an allegory of an undraped figure, perhaps a Muse, in a bank of clouds. There was an 'immense' Renaissance fireplace that occasionally smoked. There was a large Louis XIII arm-chair, where Anatole sat like a prelate, crowned probably by one of his numerous gaudy skull-caps which trailed all over the house. There was a small book-stand reserved for some favourite 'firsts.' Somewhere adjacent was a bath-tub in which Anatole dumped, it is reported, unopened packages of more recent books. (He sold them at fifty francs a tub-full.) In the bedroom and elsewhere lurked private portfolios secreting 'gallant' drawings *à la* Brantôme, to say nothing of a Florentine cabinet housing souvenirs of a similar quality. Other Italian relics, from Venice or Rome or Naples, were not lacking; and there was the usual mixture of small *bibelots* and heavy old furniture. When the Villa was remodelled, much of the early stuff vanished, including the huge bed; a marble Louis XVI chimney-piece was substituted for the Italian one; Ingres and Prud'hon appeared to dislodge their predecessors. Anatole even expressed a lively dislike for the heavy oaken pieces of the Valois period.[75]

The rooms above were less important. But one should not ignore the 'cabinet gothique,' whither the Master retired for his more intense labours and where, on Wednesday and Sunday mornings, he usually received his friends. As became a work-room, the furnishings here were fewer in number, though still choice in quality. An old leather arm-chair was the favourite seat of Sylvestre Bonnard. The Gothic note predominated and, once more, was enhanced by discreet light penetrating through stained glass. Other rooms, *mansardes* and the like bulged with the overflow from the whole museum.

A number of the medieval articles mentioned above presently took their way to the residence near Tours, where they may still be seen in the main building and outhouses of La Béchellerie. As early as 1908, France began experimenting with alterations at the Villa Saïd, especially regarding his bedroom, which was converted from the Renaissance into the Directory style. This was symptomatic of later changes, which occurred after the death of Egeria. This event released all the pent-up enthusiasm of Anatole for the more modern periods ; gradually the Gothic, the Renaissance, the baroque yielded place to the eighteenth century in all its rococo glory. Furthermore, from 1914-20, the Villa was practically rebuilt, inside and out, to provide a Parisian *pied-à-terre* for France and his new wife. It became a modern and a more standardized affair. We cannot follow all these avatars, but one spiritual effect, which was almost a visitation of Nemesis, may be noted. Much lighter and much whiter, the Villa was also less picturesque and less haunted by souvenirs of every kind. And Anatole, having worked to bring all this about, cared but little for the new place, when completed. It had too thin an aroma of the past.

But when the old Villa was in its illustrious prime, it must have offered a rare spectacle. The collector's mania which France professed—and possessed—had served him well. From far and wide, material had been acquired, assorted, and made his own by intimate acquaintance. We shall see in a moment how his travels aided him, how he would return laden with spoils from the provinces, from Italy and Greece ; in Paris itself the *bibelotier* in him was hardly less active. About once a week he would return to his former domain—the Quarter of antiquities, engravings and old books. With the elder or the younger Calmettes, with other acolytes, with Madame Arman herself, he would prowl around for hours. He had his corner *chez* Prouté on the Rue de Seine and would spend a long time fingering the prints and drawings which came to form such a large part of his collection. He would frequent what was almost the 'paternal' book-shop, the Librairie Champion, now installed on the Quai Malaquais, and it seems that he even assisted in its removal from the Quai Voltaire. Close were the ties that linked him with Honoré Champion, and the sons of Honoré have many recollections of Anatole.[76]

Home again, he would occupy himself with placing or hanging his acquisitions, which was one aspect of his 'great passion' ; still another was to exhibit his best things to those who were qualified to judge them. But it is recorded that he would abandon even this pleasure to hasten to meet an antiquity-dealer or a picture-merchant ; for these gentry often pursued him to the Villa. He could rarely be persuaded to open the letters which came to him in ever increasing quantity. But opening parcels which contained *objets d'art* and viewing their contents was an inexhaustible delight. Undoubtedly, his repute as a collector added to his general prestige.

Some people hold that the miscellany thus obtained, whether in the art-realm or the book-world, was not collected or arranged with the highest possible taste.[77] It hardly becomes a foreigner to pass on this delicate matter. But such is not the opinion of the majority of those cited above who knew and described the Villa Saïd, although these regret some of the mixtures of genres and periods already hinted at. More to the point, perhaps, is the query once put by Maurice Barrès after surveying many of the treasures. He wanted to know what a Communistic State would do with all this parade of wealth.[78]

Since France kept practically open house, especially on Wednesday and Sunday mornings, it would be impossible to list all the people — mostly men — who came to the Villa. Among the writers of reminiscential volumes, Ségur, Brousson, and Gsell were assiduous in attendance, but for the most part after our period. Such a neophyte as Henri Massis (*æt.* 18) would appear in fear and trembling, dropping the volume of Zola which he had under his arm. Pierre Champion would call and be cordially received. Abel Lefranc would start an amicable controversy about Rabelais. There was no reason for any novice to stand in awe of France, who welcomed all, even 'les indifférents,' with a sort of bland effusiveness. He would envelop them in affectionate embraces. Yet it is thought that often he did not really know whom he was greeting, or had forgotten his 'cher ami' the next moment. Such mild hypocrisy would be pardonable in a *milieu* which was thronged and which seems to have included at times rather second-rate people, a number of whom had favours to ask. Whether they knew it or not, they were there chiefly as listeners, and the monologues would presently begin. The discussions were usually about literary or artistic matters, and one difference between the Avenue Hoche and the Villa Saïd is that in the latter we are in a more professional atmosphere. Writers abounded, while men of the world were less numerous. Whoever they might be, they had the pleasure of witnessing something rare. The Master would receive in his

'Gothic cabinet,' reclining like a cardinal in his high-backed leather chair. The scene has been reconstructed by Pierre Calmettes:

His close-fitting dressing-gown of dark wool, his scarlet skull-cap, of silk, satin or velvet, fitted well with the tall andirons that held the blazing logs, with the chimney-piece whose columns framed a variegated display of Italian porcelains, with the Louis XIII table on which he leaned at ease. Those who saw him thus must have had the same thought. In this setting, the legacy of former ages, it was not really Anatole France who received, but rather the Abbé Jérôme Coignard, wafted into the twentieth-century Bois de Boulogne by the subtle and freakish wand of a magician.[79]

§ 10

It is apparent that many of France's furnishings were the spoils of his travels, especially into Mediterranean lands. During our period and after, those travels become more and more frequent. The editor of the *Echo de Paris,* for which Anatole wrote intermittently, would repeat his notice to his readers: 'Our illustrious friend, having returned to Paris after a long absence, will soon resume his collaboration.'[80] Where had he been and how had he been occupied?

We have witnessed his flights into Normandy and Brittany, Avranches, the two St. Valery's, and the watering-towns on the coast. One July he pushed as far as Finisterre, with results recorded in *Pierre Nozière,* where also we find an account of the cathedral town of Liesse. He had visited, in the Aisne valley, Soissons and Laon; and he loved Rheims, where, as he wrote Mme. de C. (1890), 'j'ai vécu avec les pierres.'[81] Several times, certainly in 1892, 1893, and 1894, he would spend part of the late summer with the Comtesse de Martel at Lion-sur-mer. He had been in England. He had visited Bordeaux. He came to know the countryside around that city through his prolonged sojourns at Capian. He was there every year after 1890 or 1891, and the mistress of the house, while providing an excellent table, saw to it that his régime of labour was also maintained.

When their relations had become a settled matter, the two lovers planned trips together. Or, failing that, Anatole wrote his Egeria of what he found at Lyons and declared gallantly that she has formed him to such an extent that now he really 'knows how to travel and takes pleasure in it only when with her.' [82]

But before going on his more famous journeys with Egeria, France was to have a final bacheloric fling. In August, 1890, he made one of a party that attended in the Midi the 'fêtes des Félibres,' or the celebrations in honour of the Provençal poets. In various forms, Anatole recorded the pleasure that he derived from this experience or prolonged the connexions then formed : articles in *Le Temps ;* the same, collected and commented upon by Louis Barthou ; an article on Paul Arène in the *Vie littéraire ;* and a preface to Arène and Tournier's book of travels.[83] This Arène, who was the author of various tales of Provence, is supposed to have influenced Alphonse Daudet and even France himself. He was one of the companions in this literary pilgrimage ; so was the sculptor, Amy ; so were Charles Maurras and Louis Barthou, whom A.F. met for the first time at the station of Agen. Starting from that town, the 'junket' proper covered Montauban, Auch, Tarbes, Bagnères-de-Bigorre, and Pau. Some of the travellers, including Anatole, pushed as far as Saint Sebastian across the Spanish border. Here and there, A.F., who had his own personal way of gleaning *impressions de voyage,* left vivid word-pictures of these various sites, telling how the delegation was received in each. He saw Agen couched cosily on the brow of its hill. It is hard to say whether he was more interested in the Roman tower or in the pretty girls who wore their beauty like an antique heritage. The Vénus d'Agen, in the Museum, symbolizes their loveliness. In Tarbes, our tourist is interested chiefly in the bust of Gautier, who was born there. In Bagnères, A.F. plays truant from the inauguration of *plaques* and the speech-making : he would rather follow a meandering brook, which led him considerably astray. He is attracted by mountain streams and picturesque costumes, as he gets on toward the Pyrenees. At Lourdes he utters the famous *mot,* which he attributed to another : that all these votive tablets at the grotto are less convincing testimonials to the miraculous than would be a single wooden leg abandoned by a cured cripple.[84] He admires the white loveliness of Saint Sebastian, but is revolted by the blood and cruelty of the bull-fights.

Altogether, he recalls a gay and delightful experience, dampened neither by the frequent rain nor by the official speeches from which he usually walked away. If he had been over-earnest, he could easily have been stunned by the ten days of eloquence, fanfares, and locomotives. He admired the oratorical efforts of Louis Barthou or of the 'distrait' Pierre Lafitte, but he preferred chatting with them privately, during the warm and lazy Southern nights, when the spirit of song was in the air. . . Sometimes they were too warm, he wrote Mme. de C. He also expanded to her on the notable cathedral-choir at Auch, the blossoming century-plant at Pau, and 'the valley of the Argelès, where the running stream was of a passionate and mysterious blue.' It was all very lovely—yet he missed her more than words can tell.

But the Midi left no effect upon France's mind and work comparable with the numerous and ineffaceable impressions that he derived from Italy. When did he become acquainted with this country of his choice? Before the present period there are few indications in his writings that would even suggest a first-hand knowledge. The touches that one finds in *Sylvestre Bonnard* and in a review of Bourget's *Sensations d'Italie*[85] may well be due to a clever use of printed matter. If France is correctly reported, he once said that as early as 1874 (he thinks) he dined at Rome with the historian Mommsen and other distinguished guests; the statement has been repeated by others.[86] But apart from this one source there is no further mention of such an early journey in any of Anatole's writings or utterances. The statement cannot be taken as proved; and moreover it seems quite unlikely that A.F., in his thirtieth year and still a gosling poet, was in any position to undertake a trip to Rome and to dine with Mommsen. We hold to the accepted view that it was Mme. Arman who in the Spring of 1893 introduced Anatole to that Italy which he was destined to love all the rest of his life.

Travelling with her son and his young wife (now Mme. Pouquet), Egeria gathered up A.F. and his carpet-bag at Avignon, from which centre he had been again prowling in Provence. The ostensible reason for the joint journey was to collect material for *Le Lys rouge;* and we shall find in that novel certain Florentine souvenirs. The tour, however, spread out over Tuscany and Umbria. Genoa, Pisa, and other towns were visited. France seems to have exerted himself as a conscientious sight-seer, although he claimed his periods of rest and wanted meals at fixed hours. The ladies of the company found him an entertaining companion. In various combinations they saw 'les monuments,' churches and galleries, palaces and, of course, antiquity-shops. Is it symbolic that A.F. brought back from Florence the bronze door-knocker which soon decorated the Villa Saïd? Truly the whole journey opened the door for him into a new world of pleasure and culture. 'Nothing Italian was henceforth to remain foreign to the illustrious writer . . .' and Anatole France was certainly thinking of himself when he said of the hero of *Le Lys rouge*: 'He always returned to Italy, as to the true country of his soul.' [87]

Anatole also returned, year after year. It came to be a regular Spring pilgrimage, usually with Mme. de C., until Greece presently asserted her rival claims. For instance, he was in Sicily, when in October, 1896, he wrote his 'Lettre de Sicile' as a preface to *l'Oaristys*; and we have seen how memories of Theocritus blended with the pastoral landscape.

Not only did he bring back, sooner or later, a number of the treasures and trophies that adorned his Villa. He brought back (as will appear in our next chapter) much of the material that underlies at least two volumes of this period. And he brought back, what gives true significance to all these things, a deep affinity with the land of art. It has been said (by Rodes) that in his home-surroundings and with this spirit in him, Anatole came to resemble one of the great figures of the Italian Renaissance; certainly he admired the long traditions and the superpositions of a culture so congenial to him. Further reasons for his 'grateful fervour' have been thus summarized.—Italy manifests abundantly those traits which are among his own abiding tastes: love of antiquity and its revival in the Renaissance; love of beauty in form; and a frank sensuality of outlook.[88] During the Great War France paid perhaps his most glowing tribute to Italy. He has loved the land all his life, and he has loved it no less for its natural beauties of seashore and hill-side, its marble capitals and its rock-ribbed citadels, than for its poets, artists, and learned men, still vibrant with the impulses of the Risorgimento. He has 'loved it, finally, with all the transports of passion, all the delights of *la volupté,* all the meditations of the philosophic mind.' [89] More than this can no man say.

§ 11

EVIDENTLY, all these factors—his social life, his splendid house, his travels at home and abroad—would contribute, along with the increasing vogue of his works, toward making France more widely known and honoured. Something like fame is coming to be his lot. Not yet do his journeys call for great demonstrations on the part of the native inhabitants—demonstrations that often fatigued their victim.[90] Not yet has his reputation become 'mondiale' or world-wide, as it did in the twentieth century, nor is his name (like that of Proust after him) yet used as a kind of literary shibboleth or touchstone. All this will come in time. But even in the early nineties he became pretty well known in Paris as a novelist and as a personage. Impossible as it still is to trace the complete curve of his ascendency, let us indicate some of the high points.

As his star rises to its apogee, it is hailed more frequently by discriminating critics. Each volume, as it comes out, is made the subject of an adequate review in one or more of the leading journals. For instance, Georges Pellissier writes a series of *comptes-rendus* for the *Revue encyclopédique*. In some cases, France's most recent volume is made the excuse for an essay which will review his total work to date. Thus Edouard Rod brought out a long, penetrating, moralistic study in the *Revue de Paris* (1894); and René Doumic followed suit just when Anatole entered the Academy.[91] Letters have been preserved in which A.F. thanks still other critics, e.g., Octave Uzanne, Francisque Sarcey, and Maurice Spronck, for favourable articles.

France's increasing mail often brought him personal or professional tributes from other writers. We shall see how and why this concert of praise reached a climax in 1896. But before that, admiring letters are on record from Mirbeau, from Schwob and from Heredia, among others. The last-named called his former brother-poet 'le Prince des Prosateurs.' France became inured to such eulogies and presently made little of them.

And since the themes of *La Rôtisserie* and of *Le Lys rouge* could be understood at least by the élite of every country,[92] our author's name began to be known abroad. His slow penetration into Germany and other Continental countries would require a separate investigation. In England, his critical method and the slogan about the 'adventures of one's soul among masterpieces' met with isolated approbation as early as 1892.[93] The first article devoted to A.F. in an English periodical was by Maurice Baring. It appeared, appropriately enough, in the rather 'advanced' *Yellow Book* in 1895, and it is thoroughly appreciative.[94] Thus Anatole was presented to the æsthetes who had admired Burne-Jones and were turning to Aubrey Beardsley. But his vogue soon extended beyond such limited circles. He became the favourite author of Sir Henry Campbell-Bannerman, while Arthur Balfour's philosophic pose certainly took hints from the *Jardin d'Epicure*. Not until about 1908, as noted by Arnold Bennett, did France's fame across the Channel begin to dwindle.[95]

Just why both countries were ready for Anatole in the nineties would require lengthier explanations than we can here allow ourselves. There was doubtless something in the *Zeitgeist* that responded to the kind of mannered thought that we are striving intermittently to analyse. And it responded not only to Anatole, but to such *fin-de-siècle* compeers as Bourget and the earlier Barrès, who were then as much in the mode as they are now outmoded. Although France too soared to some extent *via* the 'snob appeal,' there were other elements that helped his triumph. One of these would be the implication of his pen-name and the fact that many considered him, even to his dying day, as the incarnation of his country. Another was the fact that many young men (and not only in France) really considered him as their intellectual initiator. Around this hive of sweetness and light the bees came to swarm in such numbers that the hive for them was enlarged into something like a palace. Anatole came to occupy, for a generation, an eminence loftier than he rightfully merited ; and it is probable that his avoidance of too-blatant celebrations was due in part to an uneasy consciousness of this fact.[96] Still, he had to get used to 'la gloire.'

§ 12

THERE is one aspect of France's life and converse about this time that deserves to be considered separately. I refer to the formation, and possible alteration, of his whole personality, without and within. And first, what sort of general social stir did he arouse ?

He left a more definite, sharply defined impression than ever before. Mme. de Caillavet made of him a personage; and also, as already hinted, she converted him into a Mask. It is formidable, it is point-device, it is boulevardier to the last glossy hair on its imperial. It is composed of a finely moulded head, magnetic eyes, a brisk allure, and a discreetly courteous manner. It can adorn the amphitheatre of the Academy or figure in the drawing-rooms of the élite. There, says Bertaut, it can address the ladies with a 'respectful gallantry,' it can attract with an enveloping charm.[97] . . . Evidently, the Mask makes a perceptible impact, more seductive than dynamic.

There are those who hint that this benign *persona* was a precaution and defence that he took against the world; that the Master was not truly at ease in his 'mundane uniform,' where he became indeed a galvanized mummy; or that the true name of the Mask was Disillusionment.[98] . . Hush! Let us not build up merely to destroy, not even if our subject sets us the example. We are observing now the fashioning of the outer man and the aura that he gave forth. Let us grant that he 'knew how to organize his own legend'; and that he looked upon Society's parade as a sort of comedy in which he must play his part.[99] The fact is that he played it and spoke his lines convincingly.

For when suitably posed and presented by Egeria, the Mask could monologue admirably on everything from Nineveh to Napoleon. To the ladies it could murmur voluptuous parentheses, with Monseigneur the Archbishop it could exchange sharp but veiled repartee. At times he would 'seem to recite whole chapters of his books,' thus provoking some doubt as to spontaneous sincerity, while the repetition of certain phrases and *motifs* indicated pretty clearly that the screeds were prepared in advance.[100] Indeed, they seemed to some auditors to consist mostly of phrases, *jeux de mots,* esoteric brilliance of various kinds. But for Hovelaque these fireworks staged by Mme. Arman were so many

> *morceaux de bravoure* . . . which infinite rehearsals had brought to perfection. For this monologuing conversation, the marvel of our age, was, like that other pellucid marvel, his written prose, the result of a long toil, and that supple ease was the recompense attained by a great effort.[101]

His secretary once declared that Anatole practiced two types of conversations—the public performances already illustrated, and the looser, more chatty kind usually addressed to a single auditor.[102] The former variety came to be celebrated. It was virtually a recitation, prompted by Mme. de Caillavet, at times corrected by her, replete with rhetoric, well-delivered quotations, and anecdotes. Intimates of the house could usually predict the sequence of phrases that would fall from those persuasive lips. But they were careful to applaud along with those who witnessed the display for the first time. The other kind was laborious, halting, full of contradictions, resembling the puffing of a partially disabled locomotive ; it was less monotonous than the official kind, because one never knew (France least of all) where he was going and how he would wind up. This must be the sort of chatter that Henri de Régnier found almost insupportable, because of its prolixity and digressions.[103] But it had the merit of naturalness. One might add that occasionally Anatole would direct the talk into perverse or sensual bypaths that would surprise a fellow-Academician like the Duc de Broglie or even offend Madame de C. herself.[104] And she was not easily shocked. After his *conversations d'apparat* the entertainer-in-chief probably needed a safety-valve.

After all, there were things that Anatole liked better than being a Mask. He liked to play hooky. Doubtless with savoury memories of Little Pierre's escapades, he would skip into a bookstore or a pastry-shop when he should have been somewhere else. Mme. Pouquet tells us that he forgot to attend a formal dinner, and when they found him he appeared in his shirt-sleeves, with yellow boots and unclean hands. When they corralled him into a magnificently appointed work-room at Mme. de C.'s, he might labour, but he was just as likely to go to sleep ; he was full of ruses and dodges to avoid toil. He was, at bottom, more nearly a Bohemian than a man of the world. There were times when the whole business of receptions and parades went against his grain ; but, as he said, 'Madame Arman never would abdicate.'[105]

He liked to feel at ease in his clothes, his manners, and his morals. He was still fond of prowling round the antiquity-shops, the book-stalls, the daughters of joy. So he would remove the Mask and let the underlying mutable Anatole appear ; it was more nearly his true self that presided over those intimate levees at the Villa Saïd.

Deep within his uncertain soul, he liked to drift along with eddying and whimsical currents. For after all the Mask is not to be taken as a symbol of stability or of an integration achieved within the homunculus. We have seen how the time for that had come and gone. The milk of sentiment had by now curdled within him. The tabernacle of belief was shattered. Henceforth that penetrating mind would often tower only over the wrecks of things. This Nihilism, this glance into a cheerless void would suddenly check him in the midst of a flow of conversation. One observer noted that France in talking had two habitual expressions: one of mildly ironic gaiety, with face illuminated and eyes screwed together; the other, a wide-open, contemplative, melancholy gaze, when his impenetrable eyes seemed to give you 'un avant-goût du néant.'[106]

§ 13

This change in Anatole's character, already adumbrated, is so grave a matter that it requires elaboration. The main productions of this decade, it will be seen, teem with sceptical and iconoclastic ideas which reflect the alteration of the inner man. It is the main thesis of this work that the fissure in his personality was due largely to the break in his marital relations described above. Yet it must be allowed that there were forewarnings of the fissure before 1890.

The remark of Barrès, to the effect that France really 'had no character' dates from 1889. Although their real rupture came much later, Barrès here adds that he has lost his affection for his former master, because he can no longer recognize the old Anatole. About the same time, M. Hovelaque, who later recorded his admiration for A.F.'s brilliancy, was impressed less favourably by his sensuality (which was often *polissonnerie*) and by a sort of inhuman detachment that he manifested, even with regard to his own creations. Paganism and the pointed ears of the faun were already visible. Furthermore, he evinced 'a rage for destruction. And it was with terror that I discerned in his talk a patient and incessant trend towards universal negation and a systematic lowering of standards.'[107]

Some of this has reference to the contents of *Thaïs*; and it was in that novel, as we shall develop, that A.F. publicly threw down the gauntlet against orthodoxy. Doubtless this was done partly in reaction from the sort of semi-muzzling that he experienced on *Le Temps*. But there were more profound underlying causes.

Recurring to the break in his life-line in the early nineties, we might note that several authorities have emphasized its fundamental character. It was, says M. Carias, 'an extremely important date when France, abandoning his roof-tree, threw himself, like an *outlaw,* into a free existence; but he was so unsuited to liberty that he soon fell into a new servitude.' On which M. Seillière comments that it was indeed an important date—not only for Anatole personally, but 'for French society and perhaps for civilized society in general.' We need not take A.F.'s iconoclasm quite so seriously as all that, but this critic is clearly right in maintaining that the upset in France's moral ideas (*æt.* 50) was due primarily to his marital shipwreck. What has become, asks another, of the 'good-natured, genteel, altruistic' author of *Bonnard* and *Le Livre?* [108] What, indeed?

One apparent change is that he no longer has the same heart: a chilly radiance has replaced a warm glow.[109] Again, the element of sensuality, so often displayed in his daily walk and talk, may have its titillating and even its artistic aspect, but is scarcely a source of strength.[110] *Voluptas* may be a goddess but she is hardly an ideal. Indeed, the whole shift in his life did not operate in the direction of force, except in so far as the force was furnished by Mme. Arman. Once more the spoiled child, between the ministrations of his mother and those of Joséphine, leans heavily upon feminine support. At best, he seems the 'amused victim' of Egeria's efforts to make him a 'great writer.' [111] He evolves into the great writer certainly—in fact he was almost that by 1890—but in view of his various weaknesses one is tempted to agree with those who declare: 'ce grand écrivain ne fut pas un grand homme.' [112] Perhaps one had better suspend judgment on so vital a matter.

Whatever may be thought of the man, the novelist at least gives evidence of one new virile quality during the period under consideration. He becomes much bolder. Some think this audacity is found in the later *Temps* articles,[113] and while I detect few traces of it in the published volumes of *La Vie littéraire,* the point may be conceded for the unpublished articles of 1892-93, many of which reappeared in *Le Jardin d'Epicure*. But before that time, *Thaïs* had shown 'protestant' inclinations. And around the same dates, the *Opinions de Jérôme Coignard* had seemed to many people rather unpalatable opinions. In fact, whatever A.F. wrote for *l'Echo de Paris* (1893-99), nearly all of which was reprinted in book-form, exhibits this aggressive spirit. Says M. Carias :

> France will try out on his amiable and refined public all the temptations of his mind, will become diabolical, innocent, voluptuous or destructive, will brandish the sorcery-books of the scholar, the arsenal of the disputant, or clusters of naked nymphs. . .

And the same authority alleges that as an artist Anatole is through with the theory of delicious illusions and boldly prefers a broad Naturalistic platform, whereon he may freely caper with 'soiled hands'—almost as soiled as those of Zola.[114] This is a surprising analogy and pushes matters rather far. But we shall let the works speak for themselves, bearing in mind that Anatole's mouthpieces, from Bonnard to Bergeret, through the Abbé Coignard, are supposed to become progressively more daring in their speech, more defiant and disillusioned in their attitudes.[115]

§ 14

BEFORE proceeding to these works individually, we need to reckon with certain theories advanced in a recent brilliant and provocative volume—*Le Secret d'Anatole France* by M. Charles Braibant.[116] Like Mme. de Caillavet and many another, it appears that Anatole too had his 'secret.' For M. Braibant this hinges on the hypothesis that France became a radical socio-politically around 1890-92, or earlier than generally supposed. The theory is developed with reference both to our subject's personal life and his printed utterances ; and due attention is paid to the columns of *Le Temps* and *l'Univers illustré*. It is shown that A.F.'s evolving views are closely connected with events of the day.[117] M. Braibant's work serves, indeed, as a sort of 'Défense et Illustration d'Anatole France.'

What this writer calls the 'grand virage,' or the main turnabout in Anatole's life during this period, is rightfully envisaged as extremely important. Among the causes of that *virage,* Mr. Braibant is disposed to pay less attention than we have done to the break-up of A.F.'s marriage. I cannot but consider this an error. Yet there are brought to light various other causes which contributed to France's radicalism. In the forefront of these influences are his personal connexion with the Boulanger affair and his growing interest in politics and socialism—significant matters to which we shall shortly return. Some secondary causes (in our opinion) are yet stressed by M. Braibant: Anatole's reactions to the Panama scandal; his resentment against such orthodox critics as Brunetière and Brucker, which nevertheless may have accentuated his fundamental impiety; and the so-called 'démon de midi,' or the sexual restlessness that often seizes on a man in his middle years. There was also a more spiritual restlessness, which led France to turn to the younger generation for a faith which his own had lost. Metaphysical doubts, leading to pessimism, were undoubtedly active, although I believe M. Braibant places their full impact too early (1888-89). He seems correct in affirming that Mme. de Caillavet counted for little in France's *virage* to the Left. One cannot be sure whether that alleged conversion was achieved partly because of his contempt for the Society into which Mme. de C. introduced him. Was this 'gold and silver cloud, hanging in the Heavens' of a nature to irritate the vision of Anatole and to subject him anew to the mortifications experienced of old by Jean Servien?

At any rate, M. Braibant is justified, we shall presently find, in insisting on the general iconoclasm of the *Opinions de Jérôme Coignard* (1893). This was clearly the year of Anatole's 'Terror,' one hundred years after the historical event. It may be that our critic precipitates matters rather too much before this date and that he overplays the significance of certain mildly inquiring journalistic articles. The question is connected with that of the stages that M. Braibant posits within this period of A.F.'s transitional development.

We learn that Sylvestre Bonnard, or France Number Two, was 'dead' by 1888. His death, we are told, was followed by 'an interregnum wherein we meet with France Number Two-and-a-Half, an uneasy fellow who skips lightly to the Left, but with a mincing step when he thinks people are looking.' During five intermediate years (1889-93), his piety and his conjugal felicity make equal strides—backward. It is around 1890 that Anatole in *Le Temps* looks longingly toward the young men whose faith, whether mystical or rational, had not been shattered like his own. It is within the whole five-year period, says M. Braibant:

that France, who was formerly conservative and chauvinistic . . . has become (or become again) anti-clerical, well-disposed toward political and social democracy and hostile toward the military spirit.[118]

Accepting provisionally the main points in this generalization, we may ask what régime succeeded to the interregnum. First, there was the monarch of *La Rôtisserie,* the 'vieux cochon' called Jérôme Coignard, who if not a *roi fainéant* was certainly a King Do-Not-Much. But when Coignard proffered his famous *Opinions,* when he 'took a good bath in actuality,' then indeed the socio-political evolution of Anatole was an accomplished fact. This statement, together with the parallel one that the 'grand virage' was *completed* several years before the Dreyfus Affair, seems to me entirely too absolute. M. Braibant himself admits that at least round the year 1896 there was a considerable check in the flow of France's radicalism, for reasons to be discussed later.

Such debatable issues are connected with the testimony adduced bearing on Anatole's participation in the *boulangiste* movement, his alleged conversion to the democratic idea, his attitude towards Socialism, and the scandal of the Panama canal. To these matters we should now turn.

France's conception, as observer and journalist, of Gen. Boulanger's antics has been intimated above. It is now more a question of his direct share in the popular craze for the General, although some additional opinions of Anatole as journalist have been brought forward by M. Braibant, who gives a lively sketch of this passing furor. On July 14, 1886, there was a notable military parade at Longchamp, where Boulanger received an ovation as Minister of War. In reporting this for *Le Temps,*[119] A.F. was more enthusiastic about the Army than about the General. The latter was in favour of reducing the regular army-service from five years to three. But strange as it may now seem, Anatole at that time favoured keeping the longer term of service and for over a year he considered the General too 'Republican' ! It was necessary for Boulanger to concede something if he was to please the 'reactionaries' (against Parliamentary government), among whom France was then numbered. That concession took place in the Spring of 1888, when A.F. donned the pink carnation and wrote the article, where to the tune of 'lui, toujours LUI !' he found much to commend in the General.[120] The virus has taken, and the party is organized.

France's motives in adhering briefly to this cause have been sought for. He does not appear to have been impelled by Mme. de Caillavet, who sized up the General with her usual acuteness; it is true that her salon became for a time moderately *boulangiste,* but probably that was in order to aid the career of Anatole.[121] Yet what could A.F. expect, in case the General became a Dictator? Some hint that he may have hoped for a portfolio, say of the Ministry of Education—at any rate he dines privately with Boulanger and is very complacent about this token of intimacy.[122] Without such definite hopes, there was enough in the situation and the views of Anatole to make him provisionally a *boulangiste*. Though still officially attached to the Senate, he contemned that body, together with the whole Parliamentary régime. He was not then averse to military heroes. Like many others, he wanted a strong administration, which would presumably lean neither to Royalism nor to the Church. This feeling persisted during the triumphant election of January, 1889, when the General was chosen, by an enormous majority, as a deputy from Paris itself. 'Gérôme' wrote a full article in celebration and in admiration.[123]

But soon after these triumphs comes *la débâcle*. The balloting is questioned by enemies, the General takes an absurd flight to Brussels, his secret dealings with the Royalists are unveiled, the movement gradually dwindles away, Boulanger is presently condemned to deportation by a high tribunal, and ultimately kills himself. Gone for ever are the glittering days when he pranced around on his black steed, Tunis. Thus sadly ended the hopes of the Left-Centrists. Anatole experienced a considerable disillusionment. His first venture in politics had petered out. He thought that his country must seek for 'some other broom,' with a cleaner sweep, but he did not know where to look. He was stranded in a state of ironic discontent, although it is hardly necessary to say, with M. Braibant, that without *le boulangisme* we would not have had 'either Jérôme Coignard or M. Bergeret.' Allowing for such exaggerations and a tendency to make too much of minor passages, we may agree with this authority that 'the adventure of the Black Charger had a considerable influence on his [Anatole's] *"virage."*. . Under his lighter scepticism henceforward we may detect a genuine uneasiness, an anxiety, an inner disarray, from which he will emerge with a new set of ideas on the State and the social question.'[124]

We have seen already that politics came to be not only a major topic of conversation but really a chief preoccupation of the mature Anatole ; Barrès and Braibant corroborate the view that it was his 'dada.' We may follow the latter's treatment, repeating the reserves made above as to certain over-statements and questioning the advisability of accepting as fully authentic the mass of articles signed by Anatole for *l'Univers illustré,* 1891-96. Yet from these and similar sources M. Braibant has composed a convincing picture of A.F.'s eager mingling in politics, at least through the months when *Jérôme Coignard* was first written.

The early nineties saw France's modified trend toward democracy, if not toward mob-rule, together with his renunciation of militarism and his distrust of the Russian alliance. His turnabout on these themes may now be followed as they were pushed to the fore by actual events. But let us remember (with M. Braibant) that the spirit of contradiction will appear in the heart of a credo and that the confused issues of the period often left a deposit of uncertainty in the minds of all citizens. For example, we find Anatole insisting one week on Government as the supreme art, as much finer than mere writing, yet revealing another week his disgust with the political *cuisine* or hinting that, as Morley once said, politics must always content itself with the 'second-best' in results. Frequently our journalist's individualism and his scepticism led him to distrust the efficacy of institutions, new or old, when it came to ensuring the well-being of ordinary citizens. All the more credit, then, to his awakened spirit, which began to shake off the yoke of bourgeois conformity, to take up arms against a sea of troubles, to detest any Throne-and-Altar restoration, and to take a 'firm stand regarding the independence of the mind, individual liberty, respect for competent knowledge, for justice, for the true dignity of one's country.' Thus says M. Braibant, with pardonable exaggeration, 'la question France, comme la question Victor Hugo, comme la question Zola, est avant tout une question politique.'[125] (Incidentally, this critic is among those who believe that Anatole repented early regarding Zola.)

Once in 1891, in connexion with the banning of a play by

Sardou, A.F. expressed himself indignantly against censorship from the Left. But he gave up Boulanger because of the latter's intrigues with the extreme Right. When this party indulged itself in benighted anti-Semitism — as it would do again in the case of Dreyfus — A.F. wrote, independently and eloquently, a defence of Israel for all she has given to civilization. His patriotism loses its militant character. It is not hard to see why Frenchmen of the eighties, still jealous and (though more mildly) 'revengeful' toward Berlin, would place what hopes they had in their army. Something of this spirit had appeared in Anatole's 'Vacances sentimentales,' and Gérôme had often declared his respect for the military establishment. Several articles in *Le Temps* tended in the same direction.[126] Also he was slow to relinquish the Darwinian creed that life fundamentally involved slaughter and survival. But after his disappointment in Boulanger and probably because of it, France abandoned for good what we usually call militarism and along with it any excess of chauvinistic zeal. Not all the King's horses could restore the General to his saddle. . . There are minor indications of this change of heart in A.F.'s expressed dislike for the 'Chants du Soldat' and in his blunt statement that the French people really does not care for war. Another evidence of his shift is found in his attitude toward the Franco-Russian alliance of 1891.

After nearly two decades of conscious inferiority, Anatole and his fellow-countrymen had, at the advent of Boulanger, raised their heads only to sink them again. But in ninety-one our scribe put from him the veil of Illusion. He would not be smothered by the Russian bear: he would not share in the triumphant ululations of Pecus. At the moment when Paris was prostrating itself before the Grand Duke Alexis, A.F. counselled moderation and sang-froid, the preservation of dignity and close scrutiny into just what Russia, in a strategic way, could bring to such an alliance. In fact, he foretold some of the disadvantages that she suffered from in 1914.[127] We are reminded of the coolness with which in 1887 he wrote, in the midst of alarming frontier 'incidents,' his detached and penetrating article on Bismarck. In either case, what he distrusted was popular clamour. In a third instance, he distrusted not only the people, but their representatives. This was the notable Panama scandal of 1889-93, in which the Vicomte de Lesseps was involved. In view of the probability that

'Pierre' had attended a dance at De Lesseps' house, and the fact that Anatole would succeed to De Lesseps' chair in the Académie Française, his present attitude toward Panama is of peculiar interest.

In the early eighties, De Lesseps, who had successfully conducted the Suez Canal enterprise, organized the Panama Canal Company, which four years later floated lottery shares to the amount of six hundred million francs. According to one historian, there ensued 'revelations of official corruption, of wholesale blackmail, and of the abuse of funds largely subscribed by the poorer masses.' In the following year, the company was declared bankrupt and its holdings were liquidated. Although this was the most notoriously corrupt affair of its period, so many officials were concerned, the octopus had spread its tentacles so widely that, as in a more recent episode, various obstacles delayed the slaying of the beast. Only in 1892-93 did the matter come to a head, first before the Chamber of Deputies, then before the Cour d'Appel and the Cour d'Assises. Mild penalties were imposed on a former minister, on Ferdinand de Lesseps, then a very old man, and on his son. Now in dealing with these events, Anatole makes it plain that he considers De Lesseps more sinned against than sinning. Our ironist had long known the inner workings of the scandal, which, after all, did not scandalize him so very much, as far as the officials of the company were concerned. The men who made him indignant were rather the bribe-takers and manipulators in the Chamber — one more sign of his definite anti-Parliamentarianism. We shall see that it was under the urge of this feeling that he began, for *l'Echo de Paris* (March 3, 1893), the series of articles which developed into the *Opinions de M. l'abbé Jérôme Coignard sur les affaires du temps*.

In all these cases, it is evident that France dislikes blatant and forcible-feeble demagoguery; and yet — 'a paradox, which comforts while it mocks' — he comes, more and more, to sympathize with . . . shall we say Jeffersonian democracy? So vital a matter must be fully considered later, but here we may touch upon certain aspects disclosed by M. Braibant. This writer holds that although in the *Temps* articles bearing on politics, A.F. 'has probably contradicted himself more than ever,' yet on the whole, 'he has stepped on toward democracy.' Among the texts brought forward is an incidental remark of 1888, when in reacting against antiquated Royalism, Anatole sweetly says : 'Patriotism, which is *born with democracy,* is today purer, prouder, more delicate, more exquisite than ever before.' This is powdered sugar, not of a weighty brand. There is more ponderation in another dictum where he speaks, without prejudice, of science and democracy as bearing us on to larger horizons and new destinies. But the lines are more firmly drawn in still another article of the same year, where, in the wake of older masters, he begins to use a favourite symbolization :

> M. Ernest Renan has perfectly understood that the future is Caliban's, for it is all over with Ariel.... But Caliban is a brute, and in his stupidity he finds strength. This 'moon-calf' is the whole people, and nothing but the people. In the Opposition, he is invaluable, for he knows how to destroy. . . He is hideous, but robust. He went too quickly after Miranda. But he is patient ; he is obstinate ; one day he will get another Miranda, and he will have children *less ugly than he is.*[128]

This allegory inspired M. Braibant to divide his work into such headings as 'Ariel,' 'From Ariel to Caliban,' and 'Caliban Triumphant.' But the suggestion that this alignment represents a definite evolution in the political thought of France (before 1896) can be accepted only with many reserves. In commenting on the above passage, M. Braibant himself admits, 'I know that a true Democrat does not talk like this.' Yet he thinks that Anatole is getting stirred, is getting interested as a result of the Boulanger shake-up ; and soon (in 1890), the critic of *Le Temps* is reproving those who speak only evil of the democratic fabric. We are trying to achieve solidarity, to build a new house, and if it is not so fine as a thirteenth-century cathedral, it is at least liveable. Like M. Bergeret, France finds the democratic structure a little tame, a little 'flat.' But there are more eloquent utterances about what underlies the structure. In writing up a Maupassantian heroine, A.F. admires in contrast 'the simpler and more stable manners of the toiling human multitude. In that *laborious mass* are found the true mores, the true virtues and vices of a people.' And in addressing himself that same year (1890) to Youth in search of a creed, Anatole advised him thus :

> Go, plunge into the obscure masses of the people, seek what you need there. They think, so to speak, not at all. But they unconsciously

elaborate the faith of the future and confusedly mutter together the rituals of the new religion.

Evidently, Caliban is feeling his oats.

Yet these few and some other texts which M. Braibant might have cited (e.g., the views of 'Gérôme' as stated above),[129] do not to my mind constitute a conversion. In many of France's writings, for example the 'Gospels,' and at various periods, we find him sympathetic towards the people. That is a different matter from accepting heartily 'la République,' which Anatole rarely did. For Caliban-Pecus cannot govern himself, as the Revolution and the Commune amply proved. He must have leaders; these, so far, have taken the shapes either of representatives or of a dictator. But if the deputies are corrupt nincompoops and Absolutism ends in a Louis XV or a Boulanger, we seem caught in an *impasse*. Such is the dilemma in which not only A.F., but many an observer of the body politic, finds himself in these troublous times.

We may grant, however, an increasing interest throughout this period in the affairs of the Republic, and that is apparent in still another direction—namely, in the doctrines and the spread of Socialism. We have referred briefly to A.F.'s dawning curiosity, as visible in *Le Temps;* and more broadly we have seen how, even as 'Gérôme,' he took his stand against inefficient or intolerant administrations, which could properly serve neither the country nor the city. M. Braibant makes a good deal of one case in point, i.e., the indignation of Gérôme against the expulsion of the nuns from Parisian hospitals. But on the whole, during the eighties, our Conservative is not very susceptible to popular slogans or currents.

His recognition of Socialism dates rather from the early nineties, when the creed and the party became definitely organized in France; his utterances either deal with new works on the subject or cluster around the first of May, during the years of the earliest 'manifestations' associated with that date. This was the epoch, says M. Braibant, of the 'great socialistic tide,' largely controlled by Jules Guesde, and Anatole follows closely and not adversely the surging of that tide. In connexion with some demonstrations on May 1, 1890, he says soberly that nations and individuals have to reckon with 'a new power, from which none can remove himself . . . and so I took to thinking of the hard necessities of life and the law of labour.' It would seem that from this year he begins to be impressed by the iron heel, by poverty and social injustice. The passage cited above, regarding the 'obscure masses of the people,' is of approximately the same date. These articles, admittedly, 'rest on the threshold of sympathy.' Then follows a lull, and when France again touches on the subject (January, 1892), he is less keen than before. Perhaps that is because, under the heading of 'Littérature socialiste,' he is discussing the views of Georges Renard, who had accused A.F. of dilettantism; he favours rather the *Mouvement socialiste* of Téodor de Wyzewa, a work which is considered less socialistic than Tolstoyan. Yet Anatole points out that the movement is by now a Parisian 'actuality,' causing a stir all the way from the Chat Noir to high society. He repeats this point in an article on the eve of the first of May (1892), where he declares that if he had 'any pretensions to elegance,' he would call himself a Socialist. The party is distinctly *à la mode* and is getting insensibly stronger all the time. It has not won over the peasants, but rather the mass of workmen, whose instincts are with its doctrines.

It seems to me a mistake, from these few passages, to speak of 'France acceptant franchement l'évolution vers le socialisme.' It is hard to find here more than an occasional interest, expressed in passing, in the movement proper. A more vital concern with the condition of the working-classes we *do* find; but this need not involve the acceptance of Socialism any more than it involved the full acceptance of democratic dogma.

What really happens is that, since A.F.'s thought along various lines is becoming bolder, he is equally ready to challenge the organization of the State and the tenets of the Church. This iconoclasm came to a head, when in the Spring of 1893 he resigned his position on the moderate *Temps* and began writing those drastic articles under the ægis of Jérôme Coignard. This work in its entirety will concern us a little later. But let us agree with M. Braibant that this 'bomb' would not have been hurled at Society, if Anatole had not become absorbed in affairs of the time, if he had not 'embraced warmly that lively female, La Politique.'

There are other signs that the creator of *Sylvestre Bonnard* is turning into a bustling contemporary. A.F., still in 1893, shows interest in Belgian Socialism, which was becoming rampant, and even in the Anarchism proclaimed by the Prince Kropotkin. But against all such agitators, France held firmly to the view that social evolution, like the biological kind, like the history of institutions, moves by extremely slow stages and cannot depend on much amelioration of its component units—i.e., of human beings. Slow would be the processes through which, as by 'natural law,' Society could be purged of her more manifest injustice and backwardness. Each social moment, each generation is too closely linked with what precedes it for a great upset to be probable or salutary. No—let us rather bide our time and lend a hand when possible; or in language anticipating the creed of *Crainquebille*:

> For the humble folk, the disinherited, the weak, let there be always more justice, always more pity and more brotherly kindness. That is what we should wish for unceasingly.

Although he may have continued to wish for it, the next few years show us Anatole, socio-politically speaking, rather drawing in his horns and preparing to be an Academician. True that the *Jardin d'Epicure* (1894) contains some daring speculations; but these are, in certain cases, attenuated from their earlier periodical form. True that in January, 1895, the enterprising *Echo de Paris* undertook the serial publication of certain 'Nouvelles Ecclésiastiques,' which would ultimately lead off *l'Orme du Mail*. But this series was suddenly interrupted, it may be because Egeria and Anatole had conceived Academical ambitions. This, according to M. Braibant, would simply be a truce, for his thesis is that A.F.'s social views (as later manifested in the Dreyfus Affair and subsequently) were formed permanently in 1889-93. His finale is:

> Just after the *boulangiste* adventure, a great hope struck the masses of people. He [A.F.] looked upon it first with curiosity, then with interest, and ultimately with sympathy. Little by little, freely and boldly, he carries in that direction his concept of ideal government.

It is a highly interesting, if debatable, hypothesis.[130] It cannot be pronounced upon until we have studied all the works of France's climactic period. Some of them will show us the destructive side of his spirit operating very actively. But so far we have seen little that builds toward a constructive socio-political philosophy. M. Gaffiot, who has made a thorough if rather static study of Anatole's politics, does not suggest a radical shift before the *Histoire contemporaine*.[131]

CHAPTER XVI

Works of This Period: Historical Perspectives

§ 1

WITH all their diversity, France's productions from 1886-95 exhibit certain prevailing trends. They have usually a tone of maturity and sophistication, far removed from the *douceur* of his previous phase. Irony is more conspicuous than sentiment, scepticism is more abundant than idealism. A militant spirit dispossesses the suave commentaries of 'Gérôme' or of the critic of *Le Temps*. Most of these years are spent under the ægis of Renan or in the shadow of Voltaire.

But it is a Voltaire reconstructed and brought up to date. The chief productions of this decade, such as *Thaïs* and *La Rôtisserie,* overflow with all the knowledge dammed up by their author during some twenty years,[1] and are of course monuments of learning. Yet it is a learning that bears the stamp of contemporaneity, appealing in many subtle ways to the educated reader around 1890. France the journalist is still keeping his hand in. Allusions to incidents and personages of the time are fairly frequent, graceful compliments to notable compeers are not lacking, while the dedications of stories or novels recall many of the names figuring in our previous chapters.[2] In several of these *contes* and in one novel —*Le Lys rouge*—the substance is entirely contemporary, while the *Opinions de Jérôme Coignard* reflect obliquely the actualities of French politics. To be sure, the fact that Anatole, in his semi-detached way, often contemplates the passing show, is not necessarily a recommendation. We may still find him at his best in the past. We may still agree with his first English reviewer that *Balthasar, Thaïs, l'Etui de nacre* and *Le Puits de Sainte Claire,* with all their apparent unprogressiveness, represent 'a genre which M. France has made his own.'[3] This is the genre to be considered in the present chapter.

Here, then, are four of the eight book-titles distinguishing this epoch. The other four are, in order of publication, *La Rôtisserie de la Reine Pédauque, Les Opinions de M. Jérôme Coignard, Le Lys rouge,* and finally *Le Jardin d'Epicure.* Of these eight, two are volumes of political or philosophical reflections, three are full-length novels of the past or present, while the other three are collections of miscellaneous short stories. It has been suggested that Anatole attempted this form (*conte* or *nouvelle*), because he was aware of his deficiencies in sustaining the invention and composition of a regular novel.[4] But such deficiencies, on a smaller scale, may prove equally apparent in the tales. However that may be, we can glean from either category, according to our habit, the chief manifestations of his personality, his thought, his theories and *motifs*. Such is our intention, rather than to make long and otiose analyses of the action in the more famous masterpieces.[5] Sufficient accounts of the less-known volumes will, however, be given.

§ 2

THE collection called *Balthasar* (1889) is properly rated as a 'transition' volume.[6] It contains seven *nouvelles* of varying length and value. These really date, in several cases, from the preceding years and from France's second period. Thus the story of *Abeille,* here reprinted, was first published in 1883 and has already been dealt with as of that date. The remaining six tales offer a wide and characteristic variety in the range of epochs presented: for the most part they hover around what we may style A.F.'s Quarrel of Ancients and Moderns. Two of them ('Balthasar' itself and 'Læta Acilia') have to do with the old clash between pagan and Christian ideals; one ('La Fille de Lilith') takes a bold stride from the days of Adam to those of Anatole; another ('Le Réséda du Curé') is a saintly anecdote, with something of a Franciscan flavour; while modernity, though with a supernatural or pathological bent, is represented by 'M. Pigeonneau' and 'l'Œuf rouge,' I believe that on the whole the moderns lose out in the Quarrel; the material regarding them is thin and rather ordinary as contrasted with the strong evocation of ancient times.

Since our author is forming here his first collection of short-stories proper, we should notice what influences are considered to predominate in his approach. Diplock has stated that in one or two of them he 'had the notable privilege of renewing the *conte philosophique* of the eighteenth century.' While this is true as regards a certain latent Voltairianism in raising questions of historicity, relativity, and the like, France lacks the allegorical and the widely human application of Voltaire's symbols. The smiling scepticism, to be sure, is of the same brand, with the difference that we find here what Filon calls a tenderer and 'almost Christian' Voltaire, who keeps something feminine in his brain. For we are not yet quite through with the more sentimental Anatole. That being true, it is inevitable that the name of Renan should be brought forward in this connexion ; and the tone of this milder Antichrist has been thus appraised by Seillière—intelligently, though with some over-emphasis, especially in the final adjective :

> We know that the age of Renan took delight in ironical speculations about certain Biblical notions, politely distorted : a type of irreverence less 'raw' than the Voltairian pleasantries and presented with an affectation of feigned deference.

That this is more closely applicable to a good deal of Anatole than to Renan himself will become increasingly manifest.[7]

The rather long *nouvelle* of 'Balthasar' lends its name, as was customary in the volumes of Maupassant and others, to the present collection, for which it also sets the pace. Carias believes that but for the searing touches of 'la volupté,' this tale might readily link with Little Pierre's innocent visions of the Bible.[8] In fact, Anatole himself declares that his affection for the Magi goes far back into the days of his childhood. He refers to them several times in *l'Univers illustré,* round the date of Epiphany or 'Le Jour des Rois.' One such passage is full and explicit.[9] This particular date, he says, always makes him recall the tale of Balthasar, which 'charmed my boyhood.' In the recollection, his imagination is filled with 'delicious and puerile marvels.' Follows a detailed description of Balthasar, recalled as black and kinky-haired, together with the other two Magi. He will not look at any paintings of them and he will not hear of any depiction but his own. Then he gives a short 'Histoire de Gaspar (*sic*) et de la Reine de Saba.' For the incident of the queen's visit was variously ascribed to any of the three Magi. The gist of Pierre's version is that while Gaspar was watching the stars from his tower, he saw the queen's caravan arriving across the desert. When she met him, the two fell in love forthwith. But there is no dwelling on the heart-interest, for suddenly a star appeared in the East, and Gaspar forsook his royal sweetheart. In a disappointed frame of mind, the queen turned into a jackal. (The mature Anatole does not forget the jackals, but he uses them otherwise.) The Three Magi set out together on their pilgrimage to the sacred manger. Of course much more is made of the passion of the lovers in the later story of 'Balthasar.'

Other references in *l'Univers illustré* contain some learned discussions about the names of the Three Kings. Anatole is aware that they do not occur in the Scriptures, for he mentions other authorities. He thinks that a 'joli mystère' might be confected out of the story of the Magi. And he admits that in his boyhood he often admired certain figures (*poupées*) of them, preserved in the Musée Cluny. So his mental images of what they looked like were not, after all, unassisted by art.[10]

Such is the basic material on which Anatole, in 1886, set to work ; but he elaborates it, with pomp and circumstance, into a fine story, laid in the time when Balthasar, 'black but comely,' reigned in Ethiopia. It was he who first decided to visit Queen Balkis. He sets out with a sumptuous caravan across a desert described with touches of local colour anticipating *Thaïs*—and including the jackals. When the two meet, the simple Balthasar falls desperately in love, becomes timid and tongue-tied. The perverse Balkis teases him, questions him, and confides her desire to have a good fright. They disguise themselves and go for an orgy in a low inn. Here they are assaulted, and the king performs prodigies of valour, before they escape from the dive. This raises his prestige, so that the queen, in spite of his scars, gives herself to him in a ditch. But when they are attacked by brigands and Balthasar is desperately wounded, the queen abandons him. He learns later that she has become more interested in the 'Roi de Comagène,' which is probably a reminiscence of Racine's *Bérénice*. Incidentally, the charms of 'Sheba' are probably recalled from Flaubert's *Tentation*.

Returning to his home, Balthasar consecrates himself to learning, particularly to astronomy. For some time, there is a conflict between learning and love, the image of Balkis and the spectacle of the stars. Presently his gaze fastens on a certain new star and he exclaims : 'Happy is the one who is born under its influence !'. But the return match is overdue. Balkis, having lost Balthasar, resumes her interest in him and travels to Ethiopia only to find that he is permanently lost. The mystical *motif* has overcome her fascination. She 'grew pale with despite' and returned to Sheba unsatisfied. The other two kings joined Balthasar, and their pilgrimage echoes the Evangelical account.

Evidently, we have here something of the 'hour-glass' construction that signalizes *Thaïs*. The advance and retreat between the lovers, which was not in the first version, lends symmetry to the development. In addition, there is a further see-saw, or *pro* and *con,* within the heart of Balthasar. For though he is by nature single-minded, the 'complicated sentiment' of love affects him dreadfully. The queen's passion is cruel, even sadistic, but its power is inexorable. Love is evil—but Balkis is beautiful. Man is made for learning—but he is surely made for love. Astronomy is a distraction—but Balkis is on the horizon, too, and with her comes trouble. Finally, the new star brings complete catharsis. The emphasis on astronomical study is quite Anatolian. So is the discreet exoticism, achieved by firm though slight colouring. The style is masterly and appropriate, with a good amount of Biblical background. The first publication of the story was soon followed by a sort of after-piece in *Le Temps,*[11] where Anatole alludes to the tradition (popular in the Vogüé family) that Sheba loved Melchior. Let us agree that she did so, but being a generous lady, could she not also have loved Balthasar—after her fashion? France then repeats, in a tone of assumed naïveté, a good deal that he said before, with special emphasis on the rumour that the queen had cloven feet. Balthasar knew better, but the mere existence of such a rumour added to the 'complication' of his sentiments.

The remaining five tales that concern us here were also first printed in *Le Temps* (1886-87). With one exception, they are less interesting than 'Balthasar.' That exception is 'Læta Acilia,' which serves as a polished link between the early *Noces corinthiennes* and such later tales as 'Le Procurateur de Judée' and 'Gallion.'[12] In all these, as in *Thaïs,* ancient standards come into conflict with primitive Christians and their creed. It is a curious fact that although France might wander from this theme, he would presently return to it; and this at several epochs in his career. It has been remarked that no one has written better than Anatole about 'the melancholy sunset of Paganism and the troubled moonrise of Christianity.'[13] In its essential duality, the theme filled a deep fissure in his mind. One aspect of that disturbed era, to wit the turning of pagan women to the new faith, had been shown in 'La Part de Madeleine' and 'Leuconoé' : these poems, too, have close affiliations with 'Læta Acilia,' as will appear from a brief synopsis of the tale.

In the time of Tiberius, the Christians were persecuted at Marseilles. In their behalf a Roman matron, Læta Acilia, is appealed to by no less a person than Mary Magdalen. But it seems that France is at his old game of confusing the Marys. This one is not only the repentant sinner inspired by a peculiar love for Jesus, but she is also the sister of Lazarus ; in that capacity, she was told by the Saviour that, in contrast to Martha, she had chosen 'la bonne part,' namely spiritual ardour (cf. 'La Part de Madeleine'). She now hopes that Læta Acilia will move the heart of her influential husband towards the toleration of Christ among other deities. The matron will do this, if in turn Mary will pray that Læta may become pregnant, for the Roman family wishes an heir. Both sides of the bargain are fulfilled. Then Mary visits Læta, big with child, for the purpose of instructing her in the Christian faith. The matron listens willingly. The Magdalen gives her version of the Gospel account, telling how she put the precious ointment on Jesus' feet and how she was the first to see him when he rose from the tomb. But here there is an unexpected shift in the action. Almost a proselyte, Læta has become so absorbed in the recital of Mary's religious adventures, which are also semi-amorous, that she is perturbed by a mixture of feelings, in which envy finally predominates. Accusing the Magdalen of being an 'evil woman,' who is trying to tempt the matron from her comfortable patrician habits, the latter refuses to have anything more to do with Mary or with her God. Thus it appears that, in both cases, conversion is very much a matter of personal inclination.

France concludes with a 'Note on a Point of Exegesis,' in which he defends the mixing of Marys as forming a part of Church tradition and as 'consecrated by legend.' It has been remarked that in this story he leans to the view that the Christ-legend in particular may have its beauties, as well as its virtues.[14] Certainly the attitude towards Christianity is on the whole still respectful. We have observed that while France was establishing himself on *Le Temps,* he bridled his freedom of speech. So in this story he forbears to smite the Church and merely insinuates some rationalistic suggestions. Among these are hints about the relativity of belief and the multiplicity of religions. Læta Acilia mentions what Leuconoë had previously discovered, namely that there are 'amiable gods in the Orient.' And she affably adds : 'Yours, Marie, seems to me to be of that type.' In the end it costs her little to reject one of many deities. Another bit of sceptical propaganda is that a group of primitive Christians is represented, in the manner of Tacitus or Gibbon, as a despicable, diseased, and beggarly mob. They were similarly described in France's two versions of the Thaïs legend.

Perhaps by way of indirect compliment to the master who had shown him the way into this fascinating period, Anatole dedicated 'Læta Acilia' to that scholar's son, Ary Renan. Curiously enough, the hero of another story, 'La Fille de Lilith,' is also called 'Ary.' He is not much of a figure, but the heroine is an immortal siren who tempts Ary from his duty and loyalty. For this Leila, as the daughter of Lilith, is possessed of an enigmatic charm, is freed from the idea of sin, and is the secular incarnation of *la volupté*. Ary succumbs to the ineluctable power of love and 'puts the infinite into an embrace'—two typically Francian *motifs*. Another one is found in the final prayer of the unsatisfied Leila :

> O God, promise me death in order that I may enjoy life. Give me remorse, in order that I may truly feel pleasure. God, make me the equal of the daughters of Eve.

This plea recalls the old refrain about the women who found in guilty love an added attraction, 'the pleasure of damning their souls.'

If that were all of the story, one could agree with those who rank it highly.[15] But its artistic unity seems to be marred by the amount of attention given to an old scholar, a sort of moonstruck Bonnard, who sees everything in terms of the Pre-Adamites. He is thereby enabled to interpret the race of Lilith to Ary, his former pupil, who comes to confess their criminal passion. But the garrulity of the aged scholar interferes with our acceptance of that passion on the tragic plane. And anyhow the dire consequences of an ancient myth (which may derive from Bayle's *Dictionary*) seem out of place in modern circumstances and setting.

When France becomes entirely modern, the results are still less satisfactory. It is true that he tries to retain whiffs of the preternatural :—in 'M. Pigeonneau' by dabbling once more with hypnotism;[16] in 'l'Œuf rouge' by using a mystical egg to impart delusions of grandeur to a suggestible youth. This lad, by the way, is represented as connected with the author's school-days and resembles such sensitive adolescents as Cyrille or Mouron pour-les-petits-oiseaux. But the story is a blend of the anecdotal with the clinical manner, which is nearer to Maupassant than to the true Anatole. As for 'Miss Morgan,' the enterprising young lady from Chicago, who is supposed to bend M. Pigeonneau to her wishes through the marvellous power of a cat's eyes,—she is entirely incredible.

One singular feature of 'l'Œuf rouge' is that it is preluded by a summary of France's own tale of *Jocaste;* the author declares that both *nouvelles* are built on the principle of auto-suggestion. Other such analogies are pointed out by M. Carias. Not only is Bonnard recalled by the servant in 'La Fille de Lilith,' but M. Pigeonneau is also extremely like the good Sylvestre, whose 'amiable manias' he exaggerates. 'Balthasar' may link with the pictures in Pierre's old family Bible. Even such a slight thing as 'Le Réséda du Curé'—concerning a priest who fears the beauty of flowers—anticipates the temptation and damnation of the ascetic Paphnuce.[17]

§ 3

'Now speak they, now say they, now tell they the tale.' The tale of Thaïs, the courtesan who became a saint, has been related in many countries and many tongues. Bearing traces of its desert origins, it dates back, in a Syriac compilation, to the seventh century after Christ. Still informed with the ascetic spirit, it was transcribed in late Greek monasteries and by Latin schoolmen, such as Rufinus. Reaching the heart of Germany in the tenth century, it was dramatized by Hrotswitha, the Benedictine nun who was called the 'eleventh Muse.' Nearly three hundred years later, Bishop Marbodius (a name familiar to readers of *l'Ile des Pingouins*) made a metrical version less distinguished than the rimed prose of Hrotswitha. The long-dead courtesan really became celebrated when she was embalmed in the *Legenda Aurea* of Voragine (*c.* 1260) and the *Vitæ Patrum* of Rosweyd.[18] Many renderings of her story trailed after these. She became so famous that she could be sung of by Villon; presented (under an alias) by Erasmus in his *Colloquies;* cited as an *exemplum* by Jacques de Vitry and other moralists.[19] Thus she attained her apogee in the faith-loving atmosphere of the Middle Ages, when she entered the Old French vernacular. There were also a number of manuscript versions. But during the polite centuries, Thaïs in her Latin form was again edited by learned Churchmen, such as the Pères Bollandistes. And in 1761 her tale is significantly revived and modernized in the *Vies des Pères des déserts,* compiled by a certain Marin. From 1839-45 the scholarly Charles Magnin wrote his article on Hrotswitha and published his translation of her dramas. Knowing nearly all the printed sources above-mentioned, Anatole France was well-documented for his poem and his novel. The latter (1889-90) is credited with giving to Thaïs 'a new lease on life.' Massenet's opera and various more recent versions have aided in keeping her name before the public. The name itself (as is also the case with Paphnutius) was given to more than one woman of her type—a circumstance which has led to some confusion. For example, our Thaïs is not the one treated either by Terence or by Dante or by Dryden. In 1899-1900, the mummy of a woman called 'Thaïs' was discovered, surrounded by sacred objects, in a necropolis at Antinoë. Near her lay the mummy of a certain Sarapion, a name which, in the earliest MSS. and the Greek texts, was connected with the conversion of the historical courtesan. It seems likely that this is our Thaïs and that our Paphnuce was originally this Sarapion, since the change of names was not made until the late Latin texts.

The complicated question of what Anatole used among all the legends will be considered presently. First, let us collect the facts regarding the composition and publication of his novel. After printing his early and rather sketchy poem in the *Chasseur bibliographe,* he let the subject lapse for twenty years. Then a series of events revived his interest in Thaïs and the monks of the 'Thébaïde,' i.e., the Egyptian desert. In 1888, the marionettes of a certain M. Signoret began performing in Paris a series of ancient plays, and France expressed in *Le Temps* the hope that the dramas of the Abbess Hrotswitha might be added to the repertoire. That prayer was heard: the puppets enacted the play of *Abraham* (containing the story of St. Mary the Egyptian), and France reviewed the performance most favourably. Furthermore, in examining a work on St. Anthony, A.F. gave a lengthy account of the solitary lives led in the Thébaïde, the visions and temptations of the monks.[20] In the meantime there had appeared a volume which was to furnish France with a large amount of his antidote to asceticism. This was Victor Brochard's treatise on *Les Sceptiques grecs* (1887), which in turn was reviewed in *Le Temps*. Indeed, Anatole could do no less for this courtly intimate of the house on the Avenue Hoche, and it is in a courtly manner that our author acknowledges what *Thaïs* owes to Brochard's treatment of Pyrrhonism.

With these and other stimulants, it is not surprising that A.F., according to his habit, found his imagination aided in recurring to one of his early themes. His incomplete correspondence reveals only a little about the stages of the novel's composition. By 1888 the manuscript was already under way, for in August of that year he wrote Mme. de Caillavet that he felt better in the 'hair-shirt of Paphnuce' than in the role of Gérôme. This confession is followed by an interesting letter:

> Since you want to know where your poor friend has gone, he has been at Alexandria. There he was present at a play. He saw Thaïs playing the role of Polyxena in a tragic pantomime.

After explaining that he met in the desert a naked old man, whom he lifted from Brochard, Anatole goes on:

> I am beginning to be amused by this Abbé Paphnuce. He serves as a distraction from life and things in general. He arose from our conversations and therefore it's a secret that we share. I have certainly bored you enough by relating his adventures.[21]

When completed, the novel was submitted to Brunetière, then assistant editor of the *Revue des deux mondes*. It was rejected at first, and when finally accepted, certain cuts and alterations were demanded. The exasperated author wrote of the editors as 'ces imbéciles.' The only other allusion to *Thaïs* in his letters has to do with the mounting of Massenet's opera, an arrangement to which the novelist took some exception.[22]

What were France's intentions in composing the tale? They were naturally complex, but some preliminary points may be gathered from his own statements. We may take it as understood, I think, that he desired above all to make a thing of beauty. And in addition, he wanted (as in *Balthasar*, etc.) to return to that ancient world which he had given up as hopeless at the time when he wrote *Jean Servien*. But he once told Corday that his ambitions impelled him less to scatter local colour than to 'do a philosophical novel'—a desire expressed in the sub-title of 'conte philosophique,' which *Thaïs* bore when serialized for the *Revue des deux mondes*. These and other intentions are elaborated in two important first-hand documents: an unfinished 'projet de préface,' written in answer to attacks on the novel in the *Etudes religieuses;* an explanatory article for the readers of *l'Univers illustré,* followed by several 'fragments inédits.'[23]

Anatole's incomplete preface declares that the original sub-title of 'conte philosophique' was used to warn off certain worthy magazine readers who might find the matters dealt with too complex for their simplicity. Under the protection of 'Sainte Thaïs,' he has adapted the legend to his own purposes. He mentions, as his inspirations, the 'old Coptic story,' related in Latin by Rufinus and revived in the *Vies des Pères des déserts*. The more modern Reverend Father who reviewed and excoriated him (the Abbé Brucker) is handled gently, though with veiled sarcasm: this Abbé had read *Thaïs* so carefully that he allowed himself to be inducted by Anatole into certain errors. Which proves that the devil is subtle. . . The preface comes to an abrupt end with a cryptic suggestion of headings to be developed:

> '1° dire que je n'ai pas voulu conter la vraie histoire.
> '2° la conter.
> ... ...
> 'Laissez-nous vos légendes si vous n'en faites rien.'[24]

The article of 1894 is interesting partly because (after the necessary compliments to Massenet) it amplifies the cryptic headings above. France asserts that he did *not* want primarily to 'tell the tale' of Saint Thaïs as found in sacred history; nor did he want to 'restore the Alexandrian world by means of local colour.' It was rather modern colouring and modern thought that he used to redecorate the legend, wherefore his version remains primarily a philosophical novel. Thaïs going up is balanced by Paphnuce going down, because divine justice is different from the human kind. Furthermore, if people object that there is no philosophical conclusion and too many contradictions, why, all the better. Thus is inculcated 'philosophical doubt,' leading to indulgence, pity, and all the best virtues. And in opposition to the capital sin of Pride, Anatole's story advocates (as even a prelate has noticed) 'simplicity of heart and mind.'

After these tidbits, some of which are sugar-coated, one is about ready for the main meal. But since this comes in several courses, let us glance at their array.

First, the poem of 1867 was really a *hors d'œuvre* to the feast. We have seen that while this follows the usual legend regarding the conversion of Thaïs, it contains nothing about the infatuation and the downfall of Paphnuce. Secondly, according to Couchoud, there exists 'une nouvelle de quinze pages à laquelle France avait donné le nom de *Sainte Thaïs*.'[25] Thirdly came the original manuscript or *brouillon* of the novel, which we will call MS. *A*. A later form of the manuscript (MS. *B*), which the printer may have followed, is deposited in the Bibliothèque Nationale.[26] The fifth version, in our reckoning, is the serialization in the *Revue des deux mondes,* July 1 and 15, August 1, 1889. The sixth is the 'édition originale' (*princeps* for short), published by Lévy nominally in '1891,' really on October 14, 1890. A number of pages are here added (Anatole would probably say 'restored') to the serial form. An edition of 1921, 'revue et corrigée' by the author, contains very few changes. And finally there is the definitive text of the *Œuvres complètes* (Vol.V), with its apparatus.

In this bibliographical medley, the only forms that need detain us now are MS. *A* and the serialization. The present writer is fortunate in having been enabled to make a close examination of France's working manuscript. The more technical results of this are relegated to our Appendix C, but some general points may well be presented at this stage.

The holograph manuscript of *Thaïs,*[27] consisting of 402 pages, is neither complete nor consecutive. It presents several large gaps, especially in Part I of the novel. By way of compensation many pages appear in two, or even three, reworkings. There are ten *liasses* or bundles of sheets, of which the first three are of great interest. They indicate that the grotto-scene (temptation and conversion) was France's point of departure in constructing the novel. And they show, through abundant alterations, that the banquet-scene, whether as a culinary or a philosophic feast, was truly a *pièce de résistance*. In fact, throughout the *liasses,* there are incessant stylistic revisions, evincing a constant effort toward increased elegance, precision, or effective description. Furthermore, the numerous deletions and short-cuts in the printed text make for more 'sobriety' and condensation. This first draft of *Thaïs* also confirms what we have been led to suspect elsewhere. It proves that the author composed slowly, with a loving care, by a process of fitting various bits of marquetry together. The dovetailing, or overlapping from one section to another, which involves much refashioning, shows particularly his skill as a joiner. From the standpoint of the development of his ideas, this MS. likewise offers much fascinating material.

It has been observed that the serial form of the novel omitted passages which were later restored to the *princeps*. In all, these amount to some twenty-six book-pages, found mainly in Parts I and II. The editorial intention (unfulfilled) was to compress the material into two issues of the magazine, instead of three; and the editorial view was doubtless that the 'cuts' would be mostly repetitions or elaborations of points already made—or else they were points that need not be made at all. Thus, the deletions concern the ascetic life of Paphnuce, his visions, certain incidents in the desert or in Alexandria, and some of the more boldly speculative dialogue in the banquet-scene. But from France's particular angle, it was desirable to emphasize fully both the monasticism of the Thébaïde and the contrasting Epicurean scepticism which abounded at the banquet.

A certain critic once exclaimed: 'De quoi *Thaïs* n'est-elle pas le pastiche ?'—'Is there anything that *Thaïs* does not imitate ?'[28] Indeed, next to *Salammbô,* where the background is more cumbersome, our story is the most arresting as well as the most heavily documented modern example of a fine fictional resurrection of antiquity. How does France manage this superb weaving of many materials into an even pattern ? To understand that, we must observe the quantity and variety of his sources. But some fifty authors of all periods have been brought forward as contributing streams to the placid flow of *Thaïs*. It would take a volume to discuss them all. One's treatment must be limited to stating the most plausible results of investigations made either by oneself or others.[29]

Three kinds of material may be distinguished: the story of the reformed courtesan, as found in the usual legends; embellishments regarding personages or background, drawn both from ancient and modern authors; and Anatole's own essential additions.

What we may call the standardized clerical version appears with practically no changes in Rosweyd, in Migne, and in the *Acta Sanctorum* of the Bollandist Fathers. It is likely that France knew this text, which in each edition runs only to a few hundred words and is therefore very brief as compared with his own elaboration. What we can assert positively is that he was well acquainted with the similar but smoother renderings found in the *Legenda Aurea* and the *Vies des Pères des déserts.* His frequent and familiar references to the former work need no recapitulation. In addition to Voragine's original text of the *Legenda,* he probably used Brunet's translation of 1843.[30] The 'Projet de Préface' cited above mentions the popularity in its time of Marin's *Vies des Pères,* and later A.F. acknowledges his indebtedness to the 'fifty lines' (there are really twelve pages) in this text.[31] Since this plain statement may be accepted at face-value, and since the work has the added merit of rarity, it seems best to present some appropriate passages from the *Vies de Pères* *—the fullest of all these versions. The curious reader may thereby follow France's processes.

Thus, as so often elsewhere, our author relies upon the saints' lives for his basic material, which he expands to serve his own ends. As he had already done in the poem on *Sainte Thaïs* (whose analogies with the novel have been sufficiently set forth), he draws from one or another of the standardized versions much of what he needs regarding life in the desert, Paphnuce's early career, his first interest in Thaïs, her corruption and fame as a courtesan, the bloody quarrels to which her beauty gave occasion. In the same sources are found the outlines of the monk's visit to 'a certain city in Egypt,' of the worldly disguise which he assumed there, of the conversion which he effected. Save for a few touches concerning the richness and the privacy of the retreat (where yet the eye of God could penetrate), the grotto is not described in the legends. As in the novel, the repentant Thaïs throws herself at the monk's feet and asks for a respite; but in the original, it is she and not Paphnuce who conceives the idea of burning her property. In both cases, she is docile to the monk's

* See Appendix D.

directions, is led to the nunnery, sealed up in a cell, and provided only with bread and water. (The interlude, about Paphnuce on the pillar, is elaborated partly from Little Pierre's reminiscences of St. Simeon Stylites, partly from the account of that hero in the *Acta Sanctorum.*) The standard texts contain the consultation with St. Anthony regarding the penance and absolution of Thaïs; and they contain also the vision of St. Paul the Simple, according to which the contrite sinner is, prophetically, welcomed by three Virgins into heaven. In Anatole's story, Paphnuce returns to the nunnery to find a dying Thaïs; but in the *Golden Legend* and elsewhere, her edifying end lasts two or three weeks.

People have thought that Hrotswitha's drama gave A.F. the first conception of his novel and that the latter 'follows closely' this German-Latin development of the tale.[32] Neither statement is quite correct. Mme. Pouquet does not take into account France's previous poem, and Mr. Kuehne does not admit that nearly everything that he attributes to Hrotswitha could have been found as well in the standardized versions—e.g., the *Acta Sanctorum,* whence the German version largely derives. Still, it is true that in 1888-89 the critic of *Le Temps* showed much interest in Hrotswitha's *Abraham,* as enacted by the puppets already mentioned, and he discourses likewise about her *Paphnutius.*[33] He revived this double theme in an address given before a 'Little Theatre' group in March, 1890. The conversion-scenes run parallel in these two closet-dramas, of which the *Abraham* is considered the better. Both of them, with others, Anatole read about the same time in the translation of Charles Magnin.[34] He probably used the *Callimachus* of Hrotswitha for the 'hideous' transformation of Paphnuce at the very end (which also resembles Leconte de Lisle's 'Agonie d'un Saint' in *Poèmes barbares*). But apart from occasional touches, he seems to have laid her *Paphnutius* under direct contribution only as regards the introduction of the Abbess, Albine, who receives the sinning woman into the convent and later tells the monk about her piety, in terms similar to those employed by Hrotswitha. We should concede, however, that the puppets of Signoret and Magnin's translation of these naïve Latin playlets did fan the flame of an old inspiration.

We pass to the second type of sources—those that stand apart from the legend proper. On that airy scaffolding France had to erect a solid structure; and his masonry must body forth first of all a plausible environment for his characters and action. For his colourful descriptions of the Nile valley, he seems to have used certain geographical periodicals. For the kind of life led there, he drew from the works of Amélineau and of Maspéro, the Egyptologist, to both of whom he refers several times. (The latter's *Histoire ancienne des peuples de l'orient* is responsible for the sub-titles 'Le Lotus' and 'Le Papyrus.') More particularly, for the ascetics of the Thébaïde, he adapted material not only from the *Vies des Pères* and *La Légende dorée,* but from other lives of such characters as a certain Schnoudi[35] and 'le Grand Saint-Antoine.' These lives were fully discussed in *Le Temps;* and the reviews contain numerous touches familiar to the readers of *Thaïs.* Both of these saints were exposed to temptations of the flesh, practiced rigorous penances, often fared on bread and salt, lived in deserted tombs decorated with pictures, had ecstasies or visions, and were beset either by beasts or by Satan himself. But while Schnoudi was a severe ascetic, Anthony (after Athanasius) was a joyous, healthy, authoritative kind of person, even as A.F.'s tale represents him.

Yet his chief source for much of this, as for some other matters, was rather Flaubert's *Tentation de Saint-Antoine,* without which notable precedent Anatole could hardly have got his *Thaïs* written.[36] Several times in the *Vie littéraire* the *Tentation* is mentioned, and once France expresses his interest in the album of illustrations by Henri Rivière, which may have helped inspire one or more of his own figures. Flaubert, too, had gone to the desert and portrayed the visions that haunted its saints, together with their self-inflicted privations. But his St. Anthony hardly resembles the 'grand Saint-Antoine' whom A.F. built up: Flaubert's tormented eremite is more like Paphnuce, whether as a character-study or through the nature of his temptations. The preliminary seductions are in each case of the same type; the Ammonaria of the elder saint was not without her counterpart for the younger one; and although the (oft-mentioned) jackals occur elsewhere, they abound, as symbols of carnal evil, only in the *Tentation* and in *Thaïs.* The whole account of Paphnuce's residence in the tomb, whether with regard to visions, voices, or voluptuous sirens, is closer to the *Tentation* than to anything else. Some further analogies: that extraordinary work contains several passages which probably influenced part of the dialogue in

France's banquet-scene. In both writers are found a similar apologia for Judas, similar statements regarding the rehabilitation and worship of the Serpent. Both St. Anthony and Paphnuce have a horror of Arianism. When Marcus the Arian appears at France's symposium he is described as having a pointed skull, a trait attributed to Flaubert's Gnostic, Valentin. Other likenesses could be traced in the discussions of various heresies. The figure of Zénothemis, who is France's Gnostic, emanates mainly from Renan's *Histoire d'Israël;* but the story told by him regarding Eunoia has evident resemblances to the same symbol of the *Ewigweibliches* as described by Flaubert. In each case Eunoia passes through many incarnations, the most significant of which is Helen of Troy, and in each form she submits herself to all manner of persons, whether as a scapegoat for other women or in expiation of the crimes of men. Although France's serene Helen differs from the weak tool whom the magician manages in Flaubert's episode, it seems quite likely that the latter story prompted the allegory of Zénothemis.

There are also a number of more incidental influences upon *Thaïs.* Renan again, as so often, exercises something of a pervasive discipline, especially for the usual lessons in philosophic relativity, comparative religion, and Pyrrhonism. It is held that the Scriptural language employed in *Thaïs* could be parcelled out between the author of *Les Apôtres* and the Vulgate—to say nothing of the Church Fathers. Renan is also supposed to have inspired certain 'tirades,' as well as that derogatory tone towards Jehovah (the 'Iaveh des juifs') which various speakers adopt.[37] Among other modern sources, one may mention Chateaubriand's *Les Martyrs,* as aiding the description of the secret rites and persecutions of the early Christians; Jules Soury, for the nostalgic religiosity, the mingling of cults and desires that characterized France's Thaïs no less than his Leuconoë; and Lacroix' *Histoire de la Prostitution,* for the courtesan's training and even the names of her companions. There A.F. learned much about the Alexandrian flute-players who attended the banquets of the wealthy. The scene where Paphnuce visits the theatre was suggested by one ancient and the play represented derives from another—namely the *Hecuba* of Euripides. At times the role of Polyxena, assigned to Thaïs, follows the Greek drama rather closely.

With regard to the origins of the whole tale, Anatole himself once gave an account of its 'hour-glass' construction. He told Corday that in reading about two contemporary assassins, he had been much struck by their final repentance ; they were worthy to 'sit on the right hand of the Lord,' while their unshriven victim should burn in hell. Similarly Paphnuce would achieve the salvation of his proselyte, while the monk himself should be eternally damned.[38] But this modern anecdote can hardly bear the whole weight of that conception : it could also spring naturally from the author's fondness for paradox and his hatred of monks, chemically uniting in the familiar atmosphere of saints' lives. There was much in A.F.'s past to induce him into the retelling of the Thaïs legend, while immediate stimuli were provided by the Hrotswitha-Signoret-Magnin combination.

Still in the way of sources, there remains to be considered the banquet-scene, with contingent problems.

That famous scene, quite individual and Anatolian in its total effect, yet has a luxurious family-tree. One of its ancestors is supposed to be Louis Ménard. We have already noted that this retiring figure exerted something of a silent influence among the Parnassians and that his Hellenism was much like the kind professed by France. In his critical articles for *Le Temps* A.F. barely mentions the name of Ménard, but there is strong evidence that he was acquainted with the elder writer's work.[39] In 1876, the latter published his *Rêveries d'un païen mystique,* containing two items of interest to us. The 'Banquet d'Alexandrie' is akin to the philosophical symposium in *Thaïs,* since in both places religion is the chief topic, and the interlocutors discuss ancient mythology, Christianity, and Gnosticism. The Manicheism to which France is addicted is anticipated by Ménard, while his Origen relates in germ the story of the serpent and the apple, which A.F.'s Zénothémis expands. Ménard also dwells on the identification of the deities in various cults, a favourite topic with France. Some of the considerations in each work on the creation of the world are very much alike. In general, however, the resemblances are less in particular passages than in topics and tone—and some find that Ménard has the advantage here because of the pure and lofty ethos of his discourses.[40]

This symposium, involving dialogue about favourite themes, is of the type that Anatole particularly loved. The notion of such a feast, with discussions *en extra,* seems to hark back to the *Satyricon* of Petronius, especially for the kinds of food served at Cotta's house and the hedonistic atmosphere. The general plan of the two banquets is also somewhat similar, but for the philosophical conversations in *Thaïs* we must turn elsewhere—and not only to Ménard. A good deal of the sceptical doctrine, served with Anatole's usual relish, derives from Brochard's book. In addition to the acknowledgments already mentioned, there are two plain statements of A.F.'s indebtedness: in one (if correctly reported), he told Mme. de C. that 'between ourselves, the banquet is not France's—it is Brochard's'; in another he declares that in the serialization of the novel, 'there are about ten pages which I would never have written, if I had not read M. Brochard.'[41] This last tribute is at the end of a review of *Les Sceptiques grecs,* and the review itself finds some echoes in *Thaïs.* The 'ten pages' mentioned contain principally an exposition of Pyrrhonic doubt, mainly through the mouths of Nicias and Dorion, utterances which can be matched with a number of passages in Brochard's treatise. These concern the Sceptic's attitude toward action, his difficulty in finding a rule of life, his questioning of the moral law and the perfection of the gods. Nicias (or Dorion) agrees with Pyrrho as to the uncertainty, hence the indifferent evaluation of all things: 'What are good and evil?'; in the eyes of God, 'le mal est un bien'; we cannot reach to inner essences, and trusting to our erring senses, we are often led astray. So let us suspend judgment, in the Pyrrhonic manner, and recognize that opinion is all—and nothing. There was much in this last point, as in Pyrrho's balancing of *pro* and *con,* that coincided with France's general outlook.[42]

On a more positive basis, Eucrite, the Stoic, clashes with Nicias on the question of virtue. Zénothémis echoes a phrase of Brochard's to the effect that sentiment is a surer guide than reason in seeking to attain truth. (We are reminded of like statements by A.F., during his sentimental period.) Nicias often expresses Francian themes, and these are in some cases reworded from Brochard. An ascetic and sceptical type, appearing earlier in the novel, is Timocles of Cos. He is the motionless figure, physically resembling Flaubert's gymnosophist, whom Paphnuce meets in the desert. But the character and conversation of this 'vieillard nu,' completely agnostic and apathetic, is synthesized from Brochard's depiction of Pyrrho. Further philosophical material, especially as voiced by Eucrite (who commits suicide) is drawn from Epictetus and Marcus Aurelius. Still other speakers recall writers as diverse as Irenæus, Renan, and again Louis Ménard.

Quite apart from banquets, the last-named author also wrote a tale called 'La Légende de Saint-Hilarion.' This too is found in the *Rêveries d'un païen mystique*. It has been held that 'the framework of the novel [*Thaïs*], the gist of the situation and characters' are taken immediately from Ménard's legend ; but surely this is going too far.[43] The temptation theme is the chief similarity in the two treatments. Like Paphnuce, the ascetic Hilarion tries to redeem the soul of a beautiful sinner and falls in love with his ward as he bears her away to a convent, where she is entrusted to the mother superior. (This personage may have given Anatole some further hints for his Albine.) Each of the modern authors has added a note of passion to his ancient legend : both monks regret their lost opportunities, have visions of the loved one after separation, and feel estranged from thoughts of God.[44] There are definite resemblances to Hilarion's dilemma in the remorse of Paphnuce and in the way he confuses his impure passion with the salvationist's zeal. But the former's expression of penitence and jealousy is mild when compared with that of Paphnuce, and the element of sensuality is more pronounced in the latter case. We shall find that France's conception of his monk's evolution—from asceticism and harshness to obsessions and ultimate degradation—is his own peculiar contribution. Furthermore, the *facture* and descriptive talent evinced in *Thaïs* owe little or nothing to Ménard. But the twist by which the saintly Paphnuce of the standardized legend is turned into an amorous visionary probably owes something to the story of Hilarion.

§ 4

WHAT are France's personal additions to the amalgam formed from this medley of sources ? They seem to have three main trends : he must furnish background and substance, where these are still lacking ; he must bring out what he called the 'moral idea,' or thesis ; and to that end he must alter the characters and their roles. Background is provided generally in the depiction of the seductive Alexandrian civilization, with its diverse creeds and outlooks; and more particularly through the full development of the courtesan's early religious experiences, together with the introduction of the Christian martyr, Ahmès. This preparation better paves the way for the ultimate conversion of Thaïs, which is more plausibly worked up than in the brief standardized accounts. She receives Paphnuce with a peculiar Anatolian blend of coquetry and credulity. The whole grotto-scene, so important for our author, is, barring a few details taken from the legend, his own elaboration. The care with which he composed his setting and staged his personages is attested by various corrections and addenda to the manuscript. In keeping with his enlargement of the power and prestige of Thaïs, her abode is magnified into a luxurious home, fully described.

But more power is also given to Paphnuce. In the novel, it is he and not Thaïs who orders the conflagration of her belongings and who mingles his exhortations with the accompanying riot. Both during the banquet-scene and after the exit of the now savage Paphnuce from that symposium, we are made aware of what France meant by turning the tale in a modern 'philosophic' direction. Evidently, the 'Renanizer,' the 'renegade,' as he was variously termed,[45] is interested in all the phenomena of belief. His own moral conclusion is delayed a little in transmission: it is after the monk has left Thaïs in her cell that the author's anti-clerical, anti-ascetic message becomes imperative. Paphnuce's erotic visions were not without precedent; but the acrid, unhappy character of these obsessions is underscored by Anatole. The cenobite's penance on the pillar is exaggerated into the creation of 'Stylopolis,' a sort of burlesque on Lourdes. For complete illustration of the thesis, the mad monk goes from bad to worse. In Paul's dream, while roses are ready for Thaïs, demons are lying in wait for Paphnuce's soul. With this announcement of the Damnation *motif,* France prepares to leave the legend finally. The unedifying degradation of Paphnuce, though hinted at in two parallels to *Thaïs,* is substantially A.F.'s own invention. 'This antithesis,' says Provost, 'was well fitted to tempt the ironical spirit of France.' It may also have appeased the spirit of Little Pierre and assuaged his long rancours against the priests of Stanislas. This predecessor of theirs has rashly violated natural laws and defied *la Volupté:* it is this life-force, 'Vénus toute entière,' that causes his undoing. For Anatole, pagan Nemesis is by no means outmoded.

With this main intention in our minds, certain additional points regarding the plot and characters in *Thaïs* can appear in a clearer perspective. When E. M. Forster speaks of the novel's 'hour-glass' construction, he probably wishes to indicate the rise-and-fall type of plot, the fact that as the sands of the hero's faith diminish and run out, so do those of the heroine increase. 'J'ai voulu,' says the author, 'que Paphnuce perdît son âme en voulant sauver celle de Thaïs.' [46] The paradox or topsy-turvyness involved is the first signal use of a formula to which France became more and more addicted.

It is essential to Anatole's purpose that Paphnuce should become repulsive and ridiculous ; this, together with the love-motive, is his strongest individual bias given to the legend. Otherwise stated (in modern jargon), the case of Paphnuce, like that of many anchorites in the Thébaïde, is a case of suppressed desires becoming unduly prominent ; and it seems good psychology that his 'mysticisme passionel' should gradually change its direction.[47] Two-thirds of the novel are devoted to the evolution of Paphnuce, who is thus made the outstanding character. But the author so manages that the transformation of saint into sinner is a very gradual thing. We first meet him as an earnest and worthy anchorite, and we learn that like many such he was nobly born and well-educated. His adolescent memory of Thaïs is the grain of mustard-seed which will develop into an unsightly growth, aided by the grim concentration of his temperament. In Alexandria, he becomes increasingly rude and savage, whether towards Thaïs or the kindly Nicias. His strongly ambitious nature—for desire of various sorts is his bane—succumbs to what Seillière terms 'three subtle demons : Lust, Doubt and Pride.' The doubts and miseries that bewilder and anormalize him are carefully handled to prevent his becoming a sympathetic figure. His utterly damnable finish seems a foregone conclusion, though it may be that before the end France too is obsessed by *his* mania—the hatred of the priest. It can scarcely be said that he holds evenly the scales of justice, for he has admitted, in his *Discours* to the Academy, that he could not understand the soul of a monk. Rod has pointed out the similarity in theme, but the difference in tone between 'Scolastica' and *Thaïs.* The latter shows a kind of rage, and 'one would say that the author detests his hero.' Yet, as in *Les Noces corinthiennes,* he offsets the fanatic type by simpler and sweeter Christian personages, such as Ahmès, Palémon, Paul le Simple, and St. Anthony — all of whom are believers in happiness and relatively normal ways of life.[48]

With reference to Thaïs herself, she undergoes a more human metamorphosis. Although until the banquet-scene she may appear as a symbol of the clerical idea that Woman is perdition,[49] that view is not maintained by the author, who prefers to make her an incarnation of loveliness and life. Lest this should be too abstract an ideal, she is humanized by her caprices, her superstitions, and especially her fears of old age, of losing her beauty, and of death. But she is released from these last fears even as they are fulfilled, and if the grace of the Lord is efficacious, her own grace is almost 'sufficient.' Her charm is so abounding (by the will of her creator) that her inspiriting presence binds the guests at the banquet, says Doumic, 'to speak only of love, beauty and truth.'[50] The monologue of Albine towards the end is deliberately inserted as a prelude to the apotheosis of this heroine.

Most of the themes and *motifs* in *Thaïs* have been anticipated in the preceding discussion. Those that are most closely connected with France's idiosyncrasies centre round the familiar opposition of what he considers a sensible philosophy — Epicurean or sceptical — to Christian asceticism. The recurrent *motif* of the violet-eyed beauty of Thaïs, the banquet-scene as representing Anatole's Utopia of leisurely, cultivated, classical conversations, are in the Epicurean strain, in opposition to which Paphnuce's mania is the gross discordant note. Yet it has been remarked, first that Paphnuce is not so impossible at the beginning, and also that France throughout veils his insidious attack by an apparent sympathy for certain manifestations of the early Church. The atmosphere of the old saints' lives, whether regarding Ahmès or Anthony, is consistently maintained. As for Paphnuce, before he reaches Alexandria, he is no different from a dozen others of his kind. But from then on : 'Fragile are the virtues of the anchorites.' The mild judgment of Nicias, that Paphnuce 'lacked Atticism,' is an understatement : he also secreted bile. So he execrates the nobility of Nicias, wants him to burn his books (as Thaïs did with her treasures), is rabid against Marcus the Arian, and views women, precisely because they are the torch-bearers of beauty and pleasure, as creatures to be scorned and feared. No dream of fair creations for *him!* What could be sadder than the spectacle of a human being who deliberately pulls his hood over his eyes, 'pour ne plus voir la beauté des choses' ?

The reaction thus excited in the reader is encouraged by many passages in praise of beauty and love and gracious living. The loveliness of Thaïs is conspicuous whether she appears as actress, as courtesan, or allegorically as Woman. In the first capacity, she interests Anatole, because like Isabelle Constant or Elise Devoyod, she can embody the various and mutable element in femininity; and in the role of Polyxena, 'she gave to all the spectators the tragic thrill of beauty.' This power stirred the whole city, for she seemed to clothe with her grace all the diverse forms of life. She induced in the beholders a vision of happy, well-ordered things and thus, symbolically, appeared as 'the divine centre of the world's harmonies.' As courtesan, she reaches her climax in the grotto, when she confides to her mirror that her arms are the 'true chains of love,' when she declares that she is famous because she strews *la volupté* in her path, and when her languorous, waiting, mock-modest pose drives Paphnuce almost to madness. At the banquet, in her long mauve garment, she impresses even her rivals as being harmony incarnate. In her allegorical diversity, she can remind Callicrates of the eternal feminine and seem the last avatar of Helen. In the tomb she can appear to Paphnuce as the player of the cinnor (Hebrew lyre) and tempt him as the synthesis of mysterious beauty. And in her own person, she comes to him recapitulating all her previous roles: in the voluptuous veil of the grotto; pensive in her mauve gown as at the banquet; tragically lovely as at the theatre. Indeed she would say with Marcelle and a dozen other heroines of Anatole's making: 'Je suis née pour charmer les hommes.' The love that she awakens in them, whether pagan and sensuous, as with Lollius and Nicias, or confused with apostolic fervour and alternating with repulsion, as in the case of Paphnuce, is of the most stirring kind.

The other chief manifestation of beauty is, again, in France's resuscitation of antiquity. From the Alexandrian point of view, we have a wistful *Rückblick* cast upon many things, from Greek tragedy to Roman statesmanship in the person of Cotta. The speakers at the banquet feel that the palmy days are over and that they are living in the shadow of barbarism. Their vision is obscured, their myrtles are in ashes. But better for them and for Anatole are the memories of former years than the clamours of the new superstitions. If the ancient sages are now in hell, they keep there the nobility that marked their earthly walk. Thus the banquet scene is a *clou* to France's humanism, and that is why Nicias is his mouthpiece regarding things of the flesh and the spirit.

In the large this Nicias, like the Abbé Coignard, stands for the natural unfettered life. Nature for him, as for A.F., is tolerant and all-embracing; she is so broad that she can include the ugly, as a necessary background for the beautiful. Perhaps that is why Nicias tolerates even Paphnuce in his pride. The Epicureanism and the scepticism of this spokesman are conjoined along familiar lines. Recognizing that we perceive no certain foundations for things, that opinion is a trickster, that we can apprehend only what our erring senses transmit, and that illusion is lord, the conclusion is: 'Goûtons la vie!' Let us taste life, urges Nicias, through these same deluding senses, let us taste especially its finest forms—such as Thaïs—and bear with the others, such as Paphnuce. If philosophy is stuffed with inane systems, yet there remains the 'ineffable desire,' which each pursues according to his own dream, sensual rather than intellectual. For desire is the lightning-flash which illuminates the passing cloud of beauty. And Nicias dares maintain this attitude against the sterner virtues of the Stoic. When he bids Thaïs farewell, he thanks her for the illusory happiness which she, a fleeting shadow, once brought to him, another baseless fabric, on the surface of this deceiving world.

Perhaps the best answer to such Nihilism is that *Thaïs* itself is no baseless fabric. It is in the first place, I believe—and in spite of France's protest that such was not his intention—one of the most remarkable reconstructions of antiquity done in our era. *Thaïs* alone is enough to justify the existence of the historical novel as an art-form. Its only serious rival within its period is *Salammbô;* and Flaubert, with all his merits, allowed his story to sag beneath the weight of his documentation. Not so France. The characters and the plot are sufficiently prominent, but what carries all along is his feeling for the past and his ability to weld the fifty sources into a unified whole. It would be most difficult for the general reader to find the *sutures,* the points of junction where a bit of Brochard melts with the *Golden Legend,* or where Nicias imperceptibly becomes Anatole. The chief harmonizing factor is of course the musical, individual style, which the author has by now perfected. Of this polished, 'slippery,' ornate style, with its subtle rhythms and instrumentation some examples have already been given and the whole matter will come up again in a later chapter.

What of the reception of the novel at home and abroad? Its abiding appeal may be exemplified by the fact that it has been translated into no less than eighteen languages.[51] The English, the Italians, the Americans, and the Russians have shown themselves particularly attached to the work. At home, *Thaïs* was in 1890 the book of the year. Maurel spoke of it as illustrating excellently the three major trends of Anatole as 'philosophe, érudit et poète,' and as blending a choice imagination with a voluptuous style. Benoist commented on the work as full of artistic sense-impressions which are keenly transmitted to the reader—and cleverly added that perhaps the heroine is a symbol of the essential health in Nature. Filon, with considerable acumen, brought forward an analogy between dilettantism in Alexandria and the contemporary Parisian brand; Anatole as a scholar-artist can render well 'the penetrating suavity of legends . . . and resuscitate the delicate perfume of vanished creeds'; but one grows a little weary of seeing so many Niciases around! Eugène Asse agrees with Filon as to the fine description of the desert background.[52]

In 'Gérôme's' own journal, *l'Univers illustré,* appeared a puff—presumably by O'Monroy, though conceivably 'inspired'—which stresses the popularity of the novel, mentions some of its sources, including Renan, and points significantly to France's 'aimable nihilisme moral.' It is less moral than artistic devotion that makes the superiority of *Thaïs.* Philippe Gille, in a brief notice for *Le Figaro,* observed that although the book was in all the shop-windows, its appeal was rather to 'les délicats.' Reading on the surface like a regular saint's life, it has implications that suggest one of Voltaire's philosophic tales—a point that is worth making. Its simple construction is merely a pretext for the 'ravishing' description of the pagan crossed with the Christian world.[53]

But not everybody was pleased. We have seen how Anatole paid his respects to a Jesuit Father, 'who unwittingly echoed my willing errors.' This refers to the attacks by the Reverend Père Brucker, who twice became virulent in a clerical journal.[54] His first onset, which provoked France's unpublished preface to the novel, was directed against the serialized form as it appeared in the *Revue des deux mondes*. This the Reverend Father finds simply 'detestable,' full of pornographic realism and 'philosophic' by title only. The novelist, in attempting to undermine Christianity, has learned his trade from such ravening wolves as Voltaire and Renan. The 'real' legend of Paphnutius is set off against the parody by Anatole. We are definitely informed that Paphnutius was a saint, that he did *not* seduce, nor was he seduced, and that he converted Thaïs through divine grace and not through the ignorant zeal which is attributed to him.

Before printing his second article, Brucker attacked a number of other contemporary writers, styling them all literary criminals. Then he proceeded to a general condemnation of *Thaïs* as an 'outrage against the Church, against monastic life, the honour of the saints and good morals.' Addressing himself to the least noble of our faculties (perhaps the reason ?) the author has turned a legend perfumed with Christian purity into an indecent fantasy. . . And that is that ! . . . Commenting on this aerial attack, the *Journal des Débats* remarked that the Jesuits of the *Etudes religieuses* were always bombarding writers such as France, Renan, and Lemaître.

Later opinion has not usually supported Brucker's verdict. Anatole Himself, peevishly declaring that *Thaïs* was one of his worst books (a *boutade* which we need not take seriously), admitted that along with *Le Lys rouge* it was almost universally admired.[55] The chorus of praise has swelled from the early reviewers to Carias, and from the monograph of Provost to that of Kuehne. There are many evidences that *Thaïs,* though written for an élite, has become the most widely known of France's works. Yet there remain critics with a clerical bias who, like Seillière, object to the book's pseudo-Christian impiety, or, like Giraud, to the indictment of monasticism in the person of Paphnuce.[56] But the general reader, I fancy, would be more inclined to fall in with the conclusion of M. Carias, who speaks of the abundant poetry that veils with a 'luminous innocence' the thrusts of scepticism and sensuality and reminds us how people, around 1890, replete with the brutalities of Zola, 'breathed in with a delighted surprise that "flower of warm flesh," that Thaïs of the violet eyes, whom France had decked with the double aureole of voluptuousness and holiness.' [57]

As a transitional work, *Thaïs* with its many *motifs* leads forward into the amplitude of this third period. As a personal revelation, it gives us the new and bolder France, with all his Epicurean ardour and his now unveiled scepticism. For these reasons the novel has been dwelt upon with a fulness which we cannot again allow ourselves.

§ 5

L'Etui de nacre (1892), or 'The Mother-of-Pearl Casket,' is another miscellany of tales, which the title does little to unify or explain. Perhaps the suggestion is that they are choice artistic objects, such as their author was fond of collecting. They are culled either from the columns of *Le Temps* or from *Les Autels de la peur,* which A.F. dissolved into a 'poussière de nouvelles.' [58] In their variety, the majority of these sixteen stories [59] display several of his more pronounced antiquarian bents. One of them, the most celebrated, pictures Roman Imperialism at its height; five or six reflect aspects of medieval faith, chiefly in France; six deal with the period of the Revolution; while the remaining three or four are vaguely modern. They were all composed during the eight years preceding the date of publication, the Revolutionary tales going back the farthest. Perhaps the nearest thing to a key-note is the atmosphere of legend, a kind of 'archaic grace'; or else the emphasis (in the medieval stories) on 'singleness of heart,' the endeavour of the complex Anatole to appreciate and render once more the souls possessed of a simple faith.[60]

By far the best-known title in the collection, and one which did much for France's reputation, is the remarkable 'Procurateur de Judée.' It is noted not only for its handling of the thematic discord between Rome and Jewry, but for its artistic technique, including the dexterous use of the formula mentioned in connexion with *Thaïs*. Again we find the author's paradoxical support of an idea or attitude contrary to received opinion. That Pilate in his old age at Baiae should have forgotten the Crucifixion of Christ is not only a 'surprise ending': the point is that Pilate was too busy a man to recollect an incident of minor importance in the *Weltpolitik* of a Roman governor. To that end the author must subordinate Christ and the Jews and must dwell on the responsibilities and the greatness of Pontius Pilate. Along those lines the various elements in the story are carefully arrayed and massed, so that the final surprise may come as a revelation rather than a shock.

From the beginning we are made aware of the extent of the Empire, and its cares become increasingly evident. The impressive entrance of Pilate makes us realize that here is a man who has toiled and suffered, thought and planned, for the glory of Rome. As a statesman, he resembles Cotta in *Thaïs*. His friend and foil, Ælius Lamia, is there partly to furnish an admiring audience, but still more to show how an amiable Epicureanism and a penchant for Syrian dancers meet with no approval in the stern eyes of Pilate. Bitterly does the former Procurator recall Judea—in terms of his constructive projects and how they were opposed alike by the ignorant Jews and the cabal at Rome which ultimately turned him out. That he was particularly exasperated by the Jews—their obstinacy and baseness, their tumultuous assemblies, their aversion to taxation and civic improvements, their inbred obscurantism—appears in a dozen passages. No wonder, then, that one of their many upheavals, against a certain Jesus of Nazareth, has vanished from his recollection.

Characteristically Anatolian is the suggestion that there are dozens of more or less acceptable creeds ; also the description of the beautiful landscape at the beginning ; also the more indulgent philosophy of Lamia, who reads Lucretius, muses as to the relativity of fame, and even has a good word to say for the Jews. All this is harmonized and made effective in France's best manner. He took great pains with the revision of this *nouvelle*. When it was pointed out to him that Vesuvius could not have 'smoked' some years before the great eruption, A.F. acknowledged his error and changed 'fumait' to 'riait.' And this is only one of the successive retouches which the tale underwent.[61]

The inspiration for the story as well as a good deal of the development came from Renan's *Origines du Christianisme,* especially Volume II, *Les Apôtres*.[62] Naturally, then, Renan approved of 'Le Procurateur' and of its central thesis. Following his lead, the praise has increased from that day to this. Maurras, Jean Psichari, and Edouard Rod were enthusiastic. Giraud, too, enlarges on the plausibility of the theme, while others stress the 'faultless' narrative technique.[63] True that certain critics, especially among the orthodox, look askance upon the work because of its alleged 'anti-christianisme,' which they are disposed to exaggerate.[64] While some of these cry 'Blasphemy!' others try to brush the story aside as inane and paradoxical. But even Seillière admits that it is a 'chef-d'œuvre.' That this has come to be the prevalent view is shown by the frequency with which 'Le Procurateur de Judée' is included in the short-story anthologies of various countries.

For all his sophistication, France was not ready to abandon his favourite topic of medieval legends, particularly those dealing with saints' lives and miracles. Five such tales, usually slight in structure, are found in *l'Etui de nacre*. Three of these had originally appeared in *Le Temps,* 1889-91, where two of them—'Amycus et Célestin' and 'Sainte Euphrosine'—were qualified as 'Easter Tales.' They are mostly laid in the early days of the Gallic Church when legend flourished and when the woods and fields were not yet bereft of their pagan emblems and divinities. But the conflicts of the two creeds are here handled in a mild and insinuating fashion. Anatole wishes to envelop his naïve and wonder-loving saints in the atmosphere of credulity suitable to their times. If he cannot quite become a pious scribe, he does achieve sympathy for these alien souls.[65] It is natural, however, that the unbeliever should occasionally drop his mask and expose his own very different ideals.

Typical of this opposition is the story of 'Amycus et Célestin.' As a holy hermit, Amycus celebrates Easter devoutly, though discountenanced by the heathen garlands and sundry offerings suspended from a beech-tree, or 'l'arbre des fées.' (Anatole was then writing about a similar fairy-tree and other pagan practices in connexion with Joan of Arc.) Although Amycus has spent his life in exorcising and struggling with the fairies, he feels that they are getting the better of him. In fact, they make a mock of him . . . as one of them had done with Sylvestre Bonnard. The hermit asks the Lord why he has created pagan trees and fairy fountains to excite the young. It is the moment for the advocate of Pantheism to appear. He comes in the person of Célestin, who as a jovial faun is quite willing to hail the resurrection of Christ along with that of the trees and the larks. For him the whole earth is a kind of large Easter egg. The two celebrants join forces and live happily in the hermit's abode until they both pass away and are sainted.

If there is some irony in this 'parody of hagiography,'[66] there is still more effort to write a little concordance of the creeds, which will give full value to heathen symbols. But Anatole's nostalgia for a not quite vanished paganism is more apparent in the 'Légende des Saintes Oliverie et Liberette,' whose scene is again laid in Gaul, during the fourth century. Those noble maidens, instructed by the apostle Bertauld, are persuaded to forsake the cult of Diana and lead the saintly life, in separate retreats. The lives of all three are no less edifying than vacant. Such a tale is like an empty skin which needs to be *farci:* the stuffing which France chooses is a jumble of the miraculous and the mythological. The Ardennes were then inhabited by a frightful dragon, a pleasant, spiritually-minded unicorn, together with evanescent nymphs, centaurs, and satyrs with the cloven hoof. The theme of the multiplicity of religions is again played up. Bertauld was informed by local sceptics that there were a great number of deities in the neighbourhood and that his Virgin could be paralleled by Diana, whose silver foot still trod the mountain-tops in the moonlight. Thus Anatole recalls his own beautiful stanza in *Les Noces corinthiennes.*

In 'Sainte Euphrosine,' contemporary with *Thaïs,* we move over to Alexandria. There is no diminution of holiness, but there is more sarcasm and more emphasis on what the self-made ascetics lose in this life. Euphrosine is the daughter of a wealthy citizen and receives an education which includes some startling feats in the way of celestial mathematics. She is much sought after, but despite her father's wishes, she rejects all suitors, desiring to consecrate her virginity to Christ. She has to flee from Alexandria, dressed as a boy, and finds refuge in a monastery. Curiously enough, both her father and the most persistent of her lovers presently arrive and settle down at the same monastery. It seems that they might all just as well have stayed at home. But neither of the men recognizes the disguised Euphrosine, and only the father is enlightened. It is like an eighteenth-century recognition drama. The reader is made to feel that there is little point in any of these proceedings. A mock-learned after-piece throws doubt upon the date and authenticity of Anatole's alleged source.

The better-known tale of 'Scolastica' first appeared in the

'Vie littéraire' under the title of 'Histoire des deux amants d'Auvergne.'[67] As France acknowledges, the greater part of the story was taken, without much alteration, from Gregory of Tours.[68] That part covers the narrative of how this maiden of Old France, the sister of St. Benedict, revolts against her marriage to the well-born Injuriosus and persuades him to leave her untouched throughout their lives. She even converts him to Christianity through convincing him that this life is nothing in the face of Eternity. Her persistent virginity reminds one of the plight of Saint Radegonde, in Anatole's earliest effort. Here it is again the theme of the Bride of Christ:

'When you hold out your arms to me,' says Scolastica, 'I think of the hands that were pierced with nails for the salvation of the world.'

But we have seen that our author had a personal animosity against this conception. Therefore he adds, from a supposititious manuscript, a conclusion and a moral which are not found in Gregory of Tours. Over the graves of the frustrated couple springs up a rose-bush, twining together those who kept needlessly apart in life. And a new character, Silvanus, interprets the flowers as the symbol of Eros:

> The sad Scolastica, now that she is but a vain shadow, regrets the season for loving and her lost pleasures. The roses which grow from her body and which speak for her tell us all: 'Love, ye who live. This miracle teaches us to taste of earth's joys, while there is yet time.'

A rather quaint miracle, recalling the rose-bush of St. Francis; but the lesson of *carpe rosam* is one which the Epicurean Anatole often draws, especially when confronting death.[69]

The two remaining titles of this group may be considered together, for although 'Gestas' is modern in setting, there are several reasons for bracketing it along with 'Le Jongleur de Notre-Dame' as an expression of medieval mysticism. The latter tale, which has been much admired, represents one form of a widely known 'miracle of Our Lady,' having affiliations with the story of Sister Beatrice.[70] Anatole's itinerant juggler becomes a monk and performs the tricks of his trade to honour the Virgin. In spite of the doubts of his graver brethren, the *jongleur* is rewarded when Mary steps from her pedestal to wipe his sweat-stained brow. The original twelfth-century poem ('Del Tumbeor

Nostre Dame') was retold by Gaston Paris, in *La Littérature française au moyen-âge*. Reviewing that work for *Le Temps,* in 1888, France gave a brief synopsis of the legend. His elaboration of 'Le Jongleur,' appropriately dedicated to G. Paris, includes more about Barnabé's rambling life as well as about the other monks and how they did artistic things in praise of Mary. The moral of the parable is voiced by the Prior: 'Blessèd are the simple-hearted, for they shall see God.' And others have emphasized the *sancta simplicitas* of the juggler.[71]

The fact that Anatole is in sympathy with this character, as he usually is with humble and naïve souls, is reinforced by his account of 'Gestas.' Here the setting is contemporary Paris, and the model depicted is Paul Verlaine, whose life and habits are faithfully reproduced. But the prevailing tone remains that of medieval piety, slightly travestied. This appears in various touches, bearing on Virgin-worship, purification by penance, and the like. As a motto, France uses the Saviour's words to the thief on the cross: 'Today shalt thou be with me in Paradise.' According to tradition, this thief was called 'Gestas,' and his modern namesake is to win salvation likewise by his candid faith, rather than by his 'works.' For these consist mainly of the vinous dissipations of Verlaine, who knocks about familiarly from pillar to post, from cabaret to confessional, with his heavy stick, his Socratic visage, and his air of a resurrected Silenus. He will be resurrected once more as Choulette in *Le Lys rouge*.

The sources of the more strictly medieval tales await full investigation. Apart from those already mentioned, various persons have suggested the *Acta Sanctorum,* the *Légende dorée,* the *Apologie pour Hérodote* by Henri Estienne, and even the romances of Chrétien de Troyes.

We must take a long stride to reach the stories of the Revolutionary era. One of them, the lengthy 'Mémoires d'un volontaire,' may be considered as a sort of prelude to the others. Pierre Aubier has been well educated at the Collège de Langres and arrives in Paris in time to witness the series of events occurring from the administration of Necker to the advent of the Terror. A number of touches are drawn from the real memoirs of the period and young Aubier's patron has a historical counterpart.[72] The youth is excellently situated to serve as a mirror of the age. In 1789, one could still mingle the easy pleasures of the old order with the hopes of the National Assembly. One could read Chénier, or see a tragedy by Voltaire, between following the leaders of what was still considered 'the most humane of Revolutions.'[73] Gradually came the increase of emigration, the flight of the king, and a pestilential spy-mania resulting in the denunciations which Anatole plays up in all these tales. The hatred and fear that eat into an unstable people are soon reflected in the soul of Pierre Aubier, who thinks himself fortunate to become a volunteer and abruptly leaves Paris with the army of national defence.

All of this is less story than history—with personal recollections thrown in. Throughout, there are *motifs* recalling the real 'Pierre's' adolescence: Aubier's classical education at the Collège, where with some exceptions he found his professors less admirable than the art of Virgil; the favourite passage about Dido and the myrtles, once more cited; also love of the Luxembourg and gossip with merchants in the streets. Such things are, however, subordinated, like the hero's sentimental experiences, to the more essential matter of constructing a panorama of the period, especially in terms of ordinary daily life.

The remaining tales in the Revolutionary series are, again, of interest less for their unimportant plots than for their circumambient history and their affiliations with France's other work. Since they are all adaptations from *Les Autels de la peur* (1884), let us recall certain features of that *roman-feuilleton*. Its eleven chapters, as Anatole admitted, were too loosely strung together to form a good novel. So he decided to break them up and use five of them as separate stories. Under new titles, they appeared first in various periodicals (1888-92), then as the last group of narratives in *l'Etui de nacre*. Generally in *Les Autels* we discovered some distinctive elements, together with attitudes towards the Revolution.[74] These elements are again to the fore in the stories now to be treated—which also reveal curious and disconcerting lapses due to the changes in shape which they have assumed.

As for content, A.F. shows a growing disposition to criticize severely the ferocity of the Revolutionary leaders. Even in 'l'Aube,' the dangers of half-baked Rousseauism are intimated. When the Bastille had just fallen and enthusiasm was rampant, then truly one might think:

Bliss was it in that dawn to be alive.

Yet there was already a diffused spirit of foreboding. Nothing really happens in the story: we are simply given the views of four people who meet in a young widow's cottage at Chaillot. Of these, the hero and heroine are dreamily idealistic, a doctor is non-committal in his attitude, while only an old *philosophe* is for the Revolution, root and branch. Ironically enough, it is this same *philosophe,* though altered in name and character, who appears in the next story, 'Madame de Luzy,' as hunted down like a dog by a rabid butcher. To save him from the Tribunal, the heroine (less dreamy now) secretes him between the mattresses of her bed and calls on her would-be lover to enact with her the roles of a guilty pair. The seekers apologize for disturbing the couple, make a cursory search, and depart without finding M. Planchonnet—a name that rings familiarly. But the Revolution is becoming a grim actuality. So in 'La Mort accordée,' the hero begs that as a conspirator he may be sent to the jail where his mistress is confined.[75] The next tale, 'Anecdote de Floréal, an II,' shows us a 'ci-devant comtesse' actually in prison and refusing to escape lest she might compromise the jailer's daughter. Finally, 'Le Petit Soldat de plomb' is calmer and more retrospective in tone. This was later divided into two stories, of which the second was called 'La Perquisition.' The scene is laid, apparently among Anatole's own bric-à-brac, a hundred years later than the above events. The little wooden soldier comes to life after a long trance and, having exchanged some passages with a Tanagra figurine, relates another 'Perquisition' or search similar to that which Mme. de Luzy experienced. This time (in 1793), love-letters rather than an old philosopher were hidden from inquisitorial eyes, under a sofa rather than in a bed. But the search proves equally fruitless. And A.F. himself humorously comments: 'I think I have already heard that yarn somewhere.'[76]

With regard to the form of these five or six stories, there is but little action, and usually the thin plot tapers off with a decidedly unfinished effect. Furthermore, there are startling discrepancies due to the author's carelessness in achieving consistency within his successive versions—*Les Autels, l'Etui,* and a revision of 1922. When he broke up the early novel into separate tales, the aim would naturally be to destroy all consecutiveness. Yet the above résumés may suggest to the reader the fact that there remains a common denominator in the persistence of the original hero and heroine throughout. There are also such minor links as the reappearance of the old philosopher and allusions to the Chaillot cottage. The tales thus strung along produce the effect of a train of freight-cars which have been uncoupled but are left standing in juxtaposition. That is perhaps a venial offence. But what shall we say of the following ? Late in his life, Anatole was thus taken to task by Ségur, who exaggerates the blunder :[77]

'I told him laughingly that whether by distraction or error the heroine in one *nouvelle* of *l'Etui* is called by a different name on almost every page.'

Horror and consternation on the part of Anatole : 'Why, people can't understand what I'm talking about ! I simply put together some old material, without paying much attention. How frightful to commit such blunders ! I must correct them.'

He ultimately did this. But for some time the heroine of the 'Anecdote de Floréal' was called either 'Fanny' or 'Pauline,' while the hero of several stories had, quite properly, different names, but was likely to revert unexpectedly to his original appellation of 'Marcel.' It seems as if Anatole had exhausted himself in the effort of breaking up *Les Autels* and lacked the energy to apply his new-found names consistently. We are not surprised that when he had to find a second name for his *philosophe,* he fell back on the journalist, Planchonnet, well-remembered by Pierre Nozière.

Nor did his lack of the creative vein stop there. Quite apart from the *rifaccimento* of *Les Autels,* Anatole repeats in these stories incidents and passages from still other works. After the dismemberment (1922) of 'Le Petit Soldat de plomb,' its second half, 'La Perquisition,' becomes more manifestly an echo of the essential situation in 'Madame de Luzy.' But the theme of the Search had first been sounded (long ago for us) in *Le Livre de mon ami,* where Grand'Maman Nozière briskly told of having concealed a fugitive under *her* mattress. The anecdote originally derived from the journal of Grace Elliott, written during the Revolution.[78] There are also several cases where material from *La Vie littéraire* is duplicated in *l'Etui.*

The value of the Revolutionary stories consists not in their structure but in their author's insight and delicate style. A passage from 'l'Aube,' regarding Marcel's experiences, will illustrate both these qualities: [79]

Par moments, il s'arrêtait et tendait l'oreille pour entendre le murmure léger et pourtant terrible qui s'élevait de Paris, et dans ce bruit plus faible qu'un soupir il devinait des cris de mort, de haine, de joie, d'amour, des appels de tambours, des coups de feu, enfin tout ce que, du pavé des rues, les révolutions font monter vers le chaud soleil de férocité stupide et d'enthousiasme sublime. Parfois, il tournait la tête et frissonnait. Tout ce qu'il avait appris, tout ce qu'il avait vu et entendu en quelques heures emplissait sa tête d'images épouvantables : la Bastille prise et déjà décrénelée par le peuple; le prévôt des marchands tué d'un coup de pistolet au milieu d'une foule furieuse ; le gouverneur, le vieux de Launay, massacré sur le perron de l'Hôtel de Ville ; une plèbe terrible, pâle comme la faim, ivre, hors d'elle-même, perdue dans un rêve de sang et de gloire, roulant de la Bastille à la Grève, et, audessus de cent mille têtes hallucinées, les corps des invalides pendus à une lanterne et le front couronné de chêne d'un triomphateur en uniforme blanc et bleu ; les vainqueurs, précédés des registres, des clefs et de la vaisselle d'argent de l'antique forteresse, montant au milieu des acclamations le perron ensanglanté ; et, devant eux, les magistrats du peuple, La Fayette et Bailly, émus, glorieux, étonnés, les pieds dans le sang, la tête dans un nuage d'orgueil !

It should be clear by now that France opposes to the Revolutionary doctrinaires the faith of a traditionalist.

The three remaining tales in *l'Etui* have a casual modernity of setting and use effectively the first-person 'angle of narration.' Yet two of them are similar to 'Gestas' in that they have an old-world air as well as definite associations with the past. And two of them ('La Messe des ombres' and 'Leslie Wood') have an identical underlying theme, as will soon appear.

After a succession of half-told yarns, it is refreshing to find in 'La Messe des ombres' a capital short-story, which contains suspense, *dénouement,* atmosphere, and the power of making the marvellous plausible by circumstantial detail. This is the old sacristan's story of Catherine Fontaine, a lace-maker in a retired village.[80] It was said that in her youth she had loved and lost a handsome Chevalier, after which she became an assiduous churchgoer. One midnight, the bells ring for mass. Without noticing the hour, she arises and goes to the cathedral, where she finds a good assembly of people dressed in old-fashioned costumes.

Among them is the lost Chevalier, who explains to her that these 'shadows' have loved truly but not wisely and are therefore held in Purgatory. At this hour, once a year, the rejuvenated lovers are allowed to come together ; and this rule applies also to those who are about to die. The heroine and her squire recall without shame their brief happiness. The silent mass is held with due ceremony, a collection is taken, and Catherine drops her old betrothal ring in the plate. The noise causes the whole pageant to vanish. The next morning Catherine Fontaine is found dead at her home, and her ring is discovered in the collection-box of Sainte-Eulalie. It bore as an emblem two hands for ever conjoined—a symbol of the moral that love is stronger than death.

Exactly the same phrase is used to epitomize the narrative of 'Leslie Wood.'[81] Here we may perceive once more what can be learned from *l'Univers illustré*. It was in the columns of that journal that the story was first told, and it then bore the earmarks of a real event.[82] The columnist reflects on a news-item, to wit that M. Leslie Wood, former correspondent of *The World* (London), has just died in an asylum. Gérôme is reminded that he met this 'grand vieillard' a few years ago at a social gathering. Follows the story of his life as he narrated it to the chronicler and substantially as it shortly appeared in the volume of *l'Etui*. The facts of the case are then unchanged. In our tale, certain names are altered, and the social gathering is expanded into the sort of *soirée* that A.F. frequented in the nineties. He and Wood walk home together, and the latter makes Anatole his confident.

In spite of the practical exigencies of his life, Wood has found a place, the chief place, for a semi-mystical love. Like Anatole himself, the English journalist became interested in the mediumistic enterprises of William Crookes and his Katie. Presently Wood found and loved an 'Annie' of his own, a luminous and spiritual creature. Following clerical advice, they married but remained chaste. Then Annie died, but somehow returned to the arms of Wood as a warm and loving mistress. 'L'amour est plus fort que la mort.' Anatole mitigates the possible unpleasantness of this idea by stressing the uncanny exaltation of the narrator ; a week afterwards his death took place. But the theme of the 'dead maiden' was nothing new to France. There is his adaptation of the legend in *Les Noces corinthiennes*. There is his review of Hennique's novel, *Un Caractère,* where incidents very similar to the love-life of Leslie Wood take place.[83] Anatole uses the theme of the shade-maiden to illustrate a defence of physical love as a perfectly natural and blissful consummation. That is the first characteristic thing about 'Leslie Wood.' The other is that however mundane A.F. seems to become in this period, he can never leave the other-world alone.

'Le Manuscrit d'un médecin de village' contains some significant reflections on 'pity,' while describing the reactions of a sympathetic doctor before a hopeless case of meningitis. The victim is a peculiarly bright lad called 'Eloi,' who in the story is represented as a spiritual descendant of the great physicist, Ampère. But to most readers Eloi, the 'luminous child,' will seem the literary descendant either of Petit Pierre himself or of one of those frail and ardent schoolmates mentioned above in connexion with 'l'Œuf rouge.'

What is the total impact of the stories in *l'Etui?* Perhaps not very great from the point of view of substance—most of them are pretty thin gruel—nor do they shine as examples of careful, competent narration. There are only four or five that pass this test. For the others, they might have received little notice . . . if France had not written them. But nearly all are penned in that engaging manner which by now had won him an audience that would be interested even in his lesser things. Fairly numerous were the plaudits among readers and reviewers, who laid especial stress upon his rendering of the ages of faith.[84] Perhaps these too, like ourselves, were pleased to recognize some of the familiar landmarks on the Anatolian horizon—a purview that extended all the way from the Janus-faced fourth century, through the Cathedral Age, down even to Messrs. Crookes and Company. 'The Mother-of-Pearl Casket' holds several of our author's small private jewels. Among them are ornate frames enclosing miniatures of the simple Primitives for which he shows his fondness elsewhere.

§ 6

And notably so in *Le Puits de Sainte Claire,* another volume of tales, not published in book-form until February, 1895. But it contains stories which were written in previous years and which in some respects resemble the holier portions of *l'Etui de nacre.* The chief difference, historically, is that the latter volume contains legends from the early Middle Ages, while it is usually the Pre-Renaissance (*trecento*) that is pictured in *Le Puits*. For this 'pseudo-Franciscan' collection, like *Le Lys rouge,* is largely a product of A.F.'s first visit to Italy.[85] With scant exception, all of the contents had appeared in the *Echo de Paris,* then reckoned among the foremost French dailies, during 1893-94. The exceptions included two additional chapters of the long story called 'l'Humaine Tragédie' and a Prologue which was evidently an afterthought. But these sections were also printed in a periodical (the *Revue hebdomadaire*), though only a few weeks before the book came out.[86] There the Prologue bore the title soon given to the whole collection—the fiction being that the tales were told by a certain Père Adone, at an old 'Well of Santa Clara' outside Siena. There is some appropriateness in placing the stories under the protection of the sister-saint of Francis of Assisi. But as for Père Adone, Anatole scarcely thinks of him again.

Nor is any great adroitness shown in the forging of links or cross-references between these narratives. We had better consider them first singly, for their topics and sources ; then *en masse,* with regard to the themes and *motifs* which they develop.

Anatole did not know much Italian, and in some cases Mme. de Caillavet translated for him such material as he needed.[87] He made up for this lack by his knowledge of history, art, and atmospheric background ; for most of the tales are laid in and around the chief towns of Northern Italy. Thus, in the Prologue, we find a charming description of the surroundings of Siena, while 'Saint Satyre' gives a picture of convent life at the monastery of Santa Fiora. Fra Mino experiences a voluptuous vision of fauns and nymphs, explained by the fact that a satyr is buried there. This curious type of 'saint,' not unknown to the hagiographers, depicts the twilight of the older gods and assimilates the old and the new creeds in a manner recalling 'Amycus et Célestin.'[88] 'Messer Guido Cavalcanti' revives the figure of Dante's friend, but the anecdote told about him is taken from Boccaccio. It relates how the studious youth mused among the tombs of San Giovanni and how, when merry friends tried to tempt him away, he left the tombs to them, remarking that they were really at home in such an environment.[89] Thus far Anatole follows his source. But he adds a good deal concerning Guido's humanistic tastes, his morose nature, and his Neo-Platonism. Cavalcanti appears again, with a sceptical outlook, in 'Le Joyeux Buffalmacco.' His pursuit of various ideals, ending in death, is explained by the author in a letter to Mme. de Caillavet.[90]

According to Gsell, A.F. possessed a very fine copy of Vasari's *Lives of the Painters,* on which he drew freely for *Le Puits,* always through the medium of Madame Arman. One such passage inspired the tale of 'Lucifer,' where we learn how dangerous it is to misrepresent the devil.[91] The painter Spinello had depicted him as a monster, until Lucifer appeared in person and protested. But Spinello died before he could change his ways. Anatole enlarges his source ten-fold, dwelling upon how the Florentine masters feared Satan and enhancing the latter's sceptical Epicureanism. 'Les Pains noirs' concerns a certain banker who gave artistic things to his city, but was niggardly otherwise. When summoned before the bar of heaven, his handsome gifts weighed as nothing in the scales, and only some black bread that he once gave to the poor could profit him. Passages from a number of saints' lives have been suggested as lying at the basis of this tale, which, like 'Le Mystère du sang,' appeared periodically before the author visited Italy.[92]

Mainly from Vasari, though in part directly from Boccaccio, A.F. drew 'Le Joyeux Buffalmacco' and his humorous pranks. *The Decameron* is chiefly responsible for the jests presented in a summary toward the end of this series of four tales.[93] Long ago, in *Le Globe* (October 16, 1879), Anatole had demonstrated some knowledge of Italian and had discussed various translations of Boccaccio ; he had defended the story-teller against the charge of anti-clericalism and praised him for his vivid pictures of fourteenth-century life. Now in the manner of the Florentine he ascribes to the gay apprentice, Buffalmacco, various jests directed against Tafi, the painter, or against an abbess—as well as one *beffa* (practical joke), where the tables are turned on Buffalmacco by an imitative monkey. Simply as stories, these are among the best in the volume. As usual, Anatole expands and alters his sources.[94]

'La Dame de Vérone' adapts to an Italian setting an anecdote related in Olivier Maillard's *Sermons.* It concerns a wanton who falls into an excessive self-admiration and ends up as the bride of Lucifer. 'L'Humaine Tragédie,' according to Seillière's indictment, would establish 'anarchy under the protection of St. Francis.'[95] At any rate it contains (we shall find) an abundance of striking ideas, since it is the longest of these narratives. It tells how the humble Fra Giovanni wins even his superiors by the sanctity of his life and deeds. But presently, through his defiance of a powerful 'confrérie,' he is imprisoned and rescued by the aid of a 'Subtle Doctor,' *alias* Satan. After various disputes and visions, the monk finally yields to the Tempter. The substance of all this appears to be Anatole's own, but for details and incidents a number of sources have been suggested.[96] 'Le Mystère du sang' shows how St. Catherine converted a hardened sinner (i.e., politician) condemned to the scaffold and even received his bloody head at the last. Her *Letters*[97] provide the scenario, but the rather pathological ecstasy at the end is Anatole's invention.

Two of the final three tales are, like 'La Dame de Vérone' above, conveyed from French to Italian soil, in order to preserve the unity of the general setting. 'La Caution,' from the standpoint of orthodoxy, could offend no one. A Venetian merchant, having ventured beyond his means, has recourse to a rich Jew, to whom he pledges a figure of the Madonna and child. To meet the pledge, he is obliged to entrust a sum of ducats to an unpiloted bark. But the Madonna herself is the patron of the boat and brings it safely to Venice. The direct source is found in *Les Miracles de Nostre Dame*.[98] Yet it is evident that the first part of the story offers close parallels with *The Merchant of Venice*. Again, the 'Histoire de Doña Maria d'Avalos et de Don Fabricio, Duc d'Andria' was elaborated from an anecdote in Brantôme's *Des Dames galantes*.[99] From France, the scene is shifted to Naples, and indeed, as Seillière remarks, the narrator might well be Bandello or some romancer of that kind. For this is a violent and passionate tale about two lovers who forget everything in each other's arms and are slain, with additional horrors, by the offended husband and his men. Finally, 'Bonaparte à San Miniato' combines the history of two countries in its depiction of Napoleon and his staff. Having taken over Leghorn, they dine with an old canon, who is a relative of the Bonaparte family. He desires Napoleon to push the sanctification of a still older member of the family, a certain Fra Bonaventura. The episode, derivable from well-known Napoleonic material, ends inconclusively.[100]

From the various sources ascribed to these stories, France usually takes only a hint or two which he elaborates in his own manner.

The charm of that manner, barring some echoes of Boccaccio's hilarity, is entirely his own.

The two main topics throughout *Le Puits* are Italy and the religious life. With regard to the latter, in so far as religion means humble service, A.F.'s attitude is far from unsympathetic; but we shall need to examine his views regarding a number of saints, several monks, and the devil in person. The diversity of Italian life is everywhere observable. The violence of the early prideful Renaissance alternates with the meekness of St. Francis. The interest in old legends, which we first discerned in Little Pierre, is here associated with a penchant for medieval mystics and miracles. In fact, it has been well said that Anatole used Italy as a *medium* for conveying this interest, as well as for expressing the opposed sensual trend (whether latent in himself or explicit in the *novelle*), and for voicing his customary delight in the pagan traditions. Let us consider the last point first.

Antiquity does not predominate in *Le Puits,* except in so far as Italy is necessarily antique. There are abundant classical allusions. There are repetitions of old *motifs* such as the passage on Venus and the myrtles, and the Virgilian or Sybilline prophecies regarding the coming of Christ. Fra Mino is glad to think that Virgil will not be damned; and 'Messer' Guido Cavalcanti, that ardent young humanist, reads indifferently the 'divine' Plato's treatises and Cicero's orations. But it is especially in the story of 'Saint Satyre' that we meet with Antiquity Redivivus. First comes the vision of Fra Mino, in which the naïve cenobite is regaled with an orgy of nymphs and satyrs. After tantalizing the good brother, the nymphs presently become old and horrible, in token of the passing of their race. This is explained by Saint Satyre himself, who furthermore chants in A.F.'s favourite fashion—witness the already mentioned 'récit de Nectaire'—the golden prime of the Saturnian age, and praises and laments the ancient gods. Thus he expresses the author's nostalgia for paganism.

Italy is presented first in terms of lovely landscapes and appropriate settings: the purple twilight mantling the Sienese hills; paths climbing toward 'a wood of myrtles and olives'; fireflies and great oxen, lilies and evergreen oaks, herons and the Florentines hunting cranes. And then we are given an idea of the separate communal activities. In Venice, political and commercial vicissitudes are connected with the loss of Fabio's fortune. In Siena the citizens are tough—they must be in order to withstand Florentine rivalry. At one time they formed a democratic *Signoria,* which could barely make head against the Pope and the politicians. In Viterbo, quite a different oligarchy was established. Assisi and Perugia, Arezzo and Naples are touched off more briefly. So the cities, 'calling each to each,' furnish backgrounds for diverse stories.

As for Florence, not only are her churches frequently and affectionately mentioned, not only are her painters exalted, but her history during the thirteenth century is deftly recalled. There are allusions to the warfare between Guelphs and Ghibellines, to the factions of the Whites and the Blacks, to Farinata degli Uberti, who by bringing in the Sienese to oust the Guelphs, caused the 'Arbia river to be stained with blood.'[101] Then it was that the joyous life of such artisans as Buffalmacco gave place to grim street-fighting and the City of Lilies seemed a forest full of wolves. Furthermore, the customs of the Florentines are put before us as a matter of traffic and industry, the ordinary life of home and mart. A wool-merchant or a money-changer will drive a hard bargain. A troop of lusty beggars will prowl around. A suspicious banker will surround himself with gratings and chains, no less than with frescoes and tapestries. As the *novellieri* so often relate, the upper classes promenade in meadows by the Arno or go hunting and picnicking in the country ; or they have their merry meetings in town. But the young are also taught to aspire to high office ; and they are active in the street-scuffles which may develop into civil war.

None of this is very new to the cultivated traveller or reader. Such an essay as W. D. Howells' 'Florentine Mosaic' takes us more deeply and fully into the affairs of the city. Yet A.F.'s own mosaic is sufficiently variegated to serve his purposes. Here if ever the term is appropriate, because of the addiction of such artists as Tafi to this manipulation of crushed colours and particoloured glass. On the ceiling of San Giovanni, the church where Cavalcanti heard mass, Tafi and his disciples labour to present sacred history in mosaic form. This master also paints the devil and his works, because it has been found that pictures of hell (or heaven) are more effective than sermons. Again, Spinello, we are told, depicted St. Michael's life for the church at Arezzo, while the figures in Santa Croce were traced after Dante's poem.

The Florentine painters are said to be more subtle than those of any other town. Thus art is amply to the fore in *Le Puits*. On the other hand, somewhat to our surprise, Anatole's usual bookishness is not conspicuous. Allusions to the writers of the *trecento* are not very frequent, while less is made of the humanistic movement than might well be expected. But there seems enough to warrant the statement by Ségur that A.F. felt at home in the Pre-Renaissance, and that his own personality at times appears to emerge from that age as from an avatar.[102]

The dominant figure of St. Francis is made the link between Italian culture and religion. Although Anatole might personally be nearer the type of the learned Benedictine, yet he manifests here what he never lost—a benign concern with the Franciscans and their founder. This appears in certain 'imitations' of his saintly life, as well as in references to the *Fioretti*. Material is drawn also from the *Légende dorée*. In the Prologue, which sets the tone, we find St. Francis going about doing good, until the hard-hearted Sienese chased him from their city. Follows a 'gracious miracle.' Accusing himself, as was also the practice of his disciples, weary in body and discouraged in mind, he sat on the edge of a certain 'Puits' ; seeing St. Clara's face therein he arose fortified . . . and left to Anatole the legacy of a title. In 'Saint Satyre,' he appears as the spiritual father of Fra Mino, who imitates his practices. So does Fra Giovanni in 'l'Humaine Tragédie,' which becomes 'a chronicle of a simple brother of St. Francis' Order ; and is set forth with a naïveté of style that not seldom borders on the sweet naïveté of "I Fioretti."'[103] After the saint had ascended to heaven, he left on earth the perfume of his virtues and the seed of his doctrine. This was spread widely throughout Christendom, as his Order grew in numbers and strength. His 'ladies of Poverty and Obedience' had a way of disarming even the mighty. Thus when Fra Giovanni is, for his contumacy, brought before the General of the Order, the latter has a change of heart, because of St. Francis' angelic influence : 'the example of Christ's favourite had instructed him in spiritual beauty.' And it continues so to instruct Fra Giovanni until the end of the tale.

Among other saints are Clara, the 'preferred Sister' of Francis, who partakes in his vows and through her mercy converts the condemned prisoner in 'Le Mystère du sang' ; Bonaventura, the later Franciscan ; Michael, whose entire story is in Spinello's brain and who weighs good deeds against the lack of them in 'Les Pains noirs.' With the ambiguous Saint Satyre we are in different company. This two-faced creature exemplifies Anatole's favourite *thèse* of the blending of pagan and Christian rites. Our virtuoso loves to point out how mythology and the Bible may mingle as proceeding from the same basis.[104] This 'levelling' process is applied not only with regard to Joan of Arc's environment, not only in 'Amycus et Célestin,' but in the friendly arrangements which Saint Satyre made with the early Christians. He did this in good faith, for having seen the downfall of the primeval Saturn, he thought it was now time that Jupiter should collapse. Still, the satyr as an apostle of tolerance is not wholly credible. He may be buried near an altar, but it cannot be said that he did much good in the monastery, where he caused disturbing dreams. Also the nymphs, routed from elsewhere, haunted the place, considering him as a venerable 'ancestor.' In fact, this goat-footed miscreant, when conjured by Fra Mino, has some difficulty in persuading the latter that he is a saint at all. But he assures the brother that he was accepted as an equal by the early missionaries: 'My holiness seemed as good as theirs.' Both the 'saint' and his creator appear to have their tongues in their cheeks.

Yet this is not France's prevailing mood in the volume under discussion. To begin with, two rather extreme views may be challenged. I do not believe that the Père Adone Doni, the 'doux rêveur' of the Prologue, is a second edition of the faulty Jérôme Coignard; nor that the story of 'l'Humaine Tragédie,' with its evident opposition to Dante's *Commedia,* need symbolize the 'rise and fall' of Anatole's own soul.[105] Again, we should distinguish, as he does, between primitive religion and the paraphernalia of the Church. As already intimated France (in this work) is not unfavourable toward the former, when accompanied by certain definite virtues. Among these A.F. emphasizes holy, 'celestial' and even 'extreme' simplicity, which furnishes armour of proof against the devil. With this is bound up New Testament charity or love, without which, as the Seraphic Doctor realized, knowledge is but a vain thing. Humility is also a virtue *par excellence*: it is holy to give away your clothes, to play with children, and to suffer mockery. Blessed are the poor in spirit, 'for the true poverty is that of the spirit.' The conclusion of the matter is that if the good life is to act according to the will of God, then only 'the humble, the simple, and the ignorant can know God'—and his will. I do not discern any irony in the statement of these beliefs, many of which are put into practice by Fra Giovanni. Their effect upon his political fortunes will appear shortly.

There are some references to sacred history and the like, which take on different tones according to circumstances. Several miracles are mentioned as if they were ordinary occurrences—which is the tone desired. And the personages speak in character. If Fra Mino honestly feels that he is enduring what Christ underwent on the Mount of Olives, or if another monk sincerely holds forth on the terrors of Judgment Day, such views are offset by scepticism on the part of Cavalcanti, or buffoonery on the part of Buffalmacco and his master. This Tafi turns upon the Madonna and calls her names, when she seems to be actually bearing him up to heaven, as he had often begged her to do. But the pranks of Buffalmacco are as nothing compared with the sorrows and the deeds of Satan.

There are traces of lingering but ironic Romanticism in the way the Prince of Darkness is represented as a long-suffering gentleman. When Spinello depicts 'Lucifer' as a horrible monster, the latter naturally remonstrates: 'You shouldn't do wrong to anybody, not even to the devil. Don't you see that you are insulting Him to Whom you address your prayers, when you give him a villainous toad as Adversary ?' In fact, he now bears the semblance of a beautiful black angel, just as when, he casually remarks, he once set forth on his 'illustrious enterprise' of mastering the world. Call him what you will, provided you recognize that glory is his single aim. Spinello is convinced and says he will henceforth paint him as sad, proud, and beautiful. Thus equipped, it is not surprising that Lucifer walks off with 'La Dame de Vérone,' who implored her 'sweet Satan' to take her, body and soul. He is glad to take the former, since (as a notable worker in metals) he probably fashioned it; but it seems that at times he has small use for souls. . . Or so he tells Fra Giovanni, on whose vision he dawns, just as beautiful and just as black as ever. But on this occasion he assumes the guise of the Subtle Doctor, who can out-argue the angels. He certainly out-argues the poor Frater, who finally falls a victim to what has been called the Supreme Temptation—the temptation of thought and spirit. Giovanni yields to the pride of life, to the wine of doubt, but still more to the insidious tongue, which has remade him in the devil's own image . . . 'Je t'aime parce que tu m'as perdu.' This finale is akin to the old *motif* about 'la volupté de se perdre.' There is doubtless some Manicheism in this victory of Lucifer ; but there is hardly enough to make it a record of France's spiritual life ; and there is nothing like so much as is found later in *La Révolte des anges.*

If Lucifer is played up more than ever before, A.F.'s hostility to monks and priests seems to have abated considerably in this volume. Perhaps he found Italian clerics more agreeable than French ones. Adone, Mino, and Giovanni are not only represented as sincere exponents of their faith ; in spite of some eccentricities they are attractive as human beings. The canon of San Miniato is less endearing in his charms, and we are not expected to agree with his clerical absolutism. But the only thoroughly bad priest is the Dominican who prowls around Doña Maria d'Avalos and violates her when she is dead.

The philosophy scattered through *Le Puits* follows the familiar lines of sceptical inquiry and the Epicurean search for pleasure. Such themes prevail in the discourses of the Subtle Doctor and of Guido Cavalcanti. If it is Saint Satyre who first voices the doctrine of the flux, it is the devil who tells Fra Giovanni how unstable and corruptible are the uses of this world. There is no good thing, no, not one. Why do men get themselves killed for senseless slogans ? There is only relativity, 'contrariness and contradictions.' And if I, the Contradictor, assert that only *via* contrariness may small parcels of truth be revealed, I become thereby a witness and martyr in that cause. It is most likely that here A.F. is alluding to his own thought-processes and to the accusations of inconsistency that were launched against him. Furthermore, it is intimated that the contradictions of the devil are fewer than those attributed to the Deity. The Adversary tries to enforce his argument by using the allegorical Wheel, in which the variegated colours finally merge into a uniform white—which is Truth. But can there be such a universal, if truth in particulars is denied ? For Satan declares that among men there is no such thing as justice, that wealth and happiness are but mirages ; and Fra Giovanni chimes in to the effect that all effort is vain, that wisdom is *nil,* and that thought, however much he may be yielding to its temptation, is an evil thing—in so far as we can tell good from evil, which is not very far. Fra Giovanni agrees with

Voltaire in maintaining that we are 'ignorant' about that distinction as about our own nature and destiny. Evidently man's back is against the wall.[106]

He is driven there too by the case-history of Cavalcanti. In a feverish search for truth among the ancients and among the tombs, this neophyte went through experiences with which Boccaccio had never credited him. He avowed his devotion to Dame Philosophy, until death should them part. She was made manifest by the voice of Julia Læta, who spoke from her grave, and who softly led Cavalcanti to his own end. For Philosophy begins and concludes in the tomb. Not only according to Epicurus is there no future life to haunt us (which was the more obvious scandal in Cavalcanti's credo), but from all his search for the beautiful and good, from all the vanities of effort, there remained to him at long last but one cure for the curse of consciousness. And death, still administered by his sweet Lady, came as a crowning reward and consolation.

All this is set on a high plane. But other passages in *Le Puits* put the doctrine of Epicurus on a grosser basis. Satan says: 'All good things are of the flesh and are tasted by the flesh alone.' He and others, such as Buffalmacco and the wanton nymphs, proclaim that all beauty, all force, all joy are found in *l'amour* and there only. What if love is necessarily attended by sorrow and is fostered by illusion? There is joy in illusion itself. When the lady of Verona kneels in church, like Mme. Gromance later, she inspires by her gesture ardent desires in sacrilegious man. It is useless for the holy Giovanni to urge the subduing of desire. As in the case of Jean Servien, that force will lure us on eternally. In this variety of hedonism, we are not very far from Nicias and the banquet-hall in Alexandria. Yet less space is given to this doctrine than to other matters.

A certain number of socialistic and subversive ideas are also found in *Le Puits*. To the mild Père Adone are attributed sceptical views concerning government and magistrates. The author seems to approve the reform movement in Siena when the 'artisans, leaders of a free people,' chased the Emperor beyond their walls. They were doubtless inspired by a recrudescence of the old Roman Republican spirit.

But as already hinted, most of A.F.'s socio-political philosophy is conveyed through Fra Giovanni, the Franciscan. From his social experiences Anatole had come clearly to perceive that the greatest difference in the world is that existing between the 'haves' and the 'have-nots'; or as it is quaintly put in 'l'Humaine Tragédie': St. Francis 'knew that the man who sells is the enemy of the man who buys.' And Fra Giovanni believes that those who sell, whether money-changers or bakers or druggists, are plainly not of the kingdom of heaven. The interview that he sustains with the wretched quarry-man anticipates Anatole's later sympathy with such victims of society as Crainquebille and Pied d'Alouette. Against the separative sense of possession and the madness of men who think they can own a mountain, he cites the example of St. Francis who took the stones that he needed from a certain hill-side, without any by your leave. Thereby he demonstrated the iniquity of gold and foreshadowed the communal city, where there shall be neither rich nor poor.

The quarry-man was more enlightened and pleased than were the purse-proud councillors of Viterbo when Giovanni thundered at them: 'Qu'est-ce que le bien ?' These councillors professed virtue and were all for 'le bien'—at least they encouraged the poor to be good, 'in order that no change might occur in the city.' Giovanni is seized and haled before the leader of their *confrérie,* whose profession of faith is beautifully ironic:

> The knowledge of good is within all virtuous men. And good citizens are ready to respect the laws. They approve what has been done in the city to assure to each one the enjoyment of acquired wealth. They sustain the established order and will arm themselves to defend it. *For the duty of the poor is to defend the property* (*bien*) *of the rich.**

This rather sinister pun throws some light on the syndicated 'virtue' of Viterbo. The monk sturdily declares that such man-made laws partake of man's egoism and folly. 'The powerful of this earth do their will, and that will is contrary to the will of God.' Thus governance has produced only wars and slaughter. The poor and the disinherited are nearer to God than that, for they do not put their trust in the maintenance of statutes, or of the *status quo.* The preservers of wealth and power have naturally glorified militarism and publicly honored conquerors, who are of their party. The reign of gentleness and brotherhood has so

* Italics mine.

far had no real chance on earth. . . Fra Giovanni is of course condemned, in legal rigmarole, for 'conspiring against the order established in the city.'

This interlude wins approval from Braibant, and from Carias the tribute that here indeed are pages of 'a palpitating sincerity and permeated with a deep feeling.'[107] Other remarks upon *Le Puits* are infrequent. The orthodox blame the author for his 'excessive anti-clericalism'—surely not conspicuous here—and his trend toward anarchy. But as Maurras pointed out, under the frock of a Franciscan, the author's heart was beating warmly and humanly—to confound those who insist on his 'diabolical' prepossessions.[108]

Although on its appearance *Le Puits* became the centre of a cloud of congratulatory missives,[109] these have not been printed and for some reason full critical reactions are rare. Léon Blum wrote of the tales as inspired by various Italian themes and as 'animated by a pure love and a unique truth.' Delaporte insisted upon the 'pious heterodoxy,' the atmospheric religiosity of the Sienese stories. Others have pointed out the adroit mingling of irony and tenderness in the religious tales. Truc declares that he gets a more living image of the Renaissance from *Le Puits* than from Burckhardt's conscientious tomes. Both Michaut and Giraud have admired the style of a fine passage in the Prologue, and the latter has devoted a page to the question which this collection inevitably raises: Does France succeed best as a novelist, or as a short-story writer?[110] To the challenge of this problem, one can only respond in a trite (and Francian) manner that there is much to be said on both sides.

The embattled figure of Fra Giovanni suggests that Anatole had already turned his attention to certain modern problems. Such is indeed the case. We shall now in part retrace our steps to consider those major works where, more continuously, France criticizes society in terms that are more nearly contemporary.

CHAPTER XVII

Works of this Period : on Modern Affairs

§ 1

ATTENTION has already been called to the unusual productivity of France in the early nineties, when for a time he was bringing out one or two volumes yearly, in addition to journalistic activities and intermittent labour on 'La Pucelle.' In the heat of the action, Rod expressed his admiration for this fertility :

> He published in close succession three of his most important works : *Thaïs, La Rôtisserie de la Reine Pédauque* and *Le Lys rouge,* all three representing a considerable amount of research as well as fresh artistic effort ; we should add the *Opinions de M. Jérôme Coignard,* surely no mediocre work, and the *Jardin d'Epicure,* full of daring and lofty truth.

The critic adds that, through journalism, Anatole has learned how to regulate his thought to the best advantage ; and has attained an ironic and at times a violent maturity far distant from the scholarly Bonnard.[1]

Of the five works listed above, all but *Thaïs* await our examination. But first a word as to chronological difficulties. The publication in book-form of a given title does not always indicate the year when France was occupied with that subject ; newspaper publication usually preceded, and in some cases that might run back several years. Our arrangement, then, while roughly chronological, is also influenced by other considerations. Thus we saw that *Le Puits de Sainte Claire* came out in 1895 ; but the stories therein date from 1893-94 ; and it was dealt with in juxtaposition to *l'Etui de nacre,* because of its affinities with that work. *La Rôtisserie* and *Les Opinions de Jérôme Coignard* (both appearing in 1893) offer little difficulty, since in each case book-publication closely followed upon serialization. But *Le Jardin d'Epicure*—nominally of November, 1894—contains articles which date from anywhere in the early nineties and which are often anterior to the two works just mentioned. Yet it seems best to discuss *Le Jardin* in its traditional place, near the end of our period, since it sums up the philosophy of its epoch.

La Rôtisserie de la Reine Pédauque is supposed to mark the first 'definite expansion' of France's iconoclastic talent.[2] It was composed in 1892, during the period of his greatest mental and moral disarray. After the final break with his wife he repaired to the Rue de Sontay, and it is there that we find him, probably in August, complaining to the absent Mme. Arman that his books have just been dumped messily into the new apartment. He needs these or others in order to 'determine a quantity of details' about *La Rôtisserie*. Yet he feels that the work is nearly finished, since the Abbé Coignard is 'on the road to Lyons.' This Abbé is quite a character, so he has hopes of the novel. In spite of a later spell of discouragement, it is again evident that the author's procedure is first to block out the main lines, then to fill these in with minute brush-work. And it is natural that the ups and downs of his morale should be reflected in his attitude toward his production, as well as within the novel itself.[3]

La Rôtisserie was serialized, in the inevitable *Echo de Paris,* from October through December, 1892. When it began to appear, the streets of Paris, to the author's confusion, were filled with placards which bore LA REINE PEDAUQUE in large letters. As for this part of the title, it will be recalled how in *Le Livre de mon ami* Anatole was interested in the web-footed fairy queen and connected her with the mother of Charlemagne.

The reactions of the critical public toward this philosophical romance and toward its running mate, the *Opinions* of the leading character, have been described in terms which emphasize the alleged Satanism of the author. 'About this time it was discovered in the salons that *Anatole* is the first name of the devil.' Old friends were scandalized, and even Jules Lemaître testified that Bonnard had suffered a sea-change. France himself gently remonstrated with a certain reviewer who rushed into print with exclamations while *La Rôtisserie* was still appearing as a serial. There seems to have been a general feeling, with which M. Carias agrees, that these works were 'full of anarchy and libertinism.' The book, says Seillière, 'fit éclat,' whether because of its radicalism or its coarse pleasantries.[4] More specifically:—If Philippe Gille admired the philosopher-poet who here gives rein to his fantasy, if he found that the author's 'light and amiable tone' contains echoes from the language which Voltaire assigned to Pangloss, yet Edouard Rod deprecated the fact that this amiability is attained at the expense of those everyday virtues which constitute our working-creed. People call it a 'gay' book ; but it seems to Rod fundamentally sad in its undermining of essential beliefs, whether or not one calls them illusions. Georges Pellissier agreed that the novel achieves 'the derision of all morality' ; otherwise put, what might have passed for a delicate pleasantry in a brief tale becomes an indictment of all *préjugés* when drawn out to this length ; and the reviewer is correspondingly amazed.[5] We shall see how later critics develop these themes among others.

There are in the pattern of *La Rôtisserie* three substantial threads which are interwoven with the presentation of the three chief characters ; these in turn—with their 'opinions'—derive from three principal types of sources. The first and least colourful strand concerns the occultism of M. d'Astarac, the Rosicrucian adept who engages Abbé Coignard and his pupil to assist in esoteric researches. The second and most variegated skein is that connected with the personality and fortunes of the Abbé. The third element in the pattern is the story of his disciple, Jacques Tournebroche, whose adventures run from his father's 'rôtisserie' to the time when his master is slain by Mosaïde, the jealous old Jew. In the heart of these adventures appear such light-o'-loves as Catherine the lace-maker and Jahel, the nominal 'salamander,' who is really the niece of Mosaïde. This girl plays her lover false and generally brings disaster. All these different strands are well-woven together, and for once we have a definite plot that proceeds to a climax and a catastrophe. One element in the unifying process is that the tale is told from the 'angle of narration' of Tournebroche, as pliable a youngster as Gil Blas or Candide. And that reminds us that a quantity of eighteenth-century background is deftly inserted into the course of the narrative.

The sources of the occult material have been in good part worked out.[6] Early in *La Rôtisserie* A.F. refers circumstantially to a work, well-known in its time, by the Abbé Montfaucon de Villars : *Le Comte de Gabalis, ou Entretiens sur les sciences secrètes.* This book was first published in 1670, but the edition specifically cited by Anatole, and probably used by him, is that of 'Amsterdam' (really Rouen), 1700.[7] His interest in de Villars was manifested as early as March 19, 1892, when in *l'Univers illustré* he started a sort of *enquête* regarding the death of the

Abbé. Was he 'slain by the sylphs,' as reported? Did he indiscreetly reveal their mysteries — or were there any mysteries to reveal? France is already weaving together the strands of *La Rôtisserie*. It is not surprising that he was acquainted with de Villars' book, which was known both to Voltaire and to Pope; indeed, the latter had drawn upon it for the Rosicrucian portions of *The Rape of the Lock*. The *Entretiens sur les sciences secrètes* has been called the '*locus classicus* for the kind of mystic zoology in question'; A.F. may have been led to it by Joséphin Péladan's *Victoire du Mari* (1889 and also Rosicrucian); or possibly by Bayle or Voltaire's *Siècle de Louis XIV*.[8]

France's tall adept, M. d'Astarac, is an eccentric who grows rather tiresome through his long harangues; and personally he does not resemble the attractive Abbé de Villars nor the latter's creation, the Comte de Gabalis. Furthermore, the 'cabalistic' part of *La Rôtisserie,* as Doyon points out, is more a matter of background than of action proper. Yet this part looms pretty large, and it will prove of some interest to summarize where and how Anatole has followed de Villars, mainly according to M. Morel's article.

Like d'Astarac, the Abbé has formed an occult library, wherein one day appears the figure of the German savant, the 'Comte de Gabalis.' These two indulge in dialogues about salamanders, sylphs, and kindred spirits. Again like d'Astarac, Gabalis is very rich, extremely mysterious, and addicted to sudden appearances or disappearances. The place chosen for his lengthy interview with the Abbé is near Reuil, which is just where Anatole's visionary speaks one of his longest soliloquies. The massive eloquence of Gabalis is closely imitated by A.F., who adds some ironic by-play of his own. But outwardly he keeps serious, to emulate the great seriousness of the two fictional *cabalistes,* who strangely 'mingle folly and wisdom.' They emit similar theories (often expressed in the same language) about a more ethereal way of eating, about cosmogony and elementals, and particularly about the way to evoke salamanders, their fiery nature, their love-affairs with the sons of men. Far more ravishing than mere earthly love, these affairs are benevolently fostered by either adept . . . for the greater bliss, ultimately, of Jacques Tournebroche and his Jahel, who is at first mistaken for a salamander. As might be expected, Anatole extends himself on these *amours*. But mortals must beware—the salamander readily becomes jealous of earthly women, if the occasion arises. Yet who would be so indiscriminate as to return to such, after beholding the perfect thigh of a salamander? In both texts we have theological arguments to indicate that God did not forbid such unions; and in both the famous Scriptural passage about the 'daughters of men' is made to apply to their cohabitation with sylphs or gnomes.—Of course all this is developed and dramatized by France, with his own peculiar blend of wit and colour and fancy. Yet there are some who maintain that de Villars writes better than Anatole![9]

Other works that gave hints to our author along similar lines were the *Metamorphoses* of Apuleius, the Père Androl's *Génies assistants et Gnomes irréconciliables* (for two episodes); and Cazotte's *Diable amoureux*. Still other texts, chiefly from the eighteenth century, have been cited. From Cellini's *Autobiography* Anatole drew the incident of the salamander who appeared in the kitchen fire and caused Tournebroche to be soundly slapped for his own good. It will be recalled that A.F. had shown a taste for such sprites in *Bonnard* and notably in *Abeille*. Additional sources still await discovery.[10]

But we are not yet through with the 'Comte de Gabalis' and his author. Our second strand or skein of influences concerns the Abbé Coignard. Now it seems clear that certain things about him are based on the actual life of the Abbé de Villars. Both are represented as witty and well-favoured specimens of their common type. Also the death-scene of the real priest does service for that of Coignard. In the article in *l'Univers illustré* already mentioned we find Anatole stating definitely that Villars was assassinated on the road to Lyons. But why? He seeks information from his readers. Some authorities (e.g., Voltaire) aver that he was 'slain by the sylphs'; others attribute the assassination to the revengeful feelings of certain *cabalistes* whose secrets he had revealed. Again Anatole prays for light.

Whether or not he received any, he had Coignard killed by the revengeful Jew, Mosaïde. The murder took place just about where Villars was slain, and is preceded by this bit of dialogue, as a forewarning:

'Do not scorn,' says d'Astarac, 'the example of the Abbé de Villars, who on the Lyons road was killed by Sylphs, because he had disclosed their secrets.'

'On the Lyons road,' said my good master. 'That is a strange thing!'

However, the character of Coignard, as we shall deal with it later, seems closer to the portraiture in a novel called *Compère Mathieu,* where a Bohemian sort of priest is depicted by the author, the Canon Dulaurens. Like Coignard, this prototype is a roving character who indicts society and favours the humble-minded. Incidentally, the name of 'Jahel' is found in the *Compère Mathieu* as well as the name of the goddess Astaroth, who may well have suggested 'd'Astarac.' It would appear, indeed, that this work is second only to *Gabalis* as a major source.[11] As in *La Rôtisserie,* a naïve youth tells of his adventures with his 'Master'; and Mathieu shares with Coignard certain nihilistic views, inconsistency of conduct (readily admitted by either sinner), and an edifying end. But in some respects our Abbé is still nearer to an uncle of Mathieu, namely the Père Jean de Domfront. This person led an adventurous life, was expelled from school and army, and became a Capucin monk. Père Jean, too, had trouble with fair women, and on one occasion was involved with the mistress of an inn, when the husband inopportunely returned. This incident recalls the orgy which Coignard and others indulge in with Catherine the lace-maker — even to the row which follows the return of her protector.

Mathieu's young apprentice in life seems to foreshadow Jacques Tournebroche. But the latter's essential trait of naïveté is rather derivable from *Candide,* which often suggests the general tone of *La Rôtisserie.* This takes us back into the luxuriant eighteenth-century setting for the book.

It has been suggested that some of the more scandalous substance—'the dissolute monk, and the fickle, crafty, naturally perverse woman'—might well proceed from the old *contes gaulois* of the Middle Ages.[12] And that view is probably correct in so far as this frame-work became part of the lighter Gallic tradition. But evidently here it is stuffed with highly seasoned eighteenth-century dressing. It has been a long time since we have met Anatole at ease in his favourite pre-Revolutionary period; we have seen that a certain abstinence from this field, at least as regards collecting *objets d'art,* was imposed by Mme. de Caillavet. Perhaps *La Rôtisserie* was undertaken by way of compensation. The time of the action is probably around 1725 or a little later;[13]

this would make it roughly contemporary with the appearance of *Gil Blas* and of *Manon Lescaut,* with both of which our novel has affinities. As countless allusions testify, we are in the full tide of the Old Régime, in the days when Louis XV was still the Well-Belovèd, when the beautiful Mme. Parabère and M. Lesage with his folk-theatre were present memories, when dangerous little books were imported from Holland, and Catherine the lace-maker could well be relegated, like Manon, to the *hospice* for fallen women and thence to America. There are distinct and scornful references to Fontenelle's *Dialogues* on the stars; and (to paraphrase M. Doumic), we are in the sort of environment that could later produce the amoralistic adventures ascribed to the heroes of Voltaire and of Diderot.[14]

But bookishness is not all. As already mentioned, this is the place where Anatole makes abundant and dexterous use of engravings. Picturesque scenes like the entrance of Frère Ange into the kitchen of the Rôtisserie or like the appearance of the bewigged and betrayed M. de la Guéritaude, marching along and made visible by the flaming torches of his lackeys, are cases in point. There are a score of such copies, to which no originals can be definitely assigned. Thus old Paris is resuscitated, with its tortuous, history-laden streets, its quaint gabled shops, bearing such names as the 'Little Bacchus' or the 'Image of St. Catherine' or the *rôtisserie* of the 'Royal Goose,' to say nothing of the 'Web-Footed Queen.'

It was here that young Tournebroche turned the spit. The lad's real name was Ménétrier, and his father, the honest Léonard Ménétrier, placidly kept his tavern—and bemoaned the salt-tax—on the old Rue Saint-Jacques; while his pious mother hoped that her son would not misbehave—but if he had to be a little blackguard let it be in noble company, so that 'honour may be reflected on all the family.'

There are other passages burlesquing this sort of social abasement, while the actual misbehaviour of the nobility is amply illustrated by M. d'Anquetil. This raffish aristocrat having served in the wars possesses an easy scepticism about the existence of God, the rights of property, and all prerogatives save those of his own caste. If creditors bother him, he walks off with their wives or mistresses in the most gallant manner. He peremptorily takes Catherine from M. de la Guéritaude and whips her in a lordly fashion if she complains. In terms reminiscent of his ancestors' hunting-days, d'Anquetil urges his lackeys on to beat up Frère Ange; he presently indulges in a street-row with the aforesaid financier and ends by killing a man. Will they put him in the Bastille? Bah! His family will soon get him out, and while in durance he can have his gay women and his cards. Indeed, such card-games as ombre or piquet are frequently mentioned throughout the novel, old *chansons* are sung and quoted, suitable costumes for the various classes are described, together with their proper environments. And there are occasional references to the habits of 'les philosophes.'

It has been said that A.F. rediscovered Voltaire about 1880. If so, he kept the discovery dark for some time. *La Rôtisserie* is the first work which has a decidedly Voltairian flavour, whether through its direct doses of irony and scepticism, or whether the sarcasm is insinuated more subtly through a mouthpiece. None could fail, for instance, to get the implication when Tournebroche solemnly avers: 'In so far as magic is shown to be contrary to religion, I put it from me with all my strength.' This is the mock-reverence to orthodoxy which Bayle and Voltaire had made so familiar to their readers. From the garden of Candide, as Faguet indicates, various flowers are culled. Tournebroche, we have already seen, has the 'candour' of Voltaire's hero and is as easily befooled. M. Seillière tells us that in the same vein France stages the sudden repentance of sinners, or mingles gross pleasantries with beatings and combats.[15] (One might compare what happened to Cunégonde with what happened to Catherine.) But France's masterpiece in the way of Voltairian or semi-Voltairian delineations is the ambiguous figure of the Abbé Coignard himself.

This character has been very generally admired; and it is held that of all Anatole's creations Coignard most closely resembles his author.[16] The point will bear examination. That A.F. delivers *part* of himself *via* Coignard, that the two philosophizers are alike in their wilful discursiveness no less than in their searching appraisals of terrestrial matters, is undoubtedly true. Yet be it remembered that the author is at two removes from his character, who is thus rendered doubly 'enigmatic.' First, the Abbé is viewed through the ignorant and admiring eyes of Jacques Tournebroche. Then, too, his devout expressions of faith are not such as A.F.

would exhibit in his own person. However engaging a rascal, Coignard is still a misbehaving priest, whose lip-service to his religion is therefore likely to glisten with the salt of Anatolian irony. One side of his family-tree mounts up to such ne'er-do-wells as Hyacinthe Dufour and the Marquis Tudesco. Like the former he has led an adventurous life and was at one time a public writer with his own *échoppe*.[17] Like the latter, he is a plausible scapegrace with slight sense of responsibility, who takes his ease with the classics (particularly Boethius) and imposes himself upon a small bourgeois family as tutor to their very green son. The degree to which the Abbé won the esteem of his pupil will appear from this final admiring tribute:

> No one, in my opinion, equals in genius the good master whom I had the misfortune to lose on the road to Lyons; no rival can bring back to me his rare elegance of thought, his sweet sublimity, the astonishing richness of his soul, always abundantly flowing . . . ; no one can restore to me that inexhaustible source of knowledge and morality (*sic*), where I renewed the strength of my youth; no one can reflect even the shadow of that seductive charm, that wisdom, that power of thought so fully displayed in M. Jérôme Coignard. I consider him as the finest spirit that ever flourished on earth.

But are we to take this tribute in all literalness? Should we not remember the double veil which is interposed between us and the object, i.e., France's inmost thought? What has been the record of the recipient of this lyrical eulogy?

On the one hand he is clearly a bad egg. A parasite, he will take his profit from believers and unbelievers alike. He is ready to deceive his friends, he cheats at cards when the luck is not good enough, and he tries to steal the diamonds of M. d'Astarac. If he occasionally acts like a crook or a coward, that is because he attaches no great importance to the moral virtues as compared with blind faith and efficacious grace. When he participates in the orgy *chez* Catherine, he not only gets disgracefully drunk but in the subsequent row he is plunged into a situation—*viz.,* in water up to his neck—from which not even the *Consolations* of Boethius will rescue him. Yet nothing can unseat him permanently from his pupil's regard. He is saved by his demeanour and by his philosophy. The former, when not subjected to undue stress, remains 'noble and smiling.' His experiences have made him mild and kind, while his philosophy 'raised him so far above human passions' . . . that he could indulge in them almost without after-thought. Convinced of the weakness of himself and of mankind in general, he has applied his philosophy chiefly toward the acquisition of a benign clemency. He is indulgent and tolerant toward the numerous frailties of women,[18] toward an atheist like d'Anquetil and (what is harder) toward an errant Capucin. It is emphasized that human standards and laws seem to Coignard of slight validity when contrasted with divine grace. When *that* is obtained, through repentance, peccadilloes seem to vanish from the memory. Tournebroche bears fervent witness to the purity and durability of his master's faith. It was never weakened by mortal error or the disillusionments of life. It was the one thing not threatened by the rational analysis which he applied to all other things. For he stood firmly as 'a subtle theologian and a good Catholic.'

The extent to which Anatole personally accepts all this will shortly be questioned; but before the novel is concluded some doubt is expressed by Coignard himself as to whether he had not been, perhaps, *too* subtle as a theologian. After he has been stabbed by Mosaïde, he has some difficulty in making an edifying end, since the old Adam is still strong within him. He makes unseemly proposals to a woman in attendance, he sings gay songs — and it will all depend on what his last minutes are like. Fortunately the 'bottom of the basket' turns out to be pure gold. He pardons his assassin, his face lights up with its old majesty, and he thus admonishes the tearful Tournebroche:

> Do not listen to those, who like myself have grown over-subtle about good and evil. Do not be persuaded by the elegance of their speeches. For the kingdom of God consists not of words, but of virtues.

By such words Tournebroche *was* persuaded; he composed a Latin epitaph regarding the 'fine maxims' and 'unshakable faith' of the Abbé, and furthermore paid him the loyal tribute quoted above.

Among the minor characters, the fantastic d'Astarac is at least semi-Anatolian in his interest in the occult and in astronomy — two themes on which we need not linger.[19] He is treated with the care which A.F. accords to those choice monomaniacs who by incessant pursuit of their own ideas, add to the comedy of cross-purposes. He too, in his more ironic moods, has been esteemed a mouthpiece of the author [20] and it may be that we shall need him in that capacity. But now we must return to Coignard who, in spite of the cautions suggested above, is closer to Anatole than anybody else could be.

Author and personage are alike, first, in their attachment to books and learning. Coignard once goes so far as to say that the pleasures of the scholar are preferable to the fleeting caresses of women. The long conflict between these two major passions was symbolized quite early by an event in his youth when he used to browse in a book-shop kept by a Mme. Pigoreau. She tempted the studious cleric and he fell . . . among the volumes. Nineteen ancients, ten saints and scholars, nine miscellaneous writers (all named) 'were the witnesses of our embraces.' A very similar catalogue is used on a similar occasion in *La Révolte des anges*.[21] Having received this double initiation, Coignard became the secretary of a bishop and drew up an inventory of his precious MSS.; near 'La Reine Pédauque' he passed the time (quite *à la* Anatole) by leafing through the volumes of a book-dealer ; naturally, then, he was in clover when made the curator of the 'Astaracienne' library, which he considers a superb collection. He converses learnedly with its proprietor about Oriental manuscripts and other lore, and is finally set to the congenial task of translating a papyrus. Reflecting A.F.'s favourite phrase, he will now abandon himself to the 'silent orgies of meditation' [22] and forget the women.

Another trait that the Abbé shares with Anatole and Bonnard is the conversational habit of taking any casual matter, say a game of cards, back to its historical origins. Furthermore, he is as keen on the ancients as either of those gentlemen. He claims to have read all the surviving Greeks and Latins. He discriminates between their talents and compares them, for better or worse, with the moderns — an eighteenth-century habit. He alludes to over a dozen ancient authors, the oft-mentioned Boethius rivalling the allurements of such profane poets as Homer and Ovid. He turns Tournebroche into a good Latinist and humanist, cautioning him that 'humanities mean elegances.' Surely it is appropriate that the pupil should construct a resounding Latin epitaph for the master, and that the old church near the scene of his murder should today bear a tablet in honour of the Abbé's passing.[23]

Preceding this grim event, Coignard seems to have had vague

presentiments. Just before he was attacked on the road, he paid his last tribute to the life of the mind and learning. Fortunate are the Benedictines, with their serene Rule and their admirable libraries ! 'I desire more ardently than ever to sit in some venerable gallery, where choice and numerous books are silently assembled. I would write histories, preferably that of Rome during the decline of the Republic.' For of all ways of spending life the best is still the studious Way—'to prolong the brevity of our days by the spectacle of ages and empires.' . . Coignard's preachments, at any rate, dispose Tournebroche to carry on the torch. His parents install him as clerk in the same bookstore that his master had haunted, and there he finds fit companionship among the frequenters.

In his general philosophy, Coignard is again like Anatole—at least up to the point where the distrust of man ends and the love of God begins. In a discursive manner, the Abbé makes plain certain fundamentals. He scorns mankind (not excepting himself) as a prey to the clouds of illusion and all manner of vicissitudes and weaknesses. The destinies of our souls depend upon the capricious winds of Nature, of whom we are the plaything. She manages us by the double rein, the 'double concupiscence' of Hunger and Love. This *motif* is by now outstanding amid the dissolving harmonies of A.F.'s orchestration. Mortal life vibrates between these two poles, but at bottom Hunger or possessiveness is the more compelling force. Men are in essence 'hideous and ferocious creatures, intent only on devouring or embracing one another' ; yet they are restricted in their appetites by certain laws. These are not always to be respected and they are often eluded, because they are mostly the products of prejudice and self-interest on the part of a given class (cf. Fra Giovanni). Such is not the case, the Abbé interposes, with divine laws ; the justice of God is beyond our justice ; and divine stability is likewise opposed to the fleeting illusions and vain images of mankind. We shall return in a moment to this pious and constant counterblast. The point just here is that the Abbé and Anatole, for all their surface indulgence, are almost completely contemptuous of human activities and capacities. This debonair nihilism was emphasized by critics soon after the appearance of *La Rôtisserie*.[24]

Coignard does not except human reason from his indictment and points to the cloud-castles of d'Astarac as a capital illustration of reason gone wrong. But this adept, who has similar opinions regarding the lowly instincts of man, happens to be an atheist. He can therefore crow more loudly than Coignard. He has no belief in immortality. He ascribes the creation of the universe not to God, but to the fortuitous efforts of a number of Genii. Equally sceptical about the existence of the Devil or of the Other One, he is willing to discuss both of them with believers, for they are both interesting 'characters.' Jehovah, indeed, with all his violence and capriciousness, may be considered too intelligent a demi-urge to have bothered much about Adam, or about Eve and her apple. Of course he did not fashion the universe, but he may have arranged a little section of it, where he showed his skill as an ingenious potter. If people would only take the Bible as an allegory and refuse to be muddled either by theologians or by Capucins, we should hear more sensible views.

In fact, this sinister Advocatus Diaboli declares that it is ridiculous for the theologians to maintain that the Universe has man as its main object. That the idea of God as both 'a perfect and a creative being is only a Gothic dream.' That far from being God, Jehovah was really 'a great Demon [δαίμων] since he did create the world.' That on this basis he showed a certain intelligence and even a *vis comica*. That he may be indifferently called 'Adonaï, Tetragrammaton, Jéhovah, Theos, Athanatos.' And that 'the unfortunate demi-urge,' dissatisfied with his work, tried to drown humanity in the Deluge, and then gave us up as a bad job. Most of which, even to the comparative-religious standpoint, resembles A.F.'s other utterances regarding 'Iahveh.'

If d'Astarac thus complements Coignard, the author, through Jacques Tournebroche, exercises a control over both philosophizers. The pupil more than suspects that there is much illusion and vanity about occultism ; and he wonders if the nihilism of the Abbé, practically applied, would not lead to great disorders and disasters. His master's final recantation, already mentioned, seems to concede the point, for he advises Jacques to discount his clever 'maxims' in favour of humbleness and virtue.

We return to the subject of France's penetration into Coignard's religious faith. To reach the root of the matter, we may leave aside his handling (which runs true to form) of the usual orthodox paraphernalia of saints, monks, the devil, churchly ritual and the like.[25] It has been seen that the Abbé constantly opposes the law of God to the law of man. He insists that the former is to be apprehended and salvation is to be attained by docile faith rather than by reason. The latter may be our best guide in human affairs, which are in a bad way anyhow. But in this vale of tears Coignard willingly turns from the spectacle of iniquity to the one ray of beatitude that shines down from the firmament. Bliss is attainable, not through our miserable efforts, but through repentance ; not through the light of reason, but through humbly accepting divine grace and universal Providence, even in what may appear ridiculous manifestations. Dogma, of course, should be observed to the letter. 'Je me pique de délicatesse en matière de foi.'

Now here is where Anatole parts company from his mouthpiece. And it has not been sufficiently observed, perhaps, that regarding religion he is using that mouthpiece inversely and absurdly, somewhat as he had used Paphnuce, to indicate by contrast his own standpoint. The insinuative method, particularly as regards the opposition of the domains of faith and reason, goes pretty far back. For the great churchmen of the seventeenth century, Bossuet and especially Pascal, had declared this divorce, had deliberately subordinated the reason in favour of obedience to dogma or intuitive perception. Later sceptics, Bayle and the *philosophes,* had accepted the separation of the two domains, but had added a dialectical twist which put the matter in another light. Many points of faith (they say) such as miracles or Old Testament crudities appear absurd to a reasoning person ; but since faith is admittedly *un*reasonable, we can only bow our heads in mock-ironic submission. It is this eighteenth-century tradition, this dialectic, which Anatole follows. The fact is apparent not only in Voltairian reminiscences, not only in Coignard's reprobation of the 'redoubtable' Bayle, but in the subdued irony with which France treats some of the Abbé's predicaments. When oppressed by his sins, when 'all my impurities arise against me,' he hastily switches his thought to the road that leads to Paradise. When he and his companions have indulged in an orgy and slain a man (as the Abbé de Villars had also done), the best thing is to forget that act and symbolically to wash one's hands. If Peter had not betrayed Christ, a particular prophecy would not have been accomplished and he would not be today the greatest saint in heaven. 'O salutary example, leading men on the way to salvation! O wise economy of religion . . .!' For redemption is obtainable by repentance alone, not by behaviour. . . The behaviour of Coignard is, naturally, a great testimony to this doctrine. But from a poor human point of view, we find it difficult to accept his professions as we accept those of Fra Giovanni or of Père Adone.

Coignard occasionally expresses a random doubt: as to the authenticity of certain saints, as to whether the Jews are as bad as their enemies represent, or whether one can really transmute metals. But more usually it is he who affirms and the author who supplies the interlinear scepticism. For instance, this Voltairian bit concerning an early *amour* of the Abbé's:

> We have then, monsieur, a young priest, a kitchen lass, a ladder, a bundle of hay. What a logical succession, what an arrangement, what a concourse of pre-established harmonies, what a chain of cause and effect, what a proof of the existence of God!

When Master Jérôme waxes bitter against the Jesuits, but shows indulgence toward atheists and even Huguenots, we can fancy Anatole smiling up his sleeve. Indeed, that is his, and our, final attitude toward the peccadilloes of Coignard. It is appropriate to find him arguing that the greatest sinners 'provide the stuff for the greatest saints': one has only to take this abundant raw material and rework it, according to a certain 'theological art' into a very handsome repentance.[26]

There is not much in the present volume bearing on politics and the social order; most of that is reserved for the *Opinions de Jérôme Coignard*. Occasionally d'Astarac will peer at war, as largely a matter of robbing hen-roosts; or the unclassed Abbé, from the depths of his Bohemian soul, will declare that 'respectable' people are no better than others and much less agreeable. When he once sat at a bishop's table, he found that his neighbours were Mr. Constraint and Mrs. Ennui. What he chiefly resents on the part of the aristocracy is its insolence. And surely this is the forward-nodding plume in the equipment of that fresh young nobleman, d'Anquetil. Coignard further believes that pride is at the root of much social suffering. Who are we to impose our measure of justice, or of honour, upon others? Penalties and violence should be displaced by tolerance. In one screed, not long before his death, he rivals Fra Giovanni in his view of the worthlessness of human institutions. God made nature and primitive society, but man has spoiled his handiwork. All government should then be theocratic, in order to re-establish the purity of institutions. 'The city was once divinely instituted.'

It should be noted that *La Rôtisserie* is the first volume by France in which the vein of sensuality is conspicuous. Less discreet and less closely associated with beauty than in *Thaïs,* this theme is deliberately made prominent and is on the whole overstressed; the same is true of subsequent novels. When Coignard sings the pleasures of bed and table, when the characters indulge in an orgy of wine, song, and Catherine the lace-maker, it is all part of the author's professed Epicureanism. *L'amour,* easily taken and easily shared, is represented, in spite of certain reserves, as the chief preoccupation of man and woman. It has been remarked that Anatole sticks, appropriately, to the eighteenth-century attitude: love-gallantry rather than love-passion is the goal.[27] We need not unravel the whole tangle of 'affairs' in which the personages are involved. Even d'Astarac repeats France's old *motif* about the feminine shape as a harmonious amphora. Even Coignard, though age has forcibly 'amended' him, recalls lusciously his former pleasures and maintains (another *motif*) that a woman who is all compact of beauty has no place in her body where a grain of virtue might lodge. He is not disposed to make much of the sexual act and approves Saint Mary the Egyptian (often cited by France) for losing her virtue in a worthy cause. Tournebroche's sentimental education rises from timid passages with Catherine to the heights of *la volupté* with Jahel. In his descriptions of such moments, Anatole is unashamed and almost lyrical. But he insists, through the mouth of Jahel herself, that we surround the desired object with the seven veils of illusion, and the Abbé sorrowfully feels that at the core of pleasure there is a 'néant cruel.'

For the Epicurean is also a sceptic, and a cynical view is naturally induced by the feeble and faithless types of women here portrayed. 'There is none so ugly who cannot misbehave when she has a mind to.' Or, as the Abbé puts it—and here the tradition flows back to the earliest *contes gaulois*—: 'You have no idea, my boy, of what the ruses of women are like.' Indeed, the prettiest ones seem full of trickery. Catherine attempts to deceive her young nobleman even in his presence, but succumbs happily to his brutality; she also treacherously denounces Tournebroche to the police. Jahel fools everybody and passes from lover to lover without the slightest scruple. If put to the question, they will both defend their faithlessness with the arguments of Manon Lescaut: they must have food and drink, purple and fine linen. In short, like other human necessities, women are here presented (if one analyses) in a most unfavourable light. And if one listens sharply, the repercussions of France's marital infelicity are audible. But the whole story is carried off with so much verve and gaiety that for many readers moral problems hardly arise.

Yet the earlier critics, we have seen, were sufficiently aware of France's new boldness. An unexpectedly favourable reaction, considering the not very friendly relations of the two men, was that of Emile Faguet.[28] He candidly avows that he would have liked to condemn the book, but since it is an amusing little masterpiece, he cannot go against his convictions. Charming and witty, variegated and yet unified, replete with knowledge of old Paris, *La Rôtisserie* recalls for Faguet the best tales of the eighteenth century and especially Voltaire. To be sure, it is not adapted to children nor, perhaps, to ladies, but the only real fault that he can find with it is that, being in the manner of a *conte,* it is too long drawn out. Later writers have discerned the strong undercurrent of anti-clericalism, of general iconoclasm.[29] But even those who have orthodox proclivities say little in dispraise of *La Rôtisserie,* finding it 'fort gracieux,' or recognizing the vital qualities of Coignard.[30] Nearly all agree that the Abbé is in many ways a faithful embodiment of his creator's ideas. And Michaut, so frequently censorious, though he deprecates the sustained note of sensuality, seems almost to smile upon 'the abundant and flowery language, both learned and profound, both Epicurean and subtle' of this 'bon maître.' Among the few outright condemnations is that of Cerf, who in accordance with his general thesis finds that the passage from the *Livre* and *Bonnard* to the *Reine Pédauque* marks the first step in that 'descent' which though gradual was unswerving in France's career.[31]

§ 2

Profiting by the success of *La Rôtisserie,* Anatole could now turn his attention to politics—and with a vengeance. What was originally known as the 'Opinions de M. l'Abbé Jérôme Coignard sur les Affaires du temps' first appeared in the very liberal *Echo de Paris* from March 22—July 19, 1893. In October the book was published with some additions and under its present abbreviated title. As usual, France was bothered by lacking a number of pages in order to fill out the volume. Ultimately he revamped, mostly from 'La Vie littéraire,' material dealing with St. Abraham, the story of 'Docteur Zeb,' and other miscellanea.[32]

The *Opinions de Jérôme Coignard* have a double aspect: they are early eighteenth century; or they are late nineteenth. On the one hand, as a semi-sequel, they connect with *La Rôtisserie* by means of reappearing characters and references to previous incidents. Again the admiring Tournebroche records the utterances of his master, and in each case the fictional subterfuge is that A.F. found the pupil's MS. by a lucky chance.[33] The *Opinions* are supposed to begin where the *Rôtisserie* leaves off, namely at Blaizot's book-shop; and the links between the two works are numerous and apparently consistent. But although outer events are still reflected through the Abbé's eyes, little actually happens within the *Opinions*. It is a question of ideas exchanged through dialogue mostly in France's favourite setting of a bookstore.

These views and conversations ostensibly arise from 'affairs of the time,' i.e., of the Old Régime. But actually there is much criss-crossing between the past and the present. Anatole uses the veil of the past (as his eighteenth-century masters had taught him to do) in order to express thoughts on very present discontents. The various disguises employed will appear in the course of our exposition. Leaving the Church aside, as a rule, the author has Coignard discourse on Ministers of State, the 'Mississippi Affair,' the new government, science and history and the Academy, military matters and Justice. The intention is to make such a review of current institutions as we find in La Bruyère or Montesquieu. And like the *Lettres persanes,* the *Opinions* have been styled a 'most radical breviary of scepticism.'[34] The publishers naturally took a brighter view of the matter and announced the work to expectant readers in the following terms:

> The excellent Abbé, whose extraordinary theories gave so much delight in *La Rôtisserie,* triumphs afresh in this volume—through his fantasy based on good sense, through the subtle gaiety of his insight and his judgment.[35]

The fact is that the volume constitutes an indictment of its time, on a fairly extensive scale. It is full of socio-political dynamite. This is something new and something to be reckoned with.

Some have thought that A.F.'s reactions against the social hierarchies may have been induced by a certain weariness of the people whom he encountered in the salons. It is true that he was to carry on the derision of the privileged classes in the *Histoire contemporaine* as well as in *l'Ile des Pingouins*. But the roots of his criticism go deeper than that and, as M. Braibant has shown, they plunge into the mire of contemporary scandals. Not only was he 'disburdening his heart and mind' of things that had gathered there for several years; his pen leaped into life under the immediate impulsion of events occurring that very Spring and Summer of 1893. These were mostly connected with the Panama scandal and its consequences. Indeed, France began his chronicles just three days after the deposition of a certain Mme. Cottu, which threatened to shatter the government; and he continued for some time in this vein of political journalism, apparently without thought of making a volume.[36] While we have differed from M. Braibant as to the completeness of the 'evolution' described in the *Opinions de Jérôme Coignard,* we must agree with him as to two things: first, that Anatole began his writing from strong and indignant convictions; and that their expression and continuation show to what an extent politics are now uppermost in his mind. It may well be that he emerged from this 'full bath of actuality' with Socialistic leanings, which became visible a few years later; for such seems to have been the effect of the Panama mess on a number of people. At any rate, the journalistic origins of the *Opinions* dispose of Seillière's theory that these pages were, so to speak, relics of *La Rôtisserie,* assembled and furbished under the urging of Mme. de Caillavet.[37]

With these considerations in mind, we may summarize the chapters of the work, for the most part in their present order.[38] In 'Les Ministres d'Etat,' we find Coignard turning over the books at the *Image Sainte-Catherine.* He prefers the subtleties of Racine to the declamations of Corneille, who has an exaggerated idea of human sublimity. The 'race of Adam' would be as ridiculous as it is miserable, were it not for the intervention of the Saviour. In ourselves, holds the Abbé, we are fierce and repulsive animals. A historian, M. Roman, objects that certain states are well-governed and show signs of progress. But Coignard retorts that the apparent order in history is mostly put there by writers like M. Roman, and that the numerous upsets in France have done little to alter the condition of individuals.

'How can you say so,' exclaimed the historian, 'just after the death of our experienced and distinguished Minister ?'

Coignard admits the honesty, the application, the strength of the Minister . . . who is evidently Jules Ferry.[39] Since this patriot was an early advocate of the separation of Church and State, Anatole approves him for expelling the 'Jesuits,' but remarks that they have come back. As for his colonial enterprises, they are minimized and are viewed rather as collective undertakings. The Abbé concludes that human actions, whether by leader or people, only present a show of force, a 'vain appearance,' and are really the effect of invisible causes.[40] All of which is characteristic historical Pyrrhonism.

After an interlude about the coquetry of Catherine the lacemaker, the Abbé's dislike for Capucins, and his recital of the old story of St. Abraham and his niece Mary,[41] we return to the more absorbing question of statesmancraft. In this third chapter Coignard breaks out against the government of Cardinal Fleury and has a fancy for writing pamphlets against the rascals who held high place under the Old Régime. The author is really indicting the corruption prevalent in the Panama affair. But Jérôme has no hope of altering the nature of men by changing their governors ; this point is repeated, especially with reference to the government by Councils, which was tried under the Regency.[42] Furthermore, he fears the 'astringent novelties of Republics,' and he does not believe that (save in religion) there are any solid principles to be put into operation.

Chapter IV, as we have seen, was the first-written of this series, when all Paris, including Anatole, was much stirred by a particularly flagrant case of corruption. Under the guise of 'l'Affaire du Mississippi'—that old bubble of the Regency—A.F. deals with a side-issue of the De Lesseps flotation. 'The Company was accused,' in Coignard's paraphrase, 'of having bribed the officers of the kingdom,' enumerated in eighteenth-century terms. In the thick of the proceedings the actual Mme. Cottu ('Mme. de la Morangère') had deposed before the Tribunal that Soinoury, head of the Sûreté ('le sieur Lescat') had promised immunity to her condemned husband, if she would implicate any deputy of the Right. Her confrontation with Soinoury is dramatically described. The latter broke down, the scandal was bared, and Mme. Cottu became a heroine overnight.[43] In the (prophetic) discussion of this event in Blaizot's bookstore, M. Roman alleges the *raison d'Etat* as a good reason for hushing the matter up. Does M. l'Abbé expect virtue in political matters ? M. l'Abbé does not. But for once he abandons his attitude of sceptical detachment and declares that such villainy can be pushed just so far, that presently the people will quite properly rebel. Before this time (nominally 1722) revolutions have been caused by the wickedness of rulers. The new ones could not be worse than the old ones, so why not try a change ? . . . After which, he apologizes charmingly for contradicting his previous utterances and leaves us under the impression that antinomies are the most natural things in the world.

In the next chapter (another interlude), the Abbé takes Easter dinner with the parents of Tournebroche and gives vent to theological and other reflections arising from the Church festival. There is a reminder of the superstition about the coloured egg and Alexander Severus, used in the tale of 'l'Œuf rouge.' The pagan origins of the symbolism attaching to Easter eggs are also recalled by a certain scribbler, who maintains that Nature, in her teeming and monstrous productiveness, is not 'sufficiently theological and Christian.' Coignard has small difficulty in meeting this impious opinion—until a long drink stirs in him the bright idea that Nature may be an atheist after all.

Chapters VI and VII ('Le Nouveau Ministère') contain some searching criticisms on government, indirectly suggested by the fall of the Ribot cabinet, which had the noisome task of cleaning up the residues from the Panama affair. If Anatole, as a result of long previous observation, has become anti-parliamentarian, and if that feeling has been accentuated to the point of bitterness and pessimism by the notorious scandal, yet we agree with M. Braibant that only a superficial reading of the evidence could make of him a Royalist reactionary.[44] The State is pessimistically viewed, the Republic is at a low ebb, but would any other system do better ? In any government, holds the Abbé, the imbeciles and the self-seekers persist. In terms of the Old Régime, it avails little to experiment with administrative Councils or with English illusions about liberty; for if the State somehow stumbles on, it is mainly through the needs and the activity of the body of workers —a passage which has a distinctly Socialistic trend. But if according to Coignard's secret wish a popular government is ever established in France, his clairvoyance foresees certain dangers. The ministers then, as agents of Demos, will partake of his instability and can prosecute no far-reaching plans. They will truckle to the crowd; mediocrity, uncertainty, and the chatter of Deputies will prevail; corruption will merely have changed its face. Though we may have moved on from monarchical wars and wickedness, though secret diplomacy may happily come to be a dead letter, yet there will be far too much hasty law-making and general demagoguery. It may be, however, that the mass of the people will be less miserable than today (*sc.* in 1725).

Their representatives are not great men at any time. Whether as bewigged and ineffective municipal magistrates under Louis XV, or later as nominally delegates of the popular will, they become playthings of private interests and centres of turbulence. (Here there is woven in a plea for the rights of the humble peddlers, the ancestors of 'Crainquebille.') The general good is made of a number of particular evils; the public peace is founded on reciprocal fear of injury.

Scattered chapters discuss such loftier topics as 'La Science,' 'Les Académies,' and 'L'Histoire.' The opinions on these matters are mostly those to which we have grown accustomed. Though the Abbé is as fond as anybody of haunting the book-stalls near the Pont-Neuf, he is aware that the old volumes there exposed are full of foolish lies. Human knowledge is always 'illusory and deceptive.' The *philosophes* who think they have found out something about nature have merely prolonged their ignorance through the use of such scientific 'spectacles' as microscope and telescope—a simile borrowed from Voltaire. 'I hate science, because I have loved it too well. And in all this array of vain phenomena, I could throw myself from yonder parapet into the Seine . . . were I not persuaded of the truths of our Holy Religion.' How happy would Coignard be, if he could have remained in a state of boyish ignorance!

Academies for the most part have kept in that state, for they have quite rightly mingled mediocrity with an amiable politeness which has carried their fame as far as Muscovy. In view of the 'nothingness of all,' it is of course equally vain to be or not to be an Academician. This and similar considerations spring from the 'silent orgies of wisdom' (A.F. is now varying the *motif*), wherein Jérôme likewise discovers what a role chance and fantasy play in this world. The development of the theme is quite according to Voltaire. As for history, there are echoes of the old complaints about the mendacity of Clio, the contradictions of sources, the danger of attempting to learn moral truths from such a record. Eloquence and art may be found there, but not the continuity and logic which the historians fabricate. The story of 'le docteur Zeb,' who reduced to three words the history of Persia, is again related with approval. Anecdotes and tales are better than pretentious philosophizings. In short Anatole still prefers his Clio in négligée.

A curious pendant to this chapter has to do with the case of 'Monsieur Nicodème,' a gentleman who went about protesting against the exposure of nudities in public places. In actual life he was the Senator René Bérenger, known as 'Père la Pudeur'; but he does not seem to have quite merited the lowering treatment to which France has subjected him.[45] 'Nicodème' is depicted as a sort of Paul Pry who goes around finding indecencies where none are intended, objecting to a nude engraving as a frontispiece to Ronsard, and contriving absurd devices for the nuptial chamber. He exposes himself to the easy ridicule of Coignard, who points out to what extent modesty is relative and considers Nicodème as prurient as a Father of the Desert—thus recalling the temptations of Paphnuce.

We retrace our steps to consider the chapters on institutions, and notably those on the Army (X-XII). There are two sides to this question. For a while Coignard's hostility to militarism is so marked that some have seen little else in these 'terrible pages which best reveal the reversal in France's ideas.'[46] It is true that the Abbé, moved to expression by the rolling of the recruiting drums near the Pont-Neuf, is opposed to war not only as contrary to his personal habit, but as the greatest scourge of mankind. Almost everything is said that could be said against it—and Coignard is particularly strong against its concomitants of disciplined 'servitude, false glory and cruelty.' These are the features, suggests Braibant, that particularly move Anatole to a 'sensual and carnal pity'—a telling bit of divination. One may admire, according to the Abbé, the capacity of a Cæsar or the subtlety of a Macchiavelli ; but it is a sad reflection that war which is our chief shame and the proof of our inveterate wickedness should be converted into a matter of glory and pride.

Yet, since man was not made to think, perhaps the soldier-trade is by heredity and custom the nearest to his true level. As in the case of Justice, the nihilistic and defeatist view must also be heard. In spite of which, Coignard proceeds to demolish military arguments based on the development of courage, the necessary (?) extension of territory, the defence of a 'just' cause, the 'honour' of princes or of states used as a vile excuse for the murder of millions. Here the humanitarian note rings out strongly. The only argument which he can accept is that man is naturally so bad that his animal ferocity will keep him a fighter, though he may seek to disguise the instinct with high-sounding words. The only hope is that some day the rival armaments may grow so large that the 'monster will burst of his own obesity.' Perhaps this is the most significant prophecy in all the *Opinions.*

In the chapter on 'Les Séditieux,' appears the turbulent 'M. Rockstrong,' easily recognizable as Henri Rochefort, editor of *l'Intransigeant.* He had been condemned in connexion with the Boulanger affair, and he is again condemned by the voice of Coignard, who makes short work of his professions of probity and his ideals of reform. The Abbé falls here into his most cynical vein, as to the absurdity of attempting anything, the supremacy of the *raison d'Etat,* the slight differences between pure and impure politicians, namely, the 'ins' and the 'outs.' When he becomes defeatist to this extent, he is usually rebuked by one of his interlocutors, Rockstrong, or M. Roman or even Jacques Tournebroche, who fail to understand his perversity and his indifferent *laissez-faire*. That does not perturb him, for he feels that it is the lot of the *philosophe* to irritate the rest of mankind.

This shock-proof attitude reaches a climax in the five chapters on Justice, which occupy the remainder of the book. Their content had been partly anticipated by some remarks in an earlier chapter (X), where the Abbé insisted to the surprised Tournebroche that *human* justice was but a juggling of words, that the Palais itself had an historical foundation of lies and sophistries, and that it was useless to appeal to non-existent general principles. Now two illustrations to the point are exhibited. On a lovely

Spring day there passes by a cart containing a servant-girl who is about to be hanged for petty larceny. She stole some lace from her mistress and confessed the crime under torture. In spite of his scepticism, the Abbé's heart cannot be indifferent to this spectacle, which robs him of his joy in the fine day and in his food. His neighbour, a little *huissier,* is more tough-minded and tells a tale which serves as the second example of miscarriages of justice. (This 'Récit,' found by A.F. in the old *Mercure de France,* had, as the 'Histoire véritable d' Hélène Gillet,' already been narrated in *l'Echo de Paris.*[47]) A girl who had been forcibly made pregnant and was wrongly convicted of infanticide was nevertheless sent to the scaffold. The executioner himself was so conscience-stricken that he botched his job. Though dreadfully wounded, she survived and was finally pardoned by his gracious Majesty, 'Louis le Juste.' Naturally she retired to a convent, to expiate her sins.

The *huissier* hopes that Coignard has been diverted by this story. On the contrary, it has revolted him even more strongly than the execution of the servant-girl, a point of view which the callous *huissier* cannot understand. His remark that 'Gothic barbarity' has been removed from French laws and customs is indignantly rebutted by the Abbé, who believes rather that the codes are still full of horrors which will cause future Frenchmen to blush for shame. Thus is launched a 'ferocious' attack on the very foundations of justice—an attack which may well be associated with some of the windings of the Panama complication.[48] What is this justice that protects the powerful against the weak, that is all for vested interests, that rhetorically glorifies the defence of property (originally won by robbery) and of baseless conventions ? It is primarily utilitarian. It does not often pretend to fit the punishment to the actual crime, and when it does, who are we to pass in the name of 'virtue' on what is due to sinners like ourselves ? Seillière has noted that France often uses incidents and cases, in the manner of Voltaire, to drive home his point.[49] A.F. now cites, probably from *Zadig,* the well-known story of the Angel and the hermit, in order to show the relativity of human or 'temporal' judgments. When is a thief not a thief ? Evidently, when he steals a cup for some higher purpose. And if this is Voltairian, the Abbé becomes practically Rousseauistic in challenging the rights of mere property-holders, who are themselves the prime offenders, to act as if they were delegates of the Deity.

The whole judicial system is one of iniquitous banditry, and the responsibility falls heavily upon Society.[50]

Needless to say, the actual judges, for all their ermine, are as blind, as prejudiced, as corruptible as the rest of humanity. Coignard concludes that no reason can guide us in the application of laws derived from a mass of superstitions, ignorance, and egotism. Only actions and judgments that are prompted by true sentiment, by humanitarianism, by 'l'enthousiasme,' can do some good in this world.

Thus far the Abbé, in the *Opinions* proper. But the original series of articles was followed by a tail-piece or 'Conclusion,'[51] which was presently enlarged and adapted as a preface to the volume; the purpose was to introduce 'l'Abbé Jérôme Coignard' to fresh readers. Those who were horrified by the 'anarchical' passages on Justice are equally virulent against this Introduction, which they attack in detail; others accept more equably A.F.'s scorn for the 'traditional pomp of customs and beliefs,' or insist on the value of these deeply meditative pages.[52] But all acknowledge the importance of France's message as here delivered. Its dedication to the 'advanced' Octave Mirbeau was considered as a sort of challenge to the established order.

However, the opening pages are harmless enough and mostly serve to recapitulate the chief events in *La Rôtisserie,* while maintaining the fiction that Jacques Tournebroche collected these various remains regarding his master. Although a bookseller, Tournebroche did not publish them himself, because he best knew the vanity of authorship and of all the works that lie rotting in the sun. France maintains that literary glory is a mirage and that survival often depends upon accidents. The insistence on this *motif* reminds us that A.F. is speaking mainly in his own person throughout the Introduction. In spite of disclaiming responsibility for the Abbé's political and ethical views, he calls attention to their excellence and credits his character with revealing, in the following dialogues, his usual 'indulgent wisdom and magnanimous scepticism.' Save in the matter of religious faith (where neither Tournebroche nor France could follow him), Coignard braved the traditional opinions current in his century. The reason alleged for this nonconformity is that he could not hold with mediocre minds and accepted commonplaces. Observing men with a singular mixture of scorn and sympathy—a 'split' in his psychology to which we must later return—he saw no reason for supporting their ill-founded *préjugés*. He was that rare thing—'a free mind in a humble position.' Sharing the Voltairian, and the Anatolian, aversion to system-makers in philosophy, he yet composed a 'marvellous' blend of Epicurus and St. Francis—the two best friends of mankind. On these models, he endeavoured to root out the horrors of hell from people's minds. Although orthodox, he 'drew some original conclusions' from the credo, including, we may think, some Deistic trends. His God is not a 'profitable' and official superintendent, with whom worldlings find it well to keep on good terms; he is more like a vast intelligence that guides the cosmos. The author declares, indeed, that the Abbé thought of divine goodness as large enough to make the world more like the gardens of Epicurus than the deserts of the Thébaïde—an antithesis which carries us both backwards and forwards in France's work. Equally characteristic is Coignard's emphasis upon pity as the greatest among the 'indulgent and voluptuous virtues,' and his hatred of pride as our worse vice. If we attain to commiseration through a just idea of our small statures, we become vainglorious through too much trust in our 'imbecilic' mental constructions. Laws and empires themselves are but castles in the sand; and it is foolish for man to set his 'glory' or his 'honour' before his repose. The oppression of the poor is largely to foster the condescension of the rich; and Coignard again frankly prefers the former as the better company.

Our Abbé, Anatole continues, was quite lacking in the sense of veneration. His distaste for the Pharisees comports also a distaste for the major prophets, which would probably have included those of the Revolution. If you are firmly persuaded of the natural depravity of man, you cannot approve the Rousseaus and the Robespierres who attempt to lift him by his boot-straps. Coignard would have rejected the Declaration of Rights, 'because it sought to establish an excessive and iniquitous distinction between man and the gorilla.' It is made plain that the Abbé, whether by principle or practice, would never have been a Revolutionary. Popular will and popular sovereignty are equally myths, equally to be distrusted.[53]

But is this Anatole's final word as found in the present volume? Does he agree with his mouthpiece that, considering the frailties of human nature and of our institutions, it is just as well to keep our old clothes and patch them up ? 'Why, O Master,' asks Tournebroche, 'should you reduce to dust all the foundations of power, since you recognize that some such disciplines must always exist ?' Coignard hedges with a few general observations about cleaning out the dark corners and redding the house up so that it may in some form endure. On this uncertain note, the original article ('Conclusion') ended, and even Braibant considers this as representing A.F.'s true position.[54]

But what now follows in the preface (thinks the same critic) shows more of an iconoclastic tendency, because these paragraphs were added under the spur of some violent Socialistic upheavals in the French elections. Let us see. Anatole continues that since the days of Coignard Prometheus has upset Jupiter several times without really getting any forwarder. There is always another Jupiter. The Titan, it seems, is still under his rock, but preliminary rumblings may indicate that he is preparing to burst forth. If we examine our present condition, we perceive still injustice, misery, avarice, and possible ruin in the heart of a plutocracy. The rich are so stupid that they do not feel the insect gnawing at their vitals. Will we always be lulled by the declamations of statesmen and the prattle of economists about the market value of a burning house ? Democracy seems in the last century to have given rise to an 'incoherent succession of insurrectionary governments.' If we would only view our modern turbulent prejudices with the calm detachment which the Abbé practiced toward those of his own time, we might acquire a 'charitable scepticism,' and dissensions would be less evident in the fairest country in the world.

I do not think that these cautious phrases, though they do contain hints of disaster, can be said to go very far as yet in the direction either of state Socialism or political optimism ; nor that they approve the work of the Revolution as half-done, while suggesting that the sociological reforms still remain to be accomplished. It seems rather that Mathiez is right in affirming that we need more clarification as to France's final attitude towards the Revolution and its consequences.[55]

Some hold that the main theme of this work is the insistence upon the badness, and the foolish pride, of mankind. Thus, the reason for the Abbé's distrust of Revolutions or thorough reforms would be his fundamental scorn for men as 'absurd, evil and ferocious' animals in every age. Seillière seems right in maintaining that this is hard to reconcile with the pity and sympathy which France also advocates. Can you love singly people whom *en masse* you despise ? And if so, another contradiction remains : how can you entrust power to this mass ? Yet we must agree with Gaffiot that in spite of all the contempt, irony, and doubt poured out upon the race in the chief volumes of this epoch, whenever Anatole has to choose between some form of absolutism and democracy, he votes for the latter.[56] The dilemma is an interesting one, because it expresses the plight of many modern intellectuals, who are drawn in both ways. Yet the solution is beyond doubt. Notwithstanding the Abbé Coignard's professed indifferentism regarding régimes, his creator evinces already a democratic trend, which presently becomes socialistic. The *Opinions* therefore anticipate the *Histoire contemporaine* in a number of respects.

Other criticisms of the work concern its comprehensive raillery and nihilism ; or the 'complete liberty of mind' found both in the author and his favourite hero ; or the notion that the political iconoclasm is that of the student rather than of the man of business ; or the contrary (and more acceptable) notion that the 'sincere indignation' here expressed is rather the product of a closer contact with affairs ; or the suggestion that 'France's future socialism' may find root here in his opposition of tolerance and the general good to ignorance and monopolism ; or finally and more generally the conviction that Anatole's successive attacks on the present order stem from his belief that it is based primitively on brutality and social injustice rather than on enlightened reason—a constant theme.[57]

§ 3

It was probably with a feeling of relief that Anatole turned from politics to more personal matters such as Italy and the search for beauty, love-making and the portraiture of individuals. All of these figure in *Le Lys rouge,* which was the main preoccupation of the author and his mistress during much of 1893. Mme. de Caillavet had persuaded A.F. to undertake this 'society novel,' this 'belle histoire d'adultère parisien,' for which he felt himself little fitted. Impatiently she assured him that many of the types and a good part of the setting could be provided by her salon ;

for the rest of the background they went to Italy in the Spring. He really began work on *Le Lys* (first called *La Terre des morts*) in the early Autumn and he must have finished it by the following Spring, for the novel appeared serially in the *Revue de Paris,* April 1-June 1, 1894. It came out in book-form shortly afterwards.[58]

Mme. de C. evidently wished her lover to rival the successes of Bourget, Hervieu, and Marcel Prévost in the *roman mondain ;* and this is the group with which *Le Lys* was presently associated. But doubtful of his ability in this line, France alleged that he had no deep acquaintance with the 'puppets' constituting Society. Mme. Arman insisted, even to the extent of 'brushing in the background' and sketching certain personages, known to them both, who might furnish amusing traits. As usual, France yielded to her importunities ; and the two of them, whether in Paris or Florence, jotted down many notes that might serve 'le roman.' If ultimately the book became an artistic success, as well as a popular one, the credit is due to Anatole's incomparable touch, as well as to his extreme care in composition.[59]

A fairly full account of the original MSS. of the story with the alterations they successively underwent, may be found in the Andrieux Catalogue, issued in connexion with the great sale of 'Franciana' in 1932.[60] Nowhere better than in these *brouillons,* says the commentator (M. Carias), 'does there exist a manuscript ensemble so ample, so diversified in its unity, so full of surprises and of the essential Anatole.' Chapter by chapter we may watch the author tempering crudities, deleting what seemed unsuitable reflections or dialogue, altering the names of characters, expanding some portions, omitting other developments and episodes. At times, there are fundamental changes, as for example in the rupture between the heroine and her first lover, Le Ménil. This scene still has its brutal aspects, but these were more marked in the primitive version. The character of Le Ménil has been modified, made less 'black' and bold, and so has the language of Thérèse, under various circumstances. It is amazing to see how many indelicacies A.F. originally allowed himself and his characters, in a novel addressed to polite society. Certain alterations were made to diminish the autobiographical element : the second lover of Thérèse (who is much like Mme. de C.) was at first a writer

AT THE TIME OF 'LE LYS ROUGE'

very like France ; in the final draft he became the sculptor, Dechartre. As usual, Anatole shows care for exactness in matters topographical or historical ; many scenes from Florentine life, such as the cobbler and his sparrow, or the letter box near Or San Michele, are actual reminiscences. He is unwearying in his search for the right word, which often ends by being the simplest. His main endeavour, as Henriot shows, was to give a unified artistic savour to the whole book. Yet after a much later revision he expressed to Ségur his dissatisfaction with the work and declared that only the first few pages were written in passable French ! [61]

In spite of Anatole's unfavourable view, of which there are other indications,[62] such was not the general opinion on the book's appearance. Having excited much gossip at tea-tables, before publication, it was the chief literary event of the Summer of 1894. Neither the author nor Mme. de C. was quite aware of its 'immense success' ; in the *cénacle* of the Avenue Hoche, Maurras and later Proust expressed their warm admiration ; while nearly thirty letters, with signatures ranging from the younger Dumas through Colette bear witness to the interest aroused.[63] It was generally agreed that the *Lys* was the answer to those ladies who complained that France had never depicted modern love-making. Now they could take their fill of that ; and if they found the novel too much like Bourget's *Mensonges,* they had certainly asked for it themselves.

It was recognized that here was Anatole's first real *roman mondain*. Some critics, like Rod, were well pleased with his choice of distinguished characters and congratulated him on keeping his ironic penetration in the midst of luxurious settings. Others, like Vandérem, were more interested in the quantity of general culture disseminated through the discussions in the novel. Pellissier, too, cared less for the love-triangle than for the characters, episodes, even the digressions. Questioning whether France was fundamentally a novelist, Pellissier hoped he would remain outside of all classifications, as the 'most ingenious, elegant and profound of present-day writers.' Lemaître, while surprised at the sensuality of people moving in such refined circles, while noting the 'bitter and strong taste' of the book, still viewed its author—famous phrase !—as the 'final flower of the Latin genius.' One should mention, too, such dissident opinions as that of Léon

Blum, who held that France's 'fluid and ornate talent' found its best expression in reviving the past rather than in the chatter of the salons and in dissecting the sensual emotions of worldlings.[64]

What, then, is the gist of this 'simple but violent' drama? The elegant Comtesse Martin-Bellème, bored by her political husband—and by many other things—has taken as lover Robert Le Ménil, a scrupulous sportsman. Thérèse is wearying of him too, when chance throws in her path the sensitive artist, Dechartre. At Florence their love is consummated. But Dechartre has a jealous nature. When Thérèse breaks with Le Ménil, and lies about it, the sculptor's suspicions are aroused; later they are confirmed; and always he will see between his mistress and himself the image of the former lover. A second tragic parting ends the book.

The main characters have been much discussed. For some, as for Lemaître, they are less convincing than several of the minor personages. But I am not persuaded that they are merely types or symbols. At least they were modelled on definite personalities: Thérèse on Mme. de Caillavet; Le Ménil on Gassou, the sporting character from Bordeaux, whom Anatole seems to have disliked.[65] Thérèse is analysed with an exhaustive care that makes her easily the most prominent person in the book. Like Madame Arman, this Countess comes of sturdy, acquisitive stock; the father of each was a successful financier who endowed his daughter with a certain 'brutality of temperament.' Both women had auburn hair and were gifted with a feline grace. But Thérèse was the prettier, the suppler, the more seductive of the two. Like her model, she was fond of prowling in the poorer quarters—a trait which Le Ménil could not understand. From Mme. de Caillavet Mme. Martin derived her bold, frank, downright way of facing people and difficulties. She handles the conventions as she likes; when she is through with a lover, she performs a clean-cut operation; she is easily bored, except by the most natural things; she rises superior to her husband and presently to Le Ménil, who had satisfied her for three years. Although she pursues the joys of love and life, she is as tragically ironic about them, as easily disillusioned as France himself. Her motto is: 'No regrets.' Only Dechartre can bring her to her knees, can make her weep, can inspire in her something of womanly sympathy, of reciprocal affection, even of fear for what may come. Yet when it does come, she faces it and walks away proudly from their last rendezvous. Not a lovable woman in the ordinary sense, yet 'made for love,' every inch of her — like many of France's heroines. Her conversation and ideas offer a blend, difficult to separate, of her creator's and her model's.[66] Perhaps because of her basis in reality, Thérèse has been considered the 'truest' figure in the book ; the question of the morality of her conduct is never raised.[67]

Le Ménil is a comparatively simple person. It is evident that he imitates the characteristics of the well-groomed Gassou, Nimrod and athlete, suspicious of writers and artists. It is to Le Ménil rather than to any other of the masculine characters that we would apply Giraud's remark that Anatole's heroes are well-endowed physiologically, but not psychologically.[68] Tall, supple, and swarthy, Robert is at the same time loyal, punctilious, rather dull, and far from understanding his mistress. Except when other obligations interfere, he is deeply devoted to Thérèse and expects her fidelity as a matter of course. It is this matter-of-courseness, coupled with a certain narrowness and conventionality of view-point, that alienates Thérèse. He is naturally slow to believe that she has really left him for good. When he pursues her to Florence and learns the truth, he suffers, sobs, and strikes back like a wounded animal. One speech is tragi-comically revealing : 'I will wager that *he* is not even a man of the world !' (In *La Révolte des anges,* Maurice d'Esparvieu makes the same comment regarding the conduct of the visiting angel.) Though he scarcely meets Dechartre, Le Ménil distrusts him as he does the writer-tribe of Choulette and Vence. Back in Paris, he doggedly and futilely insists that Thérèse should return to him. Some think that in this limited character the author took his revenge on the 'gens du monde.'[69]

Jacques Dechartre is quite a different, a superior, a complex personality. Comparatively an outsider, he has no definite affiliations at first with the circle of Mme. Martin-Bellème nor, apparently, with the actual people surrounding Mme. de Caillavet. Yet one may perceive certain bonds of sympathy between Dechartre and Anatole himself. Each is 'un timide et un passionné' ; each, says Lemaître, is 'a philosopher, a critic, an analyst of his own impulses.' Larroumet thinks that Dechartre has in his composition more of the writer than of the plastic artist.[70] For if, while plunging into life and love, he maintains the semi-detachment of the Watcher, if he is too far-sighted to blind himself about the nature of his passion and its probable outcome, is not this a duplication of the novelist's usual attitude? And if he is credited (by Paul Vence) with a great wealth of knowledge and feeling, with a disturbing and complicated imagination, are we not on familiar ground? Who possesses the 'uneasy and mobile mind . . . that loves itself in all the fair things found in the world'? Who returns to Italy as to the country dearest to his heart?

Thus in the gradual crystallization of Dechartre's aspirations round Thérèse—the 'fairest thing found in the world'—he wishes to share with her all his artistic dreams and admirations. He is provoked when they differ in tastes; he is charmed when they agree. As a sculptor, he is enamoured of the beautiful lines of her rhythmic body. He appreciates her dresses more convincingly than any one else she has ever known. We are not surprised that he overpowers her, in an ideal setting, with his taste, his responsiveness, his masculinity. Nor is Thérèse surprised when Desire turns all this charm into something sombre and violent, demanding, jealous, always unsatisfied in the heart of pleasure. When he finds cause for his distrust of her, he stays out all night, suffering incredibly. Ultimately he reproaches her with taking from him all the beauty in the world, which they had begun by joyfully sharing. He ends by acting hatefully toward her. It may be that this break, this decline in the personality of Dechartre, once sexual love has seized him, is as incomprehensible to most readers as it was to Lemaître. But Anatole seems to have understood it well enough, since it exemplified his theory of the passions.

The origins of Dechartre lie outside the Caillavet circle; but as the hostess herself had suggested, several of the minor characters, to say nothing of the conversations and general aura, owe much to the Avenue Hoche. To a considerable extent, *Le Lys* is a *roman à clef,* and that fact doubtless contributed to its success in 1894. Today, one cannot decipher all the personal allusions; on this account as well as because of its faded Pre-Raphaelitism, the book definitely 'dates.'[71] But at that time people could easily identify the lady who in the Louvre was always finding portraits of her acquaintances—and found replicas of M. Renan everywhere! Some may have been aware that the learned 'M. Schmoll' bore the same name as an astronomer whom Anatole elsewhere laid under contribution. Furthermore, the *chic* conversations of women like the Princesse Séniavine and the bird-like twitterings of the poetess, Vivian Bell, were probably familiar to the frequenters of the Caillavet salon.

The last-named personage, indeed, has an interesting literary history. Of her actual prototype France wrote, in *La Vie littéraire,*

> Mary Robinson, today Madame [James] Darmesteter, is an English poetess of an exquisite delicacy. Her gracious hands are skilful in the art of assembling and enveloping us with large living images.[72]

The fact that Mary Robinson is mentioned by name in *Le Lys rouge,* as on a par with 'Vivian Bell' and Vernon Lee, is simply an attempt to draw a herring across the trail. This leads directly to Mme. Darmesteter, who subsequently became Mme. Duclaux, well known for her biography of Hugo and other works. Her early volume of verse, *Marguerites du temps passé,* was sympathetically reviewed by A.F. in *Le Temps* (January 17, 1892). And on the whole his treatment of 'Vivian Bell' is sympathetic likewise.

There is, however, another claimant to the honour of posing for Miss Bell. This is 'Vernon Lee' (Violet Paget) who is also mentioned by Anatole in the passage cited above. She too was one of the Pre-Raphaelite succession, was deeply interested in Italian culture, and spent much of her life in a villa near Florence. On that basis it has been stated that she served France both as cicerone and as inspiration for his 'portrait tendrement amusé' of the æsthetic Englishwoman.[73] It may be so; but the suggestion is not as yet sufficiently supported, although quite probably the Italian villa was that of Vernon Lee.

At any rate, Miss Bell has a *cachet* all of her own, a kind of artless art, which helps to give the novel whatever of sweetness and light it may possess. A virginal Quattrocentist, Miss Bell stands apart from the darker passions of the lovers. (The fact that she will presently espouse a god-like Italian, who is occupied with unloading 'antiques' on an unsuspecting world, is hardly an exception.) Throughout most of the novel Miss Bell, entertaining her 'darling' Thérèse at Fiesole, is occupied with her ingenuous poetry, twitters about the bronze bells which she collects (to justify her name), surrounds herself with choice bric-à-brac, amuses us with her boyish form and enthusiasm, leaves a delicate impression, as of the fading Primitives whose spirit she had imbibed. What was she, in short? 'An æsthete who conveyed into her need for love the mysticism of an Annunciation.'

Vivian is repelled by the 'barbaric' Choulette, another poet of quite a different type, and at times he returns her animosity. This modern Villon, this bard of the people, half-drunkard and half-mystic, living with a prostitute whom he beats and glorifies, pleases Thérèse by his originality. Since he wishes to go to Assisi and revive the order of Franciscans, she offers to take him in her suite to Italy. He boards the train, somewhat as A.F. had boarded it at Avignon, dragging along an old carpet-bag. He makes a strange effect with his ravaged face, his high-domed forehead, his air of being at once a ruin and the Eternal Bard. When Vivian Bell later compares him physically to Socrates, we feel that our suspicions are correct: in all essentials Choulette is Paul Verlaine. And what we hear about his recent volume, *Les Blandices,* 'dealing with all sorts of love' and mostly written in uneven line-lengths, deepens the impression.

On the train, Choulette is by turns truculent and fearful. He is easily intimidated by landscape and the like, even as Verlaine shows himself in his poetry. Recovering, he begins to whittle the figure of a woman on the handle of his staff and to express downright views in opposition to militarism and the social order. As Lemaître says, the 'very living' Choulette is used to transmit the more drastic opinions of A.F.[74] In Italy, the poet is promptly at home on the popular and Catholic levels. He frequents a cobbler's shop, whittling on his staff and reciting his devout verses. At Miss Bell's villa, he is more dissatisfied, shows childish vanity, and at times is positively *méchant*. Presently he goes to Assisi, becomes fully indoctrinated with Franciscanism, and returns to Florence to march in holy processions, while teaching to the very humblest the joys of Christianity mingled with much Chianti and prophecies of a better day. Thérèse still admires him as a great, slightly charlatanesque, artist; and Anatole too has an evident predilection for this battered overgrown child, whose only faults are those of the flesh.

It was long thought that Verlaine was the only original for Choulette, as he was for Gestas. His vagabond life and the quality of his naïve poetry lent colour to this belief. A.F. had often praised that verse or commiserated that existence.[75] But in his old age, Anatole declared to Mme. Bölöni that though he was thinking partly of Verlaine, he was thinking still more of Louis Nicolardot, the Catholic journalist and Bohemian. He had been greatly attracted and amused by the strange originality, the fantasy, the *drôlerie* of this personage. It becomes of some interest, therefore, to examine a pretty full account of Nicolardot which 'Gérôme' once wrote.[76] Claiming that he was well acquainted with this 'pauvre illustre,' the chronicler depicts him as an obscure and unkempt figure, who thought himself quite a man with the ladies, considered everybody else (comparatively speaking) in the condition of Abelard, and rose to heights of self-satisfaction. In a dingy overcoat, 'he looked like a drowned dog.' Poets stood him dinners, or else he ate not. Yet he was no poet himself, but rather a dusty compiler, a 'rat de bibliothèque.' He lived mostly in the streets and seemed in fact a sort of outdoor object—we surmise, a dust-bin. He was a unique figure, a gutter Diogenes, a muddy dog who pawed at strangers. A defender of the Church, he kept a kind of proud innocence in his sincere follies.

Only the last few touches in this portrait seem to anticipate Choulette, who for all of Anatole's later assertions remains nearer the type of Verlaine.

One other character in *Le Lys* must be mentioned—the *raisonneur,* Paul Vence, who is also a novelist. He is the most direct mouthpiece of the author himself, and if we cannot quite agree that 'Vence says almost nothing that France has not said elsewhere,' yet his wit and his wisdom and the balance that he keeps between the other characters, are mostly in the Anatolian vein.[77] We shall need him in our discussion of the topics and themes in the volume, to which we may now turn.

The matters most prominently displayed are Italy and Art, luxurious Society, and (*rinforzando*) Love and Jealousy. The author's beauty-loving impulses are here given full rein, to such an extent that Carias is warranted in declaring that the peculiar charm of the book 'is in the great emphasis attached to art, the splendour of things, the preoccupation with beauty'; and it has been noted that the characters contribute, as far as possible, to this major intention. The special kind of artistic atmosphere, the rather pale Primitive light in which much of the book is bathed, has excited various comment. Lanos finds too much talk of the impressionistic variety; Bainville protests that the pseudo-religiosity which charmed the æsthetes of 1894 has become trite and insipid; too many long-fingered Virgins, too many angel-laden frescoes, too many visits to see this Pietà or that gallery. Yet one may remark that the amused Anatole never lets himself be wholly carried away. And Vaudoyer testifies to the effect that this is how cultured cosmopolitans often behaved, when Florence was swarming with self-exiled English (such as Vernon Lee), 'when Anglo-Florentine æstheticism confused in one and the same admiration the Tuscan Primitives and Pre-Raphaelites like Burne-Jones.'[78] In Fiesole, we are in the midst of pallid Sienese Virgins, flanked by a lean Magdalen, and the bells of many voices that symbolize Miss Vivian. She points out to her 'darling' that the God who made the hills round Florence was a many-sided artist. In the city itself, while we move among the frescoes of Fra Angelico or pass from the bronze St. Mark to the St. George of Donatello, Dechartre praises the artisans of yore, and Thérèse characteristically finds sensuality in the heart of the supposedly ascetic Quattrocento.

This was the period then in most repute, and *Le Lys rouge* both followed and assisted the vogue. Young men dreamed of visiting the settings described by Anatole France and Paul Bourget, with the hope doubtless that women like their heroines would prove kind in the city of the Lily. For one effect of dead beauty upon A.F.'s lovers is to 'excite their ardour for living'—and loving.[79]

We have seen how the novelist himself brought back treasures from his Italy; and we need not reiterate the variety of ways in which he rendered homage to the country. His tributes here, often put on the lips of the ladies, celebrate the light which bathes the valley of the Arno, the landscape 'arranged' like a painting, stories of old artists and their triumphs in marble, stone and oils, together with pretty vignettes of daily life. Florence lies like a jewel at the bottom of a perfect hollow cup; Florence in the rosy morning blossoms indeed like the Red Lily which is the emblem alike of the city and of passion. And on a similar jewelled lily in her bosom Thérèse Martin, allegorically, pricks her finger until it bleeds.

The matter of St. Francis is not neglected—Choulette even offers a free translation of the 'Cantico delle Creature.' The matter of erudition is amply embodied by M. Schmoll of the Institut—'a great philologist who knew all languages, except French.' But a more general matter for our consideration is the presentation of society, whether or not one capitalizes the word.

When in 1888 Mme. Duclaux ('Vivian Bell') first knew France, she found him, though strange to drawing-rooms, frequenting them with some intention of social satire. Again, it seems that he began his social career as the 'retiring and absent-minded' Dechartre, to end as the *spirituel* Paul Vence.[80] In either instance, the fictional observer must have noticed, in the luxurious 'period' settings at the Comtesse Martin's, things similar to what Anatole knew so well *chez* Mme. Arman. 'These beautiful objects,' said Vence, with a circular glance, 'go perfectly with your own style.' That style (together with her enterprising toilettes) accompanies Thérèse through afternoon teas, formal or political dinners, and an evening at the Opera. 'Society' is putting Anatole through his paces, and if he has to stretch himself to keep up, the effort is not obvious to the average reader. He lingers over his *ensembles,* breaking up his first chapter in order to describe more fully two functions; and he touches off the incidental guests (e.g., a general) by accenting their incredible platitudes and prejudices in a manner foreshadowing the *Histoire contemporaine*. As a recorder of the passing show, Anatole is not quite a Bourget or a Proust, but he will 'do' and a bit more.

It has been suggested that his own 'domestic calamity revealed to him . . . the frequent cruelty of social custom and prejudice.'[81] Not improbably it aided in this enlightenment, of which we have seen manifestations in the preceding sections of this chapter. But there were other antipathies which led him to drive a satirical pen. The novel as a whole is weak after Thérèse and her friends return to Paris; yet in this later portion there is one unforgettable *tableau:* the intriguing and chicanery connected with the above-mentioned political dinner, the poor quality of these self-interested statesmen, the 'laborious distribution of portfolios' which will not stay distributed. A.F. rather prided himself on this digression which shows his usual contempt for the ministers of Demos.

Since these are the colleagues of M. Martin-Bellème, it is not surprising that his wife finds men of this and other periods 'egotistical, violent, penurious and pitiless.' She finds further that law and custom have always been hard on the unfortunate. As a good Franciscan, Choulette quite agrees. Affiliations with Jérôme Coignard, or with Fra Giovanni in 'l'Humaine Tragédie' appear in quite a few of the poet's utterances. He is clear that to the humble belong the kingdoms of this earth ; but they have been disinherited. 'In this poisoned country, whoever loves the poor is considered a traitor to society'—defined as a collection of citizens banded together 'to sustain the rich in their power and their idleness.' And the poor are forced into the coalition. Needless to say, Choulette is opposed to all this elaborate structure, believing rather in the plain work of one's hands and the vows of St. Francis. He is equally opposed to the glorification, by the ruling classes, of conquerors and their steeds and their needless massacres : 'that is why the just man will one day refuse to draw his number in military conscription.' The slightly ironic veiling that France affects here does not disguise his real sympathy with Choulette's views.

Among the cruelties of life may be reckoned those entailed by sensual love. Choulette sets the pace when he declares—for he too was once tempted by Thérèse—that the violence of passion is a bad and bitter thing. Pure love, indeed, can do no evil. 'But sensual desire is compounded of hatred, egotism and anger as much as of love.' Now Dechartre and his creator are agreed that sensual love is the only valid kind between the sexes. The conception of ardent and fatalistic passion (of which the 'Lily' is in part a symbol) is definitely Anatolian ; and he endowed his protagonist with the same conception. A typical criticism directed against *Le Lys* concerns the daring of the bedroom scenes, the 'frequent and varied embraces' which breathe 'la plus âcre volupté.' But Lemaître, while noting this fact, implies the more searching criticism that this pleasure rapidly turns to pain, that the game hardly seems worth the candle—or the lack of one. It is a singular coincidence that France's brother-Impressionist should cite as instances of sombre passion the examples dear to France himself—Racine's heroines, the case of Dido in her grotto, even the Virgilian passage concerning *durus amor.*[82]

> Plaisir d'amour ne dure qu'un moment,
> Chagrin d'amour dure toute la vie.

This dirge-like conclusion, together with the idea that passion makes bestial puppets of us all, seems to be the moral that most reviewers drew from the story.[83] It is certainly warranted by the course of events. Le Ménil, the discarded lover, is unhappy almost throughout. Thérèse and Jacques are happy and glowing only while their love is incipient or efflorescent; only while each may 'crystallize' round the other the beautiful things in life and art; only while they share the dream of a dual solitude wherein passion itself may become a perfected masterpiece; only while *la Volupté* bears them triumphant on her wings. But soon, too soon, comes (for him) the shattering disillusionment. Swift is the change from expansive delight to narrowing distrust and rancour. The final separation of the lovers has an infinite sadness, because one is made to feel that it is a necessity bound up with the nature of things. 'All that we have been to each other,' exclaims the woman, 'was then useless! We break against one another, but we do not mingle.'

Dechartre, corrosive as France in his analysis, had felt earlier that love, however one might drown in it, was but 'the effort of a delicious despair,' another Illusion in the sum of things. He had gravely told Thérèse: 'We are never good and kind when we love.' But in his case there was a particular reason for cruelty and despair. Its name was Jealousy.

This disorganizing power had shown other manifestations. The excellent M. Marmet had been jealous of his equally excellent wife, a minor character in the novel. Perhaps France himself had been jealous of Gassou; certainly Le Ménil, though serenely free from any such feeling in Paris, displayed savage jealousy when he learned what took place in Florence. And Dechartre, in turn, becomes obsessed by suspicions, the analysis of which constitutes, for some minds, the best feature of *Le Lys rouge*. Lemaître has finely said that the very definite desire of Dechartre caused his jealous rage to be equally concrete and concentrated. It is thereby rendered unbearable and speedily turns love to hate.[84]

The incident that awakens his 'retrospective' suspicions is a recurrent *motif* that inflames them again and again. It goes back to the moment when the gloved hand of Thérèse deposited a mysterious letter in the mail-box near Or San Michele. When the sculptor saw this apparently innocent gesture, his soul cried within him, as it cried out to her later: 'You have a lover!' And that image, that act, burned into him, body and soul. When he has associated the sending of the letter with Le Ménil, when the sportsman has actually been seen in Florence, then Dechartre is a prey to the most violent tortures. He explains why jealousy is worse for a man than for a woman. The sense of possession is stronger in the former ; it leads him into greater mental and physical suffering. The passion is analysed in a manner which constitutes almost a theory, and as such it has some affiliations with an earlier article in 'La Vie littéraire.'[85] But for the sculptor the issue, though laid largely in the past, is a very practical one. Othello-like, he becomes so occupied with tormenting images, so impossible with Thérèse, that the only solution is a clean break. When for the last time he tries to take her, he imagines his predecessor doing just that thing, and he is repelled and inhibited. Another form of this dénouement is used in the *Histoire comique,* where the suicide of the first lover forbids the actress to enjoy the second. (This episode had been anticipated in the story of 'M. Chevalier,' dating, like *Le Lys,* from 1894.)

Besides these central themes, a number of minor *motifs* reappear. Among France's own memories, there figure the oft-mentioned letter-box, the recollection of Paul Arène at Arles, as well as certain traits of 'Maman,' attributed to the mother of Dechartre. It is characteristic that A.F. should make much of the 'lumière' floating over Florence, that he should allow Choulette to decry the value of thought and have Dechartre prefer simple sentiment. As repetition of old material, the story of Scolastica is summarized, the parable of the three rings is amplified from Gaston Paris.[86] Once more we find the phrase about the resemblance between the feminine shape and a beautiful amphora, and the less familiar one about Thérèse stepping to meet the moon, as one lady advances to another.[87]

Paul Vence naturally conveys much of Anatole's thought. A signal instance is found in the following dialogue :

'What is still more astonishing is that the populace can believe that it has any other leaders than its own wretchedness, its desires and its imbecility. He was a wise man who said : "As witnesses and as judges, let us give to men Irony and Pity."

'But, Monsieur Vence,' replied Mme. Martin, laughing, 'you yourself wrote that!'

He also wrote that pity emerges from the heart of the man who is 'sufficiently sensual to be human.' And, like A.F., he minimized the act of writing, of toying with syllables that betray the 'belle idée.' The reader admires not the author, but himself in the author. This did not prevent Mme. Martin from admiring Vence as an 'excellent writer,' whom she esteemed for his 'profound irony, his detached pride, his talent ripened in solitude.' These are among the things that drew Mme. de Caillavet to France.[88]

We have already quoted some outstanding critics on *Le Lys*. A.F. himself, though not enthusiastic about the book and admitting its artificiality (*qualis artifex*), yet told Ségur that the ravelled-out ending was like life. His coolness was probably in reaction against the warmth of the public's approval, for of all France's works this has easily been the most popular.[89] Its vogue may have been somewhat stimulated by the dramatization, on which France collaborated with young de Caillavet. The play, which differs considerably from the novel, was represented with moderate success in 1899 by Réjane and Lucien Guitry.[90]

There have been two storm-centres of debate regarding *Le Lys* as a work of fiction. One concerns the element of sensuality plus nihilism; the other revolves around the question whether, structurally and otherwise, it is fundamentally a novel at all. As for sensuality, we may pass over the extreme views of the cleric who held *ex cathedra* that the work is an 'impure mixture of debauchery and piety,' together with the opinions of certain moralists who run true to form.[91] What is more interesting is that Jules Lemaître, the former partisan, has mounted to a fence from which he surveys Anatole's penchants with uncertainty. If he apologizes for the scepticism (induced by Brunetière), he is like others disturbed by the blend of mysticism and fleshliness, and he wonders to what sort of a *néant* his old friend is travelling.[92] It should be said, however, that whatever the overdose of sensual nihilism—and it may well be considered disproportionate—all this is sincere and characteristic, for that is how France now thought and felt.

A number of critics opine that *Le Lys* is less a novel than—something else.[93] But several, while admitting this, defend the book anyhow for its general excellence; while others specifically praise its *hors d'œuvres,* its conversations, or its style.[94] One may grant that the plot, as usual, is not the main thing; Larroumet holds that it moves too slowly and that the dénouement is too 'rigid,' since the lovers need not have parted; yet most of the action, including this dénouement, proceeds relevantly from the character-analysis as adequately set forth. But a number of pages before the end, dealing with the personages after their return to France, were apparently written with a flagging pen. The stylistic charm and unity of the volume is certainly very great; for many critics, as for the present writer, this constitutes the more abiding value of *Le Lys*.[95] This flavour permeates the dialogue as well as the indirect discourse—a rare achievement, surely. Not in vain had A.F., whether in *Le Temps* or in the salons, perfected the 'causerie littéraire' as a choice genre. The limpid, gushing, sparkling conversation of Vivian Bell is a case in point.

As for the final 'truth' of the characters and the 'humanity' of their depiction, who can say? Henriot, Pica and Lemaître (on the whole) are *pro;* Blum is definitely *con*.[96] Several of the *pros* admit that these personages and their talk are precious or bookish—Anatole himself said 'artificial.' But these are relative terms. A character may be as strangely compounded as Dechartre, as rare a warbler as Miss Bell, and yet may be true to his or her own self.

There was one person who, quite naturally, had no doubts regarding *Le Lys rouge*. For Mme. de Caillavet Anatole made a beautiful copy of the manuscript. This was specially bound in velvet. For years it reposed, like a church Bible, on a sloping stand in the centre of her library. It may now be viewed in the Salle des Manuscrits of the Bibliothèque Nationale.[97]

§ 4

The miscellany bearing the title of *Le Jardin d'Epicure* (1894) has been considered to rival *Les Opinions de Jérôme Coignard* as 'the most radical breviary of scepticism written since Montaigne'; yet Giraud holds that it is less of a 'breviary of Epicureanism' than we are led to expect.[98] The critic and others dwell upon the jumble of materials that make up the volume—disquisitions and dialogues, essays and epigrams—in fact, a rehashing of pretty much everything that Anatole had been thinking about for a number of years. That comprehensiveness and the fact that the ideas appear unadorned by fictional veils are what give the book its final representative value as the philosophical testament of France's third phase.[99] And this in spite of the further, seemingly antagonistic, fact that the medley consists largely of a revamping of articles originally printed before 1893. It is true, as Carias says, that the thought here is more abstract, less actual and pungent, than in the subsequent *Rôtisserie* and the *Opinions*. Yet Michaut seems right in affirming that the productiveness of this whole period is 'in some sort dominated and oriented by the *Jardin d'Epicure*.' It contains the essence of the Anatolian creed. Consequently it will serve us as a vestibule through which we may enter, a little later, into a discussion of the range and quality of his thought.

Due weight should none the less be given to the circumstances of the book's composition. Nothing could be more illustrative of the author's processes.[100] The original edition of *Le Jardin* (it has been revised since) contained scarcely any novelties Apart from the usual echoes of earlier themes, nearly all the material here was reprinted either from *Le Temps* or *l'Echo de Paris* or from both journals. This is worth following in some detail.[101]

When the four volumes of *La Vie littéraire* had been published, there still remained a mine of material in *Le Temps*. Some of this was general or philosophic in nature, a fact which did not prevent the reprinting of ten articles in *l'Echo de Paris* (Dec., 1893–March, 1894). We may suppose that when Calmann-Lévy wanted another volume by France in the autumn of that year, to carry on the success of *Le Lys,* author and editor naturally thought of what was still to be found in the journals.[102] Little labour would be involved. Passages would simply be culled here and there, and shorn of their journalistic embellishments or attenuations. Barring certain retouches, and with the exception of one fresh dialogue ('Ariste et Polyphile'), there need be no new writing. Thus the material falls into two main divisions. The first half of *Le Jardin,* without sub-titles, consists of a quantity of short 'gleanings and juxtapositions' from *Le Temps,* 1886-93—emphasizing the critic's bolder speculations. With certain 'cuts' these articles had been reprinted in *l'Echo de Paris,* as indicated above. In our volume, then, they usually appeared for the third time,[103] although there are ten cases of brief 'développements' taken directly from 'La Vie littéraire,' without passing through the intermediary of *l'Echo*. But in this manner *Le Jardin* was only half-filled. The remainder of the volume contains longer extracts on specific subjects, and to these sub-titles are given, such as 'Sur les couvents de femmes,' or 'Aux Champs-Elysées.' All save one of these dialogues or essays were drawn from one or the other of the journals mentioned (usually 1892-94), but apparently not from both. In addition to an abundant use of scissors and paste, some stylistic emendations were considered necessary. These consist mainly of substitutions and shifts made in the interests of harmony or precision. Here and there sentences are added to complete the thought. Things that smacked too much of the book-review, i.e., references to particular writers and books of the day, are usually eliminated. But the general reflections are seldom tampered with to any extent.

It is these reflections in *Le Jardin* that now concern us, in spite of the repetitions that their exposition may involve. We wish to see whether France had at this stage a general body of doctrine, whether or not the term 'philosophy' is really applicable. Questions regarding the basis and coherence of his thought will for the most part be reserved for the following chapter.

Of the four mottoes which precede the work, one definitely places it under the ægis of Epicurus :

> Il acheta un beau jardin qu'il cultivoit lui-même. C'est là où il établit son école ; il menoit une vie douce et agréable avec ses disciples qu'il enseignoit en se promenant et en travaillant. . . Il étoit doux et affable à tout le monde. . . Il croyoit qu'il n'y a rien de plus noble que de s'appliquer à la philosophie.[104]

Anatole once referred to *Le Jardin* as 'ces faibles essais sur la sagesse' ; and as a 'manuel de la sagesse' it was accordingly esteemed by many, including Jacques Bainville. This Book of Wisdom then begins with a lengthy (and mostly familiar) screed on the universe, astronomically considered. It is somewhat *à la* Pascal, but obviously, as Michaut says, 'a Pascal Darwinized and well up on modern science.'[105]

The drift of the argument is that however anthropocentric we may erroneously remain, the era of geocentrism is definitely over. Rewording what he had said in the notable 'Rêveries astronimiques,'[106] France drives home the point that the simple faith in medieval 'fixity' is no longer possible: we know that the heavens are indefinitely extended; we surmise (a Pascalian touch) that all these millions of suns 'may form but a drop of blood in the body of an imperceptible insect'; we are aware that the law of restless effort applies both to the ageless harmony of the spheres and to the limited days of Man—until, indeed, his thought is extinguished with his existence, and the icy globe rolls on without him. And that is as it should be. For the last men, having forgotten all that they ever knew, 'will be just as stupid, just as dispossessed, as the first ones.' Therefore it is plain that we are not capable of indefinite progress, which depends upon varying physical conditions at a given time.

Such being the strict confines of life and thought, what room does our philosopher find for their activities? In so far as we may synthesize his scattered remarks, these are the main trends.—The deterministic view (cf. Taine) is reinforced by the consideration that, all things being necessitated, our social state is at once a cause and an effect in the long chain of phenomena. Fortunately so, since only because of this slow evolution can we be assured of a comparative tranquillity. But the use of such phrases implies, after all, some belief in progress; and in fact Anatole, rejecting the theory of present decadence, now believes that we are still struggling, bit by bit, toward 'the highest point of civilization.'

It is hard to see on what he founds his hopes, since he is suspicious about the props of civilization that are commonly reckoned with. First, regarding philosophy itself, we know from of old his Voltairian distrust of metaphysical and other 'systems.' As to their procession down the ages, here is his most general statement:

> The various philosophies are interesting only as psychological monuments well-suited to enlighten the scholar on the diverse stages of the human spirit. Very valuable for the knowledge of man, they can shed little light on what is beyond his sphere.

(Yet previously he had declared that the 'know thyself' of the old Greeks is a great piece of folly.) Such being his opinion of the sages in general, we can hardly expect him to do great reverence to individual names. The chief document here is a reprinted dialogue, 'Aux Champs-Elysées.' This begins and ends Socratically, but in between it is more like a thin parody of the banquet-scene in *Thaïs*. We may omit views assigned, with a sort of jocular emphasis on relativity, to such personages as the Polynesian, the Eskimo, and even Leatherstocking! The others indulge in a dialectical skirmish about the nature of the soul. The amused listener (he is hidden in a myrtle grove) hears Pyrrho posit the question, hears Plato assert that the soul is three-fold, while the analytical Aristotle respectfully rejoins that there are in truth five divisions. Church fathers, theologians, and transcendental philosophers carry on the dialogue (*à la* Flaubert, *à la Thaïs*) to demonstrate only that 'opinions were much opposed.' If St. Augustine, Socrates, and Albertus Magnus plump for immortality, Pyrrho goes on with his eternal questioning, 'What is life?' and 'What is death?' If there is any conclusion, it is that the words *Dieu* and *Ame* have had their meaning effaced by continual usage. The author gets even less than the reader out of this 'tour des systèmes.' Both are led to prefer the positive contributions of Auguste Comte, who definitely linked together the sciences and founded sociology. These were real conquests . . . whatever one may think of worshipping that Great Fetish called the Earth.

Yet no scientific discoveries are likely to alter human conduct or to provide a basis for ethics. Morality rests on *sentiment* and on nothing else in the world. Probably because of the variety of our sensitized reactions to conduct, life itself can be by turns good or bad, 'delicious, horrible, charming, frightful,' etc. Call it real or ideal, think of it (which A.F. does) as prevailingly sorrowful and hard, yet 'this is our Garden which we must cultivate with energy.' Thus for the moment the 'Jardin' becomes a part of the property of Voltaire. As for Anatole's playful fancy that we should be able to live like butterflies, saving the brief flare of youthful happiness for the end, that seems to have been lifted from Louis Ménard.[107]

It must be apparent that France is not fond of metaphysical inquiry; but there are still plainer indications of his feeling in this respect. The subject is discussed in 'Ariste et Polyphile, ou le langage métaphysique,' where the latter speaker waxes ironical about textbooks as compendiums of philosophic wisdom. The charge here is mainly directed against the value of abstract terms, which besides being blurred like worn coins are usually negative (e.g., the Absolute) and lacking in definite application. They do not correspond to the same realities as do the inductions based upon the sciences; they are merely individual speculations. Such concepts belong to the realm of illusion and images and have, say in Hegel, about the significance of a superior game of chess. Polyphile concedes the pity of it if this onslaught damages our notions of God and the soul, the very substance of metaphysics.

This attitude is connected with a profound dualism in France's make-up which will require later examination—I mean his Yea-and-Nay evaluation of human thought. At least the problem may be stated here, for *Le Jardin* is much occupied with this subject. On the one hand, he is personally disposed to revel in meditation and (at times) to subsume intelligence and reason as prime factors in human development. People bereft of thought, in the sense of 'intellectual anxiety,' are unattractive to Anatole. On the other hand (preponderantly so in this volume), he is inclined to make ignorance, whether in a healthy country lass or in the life of the race, a necessary condition of bliss:

> If we knew everything, we could not stand existence one hour. Our feelings make it tolerable, and these are nourished by lies and illusions. . .

Again:

> In the presence of women we are penetrated by the idea [but this is a thought!] that the dreams induced by sentiment and the shadows cast by faith are invincible, and that it is not reason which governs mankind.

The theory is stated often enough to become almost persuasive. What makes one distrustful of æsthetics? The fact that almost anything can be demonstrated by ratiocination—proving only the skill of the arguer. What makes a man inapt for action? Evidently the speculative tendency, for it is a real infirmity to see beyond the immediate subject. (A.F. could easily have tested this infirmity in his own person.) Fortunately, the author himself furnishes an answer to the charge that 'the meditative state is the cause of all our evils.' It cannot do much real damage, for it is not very prevalent. And philosophical operations are at a discount when compared with the things achieved by instinct and common sense. A gentle charity can make us happy, while 'la raison n'a point tant de vertu.' The insistence upon this tenet, in the *Jardin* and correlated works, has been pointed out by the critics.[108]

Altogether, the book is a manual of doubt. France's distrust of the efficacy of reason is accompanied by a vast and penetrating scepticism, which, flanked by such willing adjutants as Relativity and the Flux, leads us far into the morass of pessimism and even nihilism. One may distinguish two degrees of this scepticism—the greater and the less. The first, as Vandérem observes, is that of the 'idéophile,' who likes to brandish in our faces his collection of contrary opinions or solutions.[109] This is the amused or amateurish doubter who takes pleasure in mental *impasses,* demanding the free play of his intelligence and his curiosity. We have already met such a person, as early as *La Vie littéraire.* But even there at times and more forcibly here, the doubt assumes darker hues, or becomes more 'corrosive' or despairing.[110] How would the reader feel about this statement?—'There is no enterprise concerning which one may predict whether it will do more harm or good.' If that seems merely an attitude of proper precaution, let us contemplate a more sweeping generalization: 'In the darkness which surrounds us, the savant knocks his head against the wall, while the ignorant person remains quietly in the middle of the room.' Also, after objecting on principle to 'know thyself,' Anatole extends the objection to knowing everybody and everything else. 'To create the world is less possible than to understand it.' We shall see in a moment how the various fields of knowledge are likewise considered as unknowable. If you ask the author what is the purpose of the intelligence, he will answer negatively that it is not suited for the search after truth, nor for the meting out of any kind of justice.

On the right wing of Scepticism is the Flux, the gulf that Anatole had leaned over at least since the days when he read Brochard. It is not surprising to hear him repeatedly speaking of 'l'écoulement des choses' as a mire of uncertainty, in which fixed standards are likely to become submerged. Only the greatest sages can survey the mire without pain, can accept the fact that 'instability is the first condition of life.' Yet the doctrine of universal illusion, coupled with the Flux, was born in the Golden Age of Greece and has been native to civilized minds ever since. Conclusion: one thing is as vain as another in our passing show: the lad of ten may as well build castles in the sand, the virtuoso of sixty may as well collect *bibelots* . . . and (we infer) install them in the Villa Saïd.

As for Relativity, that philosophic will-o'-the-wisp flickers from many points of the Dismal Swamp of scepticism. It sheds a faltering light upon conceptions of justice and æsthetics, upon religion and all 'isms.' The gist of it, with a corollary, is thus set forth: 'Things in themselves are neither great nor small, and when we find that the universe is vast, even that is entirely a human idea.'[111] More of this will appear in connexion with Art.

These various considerations stir within Anatole prevailing moods of dire pessimism. In fact they are self-induced and unresisted—he may even prefer to suffer at the shrine of melancholy:

> Philosophic pessimism has been expressed more than once with a sad magnificence. . . The wise man may intoxicate himself with this melancholy and may forget himself in the delights of a calm despair. It is a profound and beautiful sorrow which its votaries would not exchange for the frivolous gaieties and the vain hopes of the vulgar.

In fact, the relinquishment of metaphysical solutions may open up 'sober perspectives and . . . inspire a salutary sadness.'[112] Yet it is strange to hear Anatole reproaching the gods whom he had abandoned and derided, or deploring that ignorant condition which he had heartily recommended. In this 'absolute ignorance' of our reason for being he now finds the root of 'our sadness and disgust with things'—and he proceeds to make much of physical and moral evil, with all the wretchedness that they entail. When deeply serious, France's pessimism is extremely bitter: this would be the *worst* of possible worlds, were it not that one hesitated to consider it supreme in anything, to grant it even a bad eminence; among other worlds, Mars may be equally hopeless—it is more than likely that its inhabitants are busily devouring one another; life anywhere is an 'evil dream . . . for nature makes cruel sport of our ignorance and imbecility.' As for progress, he is again found on the other side of the fence with Coignard: no increasing purpose is visible, since men are perpetually endowed with the same amount of folly. Nihilism seems the natural conclusion, or ataraxia like that of Timocles of Cos. In life peace can be attained only by the suppression of all thought and action. In death there is danger; it appears to offer a tranquil end; but it is an act, and as such may conceal unguessable portents.

This does not mean that Anatole accepts orthodox immortality; the only kind that interests him is our prolongation in the memory of mankind: 'Personal immortality,' says Giraud, 'seems to him a false bait (*leurre*), and on the impossibility of miracles, he has about ten pages which Renan would have fully approved.'[113] This attack on two strongholds of the faith indicates that our sceptic, having demolished ethics as we saw, will have little difficulty with religion. Many repetitions appear in his treatment.

His starting-point is that the heavens have been emptied of their ancient promises and phantasms and fears. God's creation no longer seems 'puerile and poetic, like an immense cathedral.' It is something worse than that, for the demi-urge in charge consulted neither A.F. nor any other philosopher. The devil did a better job with his half, for he was more of an artist and a savant (cf. *La Révolte des anges*). Yet the spectres of hell, in spite of Bossuet and St. Augustine, should disappear from our consciousness. The theological dialogue or debate about the soul simply boxes the compass of improbable beliefs. We may feel bereft without knowledge of our latter end—for the justification of religions is to provide this assurance—but such is our predicament. As for miracles, it is not wise to say that none has been proven, for the orthodox may have an answer. It is better to question their conception of the 'miraculous,' as beyond Nature, when it is merely beyond our knowledge of her. With regard to other religious matters, there is practically nothing new, whether A.F. is reminiscing about his pious upbringing, about St. Anthony and the marionettes, about visiting the monastery of St. Odile. He is not necessarily opposed to convents for the real 'spouses of Christ' (another *motif*); but he still frankly dislikes monks and occasionally portrays them in an ugly light. Intolerance and fanaticism are, as ever, his *bêtes noires*.

Now as to the fields of knowledge, France questions the foundations, not only of psychology, ethics, and history, but even of the pure or exact sciences whose value he had previously rated rather high.[114] The most sweeping passage has a familiar ring:

As a castle in the air, æsthetics are founded on nothing solid. They try to base the æsthetic principle on ethics. But there are no ethics. There is no sociology. There is no biology, either. The perfecting of the sciences has never existed except in the head of Auguste Comte, whose work is a prophecy. When biology is properly constituted, some millions of years from now, people may perhaps, long centuries afterwards, construct a sociology too. After which, when our planet is old and infirm, it will be permissible to create solid foundations for a science of æsthetics.

Some of the contradictions involved in this wholesale indictment will demand later consideration. Anatole has three grievances against the race of scientists: in spite of their pretensions, they cannot penetrate to ultimate verities; they get lost in a mass of terminology and technicalities; and their experiments are often directed toward trivial ends. Their pretensions were world-shaking and seemed to aim at a new moral order. Nothing of the sort has happened. They cannot reach the substance of things; like the rest of us, they are limited to sensible phenomena; and their instruments may get them further, but not deeper. As specialists they wear blinders and are apt to say, even of a correlated subject: 'That isn't my show-case.' As technicians, they seem to think that terminology has a value of its own, whereas the truly enlightened aim would be to generalize their findings so that the layman may follow. No adequate results may be expected from the galvanizing of a frog's legs, the display of his nerves and muscles (cf. *Jocaste*). The reproach that scientists are lacking in the broader curiosity does not agree with Anatole's final reproach that they are all wrong anyhow in stimulating the spirit of man toward understanding nature: we are not shaped to understand, and our useless brains are developed at the expense of the more vital organs which we share with the beasts. Yet France himself finds it hard to quench his interest, say in astronomy. The interplanetary spaces are still too fascinating, and he must needs admire the human intelligence which has measured them. The worst he can do is to suggest, pessimistically, that since the 'giant worlds' above are made of the same substances as ours, they probably contain an equal amount of suffering and misery. And that thought 'would suffice to disgust me with the universe.'

Anatole has already frequently expressed his radicalism regarding history and politics. Not a great deal is added in *Le Jardin*. The passages from *Le Temps* concerning the selective bias of historians, concerning history as an art, are virtually repeated.

Local colour is a myth. When the near past is falsified, say by an historical painter, how can one expect *vraisemblance* in the rendering of the Augustan Age? Thus spake the author of 'Le Procurateur de Judée'. . . On political matters, he repeats Coignard's defeatist idea that, insanity for insanity, we had as well put up with the old prejudices, for fear of worse.

Up to this point we have discovered little but weeds and desolation in the garden of Epicurus, and we wonder when that serenely smiling philosopher will make his appearance and begin to cultivate. Where, indeed, have vanished the light caresses and the perfumed breath of the ancient garden? Perhaps fairer flowers will blossom in the plots allotted to antiquity, art, womankind? But first there is some doubt as to whether Epicurus himself is really the head-gardener. He may have resigned in favour of Lucretius, whose conception of primordial physical love France usually adopted. (Lemaître has pointed out that this notion furnishes the key to *Le Lys rouge*.) So far Epicurus has hardly penetrated beyond the mottoes that mark the threshold of *Le Jardin*. Within its pages he is mentioned only in passing, though that is less important than the inquiry as to whether his spirit really informs the volume. There are those who answer Yes—because of the prevalent 'temper of ἀταραξία' (freedom from pain), because on 'nearly every page one may find an Epicurean reminiscence,' whether as regards the uses of scepticism and sensuality or the concepts of religion and virtue.[115] But surely the old philosopher has changed his tune as well as his tone? The best statement of the discrepancy is uttered by Deschamps, who declares that Epicurus may have dictated some 'pretty epigrams' to Anatole-Coignard, but that on the whole:

> he has donned an unexpected costume. He is no longer that Epicurus whom Lucretius sang, that revealer *Of the Nature of Things,* that intransigent and fiery apostle, that anti-clerical reformer, who cried on the roofs, 'Neither God nor Master!' Nor is he the Epicurus of Horace. . . He is a very modern Epicurus, indulgent toward the latest fashions, coolly aware of the mysteries of contemporary science. . . If he is in a garden, he won't stay there long.[116]

Yet in certain lights he appears to be Epicurus still. This happens when France speaks in praise of resignation, which can take the finer name of contentment. 'Great souls resign themselves with a noble joy.' It happens more significantly when towards the end of the book 'mon ami Jean' remains 'perfectly tranquil'—as France loved to remain—and for fear of consequences definitely refuses to cultivate the aforesaid garden, seeking *his* ataraxia through deliberate stupidity and stillness. It happens when A.F. brings forward the doctrine of Illusion, or of our perceptions as deriving from superficial contacts, to which the whole Epicurean school subscribed. It happens more broadly when the themes of Irony and Pity are fully sounded. Anticipations of these have been noised abroad;[117] here is the place for their development. 'Let Time,' he says in one passage, 'at least leave us pity, so that we may not be enclosed in old age as in a sepulchre.' This is the most human of virtues. A.F. applauds the books that stir us to a comprehension and commiseration for the hard lot of mankind: Bulwer's *Coming Race* and especially *Don Quixote* and *Candide,* which, rightly considered, are 'handbooks of indulgence and pity.' Perhaps we need to be reminded that the French conception of the word comports not necessarily the sentimental attitude, but rather a full understanding of others. This kind of Pity seems originally Lucretian. So far, less has been made of Irony. But A.F. repeats from *Le Temps* the passage already cited, concerning Irony and Pity as the proper judges and overseers of life, maintaining that his irony is 'not cruel,' since it mocks neither at beauty nor at love.

On the whole, this *credo* is borne out by the tenor of *Le Jardin.* The irony is sharper and more conspicuous in the Coignard volumes, but here the pessimistic view does not usually exclude fellow-feeling and (at times) some hope for the race. At times also Anatole may quit his inspissated gloom to lift the reader on the wings of idealism. Thus: 'The best thing about life is the notion that it gives us of something beyond life. The chief utility of the actual is that it may help us construct, in some sort, the ideal.'

Such Platonism is not, however, conspicuous. If Epicurus is to reappear, it may be in connexion with the doctrine of happiness *via* pleasure commonly associated with his name. There is no doubt concerning France's usual predilection for hedonism; yet in this volume it has to struggle to survive. What ways can he still find to make life agreeable? How can the votary of Melancholy still contrive to

> burst Joy's grape against his palate fine?

Although the sensualistic foundations of his philosophy are assumed rather than expressed in *Le Jardin,* there is still enough to indicate that A.F. remains faithful not only to the Epicureans, but to his 'old Condillac.' Polyphile declares that 'we are confined within our senses, which limit for us the universe.' Nor do we attain to objective perceptions: 'We think that our eyes discover the world, whereas it is really a reflection of ourselves that they transmit to us.' Much as Coignard had maintained that pity itself was a sensual virtue, so here it is held that sensuality affects the activities of man, even to his vocabulary.

May we suppose, then, that a similar basis underlies art and æsthetics? But we have seen that the latter field hardly 'exists' as a solid. The essay called 'Château de cartes' gives us the cue. In such a cloud-country, you simply wander from view to view, without ever touching terra firma. Is there any universal consent as to the value of masterpieces? As A.F. had told Brunetière, there are only 'prejudices.' Consider the errors, once widely accepted, regarding Homer or MacPherson. Consider the variations of opinion regarding *Hamlet* or *The Divine Comedy*. Ridiculous as we may find the views of preceding critics, we may be sure that our own views will seem equally ridiculous within two hundred years. Thus Relativity again protrudes his persistent proboscis. If there is any uniformity in artistic and critical ideas, it is due to the principle of imitation:

> We carry it into all our actions, and it dominates our æsthetic sense. Without this imitative trend, artistic opinions would be still more variable than they are. Thanks to this process, a work which has won some plaudits continues to accumulate them.

Here is a novel and searching inquiry into the processes of fame. But does he conclude, from all this image-breaking, that we should occupy ourselves neither with æsthetics nor with literary criticism? He will not go that far. 'Let us, however, recognize that we are dealing with an art; let us put into it the passion and the charm without which no art can exist.' We will do well to remember these essential ingredients.

Sceptical about æsthetic castle-building, France's tone grows milder when he is concerned directly with art itself—and that because his 'devotion to this religion' is almost as conspicuous in *Le Jardin* as in *Le Lys*.[118] His 'ami Jean' in the dialogue called 'Le Prieuré'[119] turns aside his deadly arrows from this target: the arts are 'games which disarm hatred.' They are more. They are supporters of the Illusion of the ideal. Which is why we may bestow upon past artists an ideal which they never had; we cannot fully admire them without creating a mirage from which they too may benefit. Indeed, the artist exists chiefly to promote in us the temporary illusion that life is lovely.

This notion of the participation of the 'subject' in the creative dream is in accord with all that we have read about A.F.'s Impressionism in *La Vie littéraire*. The theatre is of less value than poetry, because its definiteness leaves no room for the cherished prolongation of our reveries. These stem from our emotions, which in turn have been touched off by the artistic impression; for, as already laid down, a passionless race would be a race without art and incapable of poetry. Sentiment is then the prime requisite, 'in art as in love,' and along with that goes a delicate appreciation which no formalism can supply.

Other adjuncts are the larger humanism, i.e., a sympathy with the life of mankind, and a fundamental simplicity. No masterpiece exists in a vacuum, and 'the greatest has value only through its links with life. The more I understand these links, the more I am interested in the work itself.' Through this approach France, echoing Goethe, again waxes relativistic: there are only 'des œuvres de circonstance,' and one can get into them only by knowing these circumstances of conception and environment. In taking this attitude he aligns himself with Sainte-Beuve and other true humanists; he removes himself from dogmatists like Brunetière who would set up an arbitrary scale of values quite apart from the lives of men and the conditions under which they labour. But A.F., seeking 'the man in the artist,' cares for *The Divine Comedy* because of what it tells us about Dante and his Florence; just as in Ghirlandajo's *Birth of the Virgin* he sees pleasing reflections of life in the early Renaissance. Such periods, as he made plain in the *Puits de Sainte Claire,* evince a harmless and simple attachment to their reproductive arts, much as rustic imitations of objects are single-minded and without noisome admixtures of pride and glory. Those poets, too, are happiest who are strong through simplicity and ignorance. In riming as in dressmaking, modes of a season pass. What remains is the poetry founded on enduring principles, provided the poets do not discuss these principles too much.

It is evident that France, as always, remains keen on associative values. In literature, he finds it a perpetual marvel that small printed signs should 'awaken in us divine images.' Enjoyment of such images and the play of his own art are still manifest in material taken from antiquity. He grants that the admiration which we accord to the classics may be part of the cumulative convention discussed above; but for his own part he willingly accords it. Along with allusions to the 'ingenious' Ulysses, to Dido and her myrtles, to the imperishable charm of *Daphnis and Chloe,* we have in *Le Jardin* an engaging 'Entretien . . . avec un fantôme sur les origines de l'alphabet.' The phantom is that of crafty old Cadmus who comes in mythical guise to discourse on his discovery of the alphabet, his skill as a trader, his indifferent scepticism, and his variegated voyages. For its rhythm and colouring, the following passage is typical. The author tells the old Phœnician:

When you landed on a beach in Greece or in the Archipelago, you immediately spread out your garments and rich adornments; and if the daughters of the shore, drawn by an invincible attraction, came alone to look wistfully upon the desired objects, then your sailors carried off these virgins who vainly wept and lamented.

This is the sort of 'image' that would have pleased the author had it been translated into reality. For the final consolation that remains to our doubter—unless doubt becomes active in that direction too—is the love of women. He retraces the steps by which they have come to 'embellish the earth': we hear again how Christianity has increased their power; and how they offered to the anchorites of the desert dreams even more seductive than the precious reality. But industrial society is changing all that. Even in the eighties 'Gérôme' uttered the complaints which are in part echoed here. The common law of labour 'is stripping you of your mystery and your charm.' Anatole is emphasizing less household drudgery, which has always weighed hard on the sex and robbed them of cultivated leisure, than he is concerned with the new professional drives. Why on earth, he clamours, should a woman want to be a lawyer or a druggist ? A nurse ? Certainly ; to heal is her *métier*. A learned lady ? A teacher ? An authoress ? Well, after all, why not, if the vocation is irresistible ? Thus Anatole makes new and handsome concessions, due probably to the larger horizons that he had now attained. Certain other concessions were made, we have seen, to the conventual life ; yet one feels that these were dragged from him and that he is still, personally and on principle, against this death-in-life, so contrary to nature.

He holds to his old thesis—that women, more given over to instinctive sensations than the rest of us, are thereby more perfectly framed for love. And love on a positive, definite basis, even as Thérèse Martin-Bellème (and perhaps her prototype) had conceived of it. 'We put infinity into our love-making : that is not the fault of the women concerned.' This epigram was too good not to be repeated. So is the discourse on Jealousy, adapted from a review of Psichari's book bearing that title ; so is the story of the ugly but admirable priest, still a prey to the 'aiguillons du désir.' Ranging freely in his old material, France might have discovered the more disrupting maxim that 'nothing is more contrary than love to the wisdom of Epicurus.' [120] Is it then to be outlawed from the Garden ? Impossible ! But it is the more sombre type of *la Volupté* that effects an entrance—love as the counterpart of hunger, as linked with suffering, and still as one of the 'twin sources of inexhaustible beauty.'

The reflections on jealousy recapitulated the interesting case of Racine's Hermione and foreshadowed (when first printed) the case of Jacques Dechartre, as outlined above. Hermione, properly speaking, is not jealous, as men understand the term. Having no imagination, she exemplifies the aforementioned positive and practical view of love. She wishes to dominate and possess. When she fails to win Pyrrhus, 'c'est un mariage manqué,' and that's all. (This may seem an excessive simplification of Hermione.) But to the truly jealous male, 'everything brings uneasiness,' everything is added in the way of dreams, obsessions, and particularly torturing images of the woman's past and present. A civilized lover is jealous without reason and all the time. The fact that he enthrones woman makes him desire her peremptorily, exclusively, with all her accessories of emotion, memories, and charm. And doom inevitably waits upon such a monomania.

With all this wealth of diverse subject-matter, it is not surprising that *Le Jardin d'Epicure* should have provoked a variety of critical judgments. The Abbé Klein naturally finds the work lamentably lacking both in art and thought and considers it a perfect 'manual of dilettantism.' Esteeming it rather a 'manual of the Unbeliever,' and deploring the increase in cynicism and bitterness here apparent, Michaut none the less admits its essential and representative character as a *pot pourri* from the third period. It is a sophisticated synthesis of Anatole's temperament with the teachings of all his philosophic masters. As a 'beautiful breviary of disenchantment' (it is extraordinary how many kinds of 'breviaries' are invoked !), Martin-Mamy thinks that *Le Jardin* will long endure.[121]

Jacques Bainville, in accordance with his usual habit of finding things outdated, grows weary of the once pleasing sceptical tone *à la* Renan ; but he admits the presence of 'many just thoughts.' Saintsbury remarks that only in Paris could such an amount of thoughtfulness be so widely appreciated. Deschamps explains that the ideas, however heady, bold or dangerous, are perfectly adapted to the *gens du monde*. 'Never has his [France's] impiety been more elegant, nor his malice more coquettish.' Tonelli presents interesting analogies, up to a certain point, with the searching scepticism of Pascal's *Pensées*. Pellissier, finding here A.F.'s 'quintessential mind,' whether for wisdom or irony, uneasiness or tenderness, warns us that the ideas are rather for Art's sake than for that of the fugitive, unattainable Truth.[122]

Little need be added to all this array. *Le Jardin d'Epicure,* with its discharge of scattered and brilliant maxims, affords a capital example of what A.F. once called his life-work of 'putting dynamite into curl-papers.'[123] It is doubly characteristic of his development : not only do we meet again the older themes regarding dreams and illusions, art and antiquity, insinuations concerning the relativity of religions and morals ; but also a fresh emphasis is given to the frequency here below of ignorance, suffering, and evil. The balance swings toward pessimism and often toward nihilism.[124] Another fact is that of all France's works, *Le Jardin* is probably the most repetitious — much more so than would appear from the general indications given above or in the notes to the definitive edition. As one turns the pages, familiar echoes are heard, unceasingly and monotonously. Yet so much the better for our purposes ; we are thus assured that the work is by intention the 'will and testament' of this crucial period. And we may now proceed to something like a systematic examination of our author's thought.

CHAPTER XVIII

His Thought ; and His Style

§ 1

IT is thus our task to co-ordinate, so far as possible, and to condense the chief deposits that fifty years of activity left in France's mind. But since it was *one* mind, however various in its manifestations, points and illustrations must occasionally be drawn from that 'autumn of ideas' which reaches beyond 1896. It is less a question of temporal than of quantitative restrictions. A long memory, a comprehensive intelligence, lie unfolded before us in all their complexity. There is an amusing tale about how a well-known Anatolian once proposed to collect all the books to which A.F. had ever referred.[1] It would be a still more stupendous undertaking to assemble even a moiety of the recorded reflections, images, sensations that flitted across the unresting stream of our author's consciousness. We must content ourselves with certain larger issues, shunning those which, like religion or history, have already been amply treated. Furthermore, there are two preliminary provisos. Anatole himself made little pretence to consistency in his ideation. And as already seen he distrusted at times the operations of the human intelligence. This dilemma now calls for a fuller development.

It is a case, as so often, of a divided mind, and here of a mind which inquired about its own intrinsic and generic value. On the one hand we have his statement, in his 'Autobiographie,' that (without any special gifts in that direction) he was personally destined to intellectual speculation.[2] We have his assertions about the long years devoted to silent meditation and to explorations in philosophic or scientific fields. We have the testimony of his friends in the Rue Chalgrin circle that in these years he considered thought as the most essential, the most creative, the highest activity. This is supported, in numerous places, by his own language.[3] For the rights of free thought he spoke up again and again—in connexion with Bourget's *Le Disciple,* in the Dreyfus Affair, in the address *Aux Etudiants* of 1910. 'La Pensée' is the chief guardian and moulder of civilization.[4] It is the first apanage of man, it marks him off from the brute (elsewhere he declares that 'le rêve' does that), and its claims to an absolutely unhampered expression are 'superior to everything.' The implication that these claims should over-ride ethical considerations was disagreeable to Brunetière and to Seillière. Tributes to the honour in which France held the processes and powers of thought are not lacking in other critics.

But it may be noted that most of these ardent defences belong to A.F.'s second period, before the blight had descended. Later, it is as if the long dominance of Reason had turned him against her sway. 'Pensée, où m'as-tu conduit?' inquires the tortured Paphnuce. The Abbé Coignard remarks that ideas become 'impertinent' visitors, if they are allowed to extend their sojourn. In the *Vie littéraire* we learn that reflection has reduced Lemaître to a state of continuous doubt; and in speaking of *Faust* A.F. admits that this state is compounded of 'sadness and desolation.'[5] So 'thought is a frightful thing.' It led Satan to revolt; it is feared by man; it is the acid that dissolves the universe. 'If all men began to think at the same time, the world would immediately cease to exist.' Anatole may be piling it on, but Coignard in the *Opinions* repeats this notion of a possible catastrophe . . . from which we are saved by the fortunate fact that 'thought is a malady peculiar to certain persons.' Fra Giovanni is opposed to its operations, considering that they lead us nowhere, while Satan himself perceives that 'man thinks in sorrow and meditates only in sadness.'

All this smoke betokens some fire and beclouds the direct rays of that *esprit* which Anatole elsewhere lauded. What does Ségur say—he who conversed with the ageing Master apprehended as an embodiment of 'Les Mélancolies de l'Intelligence'? Apparently, the leading motive of his discourse was that thought stultifies happiness, whether in enjoying love, or in appreciating jests, or in considering the history and destiny of man. To such a pass has A.F.'s 'atrocious clairvoyance' led him at last. And he still prefers the joys of ignorance, say among Sicilian peasants, to all the depressing acquisitions of the mind.[6]

Ségur is not the only person whom Anatole impressed as ready at times to cease vain speculation and to abdicate his thinker's throne.[7] But no stony Escurial would receive the weary monarch: when he was disposed to relinquish thought, it would usually be in favour of sentiment. He would make the substitution both for himself and for others. The foundations of this intermittent preference, it must be evident, were laid in his second period ; but it would be far too simple to conclude that henceforth his heart is in the ascendant. There is rather an alternation of emphasis on heart and head ; and there were times, as manifest from our last chapter, when he became tired of both organs.

A similar alternation has been suggested as regards Anatole's conception of the power, or the inefficacy, of reason and the Idea in human history.[8] For the most part, he would vibrate 'indifferently' from the positive to the negative view, although Gaffiot thinks that the positive is more frequent after 1896. The same critic keenly observes that France's attacks on the intelligence were due to the fact that it had not done as much for the world as it should have done : he placed the mind not too low, but too high. A sort of *dépit* was thus involved. When he fell out with the intelligence, it was really a temperamental lover's quarrel —and it is significant that one of the characters in the *Histoire contemporaine* uses that very phrase in this connexion. Says Aspertini to Bergeret :

> Je m'aperçois que vous faîtes à l'intelligence une querelle d'amoureux. Vous l'accablez de reproches parce qu'elle n'est pas la reine du monde.[9]

And Durant has noted that although we find in the *Humaine Tragédie* that 'the joy of understanding is a sad joy,' yet 'those who have once tasted it would not exchange it for all the frivolous gaieties and empty hopes of the vulgar herd.'[10]

Thus, Anatole's dispute with Reason would be an unreasonable dispute. It might result from having had too much of her company the day or the week before. It would be partly due, as with Pascal, to the defiance of the renegade, who had *reasoned* his way through to elevating the heart over the head ; but in France's case the abnegation is not permanent. It would be due still more, I think, to what may be observed in similar sceptics like Montaigne and Bayle. They know that they can wage a sham-battle against Reason, because in their microcosms she will always abound, she will always be queen. But they realize that she does not dominate in the world at large. And their real onslaught is rather against the unintelligent world who will not accept her mandates. In like wise, Anatole's turnabouts (which were sometimes very rapid) regarding the power and value of thought may well be due to a disappointed idealization. In the oft-mentioned article on Lemaître, he could say, almost in the same breath, that thought is the best, as well as the worst of things—and support each asseveration.[11] Just so he debates the value of Knowledge, as a pleasing illusion.[12]

§ 2

Now even when France admits the validity of thought, which is not a constant, he is far from approving any philosophical synthesis. In fact, his warfare against the very principle of a system, as well as 'les systèmes' in particular, is as pertinacious as that of Voltaire, from whom he seems to borrow certain arguments. Anatole Himself rather ascribes his opposition to the fact that his father was in the other camp—the old gentleman would try to decide the smallest things according to general laws and maxims.[13] Among Pierre-Anatole's numerous indictments of the system-making habit we may cite again the dialogue in *Le Jardin,* where Ariste is scornful of the mental habits, the defaced language, the intrusive Absolute of metaphysicians who construct lofty schemes out of what basically are but animal cries. Therefore it has been noted that not even in *Le Jardin* has A.F. attempted to systematize his own philosophy, save only as this may stem from the denial of metaphysical entities and the like.[14] Yet a man may have, broadly speaking, a philosophy, without being committed to specific 'isms.' It is possible that France evinced, toward Epicureanism, Positivism, or Socialism, certain leanings which would dispose him to enlist as a free lance, tilting for one or another of these causes. This possibility must be temporarily relegated, while we consider the emphasis which has been attached to the variety of Anatole's views.

More than once he declared that opinion rules the world, not without the implication that your opinion is as good as mine. It seems clear that our author indulges in and enjoys a considerable intellectual *diversity*—the point, abundantly illustrated already, is driven home by half a dozen critics. He becomes gymnastic with his thought, he keeps a dozen balls in the air, he 'slips like an elusive eel' from between the fingers of the earnest reader. One is bewildered by the kaleidoscope of disparate *aperçus,* often presented on a single page. One is disposed to accept the suggestion that it is France rather than Voltaire whose mind is a 'chaos of clear ideas.' One is ready to inquire: 'Is he as loose a thinker as his master, Epicurus?' One may almost argue that where Renan is 'diverse' through intellectual conscientiousness and tolerance, Anatole's thought runs riot just for the fun of the thing.[15] And one remembers the emblematic Wheel of Truth, in which allegory Anatole's private emphasis is less on the unifying, absolute white, than on the innumerable contradictory colours symbolizing the clashing opinions of men.

To the reproach that A.F. expresses the most various views and even takes pleasure in playing up heterogeneity, he would answer that this is a great part of the spectacle of life. It is because 'the world is so full of a number of things,' that the semi-detached observer, who cannot hold by the unities of Fra Giovanni, must contemplate a welter stemming from the Flux, affected always by Relativity, and consisting fundamentally of a mass of struggling individuals. The best of men are but flaring, dying beacons over the 'océan des choses.' It has also been said that 'the central idea of his work is the infinite diversity of nature and of men, who jostle against one another without coming to know one another.'[16] This mutual incomprehension furnishes the conclusion of *Le Lys rouge*. It underlies the conversations of Coignard as well as of the philosophizers in *Thaïs*. And we shall see presently how it is used in the structure of France's stories. He finds apt illustrations of the welter all the way from Heraclitus to Renan. This broad, but not firm vision was a natural consequence of his store of learning, and it permeated his familiar talk. Corday tells us:

> Whether it were a question of a thing, an idea or a human being, his thought immediately made a circuit of the object, enveloping it as in a lasso. He revealed simultaneously its strong and its weak side, its good and bad aspects—for he perceived at once *all* the aspects possible.

Thus a personage, or a doctrine, could provoke in him, that day or the next day, divergent attitudes that might well seem contradictory.[17] His enveloping, manifold, unco-ordinated type of discourse, whether in life or in books, might often be arranged in the *pro* and *con* fashion. And here we meet with another problem.

It is for the moment less a question of inconsistencies in his thought at large than of deliberate oppositions, in fairly close connexion, between the front and the back of a given theme. That this was a conscious process is evidenced by an occasional *apologia* from A.F. himself. For instance, he knows well enough that he often proceeds by marshalling antinomies. While he is striving to reconcile two adversaries, he declares, others that will not be reconciled come in battalions, fighting furiously![18] What is to be done? Shall we simply give up by granting that the 'human soul is an abyss of contradictions' and that these contradictions are a very genuine part of us?[19] Or shall we, like the Abbé Coignard, seek support in Charron, who averred that there are in fact insoluble antinomies? The Abbé succumbs under the attacks of half a dozen of these harpies.

In one notable passage France pays his respects to Georges Renard, 'who with an exquisite indulgence has pointed out some of my contradictions.' He did well to forgive me, for how can our poor humanity always make its principles square with its sentiments? It seems a good idea to have on tap two or three philosophic doctrines; for there is little reason to believe that any single one is always right. Any well-travelled mind knows that there are contrary truths, just as there are contrary climates. And regarding the geography of the Unknown, I have vainly sought light from all the sages. Which is precisely why I have chosen the way of Beauty. And please allow me my gibe at the impeccable logicians.[20]

From another angle A.F. was quite aware (as Renan was aware) that the dialogue form offers a good medium for debate, or for that type of philosophizing which becomes a long duel 'entre le Pour et le Contre.' Or, as he told Ségur, since dialogue is by nature controversial, 'it is well adapted to the human mind, whose forte is 'deliberation—I mean making a choice between two contraries.'[21]

The trouble is that frequently Anatole did not get to the point of choosing. . . We recognize the doubter who hesitated long as to whether he should attend his father's funeral; who indifferently allowed his autograph to be written: 'The future will always realize the dreams of the sages'—or 'les rêves des fous.'[22] We recall that France, just to keep his hand in, could, with deliberate paradoxicality, define life itself as 'delicious and terrible, frightful and charming,' and could qualify reasoning as 'singular, exquisite, monstrous, malign.'

This contrariness, as we may call it, this 'seductive dualism,' as others call it, has been pointed out by many writers. Among them, Maurois emphasizes 'l'alternance des thèmes,' a kind of literary counterpoint, as France's favourite method of composing a conversation. Vandérem takes the matter into the domain of the larger issues, hinted at above. If a man lets the taste for antinomies grow upon him, if he plumps for one or the other side according to his mood or his morning breakfast, he is likely on the one hand to become merely a collection of ideas, on the other a 'sceptique fieffé' ; and there is little doubt that the ageing France, with his growing mania for black-and-white argumentation, went beyond the limits of scepticism into a sort of 'mechanical sophistry.' It is further intimated that his toying with Con resulted only in apparent paradoxes.[23]

This is a very serious indictment and demands full consideration. Is it true that France, as an 'idéophile,' carried his Pro-and-Con system into all discussions and all domains of knowledge ? Is it true that he extended the uses of scepticism into a sort of mechanical *jeu,* thus impairing our belief in his sincerity ? Before we can suggest answers to these problems, we must look into Anatole's personal conception of scepticism and sceptics.

§ 3

His famous Declaration of Rights (*c.* 1908) reads as follows:

Sceptic! Yes, they still call me a sceptic ; and what they intend as an insult I consider a compliment. All the masters of French thought—Rabelais, Montaigne, Molière, Voltaire, Renan—have been sceptics . . . and I am their humble pupil. They were often the most constructive and courageous of men. They denied only negative values. They attacked whatever hinders intelligence and free-will. . . And after much meditation concerning human misery . . . they were possessed by pity and fraternal love. He who thought himself for ever detached from the combat leaps in to succour the unfortunate. . . Truly, the poor sceptics have been much abused. Disappointed idealists, they remain idealists incorruptible. And their frequent irony is only the expression of their discouragement.[24]

Anatole embroiders the text by declaring that those so-called sceptics professed a positive and 'magnificent' creed. 'Full of fervour, they all worked to deliver their fellow-men from enslaving chains. They were saints, after their fashion.' All this evinces, to be sure, a combative strain not very perceptible before the Dreyfus Affair. But even in 1888 France offers a definition and a defence of what was becoming his counter-creed: Sceptics are that class of men who (like Lemaître) are tolerant and well-meaning and who, having no faith of their own, 'communicate with all believers.' Since they accept nothing, they must also deny nothing—i.e., they are properly agnostics. Like the rest of us, they are a prey to the illusion of the universal mirage.[25]

Let us consider certain additional analogies between France and the line of sceptics from whom he claims to descend. It has been pointed out that he shared with Montaigne an 'immense curiosity,' together with an apparent deference towards other people's ideas. But when they thought he was captured, A.F. would slip away and reappear somewhere else. 'This perpetual motion, this deceptive balancing were peculiar to him.'[26] Thus he shared with Montaigne a position of unstable equilibrium, together with the use of a very large library. Anatole would probably have approved the *frondeur* definition which Emerson gave of Montaigne's scepticism—'the attitude assumed by the student in relation to the particulars which society adores.'

A.F.'s relationship to Bayle has already been sufficiently expounded for our purposes, and the same is almost true regarding Voltaire. Let us only remember that France thought of the age of Voltaire, quite rightly, as the great liberalizing epoch in his country's history. We may also recall, as among the chief trends of either sceptic, anti-clericalism, the rationalizing of history, the addiction to the *conte philosophique,* the shifting footwork to perplex one's adversary, the distrust of Pecus and yet the willingness to serve him, together with a final ardour for social justice. Voltaire's rehabilitation of Calas is very similar to what France helped undertake in behalf of Dreyfus. His kinship to Renan would require a volume for accurate demonstration.[27]

The question of the growth of Anatole's scepticism is a complicated one. In general, one may say that there were two main stages, each of which has its own development. The first would end with the climax of his third period, as exhibited in the present volume. The child who, with a 'knowing eye,' calmly passed through the disillusionments recorded in *Le Livre de mon ami* was father to the man who would tell his intimates of the Rue Chalgrin (as a prelude to discussion), 'I deny everything in advance.' The critic of *Le Temps* who filters all ideas through his own mind and temperament,[28] is seldom in the mood to accord much to absolutes of any kind. On the other hand, it seems clear that the author of *Bonnard* and even of *Thaïs* is still disposed to grant a great deal to sentiment; and that the gradual desiccation of this principle is what marks the chief difference between the scepticism of the eighties and that of the nineties. Albert Einstein once said of France: 'His intelligence is sceptical, but not his heart.'[29] Whenever, then, the note of feeling recurs, even in the nineties, A.F. drops back into the mood of the previous period; otherwise we have noted the marked difference in tone between the *Opinions de J.C.* and most preceding works. It is characteristic of Coignard's sceptical perversity that when you think you have him safely in the Opposition, he eludes you by casting a doubt on that 'opinion' too.

Almost of the same date as the last-mentioned volume is a passage from *Le Temps,* which contains something like a revelation:[30] Intelligence, says Anatole, apropos of Taine's work, is after all a by-product of sensibility and is the 'frequently painful imprint which we receive from men and things.' (There was little reason for France to rejoice, in 1893, over such 'imprints.') Follows the familiar argument for using the mind in *jeux d'esprit* rather than in the fruitless search for truth. Reverting to the impressionistic level, Intelligence, out of Sensibility, 'by' Opportunity is as diverse and changeful as flesh and blood itself. Since there are a thousand possible ways of understanding a thing, why not allow for a thousand contradictions?

Fusing the two phases before 1896, Braibant thus sums up: 'Scepticism and tolerance, with an understratum of "rationalistic faith," these are the constants in France's thought during the years 1883-1893.'[31] As for the several phases after he became a Dreyfusard, they properly lie beyond our scope, but a few suggestions may be made. There is more of a systole and diastole in his scepticism than might perhaps be expected. That is, from the amount of nihilism already found, the straight progression would be, one might think, toward an attitude of universal blank negation. But that too would be an Absolute. And France said more than once that although he had been drawn in the direction of total scepticism, he had recoiled in horror from that gulf.[32] Consequently, we find spasmodic outbursts of socialistic or humanitarian faith (the Dreyfus Affair, the causes of oppressed nations, the revolt against war) alternating with even deeper plunges into the 'gulf'—notably in *l'Ile des Pingouins*. If Gaffiot is right about France's scepticism becoming more practical and propagandist after 1896, it must be admitted that this militancy was sporadic and was interspersed with long stretches over which little light appears to gleam. At the very last he seems nearer universal doubt than he had been at any time since 1893.[33] *Dubito, ergo sum* might have been his final motto. It appears then that, by and large, scepticism was the predominant attitude, the key-note, or at least the prologue to any 'message' which A.F. may have felt called upon to deliver.

The intermittences mentioned, as well as the differences between a man's active daily walk and his solitary broodings, may help us account for the formation of two sets of views regarding the radical nature of France's disbelief. Some who consorted with him, for instance Corday, hold that the 'legend' of his scepticism has suffered from exaggerations and that it is not fair to say that such a thinker 'believed in nothing, because he examined everything. On the contrary, it is easy to prove the constancy of his major convictions, which are in accordance with the principal actions of his life.' Similarly Curtius maintains that 'scepticism was for him only a form of the critical spirit,' or one way to fight for free thought even in the thick of action.[34]

On the other hand, an increasing number among 'les jeunes' came to believe that France represented no belief whatever. They considered him an embodiment of the spirit of negation, sterile, 'grêle et pauvre,' hesitant, unintegrated, without the courage (which Pascal had) to react against the *néant*.[35] Apparent in the years immediately preceding the Great War, this revolt against the Master, as a sort of Mephistopheles who 'dated,' mounted through 1918, through 1924, and only of late do we discern clear signs of a counter-revolution. It is not our task to follow these *péripéties,* but only to indicate that they are usually linked either with the feeling that Anatole's almost total incredulity is outworn—or with the contention that it is *not* a dead issue—or with the effort to transcend that problem and to maintain that at any rate our author has entered into the ranks of the enduring French classics. With this last position, the present writer is in entire accord.

That solution (if it be one) cannot excuse us from the task of reckoning with some further ranges of Anatole's scepticism. As said, it is not now our purpose to follow him again into certain broad domains already amply traversed.[36] It is rather a question of realizing how difficulties and dichotomies—especially the Pro-and-Con habit of mind—would beset him with reference to half a dozen particular topics. And the further question is whether this warfare of antinomies prevented his coming to adequate conclusions regarding these vital topics. If this be true, the so-called 'legend' of his ultimate scepticism may be sustained. In the examination, we might bear in mind what he and others have recognized as the Gallic way—that lightness of touch and levity of tone (cf. Voltaire) need not prevent the *fonds* from being very serious indeed. The curl-papers do not always conceal the dynamite. The briskness of the repartee need not turn the duel of Doubt into a mere game.

§ 4

LIFE itself we have seen him formulate in contradictory terms—but indeed that peculiarity is characteristic of life. What are we to say about his attitude toward the king of modern ideas, which is the idea of Progress? Are we to believe that in this respect too he merited the inscription which D'Annunzio once penned in his honour: 'To Anatole France, on whom all the faces of Truth and Error smile with equal power'?[37]

We cannot say that, with Renan, he believed in an increasing moral purpose in the universe, nor that the world is in 'mysterious travail' toward some unknown end, nor that nature needs and sides with virtue. Such a semi-devout creed was alien to France's temperament. What he shared with Renan was less his ideals than his scruples—particularly those doubts regarding Caliban and Pecus, and of what they might be capable. Now a 'tendre mépris' for mankind is not the best coign of vantage from which to appreciate his achievements. Furthermore, Anatole's long bath of determinism (*à la* Darwin, *à la* Taine) would hardly dispose him to see men as rising by moral stepping-stones or pulling themselves up by a firm resolution. As he definitely puts it in *Le Jardin*: 'L'espèce humaine n'est pas susceptible d'un progrès indéfini.' When he adds that 'science and civilization have created moral and physical evil,' and that he dares not cultivate his garden for fear of consequences, the debate would seem to be closed. For he has already made plain what he thinks of the devices of science, serving only to 'prolong our ignorance.'

Yet the debate is not really over; it is just getting under way. We still have to reckon with the heritage of the eighteenth century, the impact of Positivism, the formation of Socialism, all stirring in Anatole's mind. He has not forgotten his Voltaire. In that very same *Jardin* (whose cultivation we have seen him renounce), he declared that life itself, with all its contradictions, is the fertile spot 'qu'il faut bêcher avec zèle.' And not content with this echo of *Candide,* he suddenly avers that mankind is, after all, in the making:

> For my part, I do not find in humanity any sign of decadence. I don't believe in it. I do not even believe that we have reached the culminating point of civilization. I think that man's evolution is an extremely slow business.

Just as he wavered on this question before 1896, so did he waver concerning Positivism and the extent to which he might accept that doctrine. Is it possible to resolve these discords? Thérive has, I think, given us the key.[38] Anatole had fundamentally a beneficent tendency; therefore he '*acted* as if he believed in something and especially in progress.' This would apply notably to the first part of his fourth period, when the defence of Dreyfus and militant Socialism seemed for a time to possess him. *M. Bergeret à Paris,* the title and contents of *Vers les Temps meilleurs,* such arguments for the lifting of the proletariat as we find in his preface to Roger Marx's *l'Art social*—all bear witness to an acceptance of social democracy. He recognized that the future was there. This is the explanation of how he became a Socialist: as he told his secretary, 'Il vaut mieux être porté qu'emporté'—'It is better to be swept along willingly than unwillingly.'[39] He could not react against the aristocrats without believing—at least temporarily—'in the power of democracy to look after its own destinies.' And his speeches to workmen, particularly those that seek to amalgamate the workers by hand and by brain, ring out like an early utterance of the British Labour Party.[40]

But presently the old lassitude and the old cynicism return. Profoundly discouraged by the Great War, feeling the approach of age, France reverts to the sceptical pessimism outlined above. Indifferently he lets people say for him that the future will 'realize the dreams' of sages—or of madmen—and according to one account he allows himself almost in a state of apathy to be enrolled in the Communist party. Other evidences that his last state, philosophically speaking, was as hopeless as his first, would not be difficult to find.[41] His attitudes, then, concerning Progress, are confused and at times opposed. But which of us today is in better case ?

And what are we to do with the second great schism in France's personality ? He was, they say, a 'courtly anarchist,' a 'humanistic aristocrat' who became a heresiarch, an ironist who was hedonistic by 'instinct,' though humanitarian by 'reason.' [42] Let us note first that the problem hardly became acute until after 1896. In the last month of that year Lanson could still write of A.F. as a denizen of the ivory tower, a devotee of beauty, whose artistic vision ever availed him as a *préservatif* against the acids of pessimism.[43] Our preceding chapters will have shown that this view is substantially correct, except for certain pages that adumbrate social unrest. It is the view to which France himself presently returned—to wit, that the love of beauty had been the mainspring of his existence.[44] He had found a splendid shrine for her at the Villa Saïd ; and the problem was posed when Barrès issued his challenge as to how this luxurious living comported with the doctrines of the Left ; or, as other people put it, how could Anatole in the market-place worship the gods of progressive democracy and yet deny them at home ; how could this *raffiné* turn to Socialism and ultimately to Communism ? [45] The 'enigma' has not been resolved, save by alleging his general disgust with things as they are, *plus* the strong influence of Jaurès. The challenge, we have seen, remained unanswered and, as far as I know, has never been answered except tacitly and by implication. That is, Anatole himself may well have felt that there was no such great disharmony between a foundation of artistic tastes and a 'political superstructure' with a socialistic trend. Did not certain Greeks combine æsthetic and political ideals? Was not William Morris (whom he admired) an example of a similar blend? Do the very leaders of Labour always deny themselves the delights of fine living? May not the lover of beauty dislike the banal bourgeois rather than the proletariat?

A more serious discrepancy may perhaps be found between the tradition-loving side of France and the rebel who certainly existed for a decade after 1896. This state of mind germinated in the ponderings of Coignard and of Fra Giovanni. But until his fiftieth year Anatole gave many tokens, except regarding Church dogma, of being a Conservative. His flashes of independence in the last year of the Empire had been quenched by the Commune. Henceforward neither Jean Servien, nor Jérôme Coignard, nor their creator, can take any stock in Revolutions—a position suggested in *l'Etui de nacre* and finally confirmed in *Les Dieux ont soif*. A distrust of the masses, a hatred of their fanatical leaders, a profound doubt as to whether any sort of new régime will function better than any existing order, all co-operate towards a sceptical *laissez-faire*. And these considerations, apparently forgotten in the heat of the conflict, re-emerge in the satiric burlesque of *l'Ile des Pingouins*.

But there remains Bonnard's love of the past ('Croyez-moi, l'avenir est fait du passé') and the general dilemma as stated by Stewart—that Anatole's 'historic sense was ever standing in the way of his eager radicalism.' There remain particularly those years of conflict, the period when he hobnobbed with the defenders of Dreyfus, with the party of Combes and of Jaurès. Does this break the curve of his evolution and disorient our conception of the man entire?

It does, if we accept the thesis of Roujon and others that France was fundamentally a double-dyed Conservative.[46] But one cannot accept such a wide generalization. Among Frenchmen, a respect for their language and its traditions, a sense of historic origins, a love for the native soil, have never—fortunately!—been incompatible with advanced ideas. Anatole had dropped his Boulangism and his militarism and had shown at least an interest in Socialism before Dreyfus was heard of. Furthermore his conservatism, while it lasted, need not imply that he swallowed all his home-brew with a tender faith. 'Le scepticisme reprend toujours ses droits.' It presently got to the point that, in addressing the *Universités populaires* (night-schools), France 'was appealing for revolt against the traditional in institutions, in usages, in beliefs'—and the very foundations of belief. 'In every Francian harangue there was the definite ring of a class-war' against the privileged and their frozen forms of thought.[47]

It must be apparent that, even before 1896, he swallowed neither the Army, nor the Church, nor the Chamber of Deputies, nor *in toto* the institution known as 'Society.' Now it was particularly these 'pressure-groups' that were derided in the *Histoire contemporaine,* for most of them were illiberal. True to his own creed, Anatole indulged in no Revolution when he took his definite stand in 1898. He simply emerged at one particular point in his predestined curve ; from his study, he came out onto the balcony, and presently he addressed the crowd. How he was able temporarily to *believe* in the crowd and in the future and generally in an enlightened control of things is, in view of the usual sweep of his scepticism, the real enigma. Perhaps the only solution is that, in despair of the groups which he had known so long, he turned to the other party as evincing (at least) glimmers of social justice and humanitarianism. And here too Doubt would presently resume her empire. . .

§ 5

ALMOST none of the Pros and Cons so far developed have proved inexplicable or entirely irreconcilable. But more formidable difficulties await us. As suggested several times, it does not appear that France preserved an even balance between Irony and Pity, nor that these two conning-towers for the survey of humanity are erected along parallel lines. The cause of the disparity is found in an untranslatable criticism which the pupil, Tournebroche, once advanced against Maître Coignard :

> Or je sais bien que vous prenez les hommes en pitié ; mais ce n'est pas tout à fait la même chose que d'avoir pitié des hommes.

Paraphrase : may not a scornful pity kill the feeling at its root ?

France's persuasive statement, his major theme, indeed, regarding these dual *motifs* may be recalled : 'Irony and Pity are two good counsellors; the one, through a smile, renders life acceptable; the other, through a tear, renders it sacred.' This is preceded by a famous passage, of which an alternative version reads: [48]

> The more I consider human life, the more I think we must invoke for its benefit Irony and Pity, as the Egyptians called down upon their dead the goddesses Isis and Nephtys; and we must take these as witnesses and as judges.

Repetitions and variations of the theme are not lacking. What has been less noticed is that the maxim originally derived from Renan.[49]

In France's sentimental period, the fissure between the two *motifs* was not wide, and even later his dualism could still be considered 'seductive.' That is because his indulgence seemed still more comprehensive than his irony. It was, said Lemaître, 'so Protean and so vast that it could reach from scorn to charity and fill up the gap between.' Anatole himself more than once views this tolerant virtue as the counterpoise of the ironic outlook. Whether pagan or Christian in its origins, his *'fonds de pitié,'* says Rod, 'is readily stirred by the spectacle of injustice, of wretchedness, of sorrow.' It is a widely social virtue.[50] But it is rather the other side of the medal with which we are now concerned.

No particular date, of course, can be assigned for the shift in emphasis; the *Jardin* is usually indulgent, so early a work as *Jocaste* is ironical. But the trend is for the more sentimental attitude to be displaced after 1891-92; the difference in tone between *Bonnard,* for example, and the *Opinions de J.C.* is remarkable. And this is in accordance with the change that we have found in the man himself.

Without going so far as to say with Mr. Chevalier that centring attention upon Irony 'does make possible an organic account of the contradictory elements' in Anatole, we may agree with this critic that such a position will help us comprehend his diversity. We may agree likewise that a corresponding variety appears in his own 'types of verbal Irony' and that (as even Valéry admits) in so far as this was his prevailing tone, it was both natural and classical. We have seen how Mr. Chevalier stresses incongruity, and the awareness thereof, as the basic element: the ironist, 'confronted with the choice' of two antinomies, may apparently choose both, while really choosing neither. As for the idea of incongruity extended to a whole situation—e.g., in 'Le Procurateur de Judée'—that must await a later section.[51]

Again, there is little doubt that France is often preoccupied with other ironists, in whom he appreciates qualities similar to his own. But we part company from Mr. Chevalier when he combats the idea of a 'growing disenchantment' in Anatole's later output.[52] Here it is necessary to distinguish. One may grant irony enough in his brief realistic period (*Désirs de Jean Servien, Jocaste,* etc.); but that was followed by a long rise in hope, until he reached another period of depression in the works of 1893-94; our critic urges further that the works of this era are as 'hopeless' as *l'Ile des Pingouins,* which is debatable; and he seems less concerned with marking the ebb and flow of Irony than with insisting upon its dominance in France's thought as a whole. We have, however, significant personal reasons for reckoning with the ebb and flow.

Our immediately preceding chapters have failed in their intention if they have not demonstrated that, in the productions of Anatole's grand climacteric, *la bonté* is at a discount, while *l'ironie* is indeed predominant and destructive. *Le Jardin* and *Les Opinions de Jérôme Coignard* leave very little standing save, as Henry James once remarked of a similar iconoclastic virulence, the intellect which created such a void. Does Jérôme occasionally have a benign impulse? But he takes pleasure in letting us down just afterwards. Is *Le Puits* still tender towards Catholicism? It really wears but a thin veil, it flaunts at best, as Delaporte has already pointed out, a 'pious heterodoxy.' Will Fra Giovanni be preserved by his Franciscanism? Alas! He too, as Diplock declares, 'has learnt lessons of irony from the Subtle Doctor'—and the devil gets him at the last. Not only has the sarcastic bent become a great disturber—it begins to contain touches of grossness perceptible to such delicate spirits as Mme. Duclaux, the former Vivian Bell.[53]

Various people have commented upon this development, stressing the shift from A.F.'s second manner. Among them we may linger with a certain Monsieur Bonnard . . . who perhaps incorporates the ghost of Sylvestre. At any rate, he has recently insisted that France's perpetual and 'mechanical' mockery loses its critical value because of its all-pervasiveness. It is saved from total inadequacy only by falling back on the grossness above-mentioned.

Others emphasize A.F.'s bitter tongue, his 'spirit of malice,' and his incessant mockery.[54]

There are not lacking those who intimate that the progression from Coignard to Bergeret is a progression in satirical hardness, which in turn becomes quite pitiless in *l'Ile* and *Les Dieux ont soif*.[55] A thorough discussion of this would be outside our field. But it may be remarked that such contentions underlie the indictment of Massis, in 'l'Humanisme inhumain,' and the general impatience of the pre-and-post-war *jeunes* who discover in Anatole only perversity, negation, and despair. Naturally we do not accept such a sweeping verdict. But we can understand its motivation. And we can now establish the dichotomy between Pity and Irony. In the middle nineties a firm sword severed those twins; the elder pined and grew fragile; the younger throve and waxed strong by devouring everything that came his way.

§ 6

A PARTICULAR kind of conflict, somewhat involved with the preceding one, is that between the real world, as France was coming to know it, and the domain of dreams and fancies that he had loved so long. He had insisted too much on the doctrine of appearances, the role of illusion, whether in art or in love, to abandon it without a struggle. A passage from *La Vie littéraire* shows that Little Pierre was prolonged in the critic of *Le Temps*: 'I am only a dreamer and doubtless I perceive human affairs only in the semi-slumber of meditation.'[56] A.F.'s Illusion, though philosophically grounded and resembling Schopenhauer's, also partakes of that Folly whose encomium Erasmus had pronounced: the creative life-force which must delude its possessor. Certain of the works recently discussed, notably *Le Jardin,* together with various historical reconstructions, repose on a basis of profound revery and thereby lean towards the literature of escape. Certain works still to come also evince this recurrent trend. At times the public speaker will retreat from the balcony into his tower. At times the sage, remarks Mornet, 'weary of the vanities of reason will seek rest among the harmonious horizons which are peopled by the diaphanous phantoms of our fairest chimeras.'[57] Just as the narrator in *Marguerite* demands from passing womankind only a radiance and a perfume, so even M. Bergeret will hold with tenacity to his dreams about the beautiful Mme. Gromance. Illusion in love, in art, in the matter of literary effort and form[58] . . . but the Anatole of *Le Lys rouge* wanted more of woman than an errant perfume, the lion of the Caillavet salon wanted more of the world than dreams, the debater in *La Rôtisserie* and in *Le Puits* is at least as much interested in social and political movements as in erecting ivory towers on the ruins of the past. And the social satirist who unfolds his wings in the *Opinions de Jérôme Coignard* will fully emerge in the pages of the *Histoire contemporaine*. There does not appear to be any full record of the struggle toward and from reality which presumably took place in France's mind. *Solvitur ambulando:* it was a gradual march, occurring without formal renouncement of metaphysical Illusion, of which there are still clear traces in *Le Jardin d'Epicure* and even in the *Discours aux étudiants* of 1910.

A final opposition remains to be considered. This is the possible conflict of the senses with the intellect and the Ideal. It involves, too, the old paradox concerning Desire.

It may prove that the alleged conflict is one that exists in the moralistic, or in the Anglo-Saxon, rather than in the Latin mind. In that case it might be a dualism of which France himself was hardly aware. Before facing that issue, let us premise that, as a disciple of Voltaire and of Condillac, Anatole was a good sensationalist. Not only does he orient our knowledge according to the Lockian principles, not only will he boldly style Science a 'sublime extension of sensualism,' but throughout he is as keen on the life of the senses as on that of the intelligence. Indeed, when he grew weary of the latter, he would recur to the former with a sombre zest—witness the passage in *l'Anneau d'améthyste* where Aspertini confides to Bergeret that the scholarly life would be savourless, were it not for 'the pretty swarm of naughty thoughts' that beguile the savants.[59]

Three attitudes are possible before such avowals. There are those who defend them as proceeding from the inevitable interlacing of art with *la volupté;* those who condemn them severely, as indicative of general disintegration; and those who, without prejudice, simply accept them as part of the mixture that was Anatole. Let us consider, in reverse order, these several schools.

The simple *constatation* would be illustrated (among many others) by the remark of Lewis Galantière that psychologically Anatole 'affords the student a most interesting study of the cerebral voluptuary, [of] imaginative hedonism.' Edmund Wilson also accepts, on a factual basis, A.F. the sensualist, 'the great preacher of *volupté* as the sole solace for human futility.' But this critic is on the fringe of a more censorious group when he avers (somewhat rashly) that this side of France is 'always in conflict' with the moralist, 'the Paphnuce, the Gamelin.'[60]

The moralistic group employ no such half-way measures. From various angles, they decry A.F.'s sensuality as godless, as debasing, or at best as limiting his scope and power. We have seen sufficiently how the clerics find in his neo-paganism, his sensual impiety, the hall-marks of a modern Antichrist.[61] Jérôme Coignard is almost the devil in person for M. Seillière, who supports his general thesis by finding the roots of France's individualistic immorality in his 'naturisme.' The degeneration theory, or vice as corroding the soul of the artist, is expounded in Professor Cerf's volume. This unfavourable opinion was, in a milder way, first developed by Michaut, with whose views the reader is by now familiar. One might add two particulars, in his general indictment: sensuality is virtually the only *sensibility* that A.F. possesses—he is without true passion; and the vice also invades his style, of which it forms the distinguishing characteristic—in reading his fine passages one feels 'une sorte de volupté physique.' Many of these critics hold further that the author of *Thaïs* was hostile to the Church primarily because the Church is hostile to *la volupté*—which is very near the truth, if we remember that Anatole thought of the Church as at odds not only with the Epicurean but with the whole humanistic outlook.[62]

The case for the defence of our pagan proceeds in part from France's own contention that not only is hedonism a good thing *per se,* but that it makes its devotees—witness Coignard and Nicias—more humane and, as it were, compounded of a subtler clay. In part, these supporters amplify Anatole's hints to the effect that 'il n'est point d'art sans concupiscence' (Guehenno) and that the Master, like Lucretius, never wrote a book without invoking the Universal Venus. He himself told Gsell that sensuality is the greatest component of artistic genius. Others would make the urge less a matter of mere concupiscence than of a broad pervasive 'voluptuosidad,' spreading kindness and *génial* in the direction of constant artistic endeavour.[63]

So many men of many minds! And the ladies too take a hand, which they play with a difference. The author of one monograph on *Anatole France et la Femme* brings forward instance after instance to show that his conception of womankind was decidedly sultanesque, not to say sultry; the author of another would attribute to him a broader feminism, a reckoning with various components in such a creation as Thérèse Bellême, who has 'une grande nature de femme.'[64] But we have seen what is at the bottom of Thérèse's 'nature'; and, under their skins, Thaïs and the actress Nanteuil (in *Histoire comique*) are much the same sort of person. 'Across the centuries,' remarks Will Durant, 'Anatole France sees essentially the same thing always—a man pursuing a maid.' And another critic slyly points out that he is constantly sympathetic with Eve—'no less after than before the Fall.'[65] Women for Anatole are more peremptory than war, for after all the Earth is nearer to Venus than to Mars. If occasionally, as in *Le Jardin,* he echoes the sentiment 'Put not thy trust in Woman,' he presently retorts that she alone makes the actual world and governs it—since it is not governed rationally.

That France places a great and growing emphasis on sensual Desire cannot be denied. This has already been exploited, particularly in connexion with *Les Désirs de Jean Servien*. In accordance with his usual propensity, he has emphasized the dark as well as the glowing side of the picture. As in Virgil's time, Amor is still 'durus,' desire is 'triste' or disproportionate or too closely bound up with jealousy to give us a happy time. It has been classed among A.F.'s 'bienheureuses contradictions' that he aspires at the same time to ardour and to serenity.[66] How, indeed, could he do otherwise? He never quite reaches Schopenhauer's paradox that we cannot live with women and we cannot really live without them. He is too much of a Latin and too much of a voluptuary ('cerebral' or otherwise) thus to hold the balance. On the contrary we have heard him avow—and he repeats the avowal[67]—that he has been guided by desire all his long life and that he adores the activity, the 'joys and sorrows' of desiring. So those who, like Michaut, emphasize his devotion to *la Volupté* are not far wrong.

They may, however, be wrong if they contend that France was

devoted to nothing else, or that this obsession damaged any vital concern with more idealistic interests. It has already been stated that such is the position of the moralistic critics, who therefore affirm or imply that there was in Anatole a genuine conflict between the spirit and the flesh, in which the latter triumphed. In these delicate matters any dogmatic attitude is inappropriate. But it may be suggested that possibly the conflict has been over-simplified and that there are, in the City of Mansoul a greater diversity of inhabitants than any Bunyan has enumerated. Perhaps, too, for a Latin, no warfare need exist between an attachment to the ladies, on the one hand, and an interest in Socialism, or art, on the other. A little dissociation of ideas may be indicated. Let us try this out.

Bluntly, did France cease to be an idealist because he was a voluptuary? The term 'idealist' has a different connotation in the two languages: in English it may be applied with admiration to Lamartine, because of his spiritual quality; in French it has been applied with some derogation to Woodrow Wilson because of the supposed lack of practicality in his ideals. In France the word denotes a person who will uphold certain 'ideas,' independently it may well be of spiritual or sentimental connotations. On this basis Anatole is often classified as an 'idéaliste.' He stood on the whole and despite all cynicism for enlightenment, for liberalism, and particularly for social justice. The evidence on the last point is overwhelming;[68] it testifies to the importance which Frenchmen, so much to their honour and credit, attach to 'la Justice,' as the greatest of ideals. A.F. was not conscious of any opposition between this credo and a trend toward *la Volupté*. He passes the social test.

Nor do I believe that, like certain British poets, his soul was torn between carnal and spiritual desires, or that his predilection for the former necessarily marred his work. It should be stated that the ethical problem of the effect of sensuality upon character is one that I do not pretend to solve. We are here concerned only with the artistic results, and those mainly before 1896. Now without being a Crocean, one may see the point of view of the critics mentioned above who find a certain kinship between the sensual and the creative glow. It is so much a question of degree; and the legend of a France almost wholly given over to 'la bagatelle' has been far too much promoted by Brousson and others of his persuasion. As a matter of artistic proportion, is there an excess of sensuality in *Les Désirs de Jean Servien?* Or in *Thaïs?* Or in *Histoire comique?* Evidently not, considering the nature of their respective subjects. There are, to be sure, 'scabrous' or perverse touches in *Le Puits de Sainte Claire,* and still more in later works, snickering allusions that one could well do without. As for the books written after 1896, it may be argued that these touches are too abundant in *l'Ile des Pingouins* (which yet remains an unapproachable masterpiece of its kind) ; that on the contrary *Les Dieux ont soif* is a well-balanced portrayal of human aspirations and failings. It seems, then, that in the large the second count in the moralistic indictment should be dismissed : we do not find in France a case of 'the Degeneration of a great artist.' And in the matter of antinomies, though A.F. himself likes to play up the smiling *versus* the seamy side of Desire, it is plain that he thought both sides necessary to the full life here below.

§ 7

THERE remains the fact that in spite of all the consolations which Anatole sought and the illusions which he fostered, his outlook on the world, as it became fixed in the nineties, was essentially pessimistic. Ségur once inquired whether A.F.'s tastes as an Epicurean, a collector, and an 'appreciator' of women could not save him from the gulf. France answered :

'I have had various kinds of weaknesses. I suppose you don't mean that all that kind of thing will steadily illumine the life of a man?'

He once told Brousson that he had never been happy for one day or one hour.[69] Evidently one must allow for exaggerations, for moodiness, and for the weight of the years. Nevertheless, when once the pleasure-lover challenges the foundations of that faith, he may find himself in an *impasse.* For the beautiful moment cannot stay ; Mephistopheles resurges, sneering at the ardent Faust ; love becomes *l'amour ;* the world seems hollow, once the desire is past ; the intellect, clairvoyant still, prowls disgustedly in an empty universe. And the artist himself may be adrift between a charming Epicureanism and one not quite so charming.

We must again allow for the difference between recorded

meditations and the more casual encounters of life: in conversation, France's courteous manner often beguiled himself and others. He seems by habit to have been kind and friendly, when the analytical acids were not stirred within him. Opinions vary as to whether there was a true *fonds de bonté* in his nature. The reminiscential volumes mostly speak in favour of his goodness; but others sharply differ.[70] However this may be, his load of dark reflections increased irregularly through the years. We may briefly recall some of the chief components of this pessimism.

There are those who aver that even in Parnassian days, and as an outcrop of the Parnassian creed, Anatole was sufficiently aware of the vanity of existence, was already leaning toward *le néant*.[71] *Les Poèmes dorés* has in fact a certain scientific and fatalistic grimness; nor can *Les Désirs de Jean Servien* be considered as a very cheerful book. Presently there intervened France's sentimental decade—the era of the Restoration—to be followed by the chaotic and disorganizing period of the nineties. It has been abundantly shown how he then lost faith in nearly everything and carried his pessimistic scepticism into practically all fields of effort and knowledge. One critic has suggested that he even became weary of the play of ideas; while another severely declared that 'the subjects treated by M. France . . . shock common morality, disconcert commonly held beliefs, and condemn the behaviour usual in matters of truth, justice and goodness.'[72]

His daily life was for a time glamoured over by the successes of his worldly phase; and we shall perceive, in our final chapter, to what a height that glamour could reach. But France was not really to the manner born in 'Society,' nor did he wear accommodating blinkers. His pessimism penetrated there too, as the *Histoire contemporaine* would prove. The semi-rupture with Mme. de Caillavet, followed by her death, left him defenceless and disheartened. The Great War was well suited to encourage pessimism on a grand scale. He fled backwards in time, taking refuge in the memories of his youth. Yet even in the heart of *La Vie en fleur* we find such reflections as this:

> The new Europe will be too different from the Europe now going to pieces under our eyes to care anything about our arts and our thought.

Or as this:

> I think that men in general are worse than they seem to be. They

do not show themselves in their true colours; they hide themselves to commit actions which would cause them to be hated. . . I have hardly ever opened a door inadvertently without finding something which made me regard mankind with pity, with disgust, or with horror.[73]

The first quotation is almost prophetic, in that, as Anatole himself was quite aware, his own great vogue was already passing. This was due mainly to the fact that the new generation cared little for his futilitarian attitude, his pessimistic defeatism. Here supporting evidence will be appropriate. Among his various comments on the Master, Ségur remarked upon the constant disillusionment of this apostle of illusion, his perception of the trickeries of nature and of society, his 'vision noire et nihiliste'—in spite of which he kept calm, fatalistic, and even playfully indulgent towards ideas and persons.[74] Now this and similar passages imply a superiority of Anatole over other thinkers which Vandérem, for one, was quick to challenge. What is all this gloomy talk, he asks, about nature's hidden purposes, about relativity, our ignorance, our fated end, and the like? Surely it is no longer the sign of a superior intelligence to continue baling out that stale stuff from the common reservoir. The superior mind today (1925) would rather subsume such axioms and pass on to something more interesting and vital.[75] In like vein we hear of 'Notre Anatole France' as a person who, for a certain disparaging critic, has always had a 'science infuse' of pessimism. The stagnant waters of his latest tales (*c.* 1908) flowed from a fountain which was his 'de toute éternité.' If he seemed to smile when on *Le Temps,* it was a forced smile, and it became a *rictus* in *l'Ile des Pingouins*. He has really loved nothing, because he has believed in nothing. His only god is a 'dieu nihiliste.' He is a destroyer, a debilitator; when he tries to construct, people only laugh at his social Utopias. Society now has need of something other than Anatole—an opinion which many came to share.[76]

§ 8

SUCH indictments, of course, do not invalidate France's rank as a thinker; for philosophically speaking a man may be anything he likes, provided you know approximately where to find him. The real test is the old one of *sibi constet*. Let him be consistent, that is, within reasonable bounds and as a matter of his general position. Let him also be as broad and as deep and as high as possible. What of Anatole's comparative width and depth, as bearing on the question of persistent trends?

Concerning his width there can be little doubt. Despite the fact that neither music nor landscapes were strictly within his purview and that (according to Brousson's account) he considered the world too much as 'une vaste musée,' yet it was a museum with whose corridors he was probably more familiar than any other writer of his time. For, as Ségur says, Erudition was for him the tenth Muse—and how he boxes the compass of the ages![77] Corroborations and amplifications of this theme can hardly be needed at our present stage. We may simply note Max Hermant's statement that Anatole stood before his generation as an apostle of the new Enlightenment; he broke down the compartments between specialists, he aired thoroughly the stuffy House of Knowledge. And he presented to us his own brain (which was not of an unusual size),[78] as a sort of corrugated palimpsest with myriads of notations and superimpositions.

The more searching inquiry would be regarding his vertical rather than his horizontal range: whether because of the very multiplicity of his ideas, to which may be added his inveterate distrust of universals, we are indeed confronted with an intellectual 'chaos' similar to that attributed to Voltaire. Is it true, as Vandérem implies, that his 'universal and constant indulgence' (in his later years) suggests more receptivity than co-ordination? Or as another critic affirms, did this 'marvellous assembler' of opinions collect them less for their intrinsic than their ornamental value? Massis once said of Romain Rolland that his perpetual surrender to new notions indicated a 'lack of chastity in his thought.' Can a similar approach be addressed to Anatole? And what is the resultant of the numerous self-contradictions already discussed?[79]

It is all very well to answer this last reproach superbly, as did Walt Whitman:

> Do I contradict myself? Very well then I contradict myself.
> (I am large. I contain multitudes.)

Precisely because of the multitudinous swarming, one is led to doubt the cohesion of the swarm. And because France was a social being 'tout en rapports, tout en relations,' the absence of unifying principles in his thousands of darting reflections and utterances has been often enough predicated.[80] It may be further suggested that the exponent of the Pro and Con habit of mind is likely to cast for Con more often than necessary—I mean as a matter of deliberate paradoxicality. And finally, even when Pro and Con are well balanced, what solution do they reach? in Kantian terms, France often posits the thesis and the antithesis, but less frequently attains the synthesis.

For several of these reasons—and a number of others that have been touched upon in the course of the present study—it does not appear that France is entitled to anything like the first rank purely as a philosopher, a *penseur*. To be sure, he tossed off a great number of *aperçus* or intermediary truths, which are pleasing or plausible. But when it comes to the root of the matter, either he found too many roots, or he found none: either he lacked the organizing power or his aversion to systems betrayed him into evasions, contradictions, and mere destructiveness. It is along these lines that the chorus of dispraise has swelled, since Lanson and the early moralistic judges, almost to the present day. The first-named found Anatole's philosophy too disenchanting to be accepted as a guide to life. Others have stressed either his *sécheresse* or his wilful short-sightedness, have exaggerated his mediocrity and superficiality, or have dwelt upon his metaphysical 'feebleness,' implying, again, that the power to synthesize was not his.[81] In spite of prejudice and passion, there should be some truth in this indictment. The penultimate reproaches of senility (Chevalier *et al.*) and of 'inhuman' detachment on Anatole's part, are also understandable.[82] The temper of the times was clearly changing. When A.F. gravely enquired of his companion in 1910, 'Is not the greatest sceptic also the greatest believer?' he found but few listeners.[83] The age of paradoxes was over.

The problem of self-consistency recurs, and here even such a devoted 'Francien' as M. Carias is compelled to shake his head. As an editor, he decides that A.F.'s 'opinions have become so profoundly modified in the course of forty years' of productivity, that one can present his works only in a chronological sequence. An arrangement by subject-matter 'would have run the risk of conferring on his thought an appearance of chaos.' Furthermore, this thought was 'too full and too rich ever to be stabilized.'[84]

These are grave words and almost final, as regards the matter of *intellectual* consistency. What are we to do, then, with the people who maintain that in spite of all Anatole is less Protean than commonly believed; or that, as Loewel puts it (after Giraud), there is a 'fonds de continuité' between his earlier and his later avatars; or that, as Souday and others hold, he underwent a natural evolution in the direction of more and more liberalism; or that, in spite of this incessant evolution, 'il reste un grand penseur' (Gaffiot); or with such an impression as that of Barrès who after a long interval met France again in 1897 and found that 'behind his ideas,' there was a certain urgent drive, strangely compounded of fantasy and scepticism?[85] What are we to do particularly with our strong conviction that, although somewhat loosely integrated, Anatole remains through it all substantially himself?

One solution for these perplexing discrepancies may be tendered. There is, as Barrès intimated, something deeper than the intellectual expression in weighing a writer's total impact. There is the aggregate known as personality—and with Anatole it was a case of 'Personality Plus.' It is this glorified Anatole that admirers may speak of as 'le dernier Sage,' or as the initiator, the leader of a generation.[86] It is this enlarged Anatole whom we *do* know 'where to find' as a matter of prevailing trends. For who shall deny that he believed thoroughly in Beauty and that at least through this contact he 'rejoined humanity'?[87] Who can gainsay that, as a totalitarian Anatole, he wrought for that humanity in which he could not wholly believe? It was, very probably, a faith of the heart rather than of the head; but it existed and would help explain his shift from the merely intellectual liberty which he claimed around 1890, to the widely pervasive and militant liberalism which became his chief driving force some years later. As a feeling for social justice, it never deserted him. Surely, despite his discouragements, descending blights and tergiversations, we can often lay our finger on such and such a passage, in praise of Epicureanism, or of learning, or (it may be) of the Socialistic creed, and say: 'This is the essential Anatole.' But our conviction will be born from something that underlies the written word.

§ 9

The 'Plus' which was added to France's personality was nevertheless very much enhanced by the written word. In dealing with his style, we may stretch that elastic term to cover much that pertains to the whole presentation, whether as regards structure or stylistic qualities proper, the use of *esprit* and devices, or the glove-like fitting of the diction to the thought. In analysing such matters, a foreigner is at some disadvantage; hence more than ever we seek aid from the competent French critics who have made distinctions and chosen illustrations. For obvious reasons, the Anatolian specimens displayed should usually be preserved in their mother-tongue — the original juice.

In composition or construction, A.F. generally attains but a mediocre success. It is not that he cannot construct, as Michaut would have us believe, for there are examples that prove the contrary. It is rather that he cannot be bothered, he is too much interested in other things. His famous 'nonchalance' is again operating, even to the extent of allowing him to bestow different names upon the same character in *l'Etui de nacre* and to endow M. Bergeret at times with two daughters, at times with one.[88] A writer who thus omits elementary precautions cannot be greatly concerned with plot. And, indeed, as Michaut points out, not only is orderly progression neglected in the semi-autobiographical volumes (including *Sylvestre Bonnard*), but also in such 'regular' novels as *Histoire comique* and most of the *Histoire contemporaine*.[89] Conversations and digressions, however witty and delightful, are stumbling-blocks in the path of narration. We have seen, too, that the majority of A.F.'s short stories are far from being models of the genre. As for the larger aspects of fiction, it has been said often enough that the sustained creative urge was not his and that his best characters are mouthpieces.

Yet there are exceptions in every field. His success in reviving the *conte philosophique* is generally granted.[90] As for structural matters, why, for instance, did Anatole take pains regarding certain developments in *Thaïs*? Why do Carias and Ambrière insist on his 'patience de mosaïste' in assorting the material of *Le Lys rouge*?[91] Some of these manipulations are due to the fact that our author was more interested in passion than in action. Whatever seems to bring out better the sombre manias of Paphnuce, the jealousy of Dechartre, or the sensual nature of Thérèse Bellème, will seem to him worth the trouble of study and possible alteration. In this connexion it has been observed that Anatole's best novels are novels of fatality and that they are consequently in the modern tradition as exemplified by *Madame Bovary* and many another. They are, incidentally, in the ancient tradition as well. These well-knit successes (which are rare) may be illustrated by the greater portion of *Le Lys rouge* and, almost of necessity, by *Les Noces corinthiennes*.

Apart from this trend, there is one particular kind of structural situation that A.F. finds, and leaves, piquant. This is the type, already foreshadowed, where the element of paradox or incongruity is inherent in the *res gestae,* and is deftly extracted and set off. Says Mr. Chevalier: 'The incongruity which is the quarry of the Ironist must exist in the material.' And again, this element is 'the basis of practically all his plots from *Les Noces corinthiennes* to *La Révolte des anges.*'[92] The last-named novel will, in fact, illustrate the formula, even to the degree of paradox. What could be more incongruous than angels who conduct themselves like Parisians, whether in *amours* or in politics? What could be more topsy-turvy than that Satan should rightfully displace Iahveh—save for his fear of becoming *like* Iahveh in the end? Is there any greater mental upset than that Pilate should forget the Crucifixion? The point is that in these cases, as in others, the paradoxical attitude is, in spite of some rambling, sufficiently well maintained to lend coherency to the tale.

The *procédé* may have two corollaries, both of which are illustrated in 'Le Procurateur de Judée.' One is the surprise ending, which is reserved as a clue to all that has gone before. Occasionally this is found elsewhere, as in 'La Leçon bien apprise,' where the *memento mori* of the priest unexpectedly serves only to impel the lady into carnal pleasures. The other corollary is philosophical: in both of the above instances France was deliberately countering the 'idées reçues' of smug and godly folk. In this form of paradox he took the greatest pleasure; that it was his favourite 'perversity' is illustrated throughout *l'Ile des Pingouins* and, more cautiously, in the *Vie de Jeanne d'Arc*. It is not remarkable, then, that more strictly from the 'angle of narration' we find him presenting Bluebeard as a maligned and kindly gentleman, or achieving a table-turning 'act' in *La Comédie de celui qui épousa une femme muette,* or that in *Thaïs* the roles of saint and sinner should be reversed. These are all cases where an entire plot is affected by the author's insistence on the Con of heterodoxy. At times it seems as if Poe's creation, the Imp of the Perverse, has Anatole in his grip.[93]

There is another kind of incongruity, already hinted at, which is visible in certain minor situations and incidents. This is the type arising from social encounters, where, as the expression goes, *chacun poursuit sa propre idée.* When Bonnard is in danger of arrest for his 'crime,' he leisurely discourses on medieval penalties, to the dismay of his hostess. When in *Le Mannequin d'Osier* Mme. Worms-Clavelin is deeply occupied with private worries, her small daughter irrelevantly interrupts, to the reader's mirth, with her own concern about her schoolmates, the state of her underwear, and—of all things—the Pragmatic Sanction ! In the jostling clash of egotisms known as Society, there are times when this incapacity for mutual understanding may rise from humour to tragedy. Witness once more the final scene in *Le Lys rouge.*

§ 10

We now reach the heart of the matter—the style, or styles, of Anatole France. On the threshold of our inquiry, we are met by a challenge as to whether A.F. really had an original way of putting things. The challenger, M. Miomandre,[94] holds that his inspirations, whether in matter or manner, were too bookish and too infrequently recast by a transforming energy to make for an individual style. There are cases where this is true, where the echoes seem almost translations. But much more numerous are the cases—from *Gabalis* or the saints' lives or the *Decameron*—where the material is truly changed into something new and Anatolian. Furthermore, M. Miomandre's contention begs the question if he means that bookish sources invalidate an author's originality. Shakespeare played the 'sedulous ape' before Stevenson did ; and in neither instance has the later writer been accused of lacking originality. The analogy with Stevenson is the closer, because both A.F. and R.L.S. deliberately went in for making *pastiches* or imitations of their favourite authors, and each thereby helped form the harmonies of his own orchestration.

In this direction as in others, our author owed much to the

classics, to certain features of the French tradition, as well as to half a dozen particular French writers, and to such elements in real life as the art of conversation or *bibelots* and local atmosphere sensuously perceived. Let us try to disentangle some of these threads.

Desonay, deriving from Gregh, has declared:

> If various literatures—Greek, Latin, and French—are mingled in that style, which nevertheless emerges so well-fused and unified (like a smooth bronze), yet it is Greece which gave the novelist the best of his talent as a prose-writer.

Gregh had said that the *alliage merveilleux* which composes the style is of Corinthian metal, as proved early by *Les Noces corinthiennes*.[95] We must refer back (to Chapter VIII) for a discussion of the Hellenic qualities, e.g., subtlety, harmony, luminosity, which Anatole is believed to manifest. It is usually conceded that the 'Attic spirit' gave scent and savour to his prose. Imitations both of Greek and of Latin writers are found throughout his career, from the early article on 'Daphnis et Chloé' to *La Vie en fleur*. Enthusiastic recapturings of visions inspired by the classics gave rise to wingèd flights of apostrophe or other rhetoric. Among the Latins, Lucretius and Virgil were his chosen masters; his debt to the latter has already been recorded. Precision and purity in diction were what he chiefly owed to the Romans.

But these were not the only models to whom Anatole remained faithful. His masters were both sacred and profane. He could deliberately imitate the naïveté of the hagiographers, as is apparent in many a passage, although some think that the devil had a good deal to do with his saintliness; or he carried on the tradition and the deftness of the French short-story, whether the old *conte gaulois* or the later *conte philosophique*. Anticipating the analogy with Corinthian metal, Lemaître declared that this style was a 'precious composite . . . of Racine, of Voltaire, of Flaubert, of Renan, and yet it remains Anatole France himself.' To the first two of these influences Massis adds the names (less frequently in evidence) of La Bruyère and Montesquieu, and admits that the result is a 'subtle distillation combined with an infallible taste.'[96]

As for Racine, it has been shown how intimately his rare nature was wrought into the very substance of France's being. Stylistically, his 'echoes' recall the older master by the smooth harmonious rhythm or by the peculiar blend of psychological delicacy with seeming-simple expression. As Des Hons has developed, these things are particularly manifest in passages dealing with love. For instance, from *La Révolte des anges*:

> . . . la voix mordante et les mouvements insidieux de cette créature me jetèrent dans un trouble inconnu. Je pâlis, je rougis, mes yeux se voilèrent, ma langue sécha dans ma bouche; je ne pouvais me mouvoir.

Or when the player of the 'cinnor' thus addresses Paphnuce:

> Où penses-tu me fuir, insensé ? Tu retrouveras mon image dans l'éclat des fleurs et dans la grâce des palmiers, dans le vol des colombes, dans les bonds des gazelles, dans la fuite onduleuse des ruisseaux, dans les molles clartés de la lune. . .[97]

Another aspect of France's prose harks back rather to the *style coupé* of the eighteenth century. When he is moving rapidly, whether in narration or exposition, the short pithy sentences inevitably recall Voltaire and, though less inevitably, Montesquieu. To the former, as partially reincarnated in Jérôme Coignard, A.F. handsomely acknowledges his debt: he 'learned to write through the pages of Voltaire ; hence it could be said that at times Anatole 'spoke to the twentieth century in the language of the eighteenth.'[98] Space is lacking here to demonstrate what, at other times, the Anatolian rhythms may owe to the mellifluous rhetoric of Chateaubriand, to the unction of Renan, to the metallic lustre of Leconte de Lisle. Thus his style came to be 'a rich wine, ripened on an ancient soil.'[99]

Nor are his derivations wholly bookish. One week he may be using the burin of an eighteenth-century engraver, while next time he mimics the careful notations of a nineteenth-century realist.[100] One Wednesday he may have been so far involved in the witty conversation of a salon that the results were apparent in what he wrote on Thursday.[101]

Two indications may emerge from the above discussion. First, it is a simplification, merely a convenient synthesis, to speak of *the* style of Anatole France. He has no single instrument, he uses rather a variety of organ-pipes. This will be illustrated further on. Secondly, it has been questioned by more than one person whether his 'style' (synthetically) is an original one. In view of the quantity of influences and attachments that it has undergone or experienced, men like Mauriac and Amiot contend that originality is for A.F. an impossible virtue. Carias and a number of others hold—more reasonably, it appears to the present writer—that whatever the 'dessous' and the reminiscences, the blending is so perfect, the product so fine, that there exists surely a recognizable Anatolian manner.[102] One demonstration of this seems so nearly definitive that it will bear citation.

M. Michaut cannot be said to hold a brief for France, nor does he scant—far from it—the elucidation of bookish imitations. Chateaubriand and Flaubert, especially in *Thaïs;* Bossuet himself in a page from *Vers les Temps meilleurs;* Voltaire and Renan *passim:* all these influences are displayed by the critic. Then we are shown what is more surprising—that occasionally and in definite passages A.F. could and did mimic the Naturalists, Maupassant and even Zola. He could mingle in his alembic or closely juxtapose without a clash diverse inspirations, ancient and modern. That means that he possessed a universal solvent of his own, or that the many-coloured Wheel was functioning and that we are somehow in the presence of an 'originalité véritable.'[103]

§ II

BEFORE attempting to analyse the qualities of his writing, it will be well to indicate (and partly to recall) France's main pronunciamientos regarding style. It has been found that because of his reverence for the classical ages ('Je suis resté un classique'), he stood always for this tradition as reflected in the greatest of French periods. A properly civilized taste included for him purity of choice diction, a wisely simplified expression, making a well-nigh universal appeal. In 'La Vie littéraire,' he proclaimed his faith in *le beau* and its components, where all else is uncertain or subject to personal impressions. He recommended simplicity for all writers; sentiment, especially for poets and dreamers; taste, for those who seek the flower of life. He laid stress on the naturalness and clearness of the French language. In *Le Jardin d'Epicure,* while he evinces scepticism about fixed standards in writing, as in general æsthetics, while Impressionism is still dominant in the view that the artist is he who prolongs our delusive dreams, while passion and personality are considered the prime essentials in creation, yet the finished product must reveal, together with a fine simplicity, those natural feelings that make all mankind akin. He distrusts the worn words, the 'isms,' the abstract signs of the metaphysicians.

Apart from these recapitulations, we discover some fresh testimony. As early as 1880, we find our journalist averring (not without apparent inconsistency) that worn and polished words are excellent when they are the current coinage of the language: they do not have the angular asperities of scientific formations.[104] As late as 1920, apropos of Stendhal, he came out with an attack on nineteenth-century *prosateurs:* however lyrical, however elaborate they appear, yet they write badly, as contrasted with the pure and limpid flow of seventeenth-century style. No less a person than Marcel Proust answered this, alleging that almost the contrary is true, that people have written well *only* in the nineteenth century, because of the greater exposure of individual sensibilities and because the artist has been allowed closer contact with the object to be portrayed.[105] We may see some justice on both sides of the argument, and particularly we may see how each debater was 'conditioned' to think as he did.

From the preceding paragraphs it must now be plain what France demanded in style: naturalness and simplicity on the one hand; the expression of universal sentiments on the other. Over and over again it has been shown that his most admired authors were those who possessed these qualities and, consequently, those who partook of the classical tradition. May we therefore infer that such virtues are most visible in his own writing? We may— but there are certain complications.

If at twenty-three Anatole declared (quite classically), 'it seems to me stupid to separate form from substance,' yet he came in *Le Temps* to think of form as constituting *per se* the only distinct originality and of art itself as consisting only in 'arrangement.'[106] Surely this is more of a *fin-de-siècle,* or Alexandrian, attitude than it is purely classical. He admits, furthermore, difficulties about defining simplicity, for nature (which art must follow) is complex in her manifestations. It is rather a question of 'styles which *seem* simple' and of discerning whence comes this 'happy appearance.' It proceeds from an alliance of diverse elements into a uniform whole, just as the seven colours of the spectrum may combine into one ray of white clarity.[107] The analogy reminds us again of the Wheel of Truth in 'l'Humaine Tragédie.' The difficulty recalls his suggestive definition of style as 'infinite shades of thought.' It would be asking a good deal from a man of France's comprehension and subtlety always to enjoy—or employ—a tone of absolute simplicity.

There may be added a few points about A.F.'s attitude towards his calling. He liked to protest to his intimates that he took himself less seriously as a writer than as a thinker; and in the fragment of his 'Autobiographie' he says plainly: 'I lack and have always lacked the "literary" habit of mind. When I write, I am only a man and I do not become something else, as genuine [i.e., professional] writers do.'[108] If he took some care with his *devoirs* at school, he and others have recognized that they showed few signs of the literary vocation.[109] Later, if he has been correctly reported, he composed his early tales much as he had done his school exercises—lazily and reluctantly, forced by external pressure. This was before any ambition spurred him on, for he was 'very slow in entering upon a literary career.' And he admitted to Frank Harris that even in his old age writing remained for him 'horribly difficult.'[110]

But it was another kind of difficulty. Not so much (from the time of *Thaïs*) an aversion to the task, as a body of scruples and anxieties about achieving it in finished form. All the testimony, regarding the composition of *Thaïs* itself, the emendations in *Le Lys,* his manias in proof-correction, his scrupulosity even in correspondence, point in the same direction. They show him as immensely occupied with verbal and stylistic niceties. That such is his chief concern is evidenced by the holograph MSS. preserved in the Bibliothèque Nationale.[111]

§ 12

Anatole's prose, then, may be really simple, as it usually is in the Gospels; or it may be seeming-simple, but with undertones, as often in his middle period; or these undertones may emerge, in which case there is an orchestral elaboration of the theme.

His first characteristic manner (omitting his poetry) was formed during the eighties and was established by his association with *Le Temps,* where the writer appears as 'dépouillé, sobre, alerte, définitivement maître de sa langue.'[112] This is the France whom many people still think of in terms of the eighties, the France of *Bonnard* and *Le Livre,* who wears his style like a perfect morning-coat, who when impassioned writes as simply but as eloquently as Racine (there could be for A.F. no higher compliment), the France who is praised by one critic after another for his crystalline limpidity.[113] It is he who is quoted as declaring that French authors have three great virtues: clearness, clearness, and again clearness.[114] It is he who insisted, with Malherbe and Boileau, that written French should be *easily* clear to all *honnêtes gens.* It is he who is credited with the terseness and ease of Voltaire and a like respect for the mother-tongue, which (he proves) is still capable of everything. It is he who, in spite of the ravages of the Symbolists and the approaching shadows of a still more formless obscurity, remained at once 'a model and a warning.'[115] He won his readers by the harmonious clarity of passage after passage in the *Livre de mon ami.* Later, he refused to embellish his recollections in *Le Petit Pierre.* In his fiction, he often paralleled the pithiness of a Maupassant. In *Histoire comique,* if he wanted to express the consoling power of an actress's love, he said simply: 'Mais elle l'enveloppa d'une fraîcheur délicieuse.' In 'Le Procurateur de Judée,' as a concise and revolutionary finale, he had Pilate murmur: 'Jésus ? Jésus le Nazaréen ? Je ne me rappelle pas.' A longer example concerns Bonnard's search for the MS. of *La Légende dorée:*

> —Pourquoi, me dis-je, pourquoi ai-je appris que ce précieux livre existe, si je dois ne le posséder, ne le voir jamais ? J'irais le chercher au cœur brûlant de l'Afrique ou dans les glaces du pôle si je savais qu'il y fût. Mais je ne sais où il est. Je ne sais s'il est gardé dans une armoire de fer, sous une triple serrure, par un jaloux bibliomane ; je ne sais s'il moisit dans le grenier d'un ignorant. Je frémis à la penséee que, peut-être, ses feuillets arrachés couvrent les pots de cornichons de quelque ménagère.[116]

This paragraph is simplicity itself, but it has point, variety, and a smooth development.

But there is another kind of thing, the 'seeming simplicity,' which, says Mr. Brock, 'is no less artful than the simple style of other great artists.'[117] More artful in a double sense, more unctuous, more decorated with 'grâces fluides,' more like the pseudo-

Benedictine that we know him to have been. That Anatole was aware of this transitional manner will appear from a passage in the *Jardin d'Epicure:*

> Je dirai donc que, s'il n'y a pas proprement de style simple, il y a des styles qui paraissent simples, et que c'est précisément à ceux-là que semblent attachées la jeunesse et la durée.

He adds that the composite elements in such (so to speak) macaronic styles must be so well fused that they form an ensemble which is unanalysable. Baring spoke of the blend attained by A.F. as 'a luminous and complicated simplicity.'[118]

This subtly simple manner is most readily to be recognized in the writings based on Scripture or on saints' lives, including much of St. Joan. For here the element of parody or *pastiche* involved is most discernible. The passage regarding Little Pierre's fondness for Samson, or almost any of those cited from the more religious portions of *l'Etui de nacre* or *Le Puits de Sainte Claire,* will illustrate the tone.[119] It is carried to the extreme of parody and almost of epigram in the false virgin's prayer to the true one: 'O toi qui as conçu sans pécher, accorde-moi la grâce de pécher sans concevoir.' But in the prayer of Gestas to Mary we are nearer the average norm of this pseudo-simplicity.

It is very apparent in religious subjects, but it is by no means limited to them. It is found in a good deal of Vivian Bell's cooing and twittering. It inspires a 'dying fall' in her neo-classical idyl:

> Elle avait nom Gemma. Mais l'amant de Gemma,
> Nul entre les conteurs jamais ne le nomma.

It is compatible, as Reggio has hinted, with a certain picturesqueness of detail, which frequently—witness *La Rôtisserie*—is meant to suggest more than it directly conveys. For the undertones may be visual as well as auditory. The same critic points out that when France's style has become fully organized, through its increasing sympathies and suggestions, it charms us equally by its *souplesse* and its capacity to surprise.[120] But this sort of rhetoric, though still 'simplifié' and debonair, tends rather, through its cadenced articulations, toward elaboration and artifice—which is our next topic.

It is evidently here that the variety of France's instrumentation will be perceptible, not only because of his many-mindedness (wherein the style must fit the thought), but because of the multiplicity of artistic impulses and purposes which he wishes to serve in numberless *morceaux.* That he should usually cleave to the profound principle of unity in variety, that he could preserve, through all his wanderings, his personal *cachet,* would be esteemed a miracle, were it not performed by all great writers. Some of the components or alternations in his prose would for a lesser adept offer a difficult problem ; but difficulty was a spur to this ex-Parnassian. His form, says Reissig, is 'at times harmonious, at times harsh, now strained and dark, now lightsome,' according to the particular vision he is seeking to convey.[121] A characteristic blend, says W. J. Locke, is a phrasing 'in which beauty and irony are so subtly interfused as to make it perhaps the most alluring mode of expression in contemporary fiction.' Abundant illustrations of this process have been cited. Durant remarks that in this compound of 'tenderness and disillusionment,' there is a fluidity 'as gentle as the dew,' a pensive and 'subdued style, quiet, soft, almost languorous.' Albert Samain, in addressing France, seems to emulate the Master :

> . . . l'âme s'est bercée, très lente, aux harmonies de votre beau style déroulé à larges plis comme une étoffe magnifique et douce, comme une soie merveilleuse toute chargée de fruits, de feuillages et d'oiseaux, dans un sourire de couleurs.[122]

These tributes and other such [123] intimate that we cannot always expect, from the author of *Le Livre de mon ami,* an adolescent simplicity, that he too can indulge in what Cicero (and Sainte-Beuve after him) qualified as 'Asiatic' rhetoric—with the difference that the convolutions are not too Proustian and that the major virtue of clarity is retained. Sometimes the resultant is deliberately in the grand manner ; witness above the retreat of the Romans to Canusium, or the perspective of the Revolution quoted from *l'Etui de nacre.* Sometimes there is added to the language the deliberate reflection of the culture of a given period, 'according as his subject may be Greek, or Florentine, or French.' So in *La Rôtisserie* descriptive touches from paintings and the like are fused with Anatole's own picture. Sometimes, as Lanson again suggests, the rhythmic description leads on to a less material, more 'vaporous' harmonizing of the idea (and the person behind the idea) with the movement of the sentences, as in the fatigued stroll of M. Bergeret, when he went along with vacillating step, his soul open to every vagrant breeze or impression.[124] In this, as in so many places, the modulations in the prose music are readily discernible.

Descriptions run all the way from brief exact notations, as in A.F.'s early realistic work, to the fuller depiction of exotic scenes, as in the oft-cited fire-fly passage from the Prologue to *Le Puits* or in certain pages from *Thaïs*. For example, the account of Paphnuce's journey along the Nile:

> Au matin, il vit des ibis immobiles sur une patte, au bord de l'eau qui reflétait leur cou pâle et rose. Les saules étendaient au loin sur la berge leur doux feuillage gris; des grues volaient en triangle dans le ciel clair et l'on entendait parmi les roseaux le cri des hérons invisibles. Le fleuve roulait à perte de vue ses larges eaux vertes où des voiles glissaient comme des ailes d'oiseaux, où, çà et là, au bord, se mirait une maison blanche, et sur lesquelles flottaient au loin des vapeurs légères, tandis que des îles, lourdes de palmes, de fleurs et de fruits, laissaient s'échapper de leurs ombres des nuées bruyantes de canards, d'oies, de flamants et de sarcelles. A gauche, la grasse vallée étendait jusqu'au désert ses champs et ses vergers qui frissonnaient dans la joie, le soleil dorait les épis, et la fécondité de la terre s'exhalait en poussières odorantes.[125]

Here again we have a 'subtil alliage' between picturization and phrasal harmony. The musical quotient is in fact so high in Anatole's more impassioned prose that at times, e.g., in the *récit* of Nectaire, a definite, though variable, verse-pattern can be shown to exist.[126]

There is even a higher level of attainment. The twin values just mentioned may give a special stylistic atmosphere to a whole scene or a whole story. The cadences prevalent in *Thaïs* are not those of the *Histoire comique:* in the former, the actress creating her role is rendered *à la* Theocritus; in the latter, *à la* Marcel Prévost. In *Le Lys rouge,* whether in descriptions or conversations, La Volupté is gently murmuring in your ear.[127] Bonnard or Bergeret is best realized in a study, where the domestic pets, Hannibal or Riquet, are in tune with the mood of the scholar, where the bookish aura is maintained by a succession of lulling rhythms, which are authentically Anatolian. For example, the confession of old Sylvestre:

Puissances de l'ombre, fantômes de la nuit, si, vous attardant chez moi après le chant du coq, vous me vîtes alors me glisser sur la pointe des pieds dans la cité des livres, vous ne vous écriâtes certainement pas, comme madame Trépof à Naples : 'Ce vieillard a un bon dos!' J'entrais ; Hannibal, la queue toute droite, se frottait à mes jambes en ronronnant. Je saisissais un volume sur sa tablette, quelque vénérable gothique ou un noble poète de la Renaissance, le joyau, le trésor dont j'avais rêvé toute la nuit, je l'emportais et je le coulais au plus profond de l'armoire des ouvrages réservés, qui devenait pleine à en crever. C'est horrible à dire: je volais la dot de Jeanne. Et quand le crime était consommé, je me remettais à cataloguer vigoureusement jusqu'à ce que Jeanne vînt me consulter sur quelque détail de toilette ou de trousseau.[128]

Regarding this essential France, M. Michaut has an interesting development, in line with his general thesis. Preluding by the material already given about A.F.'s imitativeness, the critic establishes, first, that the novelist not merely juxtaposes but fuses his models in a crucible of his own. The product thus obtained is hall-marked not only by a peculiar harmony, suavity, and choice of diction ; not only are there long seductive passages, of the types already quoted ; but generally the ground-swell of this prose is propelled by sensuous impulses. Full of a languorous ardour, such passages 'sont tout ensemble délicats et sensuels, et sensuels et délicats tout ensemble sont les sentiments qu'ils font naître' . . . witness what M. Bergeret experienced for Mme. Gromance. Without accepting all of Michaut's theories about A.F.'s sensuality, we may recognize the velvet touch which it gives to his style. This has been corroborated by others, who either aver that his style has 'sensuousness, richness, warmth,' or that the inner music of this complicated soul emerges in a 'volupté supérieure.'[129]

The seductive features of France's writing are, then, due less to particular recipes than to the general *allure*. Yet there are certain stylistic devices which have been studied to advantage in monographs and portions of larger works.[130] Among these we will choose the cases which seem to accord best with his habits, mental or temperamental. Two of these effects are prominent : his taste for startling contrasts or paradoxes ; and his endeavour to make his 'copy' word-perfect.

If, as we have partly seen, 'sharp antithesis and vivid paradox are the satirist's stock in trade,'[131] we may expect that this fondness for oppositions will find verbal repercussions. If, as surmised, the unique tone of France's style is attained through personality rather than through logic, then this higher harmony may resolve many dissonances. His desire to startle by unexpected correlations is thus transferred from thought to phrase, to figure, and to epithet.[132] Nowhere is the device more apparent than in A.F.'s choice of seemingly incongruous adjectives, which, as M. Maurois has indicated, is a part of his habitual 'alternance des thèmes dissonants.' A gesture will be 'placide et menaçant'; a château will be 'alchimique et délabré'; we have noted how bitter-sweet is life and how maleficent and 'exquisite' is the power of reason. Or there may be a warfare between adjective and noun: 'une gloire crapuleuse'; 'la douceur . . . cruelle.' This kind of thing, declares Maurois, is France's 'folie réglée.'

When the Master hovered over his proof-sheets, brandishing and glorifying his scissors as the chief weapon of the warrior, we are told that he frequently spied out and abolished a refractory adjective.[133] His eye would fall on the smooth banality of 'Des prélats, magnifiques et pieux, allèrent en procession.' Halt! About face! How much rarer to say, 'Des prélats, obèses et pieux . . . !' Thus we achieve a sneer at the priests; and a sneer at virtue may be born if we contort a whole phrase, thus: 'La dame de Théroulde était riche et de bonne renommée.' A stupid remark, badly in need of the scissors, which elucidate: 'Comme la dame de Théroulde était riche, on la disait de bonne renommée.' Presently it would appear that the secretary catches the disease. He, too, finds himself alternating epithets or capping a statement by its contradiction.

Whatever the exaggerations in the above account, all are agreed that France, through his tact and judgment, did much for the adjective. We learn that this part of speech has been emphasized, particularly by the nineteenth century, with its desire for colour and the specific term. In this direction, one may add, Balzac and Hugo often went too far. But France, though unclassical in shifting with his age, yet retained the old *mesure* and became the 'prince du qualificatif.'[134] Examples of his skill may be found in almost any specimen cited above. One characteristic procedure (which Proust developed) is to mass amplifying or Homeric adjectives around a noun, until the whole idea is distended to the utmost. Thus Anatole stigmatizes certain 'discours' as 'maussades, ténébreux et mal appropriés.' Not seldom such a Rabelaisian accumulation will be found in *pastiches*.[135]

The second definite tendency, perhaps an extension of the preceding one, was toward whatever derives from the conscience of the verbal artist. I say 'verbal' advisedly, because although we have found certain exceptions, it does not appear from manuscripts and proof-sheets that Anatole was addicted to recomposing *en gros*. To begin with, he did not have the massive architectonic sense of a Balzac nor the constant strength required to swing into fresh positions whole blocks of a pyramid. Rather, as a worker in mosaic, he would occasionally shift a few tiles, to improve the delicate pattern. A favourite method of composition in his later years was to jot down on scraps of paper (menus, backs of invitations, and the like) thoughts that occurred to him in restaurants or railway trains. How did he utilize such things, together with notations in his Scrap-Book and old newspaper clippings? That is where the formidable scissors came into play. With their attendant paste, they were employed, say on successive proof-sheets, for adjectival arabesques, for removing pronominal danglings, for deleting repetitions ('respectez le mot') or mere flourishes, for operating on the adornments of the poor Pucelle, for seeking simplicity and brevity—but all in matters of detail.[136] The paragraph becomes soberer and better balanced. The sentence, shortened and sharpened, speeds more directly to the mark. Above all, the Word, the sacred Word is now chosen for all time.

Let no one think that all this is easy. To the difficulties already confessed may be added a minor one—that A.F., like many an English or American student, could never learn about the agreement of past participles; and a major one, as related by the sculptor, Bourdelle.[137] While working on his bronze bust of Anatole, Bourdelle became discouraged, had one of those sinking spells to which every artist is subject. France then showed him one of his own works, its pages laden with pencilled notes, erasures, corrections, and whispered: 'Only idiots think themselves perfect.' And only idiots cease the everlasting struggle towards perfection.

Yet, to diversify our own adjectives, it is a cruel-sweet pain. He once told a young friend:

My greatest pleasure is to purify my style, to weigh the true, the etymological meaning of each word, for each word is an individual which has its own origins, its ancestors, its birth, its ups and downs, in short its history.[138]

We recall how he admired the savoury old expressions (*papelard* or *engeigner*), in La Fontaine, and we can understand how he would use similar terms himself, whenever opportunity offered. 'Il trouve toujours le mot propre,' says Braibant. 'Et c'est ce qui donne sa mesure d'écrivain.' [139]

Perhaps France's preoccupation with the smaller units of style—the word, the phrase, the brief sentence—is as characteristic as his piecemeal way of dealing with ideas. In diction as in thought, he belongs less to the race of inventors, of profound organizers, than to that of skilled assorters. His impressions and reactions are broken up 'en mille riens' without close co-ordination. Similarly, the 'style coupé' often dispenses with connectives and transitions, yet without notable loss of smoothness.

Some additional *procédés* may be briefly mentioned.[140] The principle of condensation is illustrated by a number of practices. In descriptions (save for exotic scenes), local colour is laid on not with a trowel, but rather by quick, discreet touches. In narrative, there is often a rapid succession of phrases or periods, with more emphasis on the verbs than is commonly admitted. In dialogue, a certain whimsicality of tone may be appropriate, as when the author addresses the Tanagra figurine, in 'Le Petit Soldat de plomb':

—Blanche Pannychis, toi qui filais la laine de Milet, sous le mûrier antique, tu ne m'auras pas fait entendre en vain des paroles de bon conseil ; sur ton avis, je permets à La Tulipe d'aller partout où la tradition l'appelle.

Alors une petite batteuse de beurre en biscuit de Sèvres, les deux mains sur sa baratte, tourna vers moi des regards suppliants.

—Monsieur, ne le laissez point partir. Il m'a promis le mariage. C'est l'amoureux des onze mille vierges. S'il s'en va, je ne le reverrai plus.

Et, cachant ses joues rondes dans son tablier, elle pleura toutes les larmes de son cœur.

La Tulipe était devenu rouge comme le revers de son habit : il ne peut souffrir les scènes, et il lui est extrêmement désagréable d'entendre les reproches qu'il a mérités.[141]

In general, otiose or technical details, superfluous or clogging material is deleted. For balance or brevity, a sentence may be tightened from the compound into the complex variety ; or it may be so pivoted that a main clause becomes subordinate. Like his classical masters, France is fond of general reflections, boiled down to the essential maxim : 'Les sciences sont bienfaisantes : elles empêchent les hommes de penser.' (Compare the use of brief slogans or *mots,* like 'Mort aux vaches !' and 'Que d'art !') [142] Antithesis is rarely overdone ; similes are scattered and to the point ; apostrophes are rather too frequent, too sentimental ; euphony is the constant desideratum. Although enumeration of various types is abundantly in evidence, yet sometimes a choice or 'characteristic' detail will supplant a whole series.

The *mot juste* is perpetually sought for and is generally found :

—Hamilcar, prince *somnolent* de la cité des livres . . .
—M. Brunetière est un critique guerrier, d'une *intrépidité* rare.
—Et, *galopant* avec eux [les Frères de la Miséricorde], la Mort *importune.*
—Au ras du sol, des parfums d'herbe traînaient *lourdement.*
—Les immortels doivent plus qu'on ne croit à leurs adorateurs. Ils leur doivent *la vie.**

In alterations, the same principles hold good. The 'journal de ses campagnes' becomes the 'récit de ses campagnes,' since the latter term is more fitting. 'Savant infatigable' becomes 'savant plus zélé,' because the former term made an unpleasant jingle with 'aimable.' In the notable article on Renan's *Souvenirs* (as may be seen from our photograph), the author's manuscript substitutions are most illuminating.[143]

Merely verbal repetitions, if too close together, are naturally avoided, and synonyms are found. But repetitions of a *motif,* as in the epithet 'Marcelle aux yeux d'or,' are at times deliberate. This matter is complicated by the fact that France was, often unconsciously, the most repetitious of authors. We cannot suppose that he planned quite so many appearances of Dido, of the Uranian Venus, of religion enhancing passion. It must have been unwittingly that he made the same crew of authors witness a kiss both in *La Rôtisserie* and in *La Révolte des anges.* On the other hand, when Elodie addresses the same speech of invitation to her

* Italics mine.

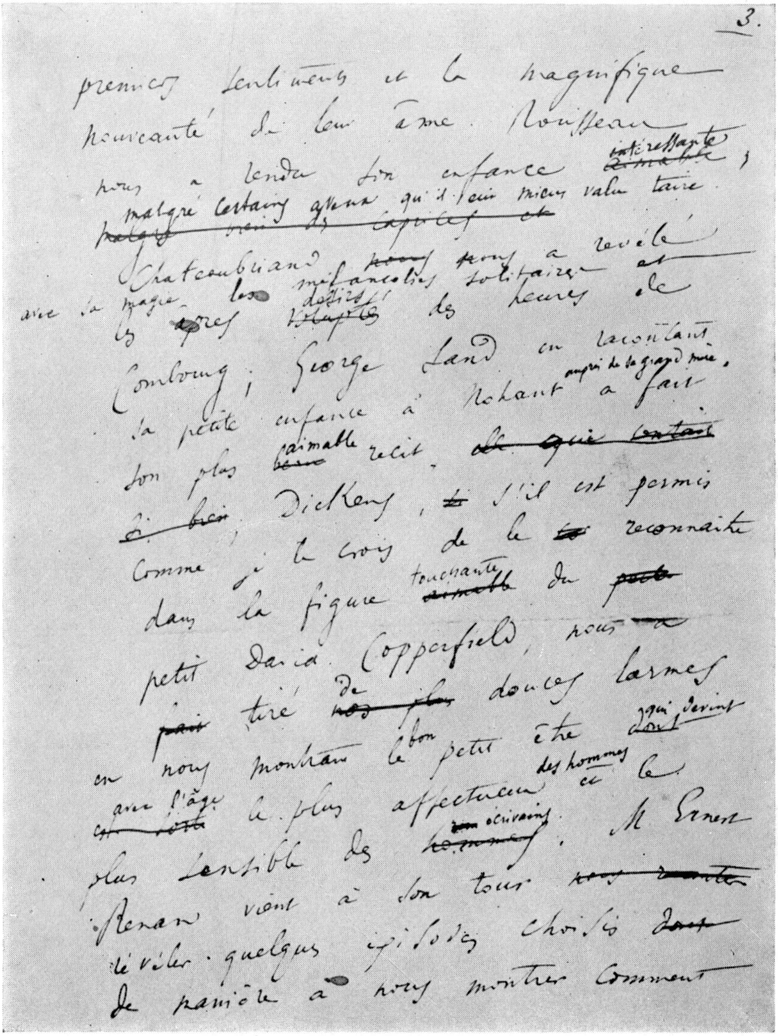

3.

premiers sentiments et la magnifique
nouveauté de leur âme. Rousseau
nous a rendu son enfance intéressante,
malgré certains aveux qu'il eût mieux valu taire.
Chateaubriand nous a révélé
avec la magie les mélancolies solitaires et
les désirs des heures de
Combourg ; George Sand en racontant
sa petite enfance à Nohant auprès de sa grand mère, a fait
son plus aimable récit.
Dickens, s'il est permis
comme je le crois de le reconnaître
dans la figure touchante du
petit David Copperfield, nous
tiré de douces larmes
en nous montrant le bon petit être qui devint
avec l'âge le plus affectueux des hommes et le
plus sensible des écrivains. M. Ernest
Renan vient à son tour
révéler quelques épisodes choisis
de manière à nous montrer comment

A PAGE OF RETROSPECT

new lover that she had addressed to Gamelin, Anatole well knew what he (or she) was doing. The effect is that of a *rentrée* in music. The passage about explorations in the Pacific, which M. Bergeret always drearily reads in the book-shop, is in the same category. Neither here nor elsewhere are we unwarranted in assuming the argument from design, for France was usually a designing person.[144]

If there is any danger in all this craftsmanship, it is the danger of over-doing. People have found *Le Lys* and *La Rôtisserie* too 'bien écrits,' monotonous in their very perfection; or else too hothouse and *livresques,* remote from the world of energy and struggle.[145] The latter reproach has been more conspicuous since the World War. Yet even today few would be found to deny that the eternal virtues of France's style remain as 'justesse, sobriété, clarté, élégance.'[146] This is in spite of the Alexandrianism, latent or overt, which perhaps has already been sufficiently discussed. Those who emphasize this feature are likely to overplay the artificial, 'secondary,' composite character of Anatole's *manière;* and they are of the opinion that this kind of thing, which is not truly Attic, has had its day. Some even declare that it is Romantic![147] But who would gainsay the compelling power of its charm?

§ 13

More impressive is the testimony of those who hold either that our author distils the essence of the best written French; or that he has found again its lost virtues and resisted barbaric invaders; or that, as the defender of its best traditions, he is himself a classic.

France the stylist perfectly represents France the country: he is the 'quintessence thereof'; he is today the 'Prince des Prosateurs'; he has not only synthesized, he has also sublimated the genius of his race. As a defender of the faith, his role has been well summarized by Edmond Jaloux:

> Various people have noted his importance in the history of French style, during the last third of the nineteenth century. He has restored to our prose its unity, its elegance, its purity. Goncourt and the Impressionists had carried it too close to the medium of painting; the Symbolists had mingled musical elements with absurd neologisms. Anatole France has rediscovered our true spirit.[148]

He discovered it, one might add, by resisting among other encroachments the crude or brutal language of the Naturalists. All this is why even the faintly disdainful M. Valéry was forced to admit that Anatole in those difficult times restored a measure of classical perfection to the art of writing. And this is why Barrès could utter his notable defence: 'Say whatever you like! But first and foremost Anatole France has preserved the French language.' Using the same verb (*maintenir*), Clouard declares that, thanks to A.F., literary art did not go under in the period 1885-1890.[149]

These and others make plain (as already developed) that Anatole then held the fort, and still lives on, mainly because of the classical finish of his style. Therefore, says Gregh, he will be 'a great classic himself,' and in fact—'c'est déjà un classique. Et c'est justice. On n'a jamais mieux écrit en français.'[150] No wonder that he has been suggested by professors at the Sorbonne as the ideal model for students seeking to obtain concinnity and smoothness in their French versions of Latin texts. In short, as Thibaudet says, although his thought progressed toward the Left, his style clearly 'belonged to the Right.' And with this consensus of the best opinion, the present discussion may well close.

CHAPTER XIX

The Triumph of Madame de Caillavet

§ 1

THE career of France, as far as the present treatment is concerned, reached its apogee in the year 1896, which also closes his third period. But before taking up his election to the Academy and kindred matters, we should recover some threads from his immediate past.

One aspect of his public life has already been touched upon—his intermittent appearances as a speaker and lecturer. Although most of his efforts in this direction belong rather to his fourth period (after he became connected with the Socialist party and the 'Universités populaires'),[1] yet some of his *discours* in the earlier nineties demand consideration. All the testimony, including his own, indicates that Anatole was no orator. Left to his own resources, he would timidly hesitate, stammer, and lose his way among his devious thoughts. The first time that he presided over a meeting, he opened the proceedings by stating, 'L'ouverte est la séance,' instead of 'La séance est ouverte.'[2] What saved him in speaking was the support of partial or complete manuscript. Naturally, then, most of his addresses smell of the lamp and are really little essays. In time and with increasing practice, he became a fairly good reader, although his voice and delivery were not always adequate.

For the last three years of the present period, we have data regarding half a dozen speeches of varying interest, excluding for the moment his *Discours de réception* at the Académie Française. In February, 1894, he was called upon (unexpectedly, it would seem) to address the antiquarian Society of Auteuil and Passy. He undoubtedly rose to the occasion. We have already cited passages from this *Conférence*,[3] which evinces his feeling for the past as connected with local monuments and celebrities. Showering compliments in his usual fashion upon the audience, Anatole is pleased to think that they all have in this *faubourg* a segment of the great city which they can cherish and preserve. In what manner ? First, by protecting the trees, which are 'the poetry of the streets.' Then by erecting statues or other memorials to noted citizens of former days. The Italians do this constantly, and why not we as well? 'Je rêve que, par votre influence, notre Passy-Auteuil prendra . . . un peu de cette noble grâce des arts.' The appeal is familiar to those who recall his campaign for Parisian monuments in *l'Univers illustré*.

There are many neighbourhood associations, he continues, with such names as Molière and Boileau. He suggests an inscription for the home of the latter, and a bust to mark the site where the charming Mme. Helvétius once held her social sway. He politely reminds his audience of other notables, all of whom, from marshals of France and medieval historians, down to Hugo and Béranger, once lived in this *arrondissement*. He waxes long on local patriotism. And still in that vein, since fresh inspiration apparently failed him, he embroidered on the tribute he had paid before to the 'petite ville' of Vernon.[4] Thus recur the interwoven themes of antiquarian *pietas* and of 'old stones.'

In the course of the same year, A.F. made a talk on feminine education before a girls' institute.[5] After tossing polite bouquets at the lady-principal and her pupils, he repeats with some variations his well-known views on this subject. Education should be diversified rather than standardized. In particular, girls should not be taught technical and scientific data. He has often told instructors: 'Teach them only the big leading ideas in science and philosophy; excite their curiosity, light the spark, but do not smother it.' After which, the said instructors made their students learn the chronology of Assyrian kings! But, young ladies, your principal is surely on my side, for I am persuaded that she can mix the useful with the sweet, the cuisine with the toilette. The chief defect in Dora Copperfield's education was that she neglected the former, while excelling in the latter. . . We are not told what Dora did with science and philosophy.

Fragments of a speech made at the Fêtes de Sceaux about the middle of the year are preserved in *l'Univers illustré*.[6] Anatole is addressing the society of Félibres and recalls pleasantly his tour of the Midi in connexion with their previous celebrations. Repeating a device he had used before the Society of Auteuil-et-Passy, he now makes the town of Arles talk as an old woman, nourishing her memories. There are side-remarks on Zola, Coppée, and especially Renan.

The record for 1895 includes apparently but one brief *discours*, delivered at a banquet of students on December 1.[7] With equal brevity, A.F. spoke a few weeks later on Molière. Shortly before his triumphal election to the Academy, he was presiding at a dinner where the guests did honour to that dramatist.[8] A letter of regret was read from François Coppée, wishing his old friend all success in the approaching Academy contest. Anatole began by saying that he was doubtless chosen as chairman because of his qualifications both as a good Parisian and as a zealous lover of Molière. He does not dwell on the latter theme, for he now believes that it is no longer necessary to defend Molière as essentially a comic poet. He will yield to none in his admiration for Paris, that masterpiece in city-building, that 'capital of the human mind.' He enumerates its various charms and urges his fellow-Parisians to preserve what they can, tree by tree, and stone by stone, in the thick of industrial vandalism.

Later in the year France was appointed as a delegate of the Academy (perhaps at the instigation of Robert de Montesquiou, president of the Committee) to a celebration in honour of Marceline Desbordes-Valmore.[9] A monument to this poetess of the Romantic era was being erected at Douai. On this anniversary our speaker falls back into his pensive and sentimental vein. He invokes the image of Marceline as she was reared in Douai: 'jeune, belle, claire comme la mémoire et les vers qu'elle a laissés.' Her poetry sprang simply from her deep capacity for love and suffering. We cannot wholly regret her numerous misfortunes, for they brought to light the genius which was recognized by the leaders of Romanticism. Yet even on a festival occasion, we can show ourselves pitiful toward her melancholy experiences. Where rigid justice may go wrong, 'la pitié ne trompe jamais: c'est un sentiment.' Once more, then, he is strongly for the poetry of feeling.

§ 2

Among evidences of France's growing importance should be reckoned the increasing sales of his volumes, of which *Thaïs* and *Le Lys* were the most popular. His standing was recognized by the government, when, midway in 1895, he was promoted to the rank of *officier* in the Légion d'Honneur; he was now entitled to wear the rosette as well as the ribbon—insignia which he later returned, when the name of Zola had been struck from the lists of the Legion.[10] But in 1895 Anatole expressed himself as gratified, and when a dinner was given in his honour, he amiably proposed a toast to the minister who had originally decorated both himself and Edmond de Goncourt.[11] This celebration was offered by the administration of the *Echo de Paris,* to which A.F. contributed abundantly during these years.

Other festivities were not lacking. According to the *Figaro,* again, the freshly elected Academician was entertained during 1896 with some profusion at luncheons and dinners. Among his hosts were the Maurice Lippmanns, the Munkacsys, and Mme. Hugo Finaly, all of whom had befriended him previously. But now he also rises to such *sommités* as the Armand Colins, the Comte and Comtesse d'Haussonville, Mme. de Porto-Riche, and the Prince Henri d'Orléans. He associated with various members of the Institute. And naturally Mme. de Caillavet was proud to show him off.

§ 3

MEMBERSHIP in the Académie Française was in those days a highly coveted distinction as well as 'good business' for a rising author. We shall treat fully Anatole's election and his subsequent reception into that body—events which stand out as twin pinnacles in his career. The first took place on January 30, 1896, but the ceremonies of the reception were postponed until Christmas Eve. It is interesting to follow the incidents preceding and accompanying his candidacy.

As early as 1892, Anatole's name had been semi-officially considered. In October of that year, Zola's possible election was viewed as quite a menace in certain circles. D'Haussonville told a friend that to combat this threat a 'very literary name was required'—to wit, that of France. But on being approached, Anatole, who had by now conceived some respect for the author of *La Débâcle,* magnanimously refused to oppose 'a man of his talent.'[12] Nevertheless, it seems that a kind of semi-candidacy on A.F.'s part was brought forward and then withdrawn. On December 2, a newspaper stated that to the three persons now competing for vacant chairs should be added the name of M. France.[13] Renan, apparently, had urged him to come forward. Not a great deal has come to light regarding this abortive affair, nor are we informed of any fresh manœuvres until late in 1895.

In the meantime, our author had taken certain precautions. He had never, as many have done (e.g., Montesquieu and Piron) spoken so contemptuously of the Institute as to jeopardize his chances there. True that in the *Opinions de Jérôme Coignard* it was suggested that entrance into the Academy (like kissing) often went by favour or by family influence, and that genius is less esteemed among these 'Immortals' than social suppleness. Jacques Tournebroche is disillusioned to hear that the members dwell in a state of amiable ignorance (save concerning the Dictionary) and that it is not of much consequence whether one becomes an Academician or not. But it seemed of consequence to Anatole shortly after Coignard's insinuations. It is probable that soon after the death of De Lesseps (December 7, 1894), A.F. was minded or 'urged by his friends' to enter the contest for the vacant seat.[14] There is little doubt that he was willing enough to cross a threshold where, as a matter of age and standing, he was somewhat overdue and where several old friends and associates — Sully Prudhomme, Lemaître, Coppée, Heredia, Bourget — had preceded him. Was it not worth while to mute for a time the pipes of protest and radicalism? If he went on as he had started in *La Rôtisserie* and the *Opinions de Jérôme Coignard,* he could not expect to appease the powerful Right Wing of the Academy. He had said what he liked, not only about that institution, but about Church and State, the judiciary and the army. Surely a breathing-spell, an era of good feeling, was in order.

It has further been opined that, in the Spring of 1895, A.F. abruptly ceased a serial publication which was likely to damage his cause.[15] The articles which M. Braibant calls France's *Lettres Provinciales* (*à la* Pascal) and which presently evolved into chapters of *l'Orme du Mail* had started on January 22; but on April 2, the *Echo de Paris* suspended their publication. Save for one lapse a few weeks later, no more of M. Bergeret's utterances appeared for slightly over a year. Why did Anatole, or his Egeria, think it necessary to call a halt? Apparently because the Academy was then composed (apart from mere men of letters) of 'a prince of the royal blood, several authentic dukes, old Orleanist diplomats . . . supporters of the Divine Right, and finally a bishop clothed in purple.' Evidently Maurras exaggerates; yet our first feeling is one of amazement. What was Anatole doing in *that* galley? And how should he comport himself during the necessary visits to 'ce vénérable tableau d'ancêtres' and their associates?

For if we ask what our iconoclast had to recommend him to the members of the Right—who in his view were often advocates of the Wrong—it is hard to make a specific answer. Some think that the fashionable aroma of *Le Lys rouge* aided him; others suggest that at least during the eighties his works had won the white flower of a blameless life. At the time it was said, by Ledrain, that there was a 'singular penury' of candidates, among whom only France had real distinction.[16] This was true. It was also true that Melchior de Vogüé, whom Anatole visited on the eve of the election, admitted to him: 'Everything in your writings, Monsieur, shocks my beliefs. But genius is a gift of God. I should then oppose the will of heaven if I did not vote for you.'[17]

But neither the divine will nor France's talent might have turned the trick, had it not been for the efforts of his friends and the fact that his election was favoured by the mysterious ways of practical politics.[18] Ludovic Halévy, especially, took hold of the situation and groomed the candidate. Says Mr. Stewart:

> At all events, the thing was worth trying. M. Halévy drilled Anatole France in the part he must play as he canvassed for votes, trusting—as he had reason to trust—that most of his books had never been read by the electors whom they might well have shocked. He was bidden to be careful with his tongue, to speak in the right quarters about the surpassing genius of Victor Hugo, to disguise under a show of compliment his real opinions about Chateaubriand, to make judicious reference to the Comte de Chambord. M. Halévy did not like his proposed letter of candidature, rewrote it for him in more diplomatic tone, and in the draft which the candidate copied *verbatim* he was pleased to observe that there were 'not more than three or four mistakes in French.' To add to the humour of the situation, it is recorded that he was chosen over the rival candidate, Ferdinand Fabre, mainly because Fabre was regarded as dangerously anti-clerical!

Much later, Anatole declared that the ineptitude of the Academicians in their writings was only exceeded by their skill in intrigue. He had to bow his head and scurry around among the dukes and the influential fine ladies. Ultimately a deal was effected by which most of the Right consented to vote for France, provided the Left would vote into another *fauteuil* a certain Costa de Beauregard, a nobleman 'de vieille souche.' Anatole agreed to everything, perhaps on the principle, as he told Ségur, that one must respect the cleverness of those fellows who had got into the Academy without any talent.[19]

This was what finally happened. But there are amusing sidelights. Apparently Jules Simon promised to vote for France, but trusted he would not be successful then, 'because I never heard of a case where a superior man was elected the first time.'

'He must,' said Anatole dryly, 'have made several applications himself.'

And Maurras solemnly observed shortly afterwards that a ridiculous cabal against France was broken up partly by the real men of letters; but partly also by certain 'colleagues of the Right,' headed by a prince of the blood![20] The Duc d'Aumale *in camera* and Prince Henri d'Orléans outside. Surely it was the least France could do to dine presently in the noble company of the latter.

§ 4

HALÉVY was not the only friend who acted in behalf of the candidate. Others undoubtedly bestirred themselves, even before the actual voting. In regretting his absence from the Molière dinner, Coppée wrote to the 'Parisiens de Paris' that he was endeavouring to get A.F. a chair in the Institute, for he might like to rest there after prowling among the near-by book-stalls.[21] A *rapprochement* with Jules Lemaître was also effected during this January. When it was all over and Lemaître had duly voted for his old friend, Anatole wrote him: 'What pleases me most about the Academy is the opportunity to see you there.'[22]

What part did Mme. de Caillavet play in all this? Needless to say, it was a considerable one and was so acknowledged by the beneficiary. 'Sans elle aurais-je été de l'Académie?' he is said to have inquired, rhetorically, of Brousson. The secretary also records the lady's statement that it was she who pinned down her prize butterfly and displayed him for the occasion.[23] This view is amply confirmed by 'Gyp,' Mme. Bory d'Arnex, and Georges de Porto-Riche. The last-named wrote Mme. de C. a congratulatory letter regarding the triumph of her campaign for A.F.: 'sa victoire est un peu la vôtre.'[24]

More than 'a little,' one is disposed to think. We are unacquainted with the full extent of Egeria's manœuvring, but it was clearly along lines of social pressure. For instance, we are informed that in her usual enveloping way, she now gave her whole attention to this crucial matter. It was the literary event of the day that France was to be considered for the unoccupied *fauteuil*. Well aware of this fact, she told a certain group, 'I shall not allow him to run unless I am certain of the outcome.' It was she herself who 'went about,' worked hard, and ensured the victory. Carias concludes that 'it was undeniably the salon of the Avenue Hoche that enabled him [Anatole] to know and to win over the majority of those who gave him their voices.'[25] It was thus that Egeria remained faithful to her inconstant lover and exalted the Mask over the man.

One other personal relationship was involved. It was to the chair of Ferdinand de Lesseps that France was succeeding, and he was bound by custom to speak lengthily of his predecessor. As a lad, he had admired this prince of finance, riding up with his family to call at the Hôtel de Chimay.[26] But as the author of the *Opinions de Jérôme Coignard,* he had expressed himself severely regarding the whole Panama swindle, although there is some reason to think that he felt leniently towards de Lesseps.[27] Now the survivors of this family, when the election was over and the time for the reception drew near, were uneasy lest France should bear too hardly on their former head. They wrote him, expressing their concern. He reassured them as to the tenor of his *Discours* and even rectified a newspaper item which rumoured that his speech would contain 'disobliging' remarks.[28] We shall see how he held to this promise.

But we have anticipated the order of events and must now turn to the unfolding of the drama.

§ 5

It was on the whole an imposing roster of names that then composed the Académie Française. This body was by no means bereft of literary talent. True that in the course of the century it had dispensed with such alien immortals as Balzac and Flaubert, just as it had formerly dispensed with Molière and Pascal. Yet at the time of France's candidacy, exactly half of the thirty-six active members were well-known as connected with *belles-*

lettres, and it is likely that most of these voted for Anatole. As poets there were Heredia, Sully Prudhomme, and Coppée—Leconte de Lisle having died in 1894; among the novelists were Loti, Bourget, Jules Claretie, and Victor Cherbuliez, who was *directeur;* the dramatists included Sardou, Meilhac and Pailleron, with several lesser names; while as for criticism, Anatole could feel at ease in the presence of such friendly enemies as Jules Lemaître and Ferdinand Brunetière. There were half a dozen historians—the Duc d'Aumale himself, with the scarcely less distinguished name of Albert de Broglie, also Albert Sorel and Thureau-Dangin, Gabriel d'Haussonville and Ernest Lavisse, who outpaced them all. Publicists and 'statesmen' (by courtesy) included Jules Simon, Mézières, and Emile Ollivier, who had been stormily received; this seems to have been the field least adequately represented. In lonely eminence stands the name of Louis Pasteur.[29]

It appears that on the first and final ballot Anatole polled twenty-one votes, while only thirteen were awarded to his opponents. These included a certain Francis Charmes and Costa de Beauregard, who later in the day was elected to another chair, amid the laughter of the populace. The news of the deal had leaked out; and it was felt that De Beauregard owed his belated victory rather to his perogative as a marquis than to his merit as a historian.[30] On that same Thursday, Anatole was visiting the Association of Students, where he was received with acclamations, the news of his election having spread abroad.[31] Triumph at the Villa Saïd that evening; triumph at the house on the Avenue Hoche.

The prophecies and comments of the periodical press are of some interest. As early as December 18, André Maurel announced that a new candidate had appeared, one who would win the approval of all French men of letters, one who was sure of success.[32] After the event, the tone of the principal newspapers—*Le Temps, Le Gaulois, Le Figaro*—is of course congratulatory.[33] Quite a few 'leaders' were written, both in and out of Paris. Some wholeheartedly recognize the power and charm of France's pen. Others credit his blossoming fame to certain 'nobles dames' of the salons. Maurras characteristically expressed his pleasure that Anatole was supported by the representatives of 'our Past,' whose traditions

A.F. himself was said to incorporate. Thus passed this 'election triomphante,' in which apparently the way was made fairly smooth for our hero.[34]

Probably on January 30, Cherbuliez as Director paid his formal visit to Félix Faure, President of the Republic, to notify him of the elections of France and Beauregard.[35] Congratulatory missives to Anatole, as we shall presently see, began to pour in. He was invited to luncheons and banquets, to join committees, to make contributions to magazines. Incidentally, he felt free, in the Spring, to resume the journal publication of *l'Orme du Mail,* including the intrigues of the Abbé Guitrel. As the year wore on, he may have experienced some of those disadvantages of glory about which he later complained. At any rate, in the early Autumn he went far afield on the Arman de Caillavet yacht, *Mélusine.* He visited Sicily once more and Egypt *via* the Suez Canal, where he inspected the work of De Lesseps.[36] After pausing at Capian, the party returned to Paris, where preparations were soon under way for the Academy reception of Christmas Eve. On December 3 a committee was appointed to pass on the two *discours* to be read by France and Gréard.[37] Of course these were formally approved. Anatole had been interviewed regarding his trip to Egypt and what he would say about De Lesseps. As the time drew near, it was evident that much curiosity prevailed on the latter head, since the notoriety of the 'Affaire du Panama' had not yet subsided. Furthermore, the personality of the new member and the circumstances of his candidacy aroused keen interest. It became apparent that the reception would be distinguished, that it would be crowded, and that tickets were at a premium. Anatole himself was besought for admission cards by friends and acquaintances.

On the fateful day, France appeared in the traditional broidered costume of green and black, with the cocked hat and the useless sword by his side. Gyp's caricature of the occasion alleges that he was accompanied by a gracious bevy of his heroines, while Paphnuce mournfully prayed in the background. In fact, Halévy and Coppée, as 'godfathers,' escorted the candidate to the daïs. The set speeches were read in a crowded amphitheatre, before the élite of Paris, who gave France a great ovation at the end. It was generally agreed that such a numerous and brilliant assembly had not been seen for years. In the *assistance* were the family of President Faure, several ambassadors, Louis Barthou as

HOW A.F. ENTERED THE ACADEMY ('GYP')

Minister of the Interior, the De Lesseps family (in mourning), together with other notables and ladies of fashion. M. Pierre Champion as a boy witnessed the scene, which he has never forgotten:

I recall the packed amphitheatre, which offered an unusual spectacle. My mother pointed out to me Mme. de Lesseps, seated in a small tribune, with the children whom I had seen around the Hôtel de Chimay. . . Then she showed me Monseigneur the Duc d'Aumale, whom we loved for his cordiality, together with various neighbours from the *quai,* such as Pailleron and Henri Houssaye. Finally Anatole France arrived in his uniform. I had glimpsed him sometimes in our book-shop, with his well-groomed and lively air, his charming courtesy. François Coppée, another of our friends, and the witty Ludovic Halévy took their places by the reading-desk. In a religious silence, France stood and read his speech, in praise of Ferdinand de Lesseps. . . I had to reread the *éloge* later, to appreciate its courage and its simple beauty.[38]

§ 6

THE text of the *Discours de Réception* deals then primarily and soberly with the life of De Lesseps.[39] After the necessary *remercîment* to his colleagues, in the course of which Anatole inquired a little about their intentions in confronting a speculative mind like his with the career of a man of action, the speaker embarked directly on his subject. While the tone of this eulogy is conventional and even conservative, it reveals quite a few of the Francian prepossessions in biographical history. Notable is the emphasis on the anecdote, on the small fact as determining a large event, in other words on the role of contingency. It was chance that De Lesseps won the favour of young Eugénie before she became the Empress. It was chance that put in his hands a memorial, prepared under Bonaparte, about the possibility of connecting the Red Sea with the Mediterranean; it was chance, coupled with a dish of macaroni, that made a fast friend of Prince Mohammed Ali, who would later support the project. The description of the enterprise is enthusiastic, for here France is treading familiar waters, the *Mare Nostrum* of antiquity, with souvenirs that included the wily Ulysses, 'le vieux Cadmus,' and Venus Anadyomene. Partially attempted under the Pharaohs, the Suez Canal had to await for its successful completion modern pertinacity and engineering skill. Anatole pays full credit to the persistence, the diplomacy, the vision, and the power of realizing his dream that were De Lesseps' qualities. His manœuvrings round Palmerston, 'ce rude vieillard,' and round Napoleon III are vividly described.

After Suez came Panama. But first there is a pause and an interlude. A.F. must have stirred many in the audience when he related the reception of De Lesseps into this same Academy in 1884. The fact that he was then received by Ernest Renan as *directeur* allowed the present orator an opportunity to descant on his favourite master. 'He showed, you will remember, that smiling humour, that frank and simple charm which went so well with his serious and profound mind. With his marvellous fecundity, he uttered on that day the thoughts of a true sage on man and nature, the configuration of the earth, the genius and destiny of races. . .' Touching upon the more personal traits of Renan, France spoke warmly of his magnetism and the supple fortitude which sustained him to the end.

De Lesseps had need of a similar fortitude. But after the above interlude, both time and discretion demanded that the Panama enterprise should be lightly brushed in. Anatole threw the blame for the tragedy on the passions of Pecus and his misguided leaders rather than on individuals. He commiserated the plight of the aged engineer, dying like a stricken Marius amid the ruins of his grandest scheme. He concluded that though De Lesseps was rash and imprudent, he was animated by large ideals and was a true benefactor to humanity.

Nothing in this speech could offend the traditionalists of any complexion ; that is why it has been much cited by those who support the legend of France's essential conservatism.[40]

The response of Octave Gréard, that imposing and devoted educator, gave an excellent appreciation of France's talent and career to date.[41] Apart from citations already made, this *Discours* further emphasized, in a slightly patronizing manner, a number of good points.[42] Directly addressing the neophyte, Gréard told him : 'Vous excellez à vous raconter'—that is, veiled autobiography is your forte, and we do not complain ; 'vous devez peu de chose au collège,' because you forged your own visions out of ancient material ; and no formal pedagogue could restrain 'votre intelligence à la fois musarde et vagabonde'—two adjectives that Anatole affected.

Yet the candidate as an adult was not without an historical flair and scholarly scruples. Gréard exaggerates in attributing to him the zeal of a *Chartiste* for sources, documents, verified data. He seems nearer the truth in averring that with A.F. the dream always haunted the historical fabric, and that Jeanne d'Arc has been 'one of the most persistent of your dreams.' That is because you are fond of the twilight zones where history can mingle with legend and where the imagination is most at home. If at times it seems that Little Pierre is still among us, with his 'fetichism' for Noah's Arks and leaden soldiers, yet we recognize occasional evidences of a realistic vein which does not run to excess ; we perceive in you a critic with the gift of self-externalization, a graceful and limpid stylist, who can hide claws under his caresses ; we perceive, too, that you are at heart 'a Pagan of the Renaissance,' while in your head you are an eighteenth-century survival, a 'disenchanted Encyclopedist.' This was one of Gréard's happiest phrases ; another was when he called Anatole a 'moment of the French conscience,' an epigram with many echoes. The most remarkable, perhaps, was when France himself, in his *Discours* at the funeral of Zola (1902), spoke of the Naturalist as 'un moment de la conscience humaine.'[43]

For Paul Valéry, Anatole was only a moment. When in his turn the former succeeded the latter in the sixteenth *fautueil* (June, 1927), a singular *Discours* resulted. In something less than his usual tortuous and sublimated manner, M. Valéry used his predecessor as a point of departure for a literary retrospect. He also preferred, for unknown reasons, never to name France and to mention him only by circumlocutions. As we have seen, he admitted what Anatole had done for the language in his time and spoke of him, though guardedly, as among the classics. Two paragraphs will sufficiently give the tone. After saying that some one was needed (in the nineties) to bring back the forgotten graces of French style, some one endowed with moderation and artistic ability, M. Valéry continued :[44]

The public was most grateful to my illustrious predecessor for affording it this oasis. His work offered a gentle and agreeable surprise through the refreshing contrast between his measured manner and the dazzling or complex styles which were displayed on every hand. It seemed that ease, clarity, simplicity, were returning to earth. *These are goddesses which please the great majority.* People immediately liked

> a language which could be savoured *without too much thought,* which allured through its natural appearance, and whose limpidity occasionally allowed the refraction of an *arrière-pensée* not too complicated; which should always be readable, though not always comforting. In his books there was manifest a consummate art of *lightly touching upon ideas* and grave problems. *Nothing caused the eye to linger,* unless it were the surprise of finding no opaque resistance.

And again:

> Your great colleague, gentlemen, the least ignorant among mankind, had no exaggerated confidence in the virtues of his readers, nor in their zeal and patience. Moreover, the effect of his constant courtesy would be never to separate the ideas to be emitted from *the smile which detaches them from actuality.* It was quite natural that his fame should not suffer from that elegant solicitude. You know to what vertiginous heights his reputation attained within a few years. Soon we were aware that this gently pervasive 'glory' had reached the point of counterbalancing the glory of the most celebrated; and we wondered how this *rather malicious spirit, exerting itself playfully,* had risen to the stature of the European colossi of that period. To the massive, brutal labours of a Tolstoi, a Zola, an Ibsen, he opposed his slight works, which *pretended only to brush* (*'effleurer'*) *dangerously* what they really grasped and shook with all their strength—the social order and the very structure of our institutions.

The italicized phrases indicate how, in 1927, a new mandarin could do more than 'hint a doubt.' It is evident that the *gloire* of the nameless one has receded since the heyday of 1896.

§ 7

It was another story when in his prime Anatole was receiving felicitations from 'Tout Paris.' There were, first, some immediate repercussions from his speech. He had maintained that De Lesseps aided the Empress Eugénie in her flight after Sedan. This was contested in a letter from the American dentist, Dr. Evans, who claimed the honour for himself and who, indeed, is generally supposed to have assisted in Eugénie's escape. But to a newspaper man France held his ground.[45] He was interviewed, in fact, by several journalists, including the famous De Blowitz, who did a leading article on A.F. in *The Times*. Photographs and caricatures began to appear in a stream which grew greater with the years.[46] And throughout the year 1896 complimentary missives of all sorts were directed to the Villa Saïd.

There exists in the Bibliothèque Nationale[47] a precious collection alphabetically arranged by the careful hands of Mme. de Caillavet. It consists of no less than 340 of these missives, addressed as a rule to France and running all the way from cordial letters to laconic visiting-cards and telegrams. It furnishes a roll-call of his acquaintance and a testimonial to the esteem in which he was held. In what follows, we shall not try to distinguish between the items that centre round his election and those that cluster more thickly in December. For they all form part of one chorus and together they constitute the signal triumph of Mme. de Caillavet. She wrote, she strove, she loved; and the event of which this collection is the fading symbol remains her best memorial.

We may be sure that the pair of them turned over these treasured papers many times. We can imagine that on some special occasion, say on New Year's Eve at the Avenue Hoche, they went through the collection, finding and pausing upon such documents as these.

They would linger—or certainly France would—upon spontaneous notes from his oldest friends. Few had survived among the intimates of 'petit Pierre.' But still the Charavays were left as witnesses of what the long years had brought. Noël, the 'little brother,' congratulated Anatole in affectionate terms, and Etienne wrote, 'this is a dream of our youth which I have seen fulfilled.' He declared that it was France's lifelong devotion to letters which had at last been rewarded, he referred to their joint passion for Racine, and mentioned that he had provided Gréard with recollections of his schoolmate's early days and of his parents.[48] As we have seen, there had been friendly services from Coppée, duly acknowledged by Anatole, before Dreyfus was to force them apart.[49] Frédéric Plessis showed that he had not forgotten the Luxembourg; and remembering their former comradeship on the Rue Chalgrin, Henry Roujon (who became an 'Immortal' himself in 1909) was brief but cordial. Louis Ratisbonne, erstwhile fellow-librarian, reproachfully sent the 'félicitations d'un oublié.'

Delving further into the collected correspondence, the explorers could find warm congratulations from Robert de Bonnières, from Pierre Calmettes ('ton petit ami'),[50] a telegram from Jules Lemaître (with the 'affectionate compliments of one of the twenty-one' electors), also from the fervent Comte de Montesquiou-Fezensac. These are written in an extraordinary peacocky handwriting, decorated with amazing arabesques and *fioriture*. Like most of his correspondence with France, or with Proust, they deal with highly æsthetic considerations.[51]

Tributes from lady-friends were not lacking—and it is likely that Mme. de Caillavet viewed these with mixed feelings, especially when they were signed by the 'petits noms' of the correspondents. Some of these epistles are charming, while others are unnecessarily long. Egeria would probably have approved the congratulations of the Baronne de Koenigswarter, since she was a member of the family. We find, too, the name of Florence Brada (connected with a colleague on *l'Univers illustré,* who also sent greetings),[52] together with the Princess Bibesco, who asked France to lunch, and a gratifying letter from 'Noémi Psichari,' once (and again in the future) Noémi Renan. She thanked Anatole for the homage which his *Discours* had rendered to her father, 'that dear figure whom you almost made live again.' Still on the personal side, the family and friends of De Lesseps thanked France for his deference to their wishes. They even presented him with a testimonial in the shape of a small bronze lion, similar to the one at the entrance of the Academy doors.

Naturally, the Left Bank was heard from. Honoré Champion, the book-dealer, wrote rather formally, requesting among many others tickets to the reception. Jules Soury, the mystical bookman, had his say. Octave Uzanne saluted A.F. in the name of the 'Académie Bibliophile,' and gracefully said that 'the newly Elected could not have failed thus to return to his home on the *quais.*' Even an alumni association of the Collège Stanislas decided to let bygones be bygones.

A number of these communications were more likely to interest France than his *amie,* in whom they could awaken no old recollections. But stirring over the pile she could savour her peculiar reward—the letters from grandees, from Academicians in general, and from those men of talent who had grown to appreciate Anatole in her own salon. The Duc d'Aumale wired his compliments from Chantilly. The Waldeck-Rousseaus did the proper thing. Prefectures were heard from, likewise countesses. From within the sacred portals, De Vogüé, Loti, Houssaye, Heredia, and others were polite ; so were, just outside, as Academicians-to-be, the scholarly Gaston Paris and the dramatist, Paul Hervieu, who wrote of 'une belle justice rendue.' Equally courteous were savants like D'Arbois de Jubainville, Gabriel Monod, or the 'très dévoué' Théodore Reinach. If he cared to do so, Anatole could finger miscellaneous cards from Henri Bordeaux, Raymond Poincaré of later fame, Boutet de Monvel (illustrator of *Nos Enfants*), Léon Bourgeois, Albert Carré (theatrical director), and even Jules Claretie ; or telegrams from Milan and Rome, from the composer Massenet, and the historian, Pierre de Nolhac—'Gaudet cum Musis Nolhac.' More specific were Henri Lavedan, with his allusions to a 'magnifique discours,' Stéphane Mallarmé, daintily 'pleased that destiny laurels your name.' Léon Dierx, ex-Parnassian, neatly congratulated the Academy on adding to its number 'le plus pur et le plus délicieux écrivain contemporain.' Edouard Rod, Paul Margueritte, and Porto-Riche were not silent. Maurice Bernhardt, the son of Sarah, expressed his pleasure and (if he knew about it) forgave France a certain article in *l'Univers illustré*.[53]

Nor in those days were the younger men lacking in enthusiasm. There were many 'chers maîtres,' notably from such admirers as the fastidious Marcel Schwob, who wrote four letters to convey fully his respects. Similar in tone were the tributes from Charles Maurras, of course, from choice critics like Maurice Spronck and Fernand Gregh, and the musician, Reynaldo Hahn. These are definite signs of a cult—a cult that was broadening into a movement and that would install Anatole France as the dominant voice in his country's literature for nearly two decades.[54]

It is observable also that astute editors are now camping on the trail of the celebrity. His previous mentor on *Le Temps,* Adrien Hébrard, regrets that the 'new Immortal' has put on invisibility as well. Louis Gandérax, of the *Revue de Paris,* is counting on him for copy. The editor of *Le Gaulois* also has hopes.

And there were many, many more, of all sorts and sizes. Pensively arranging the growing heap, Mme. de Caillavet could find but one dissident voice. It belonged to a cardinal. While offering cold felicitations, he was subacid about the chapters of *l'Orme du Mail* now running periodically and about the treatment accorded to the Abbé Guitrel therein. France answered this in the third person and in a challenging manner. It is said that he also repelled 'in a harsh burst of anger' another priest who had not found him particularly bright at the Collège Stanislas.[55]

It was not to be expected that every one would be happy; and certain cases of jealousy have been alleged. But Anatole himself was quite definitely gratified and avowed his pleasure both in the main event and in the attendant circumstances.[56] In time, he grew less pleased. Reverting to his natural iconoclasm, he made gibes at his brother Academicians and unseemly suggestions for their famous Dictionary. According to Dirick's account, he attended two elections only, although he had amusing sessions with eager candidates who sought his vote. Two characters in Goll's novel who went to see France found him chatting about the Academy and looking for his lost sword, which was finally discovered in a garret. Did he really tell prospective members that the august Forty 'never read anything'? Did he really confide to Brousson that he was glad to have won the 'false aureole, just in order to measure its inanity"?[57]

All this smoke betokens some fire. The definite fact is that France ceased to frequent the Academy with any regularity after 1898. The obvious reason is that too many of his colleagues—and especially Lemaître, Coppée, Barrès, together with the Right Wing—were hostile to Dreyfus and presumably hostile to Anatole because he signed the Protest of the Intellectuals in behalf of Dreyfus. Meetings between old friends with new faces would be painful to both parties.[58] Moreover, one feels freer to criticize an institution *in absentia.*

Anatole could afford to do all that. Since he had gained the coveted prize, he could stroll nonchalantly home through the Academy's portals and let the antiquated costume moulder. He had followed, though in a circuitous fashion, the line that he once drew on his juvenile copy-book—the arrow that pointed to the Institute. Ceasing now to be an Immortal, he could return to his relic-laden study in the Villa Saïd and confirm his hold upon true immortality.

THE END

APPENDICES

APPENDIX A (p. 289): Note on *l'Univers illustré*

Chapter XIII would be incomplete without some account of the semi-apocryphal articles written for *l'Univers illustré* from 1890-96. Even if France did not actually write all that he signed, he 'inspired' most of these articles; and many of them have his authentic hall-mark in thought or style. Yet they contain numerous repetitions of previous material, they often use (to fill space) long quotations or communications from correspondents, and during the final two or three years they run decidedly thinner in substance. What did France care? He was then making his mark in various other ways. His position on *Le Temps*, by the way, will account for the relatively small amount of literary criticism in *l'Univers illustré* after 1890. We shall simply itemize here distinctively Francian topics and themes.

Literature. Latin as a maker of men; A.F. as a lover of poetry and old songs; when Symbolists are truly poetic, they may be forgiven their queerness. Puffs: for Jean Psichari (cf. Ch. XV); for Jules Lemaître (cf. above, p. 317), his taste, intelligence, critical power; for Charavay and for Gyp. Other writers: A.F. is strong for the Dumas, father and son; reiterates with variations what he had said about Goethe's *Faust* (cf. above, pp. 283-84); is more favourable now towards Edmond de Goncourt, father of Naturalism and type of devoted man of letters; commends Heredia to Academy; pens only tribute here to Leconte de Lisle—on his death; also writes admiringly on Loti, Maupassant, Renan's style, George Sand's sentiment, and Verlaine, still as the beloved vagabond. Old books and libraries: recurrent theme; is grateful when a *bouquin* dug out of a box gives him aid in filling a column; bibliophiles are amiable folk, though surely a little mad; speaks reminiscently of the Senate library.

Personal Philosophy. Nature a hard housewife, not interested in flowers, which man cultivates and which A.F. loves; especially roses, their mystical significance. Relativity—only change is constant. Love attended by weakness and grief and commingled with death, which is often a happy ending to misery. Sciences: astronomy, Flammarion, moon and Mars probably inhabited (cf. *Le Temps*).

The Provinces and Paris (*Extensively*). At Dives, historical associations (August-September, 1892, again in August, 1895); in Brittany, saints and local colour; at Saint-Valery-sur-Somme; at Arles with the Félibres and at Pierrefonds (see France first); recalls visit to Strasbourg. Paris: numerous general tributes, his favourite vistas, mingling personal associations and art-appreciation (especially September 2, 1893, and other Septembers); the charm of old quarters, of the *quais*, of the Jardin des Plantes; her street-scenes, beggars, trees; much about her paintings now, as well as statuary; A.F. hates the Luxembourg gallery, but approves erecting statues and memorials to famous men and commends historical societies; her festivals and expositions: Fête de Neuilly, exposition of books and engravings, of decorative arts, the Musée Guimet, the Musée Carnavalet (*re* the arts, cf. above, p. 303, on Villa Saïd); the 'rentrée des classes,' students and University life.

Politics. Rather thin. Mediocrity of deputies; Socialism growing at home and abroad — first sign of A.F.'s interest in this; political leaders hardly responsible for events, rather carried along by current. A great European war would throw the balance of power over to America.

Folk-lore and History. Fine to get back to the atmosphere of *féerie* and worth-while popular tradition, whether in Brittany or Gascony. A letter to Renan and other documents on popular poetry (*noëls, amusettes,* etc.; many quoted). Scurries around Norman towns (which are like 'palimpsests') for historical data, loves to 'mingle images of the past with living forms.' Eulogy of Thierry, who 'made me see' early Middle Ages. Numerous allusions to Jeanne d'Arc, the true and the false, to the false Dauphin, to other pretenders and forgers. Still deprecates and rationalizes the Revolution, Girondins as well as Jacobins; their ridiculous fêtes.

Religion and the Supernatural. Christian and pagan elements (cf. *Noces* and *Etui*) mingled in rites and festivals of the Church, most of which are dwelt upon historically and critically. Familiar names and legends of saints. Spiritualism still out of proportion: A.F. is 'disturbed' by such phenomena, which 'solicit my imagination,' together with telepathy, hallucinations, Rosicrucians (cf. *La Rôtisserie*), apparitions, transmogrifications, and the Black Mass!

Society, Women, Actresses. Society today neither better nor worse than it used to be, say in the eighteenth century. Fashions and chiffons are one of the civilized glories of Paris; they enhance the mutable charm of women. May God save the Parisiennes from becoming Yankees and suffragettes! Tributes to such actresses of the Old Régime as Sophie Arnould and Adrienne Lecouvreur; Sarah Bernhardt gives rare interpretation of Racine; but good drama now ruined by crude cafés-concerts, which future archæologists may discover as temples dedicated to the service of some Venus of the Crossroads.

Multum in parvo. . .

APPENDIX B (p. 382): The Divorce Decree

(See Chapter XV, note 11)

Since there is some doubt regarding the legality of printing this complete document in the original, we content ourselves with translated extracts. These correspond in the main with the 'whereas' clauses outlined in the text. The name 'Gieules,' scarcely legible in the transcript, has been established by consulting the *bottins* of the period.

The Tribunal, having heard in due course of law the advocates for the plaintiff and the defence,—

Gives judgment against the said Thibault called Anatole France and against Gieules his advocate . . .

Whereas it is established in fact that since 1888 Thibault *dit* Anatole France has gradually forsaken his domestic interior [and] That in the following years, his absences became more and more frequent being prolonged at times for a period of several days

Whereas he declined to make any explanation to his wife, desiring to communicate with her only through notes delivered by the servant

Whereas finally in the month of June, 1892, he definitely abandoned their common domicile, leaving for his wife a letter in which [he] announced to her in insulting terms his absolute decision to break off henceforth all connexion with her.

Whereas being invited later to resume his place in the family, then being summonsed to do so in the interest of the child, he refused in the most downright manner accompanying his refusal by remarks most painful for his wife

Whereas this desertion and this refusal in the circumstances of the case present the character of a serious offence of such a nature as to have a divorce declared

Par Ces Motifs :

Now therefore it (the Tribunal) gives judgment and pronounces the divorce between the 'Epoux Thibault,' at the request of the wife ;

It furthermore refers the parties to appear before the proper officer of the Etat Civil . . . and whereas the divorce necessitates the dissolution of the joint-property régime (*communauté des biens*), they should also appear before a certain Brault, notary at Neuilly, to liquidate their pecuniary interests.

Follow the clauses regarding the official approbation (*homologation*) of the judgment, if demanded ; the custody and maintenance of Suzanne ; the immediate enactment of these provisions, the payment of costs by France, the proper registration of the 'injurious' letter and of the present judgment. ('Enregistré à Paris le 19 août 1893, folio 13, case 10'.)

APPENDIX C (p. 445) : The Original MS. of *Thaïs*

As hinted above, this early draft (MS. *A*) of the novel is of the greatest interest. Formerly the property of Gabriel Wells, it is now in a private collection. Unlike the bulk of the MSS. in the Nationale, it is heavily surcharged with erasures, substitutions and transpositions. It is written on all sorts of paper (backs of invitations, discarded galley-proof, etc.) in which predominates the handsome official stationery of the Bibliothèque du Sénat. The handwriting varies from Anatole's best calligraphy to a rather hurried scrawl, but it is always legible. Supplementary to the text, the writer embellished his pages with some significant drawings — the recurrent symbol of the lotus-flower, with petals symmetrically curved by means of callipers, and a Doric portico with architectural details, presumably for the grotto-scene. Likewise for this scene, A.F. drew up a list of furnishings and objects, such as a rich courtesan of the period might well possess.

About forty *per cent* of the novel, as it first appeared serially in the *Revue des deux mondes,* is lacking in these four hundred and odd pages. The gaps include nearly all of Part I and Part II, up to the meeting of Paphnuce and Thaïs ; also the conclusion regarding the transformation of the monk. Since the exposition and the previous lives of the characters are not developed here (for separate sources, see above, pp. 447-53), these omissions would seem to confirm the view that France's primary interest was in the impact of his two protagonists, with the grotto-scene as the *clou* of the spiritual drama. This will be borne out by an examination of the ten *liasses* (or twelve, if we count individually '3 *bis*' and '5 *bis*'), as compared with the *princeps* of 1890. The reason for choosing the first book-form is that this (cf. above, p. 446) more fully corresponds to MS. *A,* since the pages omitted by Brunetière for the *RDM* were here restored by the author.

In the following description of the *liasses,* the author's numeration and wording are used, whenever possible:

1. '23 feuillets. Première ébauche de Thaïs. (début, pages numérotées de 27 à 49).' This section briefly condenses the first meeting between Paphnuce and Thaïs, her conversion, and their departure from Alexandria. Thus far, and in the fact that there is no love-making, it resembles A.F.'s 'Légende de Sainte-Thaïs.' It may be the unpublished short-story mentioned in our text, or else it is the scenario ('ébauche') for the novel, from which it differs greatly.

2. Scattered pages of the novel, 72 in all, from p. 4 *bis* through p. 214. These are additions and developments, long or short, to a previous text. There is a considerable amount of pasting and piecing together. There are only ten fragmentary pages on events before the meeting of the two main characters. This scene is considerably developed (from '1' above) as regards both the grotto-setting and the dialogue (MS., pp. 132-132[5]—the last *en double* = *princeps,* 85-86 and 134-36; MS., 186-208 = *princeps,* 138-56). Some inversions of order were made later. Several important pages were reworked two, three or four times. Reductions of this section were made by 1890. It appears from sections 1 and 2 that the grotto-scene was the point of departure for the rest of the novel.

3. 'Le Banquet' (MS., pp. 215-307, with a few pages missing = *princeps,* pp. 158-226). The first full development of the famous banquet-scene. This corresponds very nearly to the first edition as regards philosophy and the general trends of the symposium, but the speeches are in some cases differently conducted and ordered. Several of them are differently assigned, in order to fit better with the character of the particular speaker. A personage called 'Diotime' is suppressed in the MS., and his role is given to Hermodore.

The scene where Thaïs burns her treasures is much altered from this MS.

3 *bis.* Ten scattered pages, containing alterations in above, working toward text of 1890.

4. (MS., pp. 239-60, plus several scattered pages = *princeps,* pp. 213-33, plus 242-44, 263-64.) This section overlaps with '3.' The bonfire scene is rewritten, and the departure of the two characters is added.

5. (MS., pp. 322-27 = *princeps,* pp. 241, 243-47.) The two versions vary considerably. This dovetails with the preceding *liasse.*

5 *bis.* (MS., p — [not numbered], plus pp. 275-79 = *princeps,* pp. 249 and 248-51.) Much reworking, some shifting and confusion. End of Part II. Condensed in book-form.

6. (MS., pp. 329 *bis*-377 [complete plus several 'doubles,' marked *bis*

and *ter*] = *princeps,* pp. 250-51 [end of II again]; and especially *princeps,* pp. 255-300.) Covering Paphnuce's return to the desert, his temptations, and his life on the pillar — which constitute the beginning of Part III.

7. (MS., pp. 279, 281, 285-89 = *princeps,* pp. 260-67.) Nine scattered pages, variations on beginning of Part III.

8. Title-page reads:

'IV

3me épisode Hélène'

A.F. speaks of this episode as requiring 'tableaux à chercher.' (MS., pp. 386-413 [complete] = *princeps,* pp. 314-33.) This covers only part of the temptation of Helen; deals also with demons, the coming of St. Anthony, and his blessings. MS. *A* as a whole does not extend beyond that point in the story.

9. (MS., pp. 329-57 = *princeps,* pp. 303 . . . 329 — scattered.) Fourteen scattered pages. Additions and variations to above. Filling out of Helen's temptation, etc.

10. 'Notes et variantes.' An interesting section, containing partly additions and variations, running throughout the novel (pages often not numbered); partly France's notes concerning developments to make and objects to describe, e.g., the scenery and details in Thaïs' garden, the *motif* of the musical instruments, "luths, théorbes, flutes,' also indications as to Paphnuce's state of 'remission' in the tomb and brief notes about Lollius, a character who does not appear in the above sections of the MS.

(A portion of the missing Part I of the MS., corresponding to pp. 31-49 in the *princeps,* was in the possession of M. Louis Barthou. It should be observed that the numeration of the above sections is neither consecutive nor consistent. Additional numberings in pencil further complicate the sequence. In several cases, pages are wrongly placed within their section; they should be transferred.)

A quantity of the original developments in MS. *A* were ultimately rejected, while others were broken up and dispersed in sundry contexts. The nature of the constant stylistic revisions has been briefly indicated in our text, but will of course bear close investigation and study. Some typical instances may be selected, particularly from the banquet-scene. Originally, Thaïs was inelegantly said to have 'lugged' Paphnuce there — 'qui te tirant par l'oreille . . .' This was improved: 'C'est elle dont la douce violence t'a amené ici malgré toi.' Cotta, who first spoke 'avec quiétude,' now speaks 'avec sérénité.' A better cadence is attained by changing 'un homme pieux' to 'un homme rempli de piété.' The other courtesans, who at first simply 'examinaient Thaïs avec attention,' ultimately 'dévoraient Thaïs des yeux.' A vague phrase about an enchanter became the familiar, 'c'est un mage,' a *motif* which Anatole applied to all and sundry. After calling the monk that, Thaïs (with some redundance) 's'assit sur un lit qui lui était assigné près de Paphnuce'— altered to '. . . un lit à côté de Paphnuce.' Nicias' blunt statement to Eucrite, 'Tu te mets au-dessus des dieux,' is veiled more ceremoniously: 'Tu t'associes à la providence céleste.' Throughout this scene, a number of insertions and amplifications give more body both to the arguments and to the interlocutors. There are also certain omissions which afford us interesting clues, among which may be mentioned the description of the 'divine Epicurus' as 'paisible, bienveillant, sans désirs, ami des dieux auxquels il ne croyait pas . . . et qu'il enseignait la sagesse dans un petit jardin.'

A comparative note may be added. The present writer has for some years been directing researches among the variations in Balzac's novels, as revealed in his manuscripts, proof-sheets, and successive editions. If asked to state the salient differences in the methods of the two men, I should say that where Balzac makes his alterations mainly in view of exactness of detail and fulness of description, France is preoccupied rather with considerations of clearness and elegance.

APPENDIX D (p. 447) : A Source for *Thaïs*

(Extracts from the *Vies des Pères des déserts,* ed. Rev. Père Marin, 9 vols., Avignon, 1761.)

In this collection we find lives of various saints in whom A.F. was interested—e.g., St. Anthony, Sts. Apollonius and Pachomius, and Ste. Marie l'Egyptienne. Furthermore, there are several Paphnutii: 'Il y a plusieurs Solitaires qui ont porté le même nom' [whether in the fourth century or later], 'car ce nom étoit fort commun en Egypte.' (T. I, p. 152.) Accounts are given of 'Paphnuce Céphale,' (T. III, pp. 11-19), of 'Paphnuce Bubole (i.e., 'lover of solitude'; T. III, pp. 26-40), and particularly of a Paphnuce who was 'Disciple de St. Antoine, Confesseur et Evêque en Thébaïde' (T. I, pp. 148-52). The last-named, be it noted, was active 'dans la basse Thébaïde' and also strongly opposed the Arians at the first Council of Nicæa. But we cannot here discuss all the 'contaminations' to which our Paphnuce was exposed.

The extract that particularly concerns us (T. I, Ch. XV, pp. 261-76) is entitled: 'Saint Paphnuce, Abbé au Territoire d'Héraclée en basse Thébaïde, et Sainte Thaïs, pénitente.' It is immediately evident where Anatole may have found his locality of 'Héraclée,' at the extremity of which (we are then told), this Paphnuce had established his monastery. He was famous for his virtues; his life was so holy that he was considered less a man than an angel. Far from being tempted and racked by demons, he was favoured by the visits of certain 'esprits bienheureux,' who bore witness to his unusual virtue. Three of his most edifying conversions are related in full, as preludes to the story of Thaïs:

> Mais on peut dire que le plus précieux fruit de sa mission, et celui en qui la magnificence de la bonté de Dieu éclata davantage, fut la conversion d'une fameuse courtisane, encore plus célèbre dans l'Eglise par sa pénitence, qu'elle ne l'avoit été dans le siècle par sa dépravation. [Her rather horrible early years give rise to the reflection that God's mercy is great.] On ne dit pas quelle fut sa patrie, ni la ville qui servit de théâtre à ses dissolutions: on sçait seulement en général que c'étoit en Egypte. Elle eut le malheur de naître d'une mère aussi méchante

qu'elle-même le devint ; car bien loin de veiller à la conservation de son innocence, elle ne lui donna que des leçons pour la perdre, et cette séduction domestique fortifiée par une beauté, qu'on peut appeller meurtrière des âmes, attira auprès d'elle tous les libertins du païs, dont la passion fut si violente, que plusieurs eurent à son sujet des querelles sanglantes, et d'autres se ruinèrent pour lui faire des présents.

This great scandal reached even to the solitudes. Providence used Paphnuce to bring back the lost lamb, by ways contrary to ordinary prudence.

Paphnuce quitta son habit de solitaire, en prit un mondain, se munit d'une somme d'argent, et dans l'équipage d'un cavalier qui lui facilitoit l'approche de la courtisane, vint se présenter devant elle comme pour grossir le nombre de ses adorateurs.

Thaïs n'avoit pas tout-à-fait éteint dans son âme les principes communs de la religion. [But her belief in the future life and in similar truths was stifled by the love of pleasure and wealth. Yet the monk reconverted her to these principles.]

Il lui demanda d'abord de l'introduire dans un endroit où il pût se dérober non-seulement aux yeux des créatures, mais aux yeux de Dieu-même ; et comme elle lui eut répondu que la chose étoit impossible, Dieu étant présent partout, il en prit occasion de lui représenter combien il étoit horrible d'oser pêcher sous les yeux de Dieu, et quel terrible compte elle auroit à rendre à son tribunal de la perte de tant d'âmes que sa conduite libertine entraînoit tous les jours dans l'abîme du péché.

At these words, Thaïs, perceiving that Paphnuce was no libertine and that God's grace was efficacious, threw herself at his feet and cried :

Mon père, ordonnez-moi telle pénitence qu'il vous plaira ; car j'espère que Dieu me fera miséricorde par vos prières ; je vous demande seulement trois heures de tems, après quoi je me rendrai où vous le trouverez bon, et j'exécuterai tout ce que vous me prescrivez.

She assembled all her belongings, which were worth forty *livres d'or ;* she had them carried to the public square and burned before all the people ; and in a loud voice she urged her companions to imitate her change of heart. Then she went to where Paphnuce, after witnessing the burning, was awaiting her. He led her to a nunnery and shut her up in a particular cell, 'dont il scela la porte avec du plomb, afin que personne n'eût la témérité de l'ouvrir sans sa permission.' He left only a small window for receiving food and ordered the Sisters to give her very little bread and water.

Thaïs, thus imprisoned, begged the monk to tell her whenever he might leave, so that she could pray to God. Paphnuce answered that she was unworthy to pronounce His name, 'ni d'élever vers le ciel ses mains souillées par tant de crimes ; mais qu'elle se contentât de se tourner vers l'Orient, et de répéter souvent ces paroles : *Vous qui m'avez formée, ayez pitié de moi.*'

Three years later, Paphnuce had compassion on her and went to ask

St. Anthony whether her sins were remitted. The monk did not at first disclose the reason for his visit to the Saint, and the latter had his disciples pray all night in order to discover it. St. Paul the Simple divined the secret. In his vision, he saw a bed in Heaven, guarded by three virgins and reserved for the converted courtesan. Accordingly, Paphnuce knew that God had forgiven Thaïs; he went back to the nunnery and told her that she might come out of the cell.

The docile Thaïs was willing either to stay in the cell or to come forth. She declared that she had done nothing there but consider and repent of her sins, all heaped up (*amoncelés*) as they were. 'It is clear that God has forgiven you,' said Paphnuce.

Thaïs survived her ordeal only fifteen days before she went to glory.

As for Paphnuce, his 'acta' do not say when he died. Always austere and penitent, he presently had a vision of an angel who invited him into Heaven, whither he went the next day. He told some visitors that we should not scorn lowly or sinful people—witness the three previous conversions that he had effected, together with that of Thaïs. He made an edifying end; and angels received his soul. He has been honoured with two different saints' days on the calendar.

APPENDIX E (p. 553 and Note 27): A.F. and Renan

The statement in the text that a volume should be devoted to the France-Renan relationship needs some amplification. In the first place, I think it can be proved that no other writer, not even Voltaire or Racine, exercised a greater influence upon A.F. than did the author of the *Vie de Jésus.* This predominance has been emphasized by various thoughtful students of Anatole, whether as regards æsthetic religiosity, the development of 'ironic potentialities,' the treatment of Iahveh, the early attitude toward science (in each case), or A.F.'s skill in covering his tracks. (See Lanson, *Pages choisies d'A.F.*, 'Notice,' p. vii; Chevalier, p. 83; Gaffiot, *Théories soc. d'A.F.*, pp. 38-39; Carias, *Gde. Revue*, 1922, pp. 530 f.) Thus, France's nickname of 'Mademoiselle Renan' is to some extent justified. Other obvious parallels would include the mutual leaning toward dilettantism, the tendency of both men to become savants of the salons, their similar rationalization of the supernatural, the fact that Anatole wrote that 'Bible of modern incredulity which Renan would have liked to write' (Doumic, p. 924).

Our intention here is simply to give some hints to the future student of this influence. Besides the numerous references to Renan above (see page-index, *s.v.*, and Notes, *passim*), there are France's personal recollections of his master, as found for example in Ségur (*Conversations*, pp. 120-26), and the more ornate tributes of the *Discours de réception* (*O. C.*, XXV, 389-90), with its allusions to *Caliban*, to Renan's charming courtesy, his maintenance of the 'necessary illusions,' particularly those of sentiment.

This of course was a high moment; but there were in previous years many other points of contact not fully emphasized in our text. The early attitude of the disciple was one of respectful homage, as shown by miscellaneous reviews. A 'notice' regarding *l'Antéchrist* (*Revue des documents historiques,* cover of No. 5, Aug., 1873) admires Renan's profundity in analyzing Nero, that 'mauvais artiste,' although the literary value of the Fourth Gospel and of the Apocalypse seems to the reviewer to be underrated. (For a chronological list of A.F.'s *aperçus* on Renan, mainly in *Le Temps,* see Antoniu, p. 89, note 2; similarly for *l'Univ. ill.*, see above, Ch. XIII, note 83.)

In those times Anatole seems to have made no secret of his discipleship, of which there are manifestations on a broad scale. For instance, *Le Crime de Sylvestre Bonnard* is permeated with Renanism of one kind or another. (See Maccone, pp. 120 ff; Huard, *Bull. du Bibliophile,* March 1, 1925, p. 138; Shanks, p. 62. The last-named suggests that Bonnard himself is modelled on Renan.) The venerated name recurs in *Le Livre* and in the 'Préface' to *Faust* (1889, 1891), where he is characterized as 'le plus grand esprit de notre temps.'

By this time the two men had become acquainted. In a letter of 1888 to Mme. de Caillavet (Renan, *Correspondance,* II, 329), the ageing savant expressed his pleasure at hearing France recite poetry in Egeria's home. There must have been many such meetings. That fairly cordial relations were established is shown by an unpublished letter from Renan to A.F. of December 28, 1891 (Bibl. Nat., Nouv. Acq. Fr., # 10805). This contains an invitation to France to visit the Renan country home ('Rosmapamon') in Brittany during the following year. In the course of the letter, Renan admiringly refers to 'Le Procurateur de Judée' as a 'little masterpiece'; in his opinion the most profound tale that Anatole has written. One sentence of this note gave France a cue for several articles and stories, and also shows the nature of the sympathy between the elder and the younger sceptic: 'Je vous montrerai combien vous avez raison, combien la couche du christianisme est mince, combien le paganisme naturaliste est là vivant, seul vivant.' . . Excursions are planned in which the two will participate. But in October of the next year death overtook the infirm scholar, and France never reached Rosmapamon.

A.F.'s sorrow at Renan's passing was, we have seen, deep and sincere. When the news was brought to him, together with a request for his necrological article, France wrote to Mme. Arman: 'C'est quelque chose de grand, c'est quelque chose de nous qui s'écroule.' (*Livres — Manuscrits — Dessins,* p. 99; cf. Pouquet, *Salon,* p. 140.) The article mentioned (see above, p. 294) expresses, particularly in the manuscript fragments which remain, a personal grief as well as a general lament. As A.F. wrote Georges Rodenbach: 'Je suis tout entier à la douleur d'avoir perdu M. Renan, que j'admirais de toute mon âme et que j'aimais de tout mon cœur' (A.L.S., in catalog of A. J. Scheuer).

Such are a few of the outstanding tributes offered by France before his grand climacteric. After 1896, although Bonnard has become Bergeret, there is for some time little diminution in the regard manifested toward Renan. The ironic sayings of Bergeret himself are often tinctured with Renanism, while one main preoccupation of the master — the conflict between Pecus or Caliban and the élite — is conspicuous in the *Histoire contemporaine.* In 1903, Anatole read his notable *Discours à Tréguier* (*Dis-*

cours prononcé à l'Inauguration de la Statue de Renan; for the curious mosaic-work in the MS., see *Chronique des lettres françaises,* V, 138). Here he saluted Renan as a brother-sceptic and a fellow-worshipper of Pallas Athene. The goddess is made to answer the supplication which Renan had addressed to her in his *Prière sur l'Acropole,* and the response blends the beautiful prose of both authors. An earlier passage on the rise of Christianity is definitely based on the *Origines.* At this time, A.F. still admired Renan's style, particularly in the *Souvenirs d'enfance,* and supported his dream of progress (*Vers les Temps meilleurs,* II, 33-57).

The tale of 'Gallion' in *Sur la Pierre blanche* is Renan with a difference and with some evasiveness regarding the obvious debt. (See Carias, *Gde. Revue,* 1922, pp. 529-66—also generally on Renan-France; cf. articles by Souday in *Le Temps,* October 23, 1924, and December 15, 1927.) It would require many pages to analyse what the *Vie de Jeanne d'Arc* owes to the *Vie de Jésus.* Very similar is the development of the central intention in each work: namely, to restore the subject of a legend to reality by dwelling on the natural background, whether historical, topographical or spiritual.

In his later years France wore with distinction the mantle of the master and was definitely considered his successor, whether for the charm of his *causeries* or for his addiction to the literary dialogue (Vandérem, *Miroir,* VII, 233-34; Guehenno, p. 211). Their reasons for liking this form were much the same: as Renan himself said (Preface to *Dialogues et fragments philosophiques,* p. vi) one could thus present the diverse facets of a problem without being forced to conclude. It is thought that France was 'renanisant' in this manner as early as the dialogue about fairy-tales in the *Livre de mon ami* (Shanks, pp. 67, 87). But the trend is more definite as he aged and grew still fonder of paradoxes and antinomies. We should recall, however, that his eighteenth-century models were also practitioners of the dialogue.

Even in Anatole's last phase, there are still echoes. M. Bellessort thinks (p. 427) that the invocation to Racine in *Le Petit Pierre* (cf. above, p. 192) has the tone and *ordonnance* of the *Prière sur l'Acropole.* As late as 1923 France read at the Trocadéro his final public eulogy, when the centenary of Renan was celebrated. The posthumous volume, *Dernières Pages inédites,* contains fragments of drama and dialogues in the old manner.

Yet there is some evidence that Anatole Himself developed a carping attitude towards his former demi-god or, as Voltaire put it under somewhat similar circumstances, he became disposed 'to bite the hand that had fed him.' That this reaction increased to the point of mockery, bitterness, and even hatred, as Brousson alleges, we do not believe. (See *Itinéraire,* pp. 179-80 and 209-10; *Nouv. litt.,* February 24, 1923.) But we may allow for some cooling off, especially regarding those works which A.F. was generally credited with imitating. (Voltaire showed a like distaste for the popularizations of Fontenelle, when he had finished using them.) Brousson exaggerates and deforms, as usual; the very pages where A.F.'s supposed diatribes are recorded evince a profound familiarity with Renan's writings. Yet we cannot dispute that he grew more critical of his 'spiritual father,' for there is other testimony to that effect (cf. Le Goff, p. 75; Barrès,

Mes Cahiers, I, 228 ; Ségur, *Conversations,* pp. 35-36 : here A.F. confides, 'je n'aime pas sa *Prière sur l'Acropole*').

Henriette Psichari (*op. cit.,* p. 208) considers that Anatole did Renan much disservice in harping mainly on his sceptical and ironical side, rather than in seeking to illuminate his more idealistic and constructive intentions. A.F. might have been more grateful for favours received : 'La mémoire de Renan a grandement servi France en lui permettant d'arriver à la notoriété littéraire.' This is at least half of the truth, for the public likes to conceive of one author in terms of another. Many of the clerical attacks upon France spoke of him as a disciple of the scholar whom they viewed as a renegade. Max Nordau, to be sure, preferred to think of Anatole as a partial 'heir' rather than as a disciple and maintains that what he inherited was an artistic instead of a philosophical legacy (*Vus du dehors,* pp. 45-47). But the larger chorus of critics, I believe, holds that it was both. It will be interesting to see if this can ever be proved in detail. (Among many other witnesses, cf. Hérenger, *Le Feu,* January, 1914, p. 6 ; Lahy-Hollebecque, p. 73 ; Poizat, pp. 379-80.)

NOTES

NOTES

(In cases where the key-number appears toward the beginning or the end of a paragraph in the text, several references may be grouped below. A little practice will enable the reader — with the assistance of the punctuation and the repetition of writers' names — to match any statement with the appropriate reference. The term 'O. C.' indicates the *Œuvres complètes* of France, 'édition définitive.' The place in this edition of any work by A.F. cited below can be determined by glancing at the Bibliography, section A I, where the contents of each volume are specified.)

INTRODUCTION

1. '. . . One of the most considerable legends of modern times.' H. I. Brock, *New York Times Book Review,* Dec. 26, 1926.
2. P. Champion, *Mon Vieux Quartier,* p. 18. But the notes alluded to were those supplied by *others,* for the *Vie de Jeanne d'Arc.*
3. Sherman, *On Contemporary Literature,* p. 169.
4. Ségur, *Dernières Conversations avec A.F.,* pp. 196-99.
5. Michaut, *A.F., étude psychologique,* 5th edition, p. 95.
6. Kingsbury, *N.Y. Times Book Rev.,* Oct. 9, 1932.
7. Blum, *En lisant. Réflexions critiques,* p. 45.
8. Chevalier, *The Ironic Temper; A.F. and his Time,* p. 13; Hovelaque, *Revue de France,* April 1, 1925, p. 573; Barthou, *Bulletin Municipal Officiel,* June 18, 1933.
9. Doumic speaks of France's 'étonnante fidélité à lui-même'— *Revue des deux mondes,* Dec. 15, 1896, p. 925.
10. On the unveiling of the commemorative *plaque,* Quai Malaquais, May, 1933; poem in *Le Lys rouge* (periodical), July 1, 1933.
11. Michaut, *op. cit.,* p. 313; Gaffiot, *Théories d'A.F. sur l'organisation sociale de son temps,* p. 9.
12. Michaut and Evelpidi (*A.F., critique social,* p. 17) have developed the contrary view.
13. *Les Théories sociales d'A.F.,* p. 12.
14. Blondheim, 'A.F.,' *Modern Philology,* July, 1916, pp. 47-48; Cerf, *A.F. The Degeneration of a Great Artist,* p. 1.
15. These reasons are well stated in Carias, *Anatole France.* For another view regarding this central period, see below, Ch. XII, note 1.
16. Michaut (p. xxv) would have the third period run from about 1892 to 1895; for various reasons, this seems quite too short a time. His views on the 'dilettante' period of the eighties are considered above, p. 374.
17. M. de Fontenay, *Bulletin Officiel,* June 18, 1933.
18. Cf. Vandérem, *Rev. de France,* Nov. 15, 1924, pp. 379-80.
19. 'Gyp' in Pouquet, *Le Salon de Mme. de Caillavet,* p. 40, note; cf. above, p. 228; Reissig, *A.F.,* p. 122; Seillière, *La Jeunesse d'A.F.,* p. 19.
20. Michaut, pp. 210-11, gives a valuable list of both types of repetition.
21. *Les Contemporains,* II, 113; cf. Michaut, pp. 147-48.
22. *L'Ile des Pingouins*; Ségur, *Conversations avec A.F., passim.*

23. J. de Gourmont, *Mercure de France,* Aug. 1, 1927, p. 652 ; Ségur, *Revue mondiale,* Nov. 1, 1924, p. 18.
24. Lemaître, *op. cit.,* pp. 87-88, 113 ; Renard, *Bulletin Officiel,* June 18, 1933. Barrès, *A.F.* (brochure), pp. 23-24 ; *Journal des Débats,* Nov. 12, 1921. Maurras, *A.F. politique et poète,* p. 8. Mornet, *Revue du mois,* July 10, 1911, especially pp. 60, 76.
25. Blum, *op. cit.,* pp. 169-70 ; Mornet, *loc. cit.* Spronck, *Les Artistes littéraires,* p. 346.
26. From 'Ce siècle avait deux ans ! . . .' in *Les Feuilles d'automne.* The comparison is found also in Truc, *A.F., l'artiste et le penseur,* pp. 114-15 ; for him France is a 'résonateur suprême.'
27. Cf. Gaffiot, *Théories soc. d'A.F.,* p. 6.
28. Michaut, p. 96 ; cf. pp. 95 and 217. Barthou, *Rev. de France,* June 15, 1926, p. 627.
29. 'A.F., der Dichter und sein Werk,' *ZfFSL,* 1927, vol. 50, pp. 85-86.
30. From Feb. 1 to Feb. 15, 1883 ; it bore the title of *Le Petit Bonhomme.*
31. Michaut, p. xvi ; cf. W. Stephens, *Madame Adam,* p. 220 ; but the latter writer is wrong in identifying *Le Petit Bonhomme* with *Pierre Nozière.* During the late eighties and early nineties, fragments of *Pierre Nozière* had appeared in *l'Univers illustré,* in *Le Temps,* and even in *Le Littoral de la Somme ;* many of these *morceaux* were utilized again in *l'Echo de Paris,* 1892-98 ; cf. notes in *O. C.,* X, 521-23 ; Michaut, p. 214 ; and a letter from Léon Bucquet in the Collection Lion.
32. *Vie littéraire, O. C.,* VI, 285.
33. I cite from the MS., which is fuller than the text as it appeared in *l'Univ. ill.,* May 12, 1883. The article properly concerns 'La Jeunesse de M. Renan.'
34. Souday, *Le Temps,* Oct. 14, 1924.
35. *Petit Pierre,* p. 265 ; cf. *Livre de mon ami,* pp. 309-10, and the preface to *La Vie en fleur,* pp. 285-86.
36. *Petit Pierre,* pp. 117 and 127 ; cf. Carez, *Auteurs contemporains,* p. 82.
37. *O. C.,* XXIII, 559 ff.
38. Descaves, *Le Journal,* Feb. 9, 1919 ; but cf. Huard, *A.F. et le Quai Malaquais,* p. 31.
39. Vandérem, *Miroir des Lettres,* VII, 224. Souday, *art. cit. ;* Morand (*Débats,* Oct. 30, 1924) takes a similar view and would playfully entitle these volumes 'les Enfances d'A.F.' Corday, *A.F., d'après ses confidences et ses souvenirs,* pp. 7-56 (the section is called 'Enfance et jeunesse') ; Masson, *A.F., son œuvre,* pp. 7-8.
40. Deschamps, *La Vie et les Livres,* V, 174 ; Prade, *Bulletin Officiel,* June 18, 1933.
41. *Miroir des Lettres,* I, 258-59 ; Delson, *Poet Lore,* August, 1920, pp. 261, 264-65 ; Gosse, *Living Age,* Sept. 16, 1922, pp. 723-24.
42. 'Le Père France,' *Mercure,* Jan. 15, 1925, pp. 349 f.
43. H. Bidou, *Revue de Paris,* May 1, 1924, p. 215.
44. *Revue universelle,* Nov. 1, 1925, pp. 295-330.
45. Roujon, *La Vie et les opinions d'A.F.,* p. 6.
46. Delson, *art. cit.,* p. 262 ; Chevalier, *op. cit.,* p. 129.
47. Le Goff, *A.F. à la Béchellerie,* pp. 237-38.
48. Reproach by Spronck, *Débats,* Oct. 11, 1893 ; refutation by Michaut, p. 71, note.
49. *Maîtres de l'heure,* II, 225.

50. E.g., Ségur, *Rev. de France,* Nov. 1, 1929, p. 77 ; *idem, Génie européen,* pp. 105-106.
51. Seillière, *op. cit.,* pp. 47, 59 ; Edmund Wilson, *New Republic,* Feb. 11, 1925.
52. Maury, *Revue politique et littéraire,* Dec. 20-27, 1919, pp. 766-67.
53. L. Lefèvre, *ibid.,* March 1-8, 1919, p. 155.
54. *Art. cit.,* p. 724.
55. Cerf, pp. 46-47, note ; Jusselin, *La Dépêche* (d'Eure-et-Loir), Aug. 6-7, 1932 ; cf. Braibant, *Le Secret d'A.F.,* p. 288.
56. Corday, *Dernières pages inédites,* pp. 194-95 — Carias, *A.F.,* p. 8.
57. *Itinéraire de Paris à Buenos-Ayres,* 1927.— The eagerly favourable reviews of these two volumes belonged mostly to the 'debunking' school and do not disprove my general contention.
58. On Brousson's inaccuracies, wilful or otherwise, see Aveline, *Chronique des lettres françaises,* 1928, pp. 201-206 and *Chantecler,* Dec. 17, 1927 ; Crémieux, *Annales,* Feb. 15, 1928 ; Souday, *N.Y. Times Book Rev.,* Jan. 8, 1928 ; I have private information to the same effect.
59. Cf. Bury, *French Quarterly,* 1924 (VI), p. 167.
60. De Gourmont, *art. cit.,* p. 653. 'Ségur' is the pseudonym for a Greek, brought up in Paris and intimate with A.F. for many years ; cf. Souday, *N.Y. Times Book Rev.,* July 10, 1927. In 1920 France wrote a preface for Ségur's *Naïs,* a study of a Greek courtesan.
61. Préface to *Conversations,* pp. 6-7 ; Le Goff, p. 247.
62. Kemp, *Rev. universelle,* Feb. 15, 1925, p. 534 ; Chevalier (*op. cit.,* p. 17) believes that Ségur has penetrated beneath the surface gaiety to France's real melancholy.
63. M. Corday's other works (see Bibliography) have also been found helpful.
64. *Op. cit.,* pp. 8-9.
65. See, for instance, the names of John Charpentier, Fourrier, etc. (in *Clarté*), Lafue, Massis, A. Breton, Soupault, etc. (in *Un Cadavre*). On the defensive side are the names of Thibaudet, Cor, Souday, Pierrefeu, André Moine, etc. (in *Le Capitole*) ; cf. Truc (*Comœdia,* Dec. 31, 1929).
66. *Rev. de France,* June 15, 1926, p. 605.
67. 'New Light on A.F.,' *Virginia Quarterly Review,* Jan., 1936, pp. 104-21.

CHAPTER I

1. Brousson, *Pantoufles,* pp. 113-15.
2. See above, p. 68.
3. Prade and Fontenay in *Bulletin Officiel,* June 18, 1933 ; Huard, *A.F. et le Quai Malaquais,* p. 13 ; Anatole himself said 'six weeks'— cf. Corday, *A.F., d'après ses confidences et ses souvenirs,* p. 15 and see *Lys rouge* (periodical), July 1, 1933.
4. Cf. Huard, *op. cit.,* pp. 6, 14-16 ; *Le Brun, A.F., Biographie . . . suivie d'opinions,* pp. 9, 45 ; *Livre de mon ami, O.C.,* III, 192 ; M. Kahn, *Père d'A.F.,* pp. 30-32.
5. Souday, *Le Temps,* Oct. 14, 1924.
6. Mouton, *Le Quai Malaquais. Le Numéro Cinq.*
7. *Pierre Nozière,* pp. 276-77 ; *Livre,* p. 286. The atmosphere of this building is well depicted by P. Champion, *Mon Vieux Quartier,* pp. 36, 84-87.

8. *L'Univ. ill.*, Jan. 19, 1884.
9. *Paris Guide*, Vol. I, p. 78 ; Prade, *art. cit.*, Ségur, *Conversations*, p. 168.
10. *Le Petit Pierre*, p. 279 and *passim*.
11. *Lys rouge*, April 1 and July 1, 1933 ; *Bulletin Officiel*, June 18, 1933. Efforts had previously been made to change the name of the Quai Malaquais to Quai Anatole France.
12. Carias, *A.F.*, p. 9 ; Roujon, *Vie et opinions d'A.F.*, p. 4 ; the birth-certificate is given in the *Chronique des lettres françaises*, 1924, p. 807. Chief authorities on Anatole's childhood and youth : Huard, M. Kahn, Girard, Giraud, Le Moy.
13. *Petit Pierre*, p. 8.
14. Carias, *loc. cit.* ; Prade, *art. cit.*
15. M. Kahn, *op. cit.*, p. 19 ; Le Moy, *Mercure*, Jan. 15, 1925, pp. 335-36 ; A.F.'s letter to a journalist on the subject is quoted in Girard, *La Jeunesse d'A.F.*, p. 34.
16. Girard, *passim* ; Corday, pp. 13-14 ; Wassermann, *A.F. vu par un Américain*, p. 83.
17. Huard, *op. cit.*, p. 6 ; cf. references in Ch. III, note 13.
18. See France's article on him, *Vie litt.*, *O.C.*, VII, 165-78. He is there described as a thorough Epicurean of taste and tact, who had cultivated the arts under three régimes. Cf. Girard, p. 29 and Giraud, *Maîtres de l'heure*, II, 181.
19. P. Champion, pp. 43-44, 194.
20. Corday, p. 15 ; *Vie litt.*, *O.C.* VII, 177, note.
21. Preface to Arène and Tournier, *Des Alpes aux Pyrénées*, 1891.
22. Most of these facts are taken from M. Ballaguy's long article. It is only in his interpretations that this writer shows a bias.
23. Letters quoted by Le Moy, *art. cit.*, pp. 341 ff.
24. *Quelques Témoignages*, p. 158.
25. Kéméri, *Promenades d'A.F.*, p. 11 ; Berton, *Vie des peuples*, Oct. 10, 1922, p. 387 ; Corday, pp. 30, 33.
26. *Scènes de la Chouannerie* (1857).
27. Le Moy, *art. cit.*, p. 336 ; Gottschalk, *ZfFSL*, 1927, vol. 50, p. 86, note.
28. Chief authorities on Père France : Ballaguy, Huard, 'Père d'A.F.,' M. Kahn, Le Moy.
29. Corday, p. 32. Huard says that Thibault belonged to the 'garde royal' rather than to the 'garde du corps.' 'Le Père d'A.F.,' *Bulletin du Bibliophile et du Bibliothécaire*, March 1, 1925, p. 121.
30. Brousson, *Nouv. litt.*, April 19, 1924. Le Moy (*art. cit.*, p. 339) is sceptical as to this prolongation of military service.
31. Huard, *art. cit.*, p. 135 ; cf. De Gramont, *Pomp and Circumstance*, p. 26.
32. *Petit Pierre*, p. 159 ; *Vie en fleur*, p. 319 ; on his Royalism, cf. P. Champion, p. 192.
33. Ballaguy, *art. cit.*, p. 320 ; cf. Huard, *op. cit.*, p. 6, and *art. cit.*, p. 123 ; Shanks, *A.F*,, p. 3.
34. Huard, *A.F. et le Quai Malaquais*, pp. 6-7 ; see following note.
35. Huard, *art. cit.*, pp. 125 ff ; Giraud, *op. cit.*, p. 183, note 3. The latter quotes Anatole himself to the effect that his father was a pathfinder on the bibliography of the Revolution.
36. *L'Univ. ill.*, Sept. 24, 1887 ; 'Autobiographie,' *Rev. de France*, Nov. 1, 1924, p. 9.
37. Letter quoted in Girard, pp. 21-23 ; cf. Carias, *A.F.*, p. 20.
38. Le Moy (p. 349) cites examples of his dreaminess ; similarly, Dr. Nozière was

lured by a certain silver-voiced promoter into an unfortunate investment with a mineral water company. *Petit Pierre,* pp. 151-56 ; cf. Stewart, *A.F., the Parisian,* p. 20.

39. In a private letter cited by Guerlac, ed. *Le Livre de mon ami,* p. xiv, note 1 ; and in *Vie en fleur* (p. 482) France speaks of his 'condition médiocre.'
40. Le Moy, *loc. cit.* ; refuted by M. Kahn, *op. cit.*, p. 45.
41. As above (note 28) ; and add : A.F., 'Un Foyer éteint,' *Chasseur bibliographe,* Feb., 1867, pp. 35-37 ; reprinted in Kahn, pp. 33-35 ; cf. Girard, pp. 95 ff.
42. *Petit Pierre,* p. 237.
43. Carias, *op. cit.*, p. 5.
44. *O.C.*, XXIII, 9-10 ; *Vie en fleur,* p. 347 ; Corday, p. 33.
45. Chevalier, *Ironic Temper,* p. 90.
46. *O.C.*, XXIII, 347.
47. Chiefly Brousson, *Pantoufles,* pp. 100, 109-11, etc. ; cf. *idem, Itinéraire,* p. 105 : 'Feu mon père, qui n'était pas un aigle. . .'
48. Stewart, p. 39 ; cf. Brousson, *Itinéraire,* p. 188.
49. May, *A.F., the Man and his Work,* p. 7 ; Carias, p. 22.
50. 'Autobiographie,' pp. 8-9 ; cf. 'Un Foyer éteint,' as above.
51. M. Kahn, p. 34 ; Huard, *op. cit.*, p. 8.
52. The 'coup de vent' passage is repeated, with variations, in *Petit Pierre,* p. 9.
53. Carias, p. 22.
54. E.g., J. Roujon, *op. cit.*, p. 5.
55. Le Moy, p. 335 ; Ballaguy, p. 311 ; Pillet, *ZfFSL,* 1930, vol. 54, p. 11, note.
56. *Nouv. litt.*, July 27, 1932.
57. *Petit Pierre,* p. 156.
58. *Ibid.*, p. 161.
59. Kéméri, *op. cit.*, p. 51.
60. *Ibid.*, pp. 52-56 ; *Pierre Nozière,* pp. 319-26 (cf. above, p. 75).
61. J. Roujon, p. 5 ; *Petit Pierre,* p. 174 ; cf. Corday, p. 35.
62. Ségur, *op. cit.*, p. 182.
63. Kéméri, pp. 154-56.
64. *Rev. de France,* June 15, 1926, pp. 614-15.
65. *Figaro,* Oct. 25, 1924 ; Léopold Kahn in *Le Petit Parisien,* Oct. 13, 1924.
66. *Alfred de Vigny,* pp. 67-69.
67. *Poèmes dorés,* p. 224.
68. *Op. cit.*, p. 151.
69. Brousson, *Itinéraire,* p. 102.
70. *Pierre Nozière,* p. 297 ; cf. Michaut, p. 119.
71. Girard, pp. 41-55.
72. *Pantoufles,* pp. 364, 220-22.
73. Cf. E. Dufour in *l'Ecole et la Vie,* May 10, 1924.
74. *O. C.*, XXIII, 10-11.
75. Cerf, *A.F.*, pp. 6-7.
76. E.g., May, *op. cit.*, p. 12.
77. Brousson, *Pantoufles,* p. 157.
78. Partly because of the character of her husband ; cf. Huard, *op. cit.*, p. 9.
79. Corday, *op. cit.*, p. 37 ; Ballaguy, p. 322 ; Kéméri, pp. 11 and 156.
80. *L'Univ. ill.*, Sept. 24, 1887 ; *Vie litt.*, Sept. 2, 1888.

81. *O. C.*, VII, 48 ff.
82. In *l'Etui de nacre* (*O. C.*, V). Cf. above, p. 468.
83. Winifred Stephens [Whale], *The France I Know*, p. 126. The title of this work refers to the country, not to the author. But Mrs. Whale has also written of Anatole, both here and elsewhere.
84. Chevalier, pp. 87-88 ; later (pp. 245-46) he considers that Giraud over-emphasizes her influence ; cf. Blondheim, *Modern Philology*, July, 1916, p. 58.
85. Giraud, p. 243 ; quoted by Chevalier, pp. 87-88.
86. This is the germ of the tale which evolved into 'Madame de Luzy.'
87. Corday, p. 38 ; *Petit Pierre, passim ; Vie en fleur*, p. 329.
88. Ségur, *op. cit.*, p. 163 ; *Petit Pierre*, p. 49.
89. Both Nanette and Madame Mathias are described in *Pierre Nozière*.
90. *Petit Pierre*, pp. 28-29.
91. *L'Univ. ill.*, Feb. 6, 1892.
92. *Pierre Nozière*, p. 295.
93. *Petit Pierre, passim.*
94. Corday, pp. 26-27.— 'Elles sont véridiques, ces figures de servantes vers qui se portait d'instinct sa tendresse d'enfant . . .'
95. Carias, ed. 'Carnets intimes,' *Nouv. litt.*, Feb. 18, 1933.
96. Dufour, *art. cit.*

CHAPTER II

1. *Rev. de France*, Nov. 1, 1924, pp. 5-9.
2. E.g., Curtius, cited in *Revue Rhénane*, Nov., 1924, p. 75 ; Bellessort, *Revue française*, Oct. 19, 1924, p. 427 ; Spronck, *Débats*, Oct. 11, 1893 ; Michaut, *A.F. Conférence*, p. 6. Cf. Ségur, *Le Génie européen*, pp. 105-107.
3. *Promenades d'A.F.*, p. 136.
4. *Living Age*, May 24, 1919, pp. 476-77.
5. *O. C.*, VIII, 5.
6. *L'Univ. ill.*, Nov. 10, 1894.
7. 'Postface' to *Vie en fleur*, p. 560.
8. 'Autobiographie,' p. 5.
9. E.g., in *Petit Pierre*, p. 31. It is the excuse of Montaigne.
10. Cf. 'Autobiographie,' p. 7.
11. *Vie litt.*, *O. C.*, VII, 462 ; *l'Univ. ill.*, March 5, 1887.
12. A case in point would be the account in *Petit Pierre* (pp. 116-17) of the vivid lady in a peignoir.
13. *Ibid.*, pp. 15-16.
14. *Nos Enfants*, pp. 72-73.
15. *Petit Pierre*, p. 144 ; *Jardin d'Epicure*, p. 436 ; *Le Temps*, April 24, 1892.
16. *Petit Pierre*, p. 8.
17. Some are reproduced in Girard, *op. cit.*, *passim*. Cf. Brousson, *Nouv. litt.*, Dec. 5, 1925.
18. Quoted by Shanks, *A.F. : The Mind and the Man*, p. 9.
19. *Petit Pierre, passim.*
20. *Ibid.*, pp. 63, 73 ff, 54 ff, 23 ; cf. Corday, *A.F.*, pp. 24, 18.
21. Other references to toys are in *Vie litt.*, *O. C.*, VI, 344 ff ; and in *Marguerite* (1920 ed.), pp. 7-9, 12.

22. *O. C.*, XXIII, 289.
23. Corday, pp. 23-24.
24. *Petit Pierre*, pp. 218-19, 48, 227.
25. *Op. cit.*, p. 53.
26. 'Une Visite à la Béchellerie,' in *Quatre Portraits*, p. 165. Cf. Huard, *A.F. et le Quai Malaquais*, p. 17.
27. *Petit Pierre*, pp. 280-81.
28. *Rev. universelle*, Nov. 1, 1925, pp. 325-27.
29. *Petit Pierre* and *Vie en fleur, passim.*
30. 'Postface' to *Vie en fleur*, p. 562.
31. Still according to Ballaguy, pp. 327-28.
32. Apparently, his name was Timothée Larade; the elder France published one of his works. Cf. Huard, 'Père d'A.F.,' *Bull. du Bibliophile*, March 1, 1925, p. 136, and *op. cit.*, pp. 11-12.
33. Souriau, *Histoire du Parnasse*, p. 373. But Pierre Calmettes (*Grande Passion d'A.F.*, pp. 36-39) believes that 'Le Bain' was addressed to him, as an infant.
34. *Petit Pierre*, p. 11.
35. In *Le Livre de mon ami*, pp. 247 ff.
36. Shanks, *op. cit.*, p. 11; Blondheim, *Modern Language Review*, July, 1918, p. 333.
37. M. Kahn, *Père d'A.F.*, pp. 24 and 29; Charavay, 'Préface' to *Documents sur la Révolution française*; A.F., *Bibliophile français*, March, 1870 and *Vie litt.*, *O. C.*, VI, 398.
38. Corday, p. 44; Girard, p. 72; *l'Orme du Mail*, pp. 71 ff.
39. Cf. Evelpidi (*A.F., Critique social*, p. 20): 'Dès le début une vérité l'étreint: la misère humaine,' etc.
40. The phrase is Ballaguy's (p. 330) and is well chosen; it is unfortunate that in the same breath he should refer to Pierre's narratives as a 'tissue of fables.'
41. *Le Temps*, Feb. 12, 1893.
42. Cf. Ballaguy, p. 329; but B. unnecessarily shortens the list.
43. *Petit Pierre*, pp. 170-71.
44. *Ibid.*, pp. 82-83, 113-22.
45. *Ibid.*, pp. 141-49; *Vie en fleur*, pp. 331-36; cf. above, pp. 71-72.
46. Corday, pp. 25-26.
47. *Petit Pierre*, pp. 8, 41 ff, 157 ff, 205-10; Corday, pp. 22-23.
48. Riquet was the fictional counterpart of Madame de Caillavet's dog of the same name — or else of her 'Mitzi'; cf. Pouquet, *Salon*, pp. 130-32.
49. Huard, *A.F. et le Quai Malaquais*, pp. 9-10.
50. *Le Crime de Sylvestre Bonnard*, pp. 285-89. Other passages in praise of dolls are to be found in *l'Univ. ill.*, Dec. 27, 1884; in *Marguerite* (1920 ed.), p. 13; and in *Petit Pierre*, p. 63.
51. Louis Barthou confirms this — *Conferéncia*, May 1, 1925, pp. 453-72. Cf. also Corday, p. 38; Pillet, *ZfFSL*, 1930, vol. 54, p. 11, note; Antoniu, *A.F., Critique littéraire*, p. 13, note 2 and references.
52. Ballaguy, p. 325. This work is thought to be the source for other anecdotes of '1830,' as recounted by A.F.
53. 'L'oncle Victor et Mathias sont deux répliques d'un même modèle.' Michaut, *A.F.*, p. 199.
54. *Ibid.*, pp. 200-201.

55. *Petit Pierre,* p. 122 ; cf. Corday, p. 27.
56. *Vie en fleur,* pp. 446-47 ; cf. Brousson, *Pantoufles,* pp. 266-67 ; Gosse (*Living Age,* Sept. 16, 1922, p. 726) refers to this 'wonderful sketch of Ingres, in his robust old age.'
57. Cf. above, p. 18 ; cf. *Vie litt., O. C.,* VII, 48 ff.
58. *Petit Pierre,* p. 12 ; transl. by Chevalier, *Ironic Temper,* p. 89 ; cf. Kingsbury, *N.Y. Times Book Rev.,* Oct. 9, 1932.
59. *Petit Pierre,* pp. 12-13 ; Chevalier, *loc. cit.*
60. *Petit Pierre,* pp. 81 ff ; cf. Corday, pp. 19-20.
61. *Petit Pierre,* p. 87.

CHAPTER III

1. *Petit Pierre,* pp. 49, 315 ; *Vie en fleur,* pp. 320-21 ; cf. *Le Temps,* Sept. 16, 1888 ; Reissig, *A.F.,* pp. 28-29, 32.
2. *Vie litt., O. C.,* VII, 165.
3. *Pierre Nozière,* pp. 321-22 ; Bourget, *Quelques Témoignages,* p. 151.
4. *O. C.,* III, 215.
5. Girard, p. 43.
6. Champion, pp. 141 ff, 173 ; Gastineau, *Nouv. litt.,* Feb. 17, 1934 ; Starrett, *Literary Observer,* Oct.-Nov., 1924, and the Parisian dailies around the former date.
7. *L'Opinion,* Oct. 17, 1924 ; cf. Carias, *A.F.,* p. 7.
8. Girard, pp. 95 ff.
9. Goncourt, *Journal,* III, 100 ; but Honoré Champion carried on this tradition — cf. P. Champion, *op. cit.,* p. 46.
10. *O. C.,* VII, 417-18.
11. Barthou, *Rev. de Paris,* Dec. 1, 1924, p. 482.
12. Brousson, *Pantoufles,* p. 100.
13. Carias, *op. cit.,* p. 15, gives a long list of Père France's clientèle ; Le Goff, p. 238.
14. *Art. cit.,* pp. 35-37. The article is signed simply 'Un Bibliophile.' Concerning its attribution to A.F., see M. Kahn, *Père d'A.F.,* p. 9.
15. 'Postface' to *Vie en fleur,* p. 560.
16. In *Bibliophile français,* March, 1870, pp. 264-65 ; cf. Antoniu, p. 13 and note 1.
17. Corday, *A.F.,* p. 41 ; Janin, *Paris Guide,* II, 946.
18. *O. C.,* VIII, 303.
19. Cited in *Le Journal* (newspaper), Oct. 13, 1924.
20. Collection Lion.
21. Quoted by Girard, pp. 98-99.
22. Brousson, *Nouv. litt.,* Dec. 5, 1925.
23. Charensol, *Nouv. litt.,* Oct. 17, 1925.
24. E.g., cf. quotations given by Gaffiot, *Théories soc. d'A.F.,* p. 7 ; he compiled for Lemerre in 1874 a *Livre du Bibliophile* (reprinted 1926).
25. Huard, *A.F. et le Quai Malaquais,* p. 18.
26. V. Jeanroy-Félix, *Fauteuils contemporains de l'Académie française,* pp. 45-46 ; Ségur, *Dernières conversations,* pp. 181-84 ; Le Goff, pp. 238-40.
27. Girard, p. 111.
28. E.g., *Petit Pierre,* p. 226 ; *Vie en fleur,* p. 322.
29. Above, p. 33 ; cf. 'Les Bouquinistes et les Quais,' *Almanach des Bibliophiles,*

1899, pp. 2-16; much of this material is found also in *Pierre Nozière.*

30. By May, *A.F.*, pp. 42-43; from *Le Livre*, pp. 312-15.
31. Ségur, *Conversations*, p. 169; cf. *Pierre Nozière*, p. 338.
32. Mme. Demont-Breton, *Les Maisons que j'ai connues*, p. 161.
33. Larguier, *l'Illustration*, May 30, 1925.
34. Cf. Brousson, *Pantoufles*, p. 104 and *passim.*
35. *Pierre Nozière*, pp. 339-40, and *l'Univ. ill.*, March 7, 1885.
36. *O. C.*, III, 193; cf. Prade, *Bulletin Officiel*, June 18, 1933.
37. C. H. C. Wright, *Background of Modern French Literature*, p. 18.
38. Michaut, *A.F.*, pp. 185-86. From time to time, France refers to such engravings—e.g., in *La Rôtisserie*, pp. 301-302.
39. De Fontenay, *Bulletin Officiel*, June 18, 1933.
40. *Livre de mon ami*, p. 279.
41. *Ibid.*, p. 286.
42. Shanks, p. 19.
43. *Petit Pierre*, pp. 49-52, 58.
44. *Vie en fleur*, pp. 287-93; *Petit Pierre*, p. 89.
45. Ségur, *Dern. conversations*, p. 157; *Vie en fleur*, pp. 321-24.
46. *Livre de mon ami*, pp. 318-19; *Vie en fleur*, p. 295.
47. *Noces corinthiennes*, *O. C.*, I, 395-97.
48. Bourget, *op. cit.*, p. 149; Bonnières, *Mémoires d'aujourd'hui*, II, 335; Bédarida, *Revue des cours et conférences*, May 15, 1926, p. 279; cf. above, p. 128.
49. *O. C.*, X, 275, 277, 340, 329, 337.
50. Cf. *Petit Pierre*, p. 221: 'Quand j'appris l'histoire des croisades, les hauts faits des barons chrétiens m'enflammèrent d'enthousiasme.'
51. In 'A Une Dame Créole':

    'Si vous alliez, Madame, au vrai pays de gloire,
    Sur les bords de la Seine ou de la verte Loire.'

    A.F. was fortunate in that he came to know both of these 'regions of glory.'
52. Cf. also *l'Univ. ill.*, Sept. 5, 1891. See above, p. 303.
53. De Fontenay, *loc. cit.*; Hanotaux, 'Discours aux funérailles,' *Le Journal*, Oct. 19, 1924.
54. E.g., March 1, 1884, where he applauds Coppée's sentiment: 'Le vrai Parisien aime Paris comme une patrie.'
55. Berton, *Vie des peuples*, Oct. 10, 1922, p. 390.
56. *Vie en fleur*, pp. 320-22. Another diatribe against the modernized Paris is found in the preface to Gérard de Nerval, *Petits Châteaux en Bohème, promenades et souvenirs*, p. xi.
57. *La Vie et les Livres*, V, 177-78; cf. *Vie en fleur*, p. 455.
58. *Pierre Nozière*, p. 268; *Paris Guide*, I, 145.
59. Ségur, *Dern. conversations*, pp. 189-90.
60. Kéméri, p. 17.
61. *Vie en fleur*, p. 455; *Pierre Nozière*, p. 275; Deschamps, pp. 178-80.
62. Cf. *Vie en fleur*, p. 324.
63. *Pierre Nozière*, p. 269; *l'Univ. ill.*, Feb. 5, 1887.
64. *Petit Pierre*, pp. 102-104.
65. *Vie en fleur*, p. 321; cf. *Petit Pierre*, p. 104.
66. *Vie en fleur*, p. 455; *Pierre Nozière*, p. 293.

67. May, p. 42 ; cf. Deschamps, p. 181.
68. *Vie en fleur*, pp. 414-15.
69. *Pierre Nozière*, p. 328 ; cf. *Almanach des Bibliophiles, loc. cit.* ; Kéméri, p. 2 ; etc.
70. *Pierre Nozière*, p. 328.
71. *Société, etc. . . . Conférence . . .* pp. 18-20.
72. Gaffiot, *op. cit.*, pp. 58 f and references ; cf. above, p. 210.
73. *Vie en fleur*, pp. 321-22, 432.
74. E.g., *Petit Pierre*, pp. 90-91, 138.
75. Quoted by Le Moy, p. 335.
76. *Sylvestre Bonnard*, p. 420.
77. *Livre de mon ami*, p. 384.

CHAPTER IV

1. *Livre de mon ami*, p. 318 ; cf. *Vie en fleur*, pp. 357-58.
2. Corday, *A.F.*, pp. 27-28.
3. Seillière, *Jeunesse d'A.F.*, p. 56.
4. *Petit Pierre*, pp. 225-35. M. Corday (p. 29) mentions another *institutrice*, Mlle. Doudet, who had been involved in a criminal law-suit.
5. M. Carias alludes to some unnamed 'aimables pensions du voisinage.'—*A.F.*, p. 11.
6. *Livre de mon ami*, pp. 277-84 ; *Revue d'hist. litt.*, XL (1933), 288-89.
7. Girard, pp. 59 f ; Huard, *A.F. et le Quai Malaquais*, pp. 17-18 ; *Petit Pierre*, pp. 245 ff.
8. *Ibid.*, pp. 246-53.
9. *Ibid.*, p. 277.
10. Kéméri, p. 54 ; cf. Corday, pp. 40-41.
11. *L'Univ. ill.*, Oct. 17, 1891 ; *Petit Pierre*, p. 268.
12. *Galignani's New Paris Guide for 1859*, p. 104.
13. Brousson, *Pantoufles*, pp. 181 f.
14. Huard, *op. cit.*, pp. 18-19 ; cf. Carias, *op. cit.*, p. 11.
15. E.g., *l'Univ. ill.*, Aug. 7, 1886. Also *Vie en fleur*, pp. 414-15 ; *Pierre Nozière*, p. 347.
16. *O. C.*, XXIII, 345 ff.
17. Corday, p. 43.
18. Guérard, *Five Masters of French Romance*, p. 52.
19. *Paris Guide*, I, 265-68.
20. Rambaud, *Hist. de la civilisation contemp.*, 6th ed., pp. 591-92 ; cf. *Vie en fleur*, pp. 346-47.
21. Du Camp, *Paris : ses organes, ses fonctions et sa vie*, V, 88-90.
22. Cf. Girard, pp. 59 ff.
23. *Petit Pierre*, p. 264 ; *Vie en fleur*, pp. 431, 435.
24. *Petit Pierre*, pp. 267-68.
25. *Pierre Nozière*, p. 340.
26. Girard, p. 81.
27. *Pierre Nozière*, p. 319 ; *Vie en fleur*, p. 354.
28. Brousson, *Pantoufles*, pp. 178-80. But see Girard, *op. cit.*, pp. 88-89 and Huard, *op. cit.*, pp. 18-19.

29. For a more recent account of this event see *Figaro artistique,* Aug. 1, 1927.
30. Brousson, *loc. cit.*
31. Cf. Michaut, *A.F.,* p. 303 and note ; Gaffiot, *Théories soc. d'A.F.,* p. 8.
32. *Livre de mon ami,* pp. 291-97.
33. Dufour, *l'Ecole et la Vie,* May 10, 1924 ; Pillet, *ZfFSL,* 1930, vol. 54, p. 11.
34. *O. C.,* III, 299-302.
35. *Institut de France. Académie française. Discours prononcés . . . pour la réception de M. A.F., le 24 décembre 1896.*
36. Le Goff, p. 215.
37. *Le Temps,* Aug. 6, 1886 ; Giraud, *op. cit.,* pp. 185-86 ; cf. Carias, p. 11.
38. *Le Temps,* Aug. 6, 1886 ; quoted by Giraud, p. 186, note 1.
39. Anon. [H. de Lacombe], *Centenaire du Collège Stanislas.* 1905. Chapter II (by Evian) concerns Lalanne's directorship (1855-71).
40. Gottschalk *ZfFSL,* 1927, vol. 50, p. 89, note 13 ; cf. above, p. 239.
41. *Livre de mon ami,* pp. 306-307. The passage first appeared in a tale ('nouvelle') called 'Le Stratagème,' in *La Jeune France,* Nov. 1, 1880.
42. Giraud, p. 186 ; Huard, *op. cit.,* p. 19 ; Carias, p. 11 ; and see below, note 48.
43. Taken mainly from Huard, pp. 18-19.
44. *O. C.,* XXIII, 368, 412, 358 ff, 287, 398-99, 374, 353, 315 ff, etc. Anatole is frequently off on dates.
45. Berton, *art. cit.,* p. 387. M. Berton speaks of this figure as 'Crottin . . . nom grotesque,' but I have been unable to find this form elsewhere.
46. *Vie litt., O.C.,* VI, 585-86.
47. *Vie en fleur,* pp. 412-13, 361-62, 318.
48. *L'Univ. ill.,* Sept. 6, 1884 ; July 11, 1885 ; Oct. 3, 1885 (cf. Oct. 17, 1891) ; March 6, 1886 ; cf. (on Chéron) Oct. 17, 1891.
49. *Ibid.,* Oct. 17, 1891, and cf. Sept. 30, 1893. Characterizations similar to the above (together with a more favourable opinion of Stanislas) had appeared in *Le Temps* (series called 'La Vie à Paris') during 1886. Cf. also Parigot, *Le Temps,* Oct. 29, 1924. Anatole seems to have made another recantation in 1904.
50. May 17, 1890 (cf. above, pp. 75-76) ; May 21, 1887 ; Oct. 17, 1891 ; Sept. 30, 1893 ; cf. *Vie litt., O. C.,* VII, 507, 594, 604.
51. *Vie en fleur,* pp. 417-26.
52. Morand, *Débats,* Oct. 15, 1924.
53. Letter from J. Calvet of July 1, 1915 (Collection Lion) ; *idem,* 'Enfances,' in *Les Lettres,* March 1, 1922, pp. 449-72.
54. Called *Souvenirs du Collège de Stanislas.*
55. Barthou, *Conférencia,* May 1, 1925, pp. 470-71 ; *idem, Rev. de France,* June 15, 1926, p. 617 ; Barthou and Calvet cite fully from the *Méditations ;* cf. *Le Temps,* Oct. 29, 1924.
56. *Mercure,* July 15 and Aug. 15, 1925 (p. 575 ; pp. 278-79). Volney spoke of his work as a 'Méditation.' The parallels between him and A.F. are developed in an article by Vaganay (see Bibliography).
57. Cf. Parigot, *art. cit.*
58. *Vie en fleur,* p. 364.
59. Cf. above, p. 59 ; *Vie en fleur,* p. 412.
60. Gsell, *Propos d'A.F.,* pp. 190, 60.
61. *Vie en fleur,* pp. 428-29.

62. *Le Temps,* August 6, 1886 ; cited by Giraud, p. 186.
63. *O. C.,* XI, 14-21.
64. Cf. Michaut, 'Préface,' p. vii, and Seillière, *op. cit.,* p. 11.
65. Wilson, *New Republic,* Oct. 24, 1934.
66. *Vie en fleur,* p. 427.
67. The education of Voltaire and of Montesquieu at such *collèges* would be cases in point.
68. *Le Temps,* Aug. 7, 1887 ; *Vie litt., O. C.,* VI, 253.
69. *Vie en fleur,* p. 445.
70. This was when the family was occupied with moving to the Quai Voltaire. Huard, *op. cit.,* p. 17.
71. *Livre de mon ami,* p. 310.
72. Girard, pp. 113-40.
73. *Vie en fleur,* pp. 405 ff ; cf. Huard, 'Origines de la *Cité des Livres* ou A.F. dans l'Avranchin,' *Normannia,* Sept., 1888, pp. 87 ff ; *l'Univ. ill.,* Nov. 10, 1883.
74. See above, p. 77.
75. *Art. cit.,* pp. 89-91.
76. As another example of France's economy regarding names, it may be mentioned that a character in *Les Dieux ont soif* is called 'Rauline.'
77. Cf. Girard, pp. 113 ff. He reproduces a sketch of Mme. Foulon, drawn by Anatole in 1858.
78. Cf. Hovelaque, *Rev. de France,* April 1, 1925, p. 560—'Avant tout, il était homme de lettres,' etc.
79. Girard, *passim ;* Brousson, *Itinéraire,* p. 190 ; Vandérem, *Miroir des Lettres,* VII, 224. Cf. Carias, *op. cit.,* p. 10 ; this view is however qualified in *Nouv. litt.,* Jan. 7, 1933.
80. As Huard has shown (*art. cit.,* pp. 92-95) the letter is lifted from E. Le Héricher's popular guide-book, *Itinéraire descriptif et historique du voyageur dans le Mont-Saint-Michel* (1st ed., 1857). A.F. makes few changes in wording. He also owned another such guide, now in the Collection Lion : Boudent-Godelinière, *Notice historique sur le Mont-Saint-Michel,* 2me. éd., Avranches, 1842.
81. Cf. chapter in the *Génie du christianisme* called 'Du Vague des passions'; and the well-known passage in *René :* 'Je descendais dans la vallée,' etc.
82. *Pierre Nozière,* pp. 347 ff.
83. *Livre de mon ami,* p. 310.
84. *Vie en fleur,* pp. 398, 296, 437. And cf. Berton, *art. cit.,* p. 392.
85. Barthou, *Bull. Officiel,* June 18, 1933.
86. Girard, pp. 71ff.
87. For references on these children, see *Vie en fleur,* pp. 296, 325-30, 362, 366-72, 397, and *Petit Pierre,* pp. 131-35, 118, 21-25, 251, 255-61.
88. Girard, pp. 141 ff. Much of Girard's material had belonged to Etienne before it passed on to his brother, Noël Charavay.
89. A.F.'s reference in *Pierre Nozière* (p. 347) to taking his baccalaureate at seventeen is fiction or fancy. He really got the degree on November 5, 1864. Cf. Carias, *A.F.,* p. 21 and illustration xxxii ; Shanks, p. 27 ; Seillière, *op. cit.,* p. 11.
90. Huard, 'Père d'A.F.,' *Bull. du Bibliophile,* March 1, 1925, p. 139.
91. *Pierre Nozière,* pp. 319-26.
92. *Le Temps,* Oct. 18, 1891.

93. *Pierre Nozière,* pp. 341 ff.
94. Ballaguy, p. 320 ; Anatole's portrait of La Bédoyère is reprinted in M. Kahn, *Père d'A.F.,* pp. 25-26.
95. *O. C.,* X, Ch. X : 'Les Deux copains' ; Ch. XI : 'Onésime Dupont.'
96. *Ibid.,* pp. 347-55.
97. June 9, 1894.
98. Michaut, pp. 197-98.
99. Similar moods of love-longing and exaltation in the midst of Nature are exhibited in *Petit Pierre,* pp. 93-94, 244 and *Vie en fleur,* pp. 324, 405-409, 441. Cf. Carias, *op. cit.,* p. 10.

CHAPTER V

1. *Le Crime de Sylvestre Bonnard,* pp. 271, 342.
2. *Nos Enfants,* pp. 67-75.
3. *Petit Pierre,* p. 57 ; Ségur, *Conversations,* p. 144.
4. Pellissier, *Nouv. essais de littérature contemporaine,* p. 340.
5. Ginisty, *Petit Parisien,* Oct. 13, 1924.
6. Ségur, *op. cit.,* p. 181.
7. Le Brun, R., *A.F., Biographie . . . suivie d'opinions,* p 25.
8. *O.C.,* XXIII, 281.
9. Cited in Ségur, *Dern. conversations,* p. 202.
10. Henning, ed., *Representative Stories of A.F.,* p. xvii ; cf. Dufour, 'Les Usagers de l'éducation.'
11. *Pierre Nozière,* p. 297.
12. E.g., *l'Ile des Pingouins,* p. 53 ; cf. above, p. 86 ; Lahy-Hollebecque, *A.F. et la Femme,* p. 36.
13. Turquet-Milnes, *Some Modern French Writers,* p. 132 ; Pellissier, *op. cit.,* p. 343 ; Baring, *Yellow Book,* April, 1895, p. 264 ; *Petit Pierre,* p. 221 ; Barthou, *Rev. de France,* June 15, 1926, p. 614.
14. Michaut, pp. ix, 119-22.
15. *Pierre Nozière,* pp. 283-84, 274.
16. *Ibid.,* pp. 268, 282, 292, 308, 309.
17. *Petit Pierre,* pp. 94, 17-18, 104-105, 111, 103, 144. Cf. the account of a 'horrible dragon,' which ornamented the passage of that name. *Vie en fleur,* p. 299.
18. Corday, pp. 16-17.
19. *Livre de mon ami,* pp. 193, 211-15, 221, 252.
20. *Ibid.,* pp. 242-43, 269-70, 312.
21. *Marguerite* (1920 ed.), p. 9.
22. Barthou, *art. cit.,* p. 609.
23. *Livre de Suzanne,* pp. 352-54. The poem appeared first in the *Poèmes dorés,* where it was called 'Ames obscures.'
24. *O. C.,* IX, 457.
25. *Livre de Suzanne,* pp. 395 ff.
26. Much of this argument is repeated in *Le Temps,* March 21, 1886.
27. *L'Univ. ill.,* Aug. 21, 1886.
28. Preface to R. Hesse, *Riquet à la Houppe et ses compagnons,* 1923.
29. *Le Crime de Sylvestre Bonnard,* p. 359.
30. E.g., in *Thaïs* and *Sur la Pierre Blanche.*

31. Pillet, p. 18.
32. *Marguerite, loc. cit.*
33. Bidou, *Comœdia,* Oct. 13, 1924.
34. Dirick, *Franciana,* p. 83.
35. Published first by Etienne Charavay, in 1883.
36. Anatole says elsewhere that in *Abeille* he deliberately used these two varieties of sprites — the 'Korigans' and the 'ondines,' (*l'Univ. ill.,* Aug. 21, 1886).
37. Henning, *op. cit.,* p. 2 ; Mrs. Lane's translation of *Abeille,* p. vii.
38. Michaut, p. 163.
39. The phrase was applied to Renan by Andrew Lang.
40. In the *Contes de Jacques Tournebroche,* pp. 91 ff.
41. Brousson, *Pantoufles,* pp. 162-63. A contrary view is maintained by Pellissier, *Rev. pol. et litt.,* July 21, 1894, p. 83.
42. Contrast the cold and selfish view expressed in *La Vie en fleur,* p. 532 ; cf. Henning, *op. cit.,* p. 203.
43. *Petit Pierre,* p. 237.
44. *O. C.,* VIII, 28.
45. *Pierre Nozière,* p. 266.
46. *Ibid.,* pp. 266-67.
47. *Petit Pierre,* pp. 237-38.
48. Much of this material was also in the *Vie litt.* (*O.C.,* VI, 620-22 ; VII, 20). Cf. *Le Temps,* April 23, 1893.
49. Bidou, *art. cit.*
50. *Pierre Nozière,* pp. 273-74.
51. *Livre de mon ami,* pp. 240-42.
52. Brousson, *op. cit.,* p. 44.
53. *RDM,* Dec. 15, 1896, p. 926.
54. Bellessort, *Rev. française,* Oct. 19, 1924, p. 428.
55. Carias, *A.F.,* p. 13.
56. Girard, pp. 47-48, 51.
57. This *Légende* has never been printed in full. Through the courtesy of M. Noël Charavay I was enabled to examine one of the few remaining calligraph copies.
58. *Conférencia,* May 1, 1925, pp. 468-70 ; cf. Morand, *Débats,* Oct. 15, 1924 and Halsey, *Le Journal,* same date (errors).
59. Cf. France's praise of Thierry's style, *Vie litt., O.C.,* VI, 227.
60. *O. C.,* IX, 400.
61. Deschamps, II, 229.
62. Ségur, *Conversations,* pp. 112, 165.
63. Michaut, pp. 100-101.
64. Brousson, *op. cit.,* pp. 141-44, 210.
65. *N. Y. Times,* Oct. 14, 1924.
66. *Livre de Suzanne,* pp. 364-66 ; cf. Ségur, *Rev. de France,* Nov. 1, 1929, p. 81.
67. May, p. 8.
68. Brousson *et al.* Cf. above, pp. 359-60, on the Chénier hoax.

CHAPTER VI

1. *Alfred de Vigny* (first ed.), pp. 85-86.
2. Champion, pp. 93-94.
3. Cf. articles on 'Les Dernières Echoppes' and 'Les Petites Industries,' *Paris Guide,* Vol. II, *passim.*
4. *Vie en fleur,* p. 526.
5. *Vie litt., O. C.,* VII, 403.
6. *L'Orme du Mail,* pp. 164-68.
7. In 'l'Expiation' (*Les Châtiments*).
8. Girard, pp. 159-61.
9. Ségur, *Dern. conversations,* p. 18.
10. Simone de Caillavet (Mme. Maurois), *Nouv. litt.,* April 19, 1924.
11. Corday, pp. 44-46 ; cf. above, p. 57 and references.
12. *Vie en fleur,* p. 415 ; Corday, *loc. cit. ;* Huard, *A.F. et le Quai Malaquais,* p. 19 (note 1). Cf. Pitollet's monograph (Bibliography).
13. Cf. a letter (of 1868) quoted by M. Kahn, *Le Père d'A.F.,* p. 16.
14. *Vie litt., O.C.,* VI, 446. On A.F.'s loafing and his lack of ambition during this period, see Vandérem, *Miroir des Lettres,* VII, 225-26.
15. *Vie en fleur,* p. 480.
16. *Ibid.,* pp. 485-93, 501-507.
17. *Ibid.,* pp. 479-80 ; 'Le Concours hippique,' *l'Univ. ill.,* March 30, 1895.
18. *Vie en fleur,* pp. 509 ff.
19. He discussed her in *Le Temps,* June 12, 1887 (*O.C.,* VI, 155-63) ; cf. Berton, p. 398.
20. *Vie en fleur,* pp. 480-82, 525.
21. *Ibid.,* pp. 445-47, 518 ; *l'Univ. ill.,* August 18, 1883.
22. *Vie en fleur,* pp. 458-68, 531 ; *Pierre Nozière,* pp. 357-65.
23. Huard, 'Père d'A.F.,' *Bull. du Bibliophile,* March 1, 1925, p. 134.
24. Carias, *A.F.,* pp. 19-20 ; cf. above, p. 76.
25. The work is in octavo, xvi + 685 pages ; interesting historical preface ; 3129 items ; cf. Kahn, *op. cit., passim ;* several documents, including the frontispiece, are here reproduced. There was another more general 'Catalogue raisonné' of La B.'s other books. This too is a fairly stout volume (over 400 pp., 2846 items). One copy (Collection Lion) shows prices marked in ink, presumably by Noël France.
26. Brugmans, *Georges de Porto-Riche,* p. 81 and references ; cf. p. 83. Carias, *loc. cit. ;* A.F., article in *Bibliophile français,* March, 1870, as reprinted by Kahn, *op. cit.,* pp. 2-5, 25-26.
27. Corday, p. 46 — cf. Le Goff, p. 241 ; *Le Bouquiniste français,* May 30, 1925.
28. E.g., Rod, *Rev. de Paris,* Dec. 15, 1894, p. 732 ; May, p. 59.
29. Girard, p. 153 ; Huard, *art. cit,* p. 138, note.
30. Cf. Carias, p. 21 : 'Laisser venir sera son grand secret.'
31. *Vie en fleur,* p. 481 ; *Le Temps,* April 11, 1886.
32. *Leconte de Lisle et ses amis,* pp. 298 f.
33. *Vie en fleur,* pp. 431-43.
34. Stewart, *A.F., the Parisian,* p. 38.

35. Carias, p. 29 ; Désonay, *Le Rêve hellénique,* p. 319 ; 'Nos échos,' *Nouv. litt.,* Oct. 18, 1924.
36. Lemerre, *Le Livre du Bibliophile,* p. 11.
37. In the sixties, however, the Charavay firm was in the Rue des Grands-Augustins, No. 26 ('ci-devant rue des S. Pères, 18').
38. Private information. He called Noël 'mon vieux coco.'
39. M. Tourneux et A.F., *Etienne Charavay, sa vie et ses travaux,* extrait de *l'Amateur d'autographes,* 1899.
40. Collection Noël Charavay ; cf. Huard, *art. cit.,* p. 137 and note.
41. *L'Univ. ill.,* May 4, 1889.
42. Cf. E. Charavay, 'Le Centenaire de 1789 et le Musée de la Révolution,' *La Révolution français. Revue historique, X,* 961-83 ; and above, p. 295.
43. Tourneux et France, *art. cit.,* pp. 3-5 ; Le Brun, *A.F. Biographie . . . suivie d'opinions,* p. 16.
44. The Preface to the Charavay *Catalogue* emphasizes that the two works are counterparts.
45. E.g., Mme. Lahy-Hollebecque, *A.F. et la femme ;* Borély, *La Femme et l'amour dans l'œuvre d'A.F.*
46. *Vie en fleur,* p. 432.
47. *Ibid.,* pp. 480, 526, 529-34 ('Marie Bagration') ; Pilon, *Rev. pol. et litt.,* Oct. 31, 1903, *passim ;* Corday, pp. 218-19.
48. 'Vie litt.,' Oct. 5, 1890 ; *Vie en fleur,* pp. 388-91.
49. Corday, p. 156.
50. Brousson, *Itinéraire,* p. 259.
51. *Petit Pierre,* p. 277.
52. Berton, *Nouv. litt.,* April 19, 1924 ; *Livre de mon ami,* p. 279.
53. Brousson, *Pantoufles,* p. 197.
54. *Vie en fleur,* pp. 547-56.
55. Private information.
56. *Chasseur bibliographe,* Jan., 1867, p. 23 ; *Vie en fleur,* p. 326.
57. *Grande Encyclopédie, s. v. ;* 'C. P.' in *Mercure,* April 1, 1927, p. 253 ; Samary, *Nouv. litt.,* July 21, 1934.
58. *L'Univ. ill.,* Nov. 19, 1887 ; *Le Temps,* Jan. 23, 1887 ; cf. *Vie en fleur,* pp. 383-93 and Huard, *Figaro,* Dec. 4, 1926. The details are a little 'arranged,' but the substance is true.
59. This recalls the disillusionment about Gérard's 'Psyche.' See above, p. 100.
60. *L'Univ. ill.,* June 29, 1889.
61. *Ibid.,* Sept. 20, 1884. A.F. says that he knew this actress 'twenty years ago'—i.e., about 1864.
62. Shanks, p. 24 ; Gautier, as quoted by Huard, 'Elise Devoyod et A.F., *Figaro,* Oct. 2, 1926.
63. Girard, Chs. VII and VIII. Material originally in the Charavay collection.
64. This would place his first glimpse of Elise in 1861.
65. Huard, 'Elise Devoyod et A.F.'
66. Exceptions are H. Bahr, *Studien zur Kritik der Moderne,* p. 143, and Edmund Gosse, who recognizes the 'yeasty condition' permeating the *Vie en fleur* (*Living Age,* Sept. 16, 1922, p. 726).
67. *Vie en fleur,* pp. 405-409.

68. *O. C.*, XXIII, 244.
69. *Vie en fleur*, p. 482 ; *Petit Pierre*, p. 61 ; Irving Babbitt, *Rousseau and Romanticism*, p. 79.
70. L.-X. de Ricard, *La Revue*, Feb. 1, 1902, pp. 302 ff ; M. Kahn, "Un Projet de jeunesse d'A.F.,' *Figaro*, Jan. 24, 1925 ; Girard, pp. 165-66.
71. The three influences are interwoven ; cf. M. Kahn, *Père d'A.F.*, p. 13.
72. This 'Prospectus et circulaire' appeared in the *Amateur d'autographes*, July 1 and 15, 1868. In condensed form, it was reprinted by Walder (as *Encyclopédie de la Révolution*, 4to., 1868). Both texts are found in Kahn, *op. cit.*, pp. 36-42.
73. Among his Parnassian friends, France would prick up his ears whenever the Revolution was mentioned.
74. Ginisty, *Souvenirs de Journalisme et de théâtre*, p. 178, note ; Anon., 'Une collaboration d'A.F.,' *Mercure*, Aug. 1, 1927, p. 763.
75. (*Revue des Revues*), July 15, 1903, pp. 175-92 ; with prefatory footnote by Ricard.
76. Lion, *Nouv. litt.*, June 2, 1934, and *Le Lys rouge* (periodical), July 1, 1934.
77. Cf. above, pp. 262 and 274.
78. Brousson, *Pantoufles*, pp. 192-93 ; cf. Stewart, p. 25.
79. *Gazette rimée*, June 20, 1867, pp. 75-78 ; *ibid.*, March 20, 1867, pp. 28-30.
80. Ricard, *art. cit.*, p. 314 ; cf. Schaffer on Ricard, *PMLA*, Dec., 1935, pp. 1191-99.
81. Some say Marshal Bazaine is indicated.
82. E.g., in 'L'Expiation' and in 'Sacer Esto.'
83. Calmettes, *op. cit.*, p. 297.

CHAPTER VII

1. Corday, p. 50.
2. See above, pp. 293 and 359 ff.
3. *Vie en fleur*, p. 436 ; *Jardin d'Epicure*, p. 455 ; cf. *O.C.*, I, 34, note 2.
4. Brousson, *Pantoufles*, p. 134.
5. Charpentier, *Mercure*, March 15, 1925, p. 605, note.
6. The derogatory remarks of France himself are quoted on the first page of the interesting monograph of Claude Aveline, *Sur l'Alfred de Vigny d'A.F.*— with facsimiles of Anatole's corrections and additions.
7. *Alfred de Vigny*, *O. C.*, I, 8.
8. *Alfred de Vigny, Edition revue et corrigée par l'auteur*. Publ. by Aveline, 1923 [1924] ; cf. *Chronique des lettres françaises*, 1924, pp. 145-46.
9. Alterations are given *in extenso* in Aveline, *Sur l'Alfred de Vigny d'A.F.* ; more briefly in *O. C.*, I, 7-116.
10. *Ibid.*, pp. 63-64.
11. Racot, *Chasseur bibliographe*, March, 1867, pp. 69-71 ; Vandérem, *Miroir des Lettres*, I, 47.
12. Racot, *art. cit.* ; *Le Temps*, Jan. 27, 1889 ; *Chasseur bibliog.*, Feb., 1867, pp. 51-52.
13. Peyre, *Louis Ménard*, pp. 333, 469, 509.
14. Carias, *A.F.*, p. 34 ; *Le Temps*, *art. cit.* and July 24, 1892.
15. Maurras, *A.F., politique et poète*, p. 15.
16. Martino, *Parnasse et Symbolisme*, p. 67 ; Charpentier, *art. cit.*, p. 594. Mendès and Ricard also edited the first volume of the *Parnasse*.

17. Souriau, *Histoire du Parnasse,* p. 408 ; Le Meur, *La Vie et l'œuvre de François Coppée,* p. 61.
18. A. Lemerre (the second), *Opinion,* Oct. 17, 1924, (he declares that A.F. was only eighteen, which is quite unlikely) ; Ricard, *La Revue,* Feb. 1, 1902, p. 302 ; F. Calmettes, p. 299. On Ricard's relations with A.F., see Schaffer's articles.
19. Bergerat, *Souvenirs d'un enfant de Paris,* II, 164 ; Gottschalk, p. 92 ; J. Roujon, *Vie et opinions d'A.F.,* p. 9.
20. *Op. cit.,* p. 2.
21. Berton, *Vie des peuples,* 1922, p. 386.
22. F. Calmettes, pp. 166, 304.
23. Souriau, p. 139 ; Bergerat, p. 165.
24. *Le Temps,* Sept. 16, 1888.
25. *Ibid.,* Oct. 30, 1892.
26. Flottes, *Le Poète Leconte de Lisle, documents inédits,* p. 170 ; Spronck, *Les Artistes littéraires,* p. 228.
27. H. Psichari, *Ernest Psichari, mon frère,* p. 69.
28. Mme. Demont-Breton, *Maisons que j'ai connues,* Vol. II, p. 129 ; Martino, p. 61 ; Flottes, p. 208.
29. Demont-Breton, p. 151 ; *Chasseur bibliog.,* Jan. 1, 1867, p. 19 — cf. Giraud, *Maîtres de l'heure,* II, 194 ; *Bibliophile français,* Feb., 1872, pp. 48-50 ; Carias, *op. cit.,* p. 31 ; and cf. Bonnières, *Mémoires d'aujourd'hui,* II, 332-33.
30. F. Calmettes, pp. 295-96.
31. Bourget, p. 153 ; *l'Intermédiaire des chercheurs et curieux,* Vol. XX (1887), p. 182 ; Demont-Breton (for portrait), *op. cit.,* pp. 129-39 ; cf. Souriau, pp. 372-75.
32. The article was published (1874) through the offices of Leconte de Lisle in a periodical of the Ile-Bourbon (now Réunion). F. Calmettes, pp. 210-18.
33. For a nearly complete list of A.F.'s friends (*c.* 1870), see Chevalier, pp. 147-48.
34. Gsell, pp. 165-66 ; Ibrovac, *José-Maria de Heredia : Sa Vie — son Œuvre,* p. 114, note 3.
35. *Ibid.,* pp. 119-20 ; *Le Temps,* Feb. 19, 1893.
36. Régnier, *De Mon Temps,* pp. 38-39.
37. *Le Temps,* Oct. 30, 1892. The article is a tribute both to Mendès and to the Parnassian technique. Régnier, *op. cit.,* p. 48.
38. *Amateur d'autographes,* Jan. 16, 1869 ; cf. Girard, pp. 162-63.
39. Monval, *Rev. de France,* May 1, 1924, pp. 179, 184-85.
40. *Ibid.,* pp. 178-79 ; A.F., *Le Temps,* Feb. 10, 1889.
41. Ibrovac, *op. cit.,* pp. 86-87.
42. Dufay, *Mercure,* June 1, 1927, pp. 324-52 ; Bersaucourt, *Au Temps des Parnassiens : Nina de Villard et ses amis,* pp. 7-8, 17, 134 ; Souriau, pp. 104-105 ; Estève, *Sully-Prudhomme,* p. 37 ; Le Meur, p. 33.
43. Dufay, pp. 336-39 ; Anon., 'Une Collaboration d'A.F.,' *Mercure,* Aug. 1, 1927, p. 763 ; P. Calmettes, *Grande Passion d'A.F.,* pp. 59-72.
44. Girard, pp. 197-215.
45. *Le Temps,* June 26, 1892 ; *Vie litt., O. C.,* VI, 611 ; Corday, pp. 51-52 ; Ségur, *Dern. conversations,* pp. 44-45 ; Gsell, pp. 253 ff ; cf. Champion, pp. 25-26.
46. Collection Lion. On all this cf. P. Calmettes, *op. cit.,* pp. 30-35.
47. F. Calmettes, p. 161.

48. Carias, 'Le Journal de Noël France' (followed by selections from the diary), *Grande Revue,* Dec., 1930, pp. 265-70.
49. *Vie litt., O. C.,* VI, 647-48.
50. Carias, *art. cit.,* p. 265 and cf. p. 267.
51 Corday, p. 54.
52. Cf. Girard, pp. 29-30 ; Huard, *A.F., et le Quai Malaquais,* p. 6.
53. Shanks, p. 32 ; F. Calmettes, *op. cit.,* p. 166. M. Girard (p. 232) assumes that this was in the post-war period ; but cf. Corday, p. 34. The letter is in Demont-Breton, p. 151. Cf. P. Calmettes, *op. cit.,* p. 143.
54. M. Kahn, *Père d'A.F.,* p. 16 and note ; Corday, pp. 48-49.
55. Brousson, *Pantoufles,* pp. 295-96.
56. Anon., *Collectors' Books on Many Subjects,* p. 13 ; an autograph inscription to the *Jardin d'Epicure.*
57. Le Goff, p. 130 ; Brousson, *loc. cit.*
58. Corday, p. 34 ; Barrès, *La Jeune France,* Feb. 1, 1883, p. 594 ; Girard, p. 227 ; Carias, *A.F.,* p. 23.
59. Desonay, *Le Rêve hellénique chez les poètes parnassiens,* pp. 365 ff ; Catulle Mendès, *Rapport sur le mouvement poétique français,* as cited by Martino, *op. cit.,* p. 91. Cf. P. Calmettes, pp. 19-20.
60. Leblond, *Nouv. litt.,* June 9, 1934 ; Estève, *Leconte de Lisle, l'homme et l'œuvre,* p. 237.
61. F. Calmettes, *op. cit.,* pp. 308-10 ; cf. Ibrovac, p. 97.
62. Bersaucourt, pp. 161-63.
63. F. Calmettes, pp. 307, 166-69 ; Bourget, p. 152.
64. *Le Temps,* Feb. 6, 1887 and Nov. 6, 1892 ; cf. *l'Univ. ill.,* June 23, 1894.
65. Bourget, p. 152.
66. Carias, *op. cit.,* pp. 23-24.
67. Monval, p. 183 ; cf. *Le Temps,* Feb. 10, 1889.
68. Demont-Breton, p. 153.
69. *Vie en fleur,* p. 391 ; *Le Temps,* Oct. 5, 1890.
70. Bonnières, pp. 329-31 ; transl. by May, pp. 54-57 ; cf. Lepage, *Rev. pol. et litt.,* Feb. 8, 1896, p. 191.
71. They are in the collection called *Poésies complètes,* 1904.
72. May, pp. 56 ff ; these date from about 1874.
73. Huard, *Normannia,* Sept., 1888, p. 97.
74. Girard, pp. 227-29.
75. *Bouquiniste français,* June 6, 1925.
76. Girard, pp. 217 f ; Barthou, *Rev. de Paris,* Dec. 1, 1924, pp. 481-90.
77. J. Roujon, *op. cit.,* pp. 8-9 ; Girard, p. 233 and private information ; Corday, p. 56 and Souriau, p. 383.
78. Calmettes, *op. cit.,* pp. 216-17.
79. Leconte de Lisle and Lacaussade were antipathetic ; cf. Corday, p. 55.
80. Barthou, *art. cit.,* pp. 486-87 and *passim ;* Souriau, p. 383. See above, p. 364.
81. Bourget, p. 150.

CHAPTER VIII

1. Clerc, *Le Génie du paganisme,* p. 100 ; Gouhier-Barrès, *Nouv. litt.,* May 14, 1927.
2. Corday, p. 99 ; Hovelaque, *Rev. de France,* April 1, 1925, p. 551.
3. *O. C.,* XXIII, 338, 460 ff, 449 ff, 411, 456.
4. His real name was Dubois-Dubé (Corday, p. 39) ; he should not be confused with the writer, Louis Dubois, who also knew the Thibaults. Cf. Huard, *Bull. du Bibliophile,* March 1, 1925, p. 136, and *Le Temps,* July 31 and Aug. 28, 1892.
5. Cf. Chevalier, pp. 92-96 ; Seillière, *La Jeunesse d'A.F.,* p. 75. Others who stimulated Pierre's taste for the antique were probably Jules Lacroix (cf. *l'Univ. ill.,* Nov. 19, 1887) and certainly Louis Ronchaud. See *Le Temps,* July 31, 1887 ; *Vie en fleur,* p. 442 ; Peyre, *Louis Ménard,* pp. 142-43.
6. *Livre de mon ami,* pp. 317-18.
7. *Le Temps,* Aug. 7, 1887. The passage about Thetis and Nausicaa is here repeated.
8. *Le Globe,* Aug. 7, 1879.
9. *Livre de mon ami,* pp. 303-308.
10. *Ibid.,* pp. 307, 397.
11. *O. C.,* X, 497, 491, 498, 334.
12. *Petit Pierre,* pp. 247-49, 79.
13. *Vie en fleur,* pp. 539-40.
14. *Ibid.,* pp. 457, 356, 543.—I learn elsewhere that this work was the *Dictionnaire des antiquités grecques et romaines,* compiled by Daremberg and Saglio. To this France contributed, in 1873, and again in 1881, three quite learned short articles on 'Agamemnon,' 'Cassandre,' 'Cécrops.'
15. Clerc, p. 117.
16. *Ibid.,* p. 98.
17. *O. C.,* IX, 393-94, 475, 504, 499.
18. *Vers les Temps meilleurs,* I, 35.
19. E.g., his Préface to *Machado de Assis et son œuvre litt.,* by Oliveira Lima and others (1909).
20. *O. C.,* XXII, 166-67.
21. Mme. Demont-Breton, *op. cit.,* II, 154.
22. Preface to Michel Psichari's *Index raisonné de la mythologie d'Horace,* 1904, pp. 7-8.
23. Crucy, *l'Illustration,* Jan. 7, 1922, p. 18.
24. *Les Contemporains,* VI, 375.
25. E.g., Michaut, *A.F.,* p. 57 ; Stapfer, *Humour et humoristes,* p. 158.
26. Blondheim, *Modern Philology,* July, 1916, p. 59.
27. A. Croiset, *Discours aux étudiants,* 1900, p. 21.
28. Cf. Invocation in the *Livre de mon ami,* p. 312.
29. Cor. *A.F. et la pensée contemporaine . . .,* p. 58 ; Doyon, *Conférence sur A.F.,* pp. 2-3.
30. The probable influence of Ménard upon A.F. cannot be discussed here. See Peyre, *op. cit.,* pp. 391, 511 (and refs.) ; Ibrovac, p. 249 ; *Jardin d'Epicure,* pp. 50-51. Cf. above, p. 451.
31. Lemaître, *Les Contemporains,* I, 131, 132-33, and *passim ;* cf. W. Stephens, *Madame Adam,* pp. 208-209.
32. Turquet-Milnes, *Some Modern French Writers,* pp. 138-39.

33. Plessis, 'À Anatole France' in *Poésies complètes,* pp. 110-11 ; Souday, *Livres du Temps,* II, 333.
34. L.-X. de Ricard, *La Revue,* Feb. 1, 1902, p. 306. Cf. Clerc, p. 97.
35. F. Lefèvre, *Une heure avec . . . ,* III, 160.
36. According to the *Chronique* in the *Revue de litt. comp.,* January-March, 1925, pp. 165 and 168.
37. Ginisty, *Petit Parisien,* Oct. 13, 1924.
38. Babbitt as cited by Blondheim, *art. cit.,* p. 60 ; Brousson, *Vient de Paraître,* Jan.-March, 1928, p. 5 ; Stewart, p. 78 ; Carias, *Nouv. litt.,* Feb. 25, 1933. Cf. Truc, pp. 16 and 47 ; Chevalier, pp. 201 ff.
39. Thibaudet, *NRF,* June 1, 1924, p. 735 ; Souday, *Nouv. litt.,* April 19, 1924 ; cf. Pierre Dominique, as quoted by Brousson, *art. cit,* pp. 1-2.
40. Gregh in *Le Lys rouge* (periodical), July 1, 1933.
41. Croiset, *loc. cit.* ; Poizat, *Muse française,* April 10, 1924, p. 375.
42. *Op. cit.,* pp. 101, 116, 118. (The passage on the 'Attic spirit' is cited from Michaut, p. 241.)
43. Amiot, *Rev. hebd.,* Oct. 10, 1925, pp. 131-46 ; cf. Cerf, pp. 98 ff, and Lanson, *Pages choisies d'A.F.,* 'Notice,' p. v.
44. Amiot, p. 146. Cf. Corday, p. 104.
45. This is the view taken by Professor L. B. Walton, in his (unpublished) study on 'Anatole France and the Ancient World.' My subsequent debts to this dissertation will be indicated by the initial 'W.'
46. *Livre de mon ami,* p. 317.
47. *Ibid.,* p. 318 ; Pouquet, *Salon,* p. 83. His copy of Sophocles (dated '1864') is in the Collection Lion.
48. 'La Rame d'Ulysse,' *Vie litt., O. C.,* VII, 562 ff.
49. Cf. Jean de Gourmont, *Mercure,* Aug. 1, 1927, p. 651.
50. By Lancelot and De Sazy. See *l'Univ. ill.,* Sept. 30, 1893.
51. May, p. 24.
52. Girard, p. 177.
53. *O C.,* XXI, 11. Further admiration for Longus is expressed in Ségur, *Conversations,* p. 53.
54. *Pages choisies d'A.F., loc. cit.* ; and *Annales,* Oct. 19, 1924. Cf. Verlaine, as quoted by Giraud, p. 204 ; this poet agrees with Lanson in emphasizing A.F.'s 'noble Alexandrian decadence.'
55. Lemaître, *art. cit.,* pp. 140, 145.
56. Ibrovac, p. 249.
57. Clerc, pp. 103, 106, 116.
58. Bidou, *Comœdia,* Oct. 13, 1924 ; Hovelaque, p. 574 ; Chevalier, p. 203.
59. Michaut, p. 54 ; Giraud, pp. 189-90, 207, 309.
60. Cf. Lanson, *l'Art de la Prose,* pp. 273 ff ; Chevalier, p. 206 ; Dubeck, *Revue critique des Idées et des Livres,* March-May, 1924, p. 192 ; and many others.
61. *O.C.,* I, 253-54.
62. Several critics apply the terms 'luminous' and 'radiance' to A.F.'s style.
63. May, p. 83.
64. June 19, 1892.
65. E.g., Ségur, *op. cit.,* p. 42 ; Brousson, *Pantoufles,* p. 321.
66. Stewart, p. 367. It is emphasized (by W.) that although France admired at a dis-

tance the stern virtues of the Republic, he is chiefly affected by those later Romans who came under the Greek influence.

67. Clerc, p. 99.
68. E.g., in *Le Jardin d'Epicure* and the treatment of passion in *Le Lys rouge*; also the character of Brotteaux in *Les Dieux ont soif*.
69. Brandes, *A.F.*, pp. 19-20.
70. Dirick, pp. 47-48.
71. *O.C.*, II, 303.
72. *Le Temps*, Jan. 5, 1875; cf. above, p. 159.
73. Brousson, *op. cit.*, p. 316.
74. *Le Temps*, April 18, 1886; quoted by Giraud, pp. 189-90.
75. See above, pp. 302-303; cf. Pierre's tribute to Spartacus (*Vie en fleur*, pp. 310 f) and A.F.'s Preface to *Faust*, *Rev. pol. et litt.*, Aug. 3, 1889, p. 149.
76. Ricard, pp. 314-16.
77. John Morley, *Life of William Ewart Gladstone* (1903), III, 19.
78. *O.C.*, III, 325 ff. Cf. *Vie en fleur*, pp. 405-409.
79. *Livre de mon ami*, p. 326, *cf. Vie en fleur*, p. 495; *Petit Pierre*, pp. 156, 33; Girard, pp. 82 ff, 115; *Le Globe*, July 24, 1879.
80. *Vie en fleur*, pp. 450, 338, 495 ff.
81. Maurras (Bourget-Pailleron, 'Le Jubilé d'A.F.'), *Opinion*, April 11, 1924.
82. *L'Univ. ill.*, Sept. 30, 1893.
83. *Mannequin d'Osier*, pp. 226 f, 262, 412-16. The real work by Jal is called *Virgilius Nauticus. Examen des Passages de l'Enéide qui ont trait à la Marine* (1843).
84. *L'Anneau d'améthyste*, pp. 107-13.
85. E.g., Brousson, *Pantoufles*, p. 285.
86. Other references may be found in *Æneid*, II, 23 and V, 72; *Georgics*, I, 28. Cf. Sellar, *The Roman Poets of the Augustan Age: Virgil*, p. 308, note 1; Prescott, *The Development of Virgil's Art*, p. 352.
87 *O. C.*, V, 355-60; *Jardin d'Epicure*, p. 423; *Sur la Pierre blanche*, p. 400; *Génie latin*, p. 247.
88. Cf. *Mémoires*, I, 93 (Biré ed.). But M. Giraud believes (*op. cit.*, p. 190, note) that Chateaubriand and France shared the same 'état d'esprit.'
89. *O.C.*, XXIII, 353; transl. by May, pp. 62-63.
90. *Ibid.*, pp. 246-47.
91. *Génie latin*, p. 145; other references to V. and myrtles are found here, pp. 7 and 247.
92. E.g., in *Jean Servien*, pp. 141-42; cf. above, p. 242.
93. *L'Ile des Pingouins*, pp. 156 ff.
94. *Op. cit.*, pp. vi and 226.
95. It is quite possible that Virgil's humanitarianism owes something to Lucretius, and that the two influences are amalgamated in France's sense of pity (W.).
96. Sellar, pp. 337-38.
97. Prescott, pp. 247-52.
98. Shanks, p. 29.
99. Sellar, pp. 305-306, 317 f, 417, 121, 84-85, 77; cf. Prescott, pp. 330, 167, 350.
100. France was aware of Virgil's 'derivative' character, as a collector of legends; cf. *l'Anneau d'améthyste*, pp. 109-10.

CHAPTER IX

1. *Chasseur bibliographe,* March, 1867, pp. 80-87. The poem (of about 280 lines) was signed in full. Although a footnote declared that the verses would form part of 'un recueil actuellement sous presse,' they have never been reprinted, and I do not know what collection is indicated — possibly *Statues et Bas-Reliefs.*
2. Italics ours. Cf. Provost, *Grande Revue,* Nov., 1921, pp. 16-55.
3. In 'La Fille de l'Emyr' (*Poèmes barbares*). I am indebted to Miss Jennie Shipman for this suggestion, as well as for the discovery of the Lacroix source.
4. See above, pp. 441 ff.
5. Six vols., Paris, 1851. Cf. especially Vol. I, pp. 133, 142-43, 175; Vol. III, pp. 69-76 and *passim.*
6. Shipman, (MS. study) *Some Sources of Thaïs: Novel by A.F.*
7. Cf. Bidou, *Rev. de Paris,* 1924, p. 210; Ricard (p. 311) speaks of these verses as 'more sensual than edifying'; Ibrovac (p. 223) suggests the influence of two of Musset's *Contes en vers.*
8. *O. C.,* I, 417-20 ('Bibliographie'); cf. Souriau, pp. 375-76.
9. *Re* the Gautier poem, see above, p. 163 f; on 'Diane de Noirlys,' cf. Ambrière, *Nouv. litt.,* March 21, 1931. Barthou (*Conferencia,* May 1, 1925, p. 459) adds three manuscript poems — none of them very good.
10. Among the fugitive poems thus added were 'La Perdrix,' 'Ames obscures,' and the two poems to Gautier. Among those found first in *Les Noces* were 'Leuconoé,' 'La Pia,' 'La Prise de Voile,' 'l'Auteur à un ami.' These four were restored to *Les Noces* in the definitive edition. For full details, see *O. C., loc. cit.*; cf. Giraud, p. 206.
11 It forms today a separate section in *O. C.,* I, 185-246.
12. *Ibid., passim* (for dating); Clerc, p. 100, note.
13. *Jardin d'Epicure,* p. 423.
14. *Le Temps,* Sept. 16, 1888.
15. *PMLA,* March, 1932, p. 281; cf. *ibid.,* p. 277; and Reynaud, *Muse française,* April 10, 1924, pp. 241 ff.
16. Schaffer, *art. cit.,* p. 273.
17. Mme. Demont-Breton, p. 132.
18. F. Calmettes, pp. 210-15, 170.
19. *Bibliophile français,* 1868, Vol. I, p. 41; Désonay, p. 351, and note 1.
20. I am informed that this confusion is in the Church tradition. France himself waxed ironic at the expense of the literalists who reproached him with the ambiguity — and took the same liberty in 'Læta Acilia' (*Balthasar, O. C.,* IV, 211-12); cf. Désonay, *loc. cit.*
21. Bidou, p. 208; cf. Giraud, p. 206.
22. Carias, *A.F.,* p. 32.
23. *O. C,* I, 411, note; Peyre, pp. 510, 512 and note; Michelet, *La Bible de l'Humanité.*
24. *Sur la Pierre blanche,* p. 435; cf. Souriau, pp. 376-77; Bidou, p. 209; Désonay, p. 352.
25. This had appeared in *Le Temps,* Jan. 5, 1875. (The theme is also developed in *A.F.'s* preface to P.-L. Couchoud's *Sages et Poètes d'Asie,* 1916.) He seems to have followed an article by Soury, *RDM.,* 1872.

26. Demont-Breton, p. 151 ; letter of Taine, as quoted by Pouquet, *Salon,* pp. 60-61 ; Maurras, *A.F., politique et poète,* p. 23. Seillière (*Jeunesse d'A.F.,* p. 101) is less favourable.
27. E.g., Ségur, *Rev. mondiale,* Nov. 1, 1924, p. 16.
28. See above, p. 72.
29. Cf. Vigny, 'l'Esprit pur.'
30. Maurras, *Nouv. litt.,* April 19, 1924.
31. Cf. G. Kahn, *Rev. blanche,* 1899, Vol. XX, p. 497. The critic finds France 'instruit et froid.'
32. 'Un Poème inédit d'A.F.,' *Rev. de Paris,* March 15, 1926, pp. 439-42. This original eulogy, 'À Théophile Gautier,' was destined for the *Tombeau* volume (1873), where 'Au Poète' actually first appeared.
33. As already said (p. 128), this is a reminiscence of gatherings in the Luxembourg and may be addressed to Frédéric Plessis.
34 Rod, *Rev. de Paris,* 1894, pp. 732-34 ; Michaut, pp. xii, 252.
35. Larroumet, *Etudes de litt. et d'art,* III, 190 ; Poizat, p. 371. Cf. Seillière, *op. cit.,* p. 97.
36. Mongrédien, *Rev. mondiale,* May 15, 1921, p. 187.
37. Those made for the 1920 edition are in the interests of simplicity, smoothness, and more fitting imagery.
38. E.g., Ricard, p. 311 ; Thérive, *Le Parnasse,* p. 130 ; Maurras, *op. cit.,* p. 10 ; *idem* (in Bourget-Pailleron), *Opinion,* April 11, 1924.
39. E.g., Désonay, Barrès, Thérive. Cf. Comtesse de Noailles, *Nouv. litt.,* April 19, 1924 ; Clerc, pp. 117-18.
40. Bainville, *Au Seuil du siècle,* p. 142 ; perhaps he comes nearer the mark in speaking (*loc. cit.*) of 'ces poésies languides et chartistes'— i.e., erudite.
41. Schaffer, *Parnassus in France. Currents and Cross-currents in Nineteenth Century Lyric Poetry,* p. 113 ; Lanson, *Pages choisies d'A.F.,* 'Notice,' p. viii.
42. Thérive, *loc. cit.* ; Vandérem, *Miroir des Lettres,* I, 45 ; L. Thomas, *Nouv. litt.,* Feb. 11, 1928 ; and see next note.
43. M. André, *Rev. hebd.,* April 26, 1924, p. 478 ; Mendès, *Le Mouvement poétique français de 1867-1900,* p. 159.
44. Vandérem, *Rev. de France,* Nov. 15, 1924, p. 365 ; Prévost, *Rev. de l'Université,* Nov. 15, 1924, p. 1200.
45. Gsell, p. 161 ; Maurras, *op. cit.,* p. 13.
46. Robert-Sigl, *Belles-lettres,* April, 1924, pp. 300-301.
47. *Op. cit.,* pp. 205-206.
48. Cf. A.F.'s 'Notes,' *Noces corinthiennes,* p. 402.
49. Aron, 'A.F. and Goethe,' *Studies in German Literature* (Univ. of Wisconsin Studies, Dec. 29, 1925) ; Rosenberg, 'Goethes "Braut von Corinth" in Frankreich,' *Archiv für das Studium der neueren Sprachen u. Literaturen,* Vol. 139, pp. 193-97 ; Fauconnet, *Mercure,* Feb. 1, 1927, pp. 521-28 ; cf. Anatole's later allusion to his sources in *Le Temps,* March 6, 1892.
50. A.F., 'Notes,' p. 405.
51. Cf. Gottschalk, p. 94 and note.
52. *Art. cit.,* pp. 735-36.
53. Cochin, *Vie catholique,* Nov. 1, 1924.

54. The Abbé Bethléem, *Romans à lire et romans à proscrire,* p. 81 ; cf. *Acta Apostolicae Sedis. Commentarium Officiale,* July 1, 1922, p. 379.
55. Mongrédien, p. 184.
56. Cf. Kéméri, pp. 103-104.
57. 'Leuconoé,' 'Prise de Voile,' 'Adieu.' Cf. Michaut, p. 72.
58. *On Contemporary Literature,* p. 170.
59. Even in *l'Ile des Pingouins ;* cf. Corday, ed., *Dernières pages inédites,* pp. 78-80.
60. Cf. Ahlstrom, *Le Moyen Age dans l'œuvre d'A.F.,* pp. 159-60 and references. This contention would be supported by several stories in *l'Etui de nacre* and by much of the *Vie de Jeanne d'Arc.*
61. E.g., André (*art. cit.,* pp. 478-79) thinks that France reaches here 'la perfection de son art' and dwells on the healthiness of his imagination.
62. Letter quoted by Ambrière, *Nouv. litt.,* April 23, 1932.
63. Désonay, p. xxv and cf. p. 62 ; Poizat, pp. 371, 373.
64. *Op. cit.,* p. 19.
65. Michaut, p. 31.
66. Bonnières, *Mémoires d'aujourd'hui,* II, 327 ; Souriau, p. 381 and references.
67. P. Calmettes, *La Grande Passion d'A.F.,* pp. 72-73 ; Reissig, *A.F.,* pp. 56-57.
68. *L'Univ. ill.,* Aug. 25, 1888.
69. Ginisty, *Souvenirs de Journalisme et de Théâtre,* pp. 174, 177-78 ; *idem,* in *Petit Parisien,* Oct. 13, 1924 ; cf. Simone de Caillavet, *Nouv. litt.,* April 19, 1924. For the casts, see *O. C.,* I, 421-23.
70. Corday, *A.F.,* pp. 150-51 ; Le Goff, p. 169 ; Souriau, p. 382.
71. Vandérem, *Miroir,* I, 46.
72. Michaut, p. 252 ; Prévost, *art. cit.,* p. 1205 ; Ibrovac, p. 249. Brugmans, (*G. de Porto-Riche,* pp. 82-85) would add that writer to the list.
73. Peyre, *passim ;* Désonay, pp. 62, 419.
74. E.g., André, pp. 481, 486.
75. Michaut, pp. 152 ff.
76. Cf. Ibrovac, p. 249 ; F. Calmettes, p. 210.
77. J. Tellier, *Les Ecrivains d'aujourd'hui. Nos Poètes,* p. 133 ; Mongrédien, p. 179.
78. Souriau, p. 377 and Michaut, pp. 152-53 ; Barrès, *A.F.,* p. 10.
79. Mongrédien, pp. 182-83.
80. Désonay, p. 419 and cf. Poizat, p. 373.
81. Vandérem, *art. cit.,* pp. 362-63 ; Prévost, p. 1205 ; Giraud, p. 203.
82. Michaut, p. 152.
83. Souriau, p. 379.
84. André, pp. 478-79 ; Vandérem, *Miroir,* I, 45.
85. Ascoli, *Rev. de synthèse hist.,* Dec., 1925, p. 171 ; but cf. Poizat, p. 371 ; and Maurras believes that France was the first Parnassian to put Racine in his proper place.

CHAPTER X

1. *Institut de France. Académie française. Discours prononcés . . . pour la réception de M. A.F. ; Vie littéraire, O. C.,* VII, 508.
2. Shanks, p. 30.

3. E.g., Pierre Champion in Lefèvre, *Une Heure avec . . .*, II, 71 ; *idem, Mon Vieux Quartier*, p. 206.
4. 'Vacances sentimentales,' *Rev. pol. et litt.*, Oct. 14, 1882, p. 490 ; quoted by Michaut, *A.F.*, p. 52. (Italics ours.)
5. *Vie litt., O. C.*, VI, 646 ; *La Société historique d'Auteuil et de Passy. Conférence faite . . . par A.F.*, p. 7.
6. Thérive, *Marianne*, Oct. 10, 1924 ; cf. Mauriac, *Le Roman*, pp. 96-97 ; Wilson, *New Republic*, Oct. 24, 1934.
7. Jullian, *Nouv. litt.*, April 19, 1924 ; cf. Truc, *A.F., l'artiste et le penseur*, p. 115.
8. E.g., in *Portraits in Miniature* (New York, 1931), p. 158.
9. *Opinions de Jérôme Coignard*, p. 460.
10. Cf. Gaffiot, *Théories soc. d'A.F.*, pp. 54, 59, 62.
11. *Vie. litt., O. C.*, VI, 5, 491, 444-45 ; cf. Gaffiot, *op. cit.*, pp. 48-51. I think that A.F. varied less in this artistic approach than M. Gaffiot would have us believe.
12. J. Roujon, *Vie et Opinions d'A.F.*, pp. 107, 113 ; *Mannequin d'Osier*, p. 381.
13. Chaumeix, *Rev. hebd.*, March 23, 1912, pp. 570 ff. The procedure is evident as early as *Les Désirs de Jean Servien ;* but Flaubert had already used it in *l'Education sentimentale.*
14. *Rev. de France*, 1925, p. 553.
15. Michaut, pp. 53-54 ; Gaffiot, *op. cit.*, p. 49. G. would add the Middle Ages.
16. *Guide artistique et historique au Palais de Fontainebleau ;* quoted by Giraud, p. 212. Cf. *Jardin d'Epicure*, p. 454.
17. Jullian, *art. cit.* ; Roujon, p. 118 ; Gaffiot, *op. cit.*, p. 96.
18. *A.F., critique littéraire*, pp. 55-58 ; and see above, p. 267.
19. *Amateur d'autographes*, April, 1868, pp. 278-79 ; quoted by Antoniu, p. 58.
20. By Miss Ahlstrom. See especially pp. 12-15, 154-55, 193-94, 76-77, 189, and *passim.*
21. Cf. Ernest-Charles, *Littérature française d'aujourd'hui*, p. 40 ; J. Roujon, p. 97.
22. Cf. the article on Gaston Paris, *Vie litt., O. C.*, VI, 570 ff.
23. Antoniu, p. 58 ; and her citations from the *Amateur d'autographes*, etc.
24. Private information ; F. Lefèvre, *Nouv. litt.*, April 19, 1924.
25. *Les Œuvres de Bernard Palissy, publiées d'après les textes originaux, avec une notice . . . par A.F.*, Paris, Charavay Frères, 1880 ; *Le Globe*, Oct. 9, 1879.
26. See, however, some later references in *Le Temps*, etc. ; above, p. 268.
27. Gaffiot, *op. cit.*, pp. 97-98.
28. Carias, *Chronique des lettres françaises*, 1926, pp. 216-18.
29. Ségur, *Conversations*, pp. 115-16 ; *idem, Dern. conversations*, p. 76 ; cf. above, p. 274.
30. The phrase is, 'grotesque and hateful' : Antoniu, p. 59 ; Wilson, *art. cit.*
31. Le Goff, pp. 11-12 ; J. Roujon, p. 238.
32. Antoniu, *loc. cit.*
33. Brousson, *Itinéraire*, p. 12 ; *Pantoufles*, p. 287.
34. Hovelaque, p. 567 ; P. Calmettes, p. 219 and *passim.*
35. Ségur, *Rev. de France*, Sept. 15, 1929, p. 237 ; repeated in *idem, A.F. anecdotique*, pp. 28-29.
36. *Amateur d'autographes*, May 16, 1896 ; quoted by Gaffiot, *op. cit.*, p. 35 ; cf. Antoniu, pp. 60-61.
37. *Vie litt., O. C.*, VII, 430 ; quoted by Giraud, p. 243.

38. Gaffiot, *op. cit.*, p. 34 ; Stewart, p. 359 ; Michaut, p. 54, note 2 ; Gottschalk, p. 91 ; Lemaître, *Contemporains,* VI, 373. Cf. Antoniu, p. 60.
39. Girard, p. 159.
40. *Amateur d'autographes,* 1869, p. 173 ; quoted by Antoniu, p. 60.
41. Stewart, p. 328 ; Jullian, *art. cit.*
42. Antoniu, pp. 60-62.
43. Gaffiot, *op. cit.*, p. 98 ; citing *Le Génie latin* (1913), pp. 273-74.
44. See above, pp. 101, 109 ff. Père France had published ten books on the period, including two by Louis Dubois.
45. Lanson, *Pages choisies d'A.F.,* 'Notice,' pp. iii-v.
46. Michaut, p. 57 ; cf. J. Roujon, p. 124.
47. *Chasseur bibliog.*, Feb., 1867 ; cited by M. Kahn, *Père d'A.F.,* pp. 33-35. See above, p. 109.
48. Giraud, p. 196 and note ; J. Roujon, p. 125.
49. Le Goff, pp. 252-53, 103, 64.
50. J. Roujon, pp. 125-26.
51. Summary by Gaffiot, *op. cit.*, pp. 100-101.
52. *Petit Pierre,* p. 10.
53. Brousson, *Pantoufles,* p. 175.
54. 'Avertissement' to *Le Génie latin* (1913), pp. i-iii. (Little is left of this preface in the *O. C.* edition, but this particular passage is kept.)
55. A somewhat more favourable opinion is expressed by Giraud, pp. 210, 213 ; and by Carias, *A.F.*, p. 36.
56. Especially in the cases of Marguerite de Navarre, La Fontaine, Racine, Prévost, Bernardin de Saint-Pierre, Chateaubriand and Lucile. Four of these articles had actually appeared in whole or in part, in periodical form. See notes by Carias, *O. C.*, XXI, 381 and *passim.*
57. Carias, *A.F.*, p. 39.
58. E.g., Giraud, pp. 214, 215.
59. France acknowledges, however ('Avertissement,' p. ii), omissions in the Racine article, and Carias shows that the *plaquette* on *Lucile de Chateaubriand* was radically revised (*O. C.*, XXI, 382, 385).
60. *Le Globe,* Oct. 2, 1879. The passage is deleted in *Le Génie.*
61. *Amateur d'autographes,* passage quoted by Girard, p. 158 ; Dirick, p. 24.
62. France had already collaborated (1881) on Charavay's edition of the *Fables ;* a number of his 'Remarques' in the present article are based upon Marty-Laveaux, *Essai sur la langue de La Fontaine,* a copy of which was in Père France's library. Anatole dealt with the fabulist several times — e.g., in *Le Temps,* March 8, 1891.
63. Lion and Marx, *Chronique des lettres françaises,* 1929, p. 169.
64. *Génie* (1913), p. 145 ; *Vie litt., O. C.*, VII, 687 ff.
65. Sellar, p. 7.
66. A.F., *Tableau de la poésie française,* in *Anthologie des poètes français, jusqu'à la fin du XVIIIe siècle,* p. 21.
67. Bidou, *Comœdia,* Oct. 13, 1924, and cf. *Rev. Rhénane,* Nov., 1924, p. 69 ; Ségur, *Rev. de France,* Sept., 1929, p. 237.
68. First appeared in the *Amateur d'autographes,* Oct.-Dec., 1873 ; publ. by Lemerre, 1874.

69. See above, p. 150. The phrase is exactly repeated in *Jean Servien,* p. 124. Not content with that repetition, France quotes the whole Dido passage again in the article on Sainte-Beuve, *Génie latin,* p. 302.
70. *Génie,* p. 145.
71. *Petit Pierre,* p. 275.
72. *O. C.,* I, 84 and *O. C.,* IV, 342.
73. Bauer, *Echo de Paris,* Oct. 8, 1925 ; Kéméri, p. 3.
74. Letters to P.-L. Couchoud, Collection Lion ; cf. Morand, *Journal des Débats,* Jan. 18, 1927.
75. Brousson, *Pantoufles,* p. 216.
76. *O. C.,* XXIII, 276.
77. *O. C.,* I, 53 ; Brousson, *Pantoufles,* pp. 36-37 ; letter to Couchoud cited above.
78. E.g., (*Génie latin,* pp. 100-101) his praise of the adjective in :
    'Par un chemin plus lent descendre chez les morts.' (*Phèdre*)
79. Bauer, *art. cit.* ; cf. Ségur, *Rev. mondiale,* 1927, p. 78.
80. *Ibid.,* p. 77 ; Brousson, *Nouv. litt.,* July 3, 1927.
81. *O. C.,* VII, 406.
82. Girard, p. 158.
83. Lanson, 'Notice,' p. iii.
84. *Génie,* pp. 243-44, 258-59.
85. *Amateur d'autographes,* April 16, 1868 ; cited by Gaffiot, *op. cit.,* p. 35.
86. Cf. Michaut, p. xii ; *Pierre Nozière,* p. 381.
87. Le Goff, pp. 137-38 ; but cf. Shanks, p. 101.
88. *Amateur d'autographes* (1868-69) cited by Gaffiot, *op. cit.,* pp. 35-36.
89. *Ibid.,* p. 37 ; *Discours aux étudiants* (1910), p. 34.
90. Gréard, p. 48.
91. Ségur, *Rev. mondiale,* Nov. 1, 1924, p. 16 ; Guérard, *Five Masters of French Romance,* p. 46 ; Gaffiot, *op. cit.,* p. 37 and references.
92. Gréard, p. 44.
93. Lanson, *Art de la Prose,* pp. 279-80.
94. Lahy-Hollebecque, pp. 6-7 ; Corday, p. 222.
95. See especially *Lucile de Chateaubriand* (*plaquette*), pp. xxii-xxxi ; *Génie,* pp. 273-76.
96. *Ibid.,* p. 289.
97. The following quotations (in the text) will be found in Girard, pp. 183, 177, 181, 179.
98. *O. C.,* I, 54, 46.
99. *Génie,* p. 312.
100. Part of this article had appeared (*Amateur d'autographes* and *plaquette*) in 1875 ; *O. C.,* XXI, 234, 376, 381.
101. Part of an unpublished letter quoted in *Rev. d'histoire litt.,* XL, 151.
102. *Génie,* pp. 243-44.
103. *Ibid.,* pp. 249-50 ; cf. Souday, *Le Temps,* July 15 and 16, 1913. It should be noted that Mme. de Caillavet claimed to have written this preface for *Adolphe* (Pouquet, *Salon,* p. 97).
104. These papers had been disinterred by Sainte-Beuve ; cf. *Rev. pol. et litt.,* July 19, 1879, p. 69.
105. *Lucile de Chateaubriand* (*plaquette*), pp. xi, xv, xxxviii, lv ; *Génie,* pp. 268-69.

106. In 1908 he praised the *Génie du Christianisme* to an Abbé (*Vie catholique,* Oct. 25, 1924); and see above, p. 292.
107. Brousson, *Pantoufles,* pp. 109-11; cf. above, pp. 11-12.
108. *Génie,* p. 18, note; *Sylvestre Bonnard,* pp. 375-76.
109. Brousson, *Pantoufles,* p. 175.

CHAPTER XI

1. Carias, *A.F.,* p. 35. See above, pp. 125-26 and notes.
2. Le Moy, p. 348; Le Goff, pp. 142-43. Their tombs are at Neuilly, by the side of their son. Cf. Champion, p. 190 (epitaphs).
3. Corday, pp. 34-35; *O. C.,* XXIII, 560.
4. Carias, *op. cit.,* pp. 37-38.
5. *Rev. des documents historiques,* July-August and September-October, 1879.
6. This *Journal* is quoted in *l'Univ. ill.* (Dec. 8, 1883), in connexion with the funeral of Mirabeau; it is also cited at some length in the article called 'Vacances sentimentales.'
7. *O. C.,* XI, 316.
8. See above, p. 273 and note.
9. Carias, *op. cit.,* p. 38; Mme. de Martel quoted in Pouquet, *Salon,* p. 57, note; Mme. Demont-Breton, pp. 157, 152; P. Calmettes, p. 145.
10. July 20, 1878 (Lion Collection).
11. P. Calmettes, p. 46; J. Roujon, pp. 11-12; Shanks, pp. 55-56; Dirick, pp. 13-15; Demont-Breton, pp. 155-56; Docquois, *Bêtes et gens de lettres,* pp. 74-80.
12. Missoffe, *Gyp et ses amis,* p. 74; Brousson, *Pantoufles,* pp. 98-99.
13. Ségur, *Dern. conversations,* p. 58.
14. Bonnières, p. 339; private information.
15. Demont-Breton, p. 161; *O. C.,* III, 186.
16. Pouquet, p. 55.
17. *Rev. pol. et litt.,* Oct. 14, 1882. See above, pp. 280-81.
18. J. Roujon, pp. 16-19; on the significance of the article, cf. Barthou, *Rev. de France,* June 15, 1926, pp. 609-11; and Bergner, *Nouv. litt.,* Oct. 18, 1924.
19. Pouquet, p. 76; Ségur, *Rev. de France,* Nov. 1, 1929, p. 81; J. Roujon, pp. 20-21.
20. Missoffe, *op. cit.,* p. 72.
21. Huret, *Enquête sur l'Evolution littéraire,* pp. 5 and 9.
22. *O. C.,* III, 361-66; and *passim.*
23. Cor, *A.F. et la pensée contemporaine,* pp. 49-50.
24. *L'Univ. ill.,* Aug. 22, 1885; cf. *ibid.,* Aug. 23, 1884.
25. *O. C.,* VI, 111-23. This novel was dedicated to A.F.
26. It was inaugurated, with some ceremony, on Aug. 15, 1927. M. Lomier delivered the principal address.
27. *Le Temps,* Aug. 15–Sept. 12, 1887 (see below, Ch. XIV, Note 8); *Pierre Nozière,* pp. 423-59. On Anatole's sojourn in this town, cf. Lomier, *A.F. à Saint-Valery-sur-Somme, passim;* also Fornand and Mouquet (see Bibliography).
28. Cf. Potez, *Rev. pol. et litt.,* Oct. 15, 1910, pp. 503-506.
29. *L'Univ. ill., passim;* he was almost certainly there in 1894.
30. *Ibid.,* Sept. 10, 1887.

31. *Gazette de Pierrefonds,* Sept. 21, 1884 ; *l'Univ. ill.,* Sept. 15, 1883 ; *O. C.,* X, 397-403.
32. *Le Temps,* Sept. 12, 1886 ; the visit occurred in 1884.
33. *Ibid.,* Aug. 14, 1887 ; *O. C.,* X, 407-22 ; letters in *Livres — Manuscrits — Dessins,* p. 90.
34. J. Roujon, pp. 12-13.
35. H. Roujon, *Au Milieu des hommes,* pp. 71 ff.
36. Léon Daudet, *Salons et Journaux,* p. 65 ; *l'Univ. ill.,* Oct. 31, 1891.
37. E.g., *Le Livre de mon ami, l'Ile des Pingouins,* etc.
38. Barrès, *Mes Cahiers,* I, 241 ; private letter from M. Grandjean. Ségur, too, later emphasized his 'merveilleuse et atroce clairvoyance' (*Conversations,* p. 15).
39. Guérard, *Five Masters of French Romance,* p. 44 ; Demont-Breton, p. 154 ; H. Cochin, *Vie catholique,* Nov. 1, 1924.
40. His appointment dated from August 3, 1876 (Lion, *Chronique des lettres françaises,* March-April, 1929, p. 145). On salary, cf. Shanks, p. 46 ; Coppée had received about the same amount.
41. To Catulle Mendès ; quoted in *O. C.,* XXIV, 397-98.
42. 'Gérôme' in *l'Univ. ill.,* Jan. 24, 1885 (cf. *ibid.,* Aug. 23, 1884) ; Monval, *Rev. de France,* 1924, p. 182.
43. Pillet, p. 14 ; Brousson, *Pantoufles,* p. 300.
44. He was evidently under Leconte de Lisle, who was 'conservateur.' Cf. Gsell, p. 42 ; Carias, *A.F.,* pp. 36, 39 ; Souriau, p. 139 and note ; Cerf, p. 13 ; Wassermann, 'A.F. vu par un Américain' in Lacretelle, *À la Rencontre de France,* p. 74 and A. Lemerre (the second), *Opinion,* Oct. 17, 1924.
45. *Rev. des Grands Procès contemporains,* July, August and September, 1912 ; cf. Le Goff, p. 134. The actual proceedings took place in the Palais de Justice, Oct.-Nov., 1911.
46. Le Goff, *loc. cit.*
47. Apparently, this is the article that finally appeared in the *Génie latin* — see above, p. 188. Cf. Dirick, p. 57.
48. Vandérem, *Miroir,* VII, 225.
49. See above, p. 265.
50. *L'Univ. ill.,* Jan. 24, 1885.
51. J. Roujon, pp. 29 ff ; Chevalier, pp. 144-45 ; Giraud, pp. 225-26.
52. Cf. Corday, *op. cit.* — chapter on 'Sa Modestie' ; Chevalier, p. 140 ; Ségur, *Conversations,* p. 173 and *A.F. anecdotique,* pp. 135-36 ; *Le Lys rouge* (periodical), Oct. 1, 1935.
53. It appeared in *La Jeune France* ('Les Hommes de la Jeune France. XIII. Anatole France'), February, 1883 ; reprinted as a brochure by Charavay, 1883 ; reprinted in part, with comment by Henri Gouhier, *Nouv. litt.,* May 14, 1927 ; cf. *ibid.,* Sept. 17, 1932.
54. Barrès, *op. cit.* (brochure), pp. 26-29 ; *idem, Annales politiques et littéraires,* Oct. 19, 1924 (posthumous) ; letters cited in Carias, *A.F.,* p. 43 and *Livres — Manuscrits — Dessins,* p. 20 ; cf. Brousson, *Nouv. litt.,* Dec. 27, 1930.
55. It first appeared in the *Rev. pol. et litt.,* Sept. 12, 1885 ; reprinted in *Les Contemporains,* II, 83-114.
56. Shanks, p. 74 ; Comtesse de Gramont, *Pomp and Circumstance,* p. 26 ; letter from Taine in Pouquet, pp. 62-63.

57. *L'Univ. ill.*, Jan. 10, 1885. Fallières, as Minister of Education, bestowed the honour, and A.F. was grateful; cf. J. Roujon, p. 64.
58. Ségur, *Rev. mondiale*, Nov. 1, 1924, p. 21.
59. Hovelaque, pp. 548-49.
60. *Art. cit.*, p. 607; Barthou adds, however, that A.F. avoided neither repetitions nor digressions.
61. Hovelaque, pp. 549, 550.
62. J. Roujon, p. 40; Blondheim, *Modern Philology*, July, 1916, p. 55.
63. Quoted in Pouquet, pp. 39-40, note.
64. Ségur, *Conversations*, pp. 23, 51; Du Bled, *Rev. illustrée*, September 1, 1887, p. 184.
65. Cf. *Les Opinions de Jérôme Coignard* — and of course the *Histoire contemporaine*. For a more detailed exposition of his political views, see above, pp. 303 and 422 ff.
66. *Nouv. litt.*, March 10, 1934.
67. Régnier, in Mille, *Nouv. litt.*, Oct. 18, 1924. Cf. Carias, *A.F.*, p. 71; Vandérem, *op. cit.*, pp. 242-43; Preface to *Marguerite* (Engl. transl., Lane, 1921). In *l'Univ. ill.* (April 30, 1892), A.F. explains his distrust of parliamentarians as gained from a close association with them during several years — presumably at the Senate Library.
68. Cf. Vandérem, *loc. cit.*; J. Roujon, p. 27; Dirick, p. 16; Pouquet, p. 87.
69. *L'Univ. ill.*, Jan. 10, Feb. 21, 1885. Cf. above, pp. 394 f; Du Bled, *La Société française depuis cent ans*, II, 188-91; Henriot, *Le Temps*, May 8, 1926; Chevalier, p. 152, note.
70. Cf. Du Bled, *op. cit.*, pp. 158, 159, 175; Galantière, *The N.Y. World*, May 1, 1927; Ségur, *Conversations*, pp. 120-24; Shanks, p. 93; Vandérem, *op. cit.*, p. 232.
71. The authoress' defence of the lack of dates may be found in *The New Republic*, March 7, 1928.— The English translation of the book bears the title of *The Last Salon*.
72. Cf. Galantière, *art. cit.*; Montfort, *Vingt-cinq ans de littérature française*, II, 174-76; Rascoe, *New Republic*, March 16, 1927; Henriot, *art. cit.*; Princess Radziwill, *The Forum*, Dec., 1924, pp. 826-27; Seillière, *Jeunesse d'A.F.*, p. 209.— Some of these references are subject to caution.
73. At the time of the purchase and for several years thereafter, this was known as the Avenue de la Reine-Hortense.
74. As above, note 72; Maurel, *Souvenirs de littérature*, in *Les Œuvres libres*, Vol. 44, pp. 358-61; on their relations, cf. Mme. Scheikévitch, *Time Past*, pp. 70-75.
75. Robert de Flers, in 'Préface' to Pouquet, p. i; *ibid.*, pp. 38 ff; Henriot, *art. cit.*
76. Pouquet, *passim*; Carias, *A.F.*, pp. 54-55.
77. Cf. Brousson, *Itinéraire*, p. 257; Carias, *loc. cit.*, Reissig, *A.F.*, p. 122.
78. 'Gyp' in Pouquet, pp. 39-40, note.
79. Carias, *A.F.*, p. 53.
80. Shanks, pp. 97, 98; see above, p. 383.
81. Cf. Du Bled, pp. 188, 192, 233 and *passim*; Pouquet, pp. 50-54; Henriot, *art. cit.*; *l'Univ. ill.*, April 20, 1889.
82. Maurel, p. 358; Daudet, pp. 15-19, 88-89.
83. Pouquet, pp. 47-48; A. Meyer, *Ce que je peux dire*, p. 154 and *passim*; Barrès, letters in *Rev. d'hist. litt.*, XL, 154; Cerf, p. 20. On Lemaître and

Loynes, see Scheikévitch, *op. cit.,* pp. 113-53; and A. Hermant, *Souvenirs,* pp. 161-64.

CHAPTER XII

1. Gottschalk, pp. 96, 100. This writer holds that the next decade (1881-90) is the first of France's *Hauptepochen;* it is characterized by tolerant kindliness and humour.
2. Carias, *A.F.,* p. 44.
3. See above, pp. 275 ff; also pp. 331-32.
4. *Vie litt., O. C.,* VII, 293.
5. *Vie en fleur,* pp. 509-10.
6. Flottes, *Le Poète Leconte de Lisle,* p. 157 (citing Fusil); Stewart, p. 48; *Vie litt., O. C.,* VII, 64-67; Ségur, *A.F. anecdotique,* pp. 140-41 and *Dern. conversations,* p. 217; Mornet, *Rev. du mois,* July 10, 1911, pp. 62-63.
7. Ségur and Mornet, as above; also Ségur, *Rev. de France,* Sept. 15, 1929, pp. 247-48.
8. Ségur, *Dern. conversations,* pp. 218-19; Sherman, *On Contemporary Literature,* p. 186.
9. *Discours aux étudiants,* Dec. 1, 1895, pp. 118-19; cf. Gouhier-Barrès, *Nouv. litt.,* May 14, 1927.
10. Cf. above, pp. 275 ff; *Le Temps,* April 14, 1876.
11. Gaffiot, *Théories soc. d'A.F.,* p. 38.
12. Michaut, *A.F.,* pp. 73, xiv-xv, 49, 56 and note 6; Bonnières, p. 336; Gsell, p. 158.
13. Pouquet, *Salon,* pp. 60-63; *Livres — Manuscrits — Dessins,* p. 127; Shanks, p. 50.
14. *Le Temps,* March 12, 1893; quoted by Giraud, p. 191, who wrongly dates the article '1913.'
15. 'Préface' to first edition of *Jean Servien* (1882), p. v; Barrès, *A.F.* (brochure), p. 23; Shanks, p. 51; Giraud, pp. 217-18. Rod (*Rev. de Paris,* Dec. 15, 1894, pp. 741-42) says the work was composed just after the Commune.
16. Pillet, p. 17; Barrès, *loc. cit.,* quoted by Carias, *A.F.,* p. 43; Michaut, p. 106.
17. Gottschalk, *art. cit.,* pp. 98-99; Coulon, *Témoignages,* II, 190; Giraud, p. 218; Pellissier, *Rev. pol. et litt.,* July 21, 1894, p. 81.
18. Michaut, pp. 76-79, 288-90; Bourget, p. 158.
19. Giraud, *loc. cit.;* Carias, *Nouv. litt.,* Feb. 25, 1933; Coulon, *Témoignages,* I, 124.
20. Seillière, *Jeunesse d'A.F.,* p. 20; Lemaître, *Contemporains,* II, 88. But A.F. says ('Autobiographie,' *Rev. de France,* 1924, p. 8) that the elder Servien was not like the elder Thibault.
21. *Loc. cit.* Garneret emphasizes this same point regarding his friend, Servien.
22. Michaut, p. 79 and references.
23. Cf. Bourget, p. 152: 'France a bien compris ce qu'il a dû aux braves gens qui entourèrent son enfance et sa jeunesse.'
24. Corday, *A.F.,* p. 53.
25. *Op. cit.,* pp. 73, 79; cf. *Vie litt., O. C.,* VI, 166 f. On the Coignard-Dufour hypothesis, see Seillière, *op. cit.,* pp. 21, 37-38.
26. *O. C.,* VI, 611; cf. Ségur, *Dern. conversations,* pp. 44-45.
27. E.g., on June 30, 1888; cf. above, p. 302.

28. *Vie litt., O. C.,* VII, 555. Reissig (*A.F.,* p. 36) thinks that Jean's adolescence was like that of Daudet's 'Jack.' Cf. above, p. 249.
29. Lemaître, *op. cit.,* pp. 88-89. The 'desires' and the general situation of the hero are very similar to those of Hyacinthe Robinson in Henry James' *The Princess Casamassima.*
30. *O. C.,* XXIII, 557-58 ; *ibid.,* pp. 61, 232, 272-73 ; Michaut, p. 313 ; cf. Seillière, *op. cit.,* p. 56 and Reissig, p. 158.
31. See above, p. 105 and references ; *l'Univ. ill.,* Sept. 19, 1885.
32. *Grande Encyclopédie,* s. v.
33. Huard, *Figaro,* Oct. 2, 1926 ; cf. *Le Temps,* Jan. 23, 1887 ; but the epithet of 'grande perche' is transferred by M. Huard from Isabelle Constant to Elise.
34. *L'Univ. ill.,* June 9, 1883.
35. Cf. the character of Chevalier in *Histoire comique.*
36. Brousson, *Pantoufles,* p. 208. This becomes a *motif* and a *cliché.*
37. *O. C.,* XXIII, 256-57 ; cf. above, pp. 74-75.
38. Cf. Gottschalk, p. 96 ; Michaut, p. 253.
39. Michaut, *loc. cit. ;* Wyzewa, *Nos Maîtres,* p. 219 (quoting original preface to *Jocaste*) ; Pellissier, *art. cit.,* p. 81 ; autograph inscription quoted in *Collectors' Books,* p. 13. In his original 'Lettre-Préface à Charles-Edmond,' A.F. spoke of the tale as an 'histoire scélérate . . . pleine de trouble et de violence.'
40. Anatole had previously revealed his acquaintance with the bathing-boat of 'La Belle Samaritaine.' A similar suicide-*motif* is found later in 'l'Œuf rouge,' (*O. C.,* IV).
41. Michaut, p. 138. He styles the work the 'worst sort of *roman-feuilleton.*'
42. Stewart, pp. 46-47.
43. Michaut, p. 73 and Bonnières, *loc. cit. ;* Gaffiot, *Théories d'A.F. sur l'org. soc. de son temps,* p. 11.
44. Boillot, *l'Humour d'A.F.,* p. 6.
45. Michaut, pp. 254, 156-58.
46. 'Préface' of 1879, p. iv ; above, pp. xxi, 294 and 357 ; cf. Delattre, *Dickens et la France,* pp. 122-23.
47. Boillot, p. 22 ; Darmesteter, *Contemp. Review,* LXXV (1899), 802 ; Courtney, *The Bodleian,* Jan., 1921.
48. Cf. Baldensperger, *Etudes d'hist. litt.,* I, 176-222.
49. Boillot, pp. 6, 22-23 ; Stapfer, *Humour et humoristes,* pp. 172-73 ; Chevalier, p. 47 ; Larroumet, *Etudes de litt. et d'art,* III, 191.
50. Cf. Barrès, *op. cit.,* p. 27.
51. *Le Globe,* Sept. 4, 1879 (cited by Michaut, p. 59, note 1) ; Fontaine de Resbecq, *Voyages littéraires sur les Quais de Paris,* p. 187.
52. Others are *La Cicogne, La Truie qui file,* etc. ; see *l'Univ. ill.,* Jan. 8 and April 16, 1887.
53. Lemaître, *op. cit.,* pp. 93-94, 97 ; Gsell, pp. 245-48 ; Schaffer, *PMLA,* March, 1932, p. 268.
54. Potez, *Mercure,* March 1, 1910, p. 11 ; Michaut, p. 158. The latter thinks (pp. 253-55) that the *procédés* of Dickens are again imitated.
55. Pillet, *art. cit.,* p. 17.
56. 'Préface' of 1879, pp. iii-iv ; Michaut, p. 19.

57. *A.F., critique de son temps,* p. 9.
58. Several other fragments, including 'La Fée,' had appeared in the *Rev. alsacienne,* 1879-80. Cf. Carias, *A.F.*, p. 41 and *idem,* in *O. C.*, II, 512.
59. Cf. Carias, *A.F.*, p. 65 ; Henriot, *Livres et portraits,* I, 297 ; Cerf, p. 23. Calmann-Lévy had vainly urged France to write a third episode in order to fill out the volume.
60. Michaut, pp. 159-60.
61. Huard, *A.F. et le Quai Malaquais,* pp. 23-24.
62. Le Héricher, *Itinéraire descriptif et historique du voyageur dans le Mont-Saint-Michel,* p. 15 ; see Huard, *Normannia,* Sept., 1898, pp. 86, 95 ; cf. above, p. 73.
63. Larroumet, p. 195 ; Barrès, *op. cit.*, p. 19 ; Reissig, p. 189.
64. Potez, *art. cit.*, pp. 8-9.
65. Maccone, *Nuova Antologia,* March 1, 1927, pp. 120-23 ; cf. Bédarida, *Rev. des cours et conférences,* May 15, 1926, p. 284. Huard ('Sylvestre Bonnard et la Légende Dorée' in *Les Trésors des Bibliothèques de France,* IX, 25-40) accepts in part Maccone's suggestions, but adds other sources for A.F.'s composite 'Polizzi' as well as for his knowledge of Naples, etc.
66. *Ibid.*, pp. 27-29 ; cf. pp. 38-40.
67. *Miroir des Lettres,* VII, 228 ; for other possibilities cf. Mornet, *Nouv. litt.*, July 3, 1926.
68. Cor, *Mercure,* July 1, 1920, p. 95, note ; cf. Lemaître, *op. cit.*, p. 106.
69. Mornet, *Nouv. litt.*, July 3, 1926 ; he is supported by Van Roosbroeck, *MLN,* April, 1922, p. 249. Michaut, *op. cit.*, p. 160 ; Potez, p. 14.
70. Giraud, p. 211 ; on the *pro* and *con* of Anatole's erudition, see Michaut, p. 55 and notes.
71. G. Kahn, *Rev. blanche,* XX (1899), 498-99 ; Lanson, *Pages choisies d'A.F.*, 'Notice,' p. xiii.
72. Lemaître, *op. cit.*, pp. 95, 101 ; Gouhier-Barrès, *art. cit.* ; Taine in Pouquet, pp. 62-63.
73. *O. C.*, II, 375-76 ; cf. *l'Univ. ill.*, Feb. 16, 1884 and above, p. 275.
74. Lemaître, *op. cit.*, p. 105 ; Mornet, *Rev. du mois,* July 10, 1911, p. 73 ; Huard, *Bull. du Bibliophile,* March 1, 1925, p. 138.
75. *Nouv. litt.*, Jan. 7, 1933.
76. Lahy-Hollebecque, p. 33 ; Bourdelle, *Rev. Rhénane,* Nov., 1924, p. 72. The sculptor says, in effect, that *Bonnard* lighted his youth like a beacon.
77. Seillière (*Jeunesse,* pp. 120-21), shows links with Pierre's own youth.
78. Gottschalk, p. 97 ; Lemaître, *op. cit.*, pp. 102-103, 114 ; Pellissier, *art. cit.*, p. 82.
79. Report quoted by Giraud, p. 220 and note 2 ; Lemaître, *op. cit.*, p. 96 ; Gouhier-Barrès, *art. cit.*
80. Vandérem, *op. cit.*, p. 224.
81. Brousson, *Pantoufles,* p. 352.
82. On Jan. 10 and March 7, 1885 ; cf. above, p. 295.
83. 'Postface' to *Vie en fleur,* p. 560 ; *Vie litt., O. C.*, VI, 283 (*Le Temps,* Oct. 23, 1887).
84. Shanks, pp. 67, 87 ; Michaut, *op. cit.*, p. 240 and references ; cf. above, pp. 338 and 620-23.
85. Cf. above, Introduction, p. xxi.
86. *O. C.*, III, 309-10 ; *David Copperfield,* Ch. XVIII.

87. 1920 edition, p. 25.
88. Lemaître, *op. cit.*, pp. 107-108.
89. Carias, in *O. C.*, IV, 353-54.
90. E.g., Noussanne, *A.F., philosophe sceptique*, p. 38.
91. Cf. Mlle. de Doucine in *Jacques Tournebroche*.
92. Barthou, *Rev. de France*, June 15, 1926, p. 609 ; Pellissier, *art. cit.*, p. 83.
93. First appeared in *Les Lettres et les Arts*, December, 1886. It was reprinted in 1920 by André Coq. I cite from this edition.
94. *Débats*, March 2-16, 1884. Full details given by Carias in *O. C.*, V, 478-80 ; his information is copied (without acknowledgement) in an anonymous article in *Nouv. litt.*, Nov. 28, 1925. A. Chénier, *Œuvres en prose* (ed. Moland, 1879), p. 73.
95. Anon., *Nouv. litt.*, *art. cit.* ; Carias, *A.F.*, p. 47.
96. Ambrière, *Nouv. litt.*, April 30, 1932. M. Claude Aveline seems to have perpetrated the hoax.
97. In *Vogue parisienne*, Aug. 19, 1870 and in *Amateur d'autographes*, Nov.-Dec., 1873, pp. 176-79.
98. Huard, *Mercure*, June 15, 1928, pp. 600-615 ; Henriot, *Le Temps*, Jan. 15, 1931. A.F. also used the *Journal* of Grace Elliott.—I am indebted to Miss Grace Sproull for research on various points connected with *Les Autels*.
99. *Débats*, March 2, 1884 ; cited in *O. C.*, V, 480.
100. *Ibid.*, pp. 482-96.
101. Ambrière, *Nouv. litt.*, April 16, 1932.
102. *Les Dieux*, pp. 99-100.
103. Referred to in *ibid.*, p. 6. Gamelin belongs to the 'section Pont-Neuf,' *ci-devant* Henri IV.
104. *Lucile de Châteaubriand* (*plaquette*), pp. xxxi-xxxiv.
105. Cf. *Les Dieux*, pp. 189, 274.
106. *Ibid.*, pp. 8, 10, 12 and *passim*.
107. Ségur, *A.F. anecdotique*, p. 126 ; *idem*, *Dern. conversations*, pp. 205-206 ; Brousson, *Itinéraire*, pp. 3-4 ; cf. Vandérem, *op. cit.*, p. 242.

CHAPTER XIII

1. Preface to *Vie litt.*, *O. C.*, VI, 11.
2. Antoniu, *A.F., critique littéraire*, p. 41. I am indebted to this volume for material on the bibliographical journals. But the authoress omits from consideration *Le Globe*, *La Revue illustrée*, and the important *Univers illustré*.
3. Corday, p. 160 ; Pillet, p. 19.
4. Antoniu, p. 53.
5. G. Picard, *Renaissance pol., litt. et artistique*, Oct. 18, 1924, p. 13.
6. He is referring to Asselineau's *Bibliothèque romantique* (1866).
7. Antoniu, p. 49, note ; *Manuscrit autographe*, March-April, 1928, pp. 72-73.
8. *Chasseur bibliog.*, February, 1867, pp. 35-37 ; see above, p. 41.
9. On Sept. 17, 1869 ; cf. Carias, *Gde. Revue*, Dec., 1930, p. 266 and note.
10. *Op. cit.*, pp. 52-65. She also gives in her 'Bibliographie' (pp. ix-xii) a full list of A.F.'s contributions to these journals.
11. *Vie litt.*, *O. C.*, VI, 446.

12. Tourneux et France, *Etienne Charavay, sa vie et ses travaux*. Extrait de *l'Amateur d'autographes,* 1899, p. 4.
13. 'Vie litt.,' *Le Temps,* Dec. 19, 1889.
14. *Bibliophile français,* June, 1870, p. 122. Cited by Antoniu, pp. 37-38.
15. Cf. Michaut, pp. 193-216.
16. Antoniu, p. 65.
17. Cf. *Bibliophile français,* Feb. 15, 1872, pp. 48-50.
18. Ségur, *Rev. de France,* Sept., 1929, p. 248 ; *O. C.,* XXIV, 154.
19. *Rev. des documents hist.,* July-Sept., 1873, and *ibid.,* Jan.-Feb., 1874. The article on 'La Fauconnerie' was done in collaboration with Fernand Calmettes.
20. In his Introduction to Mme. de La Fayette's *Henriette d'Angleterre.* See above, pp. 281-82. On the attribution of this article to A.F., see *O. C.,* XXIV, 374.
21. July-August and Sept.-Oct., 1879.
22. *Le Temps,* April 18, 1876.
23. *Ibid.,* Nov. 24, 1875.
24. June 27, 1877. I cite after Maurice Kahn's résumé, in his *A.F. et Emile Zola,* pp. 53-62.
25. Other early articles in *Le Temps* are as follows : 'Les Femmes d'Horace,' Jan. 5, 1875 (repeated in part, as a note to 'Leuconoé'— see above, p. 160) ; 'Romanciers contemporains : Ivan Tourgueneff,' Jan. 15 and 16, 1877 ; 'Romanciers contemporains : Ferdinand Fabre,' June 12, 15, 1878 ; 'Les Poètes contemporains : M. Sully Prudhomme,' Jan. 1, 1878 (the chief points here are mostly repeated in later articles on this poet). There was also, in 1879, a series of brief notices on other contemporary poets ; see J. Roujon, p. 11.
26. They appeared under various headings in *Le Globe,* July 24-Oct. 30, 1879.
27. *Ibid.,* Aug. 7.
28. *Ibid.,* Aug. 21.
29. *Ibid.,* Aug. 15.
30. Brousson, *Pantoufles,* p. 140.
31. Vol. II, 1879.
32. *Ibid.,* Vol. V (1883), pp. 589-610. This was republished as a brochure — *see* Bibliography.
33. See Thibaudet, *Nouv. litt.,* Sept. 17, 1932. I am also indebted to Professor W. S. Hastings and one of his students for some material concerning this journal.
34. *La Jeune France,* Vol. I (1878), pp. 241-49.
35. Michaut, p. 196.
36. *La Jeune France,* III (1881), 533-45 ; and V (1882), 457-63.
37. See for details Lion and Marx, 'A.F. et Madame de la Sablière' ; the various redactions of this article-type are interestingly collated. Cf. also *O. C.,* XXIV, 5-27, 370-72.
38. F. Gaiffe, *l'Envers du grand siècle, étude hist. et anecdotique,* 1924.
39. *La Jeune France,* II (1880), 368-70, 406-10, 444-48. The title of the second article, 'La Terre et l'homme,' was later used for France's epilogue to Hesiod, *Les Travaux et les Jours* (tr. Mazon, 1912).
40. *La Jeune France,* IV (1881), p. 133.
41. Vol. IV (1882), 388-97.
42. J. Roujon, pp. 30-31.
43. These appeared on the covers of the magazine ; they were signed simply 'A.F.'

44. *Les Lettres et les Arts,* February, 1886.
45. *Ibid.,* April, 1886.
46. *Ibid.,* May, 1886.
47. A partial list, incorrect in some particulars but quite useful, is given by Le Brun, *A.F. Biographie . . .* , pp. 50 f. Cf. B. Rascoe, *New Republic,* March 16, 1927.
48. December, 1886.
49. *L'Univ. ill.,* Aug. 5, 1893.
50. The passage has been quoted in full above, p. 175.
51. For full titles, etc., of this group, see Bibliography. On their value, cf. Giraud, pp. 210, 213, and Aynard in *Journal des Débats,* Oct. 23, 1924.
52. A certain number of them are to be found in *O. C.,* Vol. XXIV (*q.v.*) and in May, *Prefaces, Introductions and Other Uncollected Papers.* With the exceptions indicated below, I cite from the original editions.
53. In the review dealt with above, p. 278 and notes.
54. Pouquet, *Salon,* pp. 97, 99. This is probably the 'page' (*O. C.,* XXIV, 139-40) ascribed to 'une femme dont j'admire l'esprit hardi et pénétrant.' Cf. Seillière, *Jeunesse d'A.F.,* p. 149.
55. 'Préface' in *O. C.,* XXIV, 125-43 ; other articles listed in *ibid.,* pp. 374-75.
56. *Rev. pol. et litt.,* Aug. 3, 1889 ; much of it was in *Le Temps,* July 18, 1886.
57. See above, pp. 304 f. An explanation of France's (temporary) militarism can be found in Corday, *Dernières pages inédites,* p. 152.
58. Cf. *Chronique des lettres françaises,* 1924, p. 730 ; Aynard, *art. cit.*
59. *Vie litt., O. C.,* VI, 257 ; Ségur, *Conversations,* p. 193 ; cf. above, p. 137.
60. Aron, 'A.F. and Goethe,' *Univ. of Wisconsin Studies in German Literature,* Dec. 29, 1925, p. 16. Other passages dealing with Goethe occur in the *Vie litt., O. C.,* VI, 464 ; VII, 334 ; and especially VI, 257, where A.F. admires the intellectual and psychological depths of *Faust* — but dwells upon its Gothic murkiness.
61. This was also published as a separate *plaquette ;* it had appeared in *Le Temps* (Oct. 20, 1889) ; *O. C.,* VII, 165-78.
62. *O.C.,* XXIV, 187-95 ; the preface is of 1891.
63. *Le Temps,* Feb. 12, 1888. Seillière (*op. cit.,* p. 175) says 1873.
64. This part of the preface had appeared in the *Rev. hebd.,* June 4, 1892 (see *O. C.,* XXIV, 393).
65. Apparently they did not cost him much effort. Cf. Pouquet, p. 156 ; *Livres — Manuscrits — Dessins,* p. 100.
66. The preface to *Le Roi Candaule* first appeared in the *Echo de Paris,* March 1, 1893. It originally took the form of a letter explaining A.F.'s intention to Mendès ; the beginning of this may be found in *O. C.,* XXIV, 397-98.
67. 'Vie litt.,' *Le Temps,* Oct. 12 and 26, 1890 (*O. C.,* VII, 492-511) ; cf. Pouquet, *loc. cit.*
68. I have not seen this. It is quoted by Lods, *l'Intermédiaire,* Nov. 10, 1924.
69. Pouquet, p. 166 ; Lalou, *Litt. fr. contemporaine,* p. 310, states that A.F. prefaced another work by Maurras ; I find no confirmation of this statement.
70. Pouquet, pp. 105-109 ; cf. Le Goff, p. 243 and Souday, *N.Y. Times Book Rev.,* Jan. 8, 1928.
71. Brousson, *Itinéraire,* p. 26 ; cf. Rascoe, *art. cit.*
72. By Aveline, *Chantecler,* Dec. 17, 1927 ; cf. Souday, *art. cit.*
73. Appeared first in *l'Echo de Paris,* Dec. 22, 1896.

74. *O. C.*, XXIV, 393; XXI, 383-84; Giraud, pp. 210, 213 (also citing Bonnières).
75. Twice during this period A.F. shifted dates with his collaborators. Up to July 12, 1884, he had been contributing to the *even* numbers of the periodical; but beginning with that date, he changed to the odd numbers (No. 1529, etc.). This continued until 'Gyp' intervened with an article on the annual Salon (May 7, 1887). In the following issue but one (No. 1678, etc.), France lapsed back into the even numbers. His own contributions in this period are unmistakable.
76. Madame Pouquet (*op. cit.*, pp. 117-18; cf. p. 81) is categorical on this point; yet of course Anatole originated the ideas, however much an amanuensis may have written them up or repeated his previous utterances.
77. On repetitions here, cf. Michaut, pp. 209, 216; and the bibliographical notes to the *O. C.*
78. Almost as many were *signed* 'Anatole France,' from 1890-96. The great number of articles cited from *l'Univ. ill.* as well as from *Le Temps*, renders it impracticable, except for quotations of some length and in other outstanding cases, to give detailed references to either of these journals.
79. *Lettres — Manuscrits — Dessins*, pp. 91-92; Carias, *A.F.*, pp. 47-48.
80. *L'Univ. ill.*, Feb. 20, 1892. The tale was told here as a real event, but as fiction in *l'Etui de nacre*.
81. *L'Univ. ill.*, Dec. 22, 1883.
82. A constant attitude; cf. *Petit Pierre*, p. 53.
83. We find *fourteen* references or treatments of Renan by 'Gérôme.' These are *seriatim*: March 17, May 12, Oct. 13, 1883; Sept. 20, 1884; Nov. 28, 1885; Dec. 11, 1886; Jan. 22, Feb. 19, 1887; Feb. 11, March 10, May 5, Aug. 11, Sept. 22, 1888; Jan. 26, 1889. There are also a number of references subsequent to 1890.
84. See above, p. xxi.
85. The manuscript elaborates considerably this digression on friendship.
86. This is above his own signature: *ibid.*, Oct. 8, 1891. The manuscript, with its frequent erasures, bears traces of his agitation.
87. It is possible that some of these may have been written by a collaborator. They include commendations of his 'patriotic' preface to Pfnor's *Guide de Fontainebleau*. (See above, pp. 282-83.)
88. *L'Univ. ill.*, July 26, 1890; privately reprinted, 1928; also in *O. C.*, XXIV, 153-58.
89. *Le Cri de Paris*, May 29, 1898.
90. This reflection was lifted from Voltaire's *Zadig*.
91. *L'Univ. ill.*, June 2, 1888.
92. Gsell, p. 81.
93. MS. of letter in Bibliothèque Nationale, *fonds* Caillavet.
94. *A.F., the Parisian*, p. 8.
95. Truc, *A.F.*, p. 16.
96. *L'Univ. ill.*, July 26, 1890, and 'Le Café Procope,' *O. C.*, XXIV, 153-58; Ségur, *A.F. anecdotique*, pp. 139-40.
97. Sept. 5, 1891.
98. Passage reproduced in *Pierre Nozière*, pp. 339-40.
99. Bergerat, *Souvenirs d'un enfant de Paris*, II, 164-65.
100. Cf. Mille, *Nouv. litt.*, Oct. 18, 1924.
101. Ségur, *A.F. anecdotique*, p. 179; cf. *idem*, *Rev. de France*, Sept. 15, 1929, p. 254.

102. Chevalier, p. 24; cf. J. Roujon, *op. cit.*, p. 27.
103. There exists (Collection Lion) a large documentary background for this long-continued interest. France owned and used an inscribed copy of L. de la Sicotière's monograph, *Les Faux Louis XVII*.
104. Especially St. Rémy, St. Labre, St. Antoine.
105. Whose *Researches in the Phenomena of Spiritualism* A.F. once owned.
106. The theme of this passage had already been developed more fully in the *Livre de mon ami* ('La Bibliothèque de Suzanne').
107. *L'Univ. ill.*, Sept. 19, 1885.
108. See Appendix A for résumé of articles attributed to France from Aug., 1890–Sept., 1896.
109. For data regarding the appearance of all these articles see Bibliography, under *Revue de famille*. Also *O. C.*, XVI, 467-73.
110. For dates and titles of these, see Bibliography under *Revue illustrée*.

CHAPTER XIV

1. Italics will be used to indicate the publication of this series in book-form — first ed., four vols., 1888-92. Our references, however, are to Vols. VI and VII of the *Œuvres complètes*. Quotation marks will indicate articles constituting 'La Vie littéraire,' as they originally appeared in *Le Temps*. With rare exceptions, articles so indicated have not been reprinted.
2. *Vie litt.*, *O. C.*, VI, 3-5.
3. Strictly speaking, France first succeeded Jules Claretie as chronicler ('La Vie à Paris,' etc.).
4. Vandérem, *Miroir des Lettres*, VII, 229. On A.F.'s success and his relation to Sainte-Beuve, cf. Souday, *Nouv. litt.*, April 19, 1924 and Stewart, p. 71. Carias, Beaunier and Maurras agree on this point.
5. Will Durant, *Adventures in Genius*, p. 261.
6. Such as *Balthasar* (Dec. 26, 1886) and *Le Roi boit* (Jan. 8, 1893). Material appearing in 'La Vie littéraire' and later gathered into *Le Jardin d'Epicure* is treated under the latter heading.
7. The volumes of *La Vie littéraire* include, however, three articles of 1886 (Oct. 3, Dec. 12 and 19) that originally appeared under the caption of 'La Vie à Paris.' I am indebted to Mr. W. L. Crain for listing and securing photostats of the 169 articles that were not reprinted. These photostats are now accessible in the University of Chicago Libraries.
8. Several of this series (Aug. 15, 22, 29, 1886) were reprinted in that section of *Pierre Nozière* which was called 'Promenades de P.N. en France.'
9. A total of thirty-five articles. With the exceptions stated, none of these, so far as I know, has been reprinted.
10. This is under date of March 21, 1886. Thereafter the references to the chronicle-series would run consecutively into December of that year.
11. Among others, M. Michaut, M. Giraud, and Mlle. Antoniu have been forced, like the present writer, to have recourse to the columns of *Le Temps*.
12. Preface to Vol. II (1890): *O. C.*, VI, 325.
13. Preface to Vol. IV: *O. C.*, VII, 383 ff. Cf. 'Vie litt.,' Jan. 22, 1893.
14. Preface to Vol. II: *O. C.*, VI, 327.

15. Preface to Vol. III: *O. C.*, VII, 14.
16. See above, p. 274 and note. A.F.'s various treatments of the lady are listed in the study there cited. The *Temps* articles (Sept. 20 and 27, 1891) reveal a severe pruning of his previous versions. Cf. *Livres — Manuscrits — Dessins*, p. 95.
17. E.g., by Mlle. Antoniu, and cf. Seillière, *Jeunesse d'A.F.*, pp. 134 ff.
18. *O. C.*, VI, 491-92. The 'Vie litt.' article of March 25, 1888, antedates the similar notice in the *Rev. ill.* See above, pp. 317-18.
19. Rod objects that it is the real critic's business to narrate rather the 'roman d'une âme étrangère.'— *Rev. de Paris*, Dec. 15, 1894, p. 731.
20. *Le Génie européen*, pp. 102 ff.
21. Cf. Blondheim, *Modern Philology*, July, 1916, p. 51; Chevalier, p. 260 (quoting Guehenno).
22. Rumsey, *Bodleian*, Jan., 1921.
23. E.g., March 30, May 18, 1890.
24. *O. C.*, VII, 77. This is apropos of Bourget's *Le Disciple.*
25. *O. C.*, VII, 204-11 ('Vie litt.,' Nov. 24, 1889). 'Preceding article' of May 8, 1887, and cf. Dec. 18, 1892.
26. Corday, *A.F.*, p. 114; *idem*, *Dernières pages inédites*, p. 165.
27. For those who like to delve, this passage will reveal a dexterous amalgam of Pascal, Renan, and Flammarion.
28. *O. C.*, VI, 407-408. This article led to a debate among the pundits. Cf. 'Vie litt.,' March 17, 1889.
29. *Ibid.*, Oct. 11, 1891. Reprinted in *Jardin d'Epicure*, pp. 421-22. We find repeated and reworked in the *Jardin* some eight passages from the 'Vie littéraire'; see M. Carias' notes, *O. C.*, IX, 541-42.
30. A *Rückblick* on this enthusiasm for science is found in the article of March 17, 1889. Cf. Stewart, pp. 48-49.— On A.F. and Bourget, see Lion, *Le Temps*, Jan. 25, 1936.
31. 'La Grande Encyclopédie,' *O. C.*, VI, 418-25.
32. Cf. 'Vie litt.,' Dec. 18, 1892 and *Jardin d'Epicure*, p. 396.
33. 'Vie litt.,' April 23, 1893.
34. Wilson, *New Republic*, Oct. 24, 1934; Gottschalk, p. 103. Pessimism is also apparent in A.F.'s 'Pourquoi sommes-nous tristes ?', March 31, 1889.
35. Shanks, pp. 97, 101. *Per contra*, cf. Lanson, *Pages choisies d'A.F.*, 'Notice,' p. xxiii.
36. A review of a book by Maxime Du Camp, bearing this title. *O. C.*, VI, 292-99.
37. Guérard, p. 68.
38. 'Vie litt.,' Feb. 3 and 10, 1889; Dec. 6, 1891.
39. *Les Sceptiques grecs* (1887). The article, 'Sur le scepticisme' (*O. C.*, VI, 446-54) dates from *Le Temps*, May 22, 1888.
40. *O. C.*, VI, 111-23. This reviews an occult novel by G.-A. Thierry, A.F.'s quondam friend of the Saint-Valery sojourn.
41. 'Vie litt.,' March 13, 1887; *ibid.*, Sept. 11, 1887 (O. C., VI, 215-28).
42. Cf. Giraud, p. 191 and note.
43. Brandes, *A.F.*, p. 97.
44. *Vie en fleur*, p. 428.
45. Cf. R. Frary, *La Question du latin*, 1885, pp. 112-38; 'Pour le latin' is in *O. C.*, VI, 251-59.

46. In the main we follow the references chronologically. They run from 1887 to 1891. Three only have been reprinted in the *O. C.*
47. *Procès de réhabilitation de Jeanne d'Arc,* 2 vols., 1888; also *Jeanne d'Arc, drame historique,* 1890.
48. Cited in *Revue Rhénane,* Nov., 1924, p. 74.
49. *O. C.,* VI, 74 ff. Cf. Morche, *Revue des Indépendants,* May, 1927, and Villette, *Opinion,* Oct. 17, 1924.
50. The articles appeared in *Le Temps,* but not under 'Vie litt.,' Aug. 12-24, 1890 (*O. C.,* XXIV, 199-221). See below, Ch. XV, note 83.
51. *O. C.,* VI, 332; 'Vie litt.,' June 19, 1892; 'M. Octave Feuillet,' *O.C.,* VI, 643-44 and cf. Huard, *Normannia,* Sept., 1928.
52. Cf. Pouquet, pp. 125-27.
53. 'Vie litt.,' Jan. 31, 1892; cf. Jan. 22, 1893.
54. Thérive, *Nouv. litt.,* April 19, 1924.
55. *O. C.,* VII, 707.
56. 'Vie litt.,' Sept. 6, 1891. On his bookishness, cf. Brousson, *Itinéraire,* p. 190.
57. This boost for Lemerre is accompanied by other 'puffs' and tributes: a long one for Calmann-Lévy (the editor who 'roused me from my indolence and timidity'); for such old friends as Coppée, Calmettes and Mendès; for Boutet de Monvel as illustrator and for Charavay as dealer in autographs; for Jean Psichari, with whom France was later to be connected by marriage, over-praised here as novelist and poet.
58. A.F. was on good terms with Asselineau, as shown by various allusions. A letter to him explains that Anatole left Paris during the Commune, because it 'threatened my serenity.' (Collection Lion.)
59. Aug. 28 and Sept. 4, 1887; also *O. C.,* VI, 204-14. Preceding this, we find only (*O. C.,* VI, 76) an admission that Zola may represent a kind of perverted idealism or symbolism.
60. The 'Manifeste des Cinq,' issued in 1887. It is probable that the manifesto precipitated the article; cf. Henriot, *Le Temps,* Sept. 27, 1927.
61. Two of these are easily found in the *O. C.* The other two, on *l'Argent* and *La Débâcle* respectively, appeared in 'Vie litt.,' March 22, 1891, June 26–July 3, 1892.
62. Notably M. Kahn, *A.F. et Zola,* p. 65 and *passim;* also Henriot, *art. cit.* Cf. Carias, *Gde. Revue,* Sept., 1927. It is there maintained that France, in *l'Univ. ill.* too, showed admiration for Zola. But the evidence does not seem to warrant this conclusion. See above, pp. 292-93; and cf. Braibant's special pleading, in *Le Secret d'A.F.,* pp. 285-300.
63. Zola's contempt dates from a contribution of the late seventies to *Le Messager de l'Europe* of St. Petersburg; reprinted in *Documents littéraires,* p. 269. Others attacking Anatole on this basis are Masson, *A.F., son œuvre,* (p. 52, note) and Jean de Gourmont; cf. Hovelaque, p. 574.
64. Ségur, *Dern. conversations,* pp. 129-30; Massis, *Evocations,* p. 11; Fernand-Demeure, *Rev. mondiale,* Sept. 5, 1930, pp. 420-22. Cf. Frank Harris, *Contemporary Portraits,* p. 341.
65. 'Vie litt.,' June 15, 1890. Some think (I do not) that Mme. de Caillavet wrote it. See M. Kahn: 'Articles oubliés. II. A.F. et Pierre Loti.' Also Pouquet, p. 81.
66. Cf. *l'Univ. ill., passim,* and Brousson, *Pantoufles,* p. 194.

67. Aron, 'A.F. and Goethe,' *Univ. of Wisconsin Studies in German Literature*, Dec. 29, 1925, p. 10 and *passim*.
68. Especially Schaffer, *PMLA*, March, 1932, pp. 264 ff, 277. We cite freely from this article.
69. As a preface for an *Anthologie des poètes français depuis les origines jusqu'à la fin du XVIIIe siècle*, Lemerre, 1905. (Not to be confused with the preceding Lemerre collection — see above, p. 360.)
70. *L'Intermédiaire des chercheurs et curieux*, Aug. 10, 1864. Cf. *Vie litt.*, *O. C.*, VI, 268-79; Robert-Sigl, *Belles-Lettres*, pp. 300-301; Barthou, *Rev. de Paris*, Dec. 15, 1923, pp. 721-27.
71. 'Vie litt.,' Aug. 26, Sept. 2, 16, 23, 1888. Only two of these have been reprinted: *O. C.*, VI, 538 ff, 559 ff.
72. Sept. 4, 11, 21 and 25, 1892. As a brochure, *l'Elvire de Lamartine* appeared in the following year. Reprinted in *O. C.*, XXIV, 267-333.
73. Pouquet, p. 138; *Livres — Manuscrits — Dessins*, p. 31.
74. *O. C.*, VI, 516-17.
75. By Antoniu, Schaffer, *et al.*
76. Heredia expressed his appreciation of the article in an interesting letter cited in the *Rev. d'hist. litt.*, Jan.-March, 1933, p. 142. Sully Prudhomme also gave thanks. On the general subject, see E. Reynaud, *Muse française*, April 10, 1925.
77. *Pantoufles*, p. 301; cf. Ségur, *Conversations*, p. 35.
78. First publ. in *Le Figaro* (suppl. litt.), Sept. 18, 1886; reprinted in *Premières armes du symbolisme*, where may be found also France's critique, an answer by Moréas, and several other documents.
79. In the early 'Vie à Paris' series, Sept. 26, 1886; reprinted in *Premières armes*, etc.
80. 'Réponse à M. A.F.,' *Demain*, 1888.
81. G. Kahn, *Silhouettes littéraires*, pp. 99 ff.
82. *Conferencia*, May 1, 1925, p. 455.
83. *L'Univ. ill.*, Nov. 29, 1890; for an account of the banquet and of A.F.'s *volte-face*, see Ghil, *Les Dates et les Œuvres*, pp. 163-64, 171-72.
84. Picard, *Renaissance pol., litt., et artistique*, Oct. 18, 1924. Souriau (*Histoire du Parnasse*, pp. 284-85) calls A.F.'s article, in praise of Moréas, 'perfidious' and 'une mauvaise action.'
85. Bergerat, p. 166; others cited by Antoniu, pp. 233-34 and Picard, *art. cit.*
86. *Rapport sur le mouvement poétique français*, p. 159.
87. *Enquête sur l'Évolution littéraire*, pp. 6-9; cf., for rancorous reactions mentioned above, pp. 139, 180, 285. The Appendix to Huret contains the correspondence regarding the Leconte de Lisle incident. The interviews originally appeared in the *Echo de Paris*, 1890-91. The original letters are (or were) in the Barthou Collection.
88. Aug. 16, 1891.
89. Barthou, *Rev. de France*, 1926, pp. 612-13; *idem*, *Conferencia*, May 1, 1925, pp. 456-57; Henri de Régnier, *De Mon Temps*, p. 37; Le Brun, *Biographie d'A.F. . . .*, pp. 37-38.
90. Mme. Duclaux, *The French Procession*, p. 339; Bondy, *Le Classicisme de Ferdinand Brunetière*, Introduction; and *passim*.
91. See above, pp. 326-27. The original articles ran from June to September, 1889.

Consult: Giraud, pp. 242-43; Carias, *A.F.*, p. 49; Cor, *A.F. et la pensée contemporaine*, p. 56; Michaut, *A.F.*, p. xxiv.

92. Vol. XIII, pp. 411 ff. Article on 'Critique (Littérature)'; reprinted in *Etudes critiques sur l'histoire de la littérature française*, Vol. IX, 1925.
93. *RDM*, Jan. 1, 1891, pp. 210-24; reprinted in *Essais sur la littérature contemporaine*, pp. 1-30.
94. *Contemporains*, I, 217-48.
95. This is in the 'article de lancement,' *ibid.*, II, 83 ff. For other sallies against Brunetière, see *ibid.*, VI, v-xii (Prefaces).
96. 'Vie litt.,' Jan. 18 and 25, 1891. Much of this defence is reprinted (with alterations and shiftings) as a Preface to the third volume of *La Vie littéraire*, where it thus assumes permanent form as a 'document.'
97. The train of 'cars' which Anatole ironically deploys here is probably a reminiscence of *Candide*, Ch. V.
98. See above, pp. 325 ff. These passages are from the Preface in question.
99. So Vandérem considers it — *op. cit.*, p. 230.
100. To Ricardou, *La Critique littéraire*.
101. *Rev. pol. et litt.*, Nov. 24, 1888. Apparently not reprinted.
102. *Contemporains*, VI, 373.
103. *Les Princes de la jeune critique*.
104. In *Essais de littérature contemporaine* and *Etudes de littérature contemporaine*, I. The latter contains the essential article on 'Dogmatisme et impressionisme.'
105. *A.F.*, pp. 48-49.
106. Spronck, *Débats*, Oct. 11, 1893; Rod, *Nouvelles Etudes sur le XIXe siècle*, pp. 41 ff. Renard and (later) Bordeaux support Rod's view.
107. Lazare, *Figures contemporaines*; Quillard, *Mercure*, Nov., 1892. Souday, *art. cit.*, admits that A.F. is severe on contemporary writers. Cf. above, note 63.
108. E.g., by Hermant (Max), by Poizat, Vandérem, (*op. cit.*), and Maurras (in Bourget-Pailleron interview). Cf. Beaunier, *Critiques et romanciers*, pp. 83 ff; Michaut, p. 70 and note 3; Seillière, *op. cit.*, pp. 184, 185; J. Roujon, *Vie et opinions d'A.F.*, pp. 103-106.
109. Belis, Giraud, and especially Peyre, *MLN*, Nov. 1927, p. 488.
110. *La critique française à la fin du XIXe siècle*, pp. 180 ff; 256-57.
111. 'Il s'est mis tout entier dans ses articles,' says Revon (*Les Marges*, Nov. 15, 1924, p. 199) in what otherwise is a superficial essay.
112. Larroumet (*Etudes de Litt.*, etc., III, 192-93) takes practically the same view; also Bahr, *Studien zur Kritik der Moderne*, pp. 140-49; Mr. Stewart (*op. cit.*, Ch. V) considers France as 'educated' by Sainte-Beuve and the Second Empire; André Beaunier (*RDM*, April 15, 1918, p. 927) points out that the critic's humanism could lead him at times to certain definite affirmations.
113. Giraud, pp. 228-33; *Bibliophile français*, May, 1870. See above, p. 266.
114. Bradford, *Journal* (Boston, 1933), pp. 84-85, 487; see also his Index.
115. On these two terms see E. Evrard, *Nos Mandarins*; Spronck and Lemaître; Ledrain, *Nouv. Rev.*, 1895, p. 871 (but the articles in *l'Univ. ill.* show that this is not quite a 'new manner'). *Autour du dilettantisme* first appeared in *Nos Dilettantes* — *see* Klein. Giraud, *op. cit.*, pp. 233, 236; *Le Lys rouge* (periodical), Oct. 1, 1934.
116. *Op. cit.*, especially Preface; previously as article, 'Le Dilettantisme et M. A.F.,'

in *Le Correspondant.* The article contains some introductory material not repeated in the Preface.

117. 'Others' are Antoniu, Ch. III ; Lecigne, *Du Dilettantisme à l'action,* p. 285 ; Audouin, *Gde. Revue,* March 25, 1913, pp. 289-90. The last-named thinks that A.F., even at the time of the Great War, was still considered as a dilettante by the majority of people. Souday, in *Le Temps,* May 15 and 16, 1913 ; reprinted as 'Le Classicisme d'A.F.' in *Livres du Temps,* II, 65-76.

118. *Histoire de la littérature française* (21st ed.), p. 1087 ; *Pages choisies d'A.F.,* 'Notice,' p. xix — dilettantism as an 'insinuating contagion.'

119. Seillière, *op. cit.,* p. 205.— An interesting appreciation of France's provocative role, from the point of view of the Spanish tradition, can be found in Reissig, *A.F.,* p. 73. Cf. also the German monograph by Schön.

120. Speech in *Bulletin officiel,* June 18, 1933.— This was the last public utterance of Barthou on A.F.

CHAPTER XV

1. The best account is that given by M. Barthou in the article already cited, *Rev. de Paris,* Dec. 1, 1924, pp. 481-90. Cf. also Pouquet, *Salon,* p. 78 ; Brousson, *Pantoufles,* p. 300.
2. Letter to Ratisbonne, 1890 (Collection Lion).
3. E.g., Brousson, *op. cit.,* pp. 177, 301.
4. P. Calmettes, pp. 46-47 ; cf. Reissig, pp. 124-25.
5. Missoffe, *Gyp et ses amis,* p. 76 ; Brousson, *op. cit.,* p. 294.
6. *L'Univ. ill.,* March 1 and June 7, 1884.
7. Brousson, *op. cit.,* p. 99 ; Missoffe, p. 74 ; *Le Mannequin, passim.*
8. According to one writer (Shanks, p. 97) she plainly called him 'cocu' ; according to another (Missoffe, pp. 75-76) she used an equally insulting term, leaving little doubt as to the status of her husband.
9. This account is based partly on private information, which I believe to be accurate ; partly on the narratives of Mme. Pouquet (*op. cit.,* pp. 122-24), 'Gyp' (*ibid.*), and Missoffe (*loc. cit.*), together with alleged conversations from Brousson (*Pantoufles,* p. 119 ; *Itinéraire,* pp. 255-56). None of these can be considered as wholly impartial.
10. P. Calmettes, p. 49. There was already a difference of opinion as to how much Anatole should allow for maintenance.
11. I have a copy (see Appendix B) of this decree, which is stored in the Archives of the Palais de Justice, 1re Chambre, No. 9 (Cour de Première Instance du Tribunal Civil). The acrimonious letter of June, 1892, is also there — but is not communicated. It would probably shed much light on the whole situation.
12. Carias, *A.F.,* p. 50 ; Corday, *A.F.,* p. 229 ; private information.
13. To Mlle. Emma Laprévotte, in 1920 ; cf. Le Goff, p. 212.
14. Reissig, pp. 126-27.
15. Above, p. 207 and references ; Ségur, *Conversations,* p. 56 ; cf. Barthou, *Lys rouge* (periodical), Oct. 1, 1933.
16. A.F.'s Scrap-Book and A. L. S. letter to an unknown friend.
17. Myriam Harry, *Trois Ombres,* pp. 204, 207.
18. Massis, *Evocations,* pp. 198, 222 ; Collection Lion ; Cerf, *A.F.,* p. 19 ; J. Roujon, p. 21.

19. Le Goff, pp. 200-204 ; Barthou, *Rev. de France,* June 15, 1926, pp. 609-11 ; Missoffe, pp. 76-77, note.
20. J. Psichari, *Ernest Renan. Jugements et souvenirs,* p. 268 ; cf. p. 108.
21. May 13 and July 8, 1893 ; especially March 31, 1894.
22. G. Picard, *Rev. mondiale,* Dec. 1, 1924, pp. 348-53.
23. H. Psichari, *Ernest Psichari, mon frère,* p. 25 ; M. Psichari, *Index raisonné de la mythologie d'Horace* — see above, p. 137 and references. Cf. 'Une Préface inconnue d'A.F.,' *Chronique des lettres françaises,* 1924, pp. 805-806.
24. Anon., *Nouv. litt.,* Oct. 17, 1931. This article serves as an announcement of the sale of A.F.'s MSS., discussed below, p. 696.
25. Twenty-four appeared (in whole or in part) in the Pouquet volume ; fragments of others, in *Livres — Manuscrits — Dessins,* which is the Andrieux catalogue of the sale just mentioned. Henceforward both of these volumes are freely used, without specific page-references, as a rule. Likewise an article by Ambrière (*Nouv. litt.,* April 23, 1932) in which the Andrieux *catalogue raisonné* is summarized and explained.
26. Bibliothèque Nationale, 'Fonds Caillavet,' Nouvelles Acquisitions Françaises, Nos. 10795-10811 and 21609-21612 — about twenty bound volumes in all. Cf. A. Martin, *Belles Editions et manuscrits d'A.F. conservés à la Bibl. Nationale,* 1925. Cf. also 'Fonds Audéoud,' same collection. These MSS. show, as a rule, fewer variants than one might expect.
27. Chevalier, p. 151.
28. Henriot, *Le Temps,* Oct. 13, 1931.
29. Peixoto, *Revista da Academia brasileira,* Jan., 1926, p. 10 ; Seillière, *Jeunesse d'A.F.,* p. 210.
30. Princess Radziwill, *Forum,* Dec., 1924, pp. 828-29 ; Brousson, *Itinéraire* and *Pantoufles, passim.*
31. Carias, *op. cit.,* pp. 54-55 ; *idem, Nouv. litt.,* Feb. 18, 1933.
32. On A.F.'s relations with Mme. de C.'s family, see Brousson, *Pantoufles, passim ;* 'Jacques Vincent' (Mme. Bory d'Arnex), *Un Salon parisien d'avant-guerre,* p. 117 ; Seillière, *op. cit.,* p. 215 ; Pouquet, pp. 105, 266 ; Simone de Caillavet (Mme. Maurois), *Nouv. litt.,* April 19, 1924.
33. Le Goff, pp. 129-30 ; inscription to *Crainquebille,* as found in Pouquet, p. 80 ; e.g., Maurras, etc. — see above, p. 392 and references.
34. *Livres — Manuscrits — Dessins,* pp. 88 ff.
35. Maurel, *Souvenirs de littérature* in 'Les Œuvres libres,' Vol. 44, pp. 362-64 and Simone de Caillavet, *art. cit. ;* anon., *Nouv. litt.,* Oct. 17, 1931 ; Brousson, *Itinéraire,* p. 17 (cf. *Pantoufles, passim*) ; Reboux, *Lys rouge* (periodical), Jan. 1, 1933.
36. Maurras, 'Lettre-Préface' to *Livres — Manuscrits — Dessins,* p. 9 and cf. Brousson, *Itinéraire,* p. 320.
37. Reboux, *art. cit.*
38. Pouquet, p. 111.
39. This intention was not fulfilled and 'Mademoiselle Roxane' was first printed in *Cosmopolis,* Feb., 1897. On the articles, cf. Reissig, *op. cit.,* pp. 133-34.
40. 'Philippe Lautrey,' *Le Roman d'une Demoiselle de modes, Rev. de Paris,* March-May, 1908 (also in book-form) ; E. Burnet, *Nouv. litt.,* Nov. 13, 1926 ; Mme. Pouquet, *ibid.,* Nov. 27, 1926. Cf. Braibant, *Le Secret d'A.F.,* p. 319.

41. Burnet, *art. cit.*
42. Especially Ségur, Brousson (*Pantoufles*) and Pouquet. Brousson's later work — *Les Vêpres de l'avenue Hoche* — contains much on the salon, but is evidently bitterly prejudiced. Cf. also Maurel, *op. cit.*, p. 375 ; De Gramont, *op. cit.*, pp. 15-19 ; Shanks, p. 104.
43. Ségur, *op. cit.*, pp. 28-29, 63 ; 'J.-H. Rosny,' *Rev. belge,* May 15, 1924, p. 289 ; J. Roujon, p. 26.
44. De Gramont, p. 19.
45. 'Jacques Vincent' (Mme. Bory d'Arnex), *op. cit.*
46. Harry, pp. 212-13 ; E. Montfort, *Vingt-Cinq Ans de littérature française,* II, 174-76 ; Scheikévitch, pp. 76-78.
47. Lowenthal, *Menorah Journal,* VII, 1925.
48. Burnet, *art. cit.* ; Carias, *op. cit.*, p. 59.
49. Ségur, *op. cit.*, pp. 65-67.
50. Pouquet, *op. cit.*, p. 81 ; M. Kahn, *Figaro hebdomadaire,* June 16, 1926. Cf. *Le Temps,* June 15, 1890 ; and *l'Univ. ill.*, Aug. 8, 1891.
51. Du Bled, p. 183, note ; Hanotaux, 'Préface' to Pouquet volume, p. iii.
52. A. Hermant, *op. cit.*, pp. 12-13. But cf. *idem, Souvenirs de la vie mondaine,* p. 222.
53. E.g., Radziwill, *loc. cit.* ; Brousson, *passim.*
54. *Idem, Pantoufles,* pp. 53-54 and 59 ; Rosny, *Nouv. litt.*, March 14, 1931 — one of the best brief accounts of her guardianship.
55. W. Stephens Whale, *Contemporary Rev.*, Nov., 1926, p. 607.
56. Radziwill, *art. cit.*, p. 827 ; Hovelaque, p. 554.
57. Cf. Chevalier, p. 151 ; Reissig, pp. 132-33.
58. Pillet, pp. 20-21.
59. These entries run from Jan. 31, 1890, through May, 1895 ; and later (Ch. XIX) all through the year 1896. For both lots I am indebted to the patience and kindness of Mr. Bernard Weinberg.
60. 'J. Vincent,' pp. 114-15, 119-20.
61. Bertaut, 'A.F. dans le monde,' *Nouv. litt.*, Oct. 18, 1924.
62. A. Meyer, *Ce que je peux dire,* pp. 243, 247.
63. *L'Univ. ill.*, June 27, 1891.
64. Anon., *Nouv. litt.*, Oct. 17, 1931 ; Missoffe, pp. 71-72.
65. Maurras, *A.F., politique et poète,* pp. 47-48 and 54.
66. Rosny, *Rev. belge,* 1924, pp. 297-98.
67. Brousson, *Nouv. litt.*, March 29, 1928 and Dec. 27, 1930. Massis, *op. cit.*, p. 19.
68. *Figaro,* Feb. 3, 1891, and May 20, 1895.
69. *L'Univ. ill.*, July 7, 1894.
70. Two of these *Discours* are in *O. C.*, XXV ; see above, p. 595.
71. E.g., Saunier, *L'Art vivant,* Jan. 15, 1928, pp. 41-42 and *idem* in *Art et Décoration,* Nov., 1907, pp. 169-72 ; Crucy, *Floréal,* Sept. 18, 1920, pp. 757-58 ; Gsell, *Matinées de la Villa Saïd* ; Massis, *Arts et Métiers graphiques,* March 15, 1929, pp. 587-94 ; Mauclair, *L'Art et les artistes,* Dec., 1907, pp. 439-41 (slight) ; Ségur, *op. cit.*, pp. 47 ff. ; A. Brisson, *Les Prophètes,* pp. 102-106 ; Brousson, *Pantoufles, passim.* Catalogues of sales at the Hôtel Drouot (June 25 and 26, Dec. 4, 1931) may apply to furnishings from the new Villa as well as the old.
72. *Op. cit.*, pp. 89, 148-52 and *passim.*

73. *Op. cit.*, p. 48.
74. P. Calmettes, pp. 155 ff. (The other rooms follow in order, in his detailed description.)
75. Harris, p. 333.
76. P. Calmettes, *op. cit.*, pp. 28-29, 146-47 ; Champion, pp. 43-46, 50, 194.
77. Hovelaque, pp. 559-60 ; Thibaudet, *Nouv. litt.*, July 21, 1934. The latter thinks of A.F. as a gourmand rather than a gourmet.
78. *Comœdia,* Oct. 16, 1924.
79. Reminiscential volumes, *passim.* J. Lefranc, 'Les Dimanches de la Villa Saïd,' *Le Temps,* Nov. 13, 1921 ; Champion, p. 185 ; P. Calmettes, pp. 146, 157, 168.
80. Carias, *op. cit.*, p. 52.
81. *Pierre Nozière,* pp. 461 ff ; Pouquet, p. 113.
82. *Livres — Manuscrits — Dessins,* pp. 93-94.
83. *Le Temps,* Aug. 12-24, 1890 (these are in the form of letters from various towns visited) ; *Promenades Félibréennes* (privately printed, 1895) ; also article by Barthou, *Le Lys rouge* (periodical), Oct. 1, 1933 ; *O. C.*, VII, 56-62 and 451-52 ; 'Préface' to Arène et Tournier, *Des Alpes aux Pyrénées,* 1891. A.F.'s articles and Preface finally reprinted in *O. C.*, XXIV, 199-221, 385-92.
84. Bourget-Pailleron, *Opinion,* April 11, 1924 ; *Jardin d'Epicure,* p. 488.
85. 'Vie litt.,' Oct. 4, 1891.
86. Le Goff, p. 250 ; Bédarida, *Rev. hebd.*, Oct. 10, 1925, p. 161.
87. *Ibid.*, pp. 167-68.
88. Rodes, *l'Aurore politique, littéraire, sociale,* June 21, 1903 ; Blum, *Rev. blanche,* Feb. 15, 1895, p. 169.
89. *Discours* in *l'Effort Italien,* 1916, p. 26.
90. Brousson, *Itinéraire ; Lys rouge* (periodical), Oct. 1, 1935.
91. *RDM,* Dec. 15, 1896. See Bibliography, under other names mentioned.
92. Mauriac, *Le Roman,* p. 102.
93. In A. B. Walkley's *Playhouse Impressions* as cited in H. Jackson, *The Eighteen Nineties,* p. 250.
94. Vol. V, April, 1895, pp. 263-79. The same volume contains by A.F. 'l'Evêché de Tourcoing,' an advance chapter of the *Histoire contemporaine.* On the role of *The Yellow Book,* cf. Richard le Gallienne, *The Romantic Nineties,* pp. 225-26. On the 'New Hedonism,' the 'New Paganism,' etc., see Jackson, *op. cit.*, pp. 23-29.
95. *Books and Persons,* p. 60.
96. Mauriac, p. 101 ; Ségur, *Rev. de France,* Nov. 1, 1929, p. 77. Another curious fact, often commented upon, is that A.F. had no notable disciples and consequently formed no 'school.' Cf. Truc, *A.F.*, pp. 72-73.
97. Rosny, *Rev. belge,* 1924, pp. 289-90 ; Bertaut, *art. cit.*
98. Bonnard, *Rev. belge,* Feb. 15, 1934, p. 314 ; Brousson, *Itinéraire,* p. 243 ; Shanks, p. 86.
99. Goll, Ivan, *Sodome et Berlin.* In this novel, two characters go to see A.F. at the Villa Saïd, where he puts on an amusing show. At home, he was always at his ease. Cf. Ségur, *A.F. anecdotique,* pp. 200-204.
100. P. Calmettes, p. 3 ; private information.
101. *Art. cit.*, p. 549.
102. Brousson, *Pantoufles,* pp. 43-47.
103. Régnier, *De Mon Temps,* pp. 41-42.

104. Chevassu, *Visages,* p. 36 ; Ségur, *Conversations,* p. 38 and *passim.*
105. Pouquet, *Rev. de Paris,* March 1, 1926, p. 64 ; Brousson, *Pantoufles,* pp. 38-42 ; P. Calmettes, p. 5. On his resistance, cf. Braibant, *op. cit.,* p. 326 and Scheikévitch, *op. cit.,* pp. 72-73, 101.
106. Brisson, *op. cit.,* p. 106.
107. Hovelaque, pp. 550-52.
108. Carias, *op. cit.,* pp. 50-51 ; Seillière, *A.F., critique de son temps,* p. 13 ; *idem, Jeunesse d'A.F.,* p. 206 ; Pillet, *art. cit.,* p. 21. On the relations with Barrès, see the latter's *Cahiers* and Braibant, *passim.*
109. Marsan, *Les Cahiers d'Occident,* 1930, pp. 81-85.
110. Displayed especially by Brousson, indicted especially by Michaut.
111. Chevalier, *op. cit.* ; 'Prologue,' p. v.
112. E.g., René Benjamin (*Valentine ou la folie démocratique*) and many of the opposition at the time of France's death.
113. Seillière, *A.F., critique de son temps,* pp. 9 and 12.
114. *Op. cit.,* pp. 52 and 72.
115. Albert-Petit, *Débats,* Oct. 14, 1924. 'When he was about fifty,' says M. Seillière, with some exaggeration (*A.F., critique de son temps,* p. 13), 'he was allowed to become wholly himself.'
116. Page-references too numerous to cite fully. M. Braibant's general thesis, with regard to the stages of France's radicalism, is presented in his 'Préface' and rounded out in his 'Conclusion.'
117. M. Braibant's opinion on the importance of journalism in A.F.'s career (pp. 12, 16, 308-309) is similar to the one expressed above, pp. 264 and 319-20.
118. *Op. cit.,* p. 332. M. Braibant prefers not to say 'militarism,' for this term according to him connotes the idea that the State should be ruled by the army, and A.F. never went that far.
119. 'Vie à Paris,' July 18, 1886. (Those were early days.) Cf. Braibant, *op. cit.,* pp. 69 ff ; he points out that some of this article was revamped in the famous Preface to *Faust.* See above, p. 283 and note.
120. *L'Univ. ill.,* May 5, 1888.
121. Carias, *op. cit.,* p. 60, and Pouquet, p. 87 ; Braibant, pp. 97-98, 100-101.
122. J. Roujon, p. 27 and cf. above, p. 304 ; Braibant, *op. cit.,* p. 90 ; Pouquet, pp. 89-90.
123. *L'Univ. ill.,* Feb. 9, 1889.
124. Braibant, p. 110.
125. *Ibid.,* pp. 24, 28.— *Re* Zola, see *idem, Nouv. litt.,* Nov. 23, 1935.
126. Especially 'Le Cavalier Miserey' (March 6, 1887) and *re* the Longchamp parade of 1886.
127. *L'Univ. ill.,* Aug. 22, 1891 (this article is almost certainly his) ; cf. Braibant, *op. cit.,* pp. 151-61.
128. Italics mine. 'Vie litt.,' Nov. 18, 1888 (mentioned above, p. 349) ; cf. Braibant, pp. 145 ff.
129. See above, pp. 223-24, 303 f. But Gérôme is less *pro* democracy than *con* demagoguery. (Also cf. later *l'Univ. ill.,* April 30, 1892 ; Jan. 20, 1894.)
130. Reviews of Braibant's work, for the most part favourable, can be found in our Bibliography under Altman, Billy and Vandervelde.

131. *Théories soc. d'A.F.*, pp. 10-11 ; an opinion modified to some extent in *Théories d'A.F. sur l'org. soc. de son temps*, p. 24.

CHAPTER XVI

1. Vandérem, *Miroir des Lettres*, VII, 233, 237.
2. Among the dedicatees are Gaston de Caillavet and his *fiancée*, Maurras, Schwob, Paul Arène, Proust, the Comte de Vogüé, the Comtesse Martel-Janville, and Mlle. Cantel, A.F.'s secretary.
3. Baring, *The Yellow Book*, p. 270.
4. Giraud, pp. 244-45.
5. Several of them appeared first in journal-form, especially in the *Echo de Paris*. For all such bibliographical data, the editorial notes to the *O. C.* may be consulted. Our analytical Table of this edition indicates the volume and pagination of all titles discussed in the text above.
6. Seillière, *Jeunesse d'A.F.*, pp. 217-18.
7. Diplock, p. 435 ; Filon, *Rev. pol. et litt.*, Aug. 10, 1889 ; Seillière, *op. cit.*, p. 219.
8. *A.F.*, p. 44.
9. *L'Univ. ill.*, Jan. 5, 1884. The 'Histoire' is reprinted in *O. C.*, IV, 358-59.
10. *L'Univ. ill.*, Jan. 8, 1887 ; Jan. 26, 1889. These are subsequent to the tale proper of 'Balthasar,' which first appeared in *Le Temps*, Dec. 26, 1886, as a 'Conte pour le jour de Noël.'
11. 'Vie litt.,' Jan. 8, 1888.
12. Seillière, *op. cit.*, pp. 220-21. 'Gallion' is in *Sur la Pierre blanche.*
13. Baring, p. 269.
14. Reissig, *A.F.*, p. 63.— Yet Rod thinks that Anatole shares in Læta's revolt against a rather overpowering deity. (*Rev. de Paris*, Dec. 15, 1894, p. 754.)
15. Filon, p. 182 ; cf. Seillière, *op. cit.*, pp. 218, 220.
16. A late rationalistic treatment of this theme is found in 'Une des plus grandes découvertes du siècle,' *Figaro littéraire*, Nov. 2, 1935.
17. Carias, *op. cit.*, p. 44.
18. Practically identical with the versions in the *Acta Sanctorum* (Oct. 8, Vol. IV, pp. 225-26 : 'De Sancta Thaïde pœnitente in Ægypto'), and in Migne's *Patrologia Latina* (Vol. LXXIII, cols. 660-63).
19. 'Ballade des Dames du temps jadis' ; Preserved Smith, *A Key to the Colloquies of Erasmus*, pp. 22-23.— Throughout this section I rely much upon the unpublished monograph by Miss Shipman and upon Kuehne's *Study of the Thaïs Legend*. The latter prints translations of Syriac and Greek versions, together with Hrotswitha, Voragine, and Rosweyd.
20. 'Vie litt.,' Aug. 12, 1888 ; *O. C., VI*, 526-37.
21. Pouquet, pp. 74-75 ; the order of the above paragraphs is reversed in *Livres — Manuscrits — Dessins*, p. 92. Mme. P. believes that France got the idea for his novel through reading Hrotswitha.
22. Pouquet, *op. cit.*, pp. 95-96, 101. Massenet's opera, with libretto by Gallet, was first staged and published in March, 1894. On A.F.'s reactions to this, see Malherbe, *Le Temps*, Oct. 22, 1924.
23. Corday, *A.F.*, p. 133.— The preface was not printed until the Carias edition

(*O. C.*, V, 467-70) ; the MS. of this was in the Barthou Collection and offers, in the phototypes, some interesting variants. The article appeared a few weeks after the successful *première* of the opera, in *l'Univ. ill.*, April 14, 1894 ; reprinted in *O. C.*, V, 471-76.

24. The photographs of the MS. contain a number of erasures and substitutions which are revealing, first, of the pains which the author expended on this matter, then of his desire to minimize Brucker's attack, finally of the pleasure which A.F. took in writing the novel : 'j'ai passé quelques mois très agréables avec mon vieux moine copte.'
25. *Opinion*, Oct. 17, 1924. Couchoud thinks that the MS. of this may belong to Mme. Roujon ; but there are reasons for considering it a part of MS. *A*. See Appendix C.
26. *Fonds* Caillavet ; see above, Ch. XV, note 26.
27. Courtesy of Gabriel Wells, who has since disposed of it. See write-up in *N.Y. Times*, Dec. 13, 1927.
28. Ernest-Charles, as cited by Michaut, *A.F.*, p. 163.
29. Additional authorities : Provost, *Gde. revue*, Nov., 1921, pp. 16-55 ; Michaut, pp. 163-67 ; Carias, *Gde. Revue*, Dec. 25, 1912 ; Jan. 10, 1913.
30. *La Légende dorée*, II, 180-82.
31. *O. C.*, V, 469, 472.
32. Pouquet, p. 75, note ; Kuehne, pp. 99-100 ; Gout, *Mercure*, Aug. 1, 1931, pp. 595-611. The last-named goes too far in declaring that without Magnin's edition, '*Thaïs* would probably not have seen the light.'
33. *O. C.*, VI, 464-68 ; VII, 23-31 ; cf. *l'Univ. ill.*, Dec. 1, 1888. Anatole himself forges a link between the two plays — the legend of Thaïs and that of St. Mary the Egyptian. He retells the latter story in the *Opinions de Jérôme Coignard*.
34. *Le Théâtre de Hrotswitha*, 1845 ; preceded by an article in the *RDM*, 1839, pp. 335-48.
35. Again by Amélineau. See *O. C.*, VII, 132-42.
36. Bertrand, *Rev. de Paris*, May 15, 1921, p. 340.
37. Brucker, *Etudes religieuses, philosophiques, historiques et littéraires*, Nov., 1890, p. 505 ; Michaut, p. 166.
38. Corday, *Dern. pages inédites d'A.F.*, p. 181.
39. Peyre, *Louis Ménard*, pp. 469, 509 ; *Rêveries d'un païen mystique* (ed. of. 1911), p. 17. Cf. above, pp. 116 and 171.
40. Peyre, *op. cit.*, p. 399. Neither Peyre (*ibid.*, pp. 391, 398) nor Michaut (p. 164) has any doubt that Ménard's 'Banquet' was France's model.
41. Brousson, *Pantoufles*, p. 112 ; cf. 'Vie litt.,' May 22, 1888 ; same in *O. C.*, VI, 454. See above, pp. 395 f, 443. Also *l'Univ. ill.*, Aug. 25, 1888, where A.F. dines with Brochard and praises him as 'le premier Helléniste de l'Europe.'
42. Brochard, *Les Sceptiques grecs*, pp. 54 ff ; see above, pp. 550 ff.
43. Michaut, pp. 163-64 ; but cf. Peyre's comment, p. 513, note, and Provost, *art. cit.*
44. Peyre, pp. 408, 431, note 7, 514-15 ; others have pointed out the likeness between the two works — cf. Desonay, *Le Rêve hellénique*, p. 77.
45. Rosenberg, Herrig's *Archiv*, CXII, 382 ; Brucker, *passim* ; cf. Braibant, pp. 132-35.
46. *O. C.*, V, 472.

47. Seillière, *op. cit.*, p. 232. Some, however, challenge the plausibility of the change; cf. a letter from Samain to A.F. in *Des Lettres*, pp. 9-10.
48. Seillière, *Jeunesse d'A.F.*, p. 231; Hovelaque, 1925, p. 550; A.F., 'Discours de réception,' Dec. 24, 1896; Rod, p. 752. On all this, see above, p. 339.
49. Lahy-Hollebecque, pp. 14-15.
50. *RDM*, Dec. 15, 1896, p. 931.
51. A. K. Griggs, *Toute l'Edition*, Oct. 29, 1932. Most of these translations are found in the Collection Lion.
52. Maurel, *Rev. pol. et litt.*, April, 1890, pp. 542-43 (cited by Brucker, *art. cit.*, p. 505); Benoist, *Rev. de famille*, Nov., 1890, pp. 369-70 (he also remarks that Renan is the 'grand Saint-Antoine' of A.F.); Filon, *Rev. pol. et litt.*, Nov. 1, 1890, pp. 565-67; Asse, *Rev. encyclopédique*, 1891, p. 291.
53. 'Courrier de Paris,' Nov. 8, 1890; *Figaro*, Nov. 5, 1890, reprinted in *La Bataille littéraire*, V, 195-96.
54. See above, p. 444 and note 37. This reviewer is also mildly mentioned (though not without irony) in *O. C.*, VII, 489-90.
55. Brousson, *Pantoufles*, p. 335.
56. Seillière, *op. cit.*, pp. 230-31, 239; Giraud, p. 250; cf. Rod, *art. cit.*, pp. 752-53.
57. *A.F.*, p. 45.
58. *Ibid.*, p. 53.
59. This is reckoned in terms of the first edition; for 'La Perquisition,' see above, p. 468.
60. Abbé Lecigne, *Revue de Lille* (reprint), 1901, pp. 11-12; Estève, *Revue d'art et de litt.*, Nov. 1, 1892, pp. 135-36 and Diplock, p. 434.
61. One MS. described in *Livres — Manuscrits — Dessins* (p. 66) is now in the Collection Lion; another, less corrected, is at the Bibliothèque Nationale. *Re* Vesuvius, the error was pointed out by a journalist called Lenglé and by a German savant who proposed to translate the tale. Cf. *l'Univ. ill.*, Jan. 23, 1892; Brousson, *op. cit.*, p. 86; private letter in the possession of Vincent Starrett, Esq.
62. Woodbridge, *MLN*, Vol. XL, Dec., 1925, pp. 483-85.
63. On Renan, see *Livres — Manuscrits — Dessins, loc. cit.*; Levaillant, *Figaro*, Dec. 27, 1931. Giraud, *op. cit.*, p. 247; Shanks, p. 80.
64. Seillière, *op. cit.*, pp. 239-40 and cf. p. 343; Noussanne, *A.F., philosophe sceptique*, pp. 30-31.
65. Estève, *loc. cit.*
66. Seillière, *op. cit.*, p. 244. S. makes the same point about 'Scolastica.'
67. *Le Temps*, Dec. 8, 1889; reprinted in *O. C.*, VII, 221-25.
68. *Ibid.*, p. 221; Mauris, letter in *Débats*, Nov. 2, 1924; cf. Noussanne, *op. cit.*, p. 30, note. See St. Gregory, *Hist. Francorum* (ed. Omont, 1886), Lib. I, p. 25.
69. Brousson, *op. cit.*, pp. 141-42; cf. 'La Leçon bien apprise,' in the *Contes de Jacques Tournebroche.*
70. In both of his versions of 'Le Jongleur,' France refers to this parallel legend.
71. E.g., Diplock, p. 434.
72. The Duc de Penthièvre. See Michaut, p. 129.
73. Much of this derives from Chapter II of *Les Autels de la peur*. The behaviour of a certain Chevalier is adapted from A.F.'s article on Florian (*O. C.*, VI, 179-82), while another article in the 'Vie litt.' (*O. C.*, VI, 49) furnished some philosophical remarks.

74. See above, pp. 260 ff and notes. There the four chapters *not* repeated in *l'Etui* were particularly discussed.
75. It is here that this 'André' [Chénier] tells the prosecutor : 'Je suis l'auteur de l'écrit intitulé : *les Autels de la Peur'* (*Etui de nacre,* ed. of 1892, p. 281). This link with the past was altered after the first edition.
76. Apart from such sources as Dauban and Grace Elliott, Huard mentions as likely parallels the monographs on the Revolution actually published by Noël France (*Bull. du Bibliophile,* March 1, 1925, p. 135).
77. *Dern. conversations,* pp. 205-206.
78. For details, consult Holbrook, *MLN,* Jan., 1932, pp. 29-31. The successive alterations made by A.F. are here discussed.
79. *O. C.,* V, 402.
80. Cf. 'Catherine la dentellière' in *La Rôtisserie ;* but she was a different sort of person.
81. Cf. Maupassant's *Fort comme la Mort* (1889). At times Anatole seems to imitate the clinical Maupassantian manner.
82. *L'Univ. ill.,* Feb. 20, 1892 ; cf. *ibid.,* Oct. 22, 1892, for Henri Rabusson's comment on the similarities between the two versions.
83. 'Vie litt.,' Sept. 22, 1889.
84. E.g., Estève, Lecigne, Rod, etc., as above cited. Also Gille, *Bataille littéraire,* VI, 183 ; Delfour (*Religion des contemporains,* I, 2-7) is less favourable.
85. Seillière, *A.F., critique de son temps,* p. 56.
86. *Rev. hebd.,* Jan. 5, 1895. For further data, see Carias' notes in *O. C.,* X, 517-19.
87. Pouquet, pp. 152, 159.
88. When Fra Mino dies, after a worse vision, his heart 'swells like a sponge'— a touch lifted from *The Golden Ass* of Apuleius (cf. *Vie litt., O. C.,* VI, 119).
89. *The Decameron,* Sixth Day, Ninth Story.
90. *Livres — Manuscrits — Dessins,* p. 100.
91. Gsell, p. 16 ; Vasari, *Vita de' più eccellenti pittori,* etc., ed. of 1791, II, 323. As often, Anatole himself indicates the source in his motto.
92. E.g., St. Brendan's *Ship of Fools ; Légende dorée,* ed. Brunet, II, 269 ; *Acta Sanctorum, passim.*
93. *The Decameron,* Eighth Day, Stories Three and Nine, and Ninth Day, Third Story ; cf. *Puits,* pp. 104-106 and 88, for references to Boccaccio.
94. Three of the four anecdotes derive from Vasari, *op. cit.,* II, 165-88 ('Vita di Buonamico Buffalmacco'). In this series Vasari usually harks back to Sacchetti's *Novelle,* but there is no evidence that France did so.
95. *A.F., critique,* p. 61.
96. These include, for the allegorical wheel of Truth, Dante, *Paradiso,* XXX-XXXI ; *Le Lettere di S. Caterina da Siena,* No. 101.
97. *Ibid.,* No. 97.
98. Ed. G. Paris and U. Robert (1876), Vol. VI, pp. 170-223.
99. *Œuvres complètes* of Pierre de Bourdeille, Abbé de Brantôme (1848), T. II, p. 217.
100. Sources : various memoirs on Napoleon, especially Las Cases, *Mémorial de Sainte-Hélène.*
101. This character reappears and defends himself in the dialogue called 'Farinata degli Uberti ou la Guerre civile,' in the *Clio* volume (O. C., XIII). Cf. *Inferno,* X, 32 ff.

102. *Le Génie européen,* p. 109. This chimes in with the view of Rodes, as cited above, Ch. XV, note 88.
103. Diplock, p. 438.
104. Rosenberg, *art. cit.,* p. 383.
105. Seillière, *A.F., critique,* p. 58 ; Durant, p. 278.
106. Only in so far as Giovanni succumbs to the *libido sciendi* could he be considered a symbol of France's 'inner drama.' Cf. Michaut, pp. 90 and 272, and Shanks, p. 119.
107. Braibant, p. 13 ; Carias, *A.F.,* p. 58.
108. Noussanne, p. 33 ; Seillière, *A.F., critique,* p. 61 ; Maurras, *Rev. encyclopédique,* April 1, 1895.
109. *Livres — Manuscrits — Dessins,* p. 50.
110. Blum, *Rev. blanche,* Feb. 15, 1895, p. 169 ; Truc, p. 29 ; Michaut, pp. 271-72 ; Giraud, pp. 244-46.

CHAPTER XVII

1. *Rev. de Paris,* Dec. 15, 1894, pp. 751-52.
2. Carias, *A.F.,* p. 55 ; cf. Seillière, *Jeunesse d'A.F.,* p. 197.
3. Pouquet, pp. 135-40 ; *Livres — Manuscrits — Dessins,* pp. 97-98.
4. Carias, *op. cit.,* p. 56 ; 'Vie litt.,' Nov. 6, 1892 ; Seillière, *op. cit.,* p. 23 ; cf. *idem, A.F., critique,* p. 14.
5. Gille, *La Bataille littéraire,* VII, 148 ; Rod, *art. cit.,* pp. 755, 758 ; Pellissier, *Rev. encyclopédique,* May 15, 1893 ; these remarks were attenuated somewhat when reprinted in P.'s *Nouveaux Essais.*
6. Especially by Morel, *Gde. Revue,* Nov. 25, 1911, pp. 225-49 ; Doyon, articles in *La Renaissance de l'Occident* (see Bibliography), reprinted in the Introduction to his edition of *Le Comte de Gabalis ;* Carias, *Gde. Rev.,* Dec. 25, 1912, pp. 725 ff ; and cf. Michaut, pp. 166 ff.
7. *O. C.,* VIII, 4. We cite, however, from the modern ed. (1921).
8. Blondheim, *Mod. Lang. Rev.,* July, 1918, p. 334 and note 5 ; Carias, *art. cit.,* p. 732, note 1 ; Voltaire, *Œuvres,* ed. Moland, XIV, 108.
9. Doyon, Introd. to de Villars, pp. xxxvi, xxxix ; an opinion somewhat modified later (p. xli). But Doyon really views Anatole as little more than a 'happy assimilator' !
10. Anon., *Débats,* Sept. 27, 1921 ; Doyon, Introd. to de Villars, p. xiv ; Morel, *art. cit.,* p. 246. Enumerations by Carias, *op. cit.,* p. 55, Michaut, *loc. cit.,* and Anon., in the *Mercure,* Aug. 15, 1924, pp. 285-86. Tracy, *MLN,* March, 1924, p. 189.
11. Carias, *Gde. Rev., art. cit.,* and cf. *ibid.,* Jan. 10, 1913, pp. 51 ff ; Blondheim, *Modern Philology,* July, 1916, p. 53. A.F. showed his knowledge of *Le Compère Mathieu* in *Le Temps,* Dec. 1, 1889.
12. Diplock, p. 443.
13. See *Opinions de Jérôme Coignard,* p. 371 ; cf. Seillière, *A.F., critique,* pp. 24 and 39.
14. *RDM,* Dec. 15, 1896, p. 952. Cf. Vandérem, *Miroir des Lettres,* VIII, 24 ; and Faguet, *Propos litt.,* III, 280, 283.
15. Seillière, *A.F., critique,* p. 36 ; cf. p. 25. A.F.'s debt to Voltaire is also emphasized by Gaffiot, *Théories d'A.F. sur l'org. soc. de son temps,* pp. 52-54.

16. Harris, *Contemporary Portraits,* p. 330 ; Carias, *op. cit.,* p. 51.
17. Michaut (p. 200) compares him further to the real Abbé Prévost as well as to the fictional P. Doni and Fra Giovanni of the *Puits.*
18. This attitude is maintained in his later appearances — cf. the tale of 'Mademoiselle Roxane' (*Contes de Jacques Tournebroche*).
19. According to Carias (*A.F.,* p. 55), there was a contemporary Rosicrucian affair which stirred Paris and turned the imagination of Anatole in this direction. For his general interest in the occult, see above, pp. 309 and 471 f, and for mention of aerial beings surrounding us, see *O. C.,* VI, 297-98.
20. D'Astarac's vision of the stars from l'Ile-des-Cygnes (where Anatole spreads his wings) recalls A.F.'s 'Rêveries astronomiques' (*O. C.,* VII, 204-11). France's Scrap-Book shows that he drew this material in *La Rôtisserie* from Wolff and Flammarion.
21. *O. C.,* XXII, 60-61.
22. Derived from the Greek Anthology, the *motif* is echoed in *Vie litt.,* VI, 636 and in the *Opinions de J. C.,* 471.
23. This 'Eglise du Villars,' near Tournus, is now a 'monument historique.' The tiny town of Villars was chosen by A.F. probably because of the identity of its name with that of the author of *Gabalis.*
24. E.g., by Rod, *art. cit.,* pp. 758-59.
25. The ignorant Capucin, Frère Ange, is scorned by everybody, including both Coignard and d'Astarac. This monk is a sort of *reductio ad absurdum* of blind faith, without 'works' and without intelligence. Yet both he and the Abbé are addicted to scriptural allusions and quotations.
26. Cf. Helen Smith, *Skepticism of A.F.,* pp. 57-58.
27. Lahy-Hollebecque, p. 81.
28. *Op. cit.,* pp. 279-84.
29. Shanks, pp. 109-10 ; Reissig, p. 193.
30. Seillière, *A.F., critique,* p. 39 ; Giraud, *A.F.,* pp. 140-41 (henceforward our citations refer to this new work, rather than to the very similar essay in *Maîtres de l'heure,* II).
31. Michaut, p. 28, cf. p. 83 ; Cerf, p. 92.
32. To swell the volume, Mme. de Caillavet had proffered 'Mlle. Roxane,' but we have noted that this was held over. See Pouquet, pp. 150-51, 156-59 ; *Livres — Manuscrits — Dessins,* pp. 102-104.
33. *Opinions de J. C.,* pp. 312-13.
34. Lemaître, *Contemporains,* VI, 373.
35. Quoted by Seillière, *A.F., critique,* p. 40.
36. Braibant, pp. 233-34, 19. Yet the articles, as immediate reactions to events, must have been interrupted by the trip to Italy in May.
37. *Ibid.,* pp. 10, 253, 251 ; Seillière, *A.F., critique,* p. 40.
38. Exceptionally, the Introduction will be treated as the 'Conclusion' of the original series. The order of the articles can be restored by consulting *O. C.,* VIII, 519.
39. Braibant, p. 240. For A.F. on Ferry, see above, p. 224.
40. Cf. Gaffiot, *Théories d'A.F. sur l'org. soc. de son temps,* pp. 145-46. This writer also comments on A.F.'s quite early aversion to politicians.
41. As related by Hrotswitha (and the *Vies des Pères*) ; lifted from *O. C.,* VII, 28-31.
42. Cf. Gaffiot, *op. cit.,* p. 142.

43. Braibant, pp. 231-34.
44. *Ibid.*, pp. 240-43.
45. *Ibid.*, p. 248 ; Giraud, *op. cit.*, p. 154 ; on the Ronsard frontispiece, see *l'Intermédiaire des chercheurs et curieux,* XXVIII (1893), cols. 88, 297 ; XXIX (1893-94), cols. 67-69.
46. Braibant, pp. 244-46 ; cf. Smith, *op. cit.*, pp. 62-63.
47. See *Livres — Manuscrits — Dessins,* p. 32 ; *Echo de Paris,* Jan. 18, 1893.
48. Braibant, pp. 249-50 ; cf. Smith, p. 64.
49. *A.F., critique,* p. 54.
50. Gaffiot, *op. cit.*, p. 72. On utilitarian justice and the rickety foundations of institutions, see *ibid.*, pp. 176-77.
51. *Echo de Paris,* July 19, 1893. But the final pages, 'les plus audacieuses,' were written and added early in October (Braibant, p. 252).
52. E.g., Seillière, *A.F., critique,* pp. 39-43 ; Smith, p. 56, and Reissig, p. 196.
53. Sée accepts all this as the more abiding view of A.F. himself. Cf. *Gde. Revue,* July, 1925, pp. 121-22.
54. *Op. cit.*, pp. 256 f.
55. *Annales historiques de la Révolution française,* Jan., 1925, p. 55. Cf. Sée, *loc. cit.*
56. Seillière, *A.F., critique,* pp. 42-46 ; Gaffiot, *op. cit.*, pp. 21, 155.
57. Giraud, *A.F.*, pp. 150-51 ; Rod, *art. cit.*, p. 764 ; Vandérem, *Miroir des Lettres,* VII, 244 ; Braibant, pp. 251-52 ; Smith, p. 61 ; Blum, *En Lisant. Réflexions critiques,* p. 49. Cf. also Spronck, *Débats,* Oct. 11, 1893, and Diplock, p. 446.
58. Pouquet, pp. 144-49 and *passim ;* cf. Reissig, p. 146.
59. Pouquet, *loc. cit.*, also pp. 160 f ; cf. Pillet, p. 20.
60. *Livres — Manuscrits — Dessins,* pp. 35-46 ; Henriot, *Le Temps,* Nov. 3, 1931 ; Ambrière, *Nouv. litt.*, April 30, 1932.
61. *Dern. conversations,* p. 206.
62. 'Mes plus pauvres livres ? Ceux que tout le monde louange : *Thaïs, Le Lys rouge.'*— Brousson, *Pantoufles,* p. 335. Cf. Corday, *A.F.*, p. 135.
63. Pouquet, *op. cit.*, pp. 160-62, 168, 193 ; *Livres — Manuscrits — Dessins,* p. 34.
64. Rod., *art. cit.*, pp. 761-63 ; Vandérem, *Miroir des Lettres,* VII, 233 ; Pellissier, *Rev. encyclopédique,* Oct. 15, 1894 (also *Etudes de litt. contemp.*, I, 278 ff) ; Lemaître, *op. cit.*, pp. 362-63, 367, 375 ; Blum, *Rev. blanche,* Feb. 15, 1895, pp. 168-69.
65. 'Cette jalousie, c'est celle du piéton pour le cavalier.'— Braibant, p. 331.
66. Mme. Pouquet (*op. cit.*, p. 163) thinks that the heroine's opinions are more like Mme. Arman's, while Lemaître (*op. cit.*, pp. 367, 370) holds that France speaks for Thérèse as for most of his characters.
67. Larroumet, *Etudes de litt.*, etc., III, 202 ; Michaut, p. xxvii.
68. Giraud, *op. cit.*, pp. 146-47.
69. Larroumet, p. 197 ; cf. Braibant, *loc. cit.*
70. J. Roujon, p. 41 — cf. *Lys rouge,* p. 14 ; Lemaître, *op. cit.*, p. 368 ; Larroumet, p. 200.
71. Cf. Deschamps, *La Vie et les livres,* II, 237, 243 ; Bainville, *Au Seuil du siècle,* p. 147.
72. *O. C.*, VII, 450. On Arsène Darmesteter's 'Vie des mots,' see *O. C.*, VI, 260 ff. Furthermore, 'Gérôme' had discussed both brothers, Arsène and James, the 'Roman' and the 'Iranian' as highly esteemed scholars (*l'Univ. ill.*, Dec. 1, 1888).
73. Vaudoyer, *Nouv. litt.*, April 20, 1935.

74. *Op. cit.*, p. 373. A discussion of Choulette as a 'mauvais saint' may be found in Seillière, *A.F., critique*, pp. 74-79.
75. Cf. above, pp. 363 f and 466 ; especially *l'Univ. ill.*, March 24, 1888, and June 23, 1894 : A.F. visits V. in his hospital.
76. Kéméri, p. 148 ; *l'Univ. ill.*, Dec. 1, 1888. Since this is the same issue in which the Darmesteters are discussed, the fact may have some bearing on the composition of *Le Lys rouge*.
77. *Livres — Manuscrits — Dessins*, p. 45 ; cf. Whale, *Contemporary Review*, Nov., 1926, pp. 607-608.
78. Carias, *op. cit.*, p. 57 ; Diplock, p. 449 ; Lanos, *Queen's Quarterly*, Oct.-Dec., 1907, p. 124 ; Bainville, *loc. cit.* ; Vaudoyer, *art. cit.*
79. Lemaître, *op. cit.*, p. 372 ; cf. Giraud, *op. cit.*, p. 147.
80. Duclaux, *The French Procession*, pp. 347-48 ; Whale, *loc. cit.*
81. Duclaux, p. 350.
82. *Op. cit.*, pp. 362-63. Lemaître, however, attributes the phrase to Lucretius.
83. Rod, *art. cit.*, p. 761 ; Chaumeix, *Rev. hebd.*, March 23, 1912, p. 581.
84. Reissig, pp. 152, 178 ; Lemaître, *op. cit.*, p. 364.
85. *Le Temps*, Dec. 13, 1891 — a review of Jean Psichari's *Jalousie*. This is indicated by Reissig, p. 178. But the more significant passages on jealousy in this article are rather repeated in the *Jardin d'Epicure*, *q.v.*
86. Cf. *Lettres et Arts*, Feb., 1886. Cf. above, p. 278.
87. Cf. *Livres — Manuscrits — Dessins*, pp. 93, 95, 106.
88. Analogies may also be found between Vence and A.F. *re* Napoleon. Again, the former speaks of Renan as 'mon maître bien-aimé' and quotes the well-known passage, 'Qu'est-ce que cela fait à Sirius ?'
89. Ségur, *A.F. anecdotique*, p. 89. A few years ago *Le Lys* had run to 398 'éditions' (in the limited French sense). Its nearest rival was *Thaïs*, with 270 printings.
90. *Livres — Manuscrits — Dessins*, pp. 47-49 and references ; *Rev. d'hist. litt.*, April-June, 1930, p. 282 ; Meyer, *Ce que je peux dire*, p. 243.
91. Bethléem, *Romans à lire et romans à proscrire*, p. 81 ; e.g., Michaut, pp. 299-300 (the lovers' passion as 'exclusively' sensual) ; cf. also Seillière, *A.F., critique*, p. 70, and Cerf, pp. 43 and 47.
92. *Op. cit.*, pp. 373-75. Cf. Deschamps, *op. cit.*, pp. 238, 243.
93. Braibant, *op. cit.*, p. 331, note, and references.
94. Rod, *art. cit.*, p. 764, also Deschamps, pp. 243-44 and Pellissier, *Rev. encyclopédique*, Oct. 15, 1894 ; cf. Larroumet, p. 208.
95. Doumic, *art. cit.*, p. 933 ; Giraud, p. 144.
96. Henriot, *art. cit.* ; Pica, *Letteratura d'eccezione*, p. 271 ; Lemaître, *op. cit.*, p. 366 ; Blum, *art. cit.*, p. 170.
97. 'Jacques Vincent' (Mme. Bory d'Arnex), *Un Salon parisien d'avant-guerre*, p. 123. This copy should be distinguished from the MS. *brouillons* above discussed. The latter were sold for 70,000 francs at the Caillavet-Pouquet Sale.
98. Carias, *op. cit.*, p. 58 (Lemaître first coined the phrase for *Les Opinions*) ; Giraud, p. 157.
99. Reissig, p. 53 ; Blondheim, *Modern Philology*, July 16, 1916, p. 56 ; Michaut, p. xxv (this contains several errors in dates).
100. It is not correct to say, as Michaut does (*loc. cit.*), that the work is 'composé tout entier de fragments écrits entre 1889 et 1892.' The dates should be

widened at either end, and not all the 'fragments' have as yet been found in the journals.

101. Mainly according to Carias, in *O. C.*, IX, 540-42. Some of the themes are similarly developed in *l'Univers illustré*; to what extent has not yet been determined.
102. A.F. himself admitted that most of *Le Jardin* was 'gleaned from *Le Temps*' (Corday, *op. cit.*, pp. 137-38). At least one essay, 'Châteaux de cartes,' had also appeared in *La Vie littéraire*, VII, 384-89.
103. In a few cases, it would be a *fourth* appearance, since the same article did double service in *Le Temps*.
104. It appears that this is wrongly attributed to Fénelon. See Deschamps, *op. cit.*, pp. 249-50.
105. A.F.'s autograph on a presentation copy; Bainville, *op. cit.*, p. 142; Michaut, p. 189.
106. See above, p. 330.
107. Peyre, *Louis Ménard*, pp. 401-402.
108. E.g., by Giraud, pp. 157-58. Wyzewa (*Nos Maîtres*, p. 227) holds that it was A.F. who communicated to his contemporaries this scepticism regarding the value of thought.
109. *Miroir des Lettres*, VII, 235.
110. Bourdeau, *Débats*, Oct. 31, 1924. This philosophy of despair A.F. attributes to the Epicurean school.
111. Voltaire's *Micromégas* closely corresponds.
112. Giraud, p. 160.
113. *Ibid.*, p. 158.
114. Cf. Wyzewa, pp. 227-29.
115. Stewart, p. 62; Gaffiot, *Théories soc. d'A.F.*, p. 31.
116. Deschamps, *op. cit.*, p. 251 — but cf. p. 225 for his 'tranquillity.' This is surely akin to the negative bliss in repose which Epicurus added to the doctrine of the Cyrenaics.
117. See above, pp. 335 and 526.
118. Cf. Deschamps, p. 260.
119. That France thought well of this dialogue is recorded in Pouquet, p. 137.
120. *Le Temps*, Dec. 13 and 20, 1891. *Ibid.*, Sept. 20, 1891.
121. Klein, *Autour du dilettantisme*, pp. 265-73; Michaut, p. xxv; Martin-Mamy, pp. 206-207.
122. Bainville, *op. cit.*, p. 142; Saintsbury, *Quarterly Review*, Jan., 1923, p. 159; Deschamps, pp. 252-58; Tonelli, *Nouv. Rev. d'Italie*, May, 1920; Pellissier, *Rev. encyclopédique*, Dec. 15, 1894. Other favourable reviews may be found in Blum, *art. cit.*, pp. 168 ff and in Gaetano Negri, *Nuova Antologia*, Jan., 1898, p. 53.
123. Brousson, *Pantoufles*, p. 356.
124. I cannot agree with M. Carias who (in *Nouv. litt.*, Feb. 25, 1933) doubts whether Anatole was ever really a 'professeur de néant.'

CHAPTER XVIII

1. Aveline, *'Les Désirs' ou le Livre égaré.* (The amateur there indicated is M. Lion.)
2. P. 7.— Only the more essential references can as a rule be given in this chapter.
3. E.g., *Discours aux étudiants*, 1910, p. 37.

4. Mornet, *Rev. du mois,* 1911, pp. 71, 74.
5. *Rev. pol. et litt.*, Aug. 3, 1889.
6. Ségur, *Conversations,* pp. 181-85, 145-47. But see Introduction above, p. xxix.
7. Cf. Mornet, *art. cit., passim ;* Lœwel, *l'Eclair,* Oct. 23, 1925.
8. Gaffiot, *Théories d'A.F. sur l'org. soc. de son temps,* pp. 91-92 ; cf. p. 100.
9. Cf. Braibant, p. 35 ; Diplock, p. 431.
10. *Op. cit.,* pp. 276-77.
11. This originally appeared in *Le Temps,* March 25, 1888. Other examples of fairly swift turnabouts may be found in *ibid.*, March 20, and May 8, 1892 (*pro* sentiment) contrasted with Dec. 4, 1892 (*pro* intelligence). And cf. Diplock, p. 441.
12. *Le Temps,* July 10, 1892.
13. 'Autobiographie,' p. 9.
14. Pellissier in Petit de Julleville, VIII, 241. Michaut and Reissig agree that A.F. had no system and belonged to no school.
15. J. Psichari, p. 208.
16. Clouard, *Revue critique des idées et des livres,* 1912, p. 260.
17. Corday, *A.F.,* pp. 79-80 ; cf. p. 84.
18. *Le Temps,* Jan. 22, 1893 ; the language here is in part repeated by Coignard.
19. *Vie litt., O. C.,* VII, 5 ; *Génie latin,* p. 248. Cited by Reissig, p. 183.
20. *O. C.,* VI, 367-27 (cf. above, p. 370). Renard's article is in *Les Princes de la jeune critique.*
21. In addition to numerous examples already dealt with, see *Le Temps,* Jan. 24, 1892. Ségur, *Dern. conversations,* p. 200.
22. The story is told by Brousson : see Dirick, p. 49. *Se non è vero è ben trovato.*
23. Maurois, 'Remarques sur quelques MSS. d'A.F.,' in *Livres — Manuscrits — Dessins,* pp. 14-15 ; Vandérem, *Miroir,* VII, 235-36.
24. Gsell, pp. 81-85.
25. *Le Temps,* March 25, 1888.
26. Champion, p. 185.
27. See Appendix E. As Reissig points out (p. 43), Anatole made abundant use of the 'superior doubt' defined in the *Dialogues et fragments philosophiques* (3rd ed., 1885, p. 6) : 'Un doute supérieur plane sur toutes ces spéculations' — because our psychological organization, 'the eye by which we see reality,' may itself be defective.
28. Cf. Carias, *Nouv. litt.,* Feb. 25, 1933.
29. Cited in Braibant, p. 179 ; for the similar opinion of Barrès, see *ibid.,* p. 338.
30. 'Vie litt.,' April 16, 1893.
31. *Op. cit.,* p. 53.
32. *O. C.,* VII, 9 ; Brousson, *Comœdia,* Oct. 16, 1924 ; cf. Giraud, *A.F.,* p. 111.
33. *Petit Pierre,* p. 39 ; *Vie en fleur,* p. 307 ; Corday, *Dern. Pages inédites, passim ;* review of same by Lœwel, *art. cit.*
34. Corday, *A.F.,* p. 84 ; Curtius, p. 75 ; cf. Kéméri, p. 5. Ségur usually takes the other side.
35. Mauriac, pp. 100-101 ; L. Daudet, *l'Action française,* 1924 ; see above, Introduction, p. xxx.
36. E.g., in the religious field, one could develop the discrepancy between his fondness for Church History and his antagonism to dogma ; or his liking for certain

individuals (St. Francis, Coignard) and his rejection of their ultimate court of appeal ; or his shifting of roles between God and the Devil.

37. Gsell, p. 202 ; Gaffiot, *Théories soc. d'A.F.*, pp. 2-3.
38. In *Marianne,* Oct. 10, 1924.
39. Brousson, *Pantoufles,* p. 335.
40. Cf. Stewart, pp. 148-52.
41. Private information. Cf. Corday, *Dern. Pages inédites, passim,* and Lœwel's review (*art. cit.*). This reviewer bases A.F.'s negations (1) on his reaction against the 'Romantic' idea of indefinite progress ; (2) on his belief that our intelligence and knowledge do not advance.
42. The phrases are from Guérard, Dubeck and W. L. George *via* Blondheim.
43. *Pages choisies d'A.F.*, 'Notice,' p. xxiii.
44. *Petit Pierre,* p. 259 ; cf. Massis, *Evocations,* p. 17.
45. See above, p. 411 ; Du Fresnois, *Une Année de critique,* pp. 143, 148 ; M. Boulenger, *Echo de Paris,* Oct. 24, 1924.
46. Stewart, p. 12 ; J. Roujon, pp. 211 ff. Thibaudet and Thérive also lean to this view. Cf. discussion by Lœwel, *l'Eclair,* April 1, 1925.
47. Stewart, pp. 134-35.
48. *O. C.,* IX, 450 ; Anatole's Scrap-Book.
49. Preface to *Drames philosophiques* (1888, p. v). We have seen (above, p. 526) that Paul Vence gives an ambiguous credit for the apophthegm : 'Il était sage, celui qui a dit : "Donnons aux hommes pour témoins et pour juges l'Ironie et la Pitié." '
50. Lemaître, *Contemporains,* VI, 375 ; Rod, *Rev. de Paris,* 1894, p. 765.
51. Chevalier, pp. 11, 31, 79, 37.
52. *Ibid.,* pp. 189-93 ; p. 38, note.
53. L. Delaporte, *Pastels et Figurines,* p. 39 ; Diplock, p. 447 ; Duclaux, pp. 339, 341 — she is supported by many others.
54. A. Bonnard, pp. 314-15. Others and 'diverse' : Doumic and Lemaître (early) ; Syveton, Gottschalk, etc. (later).
55. E.g., Chaumeix, p. 586.
56. *O. C.,* VII, 427.
57. Mornet, *Rev. du mois,* 1911, p. 70.
58. Cf. Stapfer, *Des Réputations littéraires,* II, 346, 353.
59. *O. C.,* XII, 153-54 —'Le rose essaim des pensées polissonnes.'
60. Galantière, *N. Y. Herald Tribune Books,* Oct. 30, 1928 ; Wilson, *New Republic,* Oct. 24, 1934. But these characters do not represent another facet to France : they are his opposites, his adversaries.
61. E.g., Klein, Bethléem, etc.
62. Seillière, *Jeunesse,* especially pp. 21, 23, 185 ; Michaut, pp. 299, 272-73 ; Stewart, pp. 220-21.
63. Guehenno, *Gde. Revue,* 1924, pp. 201-202 ; Gsell, p. 216 ; Reissig, pp. 162-63.
64. Lahy-Hollebecque and Borély, *passim.*
65. Durant, p. 267 ; Garnett, *Bodleian,* Jan., 1921.
66. Comtesse de Noailles, *Nouv. litt.,* April 19, 1924.
67. *L'Homme libre,* May 5, 1913 ; cf. above, p. 241 and references.
68. E.g., Lanson, *Hist. de la litt. française* (21st ed.), p. 1088 ; *Chronique des lettres francaises,* 1924, p. 731.

69. Ségur, *Conversations*, p. 183, cf. p. 195 ; Brousson, *Pantoufles*, p. 61.
70. *Pour :* Corday, P. Calmettes, Kéméri, etc. ; also Couchoud, (*q.v.*) and an article by L. Kahn in the *Revue Juive de Lorraine*, Sept. 1, 1935. *Contre :* Brousson of course, Massis, Lacretelle, and such articles as the one by Marsan.
71. Thérive, *art. cit.*
72. Martin-Mamy, p. 202 ; Lanson, *Pages choisies d'A.F.*, 'Notice,' p. xvi.
73. *Vie en fleur*, pp. 560, 563.
74. Ségur, *Génie européen*, pp. 84-93 ; cf. *Rev. mondiale*, June, 1927.
75. *Miroir*, VIII, 39.
76. Beauduin, *Les Rubriques nouvelles*, 1909, pp. 153-64 ; cf. above, p. xxx.
77. Brousson, *Pantoufles*, pp. 204-205, 262 ; Ségur, *Génie européen*, pp. 98, 101. Corroborated by Courtney, Max Hermant, etc.
78. An autopsy showed that A.F.'s brain, while below the average in size and weight, was perfect in conformation and fissures and unusually complex in its associational tracts or patterns. See *N.Y. Times*, March 24, 1929, and Bibliography under Helsey, Guillaume-Louis and Dubreuil-Chambardel.
79. Vandérem, *Miroir*, VII, 222 ; A. Hermant, *Figaro*, Oct. 13, 1924 ; Massis, *Jugements*, II, 152.
80. E.g., by Lafue, *Rev. hebd.*, 1924, p. 476. Many agree with him.
81. Lanson, *Annales pol. et litt.*, Oct. 19, 1924. 'Others' are Brillant and Brousson (naturally) ; but also Mauriac, Pierre Dominique, etc.
82. Chevalier, p. 216 ; Massis, *Jugements*, I, 145 ff.
83. Kéméri, p. 5.
84. *O. C.*, XXIV, 69-70. Stewart pithily observes (p. 7) : 'He would have regarded it as sheer waste of time, to attempt a reconciliation of his different opinions.'
85. Beauduin, *art. cit. ;* Lœwel, *l'Ordre*, Jan. 13, 1936 — cf. Giraud, *A.F.*, pp. 229 ff ; Souday, *Rev. mondiale*, 1924, pp. 4-6 ; Gaffiot, *Théories d'A.F. sur l'org. soc. de son temps*, p. 9 ; Barrès, *Mes Cahiers*, I, 230. Cf. also Braibant's book, *passim*, and a review thereof in *Vendémiaire*, June 12, 1935.
86. Guehenno, *art. cit. ;* Robert-Sigl, p. 297 and see above, p. 571. On a similar basis, Gorki could declare (*art. cit.*, p. 3) that A.F. was 'in deep communion with the spirit of his country.'
87. Hovelaque, pp. 552-53.
88. Gregh, *La Fenêtre ouverte*, p. 118.
89. Michaut, pp. 22-31.
90. Diplock, p. 440 ; Poizat, p. 381.
91. *Livres — Manuscrits — Dessins*, pp. 35 ff ; Ambrière, *Nouv. litt.*, April 30, 1932.
92. *Op. cit.*, pp. 37, 194 ; cf. 196-97. Boillot (p. 9) is on the same trail when he speaks of France's humorous sense of disproportion.
93. Cf. my article in *The Dial*, Feb. 8, 1919.
94. *Nouv. litt.*, April 9, 1932.
95. Desonay, p. 357 ; Gregh, *op. cit.*, p. 121.
96. Delaporte, *Rev. pol. et litt.*, 1899, pp. 742-44 ; Lemaître, *Contemporains*, VI, 375 ; follows the passage concerning 'la perfection dans la grâce,' etc. Massis, *Arts et Métiers graphiques*, 1929, p. 590.
97. *O. C.*, XXII, 93-94 and V, 187 ; the enumeration from *Thaïs* is partly in the manner of Chateaubriand. Cf. Des Hons, pp. 34-37 and *passim*.

98. A.F. as quoted by Brousson, *Nouv. litt.,* Feb. 24, 1923; Girard quoted by 'Charensol,' *art. cit.*
99. Thibaudet, *Nouv. litt.,* March 2, 1929.
100. Cf. Preface to *Vie en fleur* — here he is after 'les petites choses peintes avec une grande exactitude'; in the same work (pp. 551-52), there is an interesting sketch of the kind of lively conversation that he preferred.
101. Not always advantageously, if we accept Mauriac's view (p. 100).
102. *Ibid.;* Amiot, p. 145; Carias, *A.F.,* p. 81.
103. Michaut, *op. cit.,* pp. 256-64.
104. *La Jeune France,* Feb., 1880, p. 369.
105. *O. C.,* XXV, 161 ff.; Proust, Preface to Morand, *Tendres Stocks, passim;* cf. Ségur, *Rev. mondiale,* 1921, pp. 208-11.
106. *Le Chasseur bibliographe,* Feb., 1867, as cited by Reissig, p. 66; *ibid.,* p. 169; the same author shrewdly remarks (p. 69): 'Su afán de ser claro y de optar por la expresión más sencilla y más breve no es [solamente] paciencia de estilista sino finura de voluptuoso.'
107. *O. C.,* IX, 442-43.
108. Private information; 'Autobiographie,' p. 7.
109. *Vie en fleur,* p. 360; Thérive, *Nouv. litt.,* April 19, 1924.
110. Brousson, *Pantoufles,* p. 99; Harris, pp. 339, 341.
111. Nouvelles Acquisitions Françaises, Nos. 10802-10803; 10806-10808; 21609, etc. It is true that several of these present a later stage than the first *brouillon.*
112. Carias, *op. cit.,* p. 49.
113. Wendel, cited in *Revue Rhénane,* 1924, p. 77; cf. Bidou, *ibid.,* p. 68; even the hostile Brousson (in *Les Vêpres de l'avenue Hoche*), Mauriac, Thérive, A. Hermant, etc., bear similar testimony.
114. Cited by Brandes, *A.F.,* p. 107.
115. *N.Y. Times Book Review,* Oct. 14, 1924.
116. *O. C.,* II, 278.
117. *N.Y. Times Book Review,* Dec. 26, 1926.
118. *O. C.,* IX, 443; Baring, p. 279.
119. See above, pp. 91, 466, and 479-80.
120. Reggio, *Au Seuil de leur âme,* pp. 65-66, 75 ff.
121. *Op. cit.,* p. 181.
122. Locke, *Bodleian,* Jan., 1921; Durant, p. 296; Samain, p. 11.
123. Doyon, though often unfavourable (*Conférence sur A.F.*), lists the Francian qualities as 'légèreté, finesse, subtilité et par-dessus tout, poésie.'
124. Lanson, *l'Art de la Prose,* pp. 279-81, 273-74; *O. C.,* XI, 367-68. (In this passage, the soft alliteration of the 'v's' is noticeable.)
125. *O. C.,* V, 28.
126. Becker, *Mercure,* 1914, pp. 320-25. It would be interesting to discover other such cases.
127. Cf. Giraud, *A.F.,* p. 145.
128. *O. C.,* II, 503-504.
129. Michaut, pp. 264-74; Cerf, p. 211; Chassé, *Le Capitole,* Oct., 1924.
130. E.g., R. Blanck, *A.F. als Stilkunstler in seinen Romanen;* Maurois, *art. cit.,* Chassé, *art. cit.*

131. Stewart, p.101 (apropos of the *Histoire contemporaine*).
132. Dike, Introduction to *Monsieur Bergeret. Passages from 'L'Histoire contemporaine' by A.F.*, p. xviii.
133. Brousson, *Pantoufles*, pp. 78-84 ; cf. *Itinéraire*, pp. 188, 305.
134. Truc, *A.F.*, pp. 26-27 ; cf. Chassé, *art. cit.*
135. E.g., in the story of the 'Trublions' (*M. Bergeret à Paris*) ; cf. Doyon, *op. cit.*, pp. 3-4.
136. Brousson, *Pantoufles*, pp. 78-88. There is sufficient supporting testimony.
137. *O. C.*, XXIII, 227 ; quoted in *Revue Rhénane*, 1924, p. 73 ; *cf. Trente Journées de grand travail.*
138. Demont-Breton, p. 160.
139. *Op. cit.*, p. 18.
140. Several of these are due to technical investigations made by students ; others emerge from examining A.F.'s manuscripts and proof-corrections.
141. *O. C.*, V, 448. (The final paragraph is in the early editions only.)
142. Respectively in *Crainquebille* and the Préface to *l'Ile des Pingouins*. 'Que d'art!' is said to derive from MacMahon's remark when officially visiting an inundation : 'Que d'eau !'
143. From A.F.'s Scrap-Book. *L'Univ. ill.*, May 12, 1883 ; cf. above, p. xxi, where this passage is translated.
144. It may be interesting to watch A.F. getting a sentence under way. In a MS. fragment (from his 'Notes'), an old man is talking about girls. The first form was : 'Le pis est que je ne les vois p . . .' [erasure]. He began again : 'Je ne les vois pas, parce que je suis vieux et . . .' [erasure]. Finally, he succeeded : 'Depuis que je suis vieux, je ne les vois plus guère.' The shifting of the emphasis is noticeable.
145. Giraud, *A.F.*, p. 144, and Prévost in *Le Lys rouge* (periodical), Oct. 1, 1934 ; cf. Angellier as quoted by Giraud, *Encore sur A.F.*, p. 160.
146. Bourget, p. 153.
147. See above, pp. 142-43 ; Amiot, pp. 145-46 ; Jean Psichari, in Picard, pp. 350-51 ; Cerf, pp. 207 ff.
148. Saintsbury, p. 141 ; Thebault, *La Volonté*, Nov. 16, 1898 ; G. Cohen, *l'Alsace française*, Oct. 18, 1924 ; Jaloux, *Nouv. litt.*, Oct. 18, 1924.
149. Valéry, *Discours de Réception à l'Académie française* (1927), pp. 73-74 ; Barrès, as quoted by Maurras, *A.F. politique et poète*, p. 3 ; Clouard, *art. cit.*, p. 258.
150. Gregh, *Annales pol. et litt.*, Oct. 19, 1924 ; cf. A. Hermant, *Nouv. litt.*, April 19, 1924.

CHAPTER XIX

1. Beginning with 1898, they have been collected in *Vers les Temps meilleurs* and in *Opinions sociales.*
2. Braibant, p. 60.
3. *La Société historique d'Auteuil et de Passy. Conférence faite le mercredi 28 février 1894.* See above, pp. 52 and 175.
4. In *Le Temps*, etc. ; cf. above, pp. 211-12.
5. *Discours de M. A.F. à la séance d'inauguration des cours externes de l'Institut Polytechnique de jeunes filles*, 1894.

6. July 7, 1894.
7. *Discours aux Etudiants, prononcés devant l'Association générale des Etudiants de Paris* (Colin, 1900). See above, p. 233. This should be distinguished from the much more important *Discours aux Etudiants* of 1910.
8. 'Les Parisiens de Paris. Dîner de Molière du 9 janvier 1896, (*O. C.*, XXV, 5-8).
9. *Le Monument de Marceline Desbordes-Valmore. Souvenir de la Fête d'inauguration du 13 juillet*, 1896 (Pamphlet). Also as 'Discours' in *O. C.*, XXV, 11-18. (A facsimile of the MS. is in the New York Public Library, Manuscript Division.)
10. Stewart, p. 334; Brousson, *Pantoufles*, p. 139.
11. *Journal des Goncourt*, IX, 352-53. E. de Goncourt was both surprised and pleased at his inclusion in the toast.
12. *Livres — Manuscrits — Dessins*, p. 99; Josephson, *Zola and His Time*, pp. 342, 345.
13. *Le Figaro*, Dec. 2, 1892. See also Braibant, p. 238, note and references.
14. Stewart, p. 331.
15. Braibant, pp. 237-38, 324; see above, p. 432 and *O. C.*, XI, 455-57.
16. *Le Matin*, Oct. 13, 1924; Stewart, p. 333; Ledrain, p. 870.
17. Authenticity attested; cf. Corday, *A.F.*, pp. 74-75.
18. So thinks Gaffiot, in *Théories d'A.F. sur l'org. soc. de son temps*, p. 6. The following account is condensed by Stewart (p. 333) from Brousson, *Pantoufles*, pp. 96-97, with touches from Gsell, pp. 43-46.
19. Ségur, *Conversations*, pp. 172-73; Gsell, *loc. cit.* and Stewart, p. 85; Corday, *op. cit.*, pp. 160, 163-64.
20. *Rev. encyclopédique*, March 15, 1896.
21. *O. C.*, XXV, 416. Monval, pp. 185-86.
22. Letter in Collection Lion.
23. *Itinéraire*, pp. 257, 319; cf. 'Gyp' in Pouquet, *Salon*, pp. 39-40, note.
24. Letter dated Jan. 23, 1896. In Pouquet, *Rev. de Paris*, 1926, p. 72.
25. 'Jacques Vincent,' p. 116; Carias, *A.F.*, p. 59.
26. Prade, *Bull. Officiel*, June 18, 1933.
27. See above, p. 428. Yet he told Frank Harris (p. 337) that they were 'all in it,' meaning the business of bribing.
28. Bibliothèque Nationale, 'Nouvelles acquisitions françaises,' No. 10800.
29. From material found in *Le Larousse Mensuel*, June, 1935, pp. 122-23. To complete the record, the following names and occupations should be added: Léon Say, *économiste*; Octave Gréard, *moraliste et administrateur*; Ernest Legouvé, *auteur dramatique*; Joseph Bertrand, *mathématicien*; Henry Houssaye, *historien*; Henri de Bornier, *poète dramatique* (in that capacity he was presently succeeded by Rostand); Vicomte E. M. de Vogüé, to be distinguished, as 'critique et romancier,' from another of the same family; Charles de Freycinet, *ingénieur et homme politique*; Challemel-Lacour, *philosophe et homme politique* (he tried to occupy the chair of Renan); E. Hervé, *journaliste*; Rousse, *avocat*; D'Audiffret-Pasquier, *homme politique*; Gaston Boissier, *humaniste* — also 'perpetual secretary' *à la* Fontenelle; Perraud, *cardinal* (the 'bishop' of Maurras?); Ludovic Halévy, *auteur dramatique* — and *entrepreneur* of A.F.
30. *Opinion*, Oct. 17, 1924; Maurras, *art. cit.*, Zola had thought of running, but decided to wait for the chair of Dumas *fils*; he never entered the Academy.
31. Collection Lion. The various newspaper accounts are also found here.

32. *Figaro,* Dec. 18, 1895 ; on Jan. 19 this journal announced the withdrawal of Stéphen Liégard, who had originally been favoured by Mme. de Lesseps.
33. See issues of Jan. 24 ff. Also *La Liberté, Le Siècle, La République française,* etc.
34. *L'Univ. ill.,* Feb. 1, 1896 ; Maurras, *art. cit. ; Opinion, art. cit.*
35. *Figaro,* Jan. 31, 1896.
36. *Ibid.,* Oct. 23, 1896.
37. This consisted originally of Henri de Bornier, Albert Sorel, Sully Prudhomme and Ferdinand Brunetière. Later, Vogüé replaced Bornier. *Figaro,* Dec. 4 and 18, 1896.
38. Champion, p. 214 (cf. p. 213). The newspapers for Dec. 25 and 26 are full of the event. E.g., *Le Figaro* and *Le Petit Parisien* of the former date. A.F.'s old standby, *l'Univ. ill.* (Dec. 26) paid due tribute to the occasion and ran a frontispiece containing woodcuts of France and scenes from his novels.
39. *O. C.,* XXV, 363-91. The *Echo de Paris* and other newspapers promptly printed the *Discours.* Two *morceaux* of the anecdotal type, omitted in the reading, were restored — cf. *O. C.,* XXV, 442, 447-53.
40. Braibant, p. 237 ; J. Roujon, *passim.*
41. Cf. Champion, p. 218.
42. Gréard, *Discours de Réception,* pp. 31 ff. See above, pp. 61, 174 and 196.
43. Again, Abel Hermant (*Figaro,* Oct. 13, 1924) epitomizes A.F. as 'un moment des lettres françaises.'
44. *Discours de Réception,* pp. 27-30.
45. Maurel, *Figaro,* Dec. 28, 1896.
46. Collection Lion. Illustrations to Carias, *A.F.*
47. Nouv. acq. fr., No. 10800.
48. Most of this is quoted in Carias, *A.F.,* p. 59.
49. Monval, p. 186.
50. It is rumoured that his father was not so cordial ; private information.
51. Other specimens are in the Collection Lion.
52. Cf. Anatole's preface for *Les Jeunes Madames* of Brada, 1895.
53. See above, p. 313.
54. Braibant, p. 14. He extends the domination to 'vingt-cinq ans' ; I would estimate the span as stretching from 1896 to (*c.*) 1913.
55. Edmund Wilson in *New Republic,* Oct. 24, 1934.
56. Pouquet, *art. cit.* He told a rather carping 'friend' : 'Eh bien, oui, on en est content comme de toutes les choses qu'on reçoit après les avoir désirées longtemps.' (Private information.)
57. Brousson, *Pantoufles, passim ;* Stewart, pp. 333-34 ; P. Gsell, pp. 31 ff ; Dirick, pp. 73-74 ; Goll, pp. 224-26 ; Brousson, *Itinéraire,* p. 257.
58. Maurel, *Les Œuvres libres,* Vol. 44, p. 367 ; cf. P. Champion, p. 219.

BIBLIOGRAPHY

BIBLIOGRAPHY

A. WORKS BY ANATOLE FRANCE

I. Collected

ŒUVRES COMPLÈTES ILLUSTRÉES. Paris : Calmann-Lévy, 1925 ff. XXV volumes to date, 8vo. Eds., L. Carias and G. Le Prat. (Each volume ends with a 'Bibliographie' compiled by M. Carias.)

Tome I. Pp. 7-119 : Alfred de Vigny.
Pp. 127-413 : Poésies, including :
Les Poèmes dorés (pp. 127-82) ; Idylles et Légendes (pp. 185-246) ; Les Noces corinthiennes (pp. 249-357) ; Epigrammes funéraires, Leuconoé, etc. (pp. 360 ff).

Tome II. Pp. 3-134 : Jocaste.
Pp. 137-262 : Le Chat maigre.
Pp. 267-508 : Le Crime de Sylvestre Bonnard, Membre de l'Institut.

Tome III. Pp. 3-179 : Les Désirs de Jean Servien.
Pp. 185-439 : Le Livre de mon ami.

Tome IV. Pp. 5-118 : Nos Enfants.
Pp. 123-352 : Balthasar.
Balthasar (pp. 123-48) ; Le Réséda du Curé (pp. 151-53) ; M. Pigeonneau (pp. 157-74) ; La Fille de Lilith (pp. 177-93) ; Læta Acilia (pp. 197-212) ; l'Œuf rouge (pp. 215-26) ; Abeille (pp. 229-352).

Tome V. Pp. 5-213 : Thaïs.
Pp. 219-463 : L'Etui de nacre.
Le Procurateur de Judée (pp. 219-38) ; Amycus et Célestin (pp. 241-46) ; La Légende des Saintes Oliverie et Liberette (pp. 249-59) ; Sainte Euphrosine (pp. 263-76) ; Scolastica (pp. 279-83) ; Le Jongleur de Notre-Dame (pp. 287-98) ; La Messe des Ombres (pp. 301-308) ; Leslie Wood (pp. 311-24) ; Gestas (pp. 327-35) ; Le Manuscrit d'un médecin de village (pp. 339-50) ; Mémoires d'un Volontaire (pp. 353-97) ; l'Aube (pp. 401-12) ; Madame de Luzy (pp. 415-25) ; La Mort Accordée (pp. 429-32) ; Anecdote de Floréal An II (pp. 435-41) ; Le Petit Soldat de plomb (pp. 445-53) ; La Perquisition (pp. 457-63).

Tome VI. Pp. 3-662 : La Vie littéraire (old series I and II).

Tome VII. Pp. 3-717 : La Vie littéraire (old series III and IV).

Tome VIII. Pp. 3-304 : La Rôtisserie de la Reine Pédauque.
Pp. 309-511 : Les Opinions de M. Jérôme Coignard.

Tome IX. Pp. 5-390 : Le Lys rouge.
Pp. 395-535 : Le Jardin d'Epicure.

Tome X. Pp. 5-260 : Le Puits de Sainte Claire.
Prologue (pp. 5-12) ; Saint Satyre (pp. 15-40) ; Messer Guido Cavalcanti (pp. 43-56) ; Lucifer (pp. 59-65) ; Les Pains noirs (pp. 69-73) ; Le Joyeux Buffalmacco (pp. 77-106) ; La Dame de Vérone (pp. 109-13) ; l'Humaine Tragédie (pp. 117-211) ; Le Mystère du Sang (pp. 215-22) ; La Caution (pp. 225-33) ; Histoire de Doña Maria d'Avalos

et de Don Fabricio, duc d'Andria (pp. 237-47) ; Bonaparte à San Miniato (pp. 251-60).
Pp. 625-516 : Pierre Nozière.
Tome XI. Pp. 5-222 : L'Orme du Mail.
Pp. 225-453 : Le Mannequin d'Osier.
Tome XII. Pp. 3-277 : L'Anneau d'améthyste.
Pp. 281-551 : M. Bergeret à Paris.
Tome XIII. Pp. 3-115 : Clio.
Le Chanteur de Kymé (pp. 3-23) ; Komm l'Atrébate (pp. 25-69) ; Farinata degli Uberti ou la Guerre civile (pp. 71-85) ; Le Roi Boit (pp. 87-94) ; 'La Muiron' (pp. 95-115).
Pp. 119-353 : Histoire comique.
Pp. 359-557 : Sur la Pierre blanche.
Tome XIV. Pp. 9-229 : Crainquebille, Putois, Riquet et plusieurs autres récits profitables.
Pp. 239-304 : Crainquebille (pièce).
Pp. 313-484 : Le Mannequin d'Osier (pièce).
Pp. 491-539 : Au Petit Bonheur.
Tome XV. Pp. 3-598 : Vie de Jeanne d'Arc, I.
Tome XVI. Pp. 3-464 : Vie de Jeanne d'Arc, II.
Tome XVII. Pp. 5-265 : Rabelais.
Pp. 269-95 : Auguste Comte.
Pp. 299-325 : Pierre Laffitte.
Tome XVIII. Pp. 3-420 : L'Ile des Pingouins.
Pp. 433-81 : La Comédie de Celui qui épousa une femme muette.
Tome XIX. Pp. 5-121 : Les Contes de Jacques Tournebroche.
Le Gab d'Olivier (pp. 5-16) ; Le Miracle de la Pie (pp. 19-38) ; Frère Joconde (pp. 41-59) ; La Picarde, la Poitevine, la Tourangelle, la Lyonnaise et la Parisienne (pp. 63-66) ; La Leçon bien apprise (pp. 69-82) ; De une horrible Paincture (pp. 85-88) ; Les Etrennes de Mademoiselle de Doucine (pp. 91-99) ; Mademoiselle Roxane (pp. 103-21).
Pp. 127-343 : Les Sept Femmes de la Barbe-Bleue et autres contes merveilleux.
Les Sept Femmes de la Barbe-Bleue, d'après des documents authentiques (pp. 127-63) ; Le Miracle du grand Saint Nicolas (pp. 167-213) ; Histoire de la Duchesse de Cicogne et de M. de Boulingrin (pp. 217-41) ; Lá Chemise (pp. 245-343).
Tome XX. Pp. 3-316 : Les Dieux ont soif.
Tome XXI. Pp. 7-335 : Le Génie latin.
Daphnis et Chloé (pp. 7-16) ; La Reine de Navarre (pp. 17-36) ; Paul Scarron (pp. 37-69) ; Remarques sur la Langue de La Fontaine (pp. 71-102) ; Molière (pp. 103-41) ; Jean Racine (pp. 143-69) ; Alain-René Le Sage (pp. 171-81) ; Les Aventures de l'Abbé Prévost (pp. 183-208) ; Bernardin de Saint-Pierre (pp. 209-43) ; Chateaubriand (pp. 245-70) ; Xavier de Maistre (pp. 271-74) ; Benjamin Constant (pp. 275-86) ; Sainte-Beuve Poète (pp. 287-310) ; Albert Glatigny (pp. 311-35).
Pp. 339-70 : Les Poèmes du Souvenir.

Tome XXII. Pp. 3-322 : La Révolte des anges.
Tome XXIII. Pp. 5-281 : Le Petit Pierre.
Pp. 285-564 : La Vie en fleur.
Tome XXIV. Pp. 5-367 : Pages d'Histoire et de littérature, I.
Madame de la Sablière, notice (pp. 5-27) ; Le Marquis de Sade, notice (pp. 31-46) ; Jocko, notice (pp. 49-58) ; Histoire d'Henriette d'Angleterre, étude (pp. 61-122) ; La Princesse de Clèves, préface (pp. 125-43) ; Le Palais de Fontainebleau, préface (pp. 147-50) ; Le Café Procope (pp. 153-58) ; Vieux Péchés, préface (pp. 161-63) ; Le Faust de Goethe, lettre préface (pp. 167-84) ; Le Dernier Abbé, préface (pp. 187-95) ; Promenades félibréennes (pp. 199-221) ; Hérodias, préface (pp. 225-48) ; l'Année littéraire, préface (pp. 251-55) ; Un Hollandais à Paris en 1891, préface (pp. 259-64) ; l'Elvire de Lamartine (pp. 267-333) ; Le Roi Candaule, préface (pp. 337-48) ; Le Chemin de Paradis, épigramme (pp. 351-52) ; Jeunes Madames, préface (pp. 355-59) ; Lettre de Sicile sur l'Oaristys (pp. 363-67).
Tome XXV. Pp. 5-413 : Pages d'Histoire et de littérature, II.
Diner de Molière, discours (pp. 5-8) ; Le Monument de Marceline Desbordes-Valmore, discours (pp. 11-18) ; Lorenzaccio, étude (pp. 21-31) ; Mentis, préface (pp. 35-39) ; Les Plaisirs et les Jours, préface (pp. 43-45) ; Alphonse Daudet, étude (pp. 49-60) ; Histoire du chien de Brisquet, préface (pp. 63-66) ; Index Raisonné de la Mythologie d'Horace, préface (pp. 69-71) ; Pallas Athena, étude (pp. 75-81) ; Les Arts et les Artistes, préface (pp. 85-89) ; Le Tombeau de Molière, hommage (pp. 93-97) ; P.-P. Prud'hon, étude (pp. 101-17) ; Petits Châteaux de Bohème, préface (pp. 121-28) ; Petite Histoire parlementaire, préface (pp. 131-32) ; La Reine Cléopâtre, préface (pp. 135-41) ; Pensées philosophiques, préface (pp. 145-48) ; Les Heures latines, préface (pp. 151-58) ; Stendhal, étude (pp. 161-82) ; Les Mémoires d'un rat, préface (pp. 185-88) ; La Garçonne, préface (pp. 191-93) ; Le Livre de la pitié et de la mort, préface (pp. 197-206) ; Sages et Poètes d'Asie, préface (pp. 209-19) ; Marguerite (pp. 223-51) ; Le Comte Morin (pp. 255-82); Pâques ou la Délivrance (pp. 285-93) ; Monsieur Patru (pp. 297-305) ; La Terre (pp. 309-11) ; Le Miracle de l'Avare (pp. 315-32) ; l'Escalade (pp. 335-43); Dialogue aux Enfers (pp. 347-53) ; La Terre et l'homme (pp. 357-59) ; Discours de Réception à l'Académie française (pp. 363-91) ; Une des plus grandes Découvertes du siècle (pp. 393-413).

II. Uncollected

(Only those items mentioned in our text are included here. In many cases stories or articles by A.F. have been treated above as they appeared periodically or in early editions. Full references to such publications are not usually given below. Those interested may refer to the *O. C.*, *'Bibliographies,'* under individual titles.

For translations and anthologies with editorial comment, see below, section B, I, under Dike, Henning, Lane, Lanson, May.)

Manuscripts. Widely scattered, especially since Caillavet-Pouquet sale (cf. *Livres — Manuscrits — Dessins*). No complete data available; no collected correspondence, except as indicated above, p. 607. See *O. C.*, 'Bibliographies,' *passim;* Bibliothèque Nationale, *Nouvelles acquisitions françaises,* No. 10795 *et seq.;* Collection Lion; Collection Barthou; also above, pp. 671, 687, and Appendix C.

Alfred de Vigny: étude. Bachelin-Deflorenne, 1868.
——. Edition revue et corrigée par l'auteur. Aveline, 1923.
Almanach de la Révolution française pour 1870. (Brief notices.)
Almanach du Bibliophile, Jan., 1899 ('Les Bouquinistes et les quais').
Amateur d'autographes, 1867-77. (Book-reviews for about 36 numbers, including July 1 and 15, 1868, 'Prospectus et circulaire.')
Les Autels de la peur. Débats, March 2-16, 1884.
——. Private printing, '1885' (really 1926).
'Autobiographie. Fragment.' Revue de France, Nov. 1, 1924, pp. 5-9.
Bibliophile français, 1870-73. (About 10 book-reviews.)
Chasseur biblographe, Jan., 1867—March, 1867. (Seven articles, including 'Un Foyer éteint,' Feb., 1867, pp. 35-37.)
Collection Lion. Numerous documents, as indicated above
'Le Comte Morin, Député.' Revue indépendante de littérature et d'art, Dec., 1886, pp. 261-317. *See O. C.*, XXV.
Curiosités littéraires — Les Premières Armes du symbolisme. Vanier, 1889. (Contains article by A.F.)
Dernières pages inédites, ed. M. Corday. Calmann-Lévy, 1925.
Dictionnaire des antiquités grecques et romaines (by Daremberg and Saglio). (Three short articles in 1873 and 1881.)
Discours:
La Société historique d'Auteuil et de Passy. Conférence faite le mercredi 28 février à la mairie du XVI arrondissement. Calmann-Lévy, 1894.
. . . de M. A.F. à la séance d'inauguration des cours externes de l'Institut polytechnique de jeunes filles, 1894. In *brochure,* Société pour l'éducation féminine. Institut polytechnique . . . pour jeunes filles. (s.d.), pp. 15-22.
Les Parisiens de Paris. Dîner de Molière du 9 janvier 1896. *See O. C.*, XXV.
Marceline Desbordes-Valmore. In Le Monument de Marceline Desbordes-Valmore. Souvenir de la Fête d'inauguration du 13 juillet, 1896. Douai, 1896, pp. 19-23. *See O. C.*, XXV.
Institut de France: Académie française. Discours prononcés dans la séance publique tenue par l'Académie française pour la réception de M. A.F., le 24 décembre, 1896. Firmin-Didot, 1896. *See O. C.*, XXV.
. . . aux Etudiants, prononcés devant l'Association générale des étudiants de Paris. Colin, 1900. (Includes A.F.'s *Discours* at the Tenth Annual Banquet, Dec. 1, 1895.)
Les Funérailles de Zola. Discours prononcé au cimetière Montmartre, le 5 octobre 1902. Pelletan, 1903.

. . . de Tréguier. (Discours prononcé à l'inauguration de la statue de Renan.) Calmann-Lévy, 1903.

Aux étudiants, discours prononcé à la Maison des Etudiants le samedi 28 mai 1910. Pelletan, 1910.

. . . prononcé à la Sorbonne le 22 juin 1916. In Barthou, l'Hommage français. L'Effort Italien. Bloud et Gay, 1916, pp. 25-28.

Echo de Paris, 1893-99. (Numerous articles, many reprinted.)

L'Elvire de Lamartine; notes sur M. et Mme. Charles. Champion, 1893. *See O. C.,* XXIV.

L'Etui de nacre. Calmann-Lévy, 1892.

Gazette bibliographique, 1868-69. (Three articles on libraries; also two book-notices.)

Gazette de Pierrefonds, Sept. 21, 1884.

Gazette rimée, 1867. (Includes 'Denys, tyran de Syracuse,' March 20, pp. 28-30 and 'Les Légions de Varus,' June 20, pp. 75-78.)

Le Génie latin. Calmann-Lévy, 1913.

Le Globe, July-Oct., 1879. (Fifteen book-reviews.)

L'Homme libre, May 5, 1913. ('En huitième.')

Jean Servien. Calmann-Lévy, 1882. (With preface.)

La Jeune France, 1878-84. (Articles and stories.)

Jocaste et le Chat maigre. Calmann-Lévy, 1879. (With preface suppressed later.)

Les Lettres et les arts, 1886. (Articles, stories and book-reviews.)

Livre du Bibliophile. Lemerre, 1874 (reprint 1926).

Lucile de Chateaubriand. Ses contes, ses poèmes, ses lettres, précédé d'une étude sur sa vie par A.F. Charavay, 1879. *See O. C.,* XXI.

Marguerite, in Les Lettres et les arts, Dec., 1886.

——, in book-form. André Coq, 1920. *See O. C.,* XXV.

Opinions sociales d'A.F. 2 vols. G. Bellois, 1902.

Prefaces to:

Les Poèmes de Jules Breton, étude par A.F. Charavay, 1875.

Les Œuvres de Bernard Palissy, publiées d'après les textes originaux, avec une notice historique et bibliographique et une table analytique par A.F. Charavay Frères, 1880.

Marquis de Sade, Dorci, ou la Bizarrerie du sort, avec une notice sur l'auteur par A.F. Charavay Frères, 1881. *See O. C.,* XXIV.

Pougens, C. M. de, Jocko . . . précédé d'une notice par A.F. Charavay, 1881. *See O. C.,* XXIV.

La Fayette, Mme. de, Histoire d'Henriette d'Angleterre, avec une introduction par A.F. Charavay, 1882. *See O. C.,* XXIV.

Fables de J. de La Fontaine, avec une notice sur La Fontaine et des notes par A.F. Lemerre, 1883. *See O. C.,* XXI.

Le Château de Vaux-le-Vicomte, dessiné et gravé par Rudolphe Pfnor . . ., accompagné d'un texte historique et descriptif par A.F. Lemercier, 1888.

La Fayette, Mme. de, La Princesse de Clèves. Conquet, 1889. *See O. C.,* XXIV.

Pfnor, R., Guide artistique et historique au palais de Fontainebleau. André Daly, 1889. *See O. C.*, XXIV.
Vivant-Denon, Baron, Point de Lendemain. Rouquette, 1890.
Œuvres de J.-M. Goethe. Faust. Traduction nouvelle par Camille Benoît. 2 vols. Lemerre, 1891. (Reprinted from *Revue pol. et litt.*, Aug. 3, 1889, pp. 146-50.) *See O. C.*, XXIV.
P. de Musset, Le Dernier Abbé. Ferroud, 1891. *See O. C.*, XXIV.
P. Arène and A. Tournier, Des Alpes aux Pyrénées. Etapes félibréennes. Flammarion, 1891.
Ginisty, P., l'Année littéraire . . . 7e année, 1891. Charpentier, 1892. *See O. C.*, XXIV.
Flaubert, Hérodias. Ferroud, 1892. *See O. C.*, XXIV.
Gautier, Le Roi Candaule. Ferroud, 1893. *See O. C.*, XXIV.
Gautier, Une Nuit de Cléopâtre. Ferroud, 1894.
Maurras, C., Le Chemin de Paradis ('Epigramme'). Calmann-Lévy, 1896. *See O. C.*, XXIV.
Théocrite, l'Oaristys, texte grec et traduction de M. André Bellessort, précédée d'une Lettre de Sicile, par M. A.F. Pelletan, 1896. *See O. C.*, XXIV.
Hély, L., Mentis. Poème. Fischbacher, 1896. *See O. C.*, XXV.
Proust, Les Plaisirs et les jours. Pelletan, 1896. *See O. C.*, XXV.
Psichari, M., Index raisonné de la mythologie d'Horace. Welter, 1904. *See O. C.*, XXV.
De Oliveira Lima and V. Orban, Machado de Assis et son œuvre littéraire. 1909.
Nerval, G. de, Petits châteaux en Bohême, promenades et souvenirs. E. Paul, 1912. *See O. C.*, XXV.
Les Travaux et les jours d'Hésiode, traduction nouvelle de Paul Mazan, suivis de la Terre et l'Homme par A.F. Pelletan, 1912.
Couchoud, P.-L., Sages et Poètes d'Asie. Calmann-Lévy, 1916. *See O. C.*, XXV.
Hesse, R., Riquet à la Houppe et ses compagnons. Mornay, 1923.

Promenades félibréennes. [Privately printed], 1895. *See O. C.*, XXIV.
Le Rappel, Sept. 17, 1869. ('Variétés. Les Poètes.')
Revue alsacienne, Oct., 1885, pp. 529-35. ('Les Guérin.')
Revue de famille, 1889-92. Following articles are included: Aug. 1, 1889: 'Frère Richard,' pp. 14-25; Jan. 15, 1890: 'Un Emule de Jeanne d'Arc — Le Petit Berger,' pp. 161-73; April 1, 1890: Jeanne d'Arc et les Fées,' pp. 33-42; Nov. 15, 1890: 'Merlin l'Enchanteur et la vocation de Jeanne d'Arc,' pp. 330-43; Feb. 15, 1891: 'Une Fausse Jeanne d'Arc. La Dame des Armoises,' pp. 344-62; May 15, 1891: 'Jeanne d'Arc a-t-elle été brûlée à Rouen?', pp. 315-31; Jan. 15, 1892: 'Les Voix de Jeanne d'Arc. Saint-Michel, Sainte-Catherine et Sainte-Marguerite,' pp. 153-73; April 1, 1892: 'Jeanne d'Arc et Saint Remi,' pp. 60-75.
Revue des documents historiques, 1873-76. (Book-notices.)
Revue illustrée, 1889-90. Following articles are included: Dec. 15, 1889: 'Menus Propos, p. 8; Jan. 1, 1890: 'Si Jeanne d'Arc a été brûlée à

Rouen,' p. 52; Jan. 15, 1890: 'Jules Lemaître,' p. 84; Feb. 1, 1890: 'Etudes et Portraits: H. Becque — Théâtre complet,' p. 135; Feb. 15, 1890: 'Etudes et Portraits: Papus — Traité élémentaire de sciences occultes,' p. 182; March 1, 1890: 'Le Comte d'Orsay et Lady Blessington,' p. 218; March 15, 1890: 'A Propos de la Bête humaine,' p. 250.

Scrap-Book. (Gabriel Wells Collection.)

Tableau de la poésie française, in Anthologie des poètes français depuis les origines jusqu'à la fin du XVIIIe siècle. Lemerre, 1905.

Le Temps, 1875-78. (Articles on contemporary authors.)

——, 1886-93. 'La Vie à Paris,' 'La Vie hors Paris,' March 21—Dec. 26, 1886; 'Vie littéraire,' Jan. 16, 1887-April 30, 1893.

Thaïs. Calmann-Lévy, '1891.'

'Une des plus grandes Découvertes du siècle.' Figaro littéraire, Nov. 2, 1935. *See O. C.*, XXV.

L'Univers illustré ('Courrier de Paris' by 'Gérôme'), 1883-90.

'Vacances sentimentales. En Alsace.' Revue pol. et litt., Oct. 14, 1882, pp. 481-92.

'Le Valet de Madame la Duchesse.' La Revue, July 15, 1903, pp. 175-92.

Vers les Temps meilleurs. Pelletan, 1906.

Vogue parisienne, July 15, 1870. (Book-notice.)

——, Aug. 19, 1873. ('Les Prisons de Paris sous la Terreur.')

B. WORKS CONCERNING ANATOLE FRANCE

(The titles include only those used or mentioned in our text; material dealing chiefly with A.F. after 1896 has not as a rule been included; also our record closes in 1935; within these limits, however, this list seems to be the fullest that has been printed up-to-date. Considering the great vogue of France, no such bibliography can pretend to anything like completeness. The curious reader will find additional items in titles listed under Antoniu, Bédé and Le Bail, Carias [*A.F.*], Chevalier, Cor, Gaffiot [*Théories sociales d'A.F.*], Girard ['Essai de Bibliographie'], Le Brun, Lion, Martin, Masson.)

I. Books

Anonymous. Collectors' Books on Many Subjects. From the Libraries of Mrs. Elie Nadelman . . . and the Estates of the Late Louis Guerineau Myers and Dr. Reginald H. Sayre. New York: Anderson Galleries, April 14, 1932.

——. Le Collège Stanislas. 1804-1905. Paris: Doumoulin, 1905.

——. Le Concours hippique. In 'Paris par les Parisiens.' Bureaux des Annales. [n.d.]

——. Paris Guide. Par les principaux écrivains et artistes de la France. 2 vols. Paris: Lacroix, 1867.

Acta Apostolicae Sedis. Commentarium Officiale. July 1, 1922, p. 379.

Acta Sanctorum. Ed. novissima. Brussels, 1870. (Vol. IV, Oct. 8, 1866, contains, pp. 226-28, 'Vita Sanctae Thaisidis' by Marbodius; p. 225, Rosweyd's version of Thaïs.)

Ahlstrom, A. Le Moyen Age dans l'œuvre d'A.F. Thèse. Paris : Les Belles Lettres, 1930.

Amélineau, E. Les Moines égyptiens. Vie de Schnoudi. Paris : Leroux, 1889.

Andrieux Catalogue. *See* Livres — Manuscrits — Dessins.

Antoniu, A. A.F. critique littéraire. Paris : Boivin, 1929.

Aron, A. W. A.F. and Goethe. In 'Studies in German Literature in Honor of A. R. Hohlfeld,' University of Wisconsin Studies in Language and Literature, No. 22. Dec. 29, 1925.

Aveline, C. 'Les Désirs' ou Le Livre égaré. In 'Les Livrets du Bibliophile,' No. 4. Paris, 1926.

——. Sur l'Alfred de Vigny d'A.F. Tirage à part. Paris, 1928.

Babbitt, Irving. Rousseau and Romanticism. New York : Houghton Mifflin, 1919.

Bahr, H. Studien zur Kritik der Moderne. Frankfurt : Rütten and Loening, 1894.

Bainville, J. Au Seuil du siècle. Etudes critiques. Third edition. Paris : Editions du Capitole, [1927]. (Contains 'Les Vieux Attendrissements de M. A.F.')

Baldensperger, F. Etudes d'Histoire littéraire. Vol. I. Paris : Hachette, 1907.

Barrès, M. Anatole France. Paris : Charavay, 1883. (Reprint.)

——. Mes Cahiers. Tome I : 1896-1898. Paris : Plon, 1929.

Beaunier, A. Critiques et Romanciers. Paris : Crès, 1925. (Contains, pp. 77-94, 'M. A.F., critique littéraire.')

Bédé, A. and Le Bail, J. A.F. vu par la critique d'aujourd'hui. In 'Etudes françaises,' No. 5. Oct., 1925. Paris : Les Belles Lettres.

Belis, A. La Critique française à la fin du XIXe siècle. Paris : Gamber, 1926.

Bennett, Arnold. Books and Persons. New York : Doran, 1917. (Contains, pp. 59-62, 'A.F.')

Bergerat, E. Souvenirs d'un Enfant de Paris. Vol. II : La Phase critique de la critique (1872-1880). Paris : Fasquelle, 1911-12.

Bersaucourt, A. de. Au Temps des Parnassiens : Nina de Villard et ses amis. Paris : La Renaissance du livre, 1925.

Bethléem, L. (l'Abbé). Romans à lire et romans à proscrire. Seventh edition. Paris and Lille, 1920.

Bibesco, Princesse. Quatre Portraits (Portraits d'Homme). Paris : Grasset, 1929. (Contains, pp. 145-72, 'Une visite à la Béchellerie.')

Blanck, R. A.F. als Stilkunstler in seinen Romanen. Münster, 1934. (Arbeiten zur Romanischen Philologie, No. VII.)

Blum, L. En lisant. Réflexions critiques. Paris : Ollendorf, 1906.

Boillot, F. L'Humour dans l'œuvre d'A.F. Paris : Presses Universitaires, 1933.

Bölöni, Mme. G. *See* Kéméri.

Bondy, L. Le Classicisme de Ferdinand Brunetière. Paris, 1930.

Bonnières, R. de. Mémoires d'aujourd'hui. Vol. II. Paris ; Ollendorf, 1885. (Contains, pp. 327-40, 'M. A.F.')

Bordeaux, H. Ames modernes. Ninth edition. Paris : Perrin, 1921. (Con-

tains, pp. 201-41, 'A.F.'; pp. 391-98, 'Opinion de M. Jérôme Coignard sur l'élection de M. A.F. à l'Académie française.')
Borély, M. La Femme et l'Amour dans l'œuvre d'A.F. Paris : Crès, 1917.
Bourdelle, A. Trente journées de grand travail. La Haye, 1925. Plaquette.
Bourget, P. Quelques Témoignages. Paris : Plon, 1928. (Contains, pp. 149-69, 'Réflexions sur A.F.')
Bradford, Gamaliel. The Journal of Gamaliel Bradford, 1883-1932. Ed. Van Wyck Brooks. Boston and New York : Houghton, Mifflin, 1933.
Braibant, C. Le Secret d'A.F. Du Boulangisme au Panama. Paris : Denoël et Steele, 1935.
Brandes, Georg. A.F. London and New York : McClure, 1908.
Brisson, A. Les Prophètes. Paris : Tallandier, 1903. (Contains, pp. 100-115, 'M. A.F.')
Brochard, V. Les Sceptiques grecs. Paris : Alcan, 1887.
Brousson, J.-J. A.F. en Pantoufles. Paris : Crès, 1924.
——. Itinéraire de Paris à Buenos-Ayres. Paris : Crès, 1927.
——. Les Vêpres de l'avenue Hoche. Paris : Editions du Cadran, 1932.
Brugmans, H. Georges de Porto-Riche. Sa vie. Son œuvre. Paris : Droz, 1934.
Brunetière, F. Essais sur la littérature contemporaine. Paris : Calmann-Lévy, 1892.
——. Etudes critiques sur l'histoire de la littérature française. Paris : Hachette, 1925. (Vol. IX, pp. 1-63, contains 'La Critique.')
Caillavet, Mme. A. de. Histoire d'une Demoiselle de mode. Paris : Calmann-Lévy, 1908.
Calmettes, F. Un Demi-siècle littéraire. Leconte de Lisle et ses amis. Paris : Librairies-Imprimeries réunies, 1902.
Calmettes, P. La Grande Passion d'A.F. Paris : Marcel Seheur, 1929.
Carez, F. Auteurs contemporains. Etudes littéraires. Liège : Demarteau, 1897.
Carias, L. A.F. In 'Maîtres des Littératures.' Paris : Rieder, 1931.
Cerf, Barry. A.F. The Degeneration of a Great Artist. New York : Dial Press, 1926.
Champion, P. Mon Vieux Quartier. Paris : Grasset, 1932.
Charavay, E. Catalogue d'une importante collection de documents autographes et historiques sur la Révolution française. Paris : Charavay, 1862.
Chevalier, Haakon. The Ironic Temper ; A.F. and his Time. New York : Oxford University Press, 1932.
Chevassu, F. Visages. Paris : Lemerre, 1904.
Clerc, C. Le Génie du paganisme : Essais sur l'inspiration antique dans la littérature contemporaine. Paris : Payot, 1926.
Cor, R. M. A.F. et la Pensée contemporaine, suivi de la bibliographie de l'œuvre du maître écrivain. Paris : Pelletan, 1909.
Corday, M. A.F., d'après ses confidences et ses souvenirs. Paris : Flammarion, 1927.
Coulon, M. Témoignages. Paris : Mercure de France, 1910-1911. (Vol. I, pp. 111-37, contains 'A.F., homme d'action'; Vol. II, pp. 185-202, contains 'Deux Aspects d'A.F.')

Croiset, A. *See* A.F., Discours aux étudiants, 1900.

Daudet, L. Salons et Journaux. Paris : Plon, 1932.

Delaporte, L. Pastels et Figurines. Paris : Fontemoing, 1898. (Vol. I, pp. 2-47, contains 'M. A.F.')

Delattre, F. Dickens et la France ; étude d'une interaction littéraire anglo-française. Paris : Librairie universitaire, 1927.

Delfour, l'abbé L. La Religion des contemporains. Paris : Société française d'imprimerie et de librairie, 1903. (Vol. I, pp. 1-13, contains 'Les Fantaisies théologiques de M. A.F.')

Demont-Breton, Mme. V. Les Maisons que j'ai connues. Paris : Plon, 1927. (Vol. II contains, pp. 127-50, 'La Mansarde Parnassienne' ; pp. 151-54, 'Lettres d'A.F. à Jules Breton'; pp. 155-61, 'Chez A.F. en 1877'.)

Deschamps, G. La Vie et les livres. Paris : Colin. (Vol. II [1895] contains, pp. 219-61, 'M.A.F.') ; (Vol. V. [1900] contains, pp. 143-48, 'Trois Etapes de M. A.F.')

Des Hons, G. A.F. et Racine. Un peu du secret de l'art de France. Paris : Le Divan, 1925. (Another ed., 1927.)

Desonay, F. Le Rêve hellénique chez les poètes parnassiens. Paris : Champion, 1928.

Dike, F. H., ed. Monsieur Bergeret. Passages from *L'Histoire contemporaine* by A.F. New York : Silver, Burdett, 1902.

Dirick, J. L. Franciana. Opinions — Anecdotes — Pensées de M. A.F. Brussels : Simonson, 1925.

Docquois, G. Bêtes et gens de lettres. Paris : Flammarion, 1895. (Contains, pp. 72-84, 'A.F.')

Doyon, R. Conférence sur A.F., atticiste, historien et philosophe. Algiers : Vedette algérienne, 1912.

——. Magie et dilettantisme. In Villars, Le Comte de Gabalis ou Entretiens sur les sciences secrètes (pp. v-xlii).

Du Bled, V. La Société française depuis cent ans. Vol. II, Madame Aubernon et ses amis. Paris : Bloud et Gay, 1924.

Du Camp, M. Paris : ses organes, ses fonctions et sa vie dans la seconde moitié du XIXe siècle. Sixth edition, Vol. V. Paris : Hachette, 1879.

Duclaux, Mme. Mary. The French Procession. A Pageant of Great Writers London : Unwin, 1919. (Contains, pp. 339-53, 'A.F.')

Du Fresnois, A. Une Année de critique. Paris : Dorbon aîné, 1914. (Contains, pp. 143-58, 'La Perversité d'A.F. — Les Dieux ont soif.')

Durant, Will. Adventures in Genius. New York : Simon and Schuster, 1931.

Ernest-Charles, J. La Littérature française d'aujourd'hui. Paris : Perrin, 1902. (Contains, pp. 39-47, 'A.F.')

Estève, E. Leconte de Lisle, l'homme et l'œuvre. Paris : Boivin, 1923.

——. Sully-Prudhomme, poète sentimental et poète philosophe. Paris : Boivin, 1925.

Evelpidi, C. A.F. critique social. Essai sur les tendances sociales et sur la mission des intellectuels. Paris : Messein, 1932.

Evrard, Abbé E. Nos Mandarins. Tourcoing : Duvivier, 1920. (Contains, pp. 291-321, 'A.F.')

Faguet, E. Propos littéraires. Paris : Lecène et Oudin and Société française. (Vol. I [1902] contains, pp. 9-29, 'A.F.,' 'L'Orme du Mail.' 'Le Mannequin d'osier'; Vol. III [1905] contains, pp. 279-95, 'A.F.,' 'La Rôtisserie de la Reine Pédauque,' 'L'Anneau d'Améthyste.')

Flottes, P. Le Poète Leconte de Lisle, documents inédits. Paris : Perrin, 1929.

Fontaine de Resbecq, A. de. Voyages littéraires sur les Quais de Paris. Lettres à un bibliophile de province. Paris : Furne, 1864.

Frary, R. La Question du latin. Third edition. Paris : Cerf, 1886.

Gaffiot, M. Les Théories sociales d'A.F. Algiers : Gaudet, 1923.

——. Les Théories d'A.F. sur l'organisation sociale de son temps. Paris : Rivière, 1928.

Galignani, A. and W. New Paris Guide for 1859. Paris : Galignani, 1859.

Ghil, R. Les Dates et les œuvres. Paris : Crès, 1923.

Gille, P. La Bataille littéraire. Paris : Havard. (Vol. V [1889-90] contains, pp. 195-96, 'A.F.—*Thaïs*'; Vol. VI [1891-92] contains, pp. 183-85, 'A.F.—*L'Etui de nacre*'; Vol. VII [1893] contains, pp. 106-11, 'A.F.—*Opinions de M. Jérôme Coignard*'; pp. 144-48, 'A.F.—*La Rôtisserie de la Reine Pédauque*.')

Ginisty, P. Souvenirs de Journalisme et de Théâtre. Paris : Editions de France, 1930.

Girard, G. La Jeunesse d'A.F. 1844-1876. Paris : Gallimard, 1925.

Giraud, V. A.F. In 'Temps et Visages.' Paris : Desclée et Brouwer, 1935.

——. Encore sur A.F. Paris : [s.d.] [1925].

——. Les Maîtres de l'heure. Vol. II. Paris : Hachette, 1914. (Contains, pp. 179-310, 'M. A.F.')

Goll, I. Sodome et Berlin. Paris : Emile-Paul, 1929.

Goncourt, E. de. Journal des Goncourt. Vols. III and IX. Paris : Fasquelle, 1896 and 1911.

Gramont, Elizabeth de. Pomp and Circumstance. New York : Cape & Smith, 1929. (Transl. by B. W. Downs.)

Gréard, O. *See* A.F., Institut de France.

Gregh, F. La Fenêtre ouverte. Paris : Fasquelle, 1901.

Gsell, P. Les Matinées de la Villa Saïd. Propos d'A.F., recueillis par Paul Gsell. Paris : Grasset, 1921.

Guérard, Albert. Five Masters of French Romance. London : Unwin, 1916.

Guerlac, O. G., ed. Le Livre de mon ami (Preface). New York : Holt, 1916.

Guillaume-Louis and Dubreuil-Chambardel. Le Cerveau d'A.F. Tours : Arrault, 1928.

Hanotaux, G. *See* Pouquet, Le Salon de Madame de Caillavet.

Harris, Frank. Contemporary Portraits. New York : Kennerley, 1915. (Contains, pp. 329-46, 'A.F.')

Harry, M. Trois Ombres : Huysmans, Lemaître, France. Paris : Flammarion, 1932.

Henning, G. M., ed. Representative Stories of A.F. New York : Heath, 1924.

Henriot, E. Livres et Portraits. Vol. I. Paris : Plon, 1923. (Contains, pp.

290-93, 'A.F. en marge d'A.F.'; pp. 294-98, 'Les Repentirs d'A.F.'; pp. 299-303, 'Stendhal, A.F., et le style.')

Hermant, A. Les Renards. Paris: Louis-Michaud, 1912.

——. Souvenirs de la Vie mondaine. Paris: Plon, 1935.

——. Souvenirs du Vicomte de Courpière, par un témoin. Ninth edition. Paris: Hachette, 1901.

Hrotswitha. Théâtre. Transl. C. Magnin. Paris: Duprat, 1845.

Huard, G. A.F. et le Quai Malaquais. Paris: Champion, 1926.

——. Sylvestre Bonnard et la Légende Dorée. In 'Les Trésors des Bibliothèques de France,' IX, 25-40. Paris: Editions G. Van Oest, 1929.

Huret, J. Enquête sur l'Evolution littéraire. Paris: Fasquelle, 1891.

Ibrovac, M. José-Maria de Heredia. Sa Vie — son Œuvre; documents inédits. Paris: Presses françaises, 1923.

Jackson, Holbrook. The Eighteen Nineties; a Review of Art and Ideas at the Close of the Nineteenth Century. New York: Kennerley, 1914.

Jeanroy-Félix, V. Fauteuils contemporains de l'Académie française. Paris: Bloud et Barral, 1896.

Josephson, Matthew. Zola and his Time. New York: Macaulay, 1928.

Kahn, G. Silhouettes littéraires. Paris: Editions Montaigne, 1925.

Kahn, M. A.F. et Emile Zola; avec une lettre autographe d'A.F. Paris: Lemarget, 1927.

——. Le Père d'A.F. Noël France-Thibault (1809-1890). Notes et documents. Paris: Giraud-Badin, 1925.

Kéméri, Sándor. Promenades d'A.F. Paris: Calmann-Lévy, 1927.

Klein, Abbé F. Autour du Dilettantisme. Paris: Lecoffre, 1895.

Kuehne, O. R. A Study of the Thaïs Legend, with Special Reference to Hroswitha's 'Paphnucius.' Philadelphia: U. of Pa., 1922.

Lacretelle, J. de. A la Rencontre de France, suivi de A.F. vu par un Américain, par E. Wassermann (trad. de J. de Lacretelle). Paris: Editions Trémois, 1930.

Lahy-Hollebecque, Mme. M. A.F. et la femme. Paris: Baudinière, 1924.

Lalou, R. Histoire de la Littérature française contemporaine (1870 à nos jours). Paris: Crès, 1923.

Lane, Mrs. John. Honey-Bee (Transl. of Abeille.) London: Lane, 1920.

Lanson, G. L'Art de la Prose. Paris: Librairie des Annales politiques et littéraires, 1908.

——. Histoire de la Littérature française. Twenty-first edition. Paris: Hachette, [1929].

——. Pages choisies d'A.F. ('Notice.') Paris: Colin and Calmann-Lévy, 1925. (First ed., 1897.)

Larroumet, G. Etudes de littérature et d'art. Paris: Hachette, 1895. (Vol. III, pp. 89-210, contains 'M. A.F.')

Lazare, B. Figures contemporaines, ceux d'aujourd'hui, ceux de demain. Paris: Perrin, 1895.

Le Brun, R. A.F. Biographie . . . suivie d'opinions et d'une bibliographie. In 'Célébrités d'aujourd'hui.' Paris: Sansot, 1904.

Lecigne, C. A.F. Arras: Librairie Centrale, 1901.

——. Du Dilettantisme à l'action, études contemporaines. Vol. I. Paris: Lethielleux, 1908.

Lefèvre, F. Une Heure avec. . . Paris: N.R.F. (Gallimard). (Vol. II [1924], pp. 65-83, contains 'Une Heure avec Pierre Champion.' Cf. Vol. III, 1925.)

Le Gallienne, Richard. The Romantic Nineties. New York: Doubleday, Page, 1925.

Le Goff, M. A.F. à la Béchellerie. Propos et souvenirs, 1914-1924. Paris: Léo Delteil, 1924.

Lemaître, J. Les Contemporains. Etudes et portraits littéraires. Paris: Lecène et Oudin; and Boivin. (Vol. I [1892], pp. 129-64, contains 'Le Néo-Hellénisme'; pp. 217-48, 'Ferdinand Brunetière.' Vol. II. [1893], pp. 83-114, contains 'A.F.' Vol. VI [1894], pp. 361-75, contains 'A.F. Le Lys rouge.')

Lemerre, A. Le Livre du Bibliophile. Paris: Lemerre, 1874.

Le Meur, L. La Vie et l'œuvre de François Coppée. Paris: Spes, 1932.

Lion, J. Bibliographie des Ouvrages consacrés à A.F. Paris: Giraud-Badin, 1935.

Livres — Manuscrits — Dessins, provenant des bibliothèques de Madame Arman de Caillavet et de Madame Gaston de Caillavet. Manuscrits et lettres d'A.F. Lettre-Préface by C. Maurras. Remarques sur quelques MSS. d'A.F. by A. Maurois. Paris: Andrieux, 1932.

Lomier, E. A.F. à Saint-Valery-sur-Somme. Paris: Grande Librairie universelle, 1928.

Marbodius, *see* Acta Sanctorum.

Marsan, E. Signes de notre temps. Les Cahiers d'Occident, II, No. 9. Paris: Librairie de France, 1930. (Contains, pp. 81-87, 'Brousson parle d'A.F.')

Martin, A. Belles Editions et manuscrits d'A.F., conservés à la Bibliothèque Nationale. Paris: Champion, 1925.

Martin-Mamy. Les Nouveaux Païens. Paris: Sansot, 1914. (Contains, pp. 197-214, 'Le Pessimisme de M. A.F.')

Martino, P. Parnasse et Symbolisme (1850-1900). Paris: Colin, 1925.

Massis, H. Evocations. Souvenirs, 1905-1911. Paris: Plon, 1931.

——. Jugements. Vols. I and II. Paris: Plon, 1924.

Masson, G.-A. A.F.: son œuvre. Paris: Editions de la Nouvelle Revue critique, 1924.

Maurel, A. Souvenirs de littérature. In 'Les Œuvres libres,' No. 44, pp. 325-78. Paris, 1925.

Mauriac, F. Le Roman. Paris: L'Artisan du Livre, 1928.

Maurois, A. *See* Livres — Manuscrits — Dessins.

Maurras, C. *See* Livres — Manuscrits — Dessins.

——. A.F., politique et poète (A Propos d'un Jubilé). Paris: Plon, 1924.

May, J. Lewis. A.F., the Man and his Work. An Essay in Critical Biography. London: Lane, 1924.

——. Transl. of Marguerite. New York: Lane, 1921.

——. Ed. Prefaces, Introductions and Other Uncollected Papers by A.F. London: Lane, 1928.

Ménard, L. Rêveries d'un païen mystique. Paris: Crès, 1911.
Mendès, C. Rapport . . . sur le mouvement poétique français de 1867-1900. Paris: Imprimerie nationale, 1902.
Meyer, A. Ce que je peux dire. Paris: Plon, 1912.
Michaut, G. A.F. Conférence. Fribourg, Imprimerie Catholique Suisse, 1903.
——. A.F. Etude psychologique. Fifth edition. Paris: Fontemoing, 1922.
Migne, J.-P. Patrologiae Cursus Completus. . . Series Latina, Vol. LXXIII (1879), cols. 660-63.
Missoffe, M. Gyp et ses amis. Paris: Flammarion, 1932.
Montfort, E. Vingt-cinq Ans de littérature française. Vol. II. Paris: Librairie de France, 1925.
Moréas, J. Curiosités littéraires — Les Premières Armes du symbolisme. Paris: Vanier, 1889. (Contains article by Moréas.)
Morice, C. Demain. Questions d'esthétique. Paris: Perrin, 1888.
Mouton, L. Le Quai Malaquais. Le Numéro cinq. Paris: Champion, 1921.
Nordau, M. Vus du dehors, essai de critique scientifique et philosophique sur quelques auteurs français contemporains. Paris: Alcan, 1902.
Noussanne, H. de. A.F., philosophe sceptique. Conférence. Paris: Peyronnet, 1925.
Pellissier, G. Essais de littérature contemporaine. Fourth edition. Paris: Lecène et Oudin, 1894. (Contains, pp. 327-69, 'La Doctrine de M.F. Brunetière.')
——. Etudes de littérature contemporaine. Vol. I. Paris: Perrin, 1898. (Contains, pp. 273-97, 'M. A.F.')
——. M. A.F. In Petit de Julleville, Histoire de la langue et de la littérature française. Vol. VIII, pp. 239-48. Paris: Colin, 1899.
——. Nouveaux Essais de littérature contemporaine. Paris: Lecène, Oudin, 1895. (Contains, pp. 335-82, 'A.F.')
Peyre, H. Louis Ménard (1822-1901). New Haven: Yale Press, 1932. (Yale Romanic Studies, Vol. V.)
Pica, V. Letteratura d'eccezione. Milan: Baldini, Castoldi, 1898. (Contains, pp. 245-88, 'A.F.')
Pitollet, C. Le Père Hase, histoire de la venue en France de l'Allemand qui refusa A.F. à son baccalauréat. Brussels: La Renaissance d'Occident, 1922.
Plessis, F. Poésies complètes. Paris: Fontemoing, 1904. (Contains, pp. 109-11, 'À A.F.'; pp. 151-53, 'Soirs évanouis.')
Pouquet, Mme. J. Le Salon de Madame Arman de Caillavet. (With Preface by G. Hanotaux.) Paris: Hachette, 1926.
——. The Last Salon: A.F. and his Muse. Transl. by Lewis Galantière. Introduction by Montgomery Belgion. London: Jonathan Cape, 1927.
Prescott, H.W. The Development of Virgil's Art. Chicago: University of Chicago Press, 1927.
Proust, M. Preface to P. Morand, Tendres Stocks. Paris: Gallimard, 1922.
Psichari, H. Ernest Psichari, mon frère. Paris: Plon, 1933.
Psichari, J. Ernest Renan. Jugements et souvenirs. Paris: Editions du monde moderne, 1925.

Rambaud, A. Histoire de la Civilisation contemporaine en France. Sixth edition, revised. Paris : Colin, 1901.
Reggio, A. Au Seuil de leur âme. Etudes de psychologie critique. Paris : Perrin, 1904. (Contains, pp. 63-86, 'La Manière de M. A.F.')
Régnier, H. de. De Mon Temps. Paris : Mercure de France, 1933.
Reissig, L. A.F. Ironia, Escepticismo, Ensueño, Voluptuosidad, Mme. de Caillavet. Buenos Aires : Anaconda, 1933.
Renan, E. Correspondance, 1872-1892. Vol. 2. Paris : Calmann-Lévy, 1928.
——. Dialogues et fragments philosophiques. Third edition. Paris : Calmann-Lévy, 1885.
——. Drames philosophiques. Paris : Calmann-Lévy, 1888.
Renard, G. Les Princes de la jeune critique. Paris : Librairie de la Nouvelle Revue, 1890.
Rod, E. Nouvelles Etudes sur le XIXe siècle. Paris : Perrin, 1899. (Contains, pp. 41-93, 'M. A.F.')
Rosweyd. *See* Acta Sanctorum.
Roujon, H. Au Milieu des hommes. Paris : Rueff, 1907.
Roujon, J. La Vie et les opinions d'A.F. Paris : Plon, 1925.
Samain, A. Des Lettres, 1887-1900. Fifth edition. Paris : Mercure de France, 1933.
Schaffer, Aaron. Parnassus in France. Currents and Cross-Currents in Nineteenth Century French Lyric Poetry. Texas : University of Texas, 1929.
Scheikévitch, Marie. Time Past. Memories of Proust and Others. Boston and New York : Houghton, Mifflin, 1935.
Schön, E. A.F. La Vie littéraire. Hamburg : Ernest Hirt, 1911.
Ségur, N. A.F. anecdotique. Paris : Michel, 1929.
——. Conversations avec A.F. ou les Mélancolies de l'intelligence. Paris : Charpentier, 1925.
——. Dernières Conversations avec A.F. Paris : Charpentier-Fasquelle, 1927.
——. Le Génie européen. Paris : Fasquelle, 1926. (Contains, pp. 83-110, 'A.F.')
Sellar, W. Y. The Roman Poets of the Augustan Age : Virgil. Third edition. Oxford : Clarendon Press, 1897.
Seillière, E. A.F., critique de son temps. Paris : Nouvelle Revue critique, 1934.
——. La Jeunesse d'A.F. In 'Les Essais critiques.' Paris : Nouvelle Revue critique, 1934.
Shanks, L. P. A.F. : The Mind and the Man. [Second rewritten version.] New York : Harper, 1932.
Sherman, Stuart. On Contemporary Literature. New York : Holt, 1917. (Contains, pp. 168-69, 'The Skepticism of A.F.')
Shipman, Jennie. Some Sources of Thaïs, Novel by A.F. Chicago : (Typewritten dissertation), 1931.
Smith, Helen. The Skepticism of A.F. Paris : Presses universitaires, 1927.
Smith, Preserved. A Key to the Colloquies of Erasmus. In Harvard Theological Studies, XII. Cambridge, 1927.

Souday, P. Les Livres du Temps. Vol. II. Paris : Emile-Paul, 1914. (Contains, pp. 65-76, 'Le Classicisme d'A.F.')

Souriau, M. Histoire du Parnasse. Paris : Spes, 1929.

Spronck, M. Les Artistes littéraires. Etude sur le XIXe siècle. Paris : Calmann-Lévy, 1889. (Contains, pp. 325-53, 'Ecoles et Personnalités diverses.')

Stapfer, P. Des Réputations littéraires. Vol. II. Paris : Hachette, 1893.

——. Humour et Humoristes. Paris : Fischbacher, 1911. (Contains, pp. 157-214, 'l'Union de l'Atticisme et de l'humour.')

Stephens, Winifred. *See* Whale.

Stewart, H. L. A.F., the Parisian. New York : Dodd, Mead, 1927.

Tellier, J. Les Ecrivains d'aujourd'hui. Nos Poètes. Paris : Dupret, 1888.

Thérive, A. Le Parnasse. Paris : Les Œuvres représentatives, 1929.

Tourneux, M. Etienne Charavay, sa vie et ses travaux. Paris : Charavay, 1900.

Truc, G. A.F., l'Artiste et le penseur. Paris : Garnier, 1924.

Turquet-Milnes, G. Some Modern French Writers, a Study in Bergsonism. New York : McBride, 1921.

Valéry, P. Discours de Réception à l'Académie française. Paris : Gallimard, 1927.

Vandérem, F. Le Miroir des Lettres. Paris : Flammarion. Vol. I (1919) ; Vol. VII (1924) ; Vol. VIII (1925-26).

Vasari, G. Vite de' più eccellenti pittori, scultori e architetti . . . First edition, Vol. II. Siena : Carli, 1791.

Villars, Abbé de. Le Comte de Gabalis : ou Entretiens sur les sciences secrètes. Preceded by articles by Doyon and Marteau. Paris : 'La Connaissance,' 1921.

'Vincent, Jacques' (Mme. Bory d'Arnex). Un Salon parisien d'avant-guerre. Paris : Tallandier, 1929. (Contains, pp. 114-29, 'A.F.')

Voragine, J. de. Legenda Aurea. Ed. Graesse. Dresden and Leipzig, 1846.

——. La Légende dorée. Transl. G. Brunet. Paris : 1843.

Wassermann, E. *See* Lacretelle.

Whale, Winifred Stephens. The France I Know. London : Chapman & Hall, 1918.

——. Madame Adam. New York : Dutton, 1917.

Wright, C. H. C. The Background of Modern French Literature. Boston : Ginn, 1926.

Wyzewa, T. de. Nos Maîtres. Etudes et portraits littéraires. Paris : Perrin, 1895. (Contains, pp. 215-40, 'M. A.F.')

II. Articles

(The few abbreviations used are according to the usual code : *MLN* is Modern Language Notes ; *NRF* is Nouvelle Revue française ; *PMLA* is Publications of the Modern Language Association of America ; *RDM* is Revue des Deux Mondes ; *ZfFSL* is Zeitschrift für französische Sprache und Literatur.)

Anonymous. 'Une Collaboration d'A.F.' *Mercure de France*. Aug. 1, 1927, p. 763.
——. 'Nos Echos. France-Ana.' *Nouvelles littéraires*. Oct. 18, 1924.
——. 'Les Autels de la peur : Une version oubliée des *Dieux ont soif*.' *Ibid*. Nov. 28, 1925.
——. 'Des Manuscrits d'A.F.' *Ibid*. Oct. 17, 1931.
Albert-Petit, A. 'A.F.' *Journal des Débats*. Oct. 14, 1924.
Altman, Georges. 'A.F. retrouvé.' *La Lumière*. Dec. 7, 1935.
Ambrière, Francis. *Nouv. litt*. March 21, 1931.
——. 'Grandes Ventes et grands papiers.' *Ibid*. April 16, 1932.
——. 'Le Bilan d'une grande amitié. A.F. et Mme. Arman de Caillavet.' *Ibid*. April 23 and 30, 1932.
Amiot, C.-G. 'A.F. et la Grèce.' *Revue hebdomadaire*. Oct. 10, 1925, pp. 131-46.
André, M. 'A.F. Poète.' *Rev. hebd*. April 26, 1924, pp. 477-86.
Ascoli, G. 'A.F. d'après quelques témoins de sa vie.' *Revue de synthèse historique*. December, 1925, pp. 169-81.
Asse, E. 'Article avec portrait.' *Revue encyclopédique*. 1891, pp. 290-92.
Audouin, R. 'Du Dilettantisme : A.F. et M. Barrès.' *Grande Revue*. March 25, 1913, pp. 289-94.
Aveline, C. 'Comment on écrit l'histoire "en Pantoufles."' *Chanteclere*. Dec. 17, 1927.
Aynard, T. 'Une Préface d'A.F.' *Débats*. Oct. 23, 1924.
Ballaguy, P. 'Aïeux et Parents d'A.F.' *La Revue universelle*. Nov. 1, 1925, pp. 295-330.
Baring, Maurice. 'M. A.F.' *The Yellow Book*. April, 1895, pp. 263-79.
Barrès, M. Article in *Comœdia*. Oct. 16, 1924.
——. 'A.F. La Grâce de l'artiste.' *Annales politiques et littéraires*. Oct. 19, 1924.
——. 'Les Hommes de la Jeune France. XIII. A.F.' *Jeune France*, February, 1883, pp. 589-610. (See under Books.)
——. Same article, reprinted in part with comment by H. Gouhier. *Nouv. litt*. May 14, 1927.
Barthou, L. 'A.F. *sans* la politique. Conférence.' *Conférencia*. May 1, 1925, pp. 453-72.
——. 'Sur A.F.' *Revue de France*. June 15, 1926, pp. 601-29.
——. 'Autour de dix vers d'André Chénier . . . qui sont d'A.F.' *Revue de Paris*. Dec. 15, 1923, pp. 721-27.
——. 'A.F., Commis-bibliothécaire au Sénat.' *Ibid*. Dec. 1, 1924, pp. 481-90.
Bauer, G. 'A.F. et Racine.' *Echo de Paris*. Oct. 8, 1925.
Beauduin, N. 'Notre A.F.' *Les Rubriques nouvelles*. Nov. 15, 1909, pp. 153-64.
Beaunier, A. 'A.F. critique littéraire.' *RDM*. April 15, 1918, pp. 923-34.
Becker, A. 'La Prose rythmée dans "La Révolte des anges."' *Mercure*. May 16, 1914, pp. 320-25.
Bédarida, H. 'A.F. et l'Italie.' *Revue des cours et conférences*. May 15, 1926, pp. 263-88.

——. 'A.F. et l'Italie.' *Rev. hebd.* Oct. 10, 1925, pp. 147-68.
Bellessort, A. Article in *Revue française*. Oct 19, 1924, pp. 427-29.
Benoist, C. 'Causerie littéraire.' *Revue de famille*. Nov. 15, 1890, pp. 363-72.
Bertaut, J. 'A.F. dans le monde.' *Nouv. litt.* Oct. 18, 1924.
Berton, C. 'Les Etapes d'un grand esprit.' *Vie des peuples*. Oct. 10, 1922, pp. 385-99.
Bertrand, L. 'Une Evolution nouvelle du roman historique.' *Rev. de Paris*. May 15, 1921, pp. 326-42.
Bidou, H. Article in *Comœdia*. Oct. 13, 1924.
——. 'Les 24 Ans de M. A.F.' *Rev. de Paris*. May 1, 1924, pp. 206-15.
——. 'A.F.' *Revue Rhénane*. November, 1924, pp. 68-71.
Billy, A. 'Les Livres de la semaine. De l'Abbé Jérôme Coignard au camarade Nathanaël.' *L'Œuvre*. Nov. 26, 1935.
Blondheim, D. S. 'Notes on the Sources of A.F.' *Modern Language Review*. July, 1918, pp. 333-34.
——. 'A.F.' *Modern Philology*. July, 1916, pp. 43-60.
Blum, L. 'M. A.F.' *Revue blanche*. Feb. 15, 1895, pp. 168-71.
Bonnard, A. 'L'Ironie d'A.F.' *Revue belge*. Feb. 15, 1934, pp. 313-16.
'Borgne, La Pie.' 'Le Secret d'A.F.' *Vendémiaire*. June 12, 1935.
Boulenger, M. 'L'Enigme d'A.F.' *Echo de Paris*. Oct. 24, 1924.
Bourdeau, J. 'La Philosophie d'A.F.' *Débats*. Oct. 31, 1924.
Braibant, C. 'A.F. et Zola.' *Nouv. litt.* Nov. 23, 1935.
Bourdelle, A. 'La Mort d'A.F.' *Revue Rhénane*. November, 1924, pp. 72-73.
Bourget-Pailleron, R. 'Le Jubilé d'A.F. : Conversation avec Charles Maurras.' *Opinion*. April 11, 1924.
Brillant, M. 'De M. A.F. considéré comme un penseur.' *Les Lettres*. Jan. 1, 1924.
Brock, H. I. 'A.F. Severely Taken to Task.' *New York Times Book Review*. Dec. 26, 1926.
Brousson, J.-J. Article in *Comœdia*. Oct. 16, 1924.
——. 'Renan et A.F.' *Nouv. litt.* Feb. 24, 1923.
——. 'La Jeunesse d'A.F.' *Nouv. litt.* Dec. 5, 1925.
——. Article in *ibid.* March 29, 1928.
——. 'France et Barrès.' *Ibid.* Dec. 27, 1930.
——. 'Autour de *l'Itinéraire de Paris à Buenos-Ayres*. Le Pour et le contre.' *Vient de Paraître*. Jan.-March, 1928. (Three articles.)
Brucker, Père P. 'M. A.F. et son dernier Roman.' *Etudes religieuses, philosophiques, historiques et littéraires*. November, 1890, pp. 503-10.
Brunetière, F. 'La Critique impressioniste.' *RDM*. Jan. 1, 1891, pp. 210-24.
Burnet, E. 'Le Secret de Mme. de Caillavet.' *Nouv. litt.* Nov. 13, 1926.
Bury, J. 'Les Miettes d'A.F.' *French Quarterly*. VI, 161-77.
C. P. 'Revue de la Quinzaine. A.F. et la Salamandre.' *Mercure*. Aug. 15, 1924, pp. 285-86.
——. 'Revue de la Quinzaine. Encore un Plagiat d'A.F.' *Ibid.* July 15, 1925, p. 575.
——. 'Revue de la Quinzaine. Une Source d'A.F.' *Ibid.* Aug. 15, 1925, pp. 278-79.

——. 'Revue de la Quinzaine. Les Romantiques Amours de Juan Valera et Madeleine Brohan.' *Ibid.* Jan. 1, 1927, pp. 251-52.
——. 'Revue de la Quinzaine. Notes inédites sur Madeleine Brohan.' *Ibid.* April 1, 1927, pp. 253-55.
Calvet, J. 'Enfances.' *Les Lettres.* March 1, 1922, pp. 449-72.
Carias, L. 'Un Vieil Ami d'A.F.: le duc de Penthièvre.' *Chronique des Lettres françaises.* March-April, 1926, pp. 217-18.
——. 'Quelques Sources d'A.F.' *Grande Revue.* Dec. 25, 1912, pp. 725-37 and Jan. 10, 1913, pp. 51-68.
——. 'A.F. et Renan.' *Ibid.* October, 1922, pp. 529-66.
——. 'A.F. et Zola avant l'Affaire.' *Ibid.* September, 1927, pp. 402-38.
——. 'Le Journal de Noël France.' *Ibid.* December, 1930, pp. 265-67.
——. 'Les Carnets intimes d'A.F.' *Nouv. litt.* Jan. 7, Feb. 18, Feb. 25, 1933.
Charavay, E. 'Le Centenaire de 1789 et le Musée de la Révolution.' *La Révolution française. Revue historique.* Jan.-June, 1886, pp. 961-83.
'Charensol.' 'Georges Girard et le Souvenir d'A.F.' *Nouv. litt.* Oct. 17, 1925.
Charpentier, J. 'La Réaction parnassienne et le renouveau de la fantaisie.' *Mercure.* March 15, 1925, pp. 594-633.
Chassé, C. 'L'Ecrivain et le critique.' *Le Capitole.* Oct., 1924.
Chaumeix, A. 'M. A.F. et l'Histoire.' *Rev. hebd.* March 23, 1912, pp. 568-89.
Clouard, H. 'La Sagesse d'A.F.' *La Revue critique des idées et des livres.* Aug. 10, 1912, pp. 257-71.
Cochin, H. 'A.F., Autrefois.' *Vie Catholique en France et à l'Etranger.* Nov. 1, 1924.
Cohen, G. 'Souvenirs sur A.F.' *L'Alsace française.* Oct. 18, 1924.
Cor, R. 'Charles Dickens.' *Mercure.* July 1, 1920, pp. 82-121.
Couchoud, P.-L. 'Souvenirs sur A.F.' *Opinion.* Oct. 17, 1924.
Courtney, W. L. 'The Humour of A.F.' *Bodleian.* January, 1921.
Coussange, J. de. 'Le Voyage de M. A.F. en Suède.' *Débats.* Dec. 25, 1921.
Crémieux, B. 'Les Inexactitudes de M. Brousson.' *Annales pol. et litt.* Feb. 15, 1928, pp. 163-64.
——. Same article. *Chronique.* March-April, 1928, pp. 201-206.
Crucy, F. 'A.F.' *Floréal.* Sept. 18, 1920, pp. 757-58.
——. 'Quand M. Clemenceau voyageait en Amérique.' *L'Illustration.* Jan. 6, 1922, pp. 7-8.
Curtius, E. F. 'Opinions allemandes sur A.F.' *Revue Rhénane.* November, 1924, pp. 74-77. (Anonymous article; carries digest of C.'s opinions.)
Doyon, R. 'Les Abbés Montfaucon de Villars et Jérôme Coignard.' *La Renaissance de l'Occident.* June-July-August, 1924.
Dargan, E. P. 'A.F. and the Imp of the Perverse.' *The Dial.* Feb. 8, 1919, pp. 126-28.
——. 'New Light on A.F.' *Virginia Quarterly Review.* January, 1936, pp. 104-21.
Darmesteter, Mme. James. 'The Social Novel in France.' *Contemporary Review.* June, 1899, pp. 800-813.

Daudet, L. 'Sceptiques et hésitants.' *L'Action française*. Oct. 15, 1924.
Delaporte, L. 'Portraits contemporains: M. A.F.' *Revue politique et littéraire*. Dec. 9, 1899, pp. 741-46.
Delson, S. M. 'A.F. Reminiscent.' *Poet Lore*. August, 1920, pp. 261-67.
Descaves, L. 'Le Petit Pierre.' *Le Journal*. Feb. 9, 1919.
Diplock, A. 'The Novels of A.F.' *Quarterly Review*. 1900, pp. 431-54.
Doumic, R. 'M. A.F.' *RDM*. Dec. 15, 1896, pp. 924-34.
Dubeck, L. 'Les Quatre-Vingts Ans de M. A.F.' *Revue crit. des idées et des livres*. March-April-May, 1924, pp. 190-93.
Du Bled, V. 'A.F.' *Revue illustrée*. Sept. 1, 1887, p. 184.
Dufay, P. 'Chez Nina de Villard.' *Mercure*. June 1, 1927, pp. 324-52.
Dufour, E. 'Les Usagers de l'éducation : A.F., historien de son enfance.' *L'Ecole et la Vie*. May 10, 1924.
Estève, E. 'A.F. *L'Etui de nacre*.' *Revue d'art et de littérature*. Nov. 1, 1892, pp. 134-36.
Fauconnet, A. 'A.F. et Goethe. La "Fiancée de Corinthe."' *Mercure*. Feb. 1, 1927, pp. 513-34.
Fernand-Demeure. 'A.F. et Emile Zola.' *Rev. mondiale*. Sept. 5, 1930, pp. 420-23.
Filon, A. 'Courrier littéraire.' *Rev. pol. et litt.* Aug. 10, 1889, pp. 181-82.
——. 'Courrier littéraire.' *Ibid.* Nov. 1, 1890, pp. 565-67.
Fornand, P. 'La Vie intellectuelle en province. A.F. à Saint-Valery-sur-Somme.' *Figaro*. Aug. 4, 1928.
Galantière, Lewis. 'The Egeria of A.F. as Revealed by Lewis Galantière.' *New York World*, May 1, 1927.
——. 'An Essay on A.F.' *New York Herald Tribune Books*. Oct. 30, 1928.
Garnett, Edward. 'A.F. in English.' *Bodleian*. January, 1921.
Gastineau, M. 'Un Hôte oublié du Quai Voltaire. Le Baron Denon.' *Nouv. litt.* Feb. 17, 1934.
Ginisty, P. 'Le Maître et son œuvre.' *Petit Parisien*. Oct. 13, 1924.
Girard, G. 'Essai de Bibliographie de l'œuvre d'A.F.' *Maison du Livre français*. December, 1921, pp. 5-8.
Gorki, M. 'Sur A.F.' *Revue européenne*. Dec. 1, 1924, pp. 1-6.
Gosse, Edmund. 'A.F.'s New Novel : La Vie en fleur.' *Littell's Living Age*. Sept. 16, 1922, pp. 723-26.
Gottschalk, W. 'A.F., der Dichter und sein Werk.' *ZfFSL*. Vol. 50 (1927), pp. 85-130.
Gouhier, H. *See* Barrès.
Gourmont, J. de. 'Littérature.' *Mercure*. Aug. 1, 1927, pp. 651-56.
Gout, R. 'A.F. et le Théâtre de Hrotsvitha. Une Source de *Thaïs*.' *Mercure*, Aug. 1, 1931, pp. 595-611.
Gregh, F. 'Le Style.' *Annales pol. et litt.* Oct. 19, 1924.
Griggs, A. *Toute l'Edition*. Oct. 29, 1932.
Guehenno, J. 'A.F. ou le dernier sage.' *Gde. Revue*. April, 1924, pp. 198-218.
Halsey, E. Article in *Le Journal*. Oct. 15, 1924.
Hanotaux, G. 'Discours aux funérailles d'A.F.' *Le Journal*. Oct. 19, 1924.
Henriot, E. 'A.F. en Promenade.' *Le Temps*. May 8, 1926.
——. 'Zola, les Cinq et A.F.' *Ibid.* Sept. 27, 1927.

——. 'A.F.' et Mme. Arman de Caillavet.' *Ibid.* Oct. 13, 1931.
——. 'L'Envers du "Lys rouge."' *Ibid.* Nov. 3, 1931.
Heredia, J.-M. de. Letter to A.F. *Revue d'histoire littéraire.* Jan.-March, 1933, p. 142.
Hérenger, A. 'M. A.F. et la culture française.' *Le Feu.* January, 1914.
Hermant, A. 'A.F.' *Figaro.* Oct. 13, 1924.
——. 'La Vie à Paris.' *Le Temps,* Oct. 17, 1924.
Hermant, M. 'La Candeur d'A.F.' *Débats.* Oct. 17, 1924.
Holbrook, W. C. 'A Note on the Technique of A.F.' *MLN.* Jan., 1932, pp. 29-35.
Hovelaque, E. 'Quelques Souvenirs sur A.F.' *Rev. de France.* April 1, 1925, pp. 548-75.
Huard, G. 'Le Père d'A.F.' *Bulletin du Bibliophile et du Bibliothécaire.* March 1, 1925, pp. 121-39.
——. 'E. Devoyod et A.F.' *Figaro.* Oct. 2, 1926.
——. 'I. Constant et A.F.' *Ibid.* Dec. 4, 1926.
——. 'Une Source d'A.F. Les Prisons de Paris sous la Révolution.' *Mercure.* June 15, 1928, pp. 600-615.
——. 'Les Origines de la "Cité des Livres" ou A.F. dans l'Avranchin.' *Normannia.* September, 1928, pp. 85-115.
Jasinski, R. 'Un Poème inédit d'A.F.' *Rev. de Paris.* March 15, 1926, pp. 439-42.
Jusselin, M. 'L'Ascendance chartraine d'A.F.' *La Dépêche de Toulouse.* Aug. 6-7, 1932.
Kahn, G. 'A.F.' *Rev. blanche.* Vol. XX (1899), pp. 496-506.
Kahn, L. Article in *Le Petit Parisien.* Oct. 13, 1924.
——. 'Souvenirs personnels.' *Revue Juive de Lorraine.* Sept. 1, 1935.
Kahn, M. 'Un Projet de jeunesse d'A.F. L'Encyclopédie de la Révolution française.' *Figaro* (suppl. litt.). Jan. 24, 1925.
——. 'Autour d'A.F. Articles oubliés.' *Figaro.* May 15, June 5, June 16, 1926; Jan. 22, 1927.
Kemp, R. 'Les Mémorables d'A.F.' *Revue universelle.* Feb. 15, 1925, pp. 531-34.
Kingsbury, E. M. 'A.F. and his Time.' *N.Y. Times Bk. Rev.* Oct. 9, 1932.
Lafue, P. 'Dialogue de deux générations sur A.F.' *Rev. hebd.* Dec. 27, 1924, pp. 470-83.
Lanos, J. M. 'A.F.' *Queen's Quarterly.* Oct.-Dec., 1907, pp. 118-33.
Lanson, G. 'A.F. La Vie et l'œuvre.' *Annales pol. et. litt.* Oct. 19, 1924.
Larguier, L. 'Vieilles Pierres et vieux livres.' *L'Illustration.* May 30, 1925.
Leblond, M. 'Hommage à Leconte de Lisle.' *Nouv. litt.* June 9, 1934.
Ledrain, E. 'Quinzaine littéraire.' *Nouv. Revue.* Dec. 15, 1895, pp. 869-71.
Lefebvre, L. 'L'Ironie au temps présent.' *Rev. pol. et litt.* March 1-8, 1919, pp. 155-56.
Lefranc, J. 'Les Dimanches de la Villa Saïd.' *Le Temps.* Nov. 13, 1921.
Lemaître, J. 'Causerie littéraire : La Vie littéraire.' *Rev. pol. et litt.* Nov. 24, 1888, p. 669.
Lemerre (*fils*), A. 'Souvenirs sur A.F.' *Opinion,* Oct. 17, 1924.
Le Moy, A. 'Le Père France.' *Mercure.* Jan. 15, 1925, pp. 335-52.

Lepage, A. 'Souvenirs sur M. A.F.' *Rev. pol. et litt.* Feb. 8, 1896, p. 191.
Levaillant, M. 'Courrier des Lettres. Deux contes de Noël.' *Figaro.* Dec. 27, 1931.
Lion, J. and Marx, E. 'A.F. et Madame de la Sablière.' *Chronique.* March-April, 1929, pp. 137-68.
——. 'Glossaire et Remarques sur la langue de La Fontaine.' *Ibid.*, pp. 169-73.
Lion, J. 'Une Comédie inédite d'A.F.' *Lys rouge* (periodical). July 1, 1934.
——. 'Une Comédie inédite d'A.F.' *Nouv. litt.* June 2, 1934.
——. 'A.F. et Paul Bourget.' *Le Temps.* Jan. 25, 1936.
Locke, W. J. 'The Personality of A.F.' *Bodleian.* January, 1921.
Lods, A. 'Les Préfaces d'A.F.' *L'Intermédiaire.* Nov. 10, 1924, cols. 817-18.
Lœwel, P. 'La Vie littéraire. "La Vie et les Opinions d'A.F." par Jacques Roujon.' *L'Eclair.* April 1, 1925.
——. ' "Dernières Pages inédites d'A.F."—"La Jeunesse d'A.F.," par Georges Girard.—"A.F. et Racine," par Gabriel des Hons.' *Ibid.* Oct. 23, 1925.
——. 'La Vie littéraire. "Le Secret d'A.F." par Charles Braibant. "A.F." par Victor Giraud.' *L'Ordre.* Jan. 13, 1936.
Lowenthal, Marvin. 'A.F.'s Jews.' *Menorah Journal.* Vol. VII (1925), pp. 14-26.
Maccone, G. 'Un Artista siciliano e un personnaggio di A.F.' *Nuova Antologia.* March 1, 1927, pp. 120-23.
Magnin, C. 'Hrosvita, sa vie et ses œuvres.—La Comédie de Paphnuce et Thaïs.' *RDM.* 1839, pp. 335-66.
Malherbe, H. 'A.F. et la musique.' *Le Temps.* Oct. 22, 1924.
Massis, H. 'Souvenirs sur A.F.' *Arts et Métiers graphiques.* March 15, 1929, pp. 587-94.
Mathiez, A. 'A.F. et la Révolution française.' *Annales historiques de la Révolution française.* January, 1925, pp. 46-57.
Mauclair, C. 'La Maison d'A.F.' *L'Art et les Artistes.* December, 1907, pp. 439-41.
Maurel, A. 'L'Impératrice Eugénie et M. de Lesseps.' *Figaro.* Dec. 28, 1896.
——. 'Dans le Monde des lettres.' *Rev. pol. et litt.* April 5, 1890, pp. 444-45.
Mauris, J. 'A.F. et Grégoire de Tours.' *Débats.* Nov. 2, 1924.
Maurras, C. 'A.F., poète.' *Nouv. litt.* April 19, 1924.
——. 'Le Jubilé d'A.F. Conversation avec Charles Maurras.' *Opinion* April 11, 1924.
——. 'La Vie littéraire.' *Rev. encyclopédique.* April 1, 1895.
——. 'À l'Académie.' *Ibid.* March 15, 1896.
Maury, L. 'Deux Enfances célèbres : A.F. et Pierre Loti.' *Rev. pol. et litt.* Dec. 20-27, 1919, pp. 764-67.
Michaut, G. 'Le Dilettantisme et M. A.F.' *Le Correspondant.* May 10, 1913.
Mille, P. 'Dialogue autour de France.' *Nouv. litt.* March 10, 1934.
Miomandre, F. de. 'Nonchalance coupable.' *Nouv. litt.* April 9, 1932.
Mongrédien, G. 'L'Œuvre poétique d'A.F.' *Rev. mondiale.* May 15, 1921, pp. 179-81.

Monval, J. 'A.F. et François Coppée (Lettres inédites), 1869-1896.' *Rev. de France*. May 1, 1924, pp. 178-87.

Morand, H. 'Les Débuts littéraires d'A.F. au Collège Stanislas.' *Débats*. Oct. 15, 1924.

——. 'Autographes et portraits du Petit-Pierre.' *Ibid.* Oct. 30, 1924.

——. 'Quelques Réflexions d'A.F. à propos de "Phèdre."' *Ibid.* Jan. 18, 1927.

Morche, R. 'L'Antimilitarisme d'A.F.' *Revue des Indépendants* (*Rev. littéraire et artistique*). March, 1927, pp. 78-79.

Moréas, J. Letter to A.F. *Le Symboliste*. Oct. 7, 1886.

——. 'Manifeste du Symbolisme.' *Figaro* (suppl. litt.). Sept. 7, 1886.

Morel, J.-E. 'Une Source d'A.F. : "La Rôtisserie de la Reine Pédauque" et "Les Entretiens sur les Sciences secrètes" de l'Abbé Montfaucon de Villars.' *Gde. Revue*. Nov. 25, 1911, pp. 225-49.

Mornet, D. 'Les Sources d'A.F.' *Nouv. litt.* July 3, 1926.

——. 'M. A.F. et la Science.' *Revue du mois*. July 10, 1911, pp. 60-76.

Mouquet, J. 'A.F. à Saint-Valery-sur-Somme.' *Figaro*. Oct. 22, 1927.

Murry, J. Middleton. 'The Wisdom of A.F.' *Living Age*. May 24, 1919, pp. 474-77.

Negri, G. 'A.F.' *Nuova Antologia*. Vol. 157 (1898), pp. 51-80.

Parigot, H. 'La Vie et l'école.' *Le Temps*. Oct. 29, 1924.

Peixoto, A. 'As mulheres de A.F.' *Revista da Academia brasileira de letras*. January, 1926, pp. 5-23.

Pellissier, G. 'Roman. *La Rôtisserie de la Reine Pédauque* d'A.F.' *Rev. encyclopédique*. May 15, 1893.

——. '*Le Lys rouge ;* par A.F.' *Ibid.* Oct. 15, 1894.

——. '*Le Jardin d'Epicure* par A.F.' *Ibid.* Dec. 15, 1894.

——. 'Romanciers contemporains : M. A.F.' *Rev. pol. et litt.* July 21, 1894, pp. 79-86.

Peyre, H. 'A Belis, la Critique française à la fin du XIXe siècle.' *MLN*. November, 1927, pp. 486-88.

Picard, G. 'A.F. anecdotique.' *Renaissance politique, littéraire et artistique*. Oct. 18, 1924, p. 13.

——. 'L'Influence littéraire et sociale d'A.F.' *Rev. mondiale*. Dec. 15, 1924, pp. 227-56 and 339-66.

Pillet, A. 'A.F.' *ZfFSL*. Vol. 54 (1930-31), pp. 9-36.

Pilon, E. 'Les Femmes dans l'œuvre d'A.F.' *Rev. pol. et litt.* Oct. 31, 1903, pp. 571-76.

Place, J. 'A.F. et Alfred de Vigny.' *Chronique*. 1924, pp. 145-46.

Poizat, A. 'A.F., poète et critique.' *Muse française*. April 10, 1924, pp. 370-82.

Potez, H. 'Le Diable et M. A.F.' *Rev. pol. et litt.* Oct. 15, 1910, pp. 503-506.

Pouquet, J.-M. '*Re* The Last Salon.' *New Republic*. March 7, 1928.

——. 'Madame Arman de Caillavet et ses amis.' *Rev. de Paris*. March 1, 1926, pp. 50-86.

Prévost, E. 'La Poésie d'A.F.' *Revue de l'université*. Nov. 15, 1924, pp. 1199-1210.

Prévost, M. 'A.F., Dilettantisme et littérature.' *Lys rouge* (periodical). Oct. 1, 1934.

Provost, A. 'Les Sources de "Thaïs" d'A.F.' *Gde. Revue*. November, 1921, pp. 16-55.

Pruette, L. 'Secrets of Greatness shown in Brain Study.' *N.Y. Times*. March 24, 1929.

Quillard, P. 'A.F.' *Mercure*. November, 1892, pp. 214-20.

Racot, A. 'Un Editeur de poètes en 1867.' *Chasseur bibliographe*. March, 1867, pp. 67-71.

Radziwill, Princess Catherine. 'A.F., the Genesis of his Fame.' *The Forum*. December, 1924, pp. 826-31.

Rascoe, Burton. 'A.F.'s Task-Mistress.' *New Republic*. March 16, 1927.

Revon, M. 'A.F., critique littéraire.' *Les Marges*. Nov. 15, 1924.

Reynaud, E. 'A.F. et les poètes.' *Muse française*. April 10, 1924, pp. 241-50.

Ricard, L.-X. de. 'A.F. et le Parnasse contemporain.' *La Revue*. Feb. 1, 1902, pp. 301-19.

Robert-Sigl. 'A.F.' *Belles-Lettres, revue mensuelle des lettres françaises*. April, 1924, pp. 297-308.

Rod, E. 'M. A.F.' *Rev. de Paris*. Dec. 15, 1894, pp. 731-66.

Rodes, J. 'A.F. en Italie.' *L'Aurore politique, littéraire, sociale*. June 21, 1903.

Roosbroeck, G. L. van. 'Sylvestre Bonnard and the Fairy.' *MLN*. April, 1922, pp. 248-50.

Rosenberg, F. 'Goethes Braut von Corinth in Frankreich.' *Archiv für das Studium der Neueren Sprachen*. Vol. 139 (1919), pp. 179-97.

Rosny (*aîné*), J.-H. 'L'Ange gardien d'A.F.' *Nouv. litt.* March 14, 1931.

——. 'Mémoires de la Vie littéraire dans le salon de Mme. de Caillavet.' *Revue belge*. May 15, 1924, pp. 289-301.

Rumsey, Frances. 'A.F.' *Bodleian*. January, 1921.

Saintsbury, George. 'A.F.' *Quarterly Review*. January, 1923, pp. 141-60.

Samary, M. 'Les Souvenirs de Marie Samary. Des Brohan à Sacha Guitry.' *Nouv. litt.* July 21, 1934.

Saunier, C. 'La Maison de M. A.F.' *Art et Décoration*. November, 1907, pp. 169-72.

——. 'A.F. Collectionneur.' *L'Art vivant*. Jan. 15, 1928, pp. 41-42.

Schaffer, Aaron. 'A.F. and Poetry.' *PMLA*. March, 1932, pp. 262-82.

——. 'Louis-Xavier de Ricard, Poet of Progress.' *Ibid*. December, 1935, pp. 1191-99.

Sée, H. 'A.F. et l'Histoire.' *Gde. Revue*. July, 1925, pp. 121-29.

Ségur, N. 'Propos d'A.F. : Evocations et souvenirs.' *Rev. de France*. **Nov. 1**, 1929, pp. 71-87.

——. 'Livres nouveaux.' *Rev. mondiale*. Sept. 15, 1921, pp. 208-11.

——. 'A.F. et son œuvre.' *Ibid*. Nov. 1, 1924, pp. 14-21.

——. 'Conversations avec A.F.' *Ibid*. June, 1927, pp. 258-61.

——. 'La Vie littéraire.' *Ibid*. Sept. 1, 1927, pp. 77-88.

Souday, Paul. 'A.F. and Paul Valéry.' *N.Y. Times Bk. Rev.* July 10, 1927.

——. 'A Spiteful Book on A.F.' *Ibid*. Jan. 8, 1928.

——. 'La Politique d'A.F.' *Rev. mondiale*. May 16, 1924, pp. 3-9.

——. 'Les Livres.' *Le Temps*. July 15-16, 1913.

——. 'A.F.' *Ibid.* Oct. 14, 1924.
——. 'Les Livres.' *Ibid.* Oct. 23, 1924.
——. 'Les Livres.' *Ibid.* Dec. 15, 1927.
Soury, J. 'Délia de Tibulle.' *RDM.* Sept. 1, 1872, pp. 68-104.
Spronck, M. 'M. A.F.' *Débats.* Oct. 11, 1893.
Starrett, Vincent. 'October 18, 1924' *Literary Observer.* Oct.-Nov., 1934.
Syveton, G. 'M. A.F. : *Le Mannequin d'Osier.*' *Rev. pol. et litt.* Oct. 23, 1897, pp. 235-39.
Thebault, E. 'Le Prince des Prosateurs.' *La Volonté.* Nov. 16, 1898.
Thérive, A. 'L'Actualité littéraire. Le Dixième Anniversaire de la mort d'A.F.' *Marianne.* Oct. 10, 1934.
——. 'A.F.' *Opinion.* Oct. 17, 1924.
Thibaudet, A. 'Prose et Poésie.' *Nouv. litt.* March 2, 1929.
——. 'Un Anniversaire barrésien.' *Ibid.* Sept. 17, 1932.
——. 'Une Bibliothèque de château.' *Ibid.* July 21, 1934.
——. 'A.F. en Angleterre.' *Nouvelle Revue française.* June 1, 1924, pp. 734-40.
Tonelli, L. 'A.F. et Pascal.' *Nouvelle Revue d'Italie.* May, 1920.
Tracy, T. F. 'A Source of A.F. : Benvenuto Cellini.' *MLN.* March, 1924, pp. 188-90.
Truc, G. 'Les Ennemis d'A.F.' *Comœdia.* Dec. 31, 1929.
Vaganay, L. 'Le Jeune A.F. et Volney.' *Neuphilologische Mitteilungen.* May 9, 1934, pp. 101-105.
Vandérem, F. 'Les Lettres et la vie : A.F.' *Rev. de France.* Nov. 15, 1924, pp. 361-82.
Vandervelde, E. 'Le Grand Virage d'A.F.' *La Dépêche de Toulouse.* Nov. 27, 1935.
Vaudoyer, J.-L. 'Mort de Vernon Lee.' *Nouv. litt.* April 20, 1935.
Villette, P. 'A.F. et la Politique.' *Opinion.* Oct. 17, 1924.
Wendel, Hermann. 'Opinions allemandes sur A.F.' *Rev. Rhénane.* November, 1924, pp. 74-77. (Digest of W.'s views.)
Whale, Winifred Stephens. 'The French Salon and A.F.' *Contemp. Review.* November, 1926, pp. 606-12.
Wilson, Edmund. 'The Last Phase of A.F.' *New Republic.* Feb. 11, 1924, pp. 308-10.
——. 'A.F. Decline of the Revolutionary Tradition.' *Ibid.*, Oct. 24, 1934, pp. 302-307.
Woodbridge, B. M. 'The Original Inspiration of Le Procurateur de Judée.' *MLN.* December, 1925, pp. 483-85.

Le Bouquiniste français. May 30, 1925. (Contains, pp. 1-3, 'Exposition A.F. au foyer de la Comédie Française.')
——. June 6, 1925. (Contains, pp. 1-3, 'Un Hommage à A.F.')
Bulletin Municipal Officiel de la Ville de Paris. June 18, 1933. (Contains account of unveiling of Plaque, on May 20, with speeches by Prade, Rageot, Renard, Fontenay, Barthou.)

Un Cadavre. Neuilly-sur-Seine, 1924. (Contains articles by A. Breton, L. Aragon, P. Soupault, P. Eduard, J. Delteil, P. Drieu La Rochelle.)

Le Capitole. October, 1924. (Contains, among others, articles by Henry-Marx, R. de Bendère, C. Chassé, R. Cor.)

Clarté. Nov. 15, 1924. (Contains, among others, articles by J. Bernier, E. Berth, M. Fourrier, G. Michaël.)

Débats. Nov. 12, 1921. (Contains, among others, article entitled 'A.F. et le prix Nobel.')

Figaro. Dec. 2, 1892; Dec. 18, 1895; Jan. 19, 31, Oct. 23, Dec. 4, 18, 28, 1896.

——. (Suppl. litt.) Oct. 25, 1924.

Figaro artistique. Aug. 1, 1927.

Larousse Mensuel Illustré. June, 1935. (Contains, pp. 122-23, 'Les Quarante Fauteuils de l'Académie française.')

Le Lys rouge. Jan. 1, April 1, July 1, Oct. 1, 1933; Oct. 1, 1934, Oct. 1, 1935, etc.

Le Matin. Oct. 13, 1924.

New York Times. Oct. 14, 1924. (Contains 'A.F.').

——. Dec. 13, 1927. (Contains 'France's *Thaïs* Manuscript Comes to America.')

Nouvelles littéraires. April 19, 1924. (Contains, among others, articles and sketches by C. Maurras, Comtesse de Noailles, P. Souday, C. Jullian, A. Thérive, A. Hermant, Simone de Caillavet, J.-J. Brousson, C. Berton, F. Léfèvre.)

——. Oct. 18, 1924. (Contains, among others, articles by P. Mille, A. Bourdelle, G. Bergner, E. Jaloux, C. Berton.)

Opinion. Oct. 17, 1924. (Contains, among others, articles by Thérive, Bourget-Pailleron, Couchoud, Lemerre, Villette.)

Petit Parisien. Dec. 25, 1926.

Revue d'histoire littéraire. April-June, 1930. (Contains, p. 282, 'Chronique.')

——. Jan.-March, 1933. (Contains, p. 151, 'Chronique.')

Revue de littérature comparée. Jan.-March, 1925, p. 168; pp. 164-65 ('Chronique.')

Revue des Grands Procès contemporains. (Contains 'M. Alphonse Lemerre contre M. A.F.' July, 1912, pp. 402-48; Aug., 1912, pp. 449-512; Sept., 1912, pp. 513-56.)

INDEX OF NAMES

INDEX OF NAMES